THE AMERICAN DELEGATES TO THE PEACE CONFERENCE

EDWARD M. HOUSE   ROBERT LANSING   WOODROW WILSON   HENRY WHITE   TASKER H. BLISS

THE UNITED STATES

AND

THE LEAGUE OF NATIONS

1918 - 1920

BY

DENNA FRANK FLEMING, Ph.D.

ASSOCIATE PROFESSOR OF POLITICAL SCIENCE
IN VANDERBILT UNIVERSITY

AUTHOR OF
"THE TREATY VETO OF THE AMERICAN SENATE"

ILLUSTRATED

G. P. PUTNAM'S SONS

NEW YORK AND LONDON

1932

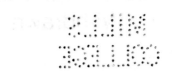

Made in the United States of America

Dedicated
gratefully
To
DORIS
AND To
HER MOTHER AND FATHER

PREFACE

THIS volume is an outgrowth of the author's study of treaties which the United States Senate has refused to approve, or to which it has given its consent conditionally. The earlier investigation encountered a mass of material dealing with the failure of the Treaty of Versailles which could not be presented without expanding the discussion to undue length, and at the same time giving a disproportionate amount of space to the consideration of one rejected treaty. The data accumulated in 1928 had, therefore, to be put aside for further development.

In undertaking to survey the highly controversial period from 1918 to 1920, the author was aware that he could not expect to present a wholly final account of the bitter struggle described. The research of future writers will be necessary to the achievement of an undertaking so difficult. The facilities for recording the acts and utterances of public men have advanced so rapidly in recent decades, however, that we should be able to give to the leaders of our own time a justice that will have something more than merely historic value, particularly when national policies of the utmost moment are involved.

The viewpoint here presented is that of one who could not believe, as a University student in 1914, that human civilization had advanced so far only to confess its impotence before the assaults of any militarized nation which chose to deny the existence of either law or right, other than its own supposed necessity. This belief was not abandoned during our own participation in the War, and it is still held. It predisposed the writer, moreover, to personal acceptance of the leadership of Woodrow Wilson, already admired for his dynamic statesmanship, in his interpretation of the permanent gains that should be wrested from the War.

While the writer makes no claim to that total objectivity of interpretation which is the supposed goal of all historical writers, he has made an earnest effort to present the available facts in proper sequence and to state both sides of the story. Attempt has been made throughout to hold to the main issues. Credit has been given where it was believed to be due; if in unfair measure, the reader's own weighing of the evidence will supply the corrective.

The author is indebted for the reading of chapters of the manuscript to Professors James W. Garner, of the University of Illinois, and Charles G. Fenwick, of Bryn Mawr College; William E. Dodd, of the University of Chicago, and Laurence M. Larson, of the University of Illinois; Arthur N. Holcombe, of Harvard University, and Arthur W. MacMahon, of Columbia University; William C. Binkley and Irby R. Hudson, of Vanderbilt University. Criticism of the text by these gentlemen from the standpoints of International Law and Relations, American History, Political Parties and Constitutional Law is gratefully acknowledged. The author alone is responsible for any errors of fact that may remain and for all opinions expressed.

He is under further obligation to his colleague, Dr. Carl S. Driver, whose careful reading of the proof has contributed to the improvement of the entire volume; to his wife for effective assistance of every kind at all stages of its preparation; to Dr. Clarence A. Berdahl and Mr. H. Maurice Darling for extensive contributions of material. Many others who have generously supplied information are all too imperfectly recognized in the footnote citations.

A short bibliography of the books principally relied upon will be found at the end of the study. If the reader desires to investigate others, he will find full bibliographical data given at the bottom of the page when each book is first referred to and sometimes thereafter.

D. F. F.

Nashville, Tennessee,
January 25, 1932.

CONTENTS

ILLUSTRATIONS

THE UNITED STATES AND THE LEAGUE OF NATIONS

1918–1920

CHAPTER I

THE RISE OF THE LEAGUE IDEA

THE idea of a League of Nations was not new in 1918. Dreams of "a parliament of man and federation of the world" began centuries ago and plans for a league to keep the peace were proposed long before the twentieth century. The "Grand Design" of Henry IV of France, published by the Duke of Sully in 1634, William Penn's "Essay towards the Present and Future Peace of Europe by the Establishment of an European Dyet, Parliament or Estates," of 1693, and the Abbé Saint-Pierre's celebrated revision of "the project for perpetual peace invented by King Henry the Great," given out in 1712, were all plans for international unions of rulers to keep the peace. [1]

The great Scotch-German philosopher Immanuel Kant, with truer vision, published, in 1795, a plan for a federation of peoples rather than rulers. He foresaw that the peace of the world could never be kept until the world was politically organized and he was equally convinced that it would be safe to organize it only after government had become representative. He therefore based his plan for "a federation of free states" on democratic government. [2]

Proposals Following the Russo-Japanese War. It apparently required the horrors of the Russo-Japanese War, however, to drive the idea of establishing peace by organization within the fringe of practical politics. That war, at least, was contemporaneous with several notable proposals for organizing the world against war. In 1905, Representative Richard Bartholdt, of Missouri, presented a plan for world federation to the Thirteenth Inter-Parliamentary Conference at Brussels, and Andrew Carnegie developed the same idea in his rectorial address at St. Andrews University, Scotland. In 1907, Señor Ordoney, Ex-President of Uruguay, submitted a detailed plan for a league of peace

[1] S. P. Duggan, *The League of Nations*, Boston, 1919, p. 27.
[2] *Ibid.*, p. 32; *The Independent*, April 25, 1907, Vol. 62, p. 977.

3

to the Second Hague Conference, [3] and Mr. Carnegie gathered a great peace conference of 1500 people in New York City, representing nearly every state in the Union and most foreign countries, which called for further steps in establishing peace. [4]

Theodore Roosevelt's Advocacy From Experience. It remained for Theodore Roosevelt to present the most thoroughgoing proposal for the curbing of war. Mr. Roosevelt, as President, had had two most unusual experiences as a peacemaker and arbiter of European politics. He had followed the Russo-Japanese War closely, repeatedly telling one belligerent or both, particularly after an important battle, that peace should be made, and finally, after exerting through the various European governments all the pressure he could command, he had succeeded in bringing representatives of the contestants together in this country. It was a remarkable feat, although even then peace would not have resulted had he not repeatedly labored most forcibly with both governments to bring them to terms. [5]

Before this great task was successfully concluded, too, the first Moroccan crisis between Germany and the Entente powers began to claim his attention. As the crisis developed he persuaded France and her supporters to accept the conference demanded by Germany. In this conference, held at Algeciras in Morocco, he had participated vigorously, both through his delegates, led by Ambassador Henry White, and by direct contact with the governments, eventually proposing the terms to Germany which she was forced to accept and putting very strong pressure on her to do so. He had recognized that American interests in Morocco were negligible, but felt that the danger of war justified his intervention in the confused political disputes with which the Algeciras Conference dealt. [6]

Roosevelt was well prepared, therefore, to make a considered statement of methods to regulate the disputes that result in war. He did so directly to Europe as the main thesis of his address before the Nobel Prize Committee, at Christiana, Norway, in May, 1910. In acknowledging the prize given him in 1906 for the services above noted

[3] *The Independent,* June 5, 1916, Vol. 86, p. 358.
[4] *The Independent,* April 25, 1907, Vol. 62, p. 976.
[5] J. B. Bishop, *Theodore Roosevelt and His Times,* N. Y., 1920, Vol. I, pp. 374–424.
[6] *Ibid.,* pp. 467–505; Allan Nevins, *Henry White,* N. Y., 1930, pp. 261–283. Roosevelt's intervention in the Algeciras Conference seemed to be decisive. For two weeks White was "busy day and night trying desperately" to arbitrate between the rival groups of powers. The result was probably a greater victory for France than President Roosevelt intended, but he did not hesitate to use his personal and official power to settle the dangerous political disputes centering in Morocco.

he first suggested the further development of arbitration, the Hague Court, and disarmament, concluding as follows:

> Finally it would be a master stroke if those great Powers honestly bent on peace would form a League of Peace, not only to keep the peace among themselves, but to prevent, by force if necessary, its being broken by others. The supreme difficulty in connection with developing the peace work of The Hague arises from the lack of any executive power, of any police power to enforce the decrees of the court. . . . Each nation must keep well prepared to defend itself until the establishment of some form of international police power, competent and willing to prevent violence as between nations. As things are now, such power to command peace throughout the world could best be assured by some combination between those great nations which sincerely desire peace and have no thought themselves of committing aggressions. The combination might at first be only to secure peace within certain definite limits and certain definite conditions; but the ruler or statesman who should bring about such a combination would have earned his place in history for all time and his title to the gratitude of all mankind.[7]

This sober statement of the American ex-President went to the heart of the problem of peace and war. The great powers had the force necessary to prevent war as well as make it. Let them use that power to enforce peace, when it was endangered, instead of continually threatening one another with it. Perhaps the whole concept could not be established at once but certain immortality awaited the statesman who could inaugurate a League of Peace.

The One Permanent Move. Under the stress of the Great War Roosevelt saw even more clearly that his proposal of 1910 was the only ultimate solution, for he wrote, in 1915: "The one permanent move for obtaining peace which has yet been suggested with any reasonable chance of obtaining its object is by an agreement among the great powers, in which each should pledge itself, not only to abide by the decisions of a common tribunal, but to back with force the decision of that common tribunal. The great civilized nations of the world which do possess force, actual or immediately potential, should combine by solemn agreement in a great world league for the peace of righteousness. [8]

He did not expect or claim everything for such an enforcement of peace. "It would be impossible to say that such an agreement would at

[7] *The Independent*, May 12, 1910, Vol. 68, pp. 1027–29.
[8] T. Roosevelt, *America and the World War*, N. Y., 1915, p. 80.

once and permanently bring universal peace. But it would certainly mark an immense advance. It would certainly mean that the chances of war were minimized and the prospects of limiting and confining and regulating it immensely increased." [9]

"What is needed in international matters," he continued, "is to create a judge and then put police power back of the judge." The time had not been ripe to do this heretofore, but surely the combatants would be willing to consider it at the close of the awful cataclysm then existing. To bring about a peace "without providing for the elimination of the causes of war would accomplish nothing of any permanent value. . . . The essential thing to do is to free each nation from the besetting fear of its neighbor. This can only be done by removing the causes of such fear. The neighbor must no longer be in danger." [10]

In his contact with European politics during the Moroccan and Russo-Japanese crises Mr. Roosevelt had more than once laughed at the great fear which England and Germany had of each other, fear which he felt to be largely groundless on both sides, but he appreciated fully the reality of such apprehensions and left no doubt about his understanding of the necessity of guaranteeing security to the members of any league. He cared not a whit either that such organization of the world for peace would be branded by reluctant followers as Utopian.

Utopia or Hell. He had no patience with the "foolish and mischievous all-inclusive arbitration treaties recently negotiated by Mr. Bryan under the direction of President Wilson," and he still wanted to exclude questions involving "honor" and "vital interest" from arbitration, but on the main issue of putting force back of the peace he gave the doubters the plain choice of "Utopia or Hell," declaring in no uncertain terms again: "My proposal is that the efficient civilized nations—those that are efficient in war as well as in peace—shall join a world league for the peace of righteousness. This means that they shall by solemn covenant agree as to their respective rights which shall not be questioned; that they shall agree that all other questions arising between them shall be submitted to a court of arbitration; and that they shall also agree—and here comes the vital and essential point of the whole system—to act with the combined military strength of all of them against any recalcitrant nation, against any nation which transgresses at the expense of any other nation the rights which it is agreed shall not be questioned, or which on matters that are arbitrable refuses to submit to the decree of the arbitral court." [11]

[9] *Ibid.*   [10] *Ibid.*, pp. 78-9.   [11] *The Independent*, January 4, 1915, Vol. 81, p. 13.

Can there be the slightest doubt about what Roosevelt as a negotiator of peace would have said to anyone who objected to the members of the league undertaking "to respect and preserve as against external aggression the territorial integrity and existing political independence of all members of the league"? In statement after statement he was ready to throw the whole force of the league against any nation which transgressed at the expense of another nation any of the rights which had been guaranteed to all; he went far beyond the guarantee of such an elemental right as safety against aggression.

He well knew, too, the type of objections that would be brought against his plan. Such a league would not "bring perfect justice any more than under municipal law we obtain perfect justice; but it will mean that at last a long stride has been taken in the effort to put the collective strength of civilized mankind behind the collective purposes of mankind to secure the peace of righteousness, the peace of justice among nations of the earth." [12]

THE CRYSTALLIZATION OF LEAGUE SENTIMENT

In this period when people everywhere were compelled to deal with the fact of war as they never are in times of peace, Roosevelt was far from being alone in recognizing that the peace could not be kept unless the world were organized for the purpose.

President Woodrow Wilson likewise had thought deeply of what was to come after the war. As early as the Fall of 1914 he had said to Dr. Stockton Axson that after the war "all nations must be absorbed into some great association of nations whereby all shall guarantee the integrity of each so that any one nation violating the agreement between all of them shall bring punishment on itself automatically." [13]

In line with this conclusion and with his repeatedly expressed purpose to admit the Latin American republics to partnership in the Monroe Doctrine Mr. Wilson proposed to them, during the period of American neutrality, a draft treaty providing that "the High Contracting Parties to this solemn covenant and agreement hereby join one another in common and mutual guarantee of territorial integrity

[12] Roosevelt, *America and the World War*, pp. 82-3.
[13] Dr. Axson, a brother-in-law of Wilson, was a visitor in the White House at the time. See his account, *New York Times*, February 4, 1924.

and of political independence under republican forms of government." [14]

The urgency of applying this principle to all nations had become apparent to ex-President William H. Taft at about the same time that President Wilson had felt its timeliness to be fully demonstrated. In October, 1914, Mr. Taft declared emphatically to a group in the Century Club, New York: "The time has come when the peace-loving nations of the world should organize themselves into some sort of society in which they should agree to settle their own disputes by amicable methods, and say to any nation that started to go to war: 'You have got to keep the peace or have all the rest of us against you!'" [15]

The idea thus forcibly expressed in similar terms by the President and two ex-Presidents was not, to be sure, a novel doctrine. It was the key provision of the Articles of Confederation, under which we had started our national existence, and the Constitution itself was founded upon a guarantee to each state of protection against invasion. It was wholly natural that the three great leaders, faced with a great international disaster flowing from the refusal of Austria-Hungary and Germany to recognize the rights of Serbia and Belgium to independence and territorial integrity, should mutually conclude that these elemental rights would have to be guaranteed as effectively as in the American Union, if civilization were to continue.

Many other Americans thought the thing through to the same inevitable conclusion with the result that there was formed on June 17, 1915, in Independence Hall, Philadelphia, a League to Enforce Peace, with a thousand distinguished Americans coöperating. A year later this organization had branches in almost every congressional district in the country. [16]

In its statement of principles the League to Enforce Peace held it to be desirable for the United States to join a league of nations binding the signatories (1) to submit all justiciable questions to an international court of justice "both upon the merits and upon any issue as to its jurisdiction of the question," (2) to submit all other questions to a council of conciliation for hearing, consideration, and recommenda-

[14] C. Howard Ellis, *The Origin, Structure and Working of the League of Nations*, Boston, 1929, p. 71. Such a Pan-American agreement was apparently first suggested to the President by Colonel House as early as December, 1914. C. S. Seymour, *The Intimate Papers of Colonel House*, Vol. I, pp. 209-10.
[15] F. H. Lynch, "Taft's Labors for International Peace," *Current History*, May, 1930, Vol. 32, p. 297.
[16] *The Independent*, June 5, 1916, Vol. 86, pp. 356-7.

tion, (3) to "jointly use forthwith both their economic and military forces" against any member committing acts of hostility against another before submitting to arbitration or conciliation, and (4) to hold periodic conferences to formulate and codify international law. [17]

Senator Lodge's Support. In pursuance of its program of education the League held a great meeting in Washington on May 27, 1916, at which both President Wilson and Senator Lodge spoke. On that occasion Lodge said in part:

> I know, and no one, I think, can know better than one who has served long in the Senate, which is charged with an important share in the ratification and confirmation of all treaties; no one can, I think, feel more deeply than I do the difficulties which confront us in the work which this league—that is, the great association extending throughout the country, known as the League to Enforce Peace—undertakes, but the difficulties cannot be overcome unless we try to overcome them. I believe much can be done. Probably it will be impossible to stop all wars, but it certainly will be possible to stop some wars, and thus diminish their number. The way in which this problem must be worked out must be left to this league and to those who are giving this great subject the study which it deserves. I know the obstacles. I know how quickly we shall be met with the statement that this is a dangerous question which you are putting into your argument, that no nation can submit to the judgment of other nations, and we must be careful at the beginning not to attempt too much. I know the difficulties which arise when we speak of anything which seems to involve an alliance, but I do not believe that when Washington warned us against entangling alliances he meant for one moment that we should not join with the other civilized nations of the world if a method could be found to diminish war and encourage peace. [18]

Little did Mr. Lodge know that some months later it would be necessary for the ghost of Father Washington to stand daily in the Senate, and in a thousand other forums, telling us that his warning of 1797 applied perfectly to the conditions of 1919. Of course the Senator could not foresee all future exigencies, but he at least had anticipated clearly the type of objections that were likely to be raised and had maintained his position for a year in the face of them, for he continued immediately: "It was a year ago that in delivering the Chancellor's address at Union College, I made an argument on this theory,

[17] T. H. Dickinson, *The United States and the League*, N. Y., 1923, pp. 14–15.
[18] H. C. Lodge, *The Senate and the League of Nations*, N. Y., 1925, pp. 131–2.

that if we were to promote international peace at the close of the present terrible war, if we were to restore international law as it must be restored, we must find some way in which the united forces of the nations could be put behind the cause of peace and law. I said then that my hearers might think I was picturing a Utopia, but it is in the search for Utopia that great discoveries have been made. 'Not failure, but low aim, is crime.' " [19]

The One Solution. The limit of voluntary arbitration had, he felt, been reached, and he thought "the next step is that which this League proposes and that is to put force behind international peace, an international league or agreement, or tribunal, for peace. We may not solve it in this way, but if we cannot solve it in that way it can be solved in no other." [20]

This was a plain statement upon which Lodge could stand permanently. He might well have expanded his idea of force to include the tremendous power of organized world opinion, but his basic conception was slowly matured and strongly reasoned. It was in line with his action of 1910 in introducing a resolution into the Senate providing for a commission to consider the expediency of armament limitation "and of constituting the combined navies of the world an international police force for the preservation of universal peace." [21]

Secretary Knox's Contribution. Mr. Lodge's position was, moreover, consonant with the thought of the best minds in the pre-war period. Secretary of State Philander C. Knox, in an address before the Pennsylvania Society of New York, December 11, 1909, had stated at length the reasons for his belief in the growing international unity and solidarity. Before the time of effective use for the radio and the airplane he saw clearly the unifying power of increasingly rapid communication. Did not the remarkable progress of international coöperation "rest upon the practically simultaneous operation of the common mind and the conscience of the world upon common knowledge?" Electricity was finishing what steam began. Each nation instantaneously felt the compulsion of the public opinion of all nations.

This, too, was before any international agency existed for focusing and expressing world opinion on political matters, and Mr. Knox did not foresee such a development, but he did see in the multitude of occasional international conferences "evidence that the common interest

---

[19] *Ibid.*   [20] *Ibid.*

[21] The resolution originated in the House as House Joint Resolution No. 223. It passed both houses and received the approval of the President. *Congressional Record,* Vol. 45, Pt. 8, pp. 8545, 8712, 8874.

of nations is being recognized as superior to their special interests and
that unity of action in international matters may yet control the unrestrained, unregulated, or isolated action of independent States."

Some Limitation of National Sovereignty Inevitable. The sweep of
events was bound to bring some limitation upon our traditional idea
of a national sovereignty giving unlimited freedom of action at all
times, but Knox did not fear that development. As complete freedom for an individual was "a thing incompatible with corporate life
and a blessing probably peculiar to the solitary robber" so the "development of commerce and industry and the necessary exchange of
commodities have caused nations to see that their interests are similar
and interdependent, and that a like policy is often necessary as well
for the expansion as for the protection of their interests. Independence exists, but the interdependence of states is as clearly recognized
as their political independence. Indeed, the tendency is very marked
to substitute interdependence for independence, and each nation is
likely to see itself forced to yield something of its initiative, not to any
one nation, but to the community of nations in payment for its share in
'the advance in richness of existence.' " [22]

President Wilson, too, during the war years, had been thinking
deeply and to the same conclusion to which the other leaders came.
While conducting his 1916 campaign to arouse the country to support military preparedness, he appealed at the same time for some
action to protect the longer future. Speaking at Des Moines, February 1, 1916, he asked: "What is America expected to do? She is expected to do nothing less than keep the law alive while the rest of the
world burns. You know there is no international tribune. I pray God
that if this contest has no other result, it will at least have the result
of creating an international tribune and producing some sort of joint
guarantee of peace on the part of the great nations of the world." [23]

President Wilson's Adhesion Secured. Though alive to the unescapable logic of the developing chaos of the war, the President had
been slow to identify himself with the League to Enforce Peace. Not
knowing where he stood, that body took its convention of May, 1916,
to Washington, with the leading purpose of securing the President's
support, if possible. Made aware of this desire, he gave no sign of
his attitude until he arose to follow Mr. Lodge in addressing the dele-

[22] *The American Journal of International Law,* January, 1910, Vol. 4, pp. 181-4.
[23] Lars P. Nelson, *President Wilson the World's Peacemaker,* Stockholm, 1919,
p. 204; *Des Moines Register,* February 2, 1916.

gates, on the evening of May 27, 1916.[24] In that address he stated it to be his belief that the people of the United States would wish their Government to favor at the close of the war an universal association of nations to preserve the freedom of the seas "and to prevent any war begun either contrary to treaty covenants or without warning and full submission of the causes to the opinion of the world"—a virtual guarantee of territorial integrity and political independence. [25]

Three days later, Mr. Wilson declared: "I believe that the people of the United States are ripe for entrance into an international league whose main object shall be to guarantee international justice and right in the whole world. George Washington warned us against mixing ourselves up in other peoples' conflicts or alliances. I shall never myself consent to any alliance that would mix us up in conflicts between other nations, but I shall be glad to join an alliance which will unite the peoples for keeping the peace of the world on the basis of universal justice. Therein is liberation; not limitation." [26]

In his campaign for re-election the President continued to voice the same belief. Speaking at Long Branch, September 2, 1916, he urged: "We can no longer indulge our traditional provincialism. We are to play a leading part in the world drama whether we like it or not. We shall lend, not borrow; act for ourselves, not imitate or follow; organize and initiate, not peep about merely to see where we may get in." [27]

Unanimity of Opinion in 1916. Up to this time there was virtually no dissent in the thinking parts of the United States from the idea of an organized peace to replace the old drifting policy which always had and forever must lead to war. The active leaders of both parties had committed themselves wholeheartedly to a league for peace which would protect the rights of all—certainly, at the very least, territorial integrity and independence.

---

[24] F. H. Lynch, "Taft's Labors for International Peace," *Current History,* May, 1930, Vol. 32, p. 298.

[25] *Messages and Papers of Woodrow Wilson,* N. Y., 1924, Vol. I, p. 275.

[26] Nelson, *President Wilson the World's Peacemaker,* pp. 205–6.

[27] Nelson, *President Wilson the World's Peacemaker,* p. 205. In speeches at Omaha, October 6, and at Indianapolis, October 12, 1916, the President repeated his belief that it would be the duty of the United States at the close of the war to join with the other nations in some kind of league for the maintenance of peace. Nelson, p. 206; *New York Times,* October 13, 1916.

The pleas of all the American leaders to date, it should be noted, were based not upon the situation arising from our decisive entry into the war, but upon their conception of our duty and self interest as a neutral at its close.

The Divergence of Wilson and Lodge

The campaign of 1916 does not seem to have produced any cleavage on the question. It did however, bring about one issue between Woodrow Wilson and Henry Cabot Lodge which removed any basis for coöperation which may have existed between them.

After the Cabinet had approved Wilson's "strict accountability" note to Germany on the sinking of the *Lusitania,* Secretary Bryan had privately persuaded the President to permit him to draft an instruction to Ambassador Gerard advising the German Government that the United States would be willing to submit the questions at issue to a commission of investigation on the principle of the Bryan treaties. The State Department at once saw the inconsistency of the instruction with the President's note and Wilson was soon besieged with requests to reconsider. He did so and on hearing the counter arguments ordered the instruction suppressed.[28]

During the campaign Senator Lodge heard in roundabout fashion of this dramatic play of forces within the Administration and attempted to show from it that Wilson was indifferent to the protection of American rights, even the right of life itself, that Germany knew he would not defend our rights because she was receiving hints that his strong words were for home consumption and that his whole policy shifted with the currents of public opinion to avoid doing anything. [29]

The considerable controversy thus aroused eventually brought from Mr. Wilson on October 30, 1916, a statement, in reply to an inquiry from the *New Republic,* in which he denied the truth of Senator Lodge's statement. He was able to do this because Lodge's information was inaccurate enough to prevent him from framing his charge in absolute accordance with the facts. From Wilson's point of view his motives in the crisis had been throughout to do what was best and his best judgment had prevailed, but Senator Lodge, not unnaturally, felt that his opinion of the President's conduct in the *Lusitania* question and others was correct and that Wilson should not have escaped from his net.[30]

Shortly after, on January 13, 1917, Wilson refused to speak from the same platform with Lodge,[31] and there is no evidence that any cordiality of relations was ever renewed between them.

[28] David Lawrence, *The True Story of Woodrow Wilson,* N. Y., 1924, pp. 145-7.
[29] *Ibid.,* 146; Lodge, *The Senate and the League of Nations,* pp. 34-56.
[30] *Ibid.*
[31] Lodge, *The Senate and the League of Nations,* p. 61.

Wilson's Address of January 22, 1917. In December, 1916, President Wilson had asked the warring powers for an avowal of their respective views with respect to peace. On January 22, 1917, after receiving their replies, he appeared before the Senate "as the council associated with me in the final determination of our international obligations, to disclose to you without reserve the thought and purpose that have been taking form in my mind in regard to the duty of our Government in the days to come when it will be necessary to lay afresh and upon a new plan the foundations of peace among the nations."

He believed it to be the mission of the American democracy to show mankind the way to liberty, and in the settlement of new world conditions he felt it could perform a great service. "That service," he said, "is nothing less than this, to add their authority and their power to the authority and force of other nations to guarantee peace and justice throughout the world. Such a settlement cannot now be long postponed. It is right that before it comes this Government should frankly formulate the conditions upon which it would feel justified in asking our people to approve its formal and solemn adherence to a League for Peace. I am here to attempt to state those conditions."

Some of the things necessary to a permanent peace were, he felt: (1) a peace without victory, because a dictated peace "would be accepted in humiliation, under duress, at an intolerable sacrifice, and would leave a sting, a resentment, a bitter memory upon which terms of peace would rest, not permanently, but only as upon quicksands," (2) the right of self determination, (3) the freedom of the seas, (4) disarmament, and (5) a league of nations to administer the peace.

The question upon which the whole future peace and policy of the world depended was this: "Is the present war a struggle for a just and secure peace, or only for a new balance of power? If it be only a struggle for a new balance of power, who will guarantee, who can guarantee, the stable equilibrium of the new arrangement? Only a tranquil Europe can be a stable Europe. There must be, not a balance of power, but a community of power; not organized rivalries, but an organized common peace." He therefore proposed "that all nations henceforth avoid entangling alliances which would draw them into competitions of power. . . ." There was no entangling alliance in a concert of power. A force must be created "as a guarantor of the permanency of the settlement so much greater than the force of any nation now engaged or any alliance hitherto formed or projected that no nation, no probable combination of nations could face or withstand it. If the peace presently made is to endure, it must be a peace made secure by the organized major force of mankind." [32]

Lodge's Reply. On February 1, 1917, Senator Lodge delivered a long speech in the Senate in reply to the President's address of January 22, in which he pointed out dangerous implications of the principles laid down by the President and definitely parted company with the idea of a league of nations.[33]

The President's hope of inducing the belligerents to stack their arms and make peace before either side had been conquered was to him a strange proposal indeed, as it was to many others. He had no difficulty in predicting, either, many of the difficulties that would arise in attempting to apply the principle of self-determination. "Who," he asked, "is to decide whether the principle is recognized under the different governments of the world with whom we are to form the League for Peace 'supported by the organized major force of mankind?' If the recognition of this principle is to be essential to the lasting peace which we are to support and every American, of course, believes in and admires the principle—what is to be done about Korea, or Hindustan, or Alsace-Lorraine, or the Trentino, or the Slav Provinces of Austria, or the Danish Duchies? Does the government of Armenia by Turkey, with its organized massacres, rest on the consent of the governed, and if it does not are we to take steps to remedy it, or is Turkey to be excluded from the league, or is the league to coerce Turkey to an observance of our principles?" [34]

The freedom of the seas, too, he thought, was a new doctrine the enforcement of which "would surely involve us, and those nations which sign the covenant with us, in every war which might occur between maritime nations."

Furthermore, the idea of enforcing the peace had lost its attraction for him. The more he thought about it the more serious the difficulties in the way of its accomplishment seemed to be. The refusal of a member of the league to abide by its decision would mean war. Every member would have to send its quota of troops. Our share in the interna-

[32] *Messages and Papers of Woodrow Wilson*, N. Y., 1924, Vol. I, pp. 348–56.
[33] *Congressional Record*, Vol. 54, Pt. 3, pp. 2364–70, February 1, 1917. Cited as given on February 28, 1917 in Lodge, *The Senate and the League of Nations*, pp. 270–296, where the speech is printed in full. Points other than those dealing with a peace league are summarized from both addresses in order to make clear the complete divergence of position which appeared in the two speeches.
[34] *Congressional Record*, Vol. 54, Pt. 3, p. 2365.

tional police force necessary would probably be 500,000 men, a force which would be inspected by the league's officers and ordered about by them. Moreover, if we adhered to the principle of equality of nations laid down by the President, a majority composed of the little nations might do the ordering.

He had done some further thinking, also, about the precepts of Washington. He still had no superstitious regard for Washington's policy, but it had been set forth "under conditions not unlike those which now exist," and after all, its wisdom, supplemented by that of Monroe, had been demonstrated for more than a century and "we should not depart from it without most powerful reasons and without knowing exactly where the departure would lead." [35]

Altogether, the stern realities had to be faced. A league for peace had a most encouraging sound but it was altogether too grave a question to be satisfied with words. A league of peace meant putting force behind peace and making war on any nation which did not obey the league's decisions. We had best consider concretely what that would mean, said Lodge, continuing:

Let me take two examples of questions which we must be prepared to face as members of a league for peace "supported by the major force of mankind." If, as I have already said, such a league is formed, it must deal with questions of vital interest and go beyond the limitations of voluntary agreements, for if it does not there will be no advance on the present conditions. Assume that such a league has been formed, with the powers which I have outlined. China and Japan, we will say, acting on the principles of the brotherhood of man which this league is to embody, come before the representatives of the league and demand for their people the right of free emigration to Canada, Australia, and New Zealand, which now practically exclude them. Suppose the league decided that the people of China and Japan ought not to be deprived of the right to migrate anywhere, and that Canada, Australia, and New Zealand, backed by England, decline to accept this decision. The league will then proceed to enforce its decision, and we shall find ourselves obliged to furnish our quota to a force which will compel the admission of Asiatic labor to Canada. Are we prepared to make war upon Canada in such a cause as this, our quota of the forces of the league perhaps being under the orders of a Japanese commander in chief? Let us turn the question the other way. Suppose the Asiatic powers demand the free admission of their labor to the United States, and we resist, and the decision of

[35] *Ibid.*, pp. 2367–68.

the league goes against us, are we going to accept it? Is it possible that anyone who wishes to preserve our standards of life and labor can be drawn into a scheme veiled by glittering and glancing generalities, which would take from us our sovereign right to decide alone and for ourselves the vital question of the exclusion of Mongolian and Asiatic labor? These are not fanciful cases drawn from the region of the imagination. They are actual, living questions of the utmost vitality and peril to-day. In them is involved that deepest of human instincts which seeks not only to prevent an impossible competition in labor but to maintain the purity of the race. Are we prepared to make any agreement which would put us in such a position as that? Before we give our adhesion to a league for peace let us consider all these contingencies. The time will not be wasted which we give to such consideration. [36]

He already heard the clamor of the peace at any price advocates arising around him "with passionate demand that we shall immediately join a league of peace—which may plunge us into war in any quarter of the globe at any moment at the bidding of other nations—but they, too, if they persist, will meet the day when words are vain, when there is no help or shelter in language, and when they must face relentless, unforgiving realities."

His Counter Program. But was he unwilling to use the power and influence of the United States for the promotion of permanent peace? Not at all. There was nothing he had so much at heart. He merely did not want to involve the country in a scheme which would create a worse situation than existed. It was better to "bear the ills we have than fly to others that we know not of." [37]

There were measures, however, which were wholly practicable, and which he commended. They were: (1) adequate national preparedness, (2) the rehabilitation of international law at the close of the war, (3) "within necessary and natural limits, to extend the use of voluntary

---

[36] *Ibid.*, p. 2369. This method of argument was not new to Mr. Lodge. He had found it satisfactory in combating the Taft arbitration treaties of 1911. The procedure was to construct hypothetical cases showing how the proposed machinery ... ng disaster in such a manner that calamity appeared quite probable. All ... al law and custom might forbid the development of the supposed situation, ... g arguments necessary for reply were not likely ever to catch up with the ... hypothesis, which to most people seemed to carry condemnation on its

closed with a solemn plea for deep reflection before it be too late, at least ... ption of something to fear was most likely to be created. ... count of the fall of the Taft treaties before the attacks of Lodge and Roose-... be found in: D. F. Fleming, *The Treaty Veto of the American Senate*, N. Y., 90–109. ...gressional Record, Vol. 54, Pt. 3, p. 2369.

arbitration, so far as possible," and mobilize public opinion behind it, and (4) to urge a general reduction of armaments by all nations.

It might be said that these were but slight improvements, "but what I purpose has at least one merit—it is not visionary." And in truth it was not.

In conclusion he wished heartily to support the resolution offered by Senator Borah committing us without reserve to the policy of Washington and Monroe in regard to foreign nations. He now saw nothing but peril in abandoning our long established policy. The statements of the fathers were "as clear as the unclouded sun at noonday, and not reflections of double meaning words under which men can hide and say they mean anything or nothing." There was "no lurking place for a league of peace 'supported by the organized major force of mankind' in the sentences of George Washington and Thomas Jefferson. . . ." [38]

The League of Free Peoples in the President's War Address

The War Message, April 2, 1917. In the excitement attendant upon the German submarine campaign, then approaching its climax, Mr. Lodge's speech appears to have attracted little attention. The President advised our own declaration of war with Germany within a month. In it he stated solemnly that he had exactly the same things in mind that he had when he addressed the Senate on the twenty-second of January preceding and that "a steadfast concert for peace can never be maintained except by a partnership of democratic nations. No autocratic government could be trusted to keep faith with it or observe its covenants. It must be a league of honor, a partnership of opinion. Intrigue would eat its vitals away; the plottings of inner circles who could plan what they would and render account to no one would be a corruption seated at its very heart. Only free peoples can hold their purpose and their honor steady to a common end and prefer the interests of mankind to any narrow interest of their own."

Then, after completing his indictment of the German autocracy, and making it clear that we fought it rather than the German people, he closed his address with the peroration which gained wider currency than any part of the message. The heart of it was: "It is a fearful

[38] *Ibid.*, p. 2370.

thing to lead this great peaceful people into war, into the most terrible and disastrous of all wars, civilization itself seeming to be in the balance. But the right is more precious than peace, and we shall fight for the things which we have always carried nearest our hearts, for democracy, for the right of those who submit to authority to have a voice in their own governments, for the rights and liberties of small nations, for a universal dominion of right by such a concert of free peoples as shall bring peace and safety to all nations and make the world itself free." [39]

Message to the Russian People. Again on May 26, 1917, the President returned to the theme in his message to the Russian people, who had lately revolted against the Czar, saying as a part of his plea to them to stand fast against Germany: "And then the free peoples of the world must draw together in some covenant, some genuine and practical coöperation that will in effect combine their force to secure peace and justice in the dealings of nations with one another. The brotherhood of mankind must no longer be a fair but empty phrase; it must be given a structure of force and reality. The nations must realize their common life and effect a workable partnership to secure that life against the aggression of autocratic and self-pleasing power." [40]

The War to End War. Through the months that followed, the President was aided by the leaders of public opinion everywhere in

---

[39] *Messages and Papers of Woodrow Wilson,* Review of Reviews Ed., pp. 372–83.

[40] *Ibid.,* p. 407–8. The President's earnest and repeated advocacy of a league of nations made little impression upon his political enemies. It was even possible for Mr. Owen Wister to say in 1930 that "Lodge, with Root, Taft, and other Republicans were strong for a league to enforce international peace in 1916, two years before Wilson would accept the idea." (O. Wister, *Roosevelt, The Story of a Friendship,* N. Y., 1930, p. 155.)

The President's complete acceptance of the league principle in his address of May 27, 1916, before the League to Enforce Peace; his clear stand in his address to the Senate on January 22, 1917, which was followed by Senator Lodge's abandonment of the cause in his speech of February 28, 1917; his moving appeal for a league of free peoples to keep the peace at the climax of his war message of April 2, 1917; the appeal to the Russian people on May 26, 1917; even the message of January 8, 1918, which contained the Fourteen Points, crowned by the league—all of these pleas failed to have any effect upon Mr. Wister. He insists that "Others persuaded him to change his mind. It was not easily done. The others were many, but chiefly Colonel House when Wilson stayed with him in 1918 at Magnolia." (Wister, *Roosevelt, The Story of a Friendship,* p. 336.)

Mr. Wilson's continued administration of the nation's affairs during one of the greatest moments in its history seems to have left many of his opponents unable to appreciate where he was going. The Rooseveltians, especially, were so intent upon demonstrating that the "words" in the President's long series of powerful addresses meant nothing, or that they meant something wrong, that they apparently left themselves for more than two years unable to credit him as an effective leader for a new international dispensation.

driving home to the peoples of the Allied and enemy countries alike that we were engaged in a crusade to end autocracy and war. The war was lifted to the highest plane to which it could be elevated, and many, indeed, who could not quite understand why the United States should settle the conflict went gladly overseas in the confidence that their service or sacrifice would help to establish a new and better order of affairs.

Addresses in Early 1918. The next official statement of our war aims came from the President in a message to Congress delivered January 8, 1918, in which he reiterated that what we demanded was that "the world be made fit and safe to live in; and particularly that it be made safe for every peace-loving nation which, like our own, wishes to live its own life, determine its own institutions, be assured of justice and fair dealing by the other peoples of the world as against force and selfish aggression." The message included the fourteen points upon which he thought the peace should be based, the last of which read: "A general association of nations must be formed under specific covenants for the purpose of affording mutual guarantees of political independence and territorial integrity to great and small states alike." [41]

Again on February 11, 1918, in an address to Congress analyzing German and Austrian peace utterances, the President declared anew: "We believe that our own desire for a new international order under which reason and justice and the common interests of mankind shall prevail is the desire of enlightened man everywhere. Without that new order the world will be without peace and human life will lack tolerable conditions of existence and development. Having set our hand to the task of achieving it, we shall not turn back." [42]

At the Climax of the War. On July 4, 1918, in summing up the allied war objectives, the President concluded with: "The establishment of an organization of peace which shall make it certain that the combined power of free nations will check every invasion of right and serve to make peace and justice the more secure by affording a definite tribunal of opinion to which all must submit and by which every international readjustment that cannot be amicably agreed upon by the peoples directly concerned shall be sanctioned." All our objects

[41] *Messages and Papers of Woodrow Wilson,* Review of Reviews Edition, pp. 464-73. Prime Minister Lloyd George had made a similar statement of British war aims three days earlier in which he had said that a great attempt must be made "by some international organization to provide an alternative to war as a means of settling international disputes." *Literary Digest,* January 19, 1918, Vol. 56, p. 12.

[42] *Ibid.,* p. 479.

in the War, he said, could be put into a single sentence. "What we seek is the reign of law based upon the consent of the governed and sustained by the organized opinion of mankind." [43]

That sentence will bear thinking through again and again. "What we seek is the reign of law based on the consent of the governed and sustained by the organized opinion of mankind." The whole program that he was later to fight for on both sides of the ocean is in that short statement.

As the End Drew Near. In late September, when the surrender of Bulgaria presaged the end of the war, the President went to New York to state as carefully as he could the kind of peace that should come after. He spoke in the Metropolitan Opera House on September 27, from a written manuscript, a thing that he rarely did, and adhered closely to the text. "At every turn of the war," he said, "we gain a fresh consciousness of what we mean to accomplish by it. When our hope and expectations are most excited we think more definitely than before of the issues that hang on it and of the purposes which must be realized by means of it. For it has positive and well defined purposes which we did not determine and which we cannot alter. No statesman or assembly created them; no statesman or assembly can alter them. The most that statesmen or assemblies can do is to carry them out or be false to them. . . . The common will of mankind has been substituted for the particular purposes of individual states. Individual statesmen may have started the conflict but neither they nor their opponents can stop it as they please. It has become a people's war. . . ."

When we entered the war the issues had become perfectly clear. Those issues were:

> Shall the military power of any nation or group of nations be suffered to determine the fortunes of peoples over whom they have no right to rule except the right of force?
> Shall the strong nations be free to wrong weak nations and make them subject to their purpose and interest?
> Shall peoples be ruled and dominated, even in their own internal affairs, by arbitary and irresponsible force or by their own will and choice?
> Shall the assertion of right be haphazard and by casual alliance or shall there be a common concert to oblige the observance of common rights?

"No man, no group of men, chose these to be the issues of the struggle," continued the President. "They *are* the issues of it; and

[43] *Ibid.*, p. 500.

they must be settled—by no arrangement or compromise or adjust-ment of interests, but definitely and once for all and with a full and unequivocal acceptance of the principle that the interest of the weakest is as sacred as the interest of the strongest."

The depth of his conviction that the peace must not be one of old-fashioned bargaining, if it were to last, was shown in the declaration that "if it be indeed and in truth the common object of the Govern-ments associated against Germany and of the nations whom they govern, as I believe it to be, to achieve by the coming settlements a secure and lasting peace, it will be necessary that all who sit down at the peace table shall come ready and willing to pay the price, the only price that will procure it; and ready and willing, also, to create in some virile fashion the only instrumentality by which it can be made certain that the agreements of the peace will be honored and fulfilled. That price is impartial justice in every item of settlement, no matter whose interest is crossed; and not only impartial justice, but also the satisfaction of the several peoples whose fortunes are dealt with. That indispensable instrumentality is a League of Nations formed under covenants that will be efficacious."

Just when the league of nations was to be formed was equally clear in his mind. He continued: "And, as I see it, the constitution of that League of Nations and the clear definition of its objects must be a part, in a sense the most essential part of the peace settlement itself."

But these general terms did not disclose the whole matter. Some details were needed. To supply them he stated five things (known later as his five points) which represented this Government's inter-pretation of its own duty with regard to peace. They were, in brief: "(1) No discrimination between those to whom we wish to be just and those to whom we do not wish to be just, (2) no settlements to the special interest of some nations that were not consistent with the common interest of all, (3) no alliances within the League, (4) no special selfish economic combinations and no economic boycotts ex-cept at the direction of the League as a means of discipline and con-trol, and (5) complete publicity of all international treaties and agree-ments."

It was a new day indeed that he looked forward to with confidence. Yet he did not wish a complete break from the past, but only an advance from it. "We still read Washington's immortal warning against 'en-tangling alliances' with full comprehension and an answering purpose. But only special and limited alliances entangle; and we recognize and accept the duty of a new day in which we are permitted to hope for a general alliance which will avoid entanglements and clear the air of the world for common understandings and the maintenance of common rights." [44]

WILSON POLITICALLY DOMINANT

In all this period there was little dissent, aside from the speech of Senator Lodge quoted above, from the often reiterated purpose to organize the peace definitely at the conclusion of the war. No disagreement with the Fourteen Points was voiced in Congress. [45]

A Coalition Cabinet Defeated. This may have been partly due to the fact that in January, 1918, the leaders of the opposition were absorbed in an effort to create a war cabinet which would take the conduct of the war largely from the hands of the President. In July, 1917, an effort had been made to create a joint committee of both houses of Congress to assist the President, which was similar to the attempt made to fasten congressional control on Lincoln during the Civil War. [46]

This movement was succeeded by a sustained campaign, beginning in September, 1917, led by Colonel Roosevelt, to create a war cabinet to conduct the war. Roosevelt first attacked the President bitterly in magazine articles, declaring that "we did not go to war to make democracy safe" and referring to Wilson as a "combination of glib sophistry and feeble, sham amiability." Then taking to the stump he continued to deny in Chicago, Detroit, New York and other great cities that we made war to make democracy safe, denounced the idea of a "soft peace" that the President might favor and urged that Wilson was to be compared to the German rulers themselves.[47]

Mr. Roosevelt's great personal following in turn stimulated him to further efforts until many members of Congress reached the conclusion that nothing less than a coalition cabinet with Roosevelt in charge as munitions head would meet the situation. The Democratic Chairman of the Senate Military Affairs Committee, Senator Chamberlain, joined the movement, which culminated in a great luncheon in

[44] *New York Times,* September 28, 1918.
[45] David Lawrence, *The True Story of Woodrow Wilson,* N. Y., 1924, p. 235; *Congressional Record,* Vol. 56, Part 2.
[46] W. E. Dodd, *Woodrow Wilson and His Work,* N. Y., 1922, p. 253; J. F. Rhodes, *History of the United States,* Vol. IV, pp. 203–5.
[47] *Ibid.,* pp. 255–57.

New York City, on January 19, 1918, held in honor of Senator Chamberlain and Representative Kahn of California and attended by 1900 people, where Mr. Chamberlain declared that the military establishment had fallen down because of wholesale inefficiency.[48]

The leaders then went to Washington. Mr. Chamberlain introduced bills creating a Munitions Department and a War Cabinet of three men and Mr. Roosevelt, on the ground, personally led the fight for their enactment. It looked for a time as if the President would be unable to weather the contest, but he countered by asking for himself even greater powers than it was proposed to give to others and won one of his most striking successes, in spite of the opposition of a number of embittered Senators in his own party. [49]

The Alignment of Forces for the Campaign of 1918. In Dr. Dodd's view, the result of this contest made certain a tremendous attempt of the older social forces in the North to regain control of Congress in the following November. These classes, representing also the great industrial wealth of the country, had been in almost uninterrupted charge of the country since the Civil War. They had grown to look upon control as their prerogative; they believed that only they were capable of ruling. They had been able to reconcile themselves partially to what seemed to them largely accidental loss of power in 1912, but they had never been able to accept the verdict of 1916. Mr. Wilson, as the representative of the equally old social classes of the agrarian South and of the newer life of the West, seemed to them ever an interloper. Moreover, his amazing program of action had transformed the scheme of things they were used to; the new tariff, the new banking system and most of all the revolution in Federal taxation coming in with the income tax had affected their interests deeply. And now, wielding power such as no President had ever had, he was in a fair way to prove that the "provincials" he had gathered around him could manage the greatest national and business effort in our history without official Republican aid.

In addition, his utterances on international questions still further disturbed deeply these same conservative classes of the North and East. He talked of a new international order and said repeatedly that our power would never be used again to aggrandize any selfish interest of our own—in Mexico or elsewhere. He "talked like a free spirit, a man

[48] Dodd, *Woodrow Wilson and His Work*, pp. 257–63. Mr. Dodd devotes a full chapter to these events. See Frederick Palmer, *Newton D. Baker*, N. Y., 1931, Vol. II, p. 62.
[49] *Ibid.*, p. 262; *The American Yearbook*, 1918, p. 4.

who would make the world over if it could be made over." People dread change, and he promised to bring about as much of it in the international field as he had in domestic affairs. Most disturbing of all, his fourteen points seemed to point to a new world order in which there would be tendencies toward free trade; we could hardly associate constantly with the other nations, as he proposed, without finding it advisable at least to mitigate our tariff policy here and there a little more than we otherwise would. And finally, if political control was to be regained it must be done soon. Wilson and the social classes that he represented had won four straight elections; soon their power would be fully consolidated. "It would have been equivalent to political suicide for the opposition to approve Wilson; and great party groups do not commit suicide, however seriously individual leaders may take the current of events. There was nothing else but a party struggle for the autumn of 1918." [50]

[50] Dodd, *Woodrow Wilson and His Work,* p. 269 and preceding.

CHAPTER II

THE CONGRESSIONAL ELECTION OF 1918

In the excitement attendant upon the crisis of the war and the resulting victories, the public was naturally less aware of the earlier stages of the campaign of 1918 than usual. There was a party debate in the Senate in connection with the war cabinet drive in January, and the atmosphere in Washington was often hardly less partisan than in peace times,[1] but the war absorbed public attention, and of course a good deal of political energy as well. The news reviews of the period comment on the tardy start of the campaign.

Preparations for it were being made, however, by both Democratic and Republican leaders. Roosevelt and Taft, whose split had inaugurated the Wilson era, had renewed a friendly correspondence and on May 26, 1918, they met publicly in the dining room of the Blackstone Hotel, Chicago.[2]

A Republican Congress Necessary. A few weeks later both addressed an unofficial Republican State Convention at Saratoga, New York, at which other national party leaders spoke. Each of the ex-Presidents agreed that events had shown the necessity of electing a Republican Congress in the approaching election. Taft conceded the ability of President Wilson in stating the country's war aims, but thought that he had not had the same success in the practical prosecution of the war. He therefore urged a Republican Congress, to stimulate the President on to victory in the war and to control reconstruction after it.[3]

The Saratoga convention, at the same time, adopted as a plank in its platform "the immediate creation by the United States and its allies of a league of nations to establish, from time to time to modify, and to enforce the rules of international law and conduct." Any nation

[1] *Congressional Record*, Vol. 56, Pt. 2, pp. 1081–87; David Lawrence, *The True Story of Woodrow Wilson*, p. 233.

[2] *New York Times*, May 27, 1918. The *Times* of May 26 carried a front page article describing the reconciliation of the two chiefs, before the meeting occurred.

[3] *New York Times*, July 19, 20, 1918. Roosevelt pleaded for beating Germany to her knees and for treating "the Hun within our gates as our greatest enemy." Paying tribute to the loyalty of millions of German-Americans, he opposed strongly the use of the German language in the United States.

26

with a responsible government which would abide by civilized standards of international morality should be admitted to the league.

Soon after, in August, 1918, Roosevelt and A. J. Beveridge held a conference with George Harvey at Beverley Farms, a suburb of Beverley, Massachusetts; at which the future publication and support of *Harvey's Weekly* was arranged for. At this meeting Roosevelt and Beveridge are reported to have guaranteed Harvey 20,000 subscribers a year for the next two years, during which period Harvey was to attack Wilson as strongly as possible on every occasion. [4]

Armistice Negotiations. Popular interest was centered in the following weeks on the victorious march of the Allied armies which resulted, early in October, in the first negotiations for peace. A wireless appeal from Germany to President Wilson came first. Then the country heard on October 6 that Austria had sued for peace "based on the fourteen points of President Wilson's message of January 8, and the four points of his speech of February 11, 1918, and those equally of September 27, 1918." [5] The end of the war was in sight.

The next day, October 7, the *Washington Post* rather strangely opposed the election of Henry Ford as Senator from Michigan on the ground that "the wrong kind of man might be able to prevent insistence by the Senate upon a peace in accordance with the aims of this government so forcibly laid down again and again by the President." The American people had elected to office "one of the greatest men who ever sat in the White House." Thousands of stand-pat Republicans were "glad that Woodrow Wilson was chosen instead of Hughes." In the same way the voters of Michigan might be trusted to hold up the hands of the President.

Two days later the same newspaper thanked God "for the firm will and clear vision of such leaders as Woodrow Wilson, who carry forward the message and the punishment necessary to redeem the world from the mastership of brute force in brutal hands." Senator Lodge, however, protested against any reply to the Germans by the President.[5a]

October 13 brought the note of the German Government saying

---

[4] A letter of July 8, 1930, from Dr. William E. Dodd, of the University of Chicago. See Professor Dodd's article in the *New York Times Magazine,* December 27, 1931, p. 15.

[5] *Washington Post,* October 6, 1918. The *Post* editorially urged "leaving the great problems to the great man who is charged with the solution of them."

[5a] *Washington Post,* October 9, 1918. The next day the *Post* thought there was no ground for fear of the elections. The possibility of a Republican Senate was so remote as to be negligible.

that it "accepted the terms laid down by President Wilson in his address of January the 8th and in his subsequent addresses as to the foundation of a permanent peace." [6]

Receipt of this news was immediately followed by a statement from Roosevelt in which he denounced the President for entering into the negotiations and sought to exert his full influence to block them. "I regret greatly that President Wilson has entered into these negotiations and I trust that they will be stopped," said Roosevelt. They were "dangerously near to treacherous diplomacy" and would merely mislead everybody—the enemy, our Allies and the American people.

So low was Roosevelt's opinion of the President's diplomacy that he called for an uprising against all of his statements of American war aims, so long unchallenged, and approved by Taft as late as July 18. He earnestly hoped "that the Senate of the United States and all other persons competent to speak for the American people will emphatically repudiate the so-called fourteen points and the various similar utterances of the President." [6a]

The President's reply to Germany, the next day, demanding the cessation of wanton destruction by the German army and, in plain terms the abdication of the Kaiser, was warmly applauded by the American Press. It fell like a bombshell in Germany. [7] His previous utterances had all pointed that way, but the Imperial Government had been all powerful to the Germans so long that its passage could hardly be visualized.

The Importance of Majority Control. As the political combat developed, the desire of the Democratic politicians to capitalize the personal prestige of the President grew. Few of them doubted apparently that the power of his name was the best asset they had and they naturally felt themselves entitled to profit by it even though some of them had been lukewarm or obstructionist toward the war. They countered charges of disloyalty in their ranks by citing the cases of Republicans who had been similarly condemned.

---

[6] *Washington Post,* October 13, 1918. The German note was dated October 12.
[6a] *Washington Post, New York Times,* October 14, 1918.
[7] Philip Scheidemann, *Memoiren eines Sozialdemokraten,* Dresden, 1928, Vol. II, p. 223.

The President was probably not aided politically by the contemporaneous praise of Marcel Cachin, the leader of the one hundred socialists in the French Chamber of Deputies, who hailed his speeches as "a new charter of international morality." They had helped to keep the French working classes steadfast because they had felt the President unbiased by imperialistic and capitalistic points of view. *Washington Post,* October 21, 1918. Such praise lent color to the charges of "socialism" made later in the campaign.

The Democratic argument was summarized by the Chairman of the Democratic Senatorial Committee, Senator Gerry of Rhode Island, on October 22. "If President Wilson is to receive whole-hearted support; if entire confidence and credit be given him; if he is to stand forth as the spokesman of a united people, it can only be done by electing to the Senate men of his political faith. To argue that a Democratic President can work with Republican Senators with the same degree of harmony, no matter how loyal they may be, is an absurdity, for a Republican majority in the Senate means reorganization of that body, with a change both in the leadership and the complexion of the various committees." [8]

The decisive importance of control of the Senate organization and committees in the period to come was probably not appreciated by any large number of voters, either then or at any later time. It has often been maintained that since Mr. Wilson was undoubtedly stronger than his party he should have appealed, if at all, for Senators and Representatives who would support his policies, welcoming Republicans as well as Democrats.

This suggestion strikes the average person as a highly sensible one. Yet aside from the storm such a policy would have roused in his own party it was not likely to succeed, even though a considerable number of Republicans specifically pledged to the President's program had been elected. Such members, most of them new, could hardly have been numerous enough to have had much influence against the Republican leaders controlling the Senate organization and dominating the Foreign Relations Committee. The number of people who foresaw that control of that one committee would enable the President's opponents to block the supreme result of his political career was in all likelihood relatively small.

Probably not even Mr. Taft anticipated that result when he united with Roosevelt, on October 23rd, in a joint appeal to the voters of Michigan to support Truman H. Newberry, the Republican nominee for the Senate against Henry Ford.[9] The fact that the President was trying to secure a supporter for his peace program from a Republican state seemed to call for heroic measures. The local popularity and influ-

---

[8] *Washington Post,* October 22. The *Post* reported the next day that the Republicans were beginning to consider the possibility of winning the Senate. It was still, however, "a long chance."

[9] *Detroit Free Press,* October 23, 1918. Roosevelt saw no reason why Henry Ford should not aspire to membership in a "Hindoo senate," if there should ever be one.

ence of the President's candidate also justified, in the minds of Republicans, the spending of such large sums of money in behalf of Mr. Newberry's nomination and election that he was later forced from the Senate by the recurrent defeat of Senators who had voted to seat him.

As both the war and the campaign drew to a close, the desire of the Republican chiefs to challenge the President's leadership increased. He was going to make a soft peace with Germany if not prevented by great pressure for the complete smashing of the enemy. While the President was replying to Germany, on October 24, that he was submitting Austria's appeal to the Allies and advising terms that would disarm Germany, Senator Lodge was urging that there be no discussion with the enemy. "The only thing now," he said, "is to demand unconditional surrender. I would leave this to Marshal Foch and the generals of the armies." [10] However, in spite of the disdain of the President's opponents for his words, his final notice to the Germans that their "Monarchial autocrats" and "Military overlords" must go, convinced the German Social Democrats, the strongest political force in Germany, that the Imperial Government must abdicate. The President, alone among the Allied leaders to distinguish between the German people and their leaders, had sealed the doom of an empire.[10a]

Repudiation of the President's Leadership Demanded. At home, however, the President was confronted with a complete revolt against his diplomacy. On October 24, Roosevelt sent a long public telegram to Senators Lodge, Johnson, and Poindexter, in which he said: "As an American citizen I most earnestly hope that the Senate of the United States, which is part of the treaty-making power of the United States, will take affirmative action against a negotiated peace with Germany and in favor of a peace based upon the unconditional surrender of Germany. I also earnestly hope that on behalf of the American people it will declare against the adoption in their entirety of the fourteen points of the President's address of last January as offering a basis for a peace satisfactory to the United States."

Referring to the President's custom of composing important state messages on his own typewriter, Roosevelt continued: "Let us dictate peace by the hammering guns and not chat about peace to the accom-

---

[10] *Washington Post,* October 24, 1918. The President's note was sent on the 23rd.
[10a] "Nun waren für Alle die letzten Zweifel und für Manche auch die letzten Hoffnungen beseitigt. Die Tage Wilhelms II. als Kaiser waren gezählt." Scheidemann, *Memoiren eines Sozialdemokraten,* Vol. II, p. 237.

paniment of the clicking of typewriters. The language of the fourteen points and the subsequent statements explaining or qualifying them is neither straightforward nor plain, but if construed in its probable sense many and possibly most of these fourteen points are thoroughly mischievous . . ."

Crying for more war, instead of urging the President to accept the capitulation of the enemy on terms that would stop the wholesale bleeding of all the belligerents, Roosevelt protested that "We ought to declare war on Turkey without an hour's delay." Failure to do so made "the talk about making the world safe for democracy look unpleasantly like mere insincere rhetoric."

Even the President's care to make it clear throughout the war that we had joined no alliance, "entangling" or otherwise, aroused Roosevelt's ire. He urged upon the Senators that "we should find out what the President means by continually referring to this country merely as the associate instead of the ally of the nations, with whose troops our own troops are actually brigaded in battle. . . . We ought to make it clear to the world that we are neither an untrustworthy friend nor an irresolute foe. Let us clearly show that we do not desire to pose as the umpire between our faithful and loyal friends and our treacherous and brutal enemies."

Unable to contemplate a peace conference led by Wilson, Roosevelt closed his message to the Senate and to the country with an appeal for the complete and utter repudiation of the President's moral leadership of the Allied cause, and of his careful statement of American purposes in the war, accepted with acclaim until the war was actually over. He besought both the Senate and the House to "pass some resolution demanding the unconditional surrender of Germany as our war aim, and stating that our peace terms have never yet been formulated or accepted by our people and that they will be fully discussed with our allies and made fully satisfactory to our own people before they are discussed with Germany." [11]

[11] *New York Times*, October 25, 1918. Knowing from all of Wilson's utterances that he was supremely interested in turning the results of the war to some constructive use for the future, and suspecting that he would not insist upon the annihilation of the retreating enemy, Lodge as early as the first of September had equipped him with a selfish motive for ending the war prematurely. Lodge wrote to Roosevelt on September 3, 1918, that he hoped a recent speech of Roosevelt's would make it "difficult for Wilson to betray the United States and the Allies by negotiating a peace with Germany with a view to the German vote in this country."—*Selections from the Correspondence of Theodore Roosevelt and Henry Cabot Lodge*, N. Y., 1925, Vol. II, p. 536.

The two need not have had any fear that ending the war would win back the votes of German-Americans to Wilson. No moderation in ending the war could at

Forgetting all his previous pleas that President McKinley's hands be upheld in making peace with Spain, Roosevelt urged the suppression of Wilson by Congress in the approaching negotiations. The threat, moreover, represented something more than the violent feelings of an embittered man, for Roosevelt was again the dominant leader of what was normally the majority party of the country, reunited and eager for power. Unmindful of what his own reactions would have been had a similar attempt been made suddenly to take from him as President the direction of foreign affairs, Roosevelt sought to challenge Wilson's leadership as completely as he could. He appealed directly to Senate leaders of his party, and to the voters, seeking in his manifesto, as he said, "to make my appeal to representatives of the American people from one ocean to another."

Carefully devised, as it evidently had been, to secure the maximum of publicity, the Roosevelt offensive was not likely to be entirely ignored. Its highly provocative nature, indeed, suggests that it may have been designed in part to draw a counter appeal to the voters from Wilson which might be turned against him. Roosevelt had already expressed his sentiments, in his statement of October 14, with sufficient clearness to make his position known to the country. His renewed assault could hardly have any further effect unless it advanced the election of a Republican Congress.

This eventuality was one which Wilson was bound to consider carefully. It was true that on the day Roosevelt's telegram was published the newspapers were full of dispatches from the Allied capitals voicing approval of the President's conduct of the negotiations with the enemy powers. The stoppage of the war was not likely to be prevented by cries of the Republican leaders for "unconditional surrender." The congressional election, however, would probably come first and the country was aroused to a pitch of war fever that made it susceptible to cries for smashing "our treacherous and brutal enemies" completely. Should the nation respond by electing a khaki Congress which would be controlled by Roosevelt and his friends, the results upon the peace settlement would be momentous indeed.

Roosevelt's appeal on the eve of the election—and of the Armistice itself—was nothing less than an invitation to the Senate to block the negotiations based on the Fourteen Points, then under way, and prevent the consummation of the President's peace program upon which

---

once neutralize in them the pain of witnessing the defeat and humiliation of the Fatherland by aid of American arms.

up to that time we had fought with apparent unanimity. It was the plainest sort of notice from the principal leader of the opposition that if control of the Senate could be gained in the impending election his influence would be used to obstruct that program in its entirety. In other words the Senate might be expected to do everything in its power to control the peace negotiations and to thwart the President's plans.

Wilson's Appeal to the Voters. The President met the open attempt of his opponents to wrest the control of the peace negotiations from him by the same means that he had defeated the campaign to take the conduct of the war out of his hands, by asking for a vote of confidence that would allow him to continue unhampered to the goal that he had set, as publicly as he could, for the nation. In the earlier crisis he had won his victory in the Congress—controlled by his party. The new attempt to nullify his leadership would succeed or fail in the new Congress—perhaps dominated by Roosevelt and Lodge.

Faced by this prospect, the President issued the next day, October 25, 1918, his famous appeal to the voters, which read:

My Fellow Countrymen:

The Congressional elections are at hand. They occur in the most critical period our country has ever faced or is likely to face in our time. If you have approved of my leadership and wish me to continue to be your unembarrassed spokesman in affairs at home and abroad, I earnestly beg that you will express yourselves unmistakably to that effect by returning a Democratic majority to both the Senate and the House of Representatives.

I am your servant and will accept your judgment without cavil. But my power to administer the great trust assigned to me by the Constitution would be seriously impaired should your judgment be adverse, and I must frankly tell you so because so many critical issues depend upon your verdict. No scruple or taste must in grim times like these be allowed to stand in the way of speaking the plain truth.

I have no thought of suggesting that any political party is paramount in matters of patriotism. I feel too deeply the sacrifices which have been made in this war by all our citizens, irrespective of party affiliations, to harbor such an idea. I mean only that the difficulties and delicacies of our present task are of a sort that makes it imperatively necessary that the nation should give its undivided support to the Government under a unified leadership, and that a Republican Congress would divide the leadership.

The leaders of the minority in the present Congress have unquestionably been pro-war, but they have been anti-administration. At almost every turn since we entered the war they have sought to take the choice of policy and the conduct of the war out of my hands and put it under the control of instrumentalities of their own choosing.

This is no time either for divided counsels or for divided leadership. Unity of command is as necessary now in civil action as it is upon the field of battle. If the control of the House and the Senate should be taken away from the party now in power an opposing majority could assume control of legislation and oblige all action to be taken amid contest and obstruction.

The return of a Republican majority to either house of the Congress would, moreover, be interpreted on the other side of the water as a repudiation of my leadership. Spokesmen of the Republican party are urging you to elect a Republican Congress in order to back up and support the President, but, even if they should in this manner impose upon some credulous voters on this side of the water, they would impose on no one on the other side. It is well understood there as well as here that Republican leaders desire not so much to support the President as to control him.

The peoples of the allied countries with whom we are associated against Germany are quite familiar with the significance of elections. They would find it very difficult to believe that the voters of the United States had chosen to support their President by electing to the Congress a majority controlled by those who are not in fact in sympathy with the attitude and action of the Administration.

I need not tell you, my fellow countrymen, that I am asking your support not for my own sake or for the sake of a political party, but for the sake of the nation itself in order that its inward duty of purpose may be evident to all the world. In ordinary times I would not feel at liberty to make such an appeal to you. In ordinary times divided counsels can be endured without permanent hurt to the country. But these are not ordinary times.

If in these critical days it is your wish to sustain me with undivided minds, I beg that you will say so in a way which it will not be possible to misunderstand, either here at home or among our associates on the other side of the sea. I submit my difficulties and my hopes to you.

WOODROW WILSON.

This letter was "received with keen elation among the great majority of Democratic Senators and Representatives. They seemed to feel that it would greatly strengthen their chances for maintaining their hold on both houses of Congress." Senator Thomas said: "The President perfectly expressed the view of the Democratic majority of the present Congress." Democratic Congressmen were reported as receiving floods of telegrams indicating confidence that the President's appeal would turn the tide in their favor.[12]

REPUBLICAN REPLIES

The Republican leaders met the appeal instantly, if not joyfully. A group of Senators assembled at once and issued a bitter statement condemning it. Senator New, of Indiana, was reported in the *New York Times,* on October 26, as saying, after the meeting, "that he had known from Democratic Senators for the past six weeks that the President had promised the Democratic National Committee to make an appeal to the voters, but that the President had qualified this promise by the condition that he would issue such a statement only in an emergency."

The emergency, deduced Senator New, must be real fear among the Democrats of Republican victory. He did not say that Roosevelt's insistent demand that Wilson's leadership in making the peace be totally repudiated had brought the President face to face with the probability that his future diplomacy would be obstructed at every step by Roosevelt partisans in control of the Senate.

Roosevelt, himself, denounced the President's letter to the people roundly. Repudiating the Fourteen Points whole-heartedly, he declared that it was "the veriest nonsense that ever partisanship can conceive" to state that failure to return a Democratic Congress would be interpreted by the Allies and Germany "as a repudiation of the war aims of this country." [13]

Other Republican leaders were almost equally incensed by the President's appeal. Charles E. Hughes asked: "Must we Republicans patriotically toil and give without seeking a voice in the national assembly, yielding our representation to Democrats, not as more worthy or more loyal, not as more sacrificing or more intelligent, but to Democrats as such simply because they are Democrats? . . .Did I not think that the Republican party would through its representatives aid . . . in the settlement of a righteous peace I should leave the party." [14] The titular head of the Party found it impossible to believe that the best Republicans should not be in power and he found it most difficult to conclude that the contemporary leaders of his party would

---

[12] *Washington Post,* October 26, 27, 1918.
[13] *Washington Post,* October 29, 1918.
[14] *Ibid.,* October 30, 1918.

obstruct the peace negotiations. Legions of his fellow party members doubtless felt the same way.

An Insult. Mr. Will Hays, chairman of the Republican National Committee, called upon all Republicans, on October 27, to accept the President's appeal as a challenge and an insult. Republicans had been good enough when they assented to the President's proposals, sent their sons into battle and largely paid for the war, but they were "not considered good enough to have a voice in the settlement of the war."

"The President," continued Mr. Hays, "wants just two things : One is full power to settle the war precisely as he and his sole, unelected, unappointed, unconfirmed personal adviser may determine. The other is full power as 'the unembarrassed spokesman in affairs at home,' as he actually demands in his statement, to reconstruct in peace times the great industrial affairs of the nation in the same way, in unimpeded conformity with whatever socialistic doctrines, whatever unlimited government ownership notions, whatever hazy whims may happen to possess him at the time ; but first and above all, with absolute commitment to free trade with all the world, thus giving to Germany out of hand the fruits of a victory greater than she could win by fighting a hundred years. . . . " [15]

Further Autocratic Power Unnecessary. On the issue of the President's leadership Taft also could not agree that Wilson's control of the Government should continue substantially unhampered. "The implied leadership which he (the President) asks," he wrote, "is autocratic power in fields in which the constitution and principles of democracy require that he should consult other representatives of the people than himself. In pursuit of his policies he consults neither his own party nor any other. He wishes a Democratic Senate, not because he would seek the assistance of Democratic Senators in the foreign

---

[15] *Congressional Record,* Vol. 56, Pt. 11, p. 11494.

The charge that Point 3 of the Fourteen Points called for unlimited free trade between all nations was especially pressed in the last days of the campaign. This declaration from the President's speech of January 8 was : "2. The removal, so far as possible, of all economic barriers and the establishment of an equality of trade conditions among all the nations consenting to the peace and associating themselves for its maintenance."

To the suggestion that every industry or individual enjoying tariff protection might expect to have that protection withdrawn in the President's proposed settlement of the war, he replied, in a letter to Senator Simmons : "I, of course, meant to suggest no restriction upon the free determination by any nation of its own economic policy, but only that, whatever tariff any nation might deem necessary for its own economic service, be that tariff high or low, it should apply equally to all foreign nations. Tariff wars are one of the most prolific breeders of the kind of antagonism that results in war." *Congressional Record,* Vol. 56, Pt. 11, pp. 11489–90.

policy concerning which by the fundamental law they are to advise and consent, but because he can mold them to his will without consulting them. He has visited his displeasure on every Democratic member of either House who has differed with him and called upon that member's constituency to reject him." [16]

Was it necessary for the country's welfare, asked Mr. Taft, that the President should be absolute ruler of the nation for two years during the period when peace would be made and reconstruction inaugurated? There would appear to be only one answer to such a question. Probably Taft never regretted asking it. But in the months that followed, as he fought shoulder to shoulder with Wilson against the leadership of his own party in the Senate for the greatest and dearest objective in the lives of both, he must have wondered whether it might have been better to have given Wilson the continued control for which he asked. Wilson was destroyed in the conflict with a Republican Congress which followed the election of 1918, and his party was demolished. From the party standpoint nothing more could be desired; in the longer view the costs of the struggle were tremendous, both in the delay of internal reconstruction which ensued and in the indefinite postponement of an international reconstruction broad and effective enough to give reasonable assurance against the continued recurrence of international anarchy.

Multifarious Corollaries. The probable attitude of the Republican leaders of the Senate toward the President's peace platform was indicated by former Secretary of State Knox, in the Senate on October 28. Congress alone, he declared, had the mandate of the people not only to declare war but to say what the aims of the war were. The President's statements of American war aims were characterized by Mr. Knox as "the multifarious corollaries and subsidiary war aims that have been proposed," as "the mesh of words that cling, some of healthy growth and some as dangerous fungi, upon the sturdy tree of America's war aims" and as "this mass of clustering ideas." They should not be allowed, he indicated, to obstruct either the war or the peace. Before the war was stopped he wanted the word of Foch and Haig, of Diaz and Pershing as to the removal of the German menace, for wars were made "by blood and bullets, not by ink and eloquence."

"As to the 'league of nations' question," he continued: "I will add

[16] *Congressional Record,* Vol. 56, Pt. 11, p. 11488, October 28, 1918.

a few words. The phrase is heard much of late. Some envisage it as a Eutopian world state. Others, less visionary, think of it as a league to enforce peace. In its most extreme form any league of nations will, I believe, have to be relegated to the future quite beyond the purview of the ending of this war or the reconstruction of peace immediately after this war. There will be no room for a task of such problematical possibility in either of the phases of negotiation that now confronts us." [17]

It seems fairly clear that there was here no flaming leadership that would burn its way to the goal of a league of nations "in its most extreme form." There was, however, a league that "now challenges our solicitude." It was "the glorious present alliance" against Germany. If we allowed this league to fall apart or be pried apart "who can say when this world will ever again be so near to having a general league to enforce peace as it is today?" The wise course was to perpetuate it "as a league for the one single purpose of enforcing peace."

While not prepared to attempt to eventuate any "problematical possibility," Knox had no objections to alliances either for war or for peace. The "glorious" alliance of the hour was to be preserved at all costs, especially against the disruptive activities of the President. Neither did he object to the idea of enforcing the peace with its necessary encroachment upon national sovereignty. "Such a league," he observed, "like any league will demand some encroachment upon the conception of complete and independent sovereignty."

The Senator could not know how "entangling" any "alliance" would soon seem to him and how urgent the preservation of total sovereignty.

Democratic Rebuttal. In the general debate which followed his speech the issue of leadership was sharply defined by Senator Pittman, of Nevada. The question to be decided, he said, was "whether or not the President of the United States, who has successfully conducted this war and who has the confidence of the world, shall continue to the end unhampered, unobstructed, uninterfered with, or whether it shall be taken out of his hands and placed in the hands of Senator Lodge and Senator Penrose."

Mr. Pittman's opinion of the nature of the Senate Republican leadership, was stated as follows: "Every Senator on that side who speaks for his party speaks for the old theories of life, for the old

[17] *Congressional Record,* Vol. 56, Pt. 11 p. 11487.

theories of nations, for force, for war, for murder, for death, for
slaughters throughout all time, and not one word for justice or humanity or peace in the future. Those thoughts are not in their souls. They
have not lived the lives that lead men to think of justice, humanity and
democracy; and yet they, by fortuitous circumstances, are today the
leaders of the great Republican Party in the United States—a party
that any one must admit has done wonderful good in its time. They
are its leaders, and no matter whom the Republicans may elect to this
body or to the House of Representatives, those leaders will dominate
and control and mould them to their way of thinking." [18]

HAD THE PRESIDENT SPOKEN FOR THE NATION?

Roosevelt's Opinion. Mr. Roosevelt endeavored to make clear his
way of thinking about the Fourteen Points on October 30. He repeated
the charge that the third point promised free trade among all the
nations "unless the words are designedly used to conceal President
Wilson's true meaning." Concerning the fourth point calling for
reduction of armaments to the lowest point consistent with domestic
safety, he declared that "Either this is language deliberately used to
deceive" or else it means that we should scrap our army and navy
and rely upon a national constabulary to prevent riot.

On the fifth point, which dealt with the disposition of colonies,
he felt that "Unless the language is deliberately used to deceive, this
means that we are to restore to our brutal enemy the colonies taken
by our allies while they were defending us from the enemy." Point
seven was entirely proper and commonplace; nine was right; ten was
so foolish that even President Wilson had abandoned it, eleven would
involve us in Balkan wars in which we had no interest; twelve proposed "to perpetuate the infamy of Turkish rule in Europe," and as
a sop to the conscience of humanity give the subject races autonomy,
"a slippery word which in a case like this is useful only for rhetorical
purposes"; a part of the thirteenth point was right and the rest "pre-
posterous."

Point fourteen, calling for a league of nations, seemed to be akin
to the Holy Alliance. If founded properly upon nationalism it might

[18] *Congressional Record,* Vol. 56, Pt. 11, pp. 11493, 11497.
Senator Williams, of Mississippi, commenting upon a Republican statement that
the state of Pennsylvania paid more income tax than "the 11 former rebel states"
observed that there was not a Mississippian but who would be glad to pay his Pennsylvania taxes if he could swap incomes, p. 11448.

do a small amount of good, but it would certainly accomplish nothing if more than a moderate amount were attempted, and probably the best first step would be to make the existing league of the allies a going concern.[19]

From Roosevelt's analysis it appeared that there was precious little statesmanship in the President's statements of American war aims. Certainly there was no disposition to urge the President to go abroad and make real the vision in Roosevelt's Nobel Peace Prize address of 1910. He was not now straining for that "Master stroke" whereby "those great Powers honestly bent on peace would form a League of Peace, not only to keep the peace among themselves, but to prevent, by force if necessary, its being broken by others." Certainly in his judgment Mr. Wilson was not to be "the ruler or statesman" who by bringing about such a combination "would have earned his place in history for all time and his title to the gratitude of all mankind." [20]

None of Wilson's statements on war aims had qualified him for this great guerdon, in Roosevelt's view. The President's four supplementary points, dated on February 11, 1918, were to him "sound moral aphorisms of no value save as they may be defined in each particular case." His five points of September 27, 1918, Roosevelt assessed as "on the whole mischievous." They either meant nothing or they meant that we were to enter a league "in which we make believe that our deadly enemies, stained with every kind of brutality and treachery, are as worthy of friendship as the allies who have fought our battles for four years." [21]

A statesmanship which looked forward to a unity of all peoples in which both victor and vanquished might hope to find relief from the deadly circle of suspicion, fear, armaments and war was beyond many Americans at the time. Mr. Roosevelt was by no means the only one who was thus gripped by the mentality of war and combat.

[19] *Kansas City Star*, October 30, 1918.
Point No. 8, said Mr. Roosevelt, revealed the President's "besetting sin—his inability to speak in a straightforward manner."
This point said: "8. All French territory should be freed and the invaded portions restored, and the wrong done to France by Prussia in 1870 in the matter of Alsace-Lorraine, which has unsettled the peace of the world for nearly fifty years, should be righted, in order that peace may once more be made secure in the interest of all."
[20] *The Independent*, May 12, 1910. See Roosevelt's address quoted in Chapter 1.
[21] *Kansas City Star*, October 30, 1918.
Mr. Roosevelt indicated the effect of the President's utterances upon him in a letter of June 23, 1915, to his friend Mr. Owen Wister. "Nothing," he wrote, "is more sickening than the continual praise of Wilson's English, of Wilson's style." O. Wister, *Roosevelt, The Story of a Friendship*, N. Y., 1930, p. 344.

Earlier Republican Comments. There is every reason to believe, however, that the President's statements of American war aims had as a whole been accepted by the American people not with mere passivity but with acclaim. The effect of the President's address of January 8, 1918, containing the Fourteen Points, had been such that Senator Lodge said of it, "It is a very able message, presenting a concrete proposition." The only note of questioning from other Senators was stated also by Frederick H. Gillett, the Republican floor leader in the House, who said, "I am in hearty accord with the President's address unless he meant universal free trade by his allusion to economic freedom, and I do not believe that could have been his intention."

Others of the minority leaders in the House added their hearty approval. "I am wonderfully pleased with the message. It contains no cheap diplomacy," said Representative Simeon D. Fess, of Ohio, while Ex-Speaker Joseph G. Cannon expressed his pleasure by saying: "The President is always strong in his addresses. I wish this one could be read by every man, woman and child and thoroughly explained in Germany and Austria." [22]

Harvey's Tribute. Colonel George Harvey, now one of the President's most caustic critics, wrote of his address of January 8 four days after it was delivered: ". . . Mr. Wilson's declaration was a veritable masterpiece. He has never done, and we doubt if anybody living could have done better. We particularly liked his definiteness. . . . His numerical summary of the fourteen war aims . . . was tremendously effective." [23]

These were strong words, but Harvey improved upon them in his comment upon the President's Fourth of July address, six months later, saying: "No such Fourth of July address as that of President Wilson at Mount Vernon ever has or probably ever again will be heard in the country's history." It was, "altogether one of the most impressive utterances that ever fell from the lips or pen of an American statesman. . . . Never did an American spokesman for the American people rise more superbly to a great occasion. . . . It was simply a masterpiece so near to being flawless in taste, in style and in virile substance that it would be probably a bootless undertaking to attempt to find a flaw in it." Commending again the state-

[22] *New York Times,* January 9, 1918; *Congressional Record,* Vol. 56, Pt. 11, p. 11489.

[23] *The North American Review War Weekly,* January 12, 1918, Vol. 1, No. 2, p. 1.

ment of war aims contained in the address, Harvey concluded: "As long as generations to come read the history of our share in the great world war just so long will this 1918 Fourth of July address of President Wilson's at Washington's tomb be read and admired as a dominant monument in our history." [24]

A Far Carrying Voice. Perhaps the President's war messages never quite gained a universal hearing but they did not miss it far. It is well known that his speeches distributed in the Central Powers in great quantities were one of the chief factors in the breakdown of morale which preceded the military collapse of the Teutonic Alliance.[25] The currency of his principles in the Allied and neutral countries was much greater. Nor did his words—those all too effective vehicles of his thought so hated by his opponents—stop even there. Travelers in the remoter regions of the earth soon began to send in reports from all quarters similar to those of the Mission superintendent of the Meerut district in India who reported that "Somehow these people have heard extracts of what President Wilson has said and it has gripped their hearts as nothing else has done since the war began." [26]

[24] *Ibid.*, July 13, 1918. Vol. 1, No. 28, p. 3.
Harvey did not then realize how soon it would be necessary to call up the shade of Father Washington to combat Wilson.
Four months later he was saying that if the time had really come "when we must submerge our independence in a World Government or, as Mr. Wilson put it at Mt. Vernon in 'a definite tribunal of opinion *to which all must submit*' we naturally want the U. S. A. to have a voice in the management." (November 23, 1918, Vol. I, No. 47, pp. 2–3.)
Only two weeks after the Mt. Vernon address, however, Harvey reported the Republican gathering at Saratoga, attended by Roosevelt, Taft and Root, and in an editorial entitled "Roosevelt: Man of Destiny" asked to whom else were the people turning as "their logical inevitable leader?" (July 27, 1918, No. 30, p. 12.)
In April he deplored partisanship in the coming election and urged that the political complexion of the House of Representatives be not changed. Could nothing be done, he plead, "to avert the calamitous effects of a bitter political contest throughout the nation, already beginning and bound to rage with increasing virulence . . . ?" (April 6, 1918. No. 14, p. 5; April 13, No. 15, p. 1.)
In November his attacks on the Democratic Congress indicated that it had committed all the possible sins. The President's appeal he branded as "a menace to all mankind. This is not exaggeration; it is sober truth. God Save the Republic." (October 26, 1918, No. 43, pp. 2–5; November 2, No. 44, p. 2.)
[25] H. D. Lasswell, *Propaganda Technique in the World War*, N. Y., 1927, pp. 216–18.
"Such matchless skill as Wilson showed in propaganda was never equalled in the world's history. . . . While he fomented discord abroad, Wilson fostered unity at home. A nation of one hundred million people, sprung from many alien and antagonistic stocks, was welded into a fighting whole, 'to make the world safe for democracy.'" The magic of his eloquence, adds Mr. Lasswell, soothed suspicions of "the Colossus of the North" among the Latin American peoples and brought most of them into the war on the Allied side. Mr. Wilson's success raised him to a lone pinnacle of power and caused his name to be "spoken with reverence in varied accents in the remotest corners of the earth."
[26] *Washington Post*, October 5, 1918.
A little later, the Associated Press reported from Trieste that "one big factor in

Writing in 1924 Dr. William T. Ellis said: "I think it is true that no other mortal man has ever attained so nearly absolutely universal fame as President Wilson. Often I have pondered the subject while in lands far outside the currents of civilized life." The illiterate millions of the backward continents know nothing of the men ordinarily called famous in civilized lands, continued Dr. Ellis, "but because of his magic appeal to the deepest sensibilities of all human life, which were given the wings of the morning by the unprecedented propaganda of the Allies, the Wilson principles quickly spread to the uttermost parts of the earth. There the innate vitality of the ideals caused them to take root and to grow. As no other wholly human man had ever done before, Woodrow Wilson voiced the basic instincts and desires of the race." [27]

Were the American people uninformed or unappreciative of these same pleas for a world in which liberty and democracy and peace might be more secure? On the contrary, press and pulpit and platform carried the President's messages to every corner of the country and evoked a response which lifted the war to a plane where almost everyone could see some positive compensations ahead for the unmeasurable agony which the chief civilized nations of the globe endured.

For a Reign of Law. In the opinion of one of the closest students of American politics there was no serious objection to the President's statement of our objectives in the war. "To have defended American participation in the World War upon the narrow ground of a mere attempt to redress the grievances arising out of the arbitrary conduct of the belligerent powers would have evoked little response from the majority of the American people. To put it upon the broader ground of a crusade to establish the reign of law in the affairs of the nations in place of the tyranny of the mailed fist was to appeal to the strongest instincts of true Americans. Throughout the struggle the President's public statements of the American war aims received the warm approval of the people. . . ." [28]

---

the disintegration of the (Austrian) empire's political fabric was the diplomatic writings of President Wilson before the United States entered the war. These were widely circulated and dozens of people have told the correspondent that Mr. Wilson's notes and speeches gave them an understanding of what a real democracy was like and encouraged their hopes for democracy." All continued "to look to him for help in solving their political problems sanely and justly so that there shall be no more war." *Washington Post*, November 8, 1918.

[27] *Literary Digest*, February 16, 1924, Vol. LXXX, No. 7, p. 1.
[28] A. N. Holcombe, *Political Parties of Today*, N. Y., 1924, p. 297.

SHOULD WILSON'S LEADERSHIP CONTINUE?

Was Mr. Wilson justified in asking for authority to carry out his peace program without having to deal with a Republican Senate? The answer must depend upon the verdict which is ultimately passed upon the character of the Republican leadership of the time in the Senate. The President knew these men and was entitled to his opinion of their probable attitude toward him in the event that they should control the Senate in a period of Republican resurgence.

Ex-President Charles W. Eliot, of Harvard University, wrote, on October 31, that the current conduct of the Republican leaders vindicated the President's judgment as to their probable action if given control of Congress. The determined drive to force the President to abandon negotiations with Germany and Austria in favor of "unconditional surrender" was immediate evidence of their general attitude.[29] "If they think and act that way in a very critical moment while they represent a minority party," asked Mr. Eliot, "how would they treat the Administration if they come to represent the majority party?" [30]

Mr. Hoover's Stand. Strong support for the President's statesmanship in dealing with both the enemy and the allied peoples came also, at the close of the campaign, from another great American who had been more detached from party politics than Mr. Eliot in his study. "If the final overthrow and surrender of autocracy can be accomplished through the Germans and their allied peoples," wrote Mr. Herbert Hoover, "the President will not only save the lives of a million American boys and countless innocent women and children, but will have attained more complete victory and a more permanent guarantee of peace than by any other means."

"I am for President Wilson's leadership," declared Mr. Hoover emphatically, "not only in the conduct of the war, but also in the negotiations of peace, and afterward in the direction of America's burden in the rehabilitation of the world. There is no greater monu-

---

[29] Even Mr. Taft, with all his love of peace and of moderate action, was reported as joining, at Portsmouth, New Hampshire, in the plea for a Republican Congress so that President Wilson could be held to demand unconditional surrender by Germany and not allowed to make a peace by negotiation. *Washington Post,* November 2, 1918.

[30] *New York Times,* October 31, 1918. On the positive side Mr. Eliot said: "He has given the United States a position in human affairs which no other nation has ever possessed or now possesses."

ment to any man's genius than the conduct of negotiations with the enemy by the President." [31]

The Administration View. Mr. Hoover, however, was not then a leader in the Republican Party. Roosevelt and Lodge were. It was their influence with which the President had to reckon. The Administration view of the meaning of their triumph was stated by Attorney General Gregory who charged, on the same day that Mr. Hoover's letter was made public, that Roosevelt had "systematically from the outbreak of the war devoted himself to carping and vicious criticism of all that had been done." He had "by every means in his power sought to destroy the confidence reposed by the people in the President and to weaken the authority with which the latter was clothed. In a more subtle way, the leader of the Republican Party in the Senate had pursued the same course." [32]

Wilson was well aware of the depth of the feeling against him in Roosevelt and his friends in the Senate and was concerned for his leadership after the elections of 1918 months before they occurred. He told Vice President Marshall in the Spring that he expected to ask for a Democratic Congress.[33] In June he asked his Secretary, Joseph Tumulty, to suggest a way of asking the country for its support without arousing party rancor. Mr. Tumulty suggested that he might reply to a letter, as Roosevelt had done in 1908, but the President finally decided that it was best to make a direct, open appeal.[34] Whatever else may be said about the appeal, it was straightforward.

It was, moreover, an expression of one of Mr. Wilson's most deep seated beliefs, that the people themselves could be successfully appealed to in a time of crisis. He had found direct appeal to the public of great assistance to him in his battle for democracy in Prince-

---

[31] *Washington Post,* November 4, 1918. Quoted from a letter to Mr. Frederic R. Coudert, of New York City.

[32] *New York Times,* November 4, 1918.

Roosevelt's bitterness toward the President long antedated our entry into the War. Panting for war with Germany many months before it came, Wilson attempting to preserve neutrality was to him "the real enemy; the demagogue, adroit, tricky, false, without one spark of loftiness in him, without a touch of the heroic in his cold, selfish and timid soul." O. Wister, *Roosevelt, The Story of a Friendship,* N. Y., 1930, p. 355. From a letter of February 5, 1916, to Mr. Wister.

After our entry into the war Roosevelt's base opinion of the President failed to improve. Discussing his leadership at one point with Mr. Wister, "He sprang to his feet like a boy, stood with his arm flung out, and exclaimed:
"'Oh—don't—let's—talk about him—any more today—at all!'" *Roosevelt, The Story of a Friendship,* p. 371.

[33] *Recollections of Thomas R. Marshall,* Indianapolis, 1925, pp. 362-3. Marshall suggested that both parties be invited merely to nominate men who were pledged to win the war and stand by the President.

[34] J. Tumulty, *Woodrow Wilson as I Know Him,* N. Y., 1921, pp. 322-26.

ton University, and again as Governor of New Jersey; he was to show his faith that the people would judge rightly, as he saw the right, on two later occasions of great importance. This fundamental principle in Wilson's political creed has been attacked as subversive of representative government. If too frequently used it might become so. At least it does not indicate a desire to accomplish things in a closet with no idea that the people as a whole would consider them to be desirable steps.

A Legislative Record Without Parallel. Up to that time, too, the American people had given Woodrow Wilson everything he asked. For six years he had required of their representatives more than any other President had ever attempted. He had never been denied. It has become a commonplace to say that the legislative record of Wilson's Administration before we entered the war is quite without parallel. The first Income Tax Law, the Clayton Anti-Trust Law, the establishment of the Federal Trade Commission, the Smith Lever Act, the Keating-Owen Child Labor Act, the Underwood Tariff Act, the La Follette Seaman's Law, the Jones Act for the government of the Philippines, the Adamson Railway Labor Law, the creation of the Federal Land Bank System, the Overman Act, the establishment of the Federal Reserve System, the National Defence Act of 1916 and other laws only less important were put through in an astonishingly rapid succession during the years before we entered the war. "Taken as a whole," in the judgment of an unusually keen political analyst, "the Wilsonian program exemplifies little short of a miracle in legislative leadership." [35]

This may be granted without endorsing in full all the laws named. But Mr. Wilson's very success was by 1918 an element of serious weakness. Nearly all of these laws had been pressed through Congresses that would never have enacted them without feeling the propulsion of the President's powerful will and influence. They had left many sore spots in Congress, in the Democratic Party as well as the Republican. Furthermore, almost every legislative success which the President achieved won him "a new group of unforgiving enemies" outside Congress. Powerful economic groups found their interests or prejudices affected. Most of them fought the proposed legislation without avail. To this day there are bankers of Democratic allegiance who would grant all the gains of the Federal Reserve System but who dislike Woodrow Wilson because he created it against their

[35] Wm. B. Munro, *The Makers of the Unwritten Constitution,* N. Y., 1930, p. 144.

opposition. "No other President since Jackson's time left such a trail of bruised and bitter feelings behind him." [36]

A Victorious War. War time legislation naturally added to the number of the President's fellow countrymen who bided a chance to bring his leadership to a close. The very act of entry into the war cost him the support of large elements who had voted for him in 1916 in the hope that he would keep the United States out of it. The war itself brought compulsion, repression, a changed way of living to everybody in some degree. People do not enjoy compulsion. The Democrats in the House of Representatives revolted at conscription by more than three to one; only a Republican vote as heavily in favor of the measure put it into operation. The President spoke truly in saying that the Republican leadership in Congress had not been anti-war.

The great majority of the people responded wholeheartedly to the war, some under one pull, some under another. But in the terrific effort to mould every individual into a contributing cog in the war machine multitudes of feelings were injured, sometimes unnecessarily. The spy fever, suspicion of sedition, the suppression of any activity, commercial or otherwise, that might give aid and comfort to the enemy, the stimulation of the lukewarm, the repression of objectors —all of these inevitable elements of modern warfare were reflected in laws which operated more harshly upon many individuals than they felt necessary or justified. The marshalling of all economic forces, too, caused large economic units to feel that others had been favored at their expense or had not borne their fair share of the burden. Some of these beliefs were unfounded, but they were held nevertheless. Inevitably, exact justice was not done.

Whatever the grievances that people had against President Wilson his election appeal for continued control made them vocal. A leading newspaper man retained the impression years later of "a roar of anger from coast to coast. An avalanche of denunciation followed." [37]

Previous Electoral Appeals in War Time

It was time for Woodrow Wilson to be concerned about his leadership in the crucial years to come when the supreme task of making a peace that would have some guarantee of permanence would have

[36] *Ibid.*, pp. 134, 135.
[37] Frank R. Kent, *A History of the Democratic Party*, N. Y., 1928, p. 433.

to be met. There were sufficient precedents, too, for an appeal to the people to permit the Administration in charge of a war to settle it. In 1864, President Lincoln had urged upon the people the unwisdom of "swapping horses in midstream." Concluding a civil war and a foreign war are not exactly analogous undertakings, of course, yet on October 11, 1898, President McKinley had plead for a Republican Congress in a speech at Boone, Iowa, saying, "This is no time for divided councils. If I would have you remember anything I have said in these desultory remarks, it would be to remember at this critical hour in the nation's history we must not be divided. The triumphs of the war are yet to be written in the articles of peace." [38]

The McKinley appeal was not so spectacularly made as that of 1918, but it was pressed as strongly by his supporters on exactly the same grounds. Ex-President Benjamin Harrison besought the people to "stand behind the President," saying: "If the word goes forth that the people of the United States are standing solidly behind the President, the task of the peace commissioners will be easy, but if there is a break in the ranks—if the Democrats score a telling victory, if Democratic Senators, Congressmen, and Governors are elected—Spain will see in it a gleam of hope, she will take fresh hope, and a renewal of hostilities, more war, may be necessary to secure us what we have already won." [39]

Sustain the President. Theodore Roosevelt, too, as a candidate for Governor of New York, in 1898, had been fully as solicitous about the impression abroad, and the success of the Administration's peace plans, as Woodrow Wilson was in 1918. In the earlier year, as candidate for Governor of New York, Roosevelt had said: "Remember that whether you will or not, your votes this year will be viewed by the nations of Europe from one standpoint only. They will draw no fine distinctions. A refusal to sustain the President this year will, in their eyes, be read as a refusal to sustain the war and to sustain the efforts of our peace commission to secure the fruit of the war. Such a refusal may not inconceivably bring about a rupture of the peace negotiations. It will give heart to our defeated antagonists; it will make possible the interference of those doubtful neutral nations in the struggle who have wished us ill." [40]

---

[38] Joseph Tumulty, *Woodrow Wilson as I Know Him*, N. Y., 1921, p. 328.
[39] *Ibid.*
[40] Lawrence, *The True Story of Woodrow Wilson*, p. 237. These appeals of 1898 were made, too, before the issue of imperialism had divided the country. In late October, when the crux of the negotiations with Spain came, President McKinley had not yet made up his mind to so far depart from our traditional policy of isola-

The Overshadowing Issue. Henry Cabot Lodge, also, speaking before the Republican State Convention in Massachusetts on October 6, 1898, had said: "But there is one question on which I do desire to say a few words and that seems to me to override all others. It is whether we shall stand by the Administration and the President at this juncture. If we give a victory to his political opponents, we say not only to the United States but we say to the world, we say to the Spanish Commissioners in Paris, that the people of the United States repudiated the result of the war and repudiated the man who has led it victoriously and is now leading us back to peace—William McKinley.

"That is the great overshadowing question to my mind. . . . Hostilities have ceased, but this war is not over. . . . There are only two parties in this country where there is a great question like this to settle; one is the party that sustains the American President who does his work well, and those who do not." [41]

Doubtless Lodge may have felt in 1918 that Wilson had not done his work sufficiently well to merit the same degree of support, but in 1898 he was in no doubt as to the duty of every American to hold up the President's hands and let him settle the war as he saw fit. The President was the "constitutional representative" in such matters. Said Lodge on October 26, 1898, there is one man who has to deal with "the extent to which we should go into the new policies involved in the war—that is the President of the United States. I have faith in him. I believe in his Americanism, and as the Constitution has charged him with this great duty, I, as one American citizen am prepared to stand back and allow the constitutional representative to deal with it in the face of Europe and of the world, and to settle it, and it is my desire, and I should think it should be the duty of every patriot, to stand behind him and to hold up his hands and not to cross him." [42]

Speaker Reed was touring the country at the same time urging "every man who loves his country to strengthen McKinley's hands," and Senator Penrose was declaring that "It is difficult to overestimate the supreme importance of sustaining the President of the United States and the Republican Party at the present critical crisis in our foreign relations." [43]

No Divided Leadership in Making Peace. These widespread

tion as to acquire a remote colonial empire in Asia. W. F. Johnson, *History of American Foreign Relations,* N. Y., 1916, Vol. II, p. 266.
  [41] *Springfield Republican,* October 7, 1898.
  [42] *Springfield Republican,* October 27, 1898.
  [43] *Philadelphia Inquirer,* October 8 and 22, 1898.

appeals of the Republican leaders of 1898 were heartily supported by the Republican press. The *New York Sun* laid upon all patriotic citizens of every political party the duty of supporting the Administration both by voice and by vote. The stream was not yet crossed. The *Chicago Tribune* plead that President McKinley was entitled to the election of a Congress that would sustain his policy. The *Topeka Capital* put it squarely "to the good sense of the country whether or not the election of a Congress in sympathy with a President who has shown himself equal to every test would be for the best interests of the country at this time." The verdict of the *Kansas City Star* was that "The people have stood together, regardless of politics, in supporting the Government in prosecuting the war, and there is sound logic in the contention of the Republicans that there should be no change in the control of Congress until the issues arising out of the war have been settled." [44]

It is not to be assumed that the conditions were exactly analogous in the campaigns of 1898 and 1918. Some contend that the Democrats had been more anti-McKinley than the Republicans had been anti-Wilson and that the danger of McKinley's peace plans being sabotaged was greater. There can be no doubt that the treaty of peace with Spain narrowly escaped defeat in the Senate, in 1899, and it seems as clearly established that it passed the Senate only as a result of the sustained exertion of the full influence of the leader of the Democratic party, Wm. J. Bryan.[45] It might well have failed even then if the Republicans had not had majority control of the Senate.

The Republicans most probably had reason to look to their leadership in 1898. Certainly they made the utmost endeavor to capitalize the war spirit of the time and continue their control on the ground of the right to finish what they had so gloriously begun. The part which the President had in that campaign was by no means so central as Mr. Wilson's in 1918. Probably Wilson erred in making his appeal so directly. He should have remembered, too, that in spite of his phenomenal successes and the great schism in the Republican Party, a majority of the people in the country had long been Republicans and that there is a mystic power in the name "Republican" which has a strong hold on those who have once responded to it.

[44] *Chicago Tribune*, November 6, 1898; *Topeka Daily Capital*, November 3, 1898; *Kansas City Star*, November 3, 1898; *New York Sun*, November 2, 1898.
[45] D. F. Fleming, *The Treaty Veto of the American Senate*, N. Y., 1930, pp. 119–123. The Treaty of Paris was approved by the Senate on February 6, 1899, 57 to 27, with two votes to spare.

Purposeless Confusion. The rank and file of the Republicans had not been so anti-Administration as the militant wing of their leaders. Moreover, the belief that the Republican Party is the one fitted and destined to rule was something to reckon with. Holding that belief it seems always the normal and natural thing for Republicans to control. Roosevelt had argued against a mid term change of Congressional control, in a letter of August 18, 1906, to James E. Watson, not on the ground that a grave crisis was in solution but that none existed. He had not felt the issues involved to be partisan and believed that a change of leadership would only give "purposeless confusion." [46] There can be no doubt that Wilson felt in 1918, particularly as Roosevelt's campaign turned against his peace proposals, that control of the Senate by the party of which the Colonel had regained the direction would mean purposeful confusion for the President's peace plans.

A Republican Senate Elected

Whether Wilson's letter to the voters lost him the election of 1918 is not wholly clear, although his critics do not have a particle of doubt about it. Democratic candidates for Congress made the most of the statement. The Republicans, on the other hand, had only to hold their normal strength in line. They did not do this if we compare the great majorities in the Roosevelt era and in the Harding-Coolidge period. The general opinion is that the letter aided the Republicans in regaining a sufficient proportion of their normal membership to enable them to control the Congress. They carried thirteen seats in the House by majorities of a few hundred while the Democrats won nine by equally small margins. For the Senate the Republicans won in Delaware 21,519 to 20,113; in Rhode Island the vote was 42,055 to 37,573; in New Hampshire 35,528 to 34,458; in Colorado 107,726 to 104,347; in Michigan 220,054 to 212,487.[47]

Since the Republican majority in the new Senate was only two it seems probable that the appeal lost the Senate to Mr. Wilson in these normally Republican states. However, lacking exhaustive evidence, it

---

[46] Joseph Tumulty, *Woodrow Wilson as I Know Him*, N. Y., 1921, p. 328.
[47] *Congressional Directory*, 67th Cong., 2nd Sess. December, 1921, pp. 149–56. Dr. C. A. Beard states that "Taking the vote state by state, the Democrats in 1918 were victorious, but the Republicans won the House; if each party had secured a number of representatives proportional to its share of the vote state by state, the Democrats would have had 231 members and the Republicans 193, whereas the tables were almost reversed." C. A. Beard, *American Government and Politics*, Fourth Rev. Ed., N. Y., 1921, p. 227.

may be that it served to cut down Republican majorities that would have been larger and at least to hold the scales quite even. When all the forces involved are considered and the normal reaction against the party in power at the mid term election, when the Presidency is not at stake, is added, the election of 1918 does not appear to have been either a great victory for the Republicans or a great defeat for the President.

The most careful analysis of the election available, after examination of the forces and questions which determined the result in each of the 37 senatorial contests, comes to the following conclusions: "The forces which determined the several elections were sometimes local, sometimes general. They included support for or hostility to prohibition; the tendency of the business interests, large and small, to back the Republican party; pressure for a high tariff in industrial districts; objection on the part of food producers and distributors to the fixing of food prices, especially as the South had profited enormously from unregulated cotton prices; resentment in the states where General Leonard Wood was popular that the administration had not permitted him to go to France; the attitude of the Non-Partisan League or of its anti-agrarian opponents, and the enthusiastic support by the women of those who appealed for their new suffrages. There was virtually no issue contested and properly discussed which arose out of the policies that were the cause of our entering the war, of the degree of efficiency with which it was conducted, of the aims announced for the United States by its official spokesman, or of the effort which the United States was to put forth in the making of a durable peace." [48]

Whatever the degree of repudiation which President Wilson and his peace program had suffered, the result of the election does not seem to have swerved him from his course in the slightest, unless it steeled a resolve not to be blocked in his greatest undertaking. It did give the ruling chiefs of the reunited Republicans the right to feel that the future was probably in their hands and an equal determination that his influence should not prevent the return of the Presidency to them two years later.

In any event the President let his electoral appeal stand for what it was worth. Faced with evidence that it was a shock to many Republican voters, he refused to issue any supplementary statement or to comment on the victory of the Republicans after the election.[49] The war

[48] Charles P. Howland, *American Foreign Relations, 1928*, Yale Press, New Haven, 1928, pp. 243–45. The attention of the reader is called to the entire chapter, pp. 239–46.
[49] David Lawrence, *The True Story of Woodrow Wilson*, N. Y., 1924, pp. 238–9.

was rushing to a dramatic close. Each day brought news of great and thrilling gains by the American and Allied armies. The German Imperial Government was collapsing, in large measure because of Wilson's steady insistence that it must go. The Armistice came within a week. Mighty celebrations, tremendous relief, ecstatic joy—the War was over!

But the Peace was not yet won.

CHAPTER III

THE PLAN OF OPPOSITION

SHORTLY before the election of 1918 the *Washington Post* observed in a leading editorial that it would be generally admitted that President Wilson was surrounded by strong men from whom he might obtain wise counsel and that when the election was over, no matter who won, the President would have united support in insisting upon "a peace with victory and the accomplishment of the aims he has so far so eloquently and so ably described."[1]

As soon as the returns were in Mr. Taft set himself to the task of inducing the President to team with Lodge and Knox, the Senate leaders who were backed by Colonel Roosevelt. He warned Wilson to consult the Foreign Relations Committee of the Senate in making the peace, specifically suggesting the appointment of Senators as his negotiators. At the same time he cautioned the new Senate leaders that "should they develop obstructive tactics while the President is attempting to carry out a policy in the interest of the country and the world the party will be made to suffer for it in the next election."

It cannot be said that Taft was able to note any swift rushing together of the opposing leaders he had sought to unite for a great common achievement. The ending of the war and the victory over Germany claimed all attention for a few days. As soon as the Armistice celebrations had subsided Senators Knox and Poindexter attacked the league proposal. The former referred to it as "a novel idea"; the latter declared it would necessitate abrogation of the Monroe Doctrine and revision of the Constitution. They were soon seconded by an opponent of the President in his own party, Senator James A. Reed, of Missouri.[2]

On November 15, the editor of the *Washington Post* was surprised

---

[1] *Washington Post*, October 30, 1918. On November 7 the *Post* thought, "The returns would seem to indicate that the voters regarded domestic questions as of more importance to them at this particular juncture than the war."
[2] *Washington Post*, November 16, 22, 1918.

to find that "Opposition has suddenly developed in this country to the proposal for a league of nations to guarantee the permanency of the peace that has been won in the war. It is unexpected, because from the beginning of America's participation in the conflict by common consent it was understood that once the issues of the war were decided steps would be taken jointly by the powers to protect against a possible repetition of it." Recalling many of the statements of the President and other Allied leaders, the *Post* concluded: "Unquestionably the United States is committed to the principle of a league of nations for the conservation of peace, and there would seem to be no more opportune time in which to put it in practical effect than the present." [3]

CRITICISM OF THE PEACE COMMISSION

No announcement was made of the President's plans during the Armistice period. How would he interpret his promise to the voters to accept their judgment "without cavil"? Would he take the Republican leaders, whose control he had asked to be delivered from, into his counsels in making the peace? The answer could not long be delayed. It was forecast by rumors that he would head the delegation to the Peace Conference himself.

Should the President Go? This prospect did not please the opposition. Reports that some of the Allied leaders would rather he did not come were eagerly quoted. To the plea that he was not wanted in Europe the *Literary Digest* replied, on December 14, 1918, that "in all fairness it must be said that the reports of an eager desire for President Wilson's presence at the peace table on the part of nearly every nation and class in Europe vastly outnumber the hints of uneasiness about his coming." It was true, according to the Roman weekly *L'Unita*, that conservative Nationalist groups in Europe were trying to boycott the league idea quietly, but they did not dare to oppose it openly, because of American advocacy and because the majority of their own soldiers had fought, "above all," in the belief that they were helping to usher in a new international régime which would make similar sacrifices unnecessary in the future. The European reactionaries therefore

[3] Two weeks later the *Post* spoke in a totally different tone. It was "quite evident that any league of nations formed in the forthcoming conference would have to be held in abeyance in America until the people could express their will." *Washington Post*, November 30, 1918.

By December 5 the *Post* was saying: "The project for a league of nations takes on dimmer outlines as it is approached, and it is particularly baffling when the question is asked, Is Germany to be a member of the League?"

smiled sardonically over the league, talked about it as little as possible and prepared to put all sorts of obstacles and quibbles in its path.

Some of the President's supporters felt it inadvisable for him to come into personal contact with these forces. They felt it better for him to remain quietly in the White House, ready to make major decisions in the calm of his study as the Conference progressed. His Secretary of State, Robert Lansing, held this view strongly. The desire to have the President at home, however, was especially keen among his opponents. It appeared that his firm guidance was wanted in domestic legislation and reconstruction. How could Congress operate without him?

Definite announcement on November 18 that he would go to France made the criticism acute. Colonel Roosevelt declared that "no public end of any kind" was to be served by President Wilson going to the Conference. "Our allies and our enemies and Mr. Wilson himself should all understand," said Mr. Roosevelt, on November 26, "that Mr. Wilson has no authority whatever to speak for the American people at this time. His leadership has just been emphatically repudiated by them. The newly elected Congress comes far nearer than Mr. Wilson to having a right to speak the purposes of the American people at this moment. Mr. Wilson and his Fourteen Points and his four supplementary points and his five complementary points and all his utterances every which way have ceased to have any shadow of right to be accepted as expressive of the will of the American people. He is President of the United States. He is a part of the treaty-making power; but he is only a part. If he acts in good faith to the American people, he will not claim any representative capacity in himself to speak for the American people. He will say frankly that his personal leadership has been repudiated, and that he now has merely the divided official leadership which he shares with the Senate." [4]

The result of the election had not changed Mr. Roosevelt's attitude toward the President and his peace program. Although none knew bet-

---

[4] *Kansas City Star,* November 26, 1918; David Houston, *Eight Years with Wilson's Cabinet,* N. Y., 1926, Vol. I, pp. 359–60.

The opposite view is that the election of 1918 was decided on local and domestic issues and not upon the President's peace program. The *Review of Reviews* for December, 1918, said editorially:

"There is no evidence at all, however, that the country intended in this election to disapprove in any manner of President Wilson or of his policies. . . . Even Presidents are mistaken at times: and Mr. Wilson was wrong in assuming that the election of Congressmen in November, in the minds of the voters, would carry the significance he suggested. Never in the history of the United States has any President been as strongly supported in his large policies, regardless of party, as has President Wilson. He may go to Europe feeling that the country is behind him with hearty and sympathetic support. . . ."

ter than he that the power to negotiate treaties had long rested securely in the hands of the President, he was now sure that a share of "the divided official leadership" belonged to the Senate. In his view the election had totally destroyed both the President's personal leadership and his capacity to speak as a representative of the American people. If so the country was indeed in a quandary. The newly elected Senate had no power to negotiate, even if it had a constructive policy and the voice to express it. Besides it could not come into existence until after March 4, 1919, before which the major decisions of the Peace Conference would probably be made.

In the meantime, the Armistice had been concluded, two weeks earlier, on the basis of the Fourteen Points. Both the Allied and enemy governments had specifically agreed to make peace "on the terms laid down in the President's address to Congress of January 8, 1918, and the principles of settlement enunciated in his subsequent addresses."[5] Every nation in the conflict had agreed to make peace on this basis. If these principles were not to be used what others would be? What possible alternative offered any hope of a peace just and stable enough to endure?

Be that as it might, Roosevelt was willing to make it clear to the foreign negotiators with whom Wilson was soon to deal that if his influence counted in the new Senate, Wilson's policies would meet with short shrift—"his Fourteen Points and his four supplementary points and his five complementary points and all his utterances every which way. . . ."

Should Senators Be Sent? Such a situation was surely without precedent. How would the President meet it? Would he attempt to secure his ends by appointing Senators as his negotiators? The general opinion probably still continues to be that he should have done so. President McKinley had inaugurated the practice on a large scale, naming Senators on at least five commissions to negotiate treaties. As a matter of tactics it had seemed to be a good plan; the treaties were approved by the Senate.

There was, however, another side to the story not so generally known. Many Senators had keenly resented the appointment of their fellow members as negotiators, on the grounds that the Senate was deprived of the services of important members for long periods and that Senators were thereby made into advocates of treaties when it

[5] Diplomatic Correspondence, *Messages and Papers of Woodrow Wilson*, N. Y., 1925, Vol. I, p. 545.

was their duty to judge them with impartial and open minds. How could a Senator come back and fail to support what he had put his name to? Moreover, when Senate leaders defended their own handiwork on the floor of the Senate was not proper criticism by their colleagues made unfairly difficult? Serious assaults were made also upon such appointments on the ground of constitutionality.

The Senate was twice at the point of taking action to condemn the practice. On the second occasion it was agreed in the Judiciary Committee that Senator Hoar, of Massachusetts, should visit President McKinley and inform him of the feeling of the Senate. He did so and received assurance satisfactory to him that Senators would not receive further appointments as negotiators in that Administration.[6]

A similar revolt against the appointment of Senators to the Commission to Negotiate Peace was not to be expected in 1918. The more immediate problem confronting the President was whom to select. Most people will probably hold that he could have selected Senators of liberal tendencies who would have given him loyal support at Paris. That they could have carried the majority leaders with them is another matter. Senator Knute Nelson, of Minnesota, would have supported strongly the principles laid down by the President, but his appointment would have been a graver affront to Lodge than the omission of all Senators. If any Senator was to be chosen, the new majority leader was entitled to invitation.

The Personnel Chosen.   No Senators were selected. The delegation, announced on November 29, was composed of the President, Secretary Robert A. Lansing, Colonel Edward M. House, Hon. Henry White and General Tasker H. Bliss.

Two of these appointments were generally expected; two were not. The choice of Secretary Lansing was natural and would have been difficult to avoid. He had been a faithful and efficient assistant, though he had as little faith in a League of Nations as Mr. Lodge or Mr. Knox and later did more to injure the President's cause than to advance it. Colonel House had long been the President's most trusted adviser. He had been in Europe much during the War and was at the moment in close confidential touch with the Allied leaders. He could be depended upon to support every effort to prevent the reconstruction of Europe on the old basis of rival alliances.

---

[6] Geo. F. Hoar, *The Autobiography of Seventy Years*, N. Y., 1903, Vol. II, pp. 47–50; D. F. Fleming, "The Advice of the Senate in Treaty Making," Current History, September, 1930, Vol. 32, pp. 1090–95.

The two remaining appointments were undoubtedly made in the belief that those chosen would give the President loyal backing in his major effort. There was every probability that it would take his whole energy to accomplish his objective, without having to deal with serious opposition in his own delegation. General Bliss, who was also in Europe, with a wide knowledge of conditions and leaders, military and otherwise, was an able soldier who was in no sense a militarist. He could be counted on to lend his full weight to a supreme effort to give the world effective legal and pacific means of settling its disputes.

No Republican Leader Taken. This was true likewise of Henry White, whose selection was in many respects the most ideal of all. Previous to his retirement by President Taft, in 1910, he had had a long and distinguished career in the diplomatic service, holding the Ambassadorships to Rome and Paris and other European posts where he had gained wide knowledge of European politics and a friendly, intimate acquaintance with nearly all of the leaders who would be influential in the Peace Conference. Moreover, as the leader of the American delegation to the Algeciras Conference he was the one American available who had been through a great international conference. He knew the maze of clashing national interests and desires which we call European politics as perhaps no man in the country did. He could be invaluable in Paris.

Furthermore, White had the recommendation of close friendship with both Roosevelt and Lodge. Entrusted by Roosevelt with his most difficult diplomatic tasks, White was regarded by him as "The most useful man in the entire diplomatic service, during my Presidency and for many years before." [7] The friendship between the two was deep, and it had continued intimately down to 1918. White had been completely behind Roosevelt in 1912 and had kept in touch with him afterwards. He had had frequent contacts with Lodge and other Republican leaders in the war years. Lodge was pleased by his appointment to the Peace Commission.[8] Roosevelt was delighted. "I am simply overjoyed that Harry White is to be on the Peace Commission," he wrote to Lodge on November 27, 1918. "If ——— had been appointed I would have felt that we had reached a lower point of infamy than has yet been attained."[9] White, when offered the appointment to Paris, did

[7] Allan Nevins, *Henry White, Thirty Years of American Diplomacy,* N. Y., 1930, Testimonial page.
[8] *Ibid.,* pp. 307, 314, 327, 335, 346.
[9] *Letters of Theodore Roosevelt and Henry Cabot Lodge,* N. Y., 1925, Vol. II, p. 548.

not accept until after he had talked by telephone with Roosevelt and Lodge.[10]

His friendship with these men was not, however, the controlling consideration in his selection. He was chosen because he stood essentially for the kind of peace the President intended to work for. This was not necessarily true of the league of nations. He had refused to join the League to Enforce Peace, in 1915, in terms as strong as could be desired. His view changed gradually, his biographer maintains, not by contact with Wilson or any of the other leaders working for a league but under the influence of the hard facts of the situation as they were borne in upon him at Paris.[11]

In whatever way his stand on the league might be modified, White's attitude toward the war had not been dominated by passion or prejudice. Keeping in close touch with the trend of events and ideas, from his home in Washington, by correspondence with relatives in Germany and in the diplomatic service at London and Rome, as well as with distinguished foreign leaders, he was also in a position to check the information received in contacts with the chief diplomats in Washington with his own wide knowledge of European conditions. Horrified at the sinking of the *Lusitania* and condemning German militarism completely, he likewise distrusted aspects of British, French and Italian diplomacy.[12]

Equipped with a broad knowledge of world events, past and present, such as few of his countrymen possessed, he had at the same time a mental poise which enabled him to understand the President's much berated proposal of "a peace without victory." He found Lord Robert Cecil and Ramsay MacDonald inclined to the same view. In the words of the latter, history had shown that "as a rule nations have had victory without peace."[13]

Knowing that White would stand for a peace not dominated by revenge, the President selected him—to act as another echo of his voice, Wilson's critics said.

Who Should Have Gone? The appointment was much condemned. Why was not a more active and prominent Republican chosen, such as Taft or Root? These two were most often spoken of, and the general feeling is still that it would have been wiser to have taken one of them.

---

[10] Nevins, *Henry White*, p. 348.
[11] *Ibid.*, pp. 362, 369. White saw little of Wilson in the early weeks and much more of Lansing, who took more of Lodge's position.
[12] Nevins, *Henry White*, pp. 327, 331, 340.
[13] *Ibid.*, pp. 342–45.

Either would have labored as loyally and as hard as Wilson for the kind of peace he wanted and for organization to preserve it. Each had a strong and sincere desire to advance the cause of world peace.

It was true that both had just taken strong partisan positions against the President. Taft's joint appeals with Roosevelt, in the campaign just closed, and Root's chairmanship of the great New York meeting of January 19, 1918, the climax of the war cabinet drive, were not likely to be forgotten. Moreover, the selection of Taft would not have won Roosevelt, and the opposition of the President's labor following to Root militated against his appointment,[14] as did the President's determination not to have lawyers drafting the treaty.[15] Taft was badly needed in the United States to campaign for the League while the President was away; Root at the Conference would have resisted, in all probability, the strong pressure from home to oppose the President and the League, in spite of his strong tendency to respond to the call of party urgency in any emergency.

Whether Root in Paris could have prevented the series of ultimatums which were to be delivered to the Peace Conference by Republican Senators, and which culminated in the Round Robin of March 4, 1919, can never be known. Nor can we know how many reservations he might have prevented later in the Senate as a returned negotiator. His influence might have been greater or less. Left in the United States, in the full confidence of the opposition, he was important later as a counselor of moderation. He did not prevent the taking of too irrevocable positions in the critical months preceding.

The President Said Little. Likewise all that passed in the mind of the President in the short interval between the Armistice and his departure overseas, on December 4, is not likely to be fully revealed. He said little, if anything, publicly about his peace plans. Whether this was due to the pressure of preparations for his absence, to a feeling that no purpose was to be served by further declarations or to reticence following the failure of his plea for a Democratic Congress, he was strongly censured for not discussing his plans in his message to Congress, on December 2, when he officially announced his departure. In spite of the fact that his full program had been before the country for a year, and prominently during the negotiations for the Armistice,

---

[14] *Ibid.,* pp. 348–49.
[15] His distrust of legal minds for such a task was later expressed to Lansing, "with great candor and emphasis." Robert Lansing, *The Peace Negotiations,* N. Y., 1921, pp. 41, 107.

he was widely criticised by Senators and newspapers for not taking the country into his confidence.

Many of the President's friends in his own party, dispirited by the election, shared in the discontent. Some felt that the taking over of the cables by Executive Order at this time was a blunder; others that the cabinet needed overhauling. Democratic morale was low as the President departed. [16]

Occasionally a Democratic leader did rise to a vigorous counter attack in behalf of his chief. Senator James Hamilton Lewis, of Illinois, addressed Roosevelt and Taft, on December 2, under the caption "Thou Art the Man!" The President had not sought to exclude the Republicans from Congress; he had only asked for a majority to support his views. Every candidate for President in living memory had done the same thing. Otherwise the head had no hands to execute its plans and purposes. "The former Presidents," charged Senator Lewis, "by appeals in marked form, have deluded the people against themselves and caused the Republican voter to stab his own children with the sword of future wars, in obedience to the demand of the former Presidents for the voter to stab the present President."[17]

Should the League Be Defeated?

Taft and Root Counsel Acceptance. If such a result of the electoral appeals threatened, Mr. Taft was now doing his best to undo the damage. On the previous day he had again urged the Senate Republicans not to make an issue of the league. Their opposition to enforcing the peace as contrary to our traditions ignored the fact that the war had happened. If this attitude were persisted in, the logical outcome would be a separate treaty of peace with Germany—an eventuality which he appeared to regard as unthinkable. "Certainly the American people," wrote Taft, "have no doubt that we are to have a full share in the settlement of all the issues. No other inference can be drawn from the messages of the President acquiesced in by all."

The imagination of Senators had been strained to conceive a situation in which the United States would resist a judgment in the international court, and in consequence face destruction by the combined military forces of the league members. If we let our imaginations run riot, said Taft, we could just as easily conceive such a union of the

[16] David Lawrence, *New York Times*, November 26, 1918.
[17] *Washington Post*, December 2, 1918

military forces of the world against the United States without a league
as with one.[18]

Elihu Root was also exerting his influence against the rejection of
the league principle in the same period. On November 26 he accompanied Henry White to Roosevelt's bedside to discuss the peace terms
to be fixed in Paris. In this conference he insisted that the great consideration must be an international organization to prevent future wars.
War must be looked upon as a breach of the peace which offended
and injured all nations. It must be dealt with accordingly. Roosevelt
was too ill to say much but he did endorse the general idea of a league
of nations.[19]

Lodge for Combat. In his final talk with Senator Lodge, White
heard no emphasis on the urgency of a league to keep the peace; that
could wait. The interview was hurried, but in the last hours before
White's departure, Lodge prepared a nine page memorandum for his
guidance in which he stood for as harsh a peace as any European
chauvinist could desire. Heavy indemnities should be exacted and the
break-up of Germany "into its chief component parts" was suggested.
Certainly if Bavaria, for example, should wish to treat separately she
should be encouraged. As for the league of nations, "It need only be said
here that under no circumstances must provisions for such a league be
made a part of the peace treaty which concludes the war with Germany.
Any attempt to do this would not only long delay the signature of the
treaty of peace, which should not be unduly postponed, but it would
make the adoption of the treaty, unamended, by the Senate of the
United States and other ratifying bodies, extremely doubtful." [20]

The Senator's mind was clear on the leading issue. The league was
going to wait. "Under no circumstances" should it be a part of the
treaty of peace. If it were created according to the President's plan it
could look forward at the best to considerable amendment in the Senate,
and, no doubt, in other ratifying bodies.

Mr. Lodge had no doubts at all, either, about his own representative capacity. The President had been and was still to be bitterly condemned for attempting to speak for the American people. His opponents no doubt were never able to believe him capable of doing so,
rightfully in any event. This naturally did not prevent Lodge from
feeling certain of his own authority. In the memorandum under dis-

[18] *Philadelphia Public Ledger*, December 1, 1918.
[19] Nevins, *Henry White*, pp. 351–52.   [20] *Ibid.*, pp. 354–55.

cussion he confidently asserted that its contents represented the views not only of the Republican party, but of the United States.

In order that the true view might prevail he proposed that White should show the memorandum, in strict confidence, to Balfour, Clemenceau and Nitti, Allied leaders known to Lodge personally. This would inform them of the real feeling of the American people "and certainly the Senate of the United States." Thus informed the foreign statesmen might be expected to resist Wilson effectually. *"This knowledge may in certain contingencies be very important to them in strengthening their positions,"* wrote Lodge. White, however, never thought of secretly undermining the President's position in this manner and kept the document wholly secret.[21]

Harvey on the Firing Line. While Mr. Lodge was thus quietly preparing a reception for the President abroad, George Harvey was doing his best to give him a fitting send off as he departed. In order to provide Wilson with a high motive, he wrote—"the underlying purpose being, we haven't a doubt, to project in striking fashion a virtual candidacy for President of the league of nations, which is destined to Dominate the Earth and ensure a Durable Peace for All Time —if it comes off."

After two columns of light ridicule, describing the probable nature of the trip, Harvey suggested that there was after all a good deal to be done at home and ended with the hope that he would "dismiss the whole silly business from his mind." But if he "really should insist upon making a holy show of himself, let him go to it."[22]

Gone were Harvey's ecstatic raptures over the President's war aims, as voiced in his great addresses. His effort to translate these aims into a peace that would substitute union and conference for rival alliances and armament races was now only "silly business," designed, of course, merely to exalt himself. Mr. Harvey appeared to share the sudden desire of many to have the President close at home and was deeply pained when he actually went. It was "the most regrettable and ridiculous performance that this country has ever had to bear up under."[23]

[21] Nevins, *Henry White,* pp. 352–53. Italics added. This *démarche* suggests that Wilson's caution in selecting the Republican member of his Commission was not without justification. It seems to dispose also of the much repeated suggestion that if the President had only taken Lodge with him to Paris the latter would have mellowed into contented coöperation with the President's chief objectives.
[22] *The North American War Weekly,* November 23, 1918, No. 47, p. 3.
[23] *Ibid.,* December 7, 1918, Vol. I, No. 49, p. 1.
The Fourteen Points, which Harvey had thought definite and "tremendously effective" in January, were now quite incapable of definition. Nobody could make out now just what "The Fourteen Commandments" came to. There was "a great deal to

Postponement Definitely Demanded. On December 3, the day before the President put to sea, Senator Sherman, of Illinois, introduced a concurrent resolution into the Senate declaring the office of President vacant. When he sat down, Senator Knox rose and offered a resolution in which he anticipated the course the President would take at the Peace Conference perfectly, as in fact everyone interested in the subject had done. After reciting that the United States had entered the war "in order to vindicate the ancient rights of navigation as established under international law and in order to remove forever the German menace to our peace" the resolution declared: (1) that our purposes in the Peace Conference should be confined to the aforesaid aims; (2) "That for the safeguarding of those aims the first essential is a definite understanding that, the same necessity arising in the future, there shall be the same complete accord and coöperation with our chief cobelligerents for the defense of civilization"; and (3) "That any project for any general league of nations or for any sweeping change in the ancient laws of the sea . . . should be postponed for separate consideration not alone by the victorious belligerents, but by all the nations if and when at some future time general conferences on those subjects might be deemed useful."[24]

There was nothing urgent about this matter of organizing the world on a peaceful and democratic basis. All that was necessary was to make peace with Germany and assure the Allies that if she broke loose again we would again help to suppress her. The creation of a league of nations could wait. "If and when at some future time general conferences on those subjects might be deemed useful," would be soon enough. The immediate necessity was to bring home the Army and Navy and to withdraw "the extraordinary powers conferred upon the President for the prosecution of the war."[25]

---

be said on both sides of every one of them, so far as any of them present sides, top, or bottom on which to erect arguments of any kind." (November 16, 1918, No. 46, p. 4.)

[24] *Congressional Record,* Vol. 57, Pt. 1, p. 23.

[25] The writer is aware that many people in Europe and some Americans (*i.e.,* Mr. Lansing) were so impressed by the danger of economic and political chaos in various European countries that they felt the peace settlement should be concluded as speedily as the great complexity of the problems would permit. This was particularly true a little later on. By that time, however, it had been demonstrated that the creation of the league could proceed side by side with the consideration of the other even more controversial problems, without appreciably delaying the final settlements. It is not doubted that many of the appeals for haste came from men anxious for the immediate safety of their countries, but it is difficult to discover any deep solicitude for the economic and political safety of the peoples of the war torn countries in the campaign in this country to divorce the league from the treaty. The great objective

The method of attack by questioning was brought into play, on December 6, by former Senator Albert J. Beveridge, of Indiana, in an address before the Massachusetts Bar Association, during which he raised almost every conceivable objection to a league of nations that could be invented. The speech in fact was one long question mark. In a comparatively short address of two pages he asked seventy-four questions. If the League bound a country to make war did it not violate the Constitution? And if it didn't it was merely an agreement to be good. It was evidently to be damned either way. "The only reason given for the proposed international super-state" was that it might prevent wars. But on the contrary didn't it contain "the very seeds of strife?"

The determination evinced by Mr. Beveridge indicated that the league was going to be deprived of that ancient right of the accused in Anglo-Saxon lands, the benefit of the doubt. Instead of being assumed innocent until proven guilty, it was to be assumed guilty on every count that could be raised against it. There was not to be the slightest presumption in its favor. If the American people accepted it, it would be in spite of every possible suspicion and fear that some of the best minds in the country could raise against it.

Yet the attitude of complete and total obstruction against the world's greatest effort at reform carried with it some unpleasant implications. Beveridge himself felt that he ought, in closing, to say a little bit about what the United States did stand for. He could hardly have forgotten the days of 1912, when as a leading Progressive he was a chief apostle of one of the most radical reform movements in our political history. His description of America's mission in the world, at the close of the world's greatest tragedy, was "no less than to create a new race on the earth and to present to mankind the example of happiness and well-being that comes only from progressive, self-disciplined liberty." That was the "faith of our fathers." Our situation was "peculiar and unique." Geographically we sat "on the throne of the world"; our resources were "greater than those of all Europe combined."[26] Our mission was to furnish to the earth an example of a free and prosperous people, no less and no more!

---

was the postponement of the league, not the formal proclamation of peace. This is proved by the fact that the Peace Conference framed the treaty in less than half the time that the Senate took to consider it—and when the Senate had done, it required still other months to procure a separate peace for this country.

[26] *Congressional Record*, Vol. 57, Pt. 3, p. 2115.

Such utterances were exceptional at this date. The declaration of the *Topeka*

There was not the slightest suggestion of the Christian doctrine of the duty of service to mankind which runs throughout President Wilson's speeches on the peace. There was no suggestion that power and responsibility inevitably go together and that wealth can not be dissociated from responsibility for its use—nor defended by steel alone.

Wilson in Europe. The President arrived in Paris on December 14 and received a welcome that was "nothing less than fanatical."[27] He was cheered by throngs, gathering since daybreak, until they packed the four miles of procession route twenty to fifty feet deep, hung from every possible perch and jammed the occasional large open spaces. The great roar of acclaim that swept along the route, said the *London Daily Mail*, was "a heart vibrating homage" to the President's countrymen, as well as to himself. Its depth and intensity was a revelation even to the venerable Clemenceau, who said of it: "I knew Paris in the glitter of the Second Empire. I thought I knew my Paris now, but I did not believe she could show such enthusiasm as this. I don't believe there has been anything like it in the history of the world."[28]

London newspaper men shared M. Clemenceau's opinion when Mr. Wilson visited the British capital some two weeks later. "Scenes of enthusiasm unprecedented in the long history of London demonstrations marked the arrival of President Wilson," said one. In Charing Cross and Trafalgar Square such dense crowds had never been seen before "and hundreds of thousands tore along the side streets to some other part of the route when they found how impossible it was to see anything of the beginning of the procession." Paris capitulated uncon-

---

Capital, Republican, is more representative: "If Mr. Wilson failed to feel that he has such an opportunity to bring peace to a confused world as will not be offered to another statesman for centuries to come, he would be without vision."

The *Wichita Eagle,* noting that there had been no opposition until lately to the President's peace program, warned that there was now much "working assiduously behind the scenes against the President's plans."

See *The Literary Digest,* December 7, 1918, Vol. 59, p. 21.

[27] David Lawrence, *The True Story of Woodrow Wilson,* p. 246.

Henry White had seen many great demonstrations, but he had never witnessed "anything like the exaltation of the crowds" which greeted the President. Nevins, *Henry White,* p. 359.

[28] *London Daily Mail,* Paris Edition, December 15, 1918. The President's foes were prepared for such news, but they discounted its practical significance as much as possible. In an article entitled "Awaiting the Revelation," Col. Harvey quoted with approval a report from abroad that "there will be much flagwaving and fine speechifying, but the things for which the President stands are now ridiculed and bespattered by the only voices one hears," and added "That is what we expected." *The North American War Weekly,* December 14, 1918, Vol. I, No. 50, p. 4.

ditionally, wrote Frederic William Wile. "London's surrender was no less complete."[29]

Immediately after the President's arrival in Paris, on December 14, the American press carried a dispatch saying that the President regarded the creation of a league of nations to be the first and foremost task of the conference. It should be the basis of the treaty. There was intimation that this course would be strongly insisted on by the American commission. Mr. Wilson's opponents at home knew what that meant.

The *New York Sun,* on December 14, professed surprise at the report. Here was "a distinct issue with and an irreconcilable divergence of opinion from" that which had been so well expressed in the Knox resolution. The *Sun* had cautioned its readers, on December 1, that "The thing to be kept in mind is that it is the final action of the Senate, not the initial action of the negotiator or negotiators, that effectuates the contract." Was it not surprising, therefore, that the President should diverge completely from the expressed wish of these final arbiters?

The Knox Substitute Offered. Senator Knox himself appeared to think so. On the 18th he spoke in the Senate in amplification of his plan for suppressing the league scheme. Recognizing that some security had to be given to the war torn countries against a recurrence of the deluge, he expanded his original substitute to propose that the United States declare that "If a situation should arise in which any power or combination of powers should directly or indirectly menace the freedom and peace of Europe, the United States would regard such situation with grave concern as a menace to its own freedom and peace and would consult with other powers affected with a view to concerted action for the removal of such menace."

If any league was to be formed, he favored a permanent entente of the Allied powers. Could we "create a league with purer conscience or higher ideals than the one called into existence by the German attack? Wise policy, as opposed to shallow empiricism, would seem to counsel us to solidify and build upon what we have tried rather than plunge headlong into a universal experiment."

His judgment as Secretary of State, in 1910, that all nations would be compelled to yield a part of their initiative (sovereignty) to the common good had evidently been superseded by more cautious counsel. In the face of the most tragic and compelling demonstration possible of the truth of his elaborately drawn judgment of the earlier

[29] *London Daily Mail,* Paris Edition, December 27, 1918.

day, he took, in 1918, the stand that no particle of sovereignty must be yielded. He was willing to give a fairly strong moral commitment, but nothing was to be agreed upon at that time.

The Meaning of Postponement. "After all, why such hurry?" he asked, and proceeded with a convincing list of examples to show that it took time to develop new institutions. The argument was plausibility itself, and would have been sufficient, if it had not been for the practical certainty that unless somebody struck hard for a beginning, while the tragedy of death and waste was still burned into men's minds, no beginning would be made—until after the next holocaust. New problems and tasks would arise, most men would become absorbed in the ordinary struggles of life, others would lose themselves in the enjoyments of prosperity, and day by day the once poignant realization that all men must stand together, if fratricidal slaughter was ever to be limited, would become less insistent, until few would be found ready to spend the energy and make the sacrifices necessary to found the new institutions of coöperation for peace. Millions felt then that today could not be too soon to begin to try to avert the next blood-letting and that if the opportunity of the moment, when ideas and arrangements were fluid, were lost it would not recur.

The Plan of Opposition Agreed Upon

Even then there were plenty of men who were not stirred by any need of a new beginning. Senator Knox himself thought it a strange idea that any one should propose giving the new league parts of the peace settlement to administer. "The practicability of such a league in any thoroughgoing sense is, to say the least, most doubtful if indeed it be not altogether chimerical at this period of civilization." How, moreover, could the treaty-making power bind the United States to declare war in the future? He put this question merely in passing.[30]

[30] *Congressional Record,* Vol. 57, Pt. 1, pp. 603-5. The speech was replied to at once by Senator Pittman. As a part of his reply he read an editorial from the *Philadelphia Inquirer,* Republican, of the same date. It said in part:

"We have no hesitation in pronouncing the Knox resolution to be mischievous in the extreme. The Senator is trifling with a most important matter. He is erecting barriers in the pathway of permanent peace, or at least an effort to secure permanence. To reject the league of nations idea is to uphold militarism—the continuance of secret alliances; the maintenance of vast standing armies. Unless the nations that have suffered from the insane ambition of German despots are prepared to prevent a similar outbreak in future, there can be no safety. . . .

"We do not pretend to say that war positively can be prevented, but we do insist that a league of nations offers the most promising preventive. What is more, we assert our belief that if there is to be such an organization, it should be created—

The Senate Must Debate and May Reject. On the 19th and 20th of December the *Chicago Tribune* published editorials urging further debate in the Senate. The *Tribune* was certain that the Senate represented the country better than any body of negotiators could. It was positive, on both days, that if the commissioners drifted or were "beguiled far from American interests, traditions, idea and sympathies" the Senate would reject what was offered it. To prevent all the troubles which would be involved in the rejection of a new scheme of international relations, "the real treaty makers" should be making their interest, purposes or demands known.

Both of these utterances were very properly phrased and might have been made without any knowledge of a purpose among the leaders of the opposition to prevent the consummation of a League of Nations under President Wilson. Even so, to require the negotiators not to trespass seriously on any American traditions, ideas or sympathies was to subject their work to very broad risks of attack in the Senate, if not to prevent altogether any innovations in international organization.

A Momentous Debate Forecast. There can be little doubt, however, that the *Boston Transcript* of December 18th spoke with knowledge of the decision that was being made. Said the *Transcript:* "One of the great debates in the history of popular government is about to begin in the Senate of the United States. It will attract the interest of the leaders of the Old World no less than of the people of the new, for it will afford our allies a barometer of sentiment in the place and among the men who, under the Constitution, have the power from the people to veto even the word and wishes of the President of the United States, whether his name be Washington or Wilson."

The debate was sure to occur at once. "Whether the (Knox) resolution is favorably reported from the committee or held back, it is certain to be debated in the Senate between now and the Christmas recess." And, "In debating the resolution the senators will serve notice upon the governments of the world that they are on their constitutional

---

not at some indefinite time in the future, but before the peace terms are written into treaties.

"Senator Knox's resolution is obstructive, and we have no patience with it."

On the other hand the *Boston Transcript* of December 19th felt that Senator Knox was "entitled to the thanks of the whole country for his clarifying speech in the Senate yesterday on the league of nations proposition." Its approving summary concluded with: "We have gone there thousands of miles and undertaken the gigantic risk of the war with only a gentleman's agreement. Why should not such an agreement suffice to keep us in peace?"

job and that the Senate never in its long life was farther from abdicating its constitutional duties."

Surely there was serious work to be done. What was it? The *Transcript* explained that "the line of cleavage will come upon an honest difference of opinion upon a mighty matter: Shall the peace treaty which will end the war provide for a series of foreign alliances popularly called a "League of Nations," or shall the latter question be deferred for decision until the wrongs of the war have been righted, the wrongdoers punished and the pillars of justice overturned by the enemy once more restored to their proper places? . . ." The purpose of the Knox resolution, which would occasion the debate, "and of its proponent and some of its supporters is to insure for the people of the United States an opportunity through their representatives in the upper house of Congress to ratify the treaty of peace without being compelled at the same time to accept a system of foreign alliances not yet subjected to the test of that 'pitiless publicity' which our President upon another occasion advised us was such an essential instrument of all 'government by discussion.' If the idea of a League of Nations is sound and feasible, if its conception is wise, if it will promote the welfare of America and the world, surely it is strong enough to stand alone, to be debated upon its merits. It is against that secret diplomacy which would attempt to ram the league down the throats of a blindfolded people, against a league capsuled in the provisions of the treaty of Versailles that the Knox resolution is aimed."

The President's opponents were beginning to be filled with a real fear that he might succeed in creating a league and that they would have to kill the peace treaty in order to destroy it. The prospect was appalling; the responsibility would be tremendous; it was not too soon to try to avert such a dilemma.

A determined drive to prevent the creation of the league was in order. It would be best for this demand to take the form of a plea for postponement, in order that no dangerous project be forced "down the throats" of the American people. Not a line of the proposed league constitution had been written and there was no reason at all to fear that the American people would not know as much about its framing as any other people. They had known for a year all that the President or anyone else could tell them about it. Nowhere, either, could the plans be so easily rejected as here. There was no reason why, if it proved to be the negation of everything it was intended to be, it should be accepted. Nobody had ever known of the Senate being moved to haste in the discussion of a treaty. What was the complaint then? Simply that it was not fair of the President to force the Senate to assume the responsibility of defeating the whole settlement in order to scotch his league. That was the "weighty matter" about which one of the great debates of popular government was to rage.[31]

Attack on the League Itself Agreed Upon. Further evidence of the advance decision of the opposition leaders to spike the Wilsonian league is to be found in the fact that the necessary amendments were agreed upon at the same time the campaign to postpone the league was launched. From past experiences it was evidently feared that this campaign would not succeed and that the President would bring the league back with him. The campaign for postponement would not be wasted, however; it would serve as a basis for direct attack on the instrument that was yet to be created. It only remained to plan the lines of attack to be used.

This was done in a conference between Roosevelt and Lodge in the middle of December, previous to the Knox speech and the utterances which preceded and attended it. One of the first accounts of this conference was given by Mrs. Douglas Robinson, a sister of Mr. Roosevelt, in the course of a speech made during the campaign of 1920, reported in the *New York Times* of October 29, 1920, as follows: "When Theodore Roosevelt was sick in Roosevelt Hospital, Senator Lodge and I went together to the hospital and there, sitting on the bedside, Senator Lodge and my brother went over every one of the reservations during a session of three hours, changing and deciding upon this one and that and finally every one of them was O.K.'d. by Theodore

---

[31] The strength of the *Transcript's* feelings was fully revealed in another editorial in the same issue declaring that the proposition to have a Christmas Eve league of nations celebration on Boston Common "must be sternly frowned upon." The star in the East on the Common would also be this year our service star. "To this star the beautiful Christmas carols will be sung, and their sentiment, their tribute will represent our idea of Peace on Earth and Good Will toward men through service. The joy which the carols will express will be that of sacrifice. No other thought can enter now. It is peculiarly not only a time for the exclusion of controversial ideas, but for the exaltation of the thought of our country. Pure Christmas in this sense, and all the lesser causes shut out."

The league of nations in its present state had far too much of controversy in it to warrant its intrusion on such an occasion. A scheme concerning which Senators had grave doubts surely had no place in Christmas rejoicings. "Intruded now, and made, as these people make it, the primary matter, the league of nations represents the denial of justice in Europe, and therefore its evocation at the Christmas season is not only impertinent but dangerous."

What was there that made the public discussion of a league of nations to keep the peace not only impertinent but dangerous? When did the birthday of the Prince of Peace become a time for the exaltation of the thought of our country? And what better time could have been chosen, when the whole world was in mourning, to pledge adherence to the prevention of future sacrifices?

Roosevelt. My brother said he had hoped something would come out of the proposed league, but had concluded that with so many nations in it with conflicting interests the League would be a war breeder rather than a peace maker."

To this statement the *Times* appended an editorial note saying that "Theodore Roosevelt died on January 6, 1919, the first draft of the league of nations Covenant was published here February 15, 1919. The Peace Conference in Paris did not hold its first session until January 18, 1919."

The next day, in a speech at the Broad Street Theater, Mrs. Robinson replied to the *Times'* implied query as to how the reservations could have been framed before the Covenant was written, saying:

> The *New York Times* has been singularly unfair to me. Today the *Times* absolutely misquoted my remarks at a quaint little meeting addressed by me last night. I don't think there was a *Times* reporter even present. I do hope there is one here now. I said that in Theodore Roosevelt's sick room on the 19th and 20th day of December, 1918, I at my brother's request, sent for Senator Lodge to talk over the tentative treaty draft with him. We all know the actual draft was hidden for some time from Senators by the President.
>
> Those men sat down for hours, and they discussed every one of those reservations of Lodge's and they were all O.K.'d by Theodore Roosevelt. The *Times* says that the treaty was not drafted until after the dates I gave and until after my brother's death. The finished draft was not over until after the Colonel's death, but there was an unfinished draft.

It will be noted that she protested only against the matter of time discrepancy and not against her statement that the Colonel had decided that the league would be a war-breeder. Some further modification was, however, necessary. At the time indicated no draft that was in any sense official, finished or unfinished, had been published. In July, 1918, the President had made a first draft of a covenant based upon an analysis of British and other proposals made by Colonel House. During the preceding spring Mr. House had had conferences on the subject with Elihu Root and, as a result, added to his scheme an International Court of Justice.[32] There is no evidence of such conference after the President wrote his first draft, however, and that document certainly was not published. Mrs. Robinson's memory had been a little defec-

[32] R. S. Baker, *Woodrow Wilson and the World Settlement*, N. Y., 1922, Vol. I, p. 218.

tive, too, as to the exact date of the conference between Roosevelt and Lodge which appears to have occurred on December 17 and 18, two days after the announcement of the President's determination to press for the League.

After reflection, these details were corrected by Mrs. Robinson in her book, published the following year, in which she wrote: ". . . and in the middle of December he asked me to telegraph our dear friend Senator Lodge to ask him to come on and discuss certain political matters with him. The Senator spent two days with me, and of those two days two whole mornings in the Colonel's room in the hospital. I was with them during the first morning when they discussed the tentative league of nations, parts of which in problematical form were already known to the public. The different reservations, insisted upon later by Senator Lodge, when the league in its eventual form was presented to the Senate of the United States, were tentatively formulated at the bedside of the Colonel. I do not mean that definite clauses in the league were definitely discussed, but many contingencies of the document, contingencies which later took the form of definite clauses, *were* discussed, and the future attitude toward such contingencies more or less mapped out." [33]

What Was Decided. These statements taken together make fairly clear what was decided in these conferences. The two gentlemen had before them only the general proposals for a league of nations contained in the President's speeches, the platform of the League to Enforce Peace, (then holding a series of great regional conferences to support the President in his purpose), and other similar proposals. They could hardly have anticipated all the reservations that were later thought of, for example: No. 3, concerning mandates, and No. 6, concerning representation on the Reparations Commission, since these institutions were not yet created. What they did decide was that the essential parts of the plan should be opposed, and they set up as many negations or

[33] Corinne Roosevelt Robinson, *My Brother, Theodore Roosevelt,* N. Y., 1921, pp. 361–2. Mr. Lodge was present in the Senate December 18 to 23 inclusive. He took part in its proceedings each day from December 12 to 16 inclusive. He was present in the early afternoon of December 16, but did not speak nor respond to roll calls (three) in the latter part of that session. This was true of the session of December 17. He was present again for Senator Knox's speech at noon December 18. (*Congressional Record,* Vol. 57, Part 1.)

In his last published letter to Mr. Roosevelt, dated December 23, 1918, he tells how much satisfaction he got from "those two talks with you," showing that the conferences had preceded that date. *Selections from the Correspondence of Theodore Roosevelt and Henry Cabot Lodge,* Vol. II, p. 550.

limitations on the proposal as they could think of.[34] They agreed in fact upon so many counter moves that later it seemed to Mrs. Robinson as if the whole fourteen Lodge Reservations were written at her brother's bedside. It was a political war council, as she states in her considered account, and its result was a decision to attack whatever League proposal the President might bring home with so many amendments and reservations that participation by the United States on the terms agreed upon by the President and the other powers would be effectively blocked.

The political consequences of permitting the President to have the credit for leading us into a new league of nations might be disastrous. All that had been won in 1918 might be lost in 1920. Therefore, if he succeeded in creating the organization and in submitting its charter to the Senate he would be presented with a set of terms that he could not accept without great loss of prestige, and such terms after his long career of power he probably would not accept. He would be too stubborn to submit the crowning achievement of his career to summary treatment at their hands. If he was too stubborn well and good. Lodge had cooled to the whole league idea long ago, and Roosevelt now agreed with him that the thing would be "a war breeder rather than a peace maker."

Defeat of the Central Principle Resolved. It would, of course, not be possible to state all of the points of the plan for opposing the unborn league which the two leaders agreed upon. Yet of the main outlines of the program, which, by the clear testimony quoted above was faithfully carried through, there can be little doubt. In all the President's addresses on the subject there had been the single purpose clearly expressed that all the members of the league should have their territorial integrity and political independence guaranteed against aggression. The corner stone in the plan of opposition was, therefore, an amendment refusing to do this very thing. All the work of the League to Enforce Peace, and all the President's thinking, pointed to the common

[34] An earlier statement of Senator Lodge, made in his Boston debate with President Lowell, on March 19, 1919, fully substantiates Mrs. Robinson's story. Mr. Lodge said:

"Two weeks before his death I was with Theodore Roosevelt for some hours, seeing him for two mornings in succession. The draft now before the country was not then before us, but we fully discussed the League of Nations in all its bearings. We were in entire agreement.

"The position that I have taken, and now take, had his full approval. The line I have followed in the Senate and elsewhere is the one he wished to have followed." *World Peace Foundation Pamphlets.* Vol. II, No. 2, p. 52, Boston, 1919.

guarantee of the safety of each. Before Article X was ever written, then, the opposition set its face against the basic idea on which the structure was to be reared and never swerved from its purpose to nullify it.

The Strategy Entailed. But could the American people be roused to support the defeat of the idea of a league for peace? Yes, a campaign of questioning and denial would do it, if time enough could be had. The thing to do was to call it an entangling alliance, stand on Washington's Farewell Address and show by countless hypothetical cases that American troops might, in this contingency or that, have to be sent to the ends of the earth. The idea of having the boys at home was very popular then. It could be further shown, moreover, that we would be in continual danger of being outvoted in the league, by the small states if equal representation was given, or by the colored races if population was to be the basis. The outcry against the votes of the British Dominions in the Assembly was a later refinement of the original idea.

At the same time an equal number of fears of interference in American affairs could be aroused. It would be easy to show that the Monroe Doctrine was endangered and millions who only dimly understood what that sacred doctrine was would rise to defend it. Other large groups could be alarmed by the old argument of the possibility of immigration being forced on us, and the new one of the danger of tariffs being affected. In short, if you raised enough questions insistently you could convince the people that instead of being a league for agreement and peace the thing was really a dangerous breeder of discord and war. If our own now immortal constitution could be pilloried in its day as "a league with death and a covenant with hell" surely this one might be damned with even greater success.

It may be said that this is not a fair characterization of the plan of campaign against the Wilsonian league that was agreed upon in mid-December, 1918. But certainly these were the shock troops which did valiant execution up to the end of the fight. Other recruits were enlisted as they appeared, as for example the deep moral indignation stirred in the senators by the Shantung clause of the treaty, but the major appeals remained the same throughout. So far as the opposition was concerned, the fate of the league in the United States was decided weeks before it was even created. The only question that remained to be settled was whether it could survive the attack and still exist.

The Plan Announced by Lodge in the Senate

On December 19, Senator Lodge gave notice in the Senate that on the 21st he would address the Senate on "the question of peace and the proposed league of nations," and if there was no routine business on that day he might be compelled to connect the speech with the revenue bill then pending.[35] As it turned out he was obliged to interrupt the revenue debate.

The Senate Would "Negotiate" in Many Speeches. His speech of December 21 was a long one. It began by asserting the right of the Senate to advise as well as consent and quoted from his article in *Scribner's Magazine,* of January, 1902, many instances where the President had asked the advice of the Senate. Aside from one occasion on which the Senate had suggested the opening of a negotiation, all the precedents cited were cases where the President had asked the advice of the Senate in advance. He did not point out this fact, but proceeded to declare that it was now the solemn and imperative duty of the Senate to give advice that had not been invited to the negotiators. "We cannot compel information but we are abundantly able to make our opinions known not only to the President but to the Allies, who have a very clear and even acute idea of the power of the Senate in regard to treaties. They must know that the Senate can and often has rejected treaties. Others the Senate has refused to ratify and held without action. Many others have been vitally amended. The Allies should not be kept in the dark as to the views of the Senate. . . ."[36]

Ratification Contingent on the Acceptance of Senate Demands. The groundwork for the future campaign was being laid. The Senate was not to respond to requests for advice made by the President; it was to influence the negotiations contrary to his desires as fully as speeches in the open Senate could do so. The drive for the postponement of the league was to be pressed, and in case it and other attempts to control the course of the negotiations failed, the country and the Allies should understand that the treaty would be drastically handled in the Senate.

The justification for this amazing course before the people was to be the astonishing argument that something was about to be foisted upon them and upon the Senate. "The plan seems to be to project upon the Senate the most momentous treaty ever made without any informa-

---

[35] *Congressional Record,* Vol. 57, Pt. 1, p. 672.
[36] *Congressional Record,* Vol. 57, Pt. 1, p. 724.

tion as to the steps which led to it or as to the arguments and conditions which brought about its adoption. This scheme, which is indicated by all the facts known to us, rests on the theory that the Senate, although possessing the power, would not and could not dare to reject a treaty of peace. This unworthy calculation is perhaps sound in practice, and yet I have seen a peace treaty bitterly opposed and ratified, after the exertion of the most powerful influences, with only two votes to spare. But if a treaty of peace might not be rejected, it can be debated and amended, and I can conceive of extraneous provisions wholly needless for a peace with Germany being unwisely added, provisions which would surely be stricken out or amended, no matter how many signatures might be appended to the treaty. Protracted opposition and amendments mean long delays, and delay is only less fortunate than rejection. All these untoward results can be avoided if the Senate frankly expresses its views beforehand on certain leading points for the consideration of the Allies and of the President himself."

Doubting whether they would receive the intimate details of every decision, disagreement or compromise that would be made in the Peace Conference, the Senators were going to be forever in the dark as to the meaning of the treaty, even after it was presented to them. But let the world understand! If certain "extraneous provisions," *i.e.* the league of nations, were found in the treaty, they would surely be struck out or amended even if every nation on earth had agreed to them.[37] No treaty of peace had ever been defeated, but one had come close enough to defeat to prove that it could be done. Drastic amendment or rejection could be avoided if the Peace Conference would heed the Senate's demand that the league be delayed—and in no other way. "Untoward results" could hardly be avoided if the Peace Conference didn't listen and govern itself accordingly.

A Proper Settlement Outlined. The Senator then proceeded to outline in detail the territorial settlements that should be made and to demand heavy indemnities, not only for vessels sunk, but for a part at least of our war expenditure. Some methods not named must be taken to safeguard the new nations, but "They involve no alliances. They are specific questions. . . ." The Russian problem was then dealt

---

[37] Clear evidence of the fact that Lodge meant his speech as a demand to the Allies that they go ahead and make peace as they desired, ignoring Wilson's League plans, is found in his letter of December 23, 1918, to Roosevelt, which said: "I am sending you a copy of the speech which I made on Saturday (*i.e.*, the speech of December 21), which was intended chiefly for the benefit of the Allies." *Selections from the Correspondence of Theodore Roosevelt and Henry Cabot Lodge,* Vol. II, p. 550.

with, and the first four of the President's Fourteen Points, upon which the powers were gathering to make peace, discarded.

Concerning the fourteenth point, we were all lovers of peace, "But we ought to be extremely careful that in our efforts to reach the millennium of universal and eternal peace we do not create a system which will breed dissensions and wars. It is difficult to discuss it at this time, because no definite plan of any kind has yet been put forward by any responsible person."

Nevertheless there were questions of great moment in the scheme which he hoped the American people would consider. First, how should the nations vote? If on an equality then the little nations could order the forces of the big ones about; if by population then China would have four votes to our one and Great Britain (for India) three. There was the Court, too; if we hadn't already bought the Virgin Islands it could permit Germany to do so, and there was still Magdalena Bay.

Then recurring to the major danger, "It is easy to talk about a league of nations and the beauty and the necessity of peace, but the hard practical demand is, Are you ready to put your soldiers and your sailors at the disposition of other nations? If you are not, there will be no power of enforcing the decrees of the international court or the international legislature or the international executive, or whatever may be established. . . . This is the heart of the whole question, but there are others which would necessarily have to be considered. Are we ready to abandon the Monroe Doctrine and to leave it to other nations to say how American questions should be settled and what steps we shall be permitted to take in order to guard our own safety or to protect the Panama Canal? Are we ready to have other nations tell us by a majority vote what attitude we must assume in regard to immigration or in regard to our tariffs? These are lesser points, but they must be met and answered before we commit ourselves to permitting an association of nations to control in any degree the forces of the United States."

We had at this moment a league of nations. Wasn't that good enough? "Is it not our first duty and our highest duty to bring peace to the world at this moment and not encumber it by trying to provide against wars which never may be fought and against difficulties which lie far ahead in dim and unknown future?" [38]

When the Continent of Europe was draped in mourning for its dead, and when the sun never set upon the saddened homes of the English speaking peoples, the Senator raised his voice only against any

[38] *Congressional Record*, Vol. 57, Pt. 1, p. 724.

"encumbrances" of the peace settlement that would "provide against wars which may never be fought."

No League for War. His cry was at once repeated by the *Washington Post* in an editorial "No Supersovereign Wanted" on December 23. The same day found Colonel Harvey making a speech in New York City, captioned "No League of Nations to Enforce War." Quoting Washington's Farewell Address extensively and lauding the Monroe Doctrine, he demanded, "Must we abruptly disregarding the beneficence of the past fare forth into foreign lands looking for trouble?" After the United States had collected indemnities from Germany let the Allies deal with her. Did anyone imagine them "incapable of affixing the guilt and exacting the penalty?" Our object in entering the war thus accomplished, the peace conference might before adjournment turn the league of nations question over to international commissions, for investigation and report to the powers for "such treaty action as they might desire."[39]

Could the President Control the Negotiations? The concerted demand thus insistently raised was heard by those for whom it was chiefly intended. A dispatch published in the *Kansas City Star,* on December 22, reported that Senator Knox's speech of December 18 had been published in the Paris papers and was being widely discussed. The American delegation feared it would encourage European opponents of the league to active opposition to the whole idea. On Christmas day Paul Scott Mowrer wrote that, particularly before the President's arrival in Paris, the speeches of such men as Colonel Roosevelt, Senator Lodge and Senator Knox were widely reproduced to prove that Mr. Wilson had lost the people's support.

On the other hand, he continued: "President Wilson's reception in Paris proved to be a signal for a great awakening throughout Europe as to the tremendous issues of peace. Before that the newspapers had only considered the peace problem in a perfunctory way, but now they began a general and healthy discussion of the topic. As for the people, the reception which they gave Mr. Wilson proved beyond all doubt what an extraordinary hold the President's idealism had obtained over them. It became apparent that Mr. Wilson was not only accepted by the liberals throughout Europe as their natural leader, but that he was looked to by the great inarticulate masses as their spokesman and guide in the struggle to end wars forever." [40]

[39] *The North American Review War Weekly,* December 28, 1918, No. 52, pp. 2–9.
[40] *Kansas City Star,* December 25, 1918. Mr. Mowrer added that "at the same

Henry White wrote to Lodge at the same time that those who knew the French political situation felt that any cabinet disagreeing with the President was likely to be overturned. Immediately after the President's reception in Paris the *Temps,* which reflected the views of the government, had said that while not much had been thought of the league previously it would be well for France to get into line.[41]

By January 1, 1919, Taft had also concluded that it was "not too much to say that he is stronger today with the people of Great Britain, France and Italy than are the respective premiers of those countries."[42]

If Mr. Wilson was as strong with the people of Europe as he seemed to be, would he be able to give them some effective protection against the institution of war before his power ebbed? Certainly if he succeeded he would have to fight simultaneously on both sides of the ocean. At the close of 1918, he was on the field where the European battle would be fought out. It has been said that in winning that conflict he lost the American campaign. Perhaps he did, but if he had remained at home to dispute the efforts of his enemies to control the negotiations he would have lost the first and vastly more important encounter.

In any event it could not soon again be said of the United States that "Politics stops at the water's edge."

---

time European leaders on coming in personal contact with him found him not to be a stubborn fanatic, as it seems they expected, but a simple democrat, quick to understand conflicting points of view and ready to be convinced by sound argument."
[41] Allan Nevins, *Henry White,* N. Y., 1930, p. 361.
[42] *Philadelphia Public Ledger,* January 1, 1919.

CHAPTER IV

THE FRAMING OF THE COVENANT

The Reversal of Party Positions. Politics certainly did not stop at the water's edge in 1918 and 1919; it never even hesitated at the ocean barrier. Nevertheless, it would not be truthful to infer that the force of partisanship determined the attitude of everyone in the United States toward the League of Nations. There can be little doubt that politics (either personal or party) settled the attitude of the majority of our people in these years. It even accounted for the attitude of many people in both parties who failed to accept the party position on the league. Of the two parties the Republican, representing more largely the commercial, banking and investing interests, had the larger natural interest in promoting a stabilized world. Their interests, and a broad vision as well, had steadily inclined the leaders of the Republican party toward a larger and larger participation in world affairs. They had smashed the tradition of American isolation resolutely in 1898, in acquiring a small colonial empire in the West Indies and a larger one in Asia. It was true that the motives advanced were largely humanitarian; they maintained that we merely assumed a trusteeship or mandate over the Spanish possessions for the purpose of leading them up to freedom. But even if this profession be questioned their outlook was broad.

The Established Republican Attitude. Republican statesmen, too, from McKinley to Taft, had worked with one accord to increase the influence of the United States among the nations and to promote institutions for safeguarding the peace of the world. We had been the pioneers in advocating and using arbitration. From the arbitration of the perilous *Alabama* claims, in 1872, on down we consistently promoted arbitration after disputes had arisen, while both Roosevelt and Taft had done what they could to induce critical Senates to agree to arbitration in advance of the disputes. Secretaries Hay, Root, and Knox had all worked for arbitration, and Mr. Root in particular had labored long to go beyond arbitration to the creation of a world court.

Little if any fear, moreover, of European "politics" had existed. The dominating Republican leader, Mr. Roosevelt, according to his own accounts, had not hesitated to exert the full power of the Presidency on two occasions to settle old world political disputes.[1] In both the Russo-Japanese and Moroccan cases he had labored for months to settle the quarrels as he thought they should be settled, never doubting that he was increasing the influence and prestige of the United States abroad and promoting the best interests of many peoples. He and multitudes of his followers would have rebelled against any suggestion that the greatest nation in the world should not exert its full influence in the councils of the nations. The person who proposed to count the United States out of world leadership in those days would have been a Democrat indeed.

So, in 1919 many Republicans refused to accept a reversal of position toward international affairs for their party and stood by the policy it had so consistently maintained. Many of them merely used the older position of the party to justify what they felt to be right, yet others were more largely animated by party motives; they thought primarily of the party and in standing for the League believed themselves the truer interpreters of the party policy and the best conservators of its future.

The Democratic Tradition. Similarly many Democrats were not able to stand on the new ground to which their leader brought them. The Democratic party had held to a strict construction of the powers and duties of government, especially when out of power, for too many generations to enable all its members to see eye to eye with Woodrow Wilson. Most of them followed unquestioningly because he was the party leader, others reluctantly, still others not at all.

Since the debate over Imperialism, in 1900, also, the Democrats had been committed against wider participation in world affairs and entanglements. They had assumed this position partly from partisan motives and now the older partisanship held a large number against the call of the new. Many used the former position of the party to justify their position when in reality the motive was dislike of Mr. Wilson, but others fully believed that the President was reversing the party policy too rapidly and that they were the wiser partisans in standing by the policy of isolation.

[1] See Chapter I above.

Much Sentiment Non-Partisan. When all the angles of partisanship have been considered, however, there were numerous Democrats who, as the debate proceeded, made up their minds wholly aside from party considerations that the new step was too dangerous, and countless Republicans ignored every appeal to partisanship and stood throughout for the League of Nations because they believed it was right.

This latter group of people, whose attitude toward the league was never determined by partisanship of any kind, was large in the country. In the Senate it must be recorded that it was small indeed. On the Democratic side the one or two Senators who opposed the league in any shape or form at all times can hardly be acquitted of personal animus toward the President. A considerable group of Democratic Senators would have been willing to see reservations attached to it at the start. Many Republican Senators, too, believed in the league at all times and would have been glad personally to see it ratified without reservation. Of them all, however, the only one who fought for the league at every step and who voted for it as it stood, and every other way, was Senator Porter J. McCumber, of North Dakota. Although later the author of one of the Lodge reservations, (No. 13), no party considerations of any kind ever swerved him from standing for the creation of the league. As time goes on the lonely but powerful stand that Mr. McCumber took will be more widely appreciated.

THE DEMAND FOR POSTPONEMENT

Senator McCumber's Plea. On January 7, 1919, Senator McCumber spoke in the Senate in reply to the speeches which had been made against the immediate formation of the league. To the counsels of caution he replied:

But, Mr. President, notwithstanding this caution, the world looks with hopeful and expectant eyes to the Peace Commission for some international arrangement that will make impossible another such war. We have seen the thunderbolt of war shot from serenest skies of peace. We have seen nations basking in the sun of tranquillity suddenly swept by the hurricane of a life and death struggle. We have seen more than four years of the most devastating and sanguinary, the most savage and brutal battles that ever blackened the earth. And as we reach its close, even the shouts of the victors are drowned by the lamentations of mothers, by the weeping of fatherless children, by the anguished sobs of millions upon millions of poor bereaved mortals. And as we look upon all this devastation and misery, and contemplate the many, many millions of brave boys to whom life was sweet and fair, who have gone to death to save the world from this bloody monster of military autocracy, their lofty hopes and ambitions entombed with their crushed and mangled bodies, and when we realize the many, many millions of young girls, whom God created to reign queen of heart and home, who must live their lives unwed, robbed of their God-given right of motherhood, and doomed to walk down life's pathway alone—we may well ask ourselves, Is it impossible for civilization to free itself from the ever impending dangers of such a scourge? Is it impossible to hold nations to the same moral code in their international relations that each enforces upon its citizens in their personal relations? Must history repeat itself over and over again? Must our children's children suffer and die as their fathers have suffered and died to propitiate the God of War?

Senator McCumber spoke with strong feeling, as befitted the situation which he faced. There had never been in any age such a demonstration of a need for new institutions as had taken place before every man's eyes. The call for reform had been sounded in every man's ears. And yet it must always be one of the astounding facts of history that men could not only shut their ears to the call but their eyes to what they had seen.

Continuing, Mr. McCumber warned the Senate that the great Teutonic empires had answered the questions he had asked in the negative. They declared that the nation could never be held to any code of Christian morals and the world had fought to the death that doctrine. If the victory could now do nothing to perpetuate the principles so hardly won "how vain have been our sacrifices, and what a mockery is our pretended civilization!" But, "I am optimistic enough to believe that great world wars can be prevented, and that the time to present and adopt the restrictive or preventive measures is now and not some indefinite time in the future—is today, when the awful horrors and consequences of war are apparent to every heart—and not when those horrors are forgotten and only the military glamour and glory remain to influence the sentiments of humanity."

The opponents of a league had painted it as a great superstate. Such a development was wholly unnecessary. It was necessary for the nations to recognize that the laws "Thou shalt not steal" and "Thou shalt not murder" applied to the relations of nations as well as of men. "The very first clause of the very first article of this agreement should, therefore, declare that each independent nation of the world as it shall exist at the time this compact shall be executed, has the right to live and work out its own destiny free from any impending danger of any mighty military neighbor." The independence and territorial integrity of the member nations must be guaranteed—that much was indispensable. Beyond that and the creation of an international court he did not see it necessary to go.

Replies to the Stock Criticisms. He then took up "the stock criticisms of a league of nations." He found in all the speeches opposing a league the assumption that it would interfere in the internal affairs of each nation, but he thought there was no possible danger of any intelligent commission ever creating such powers for the league. If they should so far forget national sentiment none of the great powers would ever ratify the treaty. No question was more clearly a domestic one than the right to regulate immigration.

With reference to the Monroe Doctrine, certainly no league founded to guarantee the territorial integrity and political independence of all its members would be a menace to the doctrine which did that very thing for the nations of the western world only. Again, on entangling alliances, "if you justify our alliance with France, Great Britain, and Italy in this war to protect the safety and civilization of the world, then how in Heaven's name can you condemn an alliance with the same and other countries to prevent another assault on civilization? How can you in one breath approve the alliance to make war to save the world and in the next breath condemn an alliance to save the world by the prevention of any savage or brutal war which might threaten it?" But of course an agreement with all the nations was not an alliance. We bound ourselves habitually in treaties to do and not to do certain things; that was exactly what we would do in the proposed treaty for a league of nations.

In reply to the cry for postponement, he gave the Senate this clear warning: "Mr. President, no matter how much we may legislate, how many resolutions we may introduce and pass, three things are certain: The first, already accomplished, is that acting within his constitutional authority the President has appointed delegates to sit with delegates from the other allied nations to agree upon the terms of peace; second, that these delegates will dictate and agree upon such terms of peace; and third, that they will not rise from their deliberations or attach their signatures to any instrument of peace that shall leave untouched or unsettled the question of the prevention of another such war. If they should do so their action would meet the condemnation of the people of all the countries who have endured the horrors and privations of this war. It will not do in one breath to say that war is wrong and in the next breath that such wrong cannot be checked." [2]

These were strong words, but William H. Taft was even more emphatic in stressing the burden of responsibility resting upon the negotiators. Holding that President Wilson faced the severest test of his career, he urged that "if he now fails to propose and secure in the treaty practical machinery for a real league of nations, which shall enforce peace, he will properly be held impotent for a lame and impotent conclusion before the world and its expectant peoples." [3]

The Relation of the Senate to the Negotiations. On January 13, Senator Sterling, Republican, of South Dakota, delivered an address which contained some new features. He began by conceding "that the treaty negotiating power is under the Constitution wholly in the hands of the President; that he can initiate the proceedings and on behalf of the United States carry them on to the point where the completed document is signed by the representatives of the high contracting parties; that up to that point he is under no legal or moral obligation to consult the Senate either as to the subject matter, the terms, or the form of the treaty. As a corollary of this the Senate has no right, legal or moral, to ask the President to disclose to the Senate his purposes or views in regard to any treaty which may be in contemplation."

And, he continued, "From the standpoint of the right of the Executive and the Senate it is of no consequence that the situation requiring a treaty is an exceedingly grave one, or that its consequences are bound to be of world importance, or that the Senate must ratify it if it is to become a binding treaty, or that harmony of thought and action between the President and Senate with the resulting public benefit would flow from some exchange of views. The President may, notwithstanding all these considerations, wholly abstain from communicating with the Senate or with its Committee on Foreign Relations or from in any way taking the Senate or any of the members of the Senate into his confidence. That is his right. The Senate may be embarrassed by disclosures made pending the negotiations or by the intermingling of the wise and unwise or the safe and the perilous in the terms of the treaty, but its right to consider any act thereon does not begin until the President

[2] *Congressional Record*, Vol. 57, Pt. 2, pp. 1084–88.
[3] *Philadelphia Public Ledger*, December 23, 1919.

lays the finished treaty before the Senate with his message requesting the ratification thereof."

That was, of course, plain statement of fact. Whether any amount of consultation by the President with his enemies in the Senate would have propitiated them is open to doubt, but there could be no question that he was not only acting within his right, but following the predominant custom. The course which the leaders of the opposition had determined upon could be immediately successful only if it compelled the President to forego in the negotiations the chief war aim to which he had committed himself and the nation. If they could enforce their will upon him, then the Senate would have in fact seized the power to negotiate; if they failed in their campaign to postpone the league, the only purpose their opposition could serve would be to form the basis for further attacks on his policies. From their standpoint the Senators may have felt themselves justified in trying to seize the power to negotiate, or in any other effort they could make to defeat the President, but certainly no serious claim of constitutional warrant could be made for their activity. It could be maintained of course that a Senator had a personal right to say anything he pleased.

The Allies Were a Sufficient League. Having demonstrated his clear knowledge of the powers and duties of the Senate, Mr. Sterling then joined in the debate on "the imminent and all-absorbing question" which was "not exactly whether we shall ever have a league of nations to enforce peace, but whether we must have it now. . . ." His thought in the first place, was "that the relations and mutual purposes of the allied nations are such as themselves to constitute an almost perfect guaranty against war as between themselves and a reasonable guaranty of the peace of the world. . . ." The President of France had said to us "We are friends forever"; what need for a formal league between France and America? And it was the same with Great Britain. The Treaty of Ghent had settled nothing that the War of 1812 was fought to settle; it had only ended the war, yet we had had enduring peace with Great Britain. Italy made four who were to be "friends forever"; we had a league already.

He then outlined a great many of the territorial and other settlements that must be made and pressed their superior urgency. There was no "acute necessity" for a league as ex-President Taft maintained. Moreover, there were "difficulties in the way of establishing a league to enforce peace that cannot at this time be overcome. . . ." No candid man who had any conception of the interests and issues involved could doubt that "many months, more probably years, would elapse before a congress assembled for the special purpose had concluded its labors and published the results to the world."

Good Will the Only Guarantee of Peace. This would, of course, have been true of the legislative body with which the Senator was familiar. Following this prediction he came to his last point which was that "in the last analysis we shall have to depend on the friendship and good faith of the nations of the world rather than force for our guaranty of peace." The decision of our constitutional convention not to provide specifically for the military coercion of a state was cited, and a distinction made between the coercion of arms and the coercion of law. Even the Civil War was not a coercion of states by arms, but a coercion of law exercised on those in armed rebellion against the laws of the United States. If less than sovereign states were not to be coerced by force of arms, then how could fully sovereign states be? "Others may see no difficulty in the way; but either there is this one mighty obstacle in the way of a league, the ultimate sanctions of which rest on force, or else I am sadly wanting in faith or vision or both."

Altogether, "We should be willing now to trust to the moral and political sympathies and kinship of the allied nations, to their example, to their kindly offices and admonitions in international disputes or when war threatens. Their influence, together with the common aversion to war intensified as it is by what the world has just passed through, ought, aside from the internal dissension of any nation, to be the harbinger and guaranty of a long peace between nations; and so we come back to the thought that good will and good faith between nations, and not force, are our only sure guarantees of international peace." [4]

This was an argument that would be heard again. There was no way to impose a coercion of law upon nations. Therefore we should have to depend on kindly offices and international good will to protect us against resorts to force that imperilled all. For the time being war weariness ought to postpone the evil day.

Roosevelt's Last Word. On the same day that Senator Sterling spoke, the last editorial written by Theodore Roosevelt was issued. It had been written on January 3, 1919, three days before the hand of death cut him off from contact with the great issue, but was not published until January 13. In it Mr. Roosevelt seemed to return to

[4] *Congressional Record,* Vol. 57, Pt. 2, pp. 1314–18.

his former belief that the thing was coming. He appeared to draw nearer, too, to the earlier friend with whom his differences had been greatest and most bitter in their consequences. "Mr. Taft," he wrote, "has recently defined the purposes of the league and the limitations under which it would act, in a way that enables most of us to say we very heartily agree in principle with his theory and can, without doubt, come to an agreement on specific details."

The Monroe Doctrine, in Roosevelt's view, was the most important of the details. It should be strictly maintained. Let Europe and Asia police the troubled areas on their thresholds and the United States treat Mexico as our Balkan peninsula. Above all we must take no position as an "international Meddlesome Matty." Such an effort, made "with utter scorn for words that are not made good by deeds," would be productive of real and lasting good.[5]

Taft, commenting on the Roosevelt valedictory two days later, saw no difficulty in securing recognition of the Monroe Doctrine as a policy in the interest of world peace "when the principles and operation of the league are really directed to the creation of a Monroe Doctrine of the world."

Recognizing that Roosevelt had "the greatest personal following in this country," Taft naturally wished his last word to carry full weight unto them. He recommended his example to all doubters and opponents of the league. "Let them treat the league," he asked, "as something in its purpose to be desired, and let them lead their thoughts not to devising and imagining objections, but to finding alternative substitutes in its structure which will not be subject to their own objections."[6]

No Satisfactory League Possible. Such an example and a like appeal were assuredly needed if the league was to have a chance in the Senate. The day which was featured by Senator Sterling's declaration and Theodore Roosevelt's final reaction to the league also brought a most significant account of the position of the Republican leaders in the Senate. The appraisal was made by Albert W. Fox, leading correspondent of the *Washington Post,* surely in the confidence of the Senate leaders. Under the declaration that no Senator was not in favor of a league in principle, he wrote: "Leaders of the opposition to the program do not see how a workable plan can possibly be evolved. They say that the league to be effective must in the last analysis employ

[5] *Kansas City Star,* January 13, 1919.
[6] *Philadelphia Public Ledger,* January 15, 1919.

armed force and that employment of this force must be compulsory upon the nations forming the league. This idea they oppose with emphasis. If the league employs merely 'moral force' they say it will not be effective and that it is merely waste of time to make it part of the peace treaty."

The opposition leaders did not intend to be denied. They might maintain themselves in favor of a league "in principle," but would refuse to accept it in practice. They did not know just what would be proposed—even the President did not yet know that—but all the signs pointed toward a strong league with real power to enforce the peace. They would oppose that "with emphasis." If, on the other hand, a strong league were not proposed they would ridicule it as ineffective, "a waste of time." The plan, whatever it might be, was to be fought *"unless it accomplishes what Republican leaders believe to be impossible."* [7]

The impossible, too, would have a liberal definition. In the event that the Conference arrived at a compromise that went to neither extreme, the thing would be condemned as being both too strong and too weak, as it actually was later on—sometimes almost in the same sentence.

Let the Enemy Be Dealt With! In justice to the Republican leaders it ought to be said, however, that there were at least some Democratic Senators who did not anticipate the successful creation of a league. Senator Myers, of Montana, thought it would take a year, if not longer, and that the settlement of the war was much more urgent. The fires of the late war were not yet entirely out, and we had better squelch them before taking steps to prevent the next conflagration. He especially wanted the league postponed until Germany had signed on the line because he did not want Germany in it. He wanted the Kaiser hanged and Germany broken up into the states which composed her. The federation should be dissolved entirely and any common government over Prussia, Bavaria and the others forbidden forever. Moreover, indemnities should be collected by the United States. [8]

Even this description of the function of the Peace Conference was restrained compared to that of Colonel Harvey, who described it as "simply a court to judge and penalize an international bandit and so to chain and bind him that the world will be immune from out-

---

[7] *Washington Post,* January 13, 1919. Italics supplied.
[8] *Congressional Record,* Vol. 57, Pt. 2, pp. 1319–22. January 13, 1919.

breaks of his congenital tendencies to barbarism and gorilla savagery for generations to come."

"Fair Warning." This tribute to the vanquished enemy was uttered to make emphatic Harvey's demand that no league be discussed at the Conference and his threat that the whole treaty might be defeated if it contained "matter certain to meet with Senate opposition." Senators Lodge and Knox, he said, were only giving fair warning from "a body in whose hands, so far as this country is concerned, the fate of the treaty rests." [9]

In a letter of February 1, Lodge gave Henry White an inkling of what that fate was likely to be, saying: "It seems here pretty clear that the League of Nations is going to be a voluntary association, and the idea of putting force behind it is abandoned. If they do put force behind it, I think it will be ill received here by the country generally and I do not believe it could pass the Senate." [10]

The *Washington Post* had expressed the same opinion of the probable nature of the league two days before. "The league as now agreed upon will be nothing more than an international association without power," said the editor. "It would be merely another advisory, statistical, rhetorical headquarters," he concluded, and added, "It is well." [11]

This was the feeling of Harvey. He had analyzed the thing and concluded that a league without force behind it would do no good and that one backed by force wouldn't do either. "The President's

[9] *Harvey's Weekly,* January 4, 1919, Vol. 2, No. 1, p. 7.
The President "of course" had no legal right to enter into a conference on the subject "unless Congress specifically authorized him to do so." After peace was made he could ask the permission of Congress if he liked.
In the same issue three pages of fun making about the President's visit to London were followed, on the short paragraph page, by one of his disarming little tributes, saying: "We doubt if any other foreign dignitary ever received in London a welcome quite comparable with that given to the President; or indeed if any other quite deserved it."
[10] Allan Nevins, *Henry White,* N. Y., 1930, p. 374.
White replied: "I can only repeat once more that no member of this Commission has the slightest intention, or ever has had, of allowing our army and navy to be placed in a position in which it can be subject to the orders of any international body; nor, so far as I have heard on the part of anyone, of abandoning or modifying the Monroe Doctrine."
Testifying to the dignity and distinction which had characterized everything done by the President in Europe, he added: "I have seen nothing but courtesy on his part to the various members of our own delegation; and in my own case he has always been ready to listen, and in several cases to accept suggestions, particularly in the phraseology of his draft of the constitution of the League of Nations. And there is no doubt that he has dealt with the other leading members of the Conference with great tact." (Pp. 375, 378.)
[11] *Washington Post,* January 30, 1919.

League of Nations," was "absolutely in the stage of rhetoric," but whatever he was aiming at the Monroe Doctrine would block it.[12]

What Must Precede a League. The hurdles in the President's way seemed to have been raised by his foes so high that there was no likelihood of his being able to scale them. Yet the ultimate was not achieved until Senator France, Republican, of Maryland, introduced, on January 14, a resolution reciting the great expense that the American and Allied soldiers were entailing and advising the peace conference to proceed with the establishment of a just peace at the earliest possible moment and that all "subsidiary questions" be postponed for later discussion at an international conference.

Under this resolution "the Senate, as part of the treaty making power of the Government," would "hereby consent to and most earnestly advise," in addition to bringing the troops home, the proper procedure for forming a league of nations. First, the President was to call, after the establishment of peace, a conference of all the powers in North and South America "to consider plans for the closer coöperation of these Governments in promoting justice, progress and friendship" among themselves.

Then, after this all-American conference, the President should call a conference of all the nations of the world to consider the same things and, in addition, plans for the removal of the economic and social causes of war. To this end particular attention was to be given to nine problems:

1. The congestion of population of some nations.
2. The underpopulation of other nations.
3. The unregulated competition between the more populous and industrial countries for the raw products and trade of the less populous and agricultural ones.
4. The exploitation of the weaker and the less advanced by the stronger and more highly organized nations.
5. A larger self determination of peoples.
6. The economic development of the backward regions.
7. Means to educate the world out of national, social, and religious antagonisms.
8. The establishment of constitutional governments throughout the world upon which could be based a permanent international order.

[12] *Harvey's Weekly,* January 25, 1919, Vol. 2, No. 4, p. 4.
The "passionate patriot" would conscribe "ten million men if necessary for our safety, but not one at alien dictation for an alien cause."

9. "The elimination of all causes of national enmities and the establishment of friendship and justice between the nations, with a view to the ultimate establishment of a league of nations or world federation of republics for the purpose of promoting the cause of progress and peace throughout the earth." [13]

If anyone still doubted that it would take a long time to create a league of nations, let him look over this proposal. Certainly there was in it no unseemly haste to organize the world against war. It would first be necessary to remove all the great economic and social causes of war, to regulate all imperialist activities, to establish representative government uniformly over the earth, and to educate the world out of national, racial and religious antagonisms. Then you could begin to consider "the ultimate establishment of a league of nations." In other words, when you arrived at the millennium you would be there. Then no league would be necessary.

Senator Borah's Direct Assault. When Mr. France sat down, Senator Borah, of Idaho, rose to deliver a direct frontal attack on the whole idea of a league. To him it was only the old Holy Alliance brought to life. It would attempt impossible tasks. He would have none of it for the further reason that it might in the future repress some desirable human movement.

Senators, you can not establish peace by force, by repression. If you have any other workable scheme or plan, bring it forward, but the scheme based on force is more repulsive and destructive of human justice and human liberty and human progress than Prussianism itself. It is Prussianism extended, amplified and denationalized. If you think you can seek out and do justice to all nations, great and small; if you think you can found an organization based upon the principles of human progress and whose decrees are enforced by public opinion; if you think you can prescribe reasonable rules for change and growth and progress; if you think you can look into the hearts of a particular people and interpret that inexplicable passion which when the appointed hour comes melts away all obstacles, rejects all restraints, and forces its way from a small to a great nation; if you think you can look upon a French Revolution cursed with apparent stupidity and steeped in blood and foretell that in a hundred years these same people, disenthralled and free will stand between civilization and organized barbarism as the French stood at the Marne; if you think you can now look upon a broken and dismembered Russia and foretell her future or point out along what paths she will

[13] *Congressional Record,* Vol. 57, Pt. 2, p. 1383.

move in order that she may realize the best that is in her; if you think you can do what the living God has not been able to do, standardize the human family; if you feel you can undo what He in His inscrutable wisdom did when He planted race prejudice in the hearts and stamped color upon the faces of men, then give us your prospectus. We will be glad to look it over. We shall be infinitely happy if we find it workable. But if you are simply going back to the old discarded league of military power with which to put out conflagration, to repress movements, and to kill off those who are dissatisfied and who in their madness and helplessness are striving for better things, we should reject it and denounce it as a menace to human liberty and a challenge to human progress.

Internationalism an Evil Force. Mr. Borah was wholly opposed to any kind of internationalism. "The fact is," he said, "we have come in contact with two evil forces from the Old World—Prussianism and internationalism. Instead of repelling and rejecting them we are yielding to their slimy maw the proudest heritage ever left to the keeping of any people." Both doctrines contemplated world dominion and the utter destruction of the national spirit everywhere. Both were "founded upon treachery, deceit, lying, repression, force, decimation, and assassination." He would have no "international superstate resting upon Prussian force, with a vast army of repression."

The thing which had won the war and beat down militarism "was the Frenchman's love of country, the Briton's love of country, the American's love of country—that which internationalism would murder." The boys who had stopped the Germans at Château-Thierry had been red blooded Americans, "not soldiers by profession, not the Hessian puppets of some superinternational tribunal nor yet the anemic minions or soulless scavengers of internationalism—God pity the ideals of this Republic if they shall have no defenders save the gathered scum of the nations organized into a conglomerate international police force, ordered hither and thither by the most heterogeneous and irresponsible body or court that ever confused or confounded the natural instincts and noble passions of a people." [14]

Senator Williams' Reply. Evidently it would be difficult to argue with a man who felt as strongly about it as that, and who could express his hatred of the idea so effectively. How would you go about it? Probably few Senators cared to undertake it spontaneously. One did. When Mr. Borah had finished, John Sharp Williams rose and

[14] *Congressional Record,* Vol. 57, Pt. 2, pp. 1383–87.

read a poem written by a woman whose sons had been killed in the
war, "by a woman whose boys were dead, not written by me or any
other man who was in the safest bomb-proof position on the surface
of the earth, to wit, the floor of the Senate of the United States. . . ."
It closed with the lines:

> This potent league of nations will send no gun nor sword,
> Its order is the law of the ever living Lord
> The law of harmony, all brutal war shall cease—
> Its corner stone is justice, its translucent walls are peace.
> Rise, citizens! Arise from the weary, blood drenched sod,
> Proclaim the league of nations—sealed with the seal of God!

"Translucent walls!" Anybody not a fool can see through them. They
are translucent—God is behind them. Ultimately you *must* see Him,
whether you will or not.

"With the seal of God," and, thank God, not with the seal of the
Senate of the United States, unless the Senate shall hereafter indicate
a sufficient degree of common sense to affix its seal, which I doubt.[15]

No better demonstration of the variety of men's minds need be
asked. Two of the keenest and most independent minds in the Senate
looked at the same proposal: one saw in it only degradation to his
beloved country and danger to human liberty everywhere; the other
saw only the hand of God himself pointing inexorably to a safer and
happier world in which there would be greater freedom and less sorrow
for all peoples.

The contrast between the views of Borah and Taft, however, was
only less marked. The latter feared that the President might rely only
on the moral sanction of justice. He felt that "if that is the only
sanction the league of nations is going to furnish for the judgment
of its court and suppression of lawless violence by recalcitrant nations,
it will be a failure and a laughing stock." [16]

Reaction from the War. Mr Taft's vision of the great object of
the war had not been dimmed by its ending, but it was clear by this
time that reaction from the high aims of the war was under way.[17]
Up to the Armistice the Allied world had been compelled to concentrate
its energies to win the war. Feeling that liberty and democracy were

---

[15] *Congressional Record,* Vol. 57, Pt. 2, p. 1388.
[16] *Philadelphia Public Ledger,* January 20, 1919.
[17] For a clear description of the "slump in idealism" see Vol. I, Chapter V, of
Woodrow Wilson and the World Settlement, by Ray Stannard Baker, N. Y., 1922.

challenged by German militarism, the people of each nation had been compelled to rise out of their ordinary ways to new heights of sacrifice and purpose. Moral endurance became as important as physical stamina. Selfish competition did not cease by any means, but an abnormal amount of coöperation was either voluntarily given or forced.

The war had to be won and any leader who put new faith and energy into the allied peoples was heard and followed gladly. Men's minds, too, were open to new appeals for better ways of doing things. Hence Wilson in his calls for a new order roused in the main only enthusiasm and support during the last year of the War. Many saw his vision, and all felt in some degree the power of his leadership.

Then the War ended and most people let down. We cannot live too long in a high state of emotional exaltation; both physical and moral reaction is inevitable. It set in at once after the Armistice. Everybody wanted to get back to normal as quickly as possible. The good old ways of doing things seemed kindly and dependable after all—even the old ways of making peace.

From his very first utterance on peace in the days of neutrality, the President had talked always of a moderate and just peace. First it was "a peace without victory," of "no annexation and no indemnities," and later it was to be a permanent peace. Nobody sounded the call to battle stronger than he. There was to be no limit to our effort, he declared in New York, on May 18, 1918. Every ship would carry every man and every supply it could move until victory was won. But before the speech was done he had reminded his hearers that "Friendship is the only cement that will ever hold the world together." It was so in almost every utterance; the peace was not to be vindictive, and it was to be permanent.

Such an objective appealed to the best that was in many of the President's countrymen; others acquiesced in it, under the stimulus of his leadership, until the hatreds stirred by the war obscured all high goals set up for the future. These feelings naturally persisted after the conflict closed. People had been given so many reasons for hating the Germans that the cry to deal with them first must have been accepted by many who were also friendly to the idea of a league.

President Wilson's Campaign for the League Abroad

How far would the reaction go? Even in the midst of preparations to go overseas Mr. Wilson must have felt some weakening of the support under him at home. The hostility of powerful groups to his going had been too marked to escape notice, but he remained confident of the support of the plain people. The wholly unprecedented popular ovation which he received in New York as he embarked must have strengthened this feeling.

A Stern Task Ahead. There could be no doubt that many European conservatives would oppose his mission. Whether or not he was aware of all the secret treaties that existed, the President also knew enough history to know how many nationalistic interests would press for place and power at Versailles. His deliberate and successful effort to pledge the Allies to a new kind of settlement had been begun a year before, in the statement of the Fourteen Points. His program had been accepted in its entirety, but he knew it was likely to be disputed at each point in its application. In the cabin of the *George Washington* he appealed to the company of experts, who had long been gathering information for the Commission, for their coöperation, saying: "Tell me what is right, and I'll fight for it; give me a guaranteed position." If a new order of affairs would not work it must be made to work. The acceptance of the poison of Bolshevism was protest enough against the way the world had been managed. It was our business at the Peace Conference to fight for a new order, "agreeably if we can, disagreeably if we must." [18] Constantly during the voyage he spoke of the 10,000,000 men killed in the war, a total which had just been announced. [19] It was a figure fit to weigh upon the mind of any man who could imagine what it meant.

Arriving in Paris the President found that the British Government had decided to secure a new lease of power from a general election, in which the slogans proved to be "Abolish Conscription," "Hang the Kaiser" and "Search their Pockets" for the last farthing of indemnity. The French Government also was not ready to begin the Conference. It maintained that the tasks of preparation were greater

---

[18] David Hunter Miller, *The Drafting of the Covenant,* N. Y., 1928, Vol. I, pp. 41–44.

Some report of this speech preceded the President to Europe and created an impression among the leaders of stormy weather ahead. Lawrence, *The True Story of Woodrow Wilson,* p. 249.

That the later fighting proved to be remarkably agreeable, considering its intensity, is attested by André Tardieu in his book *The Truth About the Treaty* (Indianapolis, 1921). After describing the forty day struggle between Clemenceau, Lloyd George and Wilson over the disposition of the left bank of the Rhine, he concluded as follows: "The long debate is over. Despite divergences of opinion, the personal relations between the three men during those forty days have never ceased to be sincere, calm and affectionate. May their fellow countrymen never forget it" (p. 186).

[19] Raymond B. Fosdick, *New York Times,* February 10, 1924.

than expected. A month of enforced waiting ensued, during which the President tried to explain to the world again why the creation of the League must be the basis of the Peace. [20]

Organized Moral Force. At the Sorbonne, on December 21, he said: "My conception of the league of nations is just this, that it shall operate as the organized moral force of men throughout the world, and that whenever or wherever wrong and aggression are planned or contemplated, this searching light of conscience will be turned upon them and men everywhere will ask, 'What are the purposes you hold in your heart against the fortunes of the world?' Just a little exposure will settle most questions." [21]

On Christmas Day he told an army of American soldiers, in a voice full of emotion, that "The world will now know that the nations that fought this war, as well as the soldiers who represented them, are ready to make good—make good not merely the assertion of their own interests, but make good in the establishment of peace upon the permanent foundations of right and justice." [22]

In his address to King George in Buckingham Palace, on December 27, he expressed again his belief that the moral forces of the world must have organized means of expression. "There is a great tide running in the hearts of men. The hearts of men have never beaten so singularly in unison before. Men have never before been so conscious of their brotherhood. Men have never before realized how little difference there was between right and justice in one latitude and in another, under one sovereignty and another; and it will be our high privilege, I believe, Sir, not only to apply the moral judgments of the world to the particular settlements which we shall attempt, but also to organize the moral force of the world to preserve those settlements, to steady the forces of mankind and to make the right and justice to

[20] Lawrence, *The True Story of Woodrow Wilson*, p. 246. Further reasons for the delay in getting the conference started are given on pp. 247–54.

Winston Churchill explains that the ministers did not invent the cries of the British election of 1918; they arose spontaneously from the people and swept the leaders along with them. According to the same writer, Lloyd George gained a huge majority, nearly five-sixths of the House of Commons, for his coalition government, but mortally injured his own Liberal party. His great following in the House was hereafter composed of Conservatives who would support him only so long as his personal prestige lasted.—Winston Churchill, *The Aftermath, 1918–1928*, N. Y., 1929, pp. 27–39.

[21] Shaw, *Messages and Papers of Woodrow Wilson*, N. Y., 1917, Vol. I, p. 577.

[22] *Ibid.*, 579.

On the same day Col. Roosevelt demanded "A Square Deal for the Man at the Front," urging the return of all troops except the regulars as soon as possible. *Washington Post,* December 26, 1918.

which great nations like our own have devoted themselves, the predominant and controlling force of the world." [23]

Here was no suggestion of the dread superstate with its gigantic armies, its dangers, and its crushing of human liberty, which the Senators in Washington were holding up before the American people.

Balanced Force Had Failed. At his Guildhall reception the next day he mentioned several factors in the singular combination of emotions that he had felt in the great crowds welcoming him to London. One element in it, surely, had been "the consciousness that the business is not yet done, the consciousness that it now rests upon others to see that those lives were not lost in vain." He felt that the armies had fought to do away with the old order, "and the center and characteristic of the old order was that unstable thing which we used to call the 'balance of power'—a thing in which the balance was determined by the sword which was thrown in the one side or the other; a balance which was determined by the unstable equilibrium of competitive interests; a balance which was maintained by jealous watchfulness and an antagonism of interests which, though it was generally latent, was always deep-seated. The men who have fought in this war have been the men from free nations, who were determined that that sort of thing should end now and forever." [24]

The President was here on sure historical ground. No attempt to maintain an equilibrium between rival groups of powers had ever succeeded; none ever would, for the reasons that one side would inevitably conclude it was stronger than the other or become obsessed with fear that the other side was about to become stronger. Certainly the United States could take little pride in a peace that offered nothing better than that, as the President pointed out at the Free Trade Hall in Manchester two days later, saying: "You know that the United States has always felt from the very beginning of her history that she must keep herself separate from any kind of European politics, and I want to say very frankly to you that she is not now interested in European politics. But she is interested in the partnership of right between America and Europe. If the future had nothing for us but a new attempt to keep the world at a right poise by a balance of power, the United States would take no interest, because she will join no combination of power that is not the combination of all of us." [25]

[23] Shaw, *Messages and Papers of Woodrow Wilson*, p. 582.
[24] Shaw, *Messages and Papers of Woodrow Wilson*, p. 584.   [25] *Ibid.*, p. 591.
Following these addresses George Bernard Shaw concluded that "After the banquet at Buckingham palace and the reception at the guildhall, no doubt remained as

But the old relation between nations was not to give way at once, either in Europe or in Washington. In spite of the fatuity of either isolation or alliance to prevent world wide war, the gray heads did not know just what the alternative would do for them. On the same day that President Wilson was speaking in Manchester, Premier Clemenceau pleaded in the French Chamber of Deputies for the making of alliances, and received a great vote of confidence. [26] The old warrior could see at least a generation of security for France in this course.

In reply, Wilson explained again, at the close of his speech to the Italian Parliament at Rome, on January 3, that the balance of power had been "tried and found wanting for the best of reasons that it does not stay balanced inside itself, and a weight that does not hold together can not constitute a make weight in the affairs of men." A thoroughly united league of nations was the substitute. "What men once considered theoretical and idealistic turns out to be practical and necessary." [27]

A Protection for Small Nations New and Old. In the same address the President also gave one of the great reasons why the league should be at the foundation of the Peace. Many new states were to be set up, some of them near that great center of intrigue, the Balkans. They had not been accustomed to being independent and it was "our duty as their friends to see that some kind of protection is thrown around them, something supplied which will hold them together. There is only one thing that holds nations together, if you exclude force, and that is friendship and good will. . . . Therefore, our task at Paris is to organize the friendship of the world, to see to it that all the moral forces that make for right and justice and liberty are united and are given a vital organization to which the peoples of the world will readily and gladly respond." [28]

There had been much talk about securing the rights of small nations. Some responsibility must now exist to safeguard those rights.

---

to who was king, by divine right of character and personality in Western Europe." *Washington Post*, February 9, 1919.

[26] Lawrence, *The True Story of Woodrow Wilson*, p. 253.

Harvey commented comfortably on Clemenceau's stand saying, that such an amazing proposal as an "omnibus league," containing all nations, "to which we have no idea that the Senate of the United States would ever for a moment assent, would be accepted . . . by European Powers was, of course, impossible." But he (Wilson) would go, so if he found himself embarrassed and defeated it was his own fault.— *Harvey's Weekly*, January 11, 1919, Vol. 2, No. 2, pp. 3–4.

[27] Shaw, *Messages and Papers of Woodrow Wilson*, p. 598.

[28] *Ibid.*, p. 597.

Especially to the new states yet to be created, the great powers that gave them birth would be under heavy obligation to see that they had a fair start in the world. No agency could do this so well as one which represented and included all.

An Agency For the Future Adjustment of Wrongs. A further powerful reason for the association of the league with the administration of the peace treaties was suggested by Mr. Wilson at Manchester. After repeating his conviction that there was a great compulsion of the common conscience in existence, the resistance of which would give any statesman the most unenviable eminence in history, he said: "We are not obeying the mandates of parties or of politics. We are obeying the mandates of humanity. That is the reason why it seems to me that the things which are most often in our minds are the least significant. I am not hopeful that the individual items of the settlements we are about to attempt will be altogether satisfactory. One has but to apply his mind to any one of the questions of boundary and of altered sovereignty and of racial aspiration to do something more than conjecture that there is no man and no body of men who knows just how it ought to be settled. Yet if we are to make unsatisfactory settlements, we must see to it that they are rendered more and more satisfactory by the subsequent adjustments which are made possible." [29]

It is becoming generally recognized now that it was not humanly possible to settle every question as it should have been settled in the midst of the storm of ambitions and jealousies, of magnified hopes and exaggerated fears that centered at Paris in 1919, but an agency that would at least make possible the later peaceable adjustment of the inevitable errors could be created. This course, it is needless to say, did not appeal to the new leaders of the United States Senate, where it was asserted, on the contrary, that article ten of the Covenant would perpetuate every injustice that existed as long as the league should last. Which was the longer view is indicated by Germany's entry into the league with the well understood intent to eventually secure by peaceful means a modification of some of the terms of the Treaty which she considers most unjust to her.

To have pressed such an argument before men who in 1919 did not appreciate or care that postponement of the league in all probability would prevent its creation, would, of course, have been of no avail; to have suggested in the atmosphere of war hatred still existing that even Germany might use the league to secure a modification of the terms im-

[29] Shaw, *Messages and Papers of Woodrow Wilson*, p. 592.

posed on her would have been to damn it even more completely. It was enough condemned in advance of its creation already.

A Sacred Pledge to be Redeemed. But the man who had led at least a section of men in a score of nations in a crusade to end once and for all the menace of military conquest could not rest his case alone on the practical advantages of a league of nations. There was a moral issue at stake which he of all men on the face of the earth was most bound to state and restate. So at Milan, on January 5, there was more than a mere play on sentiment in the following: "I was very much touched today, sir, to receive at the hands of wounded soldiers a memorial in favor of a league of nations, and to be told by them that that was what they had fought for; not merely to win this war, but to secure something beyond, some guarantee of justice, some equilibrium for the world as a whole which would make it certain that they would never have to fight a war like this again. This is the added obligation that is upon us who make peace. We can not merely sign a treaty of peace and go home with clear consciences. We must do something more. We must add, so far as we can, the securities which suffering men everywhere demand; and when I speak of suffering men I think also of suffering women." [30]

THE PRESIDENT'S STAND IN THE CONFERENCE FOR A NEW DISPENSATION

The powers were now ready to open the conference. It remained to be seen whether Mr. Wilson could actually get his plan for an organized peace into the treaty.

The Problem of Publicity. The conference opened on January 12, 1919. In this very first day the President suffered a loss of prestige that hurt him seriously. The first of his Fourteen Points had declared for "open covenants openly arrived at." It had been phrased in opposition to secret treaties, secret alliances—to the whole system of secret diplomacy that seemed to have brought on the War, or at least made it impossible to prevent Europe from drifting into hostilities. It seemed fundamental to the President to drag international business into the light of day. That was therefore his first proposal.

The idea was popular and the meaning of the phrase outran Mr. Wilson long before he got to Europe. The people, and particularly the press, took the statement literally. American newspapers alone sent

[30] *Ibid.,* p. 606.

a hundred and fifty of their ablest correspondents to see the peace made. It was apparently expected that all the meetings would be public, with the press reporting each step.

No such thing occurred. The newspaper men, keyed up to tell just how the world was being remade, waited outside, and at the end of the first day a secretary slipped out and read five lines to them saying that after a consideration of conditions necessary for the renewal of the Armistice, the delegates took up questions of procedure. [31] This was what had happened, but the indignation and disgust of the reporters is not difficult to imagine. The American newspaper men sent a vigorous protest to the President which he put before the Conference and supported, but with little result.

The French, who alone still maintained a censorship over the press, and who had many papers controlled by their Foreign Office, stood for secrecy and were backed by the Italians. Mr. Lloyd George dreaded and feared his newspaper enemies in England, particularly Lord Northcliffe. Only Wilson believed he could use the repercussions of popular opinion to his advantage, so the correspondents had to supplement the official statements with what grapevine information and rumor they could gather.

The fact was that all the delegates soon recognized that the public discussion of many of the delicate questions would arouse such diverse storms of criticism and passion in different countries as to prevent solution, and cause the fall of governments as well. Mr. Wilson, with all the opposition that was gathering in his rear, was the only chief of state who could not be overturned at once by anger or disappointment aroused at home. The atmosphere was, moreover, still that of war, and, in addition, the wall of secrecy that had surrounded diplomacy for ages could not be removed by one effort, although most of the secrets of the conference leaked into the press unofficially for weeks until the Council of Four was created. Even then much important news came through quickly, especially from the Territorial Commissions. [32] One has only to compare the American newspapers with the authentic history of the Conference now available to see how much was known at once.

Nevertheless the disappointment resulting from the failure of full

---

[31] Ray Stannard Baker, *Woodrow Wilson and World Settlement*, N. Y., 1922, Vol. I, p. 139.

[32] H. W. V. Temperly, *A History of the Peace Conference of Paris*, London, 1920, Vol. I, pp. 254–56. See also, Chapters VII to VIII in Baker.

publicity was a real loss to President Wilson. He had never meant that there should be no private discussion and settlement of delicate matters, as he had explained to the Senate on June 12, 1918,[33] but such explanations never counteracted the impression which people had formed. It gave his enemies at home a talking point which lasted them until the Conference adjourned; it fitted in perfectly with their announcement already made that something was going to be foisted on the American people. Mr. Borah and Mr. Johnson promptly expressed in the Senate, on January 17, their amazement and disappointment at the lack of complete publicity,[34] and Senators never ceased to complain that they did not know what was going on.

The Allies for Dividing the Conquests First. The degree of publicity that was to be given proceedings having been determined, and the battle for the English language having been won, a test of the President's ability to get his program adopted came at once.

The French had offered their plan of procedure at the first session of the Conference.[35] It put the league of nations last. The French leaders, too, were not the only ones present at the Conference who wanted the lands and mines and indemnities divided first. There was some sentiment for the creation of a league of nations in most of the delegations and a great deal of it in some, particularly those from the British countries. Yet even the British Dominions wanted the German colonies divided before the league was created. For others of the older diplomats, needless to say, a traditional peace treaty, based largely upon the network of secret treaties signed between them in the early years of the war was good enough.

With his long held conviction that the league and the spirit back of it must be the basis of any peace that would have a chance of permanence, the President introduced at the second session an order of procedure, prepared by the other members of the American Commission, which placed the league of nations first.[36]

Early Origins of the League Covenant. Shortly before, on January 10, he had submitted his second draft of a league agreement to the British leaders. This draft was based in part upon a first draft which Wilson had made in the summer of 1918. This in turn was an adaptation of a draft by Colonel House which the President had requested

[33] Baker, *Woodrow Wilson and World Settlement,* Vol. I, p. 137.
[34] *Congressional Record,* Vol. 57, Pt. 2, p. 1582 ff.
[35] Baker, *Woodrow Wilson and World Settlement,* Vol. I, p. 236.
[36] *Ibid.,* p. 198.

earlier, following receipt of the report of the Phillimore committee—
the first serious effort to frame definite proposals for a league.

The Phillimore draft was the result of exhaustive study by an
official committee composed of seven of the leading English authorities on International Law and politics, appointed by Foreign Secretary Balfour. It contained both scholars and representatives of the
Foreign Office. [37] Its report was submitted, March 20, 1918, and circulated confidentially to President Wilson and the Dominion governments. Being the first authoritative attempt to outline a league constitution it naturally served not only as the basis of all the earlier drafts,
American and British, but contributed many principles which found
their way into the final Covenant.

Wilson's First Paris Draft was influenced considerably also by the
sketch of another British statesman, Prime Minister Jan C. Smuts,
of the South African Union, written December 16, 1918. This outline
began with the thought that the primary and basic task of the conference was to set up a league and it proposed that the Austrian and
Turkish territories be distributed to mandatories of the league. [38]
Smuts did not suggest the German colonies in Africa for that treatment
because he thought the barbarians inhabiting these regions could not
soon arise to civilized statehood, a conviction which he still holds. [39]

"No Annexations" Insisted Upon. The idea of distributing the conquered territories under a scheme of mandates was not new to President
Wilson. He had urged its necessity during the voyage to Europe. [40]
Recalling the trusteeships we had assumed and still exercised over
Cuba and the Philippines, he thought it a good principle to apply to all
the colonial lands to be taken from the losers in the war. A distribu-
tion on this basis would not only give the league immediate and continuing work to do, it would introduce a theory of responsibility which
had always been wanting in dividing the spoils of war. It accorded, moreover, with the principle of self-determination which was the foundation of his program.

Consequently he proposed, in his draft of January 10, to apply
the mandate idea also to the German colonies in Africa, New Guinea
and the Southern Pacific. Smuts was opposed to this extension of the

[37] David Hunter Miller, *The Drafting of the Covenant*, N. Y., 1928, pp. 3–17.
Besides Sir Walter Phillimore the Committee contained Prof. A. F. Pollard, Dr. J.
H. Rose, Sir Wm. Tyrrell, Sir John Corbett, Sir Eyre Crowe and Mr. C. J. B. Hurst.
[38] Miller, *The Drafting of the Covenant*, p. 35.
[39] See Chapter 3 in his *Africa and Some World Problems*, Oxford, 1930.
[40] Miller, *The Drafting of the Covenant*, p. 43.

plan and the prime ministers of Australia and New Zealand were totally against it. The President's advocacy of drastic reduction of armaments also stirred the continental diplomats deeply.[41]

Immediate Creation of the League Decided. These divergencies of opinion, however, did not prevent agreement that the league should be a "part of the peace." A resolution to that effect, drafted by the British on January 15, was amended by President Wilson to read "as an integral part of the general treaty of peace," in order to put the matter beyond question, and passed by the Council of Ten on January 22, 1919. [42] The resolution read:

> The Conference, having considered the proposals for the creation of a League of Nations, resolves that
> 1. It is essential to the maintenance of the world settlement, which the Associated Nations are now met to establish, that a League of Nations be created to promote international coöperation, to insure the fulfillment of accepted international obligations and to provide safeguards against war.
> 2. This League should be created as an integral part of the general Treaty of Peace, and should be open to every civilized nation which can be relied on to promote its objects.
> 3. The members of the League should periodically meet in international conference, and should have a permanent organization and secretariat to carry on the business of the League in the intervals between the conferences.
> The Conference therefore appoints a Committee representative of the Associated Governments to work out the details of the constitution and functions of the League.[43]

The same resolution was unanimously accepted by the second plenary session of the Conference, on January 25. In a powerful speech on that occasion Wilson stressed again the central truth that becomes more apparent with the passage of each year. Holding the creation of the league the central object of the Conference, he said: "Settlements may be temporary, but the actions of the nations in the interests of peace and justice must be permanent. We can set up permanent processes. We may not be able to set up permanent decisions." [44]

The Issue of Annexations Fought Out. The triumph of the Presi-

[41] Baker, *Woodrow Wilson and World Settlement*, Vol. I, pp. 236–7.
[42] *Ibid.*
[43] Miller, *The Drafting of the Covenant*, p. 76.
[44] Baker, *Woodrow Wilson and World Settlement*, Vol. I, p. 239.

dent's conviction was not achieved, however, without a severe struggle, carried on simultaneously, to establish the mandate principle. On January 23, the day after the league resolution had been adopted in the Council of Ten, the British pressed for annexation of the German Colonies. British home opinion seems to have been divided as to the wisdom of expanding the empire, particularly of acquiring more African territory. [45] Mr. Lloyd George himself proposed the application of the mandatory system in the German colonial areas occupied by troops from the United Kingdom. [46]

The Southern Dominions, however, wanting outright annexation of the lands they had taken from Germany, Lloyd George moved that colonial matters be taken up and was at once seconded by Clemenceau for France and Sonnino for Italy. The President was somewhat surprised, since the questions urgently pressing were all European. Chaotic conditions in Russia, Poland and other countries had seemed to demand attention. He accordingly objected to considering the least urgent question of all and apparently won the point, for it was decided, on the 23rd, that all delegations should send in their territorial claims in writing within ten days.

On the following day, however, Lloyd George suddenly brought the British Empire, in the persons of the four Dominion Prime Ministers, in before the Council of Ten to ask for immediate annexation of the German colonies. [47] In their justification it is said that the representatives of Australia and New Zealand did not understand that only international control, not actual international administration, was intended and that Smuts regarded German Southwest Africa as so nearly unpopulated as to constitute a problem of land development rather than colonial administration. [48] The Pacific dominions were also nervous about the strategic control of the lands in question.

Their attack, led by Lloyd George and supported by similar French and Japanese annexation claims, was pushed until President Wilson declared, on January 27, that if the very first thing they did was to parcel out the helpless parts of the world a league of nations would be impossible. Speaking to the Council of Ten, temporarily enlarged to thirty-three men by the importance of the issue, the President expounded his whole conception of trusteeship for the colonial areas. Mr. Lloyd

[45] Miller, *The Drafting of the Covenant*, pp. 103-4.
[46] Temperly, *A History of the Peace Conference of Paris*, Vol. II, p. 233.
[47] Baker, Vol. I, p. 252-3.
[48] Temperly, Vol. II, p. 233.

George favored the President's principles but wanted the Dominions to have what they desired. Premier Hughes, of Australia, readily admitted that the mandatory system was suitable for territories other than New Guinea. Mr. Massey, of New Zealand, was "a great enthusiast for the league of nations," but he was anxious not to burden it too much in the beginning. Better distribute the colonies first and let the league "start with a clear sheet." The French made no pretence of believing in the new method of dealing with colonies; they argued for "annexation pure and simple."

Matters came to a showdown on the 28th, and the President refusing to yield, the French began a red hot press campaign against him, in which some British papers, led by Hughes of Australia, joined. On the 30th, the President felt compelled to tell the Council that if the attacks did not cease he would be compelled to publish his own views. The direct attacks stopped at once.

Then the British tried to persuade him that the league had in fact been created on the 25th, and proposed a mandate scheme that would be quite strict for other territories not wanted by the Dominions. This scheme was pushed to the limit of ultimatums by Massey and Hughes and of despair of agreement by Lloyd George, but after a week the battle was finally ended by turning the question over to the League of Nations Commission. Wilson had made it plain that he meant to fight for a new kind of settlement and that the league was to be created in time to influence the settlements that were to open a new epoch in the world's history. [49]

THE DRAFTING OF THE LEAGUE'S CHARTER

The President then turned as much energy as he could spare from the sessions of the Council to the preparation of the league agreement. He undertook this task without the support of his Secretary of State. Mr. Lansing had prepared a paper on December 24 entitled "The Constitutional Power to Provide Coercion in a Treaty" in which he questioned the existence of such a power. Later, on January 20, it was necessary for Wilson to tell him that a resolution designed to keep the league covenant out of the treaty was "neither necessary nor advisable." [50]

[49] Baker, *Woodrow Wilson and World Settlement*, Vol. I, pp. 268–74.
[50] Miller, *The Drafting of the Covenant*, pp. 24, 27. Mr. Miller's reply to the Lansing memorandum is that most treaties commit Congress, the courts or the Executive to some future action. The treaties whereby we purchased great areas of land

The League Commission Widely Representative. The League of Nations Commission originally contained fifteen men representing ten nations. Wilson and House sat for the United States; Lord Robert Cecil and Smuts for Great Britain; Leon Bourgeois and Ferdinand Larnaude for France. The French representatives, like the Anglo-Saxon members, had been the leaders of a vigorous league movement in their own nation. In response to it the French Chamber of Deputies had passed a resolution in favor of a league of nations on June 5, 1917. On the following July 22 a commission for the study of the problem was established at the Ministry of Foreign Affairs, and the French had a draft for a league ready to present to the Commission.

The lesser nations, represented originally by delegates from Belgium, Brazil, China, Portugal and Serbia, insisted in the second meeting of the Commission that the representation of the smaller powers be increased and, under the leadership of the able Belgian, Paul Hymans, won their point. The admission of Czecho-Slovakia, Greece, Poland and Rumania to the Commission brought to the deliberations the distinguished Greek Premier, Venizelos, and other capable leaders. This recognition of the intense interest of the smaller nations in the league was just. By the testimony of one who attended its sessions, it also contributed to the Commission a "striking group of statesmen, so keenly interested that they presented an unbroken record of attendance at the meetings and contributed to the discussion a force and vision which rivalled that of the Greater Powers." [51]

The Conference might have granted admission to spokesmen of the neutrals with equal profit, for groups of influential people in Scandinavia, Switzerland, the Netherlands and other countries had been supporting the idea as vigorously as any in the United States or Great Britain. Later, however, a committee from the Commission held meetings with representatives of thirteen neutral powers to receive their views of the completed draft of the Covenant. [52]

Realization of the desperate need for a unity of nations had been

---

notably did so. Treaties of alliance are clearly constitutional and an agreement to declare war upon a condition subsequent is equally so. "Upon the happening of the condition, it would become the *duty* of Congress to declare war and thus fulfill the treaty obligation, but it would also be within the *power* of Congress to refuse to declare war and thus breach the treaty obligation" (p. 27).

[51] W. H. Shepardson, quoted in Miller, *The Drafting of the Covenant,* p. 121.

[52] Miller, *The Drafting of the Covenant,* pp. 132, 303. Other facts stated above are taken from an unpublished memorandum obtained from the files of Mr. D. P. Myers, Research Director of the World Peace Foundation, 40 Mt. Vernon St., Boston.

THE COMMISSION WHICH FRAMED THE COVENANT

Standing, from left to right: COLONEL HOUSE, United States; M. DMOSKI, Poland; M. VESNITCH, Serbia; GENERAL SMUTS, Great Britain; PRESIDENT WILSON, CHAIRMAN; M. DIAMANDI, Roumania; M. HYMANS, Belgium; WELLINGTON KOO, China; M. REIS, Portugal; SIGNOR SCIALOJA, Italy; M. LARNAUDE, France.

Seated, from left to right: VISCOUNT CHINDA, Japan; BARON MAKINO, Japan; LEON BOURGEOIS, France; LORD ROBERT CECIL, Great Britain; PREMIER ORLANDO, Italy; PREMIER KRAMARZ, Czechoslovakia; PREMIER VENIZELOS, Greece. (M. PESSOA of Brazil, the nineteenth member, is not in the photograph.)

Photograph by Paul Thompson

Reproduced by courtesy of The Review of Reviews

keen and compelling in every civilized country. No member of the Commission, for example, contributed more sympathetically to the framing of the Covenant than Premier Orlando of Italy. His remarks in the Commission were always clear and to the point, and his point of view was that of practical common sense. President Wilson deferred greatly to his opinions and "said openly that he differed with him very rarely, and then with hesitation." [53]

President Wilson's Contribution. Beginning on February 3, ten meetings of the League Commission were held in ten days, mostly in the evening after the day's work in the Council, and several lasted into the hours beyond midnight. Knowing how much depended on completion before the other settlements had hardened, the President drove himself to the limit. [54] Years later Lloyd George said of his labor at the Conference, "The rest of us found time for golf and we took Sundays off, but Wilson, in his zeal, worked incessantly. Only those who were there and witnessed it can realize the effort he expended."

Mr. Wilson's chairmanship of the Commission has been described by two observers. Whitney H. Shepardson wrote: "He induced discussion where needed. He checked it when it ran too far or became involved in technicalities. He was sympathetic toward every view put forward. He was decisive when he spoke for the United States." [55] The notes of David Hunter Miller add: "The meetings were greatly dominated by President Wilson. The whole tone of the speeches, when differing from his views, conveyed the aim of convincing him, which indeed they sometimes did. But to his final opinions there was an unmistakable deference." [56] A lamentable deference, his American critics would have said.

The President's great contribution was not in the determination of the terms of the articles but in securing a decision of the nations to set up a league that they could all accept. While he influenced many articles and was responsible for the inclusion of several, he was the original author of few. The germ of Article 11, even, came originally from Colonel House [57] and the principle in Article 10 Wilson regarded as indigenous in the Monroe Doctrine. For that matter most of the principles adopted were already old. The Covenant merely attempted to gain for them universal acceptance and application.

---

[53] Miller, *The Drafting of the Covenant*, p. 126.
[54] *New York Times,* February 4, 1924.
[55] An account published in American newspapers Sunday, February 23, 1919. Miller, *The Drafting of the Covenant*, p. 122.
[56] Miller, *The Drafting of the Covenant*, p. 126.   [57] Miller, p. 14.

In this task the League Commission worked loyally and as faithfully as the President. Its meetings were businesslike to a high degree. "The members invariably came together on the hour." There were no formalities, no orations and no loss of time. [58] Yet there was ample opportunity for every man to make his impress upon the document. Lord Robert Cecil, notably, had great influence. "Not only his views but his manner were obviously those of a statesman of long experience." His patience and willingness to listen to argument gave his statements in reply great weight. [59] The constructive mind and practical idealism of General Smuts made him also one of the true fathers of the Covenant.

That document was not made alone, furthermore, in the thirty hours which comprised the first ten sessions of the Commission. It was the product of many keen minds and of long experience. Much groundwork had been done, moreover, before the Commission ever met. The Phillimore Committee, for example, had spent nine meetings considering the various proposals for a league, beginning with the 16th century. [60] Many conferences were held in Paris, also, while the Conference was getting under way, of which those between David Hunter Miller and Lord Cecil were notable.

The Nature of the Agreement. The President's third draft, circulated for criticism on January 10, had been revised again and then combined into the official British draft. The divergencies in the two plans were reconciled by the chief legal advisors, D. H. Miller for the United States and C. J. B. Hurst for Great Britain, and accepted by their superiors as a basis for discussion. This American-British plan was presented to the Commission at its first meeting and became the subject of its debates. The French and Italians also presented drafts. [61]

What Guarantee of Security? A fundamental divergence between the Anglo-Saxon and the Continental plans was at once manifest. The English speaking peoples proposed that the peace should be kept by close international association and coöperation and by the reduction of armaments. The fourth of the Fourteen Points had called for reduction of armaments, and in President Wilson's third draft real dis-

---

[58] W. H. Shepardson, quoted in Miller, *The Drafting of the Covenant*, p. 121–22.

[59] Miller, p. 126. From his contemporary account.

[60] *Ibid.*, p. 4. See Miller, *The Drafting of the Covenant*, Volume II. This ponderous tome of drafts and documents gives a vivid idea of the immense volume of thought that was concentrated on the framing of the Covenant.

[61] Ray Stannard Baker, *Woodrow Wilson and World Settlement*, N. Y., 1922, Vol. I, p. 231–32; Miller, *The Drafting of the Covenant*, Chapters 5 and 6.

armament was provided for, including the abolition of conscription. This was going too swiftly for the European nations and was modified in the Miller-Hurst draft to call for the reduction of armed force to the lowest point consistent with domestic safety, and to give the Council of the League the problem of trying to replace compulsory military service with voluntary.

The French and other continental nations were dominated by the fear of invasion, the horrors of which had been burned into the forefront of their minds. They felt that they could put no trust in anything except their own military power. This was even true of the new states not yet officially born and fearful for their hard won existence. The French draft therefore was almost wholly occupied with sanctions, diplomatic, legal, economic, and military. Nothing that would quickly suppress an invader was omitted. [62]

The President had recognized from the start, and particularly when he thought of France, the necessity of a mutual guarantee of territorial integrity and independence. Against the wishes of Colonel House and Secretary Lansing such a guarantee had been put into both his first drafts. In the third draft he had accepted from General Bliss the qualification "as against external aggression" to prevent any possible fear of the league being used to suppress internal disorders. At the same time, to allow the possibility of peaceful changes in the status to be established in the almost hopelessly complicated ethnic situation in middle Europe, the central idea of the present Article 11, which Mr. Wilson often referred to as his favorite article, was retained. This article established the friendly right of any member to bring to the attention of the league "any circumstance whatever" which threatens to disturb the good understanding or peace between nations. [63]

The obligation of the members of the League "to respect and preserve as against external aggression the territorial integrity and existing political independence of all members of the league" was later to prove too much for the Republicans in the United States Senate, but it was far too little to satisfy the French and others who had felt and seen the terrors of conquest. They proposed, in the French draft, in addition to all the other sanctions, an international army to be held at the disposal of the Council and controlled by a League General Staff

[62] See H. V. M. Temperly, *A History of the Peace Conference of Paris*, London, 1924, Vol. 6, pp. 452–58 for a summary of the French, Italian, Dutch, Swiss, Scandinavian and German plans for a league.

[63] Baker, Vol. I, pp. 228–30. This is the article under which the Council dealt with the Sino-Japanese Manchurian crisis in the Autumn of 1931.

which should have supervision over the training of the various state
contingents so as to weld them into a real fighting machine. Far from
abolishing conscription it was even left open to the League Council
to require everybody to adopt it. The kind of league which so aroused
the fears of American Senators would not allay the much deeper and
more poignant fears of the French.

The contest in the League of Nations Commission was from the
start between the two kinds of leagues. The French fought steadily
both to eliminate the sweeping disarmament proposals and to make the
league a military super-state with absolute power to suppress any
disturber of the peace. The proposal to disarm "to the lowest point
consistent with domestic safety" was first changed, February 6, on
motion of Baron Makino the Japanese delegate, to read "consistent
with national safety"—a far different standard. Further attack toned
down the rest of the disarmament program, though the right and duty
of the league to initiate disarmament plans was retained. On the other
side, the American-English position that it was not wise to go beyond
the obligation of Article 10 in guaranteeing security prevailed. [64]

The Minimum Guarantee Given. The completed Covenant, as
finally agreed upon on the 13th, was presented by the President to a
plenary session of the whole Conference on February 14. He spoke
to the heart of the issue. A definite guarantee of peace and against aggression had beeen created. He was clear as to the place of force in
the plan, saying: "Armed force is in the background of this programme, but it is in the background, and if the moral force of the
world will not suffice, the physical force of the world shall. But that
is the last resort, because this is intended as a constitution of peace,
not as a League of War."

It was, too, to be far more than a means of keeping the peace;
it was to be an agency and a place for daily use in coöperation upon
every kind of international problem—the phase of the league's usefulness that attracts wider and wider attention every year. "It is not
in contemplation," he said, "that this should be merely a league to
secure the peace of the world. It is a League that can be used for
coöperation in any international matter." [65]

---

[64] *Ibid.*, Chapter 20; Miller, Chapters 11–21, inclusive.

[65] Baker, Vol. I, p. 285. One of the President's Republican contemporaries, William
Allen White, has described Wilson's presentation of the Covenant from his view of
it as a journalist. It was all, he says, "typically Wilsonian, that is to say, toned down,
understated, gray, shadowless. . . . He read slowly, in an even voice which carried
throughout the room. . . . Here and there he stopped reading to explain some ambiguous line of the text or to amplify some thought, but his spoken words were as

The league was not to be a shaky machine for occasional use in putting out fire, but a flesh and blood organism with daily work of many kinds to do.

COULD THE COVENANT BE DEFEATED AT HOME?

While the Covenant was being debated in Paris further evidences of the kind of peace the President's opponents in the Senate would stand for appeared occasionally in the *Congressional Record*. Thus on January 31, Senator Lodge had noted the press attacks of the French and English on the President in their campaign to divide the German Colonies. The reports seemed to him "absolutely unbelievable." He knew that the dispatches were nearly all colored "for a certain definite purpose, yet it seemed incredible that some of the things should be pure invention." However, he continued, "We apparently are being involved in some sort of guaranty, either with force or without force, to take care of the German possessions in Africa and in the Pacific ocean. We seem to have involved ourselves already in serious differences with the Australians and the Boers of South Africa— populations with which we have always been most friendly and sympathetic. Our good relations with Australia are of enormous importance. I do not know exactly what we are doing, but we seem to be annoying them very much; and in some method we are apparently going to guarantee and sustain and watch over republics or States made up of Bantus and Hottentots, and we are to be meddling with it all the time in an indefinite future."

He said these things with hesitation, because he did not know what the facts were. The Senate was kept "absolutely in the dark." It had "nothing to go upon except these casual dispatches." How the Senate would have aided in the negotiations if it could only have had the intimate details daily! In the case of the German Colonies, Mr. Lodge would have stood most heartily for outright annexation by the

---

lifeless as his reading. Slowly as he read, his hearers realized that they were getting some new declaration of independence as well as of international interdependence. The import of the thing grew. Two or three hundred newspaper men, standing on their chairs and on tables, tiptoed to see the President's face as he read the words before him. . . ."

"Then he began speaking. What he said was well said. It was spoken from the heart, only a few typewritten headings in his hand guiding him. He improvised his paragraphs, and the stenographers took them down. Almost with a studied casualness he took the dramatics out of the day and scene."—William Allen White, *Woodrow Wilson*, N. Y., 1924, pp. 404–8.

The reader will find in White's biography effective pictures and appraisals of Wilson during the war years.

states which had captured them. Why "should we hand them over to a league of nations not yet in existence," he asked, and then be involved in guaranteeing them for an indefinite future? [66]

Taft, on the other hand, opposed the mandate plan as not going far enough and urged that the League itself take full control of the conquered colonies. [67] His voice, too, carried farther, for Mr. Lloyd George replying to suggestions in Parliament that Wilson represented only one party, cited Taft as going further than Wilson on mandates, further than Britain could follow. He had been assured by a prominent Republican also that American public opinion was not divided on the league, although there might be differences of opinion on details. [68]

The President sailed for home on February 15 to attend the closing of Congress and to present the Covenant of the League to the American people. Would they give him the support necessary to secure approval in the Senate? It would take great pressure of public opinion indeed to do so.

Mr. Taft undertook his share of the task as soon as the Covenant was published. He hailed it as a real league, not a super-sovereign but a partnership intended to secure to us and to all the only sovereignty we can properly have—"sovereignty regulated by international law and morality and consistent with the same sovereignty of other countries." The Monroe Doctrine was extended by Article 10 to the world. With so much accomplished Taft asked why the Senators could not give the President unanimous support. [69]

Was "a Tragedy to the History of Civilization" Ahead? A few days later, after describing the tremendous enthusiasm in the nine great regional conferences of the League to Enforce Peace, he stated it to be the belief of that great organization "that it would be a tragedy to the history of civilization if the Senate can be induced by the protests and narrow views of a small number of Senators who have expressed themselves to defeat this grand covenant of peace, the unanimous agreement of the representatives of fourteen nations, facing not a theory, but a real and fateful crisis for the world." [70]

The words were grave but they were not too serious to describe

---

[66] *Congressional Record,* Vol. 57, Pt. 3, p. 2420.
    The *New York Sun* of January 29, 1919, greeted "Mr. Wilson's scheme for handling the German Colonies by a league of nations" as "a footless dream without any worth while practical basis."
[67] *Philadelphia Public Ledger,* February 3, 1919.
[68] *New York Times,* February 13, 1919.
[69] *Philadelphia Public Ledger,* February 17, 1919.
[70] *Washington Post,* February 23, 1919.

the danger to the league which lay in the control of the incoming Senate organization by the men referred to. George Harvey, lauded by his biographer as the chief protagonist of the fight on the league, [71] had revealed again while the Covenant was being framed, how implacable would be the opposition to it, whatever it contained. "The League of Nations," he wrote in *Harvey's Weekly* on February 8, "as we have hitherto pointed out, must be either a strenuous body so transcending nationality as to be impossible of American approval, or a futile thing of pious aspirations and impotent achievement." [72]

He did not need the contemporary urging of A. J. Beveridge that it was of infinite importance that Lodge and Knox assail the whole thing without making the fatal error in tactics of accepting the principle. [73] Harvey's great ability as a political manipulator and his burning determination to block the path of Wilson could be depended upon to stimulate Lodge and Knox at every turn and to give no quarter to the Covenant at any time.

His greeting to the league's charter was: "It is the most impudently un-American proposal ever submitted to the American people by an American President." [74]

[71] W. F. Johnson, *George Harvey, A Passionate Patriot,* N. Y., 1929, p. 95. Giving that title proudly to Harvey does not prevent Mr. Johnson from suggesting that Harvey when called to the White House early in 1914 had planted the germ of the league in Wilson's mind (p. 236).

[72] A charge by Senator Warren G. Harding, of Ohio, that a large part of the menace of Bolshevism was due to the utterances of the President, won him the acclaim of Harvey as the Republican Senator whose name led all others as a possible candidate for the Presidency. *Harvey's Weekly,* February 1, 1919, Vol. 2, No. 5, p. 2.

[73] Johnson, *George Harvey, A Passionate Patriot,* p. 266.

[74] *Harvey's Weekly,* February 22, Vol. 2, No. 8, p. 2.

CHAPTER V

THE OPENING ATTACK

THE text of the Covenant was published in American papers on February 15 and was favorably received by the press. The *St. Louis Globe Democrat,* speaking for many newspapers, assessed it as primarily a moral force, and was "inclined to think that the main value of the League, both in the preservation of the peace and in the promotion of the welfare of mankind, will be found in the machinery of international coöperation which it creates, and in the habit of mutual consideration it will establish. It is sufficient for the moment that it is born, and no birth of history, save one, is of greater importance to mankind." [1]

An International Quilting Circle? The reception accorded by the *New York Sun,* as the leader of the small group of newspapers determined to defeat the League, was quite different. While the Peace Conference was coming together the *Sun* had repeatedly called upon the President for his League plan. [2] It had to be content with a "Phantom League" until January 25 when the decision of the conference to create the League seemed to indicate its probable nature rather authoritatively. The speeches of the President and Lord Robert Cecil on that occasion were cited by the *Sun,* on January 27, as "proof that the idea of international force has been abandoned." "Under these circumstances," continued the *Sun,* "Senators are not inclined to be unduly excited over any form which expression of principles or declarations of moral purpose may take. They assume that the nations will not find it difficult to agree on matters of abstract principle so long as the element of international force does not enter into the question. Republican Senators say that a league without force to back its decrees amounts to little more than 'an international quilting circle.' They are not concerned over the final form which any non-effective league takes."

The Senate leaders and their newspaper spokesmen were beginning to be reassured. Their matured plans gave confidence and they still

---

[1] *New York Times,* February 15, 1919.
[2] See the *Sun* from December 18, 1918, to January 4, 1919.

doubted whether after all an effective league would really be created. If only some sort of amplified Hague Tribunal, "an international quilting society" resulted, the President might have whatever credit could not be ridiculed away.

The draft of the Covenant which was published twenty days later, therefore, gave them a distinct shock. A special dispatch to the *Sun* reported, February 15, that "Republican leaders like Senators Lodge and Knox read the document in silence and amazement." [3] The *Sun,* too, was rather stunned, but it rose to the attack as best it could. The Conference seemed to have nullified the great objection which the President's foes had expected to bring against any league that had something back of its decisions. "It ingenuously and successfully avoids the constitutional objection," admitted the *Sun,* "with regard to the absolute control of Congress over the beginning of war."

The mistake of thus reading nothing dangerous into Article 10 was not often repeated by the League's opponents as soon as they had had time to gather themselves together. In the beginning the error was made even by Colonel Harvey himself. In his first readings of the Covenant he, too, could find no juggernaut where one had been confidently expected. Scrutinizing the Covenant, Article 10 and all, and recalling the President's statement in the midst of the war that a force must be created so great that no probable combination of nations could withstand it, he explained in glee: "Why, there is no force at all created, but the Executive Committee of the League is to 'recommend' to the members of the League their proportionate contribution to the armed forces to be used to protect the covenants of the League. Merely 'recommend'; and if the recommendation is not favorably received and acted upon, there will be no force at all. . . . From the President's own point of view, then, this proposed League would be hopelessly inefficient and futile." [4]

For its initial attack, the *Sun,* failing to find the right of Congress to declare war negatived, found other constitutional objections "equally fatal." Article 12, it maintained, did limit the right of Congress to

---

[3] The Washington correspondent of the *New York Times* reported that "although Republicans would not admit it, there was unmistakable evidence of concerted action on their part in opposition to expressions of opinion pending careful study of the project." Senators Lodge, Knox, Penrose and Smoot had held a conference soon after the receipt of the text of the Covenant. *Times,* February 15, 1919.

The desire of the leaders to prevent spontaneous expression of approval, or mistakes in criticism, and, if possible, to voice concerted disapproval was natural.

[4] *Harvey's Weekly,* March 1, 1919, Vol. II, No. 9, p. 10. In this and the succeeding issue the League was dubbed "a League of Nations for International Meddling," and "A League of Notions" (March 8, No. 10, p. 1).

declare war against a member of the League which complied with an arbitration award or a recommendation of the Council. (Think of it!) Article 8, urging disarmament within the limits of "national safety," was construed as a limitation upon the power of Congress to regulate armaments. Moreover, the provision for an economic boycott would require a bill for raising revenue, and Article 23, requiring the registration of treaties, added a process to those described in the Constitution and so would not do unless the Constitution were amended.

Feeling that it had found necessity for constitutional amendments —prohibitive hurdle—"the question foremost in the mind of the *Sun,*" was whether after eliminating these provisions the plan would be "anything more than another Hague Tribunal."[5]

Delay Urged. The *Washington Post* also appeared to be similarly nonplused when confronted by the Covenant. On February 20 and 22 it argued that the Senate could not decide on such mighty matters and urged the calling of a constitutional convention to pass upon them. On February 26 it reported that opponents of the League had accepted the President's challenge (referring to his Boston address) but had "a more far reaching idea in mind. They will attempt to prevent ratification before the presidential campaign of 1920, when a direct vote of the people can be had on the issue."

Something had to be done. The President was on the ocean with an actual league charter, endorsed by the representatives of many nations, and with prestige even greater than when he departed. What could be done to stop him?

The President Requested that Debate be Postponed. Before leaving Paris the President cabled an invitation to the members of the Foreign Relations Committees of the House and Senate to dine with him as soon as he returned, for the purpose of discussing the provisions of the Covenant. There was, he said, good and sufficient reason for the phraseology of each article and he requested that "I be permitted to go over with you, article by article, the constitution before this part of the work of the conference is made the subject of debate in Congress."[6]

However well meant, this request was not likely to be complied with. It would have been highly desirable to remove the misapprehensions that Senators might get on first study of the document before they had committed themselves too heavily in public, and no doubt Mr. Wilson felt so full of the subject that he believed he could answer

[5] *New York Sun,* February 15, 1919.
[6] *New York Times,* February 16, 1919.

any reasonable objection to every provision, but the Senate leaders did not want to have their objections removed. Even if he had appreciated this fact as well as he did a little later, it may well have appeared to him that it was only fair that he present the case for the Covenant to them before they condemned it. He might have known, however, that this request would only be advertised as one more evidence of a plan to stifle criticism and secure approval of the League before the people knew what was in it.

The Senators had been complaining that they did not know what was going on, but now that they had something to shoot at they did not care for sympathetic accounts of the origin of the target. After twenty-four hours' study, leading Republican Senators declared that the project appeared to surrender American independence and upset the Monroe Doctrine. Desiring to defeat the President, not to hear him, the Senators felt, too, that the President was unfair in planning to land in Boston and make a speech or two for the League before he reported to them. This feeling can be appreciated, especially among those who really felt it was their patriotic duty to save the country from any league. The European leaders had never enjoyed Mr. Wilson's direct appeals to the people, and the Senators could not be expected to, especially in Boston. They appear to have feared, moreover, that instead of being permitted to approve a Treaty of Peace, without a League, they were about to have to pass first on the League itself. They insisted that the Senate would not endorse it, even by majority vote, before the President returned to France.[7]

Poindexter's Opening Attack. Senator Poindexter, of Washington, opened the inevitable onslaught on the Covenant in the Senate on February 19, asking whether George Washington was a friend of peace, and didn't the Covenant add to the opportunity, to the cause and to the temptation for war? He found the machinery of the League similar to the Soviet Government of Russia. It was the most entangling alliance that could be conceived and there was no way to withdraw from it.

Specifically, he made five charges against the League: (1) that under it we surrendered the power of disarmament, (2) that it called for compulsory arbitration of all questions, without exception, (3) that it would compel the United States to "participate in the wars and controversies of every other nation" and to assume the burdens of a mandate over any part of Europe, Asia, or Africa that was assigned to it, (4) that the International Labor Bureau would interfere in our domes-

[7] *New York Times,* February 16, 1919.

tic affairs and (5) that the United States would surrender to other nations the power "to regulate commerce with foreign nations in arms and ammunition."[8]

Borah. On February 21, Senator Borah took the floor to maintain against Mr. Taft that the Covenant did abolish the Washington and Monroe Doctrines. He read into Article 10 a guarantee to England of possession of every foot of land then in the British Empire and hailed the League "as the greatest triumph for English diplomacy in three centuries of English diplomatic life." The Covenant had been taken almost bodily from General Smuts. It gave the British Empire five votes to our one. He began by asking for a direct vote of all the people of the nation on the question of entering the League and closed with a powerful plea for maintaining full liberty of action in the future.[9]

Reed. Senator Reed, Democrat, of Missouri, followed on the next day with a bitter excoriation of the entire Covenant. He proved at length that Great Britain would control the League and came to the conclusion that in any controversy the votes of the British Empire, France, Italy, and Japan would always be against the United States. Great Britain could protect her control by admitting new members as she chose. Colonies could easily be qualified as self-governing. Probably Japan would bring Korea in for a vote. From the first and at all times Europe and Asia would predominate over the United States. We should be forever alone; even Canada would be against us.

Moreover, the powers of the League were almost unlimited. He wanted to "burn into the brain and heart of the American people, that every nation entering the League yields to its arbitrament and decision all controversies with other countries, even though they involve the national honor and the national life." Everything, however small or domestic in nature, came under the jurisdiction of the Council, which he characterized as "nine autocrats—eight of them representing foreign countries; seven of them at least representing Asiatic or European despotisms or monarchies." "Let those who hesitate and doubt, scarcely believing that such a thing as this could be writ down in cold ink upon cold paper read Article 7"!

But there were equally unbelievable things in Articles 8 and 9. They would tell us "You shall have an army of a certain size" or "vessels

[8] *Congressional Record,* Vol. 57, Pt. 4, p. 3748.
[9] *Ibid.,* pp. 3911–15. Taft replied from San Francisco to the initial attacks saying: "These gentlemen who are sitting up with the Constitution using it to defeat the League of Nations are men whom I would not trust overnight." *New York Times,* February 20, 1919.

Permission—Keystone View Co.

WILLIAM E. BORAH
OF IDAHO

Permission—Underwood & Underwood

FRANK B. BRANDEGEE
OF CONNECTICUT

Permission—Underwood & Underwood

JAMES A. REED
OF MISSOURI

Permission—Underwood & Underwood

CHARLES S. THOMAS
OF COLORADO

IRRECONCILABLES—REPUBLICAN AND DEMOCRATIC

of a certain number" and we could not "exceed such numbers without going to Europe and asking the gracious permission of eight gentlemen, six of whom probably cannot speak our language and who have likely never set foot upon our shores!" And we would have to get a license for the private manufacture of arms from these same eight foreign gentlemen. A "sort of international smelling committee" would be around to inspect our industries adapted to warlike purposes.

The guarantee of Article 10 made us do what the Holy Alliance did. Nobody could go to the aid of an Irish rebellion and we should have to fight anybody who did. The same would be true of a Canadian revolt. Neither could we deal with Mexico as we saw fit. (Consider the enormity of it!) Under this "astounding sweep of power" from our hands into that of foreigners "a cloud of dispute as big as a man's hand may rise on the political horizon, and that could be construed into a threat or a danger. A dispute with Mexico over an oil territory, a dispute with reference to the stealing of American cattle . . . all these would be threats or dangers; and instantly this body of non-English-speaking foreigners, living 3,000 miles from here, could assume jurisdiction and could advise upon the means by which the high contracting parties would preserve the territorial and political independence of Mexico!"

But Article 11, which said that any threat of war, whether immediately affecting any of the members or not, was a matter of concern to the League, was equally astounding. "What?" cried Mr. Reed, "Do you say this League is to interfere with matters outside its own members? It is unbelievable that so monstrous a theory as that should be proposed; yet it is here plainly written down. . . ." We undertook to set ourselves up as masters of the world.

And so he went down the articles of the Covenant from one monstrosity to another. Each article contained a horrible deformity of some kind or a vital threat to our ancient rights, or both. The League would assume jurisdiction over the Monroe Doctrine, border disputes, the rights of aliens among us, the impressment of American seamen, the destruction of American ships at sea, fortifying the Panama Canal and a thousand other questions. Our antagonists (we seemed to have many of them) could put us at the mercy of the league on any question arising. Mexico could do it. It was even "entirely conceivable that such a tribunal might conclude that a simple tariff levied upon importations might become a cause of war and assume the right to command a state not to levy a tariff duty."

There were pains and penalties for non-obedience to the League; our armies would be levied by orders of the Council; the League compelled its members to commit acts of war; it was an international despotism.

Then, after quoting Jefferson, John Adams, Clay and Webster, he dramatically called the roll of all the European wars of the last century that the United States had not been in, inferred at length that war must continue in Europe forever, finished with a heroic tribute to the American soldier from Belleau Wood back to Yorktown and sat down amid applause on the floor and in the galleries,[10] which continued for five minutes while Senators crowded to shake his hand.

Lewis' Reply. He was replied to the next day by Senator Lewis, of Illinois, who observed in opening that "at the outset one would think that at a time like this any man in America could advance to a discussion of that grave question in a spirit qualifying him impartially to judge the thing as it is and to refrain from coloring it with personal animosity or political prejudice. But, sir, I deplore to have to confess that had there been a stranger from another world whose spirit in spectral form in the gallery of this Senate could have heard the attacks made on the project, he could have believed that he had returned to the Roman forum, to the senate of that imperial country, and that some Catiline by the name of Taft or Wilson was being arraigned by a Cicero on the charge of betraying his country to its enemies and for delivery of his native land to its foreign foes."

In an effort to put the League into its true setting he reviewed the tragedy and misery and suffering of the war, and the waste of "$180,000,000,000 of the earnings of ten generations of mankind gone to ashes in the nowhere." He thought it strange that in such a time any one could recite the list of European wars for a century past and "contemplate the loss of all those lives, the devastations of all those lands, the demolishment of all their homes, the widowing of all those wives, the bereaved mothers without children, and not feel that the 'dam'd manner of their taking off' is not of concern to civilization and feel that if we could lay our hands against its ever being repeated we owe to do so, not only unto ourselves, but unto the thing we profess and call religion."

He then discussed the principal fears raised, in an effort to show them unfounded in reason or fact. He laid the specter of Japanese

[10] *Congressional Record,* Vol. 57, Pt. 4, pp. 4026-33.

immigration being forced on us by pointing out the solid front that the British Dominions maintained with us on that score—the very countries whose votes had been declared so dangerous to us. As far as the six British votes went, we could more than overbalance them with the votes of the small American countries to the south of us. And if the Council could tell us how many soldiers and ships we could have, it could destroy British naval supremacy, and every one of the great powers represented on the Council would have an incentive to do that very thing. That Britain, whom it was said had dominated the creation of the Covenant, would be so blind as to sign a clause permitting such action required imagination indeed to believe.

Mr. Lewis apparently recognized the appeal to the anti-British vote as a dangerous one and did what he could to show that the League could not be used as an engine of repression on Ireland or India or elsewhere. The fact of British influence in the League was much harder to deal with. That fact, so incessantly kept to the front in the ensuing fight against the League, could not be removed by any amount of argument from the minds of millions of Irish and German Americans. Mr. Wilson had been able to create the League only by British aid; that was enough.

It was in vain to remind these groups that it was the object of those who framed the document to enable all those who would suppress an invasion of a peaceful country to bring their collective strength to bear on the offender. Did anybody imagine, asked Mr. Lewis, that if Germany had known the extent of the power she would have to face she would have ventured upon a course of destruction?

After all, the power and the usefulness of the League would be determined not by arguments over the possible meaning of this line or that, but by public opinion. "Public opinion, stimulated by public virtue, will sustain this League in what it shall undertake, or it will overthrow and defeat it in any attempt against the equities of men or the rights of countries. It will appeal to public opinion before ever it assumes to execute any policy, and on that judgment it will advance or withdraw." [11]

The President's Boston Address. To American public opinion President Wilson made his first appeal. The choice of Boston as a port for his triumphal return to the United States was naturally resented by Lodge, though it does not appear that the President planned his appearance in Lodge's city entirely to put pressure upon the questioning

[11] *Ibid.*, pp. 4125–35.

Senator. The entry at Boston was suggested by citizens of that city to Secretary of War Newton D. Baker and cabled by him to Wilson. Mayor Peters also had been urging the President to visit Boston for more than a year. Henry White cabled Lodge to this effect on February 20, saying that when the President left France he had no intention of speaking in Boston or elsewhere before meeting the Foreign Relations Committees.[12]

As the President neared Boston Harbor, the *New York Times* reported that two groups of his friends and advisers had gathered in Boston, one wishing him to give a judicial endorsement of the League of Nations with a simple explanation of what it was, and the other waiting to urge him to make a fighting speech, to strike out straight from the shoulder and challenge the opposition to the League. The latter group argued that the President's absence on his next trip would be long and that unless he reached the country in a stirring speech the anti-League campaign being organized would fan so many prejudices that it would be difficult to allay them when he returned.[13]

Both parties of the President's friends had their inning in his Boston speech, given in Mechanics Hall February 23. The group who wanted him to hit back against those who had been savagely assaulting his work in every particular, stood at the right of the platform during the first half of the speech with glum and anxious faces. He was talking ideals as strongly as he ever had, and he was not getting tumultuous applause. There was a rousing cheer when he said that the proudest thing he had to report was that this great country of ours was trusted throughout the world, and again when he explained that every interest coming to Paris sought out the representatives of the United States first, because—and he thought he was stating the most wonderful fact in history—there was no nation that suspected the motives of the United States.

But in the latter part of the speech those who wanted a challenge to the opposition got relief. The speaker took up the suggestion that America would keep her power for her own selfish purposes, and declared that "I should welcome no sweeter challenge than that. I have fighting blood in me, and it is sometimes a delight to let it have scope, but if it is a challenge on this occasion it will be an indulgence." The crowd cheered as it had not before, and continued to applaud as he asked if we were to say one day, "Here is our power to vindicate

[12] Allan Nevins, *Henry White*, N. Y., 1930, p. 388.
[13] *New York Times*, February 24, 1919.

right," and the next day, "Let right take care of itself and we will take care of ourselves." A still wilder cheer met his statement that he had no more doubt of the verdict of America than he had of the blood that was in him, and as he said, "I have come back to say to you that I have tried in all soberness and honesty to speak your thought," the applause "leaped to thunder before the words were fairly out of his mouth."[14]

The Boston public likewise was won by the address.[15] The reception given him deepened the belief of the President in turn that he still had the support of the people and that they would back him in his fight to seal the Covenant. Lodge and his colleagues were also impressed and convinced that there was very serious work ahead. The President had won approval by meeting the challenges thrown down to him so sweepingly as he neared home. One of the counter measures evolved was to condemn him for taking up the gauntlet. From then on Senators never ceased to quote his acceptance of their defiance as a justification for their own incessant attacks on the Covenant in the many weeks before that document was laid before the Senate for action.

The crowd in Mechanics Hall did not doubt his earnestness. Neither did the *New York Tribune,* the leading Republican paper of the metropolis. Speaking editorially in the issue of February 25, 1919, the *Tribune* said: "The speech of the President in Boston, neither in words nor in spirit contains anything to arouse controversy. . . . No sensible person now challenges, or has challenged, the sincerity of the President's allegiance to the idea of organizing the world for peace instead of for war. The war was to end war, or if this is not completely possible, then to set up some bulwarks for peace. If there is failure in Paris as to this, great indeed will be the failure. The discussion of the momentous problem must therefore be lifted above the plane of personalities. To do other than this is to degrade a theme almost as lofty as that contained in the new testament."

SENATOR CUMMINS' DISTRESS

Senator Cummins, Republican, of Iowa, continued the drive on the Covenant in the Senate on February 26.[16] Mr. Cummins was

[14] *New York Times,* February 25, 1919.
[15] That was the impression of an observer in the World Peace Foundation, 40 Mt. Vernon St., Boston, who is not given to exaggeration.
Applications for admission to the address ran up toward 200,000. *New York Times,* February 23, 1919.
[16] *Congressional Record,* Vol. 57, Pt. 5, pp. 4309–16.

one of the best known and most respected men in the Senate. His situation was a difficult one. He had made his reputation as a progressive and on some subjects was still liberal. That he sincerely wanted to do something effective to keep the peace there can be no doubt. He wanted a League of Nations, as he more than once said in public after all the debates were over.

A Developing Internationalism Inevitable. He was not even opposed to internationalism, but on the contrary, believed the inevitable trend was in that direction. "I cannot concur," he said, "in the argument which seems to lead to the conclusion that any form of internationalism is an unwise invasion of nationalism. I cannot agree that the highest ideals of Americanism preclude coöperation among nations looking to the abolition of war. . . . I am saying these things . . . because it is helpful just now to remember that there is an internationalism which is not only in harmony with the most exalted spirit of nationalism but which supplements and strengthens that national power which every self respecting government must exercise for itself. It must be clear to every thoughtful person that there must be in a world like ours, where an increasing intimacy among nations has been brought about by the genius of invention, the imperative demands of commerce, the drifting tides of population and with the constantly growing opportunities of conflict and controversy, a developing internationalism that will meet successfully conditions as they change from year to year."

The Desire for a Compact Universal and Urgent. Though he thought Germany and the terms of peace should be disposed of first, he was not in favor of postponing long the effort to prevent future wars, for he continued: "It is my belief that the close of the unparalleled conflict in which we have been engaged presents the most favorable opportunity that we ever have had or that is likely to occur in years and years to come to do something that will be a distinct advance in preventing war in the future." He had no doubt either that the American people felt the same way. "It requires no close inquiry into the sentiment of the American people to be certain that there is a universal and passionate desire to do something to enter into some compact to prevent war with all its deadly and destructive consequences. Nor can it be denied that at this juncture in the world's affairs they believe that something can be done to facilitate a peaceful settlement of international controversies which hitherto have led to the battlefield. It is this overwhelming conviction which finds expression in the tumultuous applause which thrills every audience as it listens to the glowing appeals for a League of Nations."

Yet the Covenant Would Not Do. Still, in spite of these deep convictions, Mr. Cummins was compelled to declare that he would unhesitatingly vote against the Covenant as it stood. There was good in it, but there was more bad. There were articles in it which were not only far beyond our authority to make but which changed the whole character of our Government and overturned the institutions upon which we had so long depended for our safety and independence.

Before discussing these fatal provisions he outlined the compact he thought ought to come out of the Great War. It would provide (1) for compulsory arbitration or adjudication of all justiciable questions, (2) for compulsory investigation of all other disputes by the league, but without award or judgment, (3) ostracism for any nation that refused to abide by either of these processes and (4) real disarmament to be agreed upon at once. The Covenant, he thought, would not bring about disarmament.

Article 10 Precluded Desirable Change. The first of the articles that would overturn our institutions was Article 10. "I am opposed to it, because it is the most destructive, unjust and reactionary proposal which was ever submitted to a patriotic and intelligent people. I predict that when the citizens of the United States thoroughly grasp the meaning of the proposed agreement and fairly understand its irresistible consequences, it will be rejected in a storm of obloquy the like of which has never been witnessed within the borders of the Republic."

This was a grave statement which in itself must influence many people to fear and suspect the entire Covenant.

But where was the evil? It was in a few men in Paris fixing the boundaries of the whole earth forever. It was proposed to gridiron the earth with an inflexible pattern. "How dare we determine what sovereignties the civilization of the next century will demand"? The statesmen in Paris might with equal propriety have ventured to set the bounds of the Heavenly Kingdom or prescribe the activities of the Prince of Darkness. At many stages in the world's history it would have been calamitous to have had all boundaries guaranteed.

Truly what were the makers of the League, or of any league, to do? The one idea that had run throughout all the discussion of means to prevent the next Armageddon had been the clear belief that every nation must be prevented from assaulting its neighbors. That could only be done by union against the aggressor. But now the Senator entirely lost sight of this simple agreement as a guarantee of security, and thought only of it as preventing future changes of territorial lines in the interest of liberty. There was not a word in the article that would prevent revolution, or the voluntary union of States, or their peaceable separation as had happened in the case of Sweden and Norway, or the purchase and sale of territory, or the gradual attainment of nationhood, independence even, as in the British Dominions, or that would prevent the League Council from deciding that a war which was widely felt to be in the interest of liberty, or of an oppressed minority, was not a war of aggression. The obligation of Article 10 did not come into force in any case until the Council advised, and there was nothing to compel the Council to exercise its discretion when the result would be to suppress liberty and justice. There was nothing, moreover, to compel any nation to accept the advice of the Council, if it felt that the crossing of a boundary was in the interest of liberty. The whole purpose of the article was to give security to liberty, not to repress it.

Was No Guarantee Possible? The Senator had quoted with deep sympathy an article describing the panicky reaction in France to the President's attitude toward the peace, saying that "as a result of what has occurred here in the peace conference, there is something amounting to real terror lest the war shall be lost after all and France left alone again across the pathway of a Germany increased in power and population by the last war." And yet Mr. Cummins was for destroying the guarantee in the Covenant which the French had felt was too pitifully small and leaving them with no protection except an agreement to "ostracize" any nation which invaded them before it had observed a prescribed cooling off period.

What was the President to do?

Indeed it may be that future Presidents will be compelled to take the Senate with them to any later peace conference in spite of all objections, constitutional and otherwise. But that would hardly have solved the dilemma in question, for the American papers for a week had been full of the French fight for a league with teeth—sanctions of all kinds up to an International General Staff. Senators knew what France demanded. Yet they refused to give her any assurance of security in the future—unless it be leave to attempt to get it by dismembering and trying to destroy the German nation. What could the President do? Must he go back to Paris and say to the French "We denied you everything you asked for and gave you instead this single promise. My Senators now say that even that was far too much. We can give you no assurance of assistance against future invasion." Such a course would have meant the end of the League before it was ever organized.

The Mandate System was Impossible. The next article that Mr. Cummins felt would overturn our institutions was Article 19 which created the mandatory system for the conquered territories. When he read Article 10 he was under the impression that "nothing could surpass it in its repugnance to good morals and to the civilization of the world," but he was bound to admit that Article 19 was the climax of the conflict. The article was not only bad in itself, but it was the grossest violation of our powers under the Constitution that had ever fallen under his observation. He accepted the assumption already laid down that the League could force a mandate over any part of the earth upon the United States, without its consent, and assumed that we would soon be commanded to take charge of the Turkish dominions, both east and west from Constantinople. There was nothing in our Constitution which authorized such an arrangement. We unquestionably had power to buy territory or conquer it, but this was neither one nor the other.

He confessed to more amazement when he reflected on this proposal than had ever filled his mind before, and when one contemplates the result of his reflection one must share the same feeling. It was as plain as day that the Constitution had never anticipated our accepting a trusteeship from a League of Nations any more than it had anticipated the submarine or the radio but neither had it authorized us to purchase territory, and there was assuredly nothing in it that would authorize us to exercise a trusteeship over the Philippines with title to territory and forbid us to exercise the same trusteeship without title. But neither was there any suggestion in Article 19 that a mandate could be forced on a nation. Such a thing was so unlikely that it had indeed not been prohibited. The powers were too intent on getting the territories, under a mandate if they could not secure them outright. On the contrary, the article named geographical position as one of the things that would entitle a nation to a mandate, a presumption against our being compelled to administer Turkey even if the power to compel us had existed.

None of these considerations deterred the Senator as he proceeded to view "this mad proposal from the standpoint of the burdens it would lay upon us." It would require an army of more than a hundred thousand men for many years to come, and an even larger civilian force. The civil service employees in Constantinople would "outnumber our employees in Washington." The fathers and mothers of America would be asked to send their sons 5,000 miles from home to keep the Turk, the Armenian, the Syrian and the Arab in order and train them for self-government. It was "safe to assume that the annual cost of this enterprise would exceed a billion dollars."

Safe to assume! When a plan for organizing the world against aggression (and land-grabbing)—a consummation, he testified, that in common with the American people he ardently wanted—when the only plan of this character that would ever come before him arrived, he created extravagant assumptions from one of its most enlightened articles that would operate powerfully to cause the American people to reject the whole plan, as he predicted they would reject Article 19.

What, again, was the President to do? He had fought against overwhelming pressure at Paris for a disposition of the conquered territories that would give a foundation for an organization of the nations against military conquest. His principle of self-determination for all peoples, a vital necessity in any federated world, was also at stake. He had based his stand on the often repeated maxim that we administered the territories conquered from Spain as a trust, a guardianship in the interests of the people concerned. Should he go back to Paris and confess that our professions were insincere and that, after all, the world was not ready to infringe upon the rights of military conquest in the least? How much better it would have been, indeed, if the Senators who in their hearts wanted what he did could have waited until they understood what was at stake and what the consequences of their hasty commitments must be.

Article 15 Would Force Immigration Upon Us. The third principal indictment which Mr. Cummins brought against the Covenant was that it might enable Japan to force upon us equal treatment of her citizens in this country and equal freedom of entry. This possibility— it was a strong probability in his illustration—arose from Article 15, which agreed that when a dispute was submitted to the Council the members of the League would not go to war with any party which accepted the Council's recommendations, and that if any party should refuse so to comply, the Council should "propose measures necessary to give effect to the recommendation."

Starting from this basis, he assumed that the Council would take jurisdiction and decide against us adversely all down the line to the point of forcing us into war with the members of the League to uphold our right to discriminate against the Japanese. "When we reflect," he said, "on the composition of the executive council, it is incredible that a provision of this character should commend itself to the American people." Yet there was Great Britain on the Council who would lose her Dominions if she voted to inflict any such course upon us, and one vote would prevent any action.

But the same thing might happen, said the Senator, in a controversy with Southern Europe over immigration or if anybody protested our protective tariffs. The fallacy here was, of course, that no questions were so universally recognized to be domestic questions as immigration and the tariff, and the other nations would never seriously consider laying themselves open to similar interference in their own internal affairs by forcing their way into ours. The others were as solicitous about their sovereignty as we could be.

The Established Need. Moreover, sovereignty is of no avail unless it preserves national life. The free and unrestrained use of international force perpetually threatens and often destroys national order and even existence. The Covenant, said Senator Owen of Oklahoma, was an effort to prevent the progressive destruction of civilization itself. This fact was being overlooked. Discussing a dozen of its articles serially, Mr. Owen pointed out the deterrent to war in each case. He emphasized Article 10 as a guarantee not only against aggression but of political independence. Here was an additional safeguard against interference with our domestic concerns if one were needed. Again, the inference of interference into our domestic affairs by the International Labor Bureau was unfounded; its purpose was to improve labor conditions, not to pull them down anywhere.[17]

It was remarkable that two high-minded and equally patriotic Senators could paint such opposite pictures of the same thing on the same day as Mr. Owen and Mr. Cummins held up before the Senate on February 26.

The First White House Conference

On the evening of that day the President discussed the provisions of the Covenant with the Senate and House Foreign Relations Committees at the White House, in a conference lasting until after midnight. The Associated Press reported that the discussion covered a wide range and that the President was questioned closely, especially by Senator Brandegee, of Connecticut. He answered all questions freely,

[17] *Congressional Record,* Vol. 57, Pt. 5, pp. 4320–25.

and especially emphasized that his guests were free to discuss the conference and its information with newspaper men and others. On the major question of surrender of sovereignty, the President was said to have taken the position that recession of American sovereignty was not a new precedent, being an incident of every treaty. The views of the Republican members of the committees remained unchanged after the discussion.[18]

"Tea With the Mad Hatter." The conference brought into prominence another of the small group of men who had determined to block Wilson in his greatest endeavor at all costs. A strong, intense man, later a suicide, Senator Frank M. Brandegee, of Connecticut, subjected the President to a keen cross examination upon the terms of the Covenant which in his opinion left Wilson in a very bad light indeed. Speaking to the *New York Sun* the next day, he said, "I feel as if I had been wandering with Alice in Wonderland and had tea with the Mad Hatter." Lodge testified also that "The President seemed actually befuddled about many most important points," and Knox, who had posed his share of lawyer questions to the President, agreed in equally strong language. Lodge wrote in his diary that the President gave no information and that his performance under Brandegee's cross examination was "anything but good."[19]

At the time the conference adjourned the correspondent of the *Sun* could obtain little from the Senators; they were so "weary and mind muddled." The next afternoon "after they had opportunity to get together to compare notes" they were able to present a clear account. The result was "indeed amazing."

"Stated With Finality." The quotations noted above were a part of the amazing result, but not more astonishing than a series of statements which the *Sun* put into the President's mouth as a part of the checking of Senatorial recollections which it reported. "Pressed by men eager for scraps of information", the President had "stated with finality":

> That the United States must surrender vital points of sovereignty.
>
> Chinese and Japanese exclusion goes out of American control into the hands of League control.
>
> Ireland is to be left to the mercies of England.[20]

[18] Associated Press, *New York Times,* February 27, 1919. "No man not entirely confident of the strength of his cause," said the *Times* editorially on February 28, "would have risked the chances of such a test."
[19] H. C. Lodge, *The Senate and the League of Nations,* N. Y., 1925, p. 100.
[20] *New York Sun,* February 28, 1919.

These statements are only samples of those purported to have been made "with finality," the *Sun* insisting that Knox, Lodge, Brandegee, McCumber, and Hitchcock all "agreed that the President actually made these statements or admissions." Hitchcock immediately denied the truth of any of the much vouched for statements from the floor of the Senate, and McCumber made it emphatically clear, in terms which will be quoted below, [21] that he had no connection with the effort thus to ridicule and falsify the President's effort to satisfy the Senators. Lodge, Knox and Brandegee kept silent as to their complicity.

A Different Account. The response to the President's explanation of the Covenant indicated that no scruples would stand in the way of the effort to discredit him and convince the country that he had betrayed it. Nothing could be more fair, however, than the records left by some of the Republicans who attended the conference. Representative John Jacob Rogers, of Massachusetts, ranking Republican in the House Foreign Relations Committee, wrote to Henry White, March 3, 1919, as follows:

> The White House dinner a week ago tonight was a most interesting one and in most respects a memorable one. I thought the President appeared extremely well. He submitted himself to quite rigorous cross-examination for two hours, answering every question, easy or difficult, as fully as possible and with apparent candor. He showed not the slightest vexation, even when Senator Brandegee was pressing him rather closely on certain of the difficulties which to his mind were of importance. I never saw Mr. Wilson appear so human or so attractive as that night. There was no suggestion of a feeling of militant arrogance about him. He apparently tried to give the impression that he was really one of the circle in the East Room, who was answering rather than asking questions only because he had been so recently in Paris, and had been a factor in the preparation of the instrument under discussion. He showed a good general familiarity with the document itself—of which, by the way, he did not have a copy at any time before him during the two hours —but I think scarcely had a letter-perfect knowledge of some of the minor details. I do not say this in criticism, for my own impression was that he was as thoroughly versed as he need have been, or indeed could reasonably have been expected to be. But some of the Senators there that night thought that he was not at all adequately informed. As I said, my own impression was quite the opposite.[22]

[21] See page 151.
[22] Allan Nevins, *Henry White*, pp. 392–3. Perhaps the most important statement made by the President after the White House dinner, from the standpoint of his

SENATOR LODGE'S PLEA FOR CAUTION

Senator Lodge, courteously observing the President's request to be allowed to present his case, had used the interval in preparing an admirable negative speech which he delivered in the Senate on February 28.[23] As the first speech for the negative it would have been a classic in any debate. The address was moderate in tone. There were strong shades of sarcasm in places, but no trace of the violence evident in other recent speeches. In fact until the end of the speech he did not oppose the Covenant; he merely raised questions and asked for deep, serious consideration of them. It was so wholly reasonable and cold blooded that it would be difficult for the defenders of the League to take hold of it.

By way of introduction, everybody hated war and longed to make it impossible. We all desired to advance toward that end and merely disagreed as to how best to do it. Of course partisan motives played no part in the discussion of such a question. "It is almost needless to say that the question now before us is so momentous that it transcends all party lines. Party considerations and party interests disappear in dealing with such a question as this." No question of equal importance had ever confronted the Senate. There should be no undue haste in considering it. "My one desire is that not only the Senate—but that the press and the people of the country should investigate every proposal with the utmost thoroughness and weigh them carefully before they make up their minds." Suspicion should be attached to any article that would not bear the most thorough public discussion; "Beware of it; be on your guard against it. Demand reasons and the facts, something more than rhetoric from both sides." That the American people should look into it with considerate eyes was all that he desired.

Then he stressed at length the importance of clearness of terms in the Covenant. It seemed to have been quite hastily drafted. The result was crudeness and looseness of expression, unintentional, he hoped. The language was often not the language of statutes and laws. The matter of form was of great importance. There would be enough disagreements over interpretation at the very best, and there was no court to pass upon them. We must be careful what we set our hands

---

opponents, was to the effect that he did not believe that the Covenant could be much amended; it would be too difficult to secure the consent of the many nations which had agreed to it.

[23] *Congressional Record*, Vol. 57, Pt. 5, pp. 4520–28.

to and then carry it out to the last jot and tittle. This was a point that he made again and again. We must not expect to refuse to do anything we agreed to; we must go through with it. And what could be more proper?

Turning to matters of substance, it was no idle thing to abandon entirely the policy laid down by Washington in his Farewell Address and by the Monroe Doctrine. Perhaps the time had come to cast aside Washington's policy, but it must at least be done respectfully and reverently. We had observed these policies a long time, probably longer than any other people had stood by a political policy. He wished now merely to point out that the American people ought to be perfectly certain that they earnestly wished to abandon these doctrines.

So with Article 10, it was "a very grave, a very perilous promise to make." It would mean fleets and armies, and that our youth would be ordered to war by other nations. He hoped the American people would take time to consider before making this promise. Likewise with immigration: were we now "ready to leave it to other nations to determine whether we shall admit to the United States a flood of Japanese, Chinese and Hindu labor"? He was "not now contending that these things must not be done." He had no intention of opposing a blank negative to propositions which concerned the peace of the world which he was as anxious to see promoted as any living man could be. "What I ask, and all I ask, is consideration, time and thought."

Then the speaker took up each and every article in the Covenant in the most judicial sort of way. Some he accepted as a matter of course and others he commended. Some he considered through a column of print; in most of them he found words or phrases which were ambiguous or which raised a doubt or a danger, but usually he did not "now" argue the case; he merely pointed to the error. For example, the words "any disputes" in Article 13 gave the League jurisdiction over immigration, and "equitable treatment for the commerce of all states members of the League" gave it authority over tariffs, said Lodge.

Eventually he had demonstrated "the uncertainties which cloud this instrument from beginning to end," and was compelled against his earnest desire to do everything that could be done to secure the peace of the world to conclude that "this machinery would not promote the peace of the world, but would have a directly opposite effect." Wasn't it "possible to draft a better, more explicit, less dangerous scheme than the one here and now presented"?

His Constructive Proposals. The burden of proof rested on the affirmative, on those who supported the present draft. He would suggest, however, certain constructive propositions which, he thought, it would be well for the peace conference to consider. Let it (1) put three lines into the draft for the League which would preserve the Monroe Doctrine, (2) exclude completely from its jurisdiction such questions as immigration, (3) provide for peaceful withdrawal and (4) state whether the League was to have an international force of its own or to have the power to summon the armed forces of the different members. If those who supported the League refused to make such simple statements in the instrument it was "impossible to avoid the conclusion that they are seeking to do by indirection and the use of nebulous phrases what they are not willing to do directly. . . ."

No League Then Practical. The future majority leader of the Senate apparently did not have much hope that the Covenant could be made over so as to be acceptable, for he continued: "Unless some better constitution for a league than that can be drawn, it seems to me, after such examination as I have been able to give it, that the world's peace would be much better, much more surely promoted, by allowing the United States to go on under the Monroe Doctrine, responsible for the peace of this hemisphere, without any danger of collision with Europe as to questions among the various American states, and if a league is desired it might be made up by the European nations whose interests are chiefly concerned, and with which the United States could coöperate fully and at any time, whenever coöperation was needed."

It seemed almost painful for the Senator to have to point out again that the League really could not be created now. That had been so plainly stated before. "To me," he said, "the whole subject is one of enormous difficulties. We are all striving for a like result; but to make any real advances toward the future preservation of the world's peace will take time, care, and long consideration. We cannot reach our objects by a world constitution hastily constructed in a few weeks in Paris in the midst of the excitement of a war not yet ended." (The results of the President's obstinate effort were of course absurd, as the Allies would come to see.) "The one thing to do, as I said in the Senate some time ago, and that which I now wish above all others, is to make the peace with Germany."

Let the Other Settlements Proceed. He then spoke warmly for the immediate creation of all the proposed new states, mentioning them all by name, even to the restoration of Schleswig to Denmark, and suggested that everybody go ahead with the collection of the indemnities, the United States, England, Italy, Belgium and particularly France whom he eulogized at length. He cautioned that Germany was lifting her head and threatening again. The invitation to go on with the other business was plain.

It was followed by a paragraph for home consumption. "That which I desire above everything else, that which is nearest to my heart, is to bring our soldiers home. The making of a League of Nations will not do that. . . . What is it that delays the peace with Germany? Discussions over the League of Nations; nothing else."

Then he remembered that the Covenant had after all been proposed and remained to be dealt with. Therefore: "Pause and consider well before you take this fateful step. I do not say that agreements may not be made among the nations which stand for ordered freedom and civilization, which will do much to secure and preserve the peace of the world; but no such agreement has yet been presented to us."

Thus did he dispose of the Covenant so casually that it hardly seemed to be worthy of consideration, although he added a final paragraph of warnings against it.[24]

It was a remarkable speech, one that would be widely quoted as an exhaustive analysis and that would cause all the questioning of the Covenant in countless minds that anyone could desire. It might still accomplish the sidetracking of the League in Paris. If it didn't, it laid down a perfect basis for as long a campaign as might be necessary to defeat the Covenant. Senate leaders had told Wilson not to attempt to make a league. He had ignored them, but he should not do so in the final showdown. Agreements that would do much to secure and preserve the peace of the world might later be made "but no such agreement has yet been presented to us," and the chiefs were never

---

[24] The effect of the speech upon one of the great lawyers of the time, Mr. John W. Davis, later Democratic nominee for President, was indicated in a letter, March 24, 1919, written from his post as Ambassador to Great Britain to Henry White in Paris. Analyzing Lodge's address he came to the conclusion that the Senator's mind, whether he realized it or not, was "bent not upon amendments which would render the present scheme acceptable but upon objections which would render it or any substitute impossible." He said this, not in criticism of Lodge's attitude but because he thought it must be borne in mind in any effort made to meet him. His own view was that "If the iron is not hot now, when will it ever be?"

Replying to Lodge's criticism that the language of the Covenant was "crude," "lacks precision," "demands interpretation," he took comfort in the fact that after much polishing our own Constitution had given the courts work for one hundred and thirty years in an effort to fathom all its meaning—and the job was not finished yet. Miller, *The Drafting of the Covenant,* Vol. I, pp. 368–74.

going to admit that the Covenant of the League of Nations was such an agreement.

An Appeal for Amendment. That many Republican Senators sincerely wanted the United States to join the League is equally clear. They all saw some imperfections in it and most of them felt that it must bear some Republican earmarks, but more than a few felt the thing itself bigger than its shortcomings. On the same day that Senator Lodge spoke his mind Senator Lenroot, of Wisconsin, made a straightforward appeal for amendment of the Covenant. "I am not opposed to a League of Nations," he said, "I favor it. I approve the general plan of the formation of the League as proposed. In my judgment the country will approve the proposed constitution if certain material modifications are made and other provisions simplified and made clear."

He then gave his conclusions as to the articles that needed change. Articles 1 to 7 were free from objection except in the one important particular of voting power. He recognized our position of vantage on the Council but felt that since Article 12 gave the Assembly jurisdiction over "any dispute," we should have heavier voting power there. Article 15 seemed to call for unanimity in voting and Article 12 for majority action only. This inconsistency should be cleared up.

Article 8 he criticised only because he feared it would not lead to disarmament. Article 9 was beneficial. He did not believe we could safely agree to Article 10 as it stood either from an American viewpoint or from that of safeguarding the liberties of mankind. "The United States should be primarily responsible for peace in the Western Hemisphere. If the European nations shall be unable to maintain peace, then they should be free to call upon us for help; but we should be left free to decide for ourselves whether the situation is such as to call for our intervention. If the peace of the world is menaced we will intervene as we did in this war, but we should not be obliged to do so. . . . The European members of the League should be primarily responsible for the peace of Europe. . . . On the other hand the United States will prevent external aggression against any of the nations of the Western Hemisphere, and will ask no aid from Europe in so doing."

In the second place, said Lenroot, Article 10 would prevent desirable changes in the future. It would have prevented the success of our Revolution, our extension into Mexico or our freeing of Cuba and would have kept Armenia under the heel of the Turk. We might be obligated to send our troops in the future to fight for despotism, and against liberty.

From both these standpoints, therefore, he suggested that Article 10 simply provide that "in case of external aggression or threatened aggression against one of its members the executive council at once take jurisdiction of the matter and advise such common action as it may deem necessary in the particular case." It might even go further and bind each member state not to extend its territory, either through force or peaceful means, without the consent of the inhabitants of the territory affected.

For the remainder, he felt that such questions as immigration needed specific exclusion from the League's jurisdiction, that the assumption of a mandate should require the legislative consent of the country accepting it, that it should be surrenderable at any time, and that members be allowed to withdraw from the League at the end of ten years.[25]

Mr. Lenroot's speech was easily the most impartial criticism of the Covenant that had so far been made. He wanted to take a prominent and active part in the orderly management of world affairs; he only asked to have the right to abstain from military duty far from home unless it was urgently necessary. It was very difficult to deny him any of the amendments he asked for, even though some of them soon proved in practice to be unnecessary. Probably on the heels of the war his interpretation of Article 10 would not have given the security which the world, and especially the Continent of Europe cried out for, but ten years after, one is strongly inclined to think it would have been equally effective.

He presumed that if the President received suggestions for amendment he would try to carry them out. If such modification could be effected he hoped to be able to support the Covenant. He would "gladly vote to ratify a treaty embodying a league having the fullest powers consistent with our own interests and our own safety."

Questions by Frelinghuysen. The speech of Senator Frelinghuysen, of New Jersey, returned to the already familiar themes. The first half of it dealt with the President's failure to interpret the Fourteen Points before he went overseas, and with his failure to keep the Senate posted after he got there. Throughout the address he insisted on examination, discussion and delay, and closed by censuring the President for his intolerance of opposition as manifested both at home and abroad.

Applying the questioning policy in orthodox debating style, he

[25] *Congressional Record,* Vol. 57, Pt. 5, pp. 4569–72.

asked thirteen questions, the probable answers to all of which seemed to indicate something wrong somewhere, or to suggest very busy times for Uncle Sam. Question 3 asked how we could give self-determination to former enemy populations and not to those who fought with us, *i.e.* the Irish. Question 4 wanted to know whether there was anything to prevent the other powers from making a deal to appoint the Secretary General. Question 11 asked what would have happened if the League had existed during our Civil War and England had had five votes. Number 13 inquired whether if Germany and Russia attacked the new Poland we must fight them both.[26]

THE KNOX ASSAULT

On March 1, Senator Knox delivered a monumental assault on the Covenant.[27] Beside it the analysis of Senator Lodge was casual and superficial. To say that his attack was weighty would be putting it mildly enough—it was massive. He had absorbed and digested the whole instrument as completely as any one could. He seldom referred to a single article; he grouped all the powers of each operative body of the League together.

He began as if the League had not been mentioned in the Senate before, referred to it as the United States of the World and called attention to the fact that M. Clemenceau had assured the peace conference that the Covenant was merely the report of a Commission and could be reviewed for debate, amendment and adoption, or rejection.

He, too, had always been against war. No man dreamed more loftily or felt more intensely than he on these matters, but after the most mature deliberation it was possible for him to give, he was convinced that you might place the case as high as you would, yet you could not in the present state of society spell out an attainable end which would justify the destruction of our great country and Government. Conjure in your mind if you could a world without us.

Having made this explanation he would discuss the plan without heat or choler and with such judicial calm and fairness as he could command. Discussion was difficult because of the looseness of expression. Article 1 either as a matter of language or of logic was sheer nonsense. Beginning with it and tracing through the use of the terms "the league" and "the high contracting parties" there seemed to be a

---

[26] *Congressional Record*, Vol. 57, Pt. 5, pp. 4569–72.   [27] *Ibid.*, pp. 4687–94.

possible double international entity. The term "league of nations" as applied to the proposed organization was a misnomer because it did not include all nations, and because that term connoted a federation, whereas the association here provided for was an indissoluble union in the full sense of that term as applied to our own political institutions. This construction of the League as a super-state he supported by inference throughout, referring to Article 10 as "the supercovenant," to the Council as "this superbody" and to the Military and Naval Commission as "the general staff of the league."

Taking up each of the organs of the League, he showed that in each case the usual provisions for appointment, removal, compensation, calling of meetings, etc., were lacking. There were "great gaps in indispensable provisions and procedure," nor could it be said that these were mere details, for our own Constitution contained them.

Four Simple Tests. After discussing Article 11 and others as creating a magnificent field for "grandiose international political manipulation by ambitious men and groups" he came to the four "simple and reasonable tests" which he proposed for the document. First, "Do its provisions abolish war and make it hereafter impossible?" There was not an important article in the document that did not specifically answer "No." And further, the scheme provided therein held out "a higher promise—nay, assurance—of a future world with war, greater than any which has gone before, than any other document in the history of recorded time." This was because the Central Powers left out would form a rival league. The proposed League was merely an offensive and defensive alliance among certain picked powers. Moreover, a detailed analysis (which he included) showed that the draft legalized war in seven cases and made it compulsory in three. Furthermore, it absolutely required that every future war be a potential world war and that we should be an active participant in every such war. "We are thus thrust fully into the terrible cauldron of European politics, and every outbreak in the Balkans—even domestic, if it threaten international war —will call for some expenditure of treasure, for some shedding of American blood, for some loss of American life."

The second test was: "Do the provisions of the proposed constitution strike down the precepts of the Constitution?" They would undoubtedly, for it took away the exclusive power of Congress to raise and support armies and navies; it provided that treaties become binding only on registration, whereas the Constitution said on ratification; and situations might arise under Articles 16 and 20 requiring the making of laws which Congress would prefer not to make. In this connection he assumed the compulsory theory of mandates and visioned our boys being ordered by the League to "the aid of Armenia, or to the sleeping death regions of central Africa, or to the wildernesses of southwest Africa, or to the inhospitable South Pacific Isles."

His third test was: "Are the provisions of the proposed covenant destructive of our sovereignty?" "Cast up in your mind the colossal powers granted to the executive council," he exclaimed, "recall the covenants, the toils, and consider the infringements on our Constitution just noted." There were the disarmament provisions, which Senator Lenroot had criticised only because he thought they would be ineffective. There was no such pacific doubt in Mr. Knox's mind; he saw the provision as all too effective. "Pause, Mr. President," he begged, "and consider what it is proposed to do—to take from the social organism not alone the right, but the power of self defense. We shall stand not only naked, but bound and helpless. Why, sir, it is contrary to the eternal course of nature, exhibited in all her works since the dawn of time for a defenseless organism to survive, whether that organism be plant, animal or social. How, then, shall we hope to live?"

Thus did the great constitutional lawyer argue, as had Senator Lodge, that the Covenant destroyed that most elemental of all rights, the right of self defense. And he went further than Mr. Lodge to arrive at the astounding conclusion that in some mysterious way the Covenant would destroy the power of self defense in us while leaving others strong enough to destroy us. In truth, if the league makers could not even give the Council power to propose disarmament without such hazardous consequences, what could they hope to do?

After so many condemnations it was hardly necessary for Mr. Knox to put the Covenant to his fourth test: "Will this plan, if put in operation, threaten our national independence and life?" The dire consequences of disarmament, repeated again, plus the loss of our sovereignty, answered this question also in the affirmative. Hadn't we lost our freedom of action? There was no glimmer of his forward looking position of 1910 when he had said that "the tendency is very marked to substitute interdependence for independence," and predicted that "each nation is likely to see itself forced to yield something of its initiative, not to any one nation, but to the community of nations in payment for its share in 'the advance in richness of existence.' " His outlook now was backward to the warnings of Jefferson and Monroe.

Why the Hurry? The plan having failed to meet each and every one of the "simple and reasonable tests" he had set up for it, why then was there this feverish anxiety for its adoption? "Why is there this racing up and down over the face of the whole land by propagandists urging its adoption?[28] What benefit is to come from such a sale of the country as is urged upon us? Who are the beneficiaries of this betrayal of our people?" War was farther away than it had been for centuries. Hadn't we rescued civilization and couldn't we be trusted to do it again? "Why then this plan to strangle and crush us? Mr. President, there is here something amiss."

He hardly needed to say more to give the impression that the men who framed the Covenant were either colossally ignorant or cunningly diabolical. But he felt the compulsion of the sentiment to "do something to avert the horrors of war" enough to lead him to propose some other alternatives. They were: (1) "compulsory arbitration of all disputes," or (2) if we felt that world power was reshaping in such a way that we would need protection or to protect others "let us form an alliance with the strongest power or two powers of the world for mutual protection—as strong an alliance as could be written," or (3) if the great majority of the people of the United States eventually decided that they wanted to establish "a true league of nations" let all the nations be convoked to declare war an international crime and set up an international court with power to call upon the members to enforce its decrees by "force, economic pressure or otherwise."

Each of these proposed substitutes for the League was a more drastic departure from all our past traditions and practices than the Covenant, and the first and third were assuredly more Utopian. The Senators who could have been found to vote for any one of these proposals would have been few indeed.

"*Let Us Have An End of This!*" It was not intended, however, that any of these should be urged, for the speaker continued: "But, Mr. President, these are not the problems which now press urgently upon us. As I have recently proposed to the Senate, let us have an end of this. Let the discussion of a league of nations be postponed for later consideration not alone by the victorious belligerents but by all the nations if and when at some future time a general conference on this subject may be both possible and useful." Meanwhile "our co-belligerents need have no anxiety, for so surely as the sun rises if the Hun flood again threatened—" we would be there to meet it.

[28] The leaders of the League to Enforce Peace, led by his former chief, Wm. H. Taft, were touring the country in favor of the League.

Here was revealed again the bottom of the situation. As the President first started overseas the Senator had publicly warned him not to attempt to create a league of nations—that could wait—before Knox knew what kind of league might be agreed upon. The President had ignored the warning, had succeeded in a remarkably short space of time in getting a draft of a plan for the League, and had brought it back to present to the American people. That it was a rough draft, far from the last word in precision, everyone admitted, but the country had hailed it as containing the essentials.

Mr. Knox then bent all the powers of a great legal mind to deny that there was anything in it but danger and calamity of every kind. It was attacked from every possible legal angle, held up to the country as the ridiculous outcome which might have been expected to result from Mr. Wilson's obstinacy, and cast contemptuously aside. "Let us have an end of this!" Let the League be postponed for later consideration as he had proposed.[29]

Once again was renewed the demand that the Allies go ahead and ignore Wilson. France need not worry about her security; the Senate would look after that.

Meanwhile the thing to do was to conclude a treaty of peace and bring the troops home. Like Lodge, Senator Knox closed his address with a warm appeal for the return of the boys, a demand which Senator Reed had also made on February 19.[30] The troops were returning as fast as ships could be found for them, but they were all homesick to come at once. The leaders therefore sought to convey the impression that the League was delaying the treaty of peace and indirectly the homecoming of the soldiers. It was a subtle suggestion that reached millions of anxious relatives effectively, and it was not lost among the troops themselves.

Senator Hardwick's Opinion

No additional Democratic speeches were made in favor of the League during the remainder of the session. The Democrats were struggling against a Republican filibuster to get the appropriation bills through. Two Democrats, however, let their opposition to the Covenant be known. One was Senator Hardwick, of Georgia, who was to be replaced in the Senate by a supporter of the Administration.

[29] He had defined later consideration in connection with his "true league of nations" as "a convenient and proper time in the relatively near future." Such a time was not likely to commend itself before the close of Wilson's term.

[30] *New York Times,* February 20, 1920.

Mr. Hardwick, speaking on the same day, March 1, protested against the supposed delay of the peace treaty on account of the Covenant as loudly as any man had, calling it an international legislative rider. His argument was practically a repetition of that of Senator Knox. He regretted that Knox was not one of our peace commissioners. He pictured the usual war in the Balkans which would take "American boys from the farm and the factory and the foundry and the workshop and the bank and everywhere else." But he had a new one. Other Senators had often suggested that we couldn't handle Mexico as we pleased in the future with reference to such matters as oil wells and border raids, but Mr. Hardwick went them one better. Mexico might well ask us to return the vast territory we took from her in the Mexican war. Then if we refused to arbitrate, or lost the award, the entire League would make war on us to restore the territory to Mexico.

Before he was half done he was denouncing the President bitterly and repeatedly as "a thoroughly impracticable man," and replying sarcastically to his Boston speech, and others. He too had a list of 32 embattled questions among which were, "Are you willing to revoke and deny and denounce the Declaration of Independence?" "Were the Tories good Americans?" "Do you believe in fairies?" "Are you willing to enter into a league for perpetual, unending, interminable and innumerable wars?"

He closed with an impassioned plea to the Senators to stand firm against an Executive who had "absorbed all power that belonged to the States," who had "taken all the rights that belonged to the citizens and lodged them here in the Federal Government" and who had broken down the independence of the three coördinate branches of the Federal Government itself, "usurped the powers of Congress and paid no attention, in some cases, to the decisions of the courts."[31]

Amendments Desired by Bryan and Gore. Senator Gore, of Oklahoma, who favored amendment of the Covenant, inserted in the *Record* on March 3, a statement by W. J. Bryan, which apparently expressed his own views. Mr. Bryan hailed the League as the greatest step toward peace in a thousand years but thought that the United States should have more votes in it, that it ought to be easier for nations to enter, that the right to reject a mandate should be plainly stated, that the Monroe Doctrine should be clearly preserved and full liberty of action in applying force or the economic boycott should be reserved.

[31] *Congressional Record,* Vol. 57, Pt. 5, pp. 4699–4705.

This was a substantial program of amendment, particularly the modification of the obligation to move against an aggressor, but Mr. Bryan urged that the risks to be run in accepting the Covenant as it stood were less than those involved in rejection.

Some Phrases of Senator Sherman. On the same day Senator Sherman, of Illinois, who was leading a filibuster, with the consent of Senator Lodge, to force the calling of an extra session so that the war on the League might continue in the President's absence, delivered another vitriolic outburst on the subject. [32] He referred to the League as an oligarchy, the worst possible form of government and as "a Pandora's box of evil to empty upon the American people the aggregated calamities of the world." It obliged us "to defend Great Britain's colonial dependencies any place in the world," and to send the angel of death to every American home.

By a decree it would "embargo our commerce, close our exchanges, destroy our credits, leave our merchandise rotting on the piers, shut the Isthmian Canal, order Congress to declare war, levy taxes, appropriate money, raise and support armies and navies, and dispatch our men to any quarter of the globe to fight and die because our alien council has so willed." It was "the death knell of the American Republic," "a fantastic idealism, a polyglot philanthrophy as vain in the realms of world philosophy and morals as it is impossible in peaceable execution."

The Senate must interpose its power against "this universal Utopia promised by the President", whom he referred to as "suffering from the autointoxication of excess in phrase making." He charged him with adroitly maneuvering "himself into the spot light as the fountain of perpetual peace and the guardian of mankind" and with aiming to make himself "the drum major of civilization." [33]

It was plain enough that if the President won any further successes, no matter in what cause he fought, it would be only because his enemies did not have the power to thwart him.

SENATOR McCUMBER'S REPLY TO THE CRITICS

At the conclusion of Senator Sherman's castigation of the League and its maker, Senator McCumber, of North Dakota, obtained the floor to defend the Covenant. [34] He did so because he "feared that the

---

[32] W. E. Dodd, *Woodrow Wilson and His Work*, p. 325.
[33] *Congressional Record*, Vol. 57, Pt. 5, pp. 4864–69.
[34] March 3, 1919. *Congressional Record*, Vol. 57, Pt. 5, pp. 4872–82.

country, after reading the arguments that have been made on this side of the Chamber against any league of nations, might be misled into the belief that the Republicans of the United States as a party were opposed to any character of a league or agreement to maintain the peace of the world." He knew that some of his colleagues were so opposed and that others took the position that since we were big enough to take care of ourselves we need not enter into such agreements, but "notwithstanding all the arguments and criticisms that have been made upon that side of the Chamber, I think it but fair to say that there are a large number of Republicans who favor a league of nations to maintain the peace of the world."

He recognized that we might go to the rescue of civilization again without any league as Senator Knox said we would, but the fact was that we would not have intervened in the Great War if Germany had let our shipping alone. He wanted the country committed so that we could stand on our agreement to prevent such another holocaust.

The Purposes of the League Could not Be Ignored. He was compelled to say that he thought some of the criticisms of the League very far fetched. He wanted to read the Covenant and show the reading public the difference between what was in it and what had been read into it. The critics had all passed over the preamble, which said: "In order to promote international coöperation and to secure international peace and security by the acceptance of obligations not to resort to war, by the prescription of open, just, and honorable relations between nations, by the firm establishment of the understandings of international law as the actual rule of conduct among governments, and by the maintenance of justice and a scrupulous respect for all treaty obligations in the dealings of organized people with one another. . . ." These were the purposes of the League and every article in the Covenant should be construed in the light of the declaration of its purposes.

Article 10 the Corner Stone. He came at once to Article 10, which had received more condemnation than all the others. "That article is the very foundation stone in the structure of a world agreement for peace." He would like to have any Senator give him a clearer and more concise declaration of an agreement to preserve peace than this agreement not to go to war for an unlawful purpose. It was a guarantee against external aggression only. "In other words, the very object and the very purpose and the only purpose of the proposed League of Nations is to prevent one great powerful nation from making a war of aggression, a war to seize territory, or to annex another nation."

"Mr. President," continued Mr. McCumber, "if we cannot have that kind of agreement, of course we cannot have any agreement to insure peace. If we do not agree that we will not make a war of aggression against another nation, then what is all this peace talk about? Again, the agreement is to protect 'the territorial integrity and existing political independence.' What does 'political independence' mean? It means simply the sovereignty, the absolute sovereign power of the nation to conduct itself politically as a complete independent entity. That is all. If we protect the territory of a nation from aggression we must necessarily protect its independence, its political sovereignty, and that is the whole purpose of this compact."

Domestic Affairs Invariably Reserved. Article 12 provided that no member should go to war without submitting its dispute either to arbitration or inquiry, waiting three months after the award or recommendation—and not then against any member which complied with the award or report. This provision had been criticised "on the assumption that we are compelled to submit internal relations, our domestic affairs, to every nation in the world which questions the propriety or the justice of any regulation which we make in reference to such affairs." He thought "one must be led far afield, indeed, by his prejudice to draw a conclusion of this character."

We had the whole history of the world, all the diplomacy of the ages, to guide us in determining what were domestic rights and what were international rights. Nowhere could we ever find any authority that would question the right of any nation to determine its purely domestic affairs.

The Covenant Could Not Be Condemned on Scattered Phrases. Speaking extemporaneously, he explained the various articles as they stood, showing what the obvious purpose was, as fast as the interruptions of Senators would let him. [35] When they pressed him insistently to make a criticism of a word or a phrase he replied: "I am not contending that we have here a perfect instrument. [As indeed no one did.] I admit that it is loosely drawn in some respects, and that it is not clear and as definite as it should be made. The only contention I am making is that much of the criticism, and most of it, is without foundation under the terms of the agreement."

He maintained throughout that what the Senators were doing was

[35] After one Senator had made two particularly long interruptions and seemed likely to argue indefinitely, Senator Bankhead, of Georgia, warned McCumber that he would lose the floor if there were any more such debates. After that the interruptions were brief.

to take merely a part of a clause and construe it as if there were nothing else left in the instrument. Every part of it must be given force and effect; we must construe its provisions together; and we must construe them as intended to carry out the main purpose enunciated. When urged to declare for amendments to safeguard domestic issues, the Monroe Doctrine, etc., he replied that he would make such additions, not that there was anything in the Covenant inconsistent with them but to stop the useless cavil.

The Monroe Doctrine Applied to Us Too. On the Monroe Doctrine he brought out that the critics were largely giving it an interpretation that was never intended. They spoke in terms of overlordship, resenting, as an interference with our prerogatives, any suggestion that the League have jurisdiction on this side of the ocean.

Many Senators had read the Monroe declaration to the Senate, noted Mr. McCumber, but all had omitted one part of it, namely, that "It is still the true policy of the United States to leave the parties to themselves. . . ." We had assumed obligations that limited our own conduct. The Doctrine simply said keep your hands off and we will do the same. It put us in the position of a big brother to the South American Republics, but it gave us no right to be the big tyrant over them. The Covenant which bound everybody to keep their hands off these countries did merge the Monroe Doctrine into a world doctrine, but did not destroy it in any respect.

Fairness and Honesty Asked. Referring to the extended ridicule of the White House conference imputed to individual Senators by the *New York Sun*, the speaker felt compelled to say a little about that conference, which he had attended. He maintained that he was as good a Republican as any member of the Senate but he did not feel that he was justified in misstating the position of a Democratic President. Because denial of these statements had come only from the Democratic side he wished to say that on the evening when the Committee on Foreign Affairs of the Senate dined with the President "nothing could have been more fair than his presentation of the case. He subjected himself to every inquiry that might be made and answered every inquiry fairly and justly and in a spirit of conciliation, with a desire to make all matters perfectly clear."

Mr. McCumber was also the first Senator apparently to mention—he barely did so—that the President had other nations to deal with at Paris. Their desires had to be considered.

He did not deny the right of any Senator to oppose the League entirely, but he insisted that what "we ought to do is to be absolutely honest with ourselves. If we do not want any kind of an agreement to maintain the peace of the world, in Heaven's name let us say so and be done with it. If we do believe that we are in honor and in duty bound, if we do believe that there is any moral obligation resting upon this great nation to assist in maintaining the peace of the world, then let us at least do what we can to assist other nations in making an agreement that we can all stand by."

CHAPTER VI

THE ULTIMATUM

SENATOR McCUMBER's plea for a forthright stand of some kind on the part of his colleagues was answered sooner probably than he expected. Senator Brandegee had been thinking deeply that the bitter and sweeping assaults made on the Covenant in the Senate were not enough. Some vigorous action should be taken, he thought, which would give positive notice to the world that there must be "an end of this." Having conceived of a striking way of achieving this purpose, he sought out Senator Lodge early in the morning on Sunday March 2, and, says Lodge, "told me that it seemed to him of the last importance that at that juncture some declaration should be made, receiving for it if possible the signatures of more than one third of the Senate, to the effect that a League of Nations such as it was understood was to be proposed, and the outlines of which had been given through the press, could not be passed." [1]

One would hardly suspect from Mr. Lodge's statement that a draft of a league charter, approved by a great international conference, had been published throughout the land and was in every Senator's hands. However, Lodge was "very much struck by the proposition, and he had no difficulty in convincing me of its essential and even vital importance." Lodge therefore accompanied Brandegee to ask Knox to draft the declaration. He did so, and Cummins agreed, after making some amendments, to sign it. The necessary number of signatures was then obtained during the next day and just before midnight of March 3, Lodge arose in the Senate and delivered the ultimatum in the following manner [2]:

MR. LODGE. Mr. President, I desire to take only a moment of the time of the Senate. I wish to offer the resolution which I hold in my hand, a very brief one:

[1] Lodge, *The Senate and the League of Nations*, p. 118.
[2] *Congressional Record*, Vol. 57, Pt. 5, p. 4974.

"Whereas under the Constitution it is a function of the Senate to advise and consent to, or dissent from, the ratification of any treaty of the United States, and no such treaty can be operative without the consent of the Senate expressed by the affirmative vote of two-thirds of the Senators present; and

"Whereas owing to the victory of the arms of the United States and of the nations with whom it is associated, a peace conference was convened and is now in session at Paris for the purpose of settling the terms of peace; and

"Whereas a committee of the conference has proposed a constitution for a league of nations and the proposal is now before the peace conference for its consideration: Now, therefore, be it

"Resolved by the Senate of the United States in the discharge of its constitutional duty of advice in regard to treaties, That it is the sense of the Senate that while it is their sincere desire that the nations of the world should unite to promote peace and general disarmament, the constitution of the league of nations in the form now proposed to the peace conference should not be accepted by the United States; and be it *Resolved further,* That it is the sense of the Senate that the negotiations on the part of the United States should immediately be directed to the utmost expedition of the urgent business of negotiating peace terms with Germany satisfactory to the United States and the nations with whom the United States is associated in the war against the German Government, and that the proposal for a league of nations to insure the permanent peace of the world should be then taken up for careful consideration."

I ask unanimous consent for the present consideration of this resolution.

MR. SWANSON. I object to the introduction of the resolution.

MR. LODGE. Objection being made, of course I recognize the objection. I merely wish to add, by way of explanation, the following:

"The undersigned Senators of the United States, Members and Members elect of the Sixty-sixth Congress, hereby declare that, if they had had the opportunity, they would have voted for the foregoing resolution.

"HENRY CABOT LODGE	WILLIAM M. CALDER
PHILANDER C. KNOX	HENRY W. KEYES
LAWRENCE Y. SHERMAN	BOISE PENROSE
HARRY S. NEW	GEORGE P. McLEAN
GEORGE H. MOSES	CARROLL S. PAGE
J. W. WADSWORTH, JR.	JOSEPH IRWIN FRANCE

Bert M. Fernald	Medill McCormick
Alrert B. Cummins	Charles Curtis
F. E. Warren	Lawrence C. Phipps
James E. Watson	Selden P. Spencer
Thomas Sterling	Hiram W. Johnson
J. S. Frelinghuysen	Charles E. Townsend
W. G. Harding	William P. Dillingham
Frederick Hale	I. L. Lenroot
William E. Borah	Miles Poindexter
Walter E. Edge	Howard Sutherland
Reed Smoot	Truman H. Newberry
Asle J. Gronna	L. Heisler Ball"
Frank B. Brandegee	

"As the Massachusetts Senator started to speak," reported the faithful *New York Sun,* "realization of the gravity of the step he was taking and that others were taking under his guidance and leadership came to him. His voice was steady, but his hand, in which he held the resolution he read from was shaking perceptibly. As he finished reading the list of names, Mr. Lodge paused a moment, then quietly left the hall of the Senate. There was not a sign of approval or disapproval from Senators on the floor or from the hundreds jammed in the galleries." [3]

The proposed resolution, records Lodge, "was clearly out of order." A vote on it indeed was not desired. Barely 33 of the sitting Senators had signed the paper. [4] It was most improbable that even with a few Democratic recruits a majority vote of the Senate could be mustered for it. To have it announced that the resolution had been defeated would not create the desired effects. It is doubtful whether the fathers of the declaration would have permitted a vote on it. It would be strange indeed though, if some Democrat did not object to consideration. One did. "The plan worked out beautifully after Senator Swanson's objection," said the *Sun.* "Our purpose, however, had been served," added Senator Lodge, "The declaration went out to the world." [5]

What was the purpose of this remarkable declaration? On its face it was a resolution of the Senate proposed "in the discharge of its

[3] *New York Sun,* March 4, 1919.
[4] Two additional signatures were added the next day, David Elkins, of West Virginia, by arrival, and Albert B. Fall, of New Mexico, by telegraph. The list included four Senators-elect, Edge, Phipps, Ball and Newberry, making a final total of 39 signatures.
[5] Lodge, *The Senate and the League of Nations,* pp. 118–9.

constitutional duty of advice in regard to treaties." Of course its de-
signers knew, as Senator Sterling had pointed out in February without
contradiction, [6] that by the practice of more than a century the Senate's
function on treaties began when the treaty was formally laid before it
by the President. Senator Lodge had said in his speech of February 28,
a week earlier, that "The Senate can take no action upon it, but it
lies open before us for criticism and discussion." [7]

It is not important, however, to dispute the pretended constitutional
orthodoxy of the document. Anybody has a right to advise the President what to do about treaties, and the Senate, which must pass judgment upon his work, does have especial leave to do so if it sees fit.

Did they Seek Revision? Much more important than the form of
the proposal are the motives back of it. What were the purposes that
may reasonably be assumed to have dictated it? The first that may be
advanced is that the Senators wished to have the Covenant revised to
protect American interests. If this motive be assumed, the document
has justification, because the President had indicated at the White
House conference that it would be very difficult to amend it, and he
had admitted no need for amendment. If the Senators had earnestly
desired to perfect the document from the American standpoint they
could have been justified in addressing a petition or a notice to the
President stating plainly that they considered the amendments suggested in Mr. Lodge's speech, or others, as indispensable to American
participation. But the character of all the speeches made by them on
the Covenant, save one, precludes this assumption, as does the wholly
irreconcilable origin of the ultimatum. The Senators had been seeking
to give the impression that the Covenant was altogether unsatisfactory in
its entirety. Only Senator Lenroot had shown a real desire to perfect it.
The Round Robin does contain the qualifying phrase, "in the form now
proposed," which left open a way of retreat if the signers later found
it impossible to risk rejection, but the whole tone of the document itself, as well as their previous utterances, shows that it was not
amendment of the Covenant the leaders were seeking. The inclusion of
the words "in the form now proposed" also made it possible for
Senator Lenroot and some other Senators to sign it. They could do so
and still hope for a chance to vote for the League. Without this clause,
it is highly probable that the thirty-three signatures necessary to defeat the Covenant could not have been secured.

[6] See page 87.
[7] *Congressional Record,* Vol. 57, Pt. 5, p. 4520.

Was Later Action by the Peace Conference Desired? Again, may it not have been the belief of the Senators that the other peace settlements were more urgent and that the League could be successfully created by the Peace Conference after all the other problems had been settled? The language of the document also permits this interpretation. That proposals for a league "should then be taken up" appeared to mean without delay. This was the first time, however, that Senator Lodge or any of his lieutenants had ever suggested the possibility of a league being created by the Peace Conference then sitting. In all their speeches there had been nothing urgent at all about this league business. In Senator Knox's resolution of December 3, the opening gun of the whole campaign, "any project for any general league of nations" was to be "postponed for separate consideration not alone by the victorious belligerents, but by all the nations if and when at some future time general conferences on those subjects might be deemed useful." In his speech of March 1 Knox had advanced only so far as to suggest the possibility of such a conference being held "at a convenient and proper time in the relatively near future." The resolution of Senator France, described above, laid down a wholly indefinite interval before a league should be formed.

No, that tardy suggestion of action just after the peace settlements had been made was not expected to be carried out. The Senators knew that after months of exhausting labor on the settlements, when everything had been divided, the delegates would not wait longer to formulate with great deliberation a league of nations. Everybody would be either satisfied with what had been obtained or disgruntled and bitter over what had not been received. Mr. Wilson would have then no leverage on the conflicting national interests of Europe; there would be little chance of giving the league work to do to give it vitality until it could become established; there would be no chance of projecting its spirit and purposes back under the settlements that had been sealed. The President would be left with only an abstract principle to promote in an atmosphere wholly unfavorable to such championship. By that time, too, the world-wide popular support which the President still had would have subsided and his prestige with the European governments would have been destroyed. The natural working of things, unaided by a steady drum-fire of opposition from his rear, would give these results.

As Senator McCumber contended for the Covenant, the Round

Robin must be construed in its entirety and in view of the spirit back of it and not on the basis of a single phrase. It was the high-water mark in the sustained demand of the Senate leaders that the Peace Conference suppress Wilson and make peace on the old basis, without reference to his plans and principles. The sponsors of the demand had made up their minds in December that he was not to have the honor and credit of creating a league of nations if they could prevent it, and the amazing success that he had had during two short months in moving toward that very consummation only spurred them on to frenzies of opposition and steeled their resolve that he must not succeed.

The proposed resolution was "a notice to the people in Paris," said Senator Penrose, on March 5. [8] Simultaneously, the *Washington Post* explained, under "How Europe Will Take the Warning," that "Necessarily those governments will shape their movements in the peace conference according to the nature of their information. If they become convinced that the proposed constitution of the league of nations will not be accepted by the United States, notwithstanding President Wilson's insistence, they will do their best to sidetrack the proposition, or to so modify it as to make its adoption or rejection a matter of no importance." [9] If Great Britain and Europe continued to ignore the notice, wrote Lodge afterwards, the consequences were their own fault. [10]

The publication of the Round Robin was a highly significant move, the counterpart of which would be difficult to discover in the history of treaty making in the United States or any other country. It was to lay its originators open through all time to the charge of attempting to strengthen the hands of reactionary forces abroad against the supreme effort of an American President to achieve international security at the close of fratricidal warfare that had all but extinguished civilization. But the authors of the Round Robin were not playing for the verdict of history, and if the venture succeeded it would spare them from the very grave danger of emasculating the Covenant, when it later came before them, in the face of an overwhelming public sentiment demanding the creation of the League. That would be relief indeed. But even if the demand failed in its immediate objective it would still support them in a war of attrition, so well prepared for by their speeches in the Senate, and it would enable them to start this

[8] *New York Times,* March 5, 1919.
[9] *Washington Post,* March 5, 1919.
[10] Lodge, *The Senate and the League of Nations,* pp. 120–122.

phase of their campaign with enough votes substantially committed to ensure their ascendency at the end.

"Woodrow Wilson's League of Nations died in the Senate tonight," chanted the *Sun*. "Henry Cabot Lodge, Senator from Massachusetts, who has bitterly opposed a League of Nations on the terms drawn up by President Wilson, read the death warrant of the League." [11] "Honor and Praise," sang Harvey, to Lodge who "fathered it," to Knox who "played the chief part in drafting it," to Brandegee who "conceived the idea and obtained the signatures." [12]

The issuance of the Round Robin was followed up by a final filibuster conducted by Senators Sherman, France and La Follette, bitter opponents of the League and its sponsor, to kill the great revenue bills and thus force the President to call the Senate and House into session during his absence. The filibuster was carried on by the three Senators from two o'clock in the morning of March 4 until eleven-thirty and succeeded in its purpose. The General Deficiency Bill which carried large appropriations for expenses already incurred by the Government in the administration of the railroads was lost, together with bills carrying huge appropriations for the army, navy and shipping board. A dozen other important measures also failed.

While the filibuster neared conclusion the President talked cheerfully with Democratic Senators in his room at the Capitol without betraying any emotions he may have felt. Would he bow to the heroic efforts of the opposition Senators to force him out of his position of leadership at Paris? All those who wondered did not have long to wait. Immediately upon the adjournment of Congress he issued a statement saying, "It is plainly my present duty to attend the Peace Conference in Paris. It is also my duty to be in close contact with the public business during a session of the Congress. I must make my choice between these two duties, and I confidently hope that the people of the country will think I am making the right choice. It is not in the interest of the right conduct of public affairs that I should call the Congress in special session while it is impossible for me to be in Washington, because of a more pressing duty elsewhere, to coöperate with the Houses." [13]

[11] *New York Sun*, March 4, 1919.

[12] *Harvey's Weekly*, March 8, 1919, Vol. 2, No. 10, p. 1. All numbers of the *Weekly* were now almost entirely filled with criticism of "the President's League of Nations Claptrap," "The Smuts League of Nations," the "League of Denationalized Nations."

[13] *New York Times*, March 5, 1919. The remainder of the statement attempted to place responsibility on the filibusterers (without naming them) for the financial embarrassment the government would be under during his absence.

The Replies of Taft and Wilson in New York

Wilson had been disturbed by the suppressed hostility of the ruling Senators which was obvious in the White House conference. He didn't like the situation and decided that he would make an important address before he returned to Europe. Realizing the necessity of Republican restraint upon the Senate leaders, he telegraphed to Taft, who was in North Carolina, asking if he would speak with him in New York on the evening of March 4. Taft was much exhausted by his great tour of the country in behalf of the League. His physicians advised him to decline, but Taft's heart was in the cause. He was waiting at the Metropolitan Opera House when Wilson arrived.

The President had been greeted by enthusiastic crowds as he left Washington and passed through Philadelphia and had received a great ovation in New York. A full share of the applause was Taft's as the two ascended the platform together.

The ex-President spoke first, dealing good humoredly with the Lodge Round Robin, but insisting forcefully that it would be the duty of the President to insert the Covenant into the treaty of peace as indispensable to the peace sought. The responsibility for postponing peace would then be on the Senators, and when confronted with it he thought they would have a different idea.

The League would stand "as the living evidence of the united power of Christian civilization to make this treaty a real treaty of peace." It was needed, moreover, to steady the new nations and hold the world level against bolshevism. No critic of the League had offered a single suggestion to meet the crisis the world faced. Therefore, "Well may the President decline to comply with the suggestions of the proposed resolution."

The bulk of Mr. Taft's address was a detailed analysis of the objections to the League—entangling alliances, Monroe Doctrine, loss of sovereignty, etc. Though certainly as good a constitutional lawyer as the critics of the League in the Senate, the future Chief Justice of the Supreme Court saw no super-sovereignty in it. On the contrary, it was "only a limited and loose union of the compelling powers of many nations to do the same thing." Certainly somebody was misinterpreting the League; it could not be an overpowering super-state and at the same time a "limited and loose union"; either Taft or the Senatorial critics of the League were wrong.

The True Meaning of Sovereignty. The League, said Mr. Taft, merely created contract obligations not different from a contract made with one nation. To argue that we could not make the contract implied that we did not have full sovereignty. Sovereignty to him was "exactly analogous to the liberty of the individual regulated by law. The sovereignty that we should insist upon and the only sovereignty we have a right to insist upon is a sovereignty regulated by international law, international morality and international justice, a sovereignty enjoying the sacred rights which sovereignties of other nations may enjoy. . . ." Sovereignty was necessarily limited by the law of nations and by the contracts entered into.

No Involvement in a Lot of Small Wars. With reference to Article 10, he suggested that force could be employed without bringing the article into effect. Secretary Seward and President Roosevelt had both held that the Monroe Doctrine did not prevent European nations from forcibly collecting debts from Chile and Venezuela, so long as these countries were not deprived of independence or territory.

Would our country "be forced by these covenants into a lot of little wars all over the face of the world? No. In the first place, the existence of the League and its covenants and the immediate self-acting boycotts will restrain most nations, especially small nations, from incurring the penalty of complete world ostracism. The background of possible limited force will be a further restraint. It will minimize war everywhere. The risk of war for the members of the League under the covenant is, therefore, not to be compared with the danger of a recurrence of general war without the League and its covenants. Into such a war we are bound to be drawn."

Furthermore, in the event that force had to be employed to settle minor conflicts it was most unlikely that the Council would habitually advise the sending of troops outside of a continent.

The Covenant Indispensable to the Peace. At the close of his speech he advised the President to accept the useful suggestions for amendment in the constructive part of Senator Lodge's speech, and concluded: "The covenant should be in the treaty of peace. It is indispensable in ending this war; if the war is to accomplish the declared purpose of this nation and the world in it. . . . We know the President believes this and will insist upon it. Our profound sympathy in his purpose and our prayers for his success should go with him in his great mission." [14]

Taft's Service in the Creation of the League. When the roll of

[14] *New York Times,* March 5, 1919.

the great founders of the League of Nations is some day compiled it will be impossible to keep from writing William Howard Taft high upon it. Under his active leadership the League to Enforce Peace had been the leading factor in moulding and expressing sentiment for a league during the major part of the war. Without its efforts the President himself probably would not have been convinced so early and so certainly that a League was not only indispensable to the future, but also demanded by the best thought of the country.

The services of the League to Enforce Peace, moreover, did not stop there. During the critical weeks of late January and February, when the fact that there should be a league was being decided in Paris, the American organization was carrying on a powerful nation-wide campaign to bring about its creation. The splendid popular response to the tour of the country which Taft and others made—not under Carnegie Peace money as the Senators charged—must have done much to convince not only Wilson but the Peace Conference that the American people wanted a new dispensation. Besides addressing a series of great regional conferences, Taft made many other speeches and assuredly did much to stir the national sentiment for a league that undoubtedly existed when the attacks in the Senate began.

He had assisted the enemies of the President to gain control of the Senate, but he strove valiantly for a long year thereafter to ward off the results of the election of 1918. When the leaders of his party in the Senate had done everything within their power either to defeat the League outright or to delay it until the chance of its creation would be slight indeed, Taft stood by his beliefs as few other national political figures have done when their party headed the other way. The effect of the Lodge ultimatum of March 3 was bound to be considerable in Europe. As we shall see, the President had lost some of the ground gained by the time he got back to Europe, through the operation of forces there, aside from the adverse influences of the Senate's opposition to him. Without the whole-hearted and generous support which Taft gave to him and to the League on the night of March 4 he might not have been able to bring the League back to the foreground when he returned to Paris. Surely it would have been more difficult. If the declaration of the thirty-nine Senators had not been counteracted in some way the forces at Paris who wished to shelve the League might have felt able to do so. But the complete support which Mr. Wilson's Republican predecessor gave him largely neutralized the effect of the Round Robin. Roosevelt was dead; Taft was exerting powerful leader-

WILLIAM HOWARD TAFT

ship in support of the League. The move of the Senators was widely assessed in European newspapers as a play in American internal politics; the action of Taft could not be so interpreted. The last thing he could be charged with was partisan motive. There was every reason to believe, in addition, that he spoke for millions of Republicans. His timely defense of the President's course had, too, probably even greater dramatic value than the action of the Senators. His prediction that when faced with the Covenant as a part of the Treaty they would see things differently seemed the reasonable thing to expect. At the very least, the fact that Taft exerted his full strength to block the action of the leaders of his party indicated that supporters of the League in America were deeply in earnest. His action also must have sent the President overseas believing that his cause would not fail.

Wilson's Belief Unshaken. Certainly the President's address, which followed Taft's, was full of conviction that the peoples of the world wanted the League and must have it. He accepted the intimation of the air played by the band, "Over there". He would not come back till it was over, over there, and the first thing he proposed to tell the people on the other side was that an overwhelming majority of American people were in favor of the League.

Continuing, he described the inspiring concurrence of purpose to make an effective working agreement that he had found in the League of Nations Commission. There was conviction that the thing must be done. Taft's picture of the need of the League to stabilize the new nations was not overdrawn. They would provide fertile ground for the old poisonous seed of intrigue—one of the things the League was intended to keep down. "Intrigue cannot stand publicity, and if the League of Nations were nothing but a great debating society it would kill intrigue."

The People Wanted Unity in Support of Justice. Vision had always been with the people. The vision necessary for great reforms had seldom come from the top in the nations of the world. The heart of the world was awake at the moment and the world must be satisfied. The uneasiness of the populations of Europe was not due for one moment to economic causes alone; something very much deeper underlay it. They saw that their governments had never been able to defend them from intrigue and aggression, and they were beginning to perceive that the fundamental cause lay in the fact that nations stood singly or in jealous groups against each other "fostering prejudice, increasing the danger of war rather than concerting measures to prevent it; and that if there is right in the world, if there is justice in the world, there is no reason why nations should be divided in support of justice."

They Must be Considered. There was warning aimed at the Senators also, uttered "not in the way of a threat; the forces of the world do not threaten, they operate. The great tides of the world do not give notice when they are going to rise and run; they rise in their majesty and overwhelming might, and those who stand in the way are overwhelmed." The peoples of the world were saying "if you really believe that there is a right, if you really believe that wars ought to be stopped, stop thinking about the rival interests of nations and think about men and women and children throughout the world. Nations are not meant to afford distinction to their rulers by way of success in the maneuvers of politics; nations are meant, if they are meant for anything, to make the men and women and children in them secure and happy and prosperous, and no nation has the right to set up its special interests against the interests and benefits of mankind, least of all this great nation which we love. It was set up for the benefit of mankind; it was set up to illustrate the highest ideals and to achieve the highest aspirations of men who wanted to be free; and the world —the world of today—believes that and counts on us, and would be thrown back into the blackness of despair if we deserted it."

The Tragedy of Their Hope. The President's critics later made merry over the idea of our breaking the heart of the world, but future students can hardly doubt the depth of the responsibility which the President felt for himself and for his country as he continued:

I have tried once and again, my fellow citizens, to say to little circles of friends or to larger bodies what seems to be the real hope of the peoples of Europe, and I tell you frankly I have not been able to do so, because when the thought tries to crowd itself into speech the profound emotion of the thing is too much; speech will not carry. I have felt the tragedy of the hope of these suffering peoples.

It is a tragedy because it is a hope which cannot be realized in its perfection; and yet I have felt besides its tragedy, its compulsion, its compulsion upon every living man to exercise every influence that he has to the uttermost to see that as little as possible of that hope is disappointed, because if men cannot now, after the agony of bloody sweat, come to their self possession and see how to regulate the affairs of the world we will sink back into a period of struggle in which there will be no hope and therefore no mercy. There can be no mercy where there is no hope, for why should you spare another if you yourself expect to perish? Why be pitiful if you get no pity? Why should you be just, if upon every hand you are put upon?

The Covenant Would Be in the Treaty. Every man in the Peace Conference knew that the treaty of peace itself would be inoperative, as Mr. Taft had said, without the constant support and energy of a great organization such as is supplied by the League of Nations. Those who doubted that it could be formed had admitted that if it could be created it would be invaluable in securing the operation of the various parts of the treaty. When the treaty came back, gentlemen on this side would find the Covenant "not only in it, but so many threads of the treaty tied to the covenant that you cannot dissect the covenant from the treaty without destroying the whole vital structure."

He could not imagine how the gentlemen could be Americans and set up "a doctrine of careful selfishness thought out to the last detail." He had heard no counsel of generosity in their criticisms, no constructive criticism—nothing except "Will it not be dangerous to us to help the world?" It would be fatal to us not to help it.

But the fact of being an American was enough to tell him that the people of the United States would support this Covenant. "Take an individual American and you may often find him selfish and confined to his special interests; but take the American in the mass and he is willing to die for an ideal." And so he was going back to his task with renewed vigor immensely refreshed by coming in contact with the spirit of the American people again. [15]

He would need to be refreshed, for he would find when he reached the other side again that he would need all his strength to maintain what had already been won.

PRESS OPINION OF THE COVENANT

Opinions Before March 1. Did the American people favor the League as much as the President believed? It would be impossible to say just how overwhelming the sentiment for it was, but the news reviews of the day indicate a clear preponderance of support for it. The *Literary Digest* reported on March 1, that "the majority of our papers regard the experiment as tremendously worth trying." The *St. Paul Pioneer Express* (Rep.) had no doubt of its final acceptance

[15] *New York Times*, March 5, 1919.

but nevertheless invoked for it the severest scrutiny. The *Duluth Herald* (Ind.) reminded its readers that in running the gauntlet of criticism it would only be repeating the experience of the American Constitution which was "roundly condemned by many statesmen as impracticable, unworkable, and a dangerous invasion of the liberties of the several sovereign colonies." The *Philadelphia Public Ledger* (Ind. Rep.) admonished that discussion distorted and perverted by selfish partisanship would be a crime against civilization. The *New York Tribune* (Rep.) agreed with the *Richmond Journal* (Dem.) that "international peace must rest on force just as domestic peace does." "It is bound to win because the enlightened sentiment of all Christendom is behind it," affirmed the *Manchester* (*N. H.*) *Union* (Ind. Rep.) "The adoption of this constitution will mark the longest step the world has taken in human government," according to the *Pittsburgh Dispatch* (Ind.).

"The plan unquestionably stands for a forward step in the advance of civilization—a step which must be taken if civilization is to endure," said the *New York Journal of Commerce,* which thought that "it has gone a long way toward providing for the peace of the world with the least possible interference with national sovereignty." It is an effort to mobilize and organize the moral forces and right thinking of the world, noted the *Baltimore Sun* (Ind.). "It may not eliminate war entirely, but it will reduce the chance of future wars to a minimum, and start the world in a new era of peace, prosperity and guaranteed liberties," declared the *Oshkosh Northwestern* (Rep.). It gave every promise of taking us a long way toward the abolition of war, thought the *Indianapolis Star* (Ind. Rep.) which added that "there is not a provision in its twenty-six articles that restricts a legitimate right of any sovereign nation or proposes a hardship on any one." As a whole it was far in advance of the Hague Conference concluded the *New York Herald* (Ind.)." [16]

The President the Storm Center. Current Opinion in its issue of March, 1919, noted in its leading article that the President was the center of the strife. "Released, by the cessation of fighting," it said, "from the obligation felt by most of us to give loyal support to the President in time of war, the political opponents of Mr. Wilson have been indulging of late in an orgy of criticism." His presence at the Versailles Conference was resented and his achievements there were either belittled or viewed with alarm. "This critical disposition is

[16] *Literary Digest,* Vol. 60, No. 9, pp. 11–13.

not very widespread or general, but as far as it goes it is intense and sweeping. . . ."

The first item in the indictment was that the President no longer represented the will of the American people. Referring to some of his statements the *Providence Journal* (Rep.) asked, "How did he know what the United States will do or will not do?" It termed his trip to Europe "a fantastic adventure" and the *New York Sun* (Rep.) insisted that he went to Europe as "the self-constituted brain and voice of the country." The *Lowell Courier-Citizen* argued with reference to his conduct at Paris that the autocracy of the Kaiser paled before that of the President. The *Brooklyn Eagle* (Dem.) contended in reply that he was President by majority vote, and that in the congressional elections recently won by the Republicans, "Not a man who had openly antagonized Wilson whether he were a Republican or a Democrat got popular favor."

On the other hand, Charles H. Grasty wrote from Paris to the *New York Times* that the President was out to gain a stupendous reform in world methods and nothing less would satisfy him. Nobody in the Conference sincerely wanted to go the whole distance with him, but there was no end to his energy, patience and wisdom. A British journalist, A. G. Gardiner, also wrote to the *London Daily News* in similar vein, saying: "His serene and powerful personality is pervading the atmosphere of negotiations with the spirit of wisdom and urbanity and is providing a solvent for all sorts of difficulties."

Western Republican Support. Equally strong support, too, was given to Mr. Wilson by another group of Republican papers at home. The *Des Moines Register* maintained that "What the American delegation is proposing at Versailles is the greatest thing the world has ever had proposed since governments were formed." President Wilson was not sitting at Versailles as a Democrat but as the representative of the American people, and "with world interests in the balance, with everything America has fought for in this war still to be won, with the President taking a great leadership for world democracy, to make mere opposition to Wilson a test of Republicanism as though the real matter of interest was who should hold the offices next year, is to make one of those blunders Talleyrand defined as worse than crimes."

The same note of warning against partisan opposition was sounded by the *Topeka Capital* (Rep.) which said of Mr. Wilson's course in Europe: "The Allied governments were against Wilson's program. It was too ingenuous. He confronted them with their people. Millions of people are burning candles to his name and success before the altars of the cathedrals of Europe." Similar defense of the President was given by the *Chicago Evening Post* (Rep.) which could find no leadership in Congress. When the President went to Europe he left Congress a *carte blanche* to deal with domestic matters. It had had two months to prove its capacity and now the cry was going up that it must have the President to tell it what to do. No constructive, hopeful voice was raised. The Democrats drifted to the end of their responsibility and the policy of the Republicans seemed to be one of objection and negation. "All they can do is froth and fret and fume."

The *Richmond Times-Despatch* observed that "If we thought we had no vital interest in the settlement of the war and in the enforcement of that settlement then we had no business in it at all." The Conference could not adjourn, after completing what seemed to be its work, said the *Indianapolis News,* "without leaving behind some authority to represent it and carry out its will." Discussing the supposed loss of sovereignty the *Newark Evening News* explained that the Senate in approving treaties and the Supreme Court in its decisions constantly imposed restrictions on our sovereign freedom of action without abandoning it or yielding it to others. No more did we yield our sovereignty if we entered the League. "The peace conference," said the *Portland Oregonian,* "will blight the hopes of the most sincere lovers of peace if it does not form a workable league of nations to keep the peace," while the *Nebraska State Journal* declared that if any party were to go before the country in 1920 "to advocate the rejection of a peace treaty because of its inclusion of a reasonable League of Nations arrangement, who that knows America could doubt that it would be overwhelmingly rebuked." [17]

But the *State Journal* did not foresee how much a year's insistent questioning of what was reasonable could cloud the issue.

Comment after the Senate Ultimatum. On March 8, the *Literary Digest* asked in its leading article, "Will the Senate defeat the League of Nations?" The criticism of President Wilson's League program in the Senate had been so violent and sweeping that some editorial observers were asking whether it was possible that this covenant against war would be wrecked at last by the nation that had been regarded as its special sponsor. The *Springfield Republican* (Ind.) declared that "the men who are now attempting to wreck the League of Nations are in reality attempting to wreck the peace of the world." "Must we, for the

[17] *Current Opinion,* Vol. 66, pp. 137–140.

absurd fear of 'entangling alliances,' become a nation to be scorned and hissed?" asked the *Philadelphia Inquirer* (Rep.), which believed it unthinkable that the United States "should be the one sulker among the nations." The *New York Evening Post* (Ind.), commenting on rumors of an expensive nationwide campaign against the League, wondered who would pay for it if not the munition makers. "We want a League of Nations to prevent war and we ought to be able to get it," declared the *Minneapolis Tribune* (Rep.), and the *St. Joseph News-Press* (Ind.) after reading the arguments of Senator Borah and others was moved to remark that "these same devotees of precedents, had they lived in earlier days, would have called the American Revolution too radical a step and would have clung steadfastly during the Civil War to State rights." By this time, however, the *New York Tribune* (Rep.) complained that "Neither league nor alliance, the plan seems to have the virtues of neither and the faults of both." [18]

The Views of Religious Publications. By the close of March the *Literary Digest* had made a survey of the church periodicals of the country and reported in its issue of March 29, as follows: "Party ambitions and party issues are plentifully charged in the lay press as explaining attitudes for or against the League of Nations. Violent language may be used in some cases, but, without violent language, just as deep conviction seems to actuate the religious press, with this difference—that not one member of it, so far as we have observed, opposes the League *in toto.*"

"Four-fifths of the opposition or indifference to the League of Nations," asserted the *Congregationalist* (N. Y.), the leading organ of that church, "is due, we believe, to prejudice against or distrust of President Wilson." It pointed to the fear of his critics and opponents "that he is going to secure some personal or political advantage if he carries through the proposition on which he is concentrating all his energies," and wondered why the "worth of a proposal affecting the destinies of mankind should be pivoted upon the character or characteristics of any one man." Americans had a right to think what they pleased of their President, provided they appraised him fairly and honestly, but they had no right to let their attitude toward him prevent them from forming a candid opinion on the League. The President could stand defeat better than this great American nation. Having once taken a man's part in the world problems of our time should we

[18] *Literary Digest,* Vol. 60, No. 10, pp. 11–13.

then "heed the counsels of those who would have the nation undertake to crawl back into a shell which has been forever shattered?"

Our own belief is that in the long view of history, the American nation will be proud of the share which its President has had in helping to frame a project designed to avert wars and bind the nations together. Men returning from foreign lands speak of the esteem felt for him around the globe and wonder why in certain circles here in America the antipathy to Mr. Wilson is so intense and deep-seated. It is comparable only to the attitude cherished by certain sections of the English population a generation ago toward Mr. Gladstone.

But the question before us at the moment is not what Mr. Wilson is today or what will be thought of him ten years hence. The truly broad-minded men and women among his political opponents should see that a great international issue, bearing upon not the future of civilization only, but of Christianity, is to be settled on a higher basis than that of opposition to, or admiration for, any one participant in the Paris Conference.

The *Presbyterian* (Philadelphia) was not so outspoken, but it reminded "every Senator" that he was "under solemn duty to give this matter most careful deliberation, and this should be in the most courteous manner." The Methodist *Zion's Herald* (Boston) saw the League as "Neither a Republican nor a Democratic proposition, but one that comes from the heart of the people, both in America and in Europe, who desire an end of all wars." It believed that Mr. Wilson interpreted aright in saying that an overwhelming majority of the American people favored the League.

Another Methodist organ, the *Christian Advocate* (New York) felt it "obviously improper to advocate any plan of such importance merely as a party measure, or because of personal loyalty to the President" and urged that politics "should be sternly relegated to the rear at this time, when the one objective of the world's effort ought to be the establishment of peace upon foundations which give the greatest promise of permanence." As Bishop Quayle had said, "It is a million years since 1914," yet some men in responsible station continued to write and speak as if the advents of 1918 were not. "They seem to forget that the Yankee soldiers died in the faith that they were thus bringing an end, not to one but to all wars."

Christian Work (New York), in showing how important it was that President Wilson should have the support of the nation, had faith that the League would arise above the clash of party turmoil: "While there are pessimists who cry that it is a Utopian idea and can never be made practicable, and while there are very grave difficulties in the way, and while nations may have to make distasteful sacrifices perhaps, still we must believe that an establishment of a workable League of Nations will surely be achieved and that it will be the only possible ending, to the victory which we have won." [19]

Not Lost, Yet Not Achieved. Much of the faith of this editor has been justified. The League was created. It has offered a steadily increasing service and protection to mankind. The League was not lost. Yet twelve years later it was, for the United States, still not achieved.

[19] *Literary Digest,* Vol. 60, No. 13, pp. 32–33.

CHAPTER VII

THE COMPLETION OF THE TREATY

IT will never be a surprise to the student of the post-Armistice period that Woodrow Wilson broke down physically before his fight for the League of Nations was finished; the only wonder must be that he did not break long before he gave way in September, 1919. That he got as far as he did was quite largely due to the four long ocean voyages that broke up the heaviest of his labors and gave time for rest between the conflicts that he faced in swift succession on both sides of the ocean.

His return voyage to France, beginning on March 5, was particularly needed. His ten-day stay at home had been as strenuous as any President had ever had. During the voyage, too, Wilson had plenty to give him anxiety as to his future course. He had felt it vitally necessary to return and report progress to the American people as well as to close the session of Congress. Returning, he had been met by a fire of opposition as concentrated as could be delivered in that short space of time. The core of the opposition in the Senate he felt to be partisan and personal and not open to conciliation. "No matter what I do," he said during the voyage, "they will continue the attack." [1] It would be of little use to try to amend the Covenant to please the leaders of this group, especially when to attempt to do so would arouse again all the fears of the French that their security was inadequately assured.

He had left the French apprehensive and afraid that the guarantees of Article 10 were too weak to afford them any real security. Yet this guarantee had been assailed in the Senate as much too strong. To weaken it would still further alarm the French, and to press for amendments on the Monroe Doctrine and other subjects might open the gates for a flood of changes from other quarters.

These considerations inclined him to fight on for the Covenant as drawn. Yet this course would so add to the charges of dictatorship

[1] Baker, *Woodrow Wilson and World Settlement,* Vol. I, p. 321.

being hurled against him that he might finally lose when he returned with the treaty. Moreover, he could not fail to heed the friendly advice being given him by the group of nationally known leaders headed by Mr. Taft. Their unselfish support was the greatest assurance of ultimate victory at home that he had. Neither could he afford to ignore the suggestions for amendment made by his loyal supporters in the Senate. He had with him a letter from Senator Gilbert M. Hitchcock of Nebraska, the retiring chairman of the Foreign Relations Committee, which expressed the opinion that a number of Republican Senators who signed Senator Lodge's manifesto would nevertheless vote for the League as a part of the peace treaty and that a still larger number would give it support if certain amendments, six of which he suggested, were made. [2] By the end of the voyage, too, practically the entire press of the United States had concluded that some amendments would be necessary out of deference to the critics of the Covenant and to lessen the doubts which had naturally been aroused in many people by their campaign. [3]

It was pretty clear, then, that the President must press for amendments even though he considered the ends sought already attained. But before the Covenant could be amended it was first necessary to rescue it from submergence at Paris. In his absence the Conference had drifted away from his great objective.

THE LAPSE OF THE LEAGUE DURING THE PRESIDENT'S ABSENCE

The Preliminary Treaty Phantom. This result does not appear to have been due chiefly to the determined effort of the Senate leaders to serve effective notice on the Conference or to any plan in the Conference to sabotage the League. It was due principally to a confusion of mind which affected the whole Conference over a proposed preliminary treaty of peace. Nobody seemed to know exactly how to end a state of war of such gigantic proportions. This was not strange; the conflict had grown beyond all experience. The drafting of the Armistice terms had not been a simple task. It had been done, but for a month only and at each succeeding renewal important questions of policy arose which led to much dispute.

The Americans and the British wished to disarm the Germans,

---

[2] Miller, *The Drafting of the Covenant*, pp. 276–77.
[3] The Washington correspondent of the *London Times* reported, on March 8, that almost no American paper of importance still maintained that no amendment was necessary.

raise the blockade for the benefit both of commerce and the underfed enemy and bring their homesick armies back as soon as possible. When the Armistice had been drawn up originally General Bliss had stood strongly for complete disarmament of Germany in order to release the Allied armies. The French, on the other hand, were opposed to immediate demobilization above all things. They had heavy scores indeed which they meant to settle with the Germans and they intended to have the force ready to compel acceptance.

This clash of policy produced several stormy sessions in the Council of Ten during the first days of February when the President was also working at the Covenant. In opposition to a particularly strenuous effort of the French to secure in the February renewal of the Armistice what would have been in effect reparations, the President proposed that the final military and naval terms be given Germany in a preliminary treaty and Allied demobilization completed. Clemenceau, remembering ever the long agonies of invasion and the deliberate economic devastation of his finest provinces by the Germans, opposed the plan because he wished to shackle Germany securely with military and economic chains that would hold for a generation at least. He knew the Germans, he maintained. The support of the British, nevertheless, secured approval on February 12 of the idea of a preliminary treaty. [4]

The consequences of such a course were not realized by any of those adopting it. When once it came to be grasped that such a preliminary treaty would be a treaty of peace, that it would have to be ratified by the Senate, that it would leave important political questions such as Alsace-Lorraine to be settled out of relation to the whole settlement, whether they were dealt with in the preliminary treaty or the final one, no one was anxious to go ahead with the idea of a preliminary treaty—least of all Wilson who would stand to lose the League.

Moreover, when the military experts came to draw up the naval, military and air terms it proved to be such an exceedingly complicated task that they were by no means finished when the President returned, and it seemed likely that the whole settlement could be made while they were completing the stipulations that finally went into the treaty as twenty pages of schedules and tabulations.

The idea of a preliminary treaty was thereupon dropped by common consent, but during the period of the President's absence, when

[4] Baker, *Woodrow Wilson and World Settlement,* Vol. I, pp. 287–91.

it was supposed to be definitely provided for, the Covenant was never associated with it. Wilson had not asked that the League be made part of this first treaty and the idea spread generally that the League was relegated to the rear. The first treaty produced by the Conference, an important one, was not to contain it and probably little more would be heard of it. [5]

Widespread Conservative Opposition Aroused. The efforts of those who wished to suppress the League naturally helped to spread this impression. At the same time that Wilson was facing the defiant Republican leaders of the Senate, Lloyd George had to deal with a stormy assertion of the conservative and militaristic end of his cabinet. Too much progress had been made for them also. Marshal Foch's grand plan for using the Allied armies to crush Soviet Russia was revived. Clemenceau, who had been wounded by an assassin, was temporarily away from the Conference and unable to exercise fully his restraining influence upon such schemes. With the leader of a new approach to world affairs also absent, the old methods naturally asserted themselves. [6]

No One to Keep the League the Central Principle. It was not the business of anyone to take any positive action about the Covenant while the President was away. Advancing it was his job. No one could be expected properly to alter or promote it even, in his absence. Nevertheless, he was unfortunate in leaving behind him no capable lieutenant to hold the ground won.

Secretary Lansing, who would normally become the chief American on the Council of Ten, had little more faith in the new order for which the President labored than Senator Knox or Mr. Lodge had. He had tried to dissuade the President from attending the Peace Conference in person "since it was manifest that his influence over the negotiations would be much greater if he remained in Washington and issued instructions to his representatives in the Conference." [7] He was opposed, too, to the President's plan for a League of Nations, and had tried repeatedly to persuade him not to include any positive guarantee of territorial integrity and independence, *i.e.*, of security, in it. He was particularly against including the constitution of the League in the Treaty of Peace, had tried in the Council to prevent it, and had told the President that in two weeks time "no plan could be

[5] Miller, *The Drafting of the Covenant,* pp. 87–100.
[6] Baker, Vol. I, pp. 296, 301.
[7] Robert Lansing, *The Peace Negotiations,* N. Y., 1921, pp. 8–15.

prepared with sufficient care to warrant its submission to the Conference." [8]

The system of mandates, too, was as strange and incomprehensible to Mr. Lansing as to any Senator. He could not figure out where the sovereignty of the mandated territories would lie, and agreed with "the more conservative thinkers at Paris" that it was "a very doubtful venture. It appeared to possess no peculiar advantages over the old method of transferring and exercising sovereign control. . . ." [9]

Lansing was hardly in charge, however, during Wilson's absence. The President had told the Council of Ten, on February 12, that he had asked Colonel House to take his place while he was away. [10] House, moreover, had no instructions from his chief. Wilson relied upon the sympathy of Colonel House with his aims to give him clear intellectual grasp of situations that might develop, a reliance, as Baker shows, which was not necessarily well founded. House's great talent, furthermore, was in conciliation and agreement. Wilson felt that House agreed too often while he was gone and that the Colonel had not safeguarded the position of the Covenant sufficiently. [11] House had also considered privately the advisability of conceding the Senate's demand that the Covenant be separated from the treaty. [12] Whether this consideration became circulated enough to influence the impression that the League was sidetracked, or whether the President heard of it, is not known.

Full Comprehension Naturally Slow. When all is said, however, it was inevitable that it should take time for many men, many leaders even, to fully understand that a new authority, a new technique, a new spirit, was really necessary to the future conduct of world affairs.

It took time for the Conference to comprehend the fact that authority had been destroyed over the larger half of the continents of Europe and Asia, that the old diplomatic system was ruined and discredited and that new machinery must be created to administer not only the peace, but the normal life of the new world which would emerge from the wide regrouping of peoples then in progress. With no stable government anywhere east of the Rhine a rigid treaty of peace could not be written. A continuous series of decisions and the machinery for executing them was required. [13]

[8] *Ibid.,* pp. 8, 118.   [9] Lansing, p. 155.   [10] Baker, Vol. I, p. 297.
[11] Baker, Vol. I, pp. 304, 307.
[12] Miller, *The Drafting of the Covenant,* Vol. I, p. 99.
[13] See Walter Lippman's stimulating essay, *The Political Scene,* N. Y., 1919, Chap. IV.

As General Smuts had shown in December, Europe was being liquidated and the League was needed as the heir to that great estate. It was imperative to avoid a settlement based on the old spoils system. Walter Lippman warned, in the same year, that "a re-partition of Europe at a moment when Europe is bleeding at every pore as a result of partitions less than half a century old, would indeed be incorrigible madness on the part of rulers, and enough to drive the torn and broken peoples of the world to that despair of the state which is the motive power behind Russian Bolshevism." In this debacle of the old Europe the League of Nations became, not an outsider or stranger, but "the natural master of the house." It was "naturally and obviously the solvent for a problem which no other means will solve." [14]

It was natural that a few world statesmen should see first that an old order had passed away; it was not unnatural that many politicians at London and Paris and Washington should be quite unaware of it. Indeed, as Professor Charles Seymour of Yale has explained, the bulk of the delegates at Paris came to see only by degrees that a new dispensation was beginning. "When the principle of the League had first been approved," writes Mr. Seymour, speaking from his close observation as one of the experts attached to the American Commission, "although the decision received the approval of the vast majority of the delegates, the idea of the League still remained something rather abstract. It was felt to be desirable that there should be a League and that the League should be the foundation for the different treaties. But many, even of those most enthusiastic, regarded it as something apart from the material stuff of the treaties. The delegates were inclined to look upon the League of Nations commission as different from the commissions, economic or territorial, upon which they themselves were serving, and the difference was not entirely due to the distinguished character of the membership. Its work was doubtless on a higher plane, but on one that seemed at first to have little relation to the practical solution of the treaty problems which formed the subject of their own discussions. Some of the delegates did not hestitate to say that, while the League was all very well and they hoped that it would work, they thought that the treaty problems ought to be solved without reference to it.

"Such an attitude was not long-lived. For when during the months of February and March, the commissions had racked their brains for weeks over the complex questions presented to them and often failed

[14] *Ibid.,* p. 33.

to find any answer, they finally discovered that the League was not merely desirable but absolutely essential to a just and satisfactory settlement. The League, they learned, was not an abstract advisibility, but a concrete necessity; it was no longer a question of the League's being able to work, but an acknowledgment that without it the treaty could not work." [15]

The League Was Dead. While this perception was developing, the sum total of all the influences here referred to was a general conviction that the Covenant was to be separated from the treaty and left to the future. M. Pichon, the head of the French Foreign Office, was saying frankly that the Covenant would not be in the treaty. [16] The French Press accepted the statement as fact and the *London Times* assumed it. Even Lord Robert Cecil admitted as much. [17] Many who were not cynics decided that the League was dead.

When Wilson returned he acted swiftly to forestall such a denouement. Long cables from Colonel House had kept him fairly well informed about the drift of things at the Conference while he was back in the White House. House met him at Brest on March 14, and completed his information as they rode to Paris, a talk which seems to have marked the beginning of the coolness between the two.

On the morning of March 15 Wilson issued the following statement: "The President said today that the decision made at the Peace Conference at its plenary session, January 25, 1919, to the effect that the establishment of a League of Nations should be an integral part of the Treaty of Peace, is of final force and that there is no basis whatever for the reports that a change in this decision was contemplated."

This brief statement was followed by a copy of the resolution of January 25 which set forth the League as a permanent means of international coöperation. The explosion of wrath which it caused in conservative British, French and American newspapers was wholehearted and genuine. All their expectations of avoiding the League by way of an expanded preliminary treaty of peace were abruptly ended.

The idea of a preliminary treaty ceased at once to be talked about. The French did not want the kind of final Armistice which the President had expected to be ready for his approval—one disarming Ger-

---

[15] Charles Seymour, "The League of Nations," *Yale Review,* October, 1919, Vol. 9, pp. 36–7.
[16] Harry Hansen, *The Adventures of the Fourteen Points,* N. Y., 1919, p. 369; Baker, *Woodrow Wilson and World Settlement,* Vol. I, p. 308; C. A. Kluyver, *Documents on the League of Nations,* Leiden (Holland), 1920, p. 117.
[17] Baker, Vol. I, p. 309.

many and demobilizing the Allied armies—and neither they nor the British Conservatives were apparently interested further in a general preliminary treaty which would include the Covenant. The President on his part considered the possibility of regarding such a preliminary statement of terms as a *modus vivendi* which would allow him to see the League set up before going before the Senate,[18] but on being convinced that the preliminary treaty could not be so regarded he of course had no desire to present two separate treaties to the Senate. He therefore urged the immediate preparation of the final treaty.

The progress made by the commissions justified the hope that the definitive treaty could soon be completed, as indeed it was six weeks later. [19]

THE AMENDMENT OF THE COVENANT

The Covenant having been rescued from the realm of things that might sometime be, the President turned to the consideration of the problem, among many others, of how to amend it to satisfy its American critics.

An Opposition Difficult to Satisfy. The task would not be easy. The Senate leaders, having repeatedly and publicly warned the President and the Peace Conference not to attempt a League of Nations, were naturally embittered when a charter for a League was not only framed but proposed as "an integral part of the general Treaty of Peace." It was bad enough to have their plain directions disregarded by the creation of a League, but it was doubly maddening to have the Covenant presented to them in a form which seemed to make it impossible for them to reject it. The Senators would not have been human if they had not felt that they were not going to be completely balked of doing something to the thing. There is no feeling much worse than

---

[18] President McKinley had effectively anticipated the action of the Senate in concluding the armistice with Spain of August 12, 1898. This "Protocol of Agreement embodying the Terms of a Basis for the Establishment of Peace between the United States and Spain" provided, in addition to the suspension of hostilities, for "the cession of Porto Rico and other islands to the United States and for the relinquishment of Spanish sovereignty over Cuba. Furthermore, it created a *fait accompli,* because it provided for the complete evacuation of Porto Rico, as well as Cuba, by the Spanish. Long before the Treaty of Peace with Spain came before the Senate, Porto Rico was held by American forces and by no one else. The legal right of the Senate to reject the proposed acquisition no doubt remained, but the practical possibility of turning back the clock had disappeared."

The extraordinary "Protocol" which accomplished all these things was, moreover, never submitted to the Senate. Miller, *The Drafting of the Covenant,* p. 90.

[19] André Tardieu, *The Truth About the Treaty,* p. 105; Lansing, p. 207; Baker, p. 312–13; Miller, pp. 90–92.

helpless anger. Action of any kind is demanded to give relief, though the leaders of the Senate opposition did not know what to do until Brandegee conceived the idea of the Round Robin ultimatum. Surely that would reach the Peace Conference! "It seemed the only way," wrote Lodge to White, "to make them understand that Mr. Wilson had against him an opposition of extreme seriousness and that he could not hope to pass through the Senate the League as now proposed." [20]

An Appeal to Lodge. Whether or not the Round Robin accomplished its purpose, it was bound to leave the opposition leaders committed against the Covenant to such an extent that they could not readily recede, if they should later wish to do so. If their desire had been to get a properly revised Covenant, an opportunity soon offered through Henry White, who had been spending himself without stint in an effort to keep Lodge informed as to the aims and purposes of the League and its provisions. He wrote many long letters to Lodge, often sitting at his desk for the purpose beyond midnight, after heavy and exacting days. Not infrequently his letters ran to ten or twelve typewritten pages. [21]

He had read with consternation in the Paris press a summary of Lodge's speech of December 21, 1918, and had thereafter omitted no effort to make clear to him the course of events in Paris. Lodge could hardly have been more fully or reliably informed than he was, but the information did not induce any change whatever in his attitude. White had painful evidence of this fact when the Round Robin arrived in Paris. Yet he did not despair; the emergency was too urgent. Writing Lodge at once he pleaded with all his power that surely the fact of the millions so lately dead, and the fate of the other millions who must struggle on "entirely incapacitated for any sort of usefulness during the rest of their lives," must make timely a strenuous effort to abolish such barbarities. There could not be the slightest doubt that similar tragedy would occur again if no agreement for a League of Nations could be made. He therefore implored his friend to send him precise amendments for the Covenant which would enable it to be accepted. [22]

Then, reflecting on the slowness of the mail, he sent Lodge a cablegram two days later, on March 9, 1919, saying:

> Should be grateful if you would cable me in cipher, through State Department, exact phraseology of amendments modifying League of Nations Covenant which Senate considers important. Our desire is to

[20] Nevins, *Henry White,* p. 400.   [21] *Ibid.,* p. 357.
[22] Nevins, *Henry White,* pp. 360, 397.

meet Senate's views as closely as it is possible to obtain acquiescence therein of other nations anxious for recognition of their own special interests which they will immediately insist upon in the Covenant if we demand exceptions in favor of ours. Wrote you fully two days ago but feel use of cable desirable, time being so important. Please send by next courier full reports your and Knox speeches.[23]

The effort, gallant and sincere though it was, was foredoomed to failure. The leaders having exchanged public defiances with the President, inevitably considered the plea from the standpoint of their political strategy. Moreover, a high degree of suspicion naturally accompanies any kind of warfare, political, personal or international. Lodge and his associates suspected even White. True enough, Wilson was on the ocean, but might he not have instigated White by wireless?

Lodge therefore at once laid the cablegram before Brandegee, Knox and Root, all of whom echoed his suspicions. Even Root considered White's plea from the standpoint of political tactics, writing that Lodge should not commit himself to a subordinate of Wilson's and that the Senate's views to be effective must reach him "as the demand of a co-equal power." [24]

Allen Nevins has stated well the fallacy in both these conclusions from the standpoint of securing revision of the Covenant. [25] From that of asserting an assumed right of the Senate to direct negotiations —a function which the Senate has never exercised except by the grace of the President, and then with comparative rarity—Senator Lodge's cabled reply to White, dated March 15, was quite correct. It read:

Have considered your cable March 9th. The President expressed no willingness to receive any communication from the Senate while that body was in session. If he now wishes to have amendments drafted which the Senate will consent to, the natural and necessary course is to assemble the Senate in the customary way. Manifestly I cannot speak for the Senate or consult its members, nor can they consult with each other, nor can the President consult them while they are at their homes in 48 states.[26]

Responsibility. The Senate leaders, having established a deadlock with the President, could hardly recede from it so early. Their ob-

[23] *Ibid.,* p. 399.
[25] *Ibid.,* p. 401.
[24] Nevins, *Henry White,* p. 400.
[26] *Ibid.*

jectives were so different from White's that his appeals could not reach them. Sensing the gulf between himself and his friends White could not refrain from writing to Representative Rogers, on March 5, while the impact of the Round Robin was keenly felt, that Lodge's speeches were hypercritical and wrong headed. They overlooked the fact that all such documents had to be matters of compromise. "If you knew the difficulties," he wrote, "which existed in bringing the various nations concerned to an agreement, you would realize what a great feat has been accomplished in bringing about the acceptance of the Covenant as it stands."

Reiterating his complete conviction that only the League could avert wars more deadly still, White concluded his letter in all seriousness, saying: "It seems to me that a frightful responsibility will rest upon any set of men who are instrumental in preventing the trial, at least, of an experiment to settle international differences in some other way than by methods involving such frightful sacrifice of human life and tending toward the destruction of civilization." [27]

White was not the only man who felt that no group of men had ever incurred, or could ever assume, a responsibility more stupendous. Yet other minds remained, and still remain, quite cold both to the abysmal devastation of that hour and to the awesome prospect of renewed carnage in a smaller, more scientific world, unorganized against war.

Suggestions from Root. Among the advisors of Senator Lodge, Elihu Root assuredly appreciated the responsibilities of the time and was desirous of seeing the great experiment tried. His proposed amendments to the Covenant were constructive in spirit. Requested by the State Department, they were supplied and cabled to Paris on March 28. [28] Mr. Root evidently did not feel that considerations of party or Senate prestige need prevent his replying to such a request. In his draft he proposed that withdrawals from the obligation of Article 10 be permitted after five years. A general revision of the Covenant at the close of the same period was also called for. These suggestions were not adopted. Others of his proposals did not go into effect because they went far beyond what any of the great powers were willing to accept. This was true of his stipulations of obligatory arbitration for all justiciable questions and of his provisions for "full power of inspection" of national armaments. Needless to say it is likely to be a

---

[27] Nevins, *Henry White*, p. 408.
[28] Miller, *The Drafting of the Covenant*, Vol. I, pp. 327-79.

long time before any United States Senate will agree to either of these ideas.

The Taft Requests. Previous to the forwarding of the Root amendments the President had received, on March 16, a cable from his private secretary, Mr. Joseph Tumulty, saying that Mr. Taft would like to make some suggestions for amendment. Taft was quoted as saying "that these suggestions do not look to the change of the structure of the League, the plan of its action or its real character, but simply to removing objections in minds of conscientious Americans, who are anxious for a League of Nations, whose fears have been roused by suggested constructions of the League which its language does not justify and whose fears could be removed without any considerable change of language."

To this Wilson replied, "Appreciate Mr. Taft's offer of suggestions and would welcome them. The sooner they are sent the better." [29]

This brought the following cablegram from Taft on March 18:

PRESIDENT WILSON, PARIS:

Following from WILLIAM H. TAFT:

"If you bring back the treaty with the League of Nations in it make more specific reservation of the Monroe Doctrine, fix a term for the duration of the League, and the limit of armament, require expressly unanimity of action of Executive Council and body of Delegates, and add to Article 15 a provision that where the Executive Council of the Body of Delegates finds the difference to grow out of an exclusively domestic policy, it shall recommend no settlement, the ground will be completely cut from under the opponents of the League in the Senate. Addition to Article 15 will answer objection as to Japanese immigration, as well as tariffs under Article 21. Reservation of the Monroe Doctrine might be as follows:

"Any American State or States may protect the integrity of American territory and the independence of the Government whose territory it is, whether a member of the League or not, and may, in the interests of American peace, object to and prevent the further transfer of American territory or sovereignty to any power outside the Western Hemisphere.

[29] Compare with Wilson's statement at the final meeting of the League Commission: "You see, the whole object of this mentioning of the Monroe Doctrine is to relieve a state of mind and misapprehension on the other side of the water; relieve the minds of certain conscientious public men in the United States who want to be assured that there is no intention in this League to interfere with the Doctrine." Miller, *The Drafting of the Covenant*, p. 459.

"Monroe Doctrine reservation alone would probably carry the treaty, but others would make it certain.

(signed)   "WILLIAM H. TAFT."
TUMULTY.

Four Changes Generally Demanded. From this statement, from the letter of Senator Hitchcock, and from the proposals made by Senator Lodge in the Senate it appeared that there was a strong American demand for changes in the Covenant specifically providing for (a) the recognition of the Monroe Doctrine by name; (b) direct statement that domestic questions such as immigration and the tariff were excluded from the League's jurisdiction; (c) withdrawal from the League; (d) the right to refuse a mandate. These were the things most often criticized. The cry against Article 10 was not yet insistently pressed.

The President felt, as Taft did, that the ends sought by the changes demanded were already attained in the Covenant. He was sure, moreover, that efforts to have them explicitly recognized would only weaken his position and lead to renewed struggles in the Conference, but he was nevertheless compelled to push for these changes. He therefore drew up, about March 22, the date when the League of Nations Commission met for the revision of the Covenant, a set of amendments covering the principal points at issue. [30]

Three Amendments Accepted. The desire for the right of withdrawal was met by an addition to Article 1 saying that any member might withdraw after two years' notice. Attempt to allay the anxiety as to interference with immigration and the tariff was made by the addition of a clause to Article 15 which said: "If the dispute between the parties is claimed by one of them, and is found by the Council, to arise out of a matter which by international law is solely within the domestic jurisdiction of that party, the Council shall so report, and shall make no recommendation as to its settlement." The fear of having a mandate forced upon us was countered by the insertion in Article 22, in describing those to whom mandates should be intrusted, of the phrase "and who are willing to accept it."

These amendments were accepted with comparatively little opposition, although the debate over the American withdrawal clause, on March 26, was so bitter that the President postponed the combat

---

[30] Baker, I, 329. See Miller, *The Drafting of the Covenant,* Vol. I, Chapter 28, for a survey of the changes proposed from the United States.

he knew would come over the Monroe Doctrine amendment until he had gathered strength from other understandings. [31] The Monroe Doctrine had never been popular in Europe, except among the English who had stimulated us to issue it and had supported it for a century to the advantage of their own commercial interest and colonial security. On the Continent it had naturally been resented as an effort to fence off a vast area which European powers might be "developing." To be asked explicitly to recognize this doctrine as valid was something which the continental Allies could not be expected really to enjoy.

French Fear of the Monroe Doctrine Addition. Yet not unnaturally it was not the positive side of the Monroe Doctrine—the "Hands off!" policy—that aroused the fears of the French; it was the negative aspect of it, the abstention from European affairs angle, more commonly associated with Washington's Address, which concerned France and her allies. With the problem of security always and forever uppermost in their minds they could not help fearing that an express reservation of the Monroe Doctrine might be interpreted to mean that the United States would in a crisis decide itself unable to participate in a European settlement.

This fear was accentuated by the fact that the Monroe Doctrine amendment had been attached to Article 10, "which was of the greatest importance to France." The President had taken the suggested amendment of Taft's cable, reproduced above, and in accordance with the suggestion of Mr. Taft's explanatory letter, which followed the cable, had added it to Article 10. When submitted first to the British members of the Commission they objected to the attempt to define the Monroe Doctrine, contending that any attempt to define it might limit or extend its application. Their real motive being probably to protect similar understandings of their own, they proposed a different statement which was finally written into the Covenant as Article 21, reading: "Nothing in this Covenant shall be deemed to affect the validity of international engagements, such as treaties of arbitration or regional understandings like the Monroe Doctrine, for securing the peace of the world." [32]

This amendment, originally added to Article 10, was removed after it had alarmed the French thoroughly for the safety of the guarantee article. They feared the effect would be to weaken Article 10 which was already far too weak to suit them.

[31] Baker, Vol. II, p. 66.
[32] Baker, Vol. I, pp. 330–32.

Was the Monroe Doctrine in Danger? The President on his part was forced to contend for a statement which he believed was wholly unnecessary. His first conception of the League of Nations had grown out of the Monroe Doctrine. Its function in maintaining the independence of the weak republics to the South and protecting their territorial integrity had always appealed to him powerfully. If the principle could only be extended between all nations real peace and security would be assured. He had proposed, as previously noted, to make the guarantee mutual between the American republics, in the projected Pan American Union of 1916. Each state was to guarantee the "territorial integrity and political independence" of the others—exactly as it had now been tentatively agreed that all members of the League should mutually protect each other. [33] Never conceiving of the Monroe Doctrine as a device for imposing our will on the other sovereign states of the new world or moulding them to our imperialistic advantage, he believed that the heart of our most revered foreign policy had been extended to the whole world. He had explained to the Senate that this was his aim as early as January 22, 1917.

Now he was compelled to ask that what he believed had become the ruling motif of the Covenant be itself protected by a reservation in that document. The Senators had said that if there was nothing contrary to the Doctrine it would hurt nothing to say so plainly— three lines would be all that was necessary—and Americans thought that mighty reasonable argument. Taft cabled again on March 28 that if the Doctrine were not specifically reserved people would conclude that there was some danger to it in the Covenant. The friends of the Covenant would be seriously embarrassed and amendment in the Senate would be certain. [34] Taft himself believed that Article 10 covered the Monroe Doctrine and extended it to all nations,[35] but the doubts aroused at home had to be satisfied.

As days passed and no news of the necessary statement came, a third plea for it was sent across the Atlantic under date of April 13:

PRESIDENT WILSON, Paris:

Following is sent at the request of Mr. Taft:

"Friends of the covenant are seriously alarmed over report that no amendment will be made more specifically safeguarding Monroe Doc-

---

[33] *Ibid.*, p. 326.
[34] Tumulty, p. 538. See also for the text of the cable of April 13 and others on the subject.
[35] *Ibid.*, p. 333.

trine. At full meeting of Executive Committee of League to Enforce Peace, with thirty members from eighteen States present, unanimous opinion that without such amendment Republican Senators will certainly defeat ratification of treaty, because public opinion will sustain them. With such amendment, treaty will be promptly ratified.

(signed)

"WILLIAM H. TAFT."
"A. LAWRENCE LOWELL."
TUMULTY.

The Struggle for Adoption. But meanwhile the President had introduced the amendment, on April 10, and after a long two-day struggle, one of the most gruelling he had during the Conference, it had been put through at the close of the last session of the League of Nations Commission.

Lord Robert Cecil had tried to explain to the French that "The amendment had been inserted in order to quiet doubts, and calm misunderstandings. It did not make the substance of the Doctrine either more or less valid. There was nothing in the Covenant which conflicted with international understandings like the Monroe Doctrine." But the French thought that "if it was not inconsistent with the terms of the Covenant it was unnecessary to refer to it." [36] Outside the Council chamber they asked, "Why were they expected to make every concession to American prejudice when the President would make none to European traditions? They had gone to the length of accepting the doctrine of Monroe for the whole of the earth, but now because American pride demanded it, they must make public confession of America's right to give orders. No! A thousand times no!" Let the President consider other people's prejudices. Other governments were at stake as well as his own. If the President asked he must be willing to give. France thereupon renewed her claim to the Rhine valley and the Saar, Italy to Fiume and Dalmatia, and Japan presented her demand for Shantung in fee simple. [37]

The British also, their naval supremacy threatened by our authorized building program, at once proposed a naval limitation agreement and stood for it some days until finally told that the United States would not bargain, that the Monroe Doctrine amendments

[36] Minutes of the League of Nations Commission, p. 96; Baker, Vol. I, p. 333. See Baker, Vol. I, pp. 324 to 328, for texts of the Taft cablegrams. See also Miller, *The Drafting of the Covenant,* p. 443 ff.
[37] George Creel, *The War, the World and Wilson,* N. Y., 1920, p. 210.

would be presented and that the British could oppose it if they saw fit. [38]

Having put his hand to the task the President exerted his full power to see it through. At the close of the first day of debate on the amendment he made a speech which Baker says was acknowledged by all who heard it as one of his greatest efforts at the Peace Conference, in which, "taking the Monroe Doctrine as a text, he set forth his vision of the new order, the need of a new attitude of mind, and the part America must play in future world relationships." [39] Of the same event David Hunter Miller says: "At the close of the debate, President Wilson replied to the French in an extempore speech of witching eloquence—a speech made after midnight, which left the secretaries gasping with admiration, their pencils in their hands, their duties forgotten, and hardly a word taken down; the proposal was then adopted." [40]

From his notes made later in his hotel, Miller records that the President, characterizing the Monroe Doctrine as the first international charter of human liberty and the real forerunner of the League of Nations, demanded whether the United States was to be denied recognition of this fact. [41]

The matter was not ended yet, however, for at the final meeting of the League Commission, held the next evening, April 11, the French endeavored to amend the new article by defining or describing the Monroe Doctrine in such a way as to limit the right of the United States to insist on its own interpretations in the future. Hoping for some advantage for their own proposals, the French representatives urged a definition until Miller "thought for a moment in despair that President Wilson would yield to the final French suggestion, which contained only a few seemingly simple words; but he stood by his position through the long discussion, and the meeting and the proceedings of the Commission ended early in the morning in an atmosphere of constraint and without any of the speeches of politeness customary on such occasions." [42]

The discussion, says Baker, came perilously near to an open break. The French persisted in their argument after midnight. They de-

---

[38] Miller, *The Drafting of the Covenant*, Vol. I, p. 425. See the whole of chapter 30, on this subject; also Nevins, *Henry White*, pp. 442-3.
[39] Baker, *Woodrow Wilson and World Settlement*, Vol. I, p. 332.
[40] Seymour and House, *What Really Happened at Paris*, N. Y., 1921, p. 416.
[41] Miller, *The Drafting of the Covenant*, Vol. I, p. 450.
[42] Seymour and House, *What Really Happened at Paris*, pp. 416-17.

Photograph by Bachrach

DAVID HUNTER MILLER

Permission—World Wide Photos

SIR CECIL J. B. HURST

BRITISH AND AMERICAN LEGAL ADVISORS

sisted only when the President abruptly declared their proposition not adopted. He was able to do this only because he had reached a personal understanding with Clemenceau on the French claims against Germany which made him willing to concede to the President on the Monroe Doctrine amendment. [43] If the security offered by the League was to be weakened, France demanded, with justice, more of the old fashioned military and economic guarantees. [44]

The Crisis of the Conference. The period from April 8 to 13, during which the Covenant was revised, was indeed the crucial week of the Conference. The President had been resisting the extreme French and Italian claims all along the line—and the League of Nations also still hung in the balance as a result. The intensity and tenacity with which "The Tiger," backed by preponderant French opinion, fought for the Rhine frontier, or a buffer state on its west bank, for the Saar valley, for heavy reparations and other guarantees, cannot be appreciated without reading extended accounts of that terrific campaign. [45]

The persistence of this struggle inevitably wore Wilson down. When Ray Stannard Baker went up to see him in the evenings he was likely to find him looking "utterly beaten, worn out, his face quite haggard, one side of it and the eye twitching painfully; but the next morning he would appear refreshed and eager to go on with the fight." [46]

It could not continue thus indefinitely. On April 3 Wilson had a sudden and violent attack of influenza which proved to be very serious. The Council of Four continued to meet in a room adjoining the President's sickroom. During these days Colonel House referred many different proposals to him without result. The President from his bed

---

[43] Baker, Vol. I, p. 337.

[44] The French could never understand how a future attack of Germany on France could be considered by the United States as anything but a matter of primary importance to ourselves. Our tremendous effort on their soil in 1918 to end one German invasion made them unable to see how the problem of their own security could be subordinated by us to traditional sentiments of aloofness that had been totally disregarded in the crisis of the war just ended. This feeling of the great concern to the world of their own security filled French thinking, wrote Miller on March 19, 1919, "in a degree which it is almost impossible to overstate." Miller, *The Drafting of the Covenant*, Vol. I, p. 300.

[45] See Baker, *Woodrow Wilson and World Settlement,* Vol. II, chapters 27 and 28.

[46] Baker, Vol. II, p. 43. Other observers thought that the President aged alarmingly in these weeks. See Vernon Bartlett, *Behind the Scenes at the Peace Conference,* London, 1919, p. 31.

Of this period Bartlett says, also: "The President did much to endear himself more than ever to his admirers by his accessibility. On one of his busiest days he had twenty-one visitors, representing seventeen different nationalities," p. 35.

invariably answered "No." [47] He would not compromise nor yield to a settlement with Germany which would violate all the understandings of the Armistice and would make future wars as certain as their past succession was. If he had yielded we should never have had the later Locarno treaties, or an effective League of Nations with a new approach to the solution of every sort of international friction. The world owes much to Woodrow Wilson's unconquerable will, as the various peoples who cursed him for it are already coming to see.

Gaining his feet again on April 7, the President ordered the *George Washington* to sail for Brest at once. He would quit the Conference rather than abandon the principles accepted for the peace. This decision had been practically made before his illness and matured during it. Clemenceau ceased at once his threats to resign, the French press changed its tone and French demands were modified sufficiently to make compromise, such as the fifteen year occupation of the Saar valley, possible—and with it final assurance of the League. [48]

In the many compromises which rapidly followed, the necessity of securing amendments to the Covenant certainly weakened Wilson's position. This does not mean that his opponents at home could not properly demand those amendments, nor that he should not have fought for them. The United States was asking little enough for itself. Neither, also, does this truth obviate the fact that having been forced into a position of asking favors of the Conference at its most critical stage, and having given himself without limit in the endeavor, he was sternly censured for yielding so much when he returned home again, and condemned for making a brutal peace, while the amendments to the Covenant secured at such cost were belittled as of no worth or consequence. [49]

THE CAMPAIGN TO CONTROL AMERICAN OPINION

An English Observer's Account. The nature of the opposition the President would have to meet at home had been early appraised by foreign observers watching the course of events. As early as February

---

[47] *Ibid.*, p. 45.

[48] Baker, Vol. II, pp. 41, 59–63. White was strongly for preparing to quit the Conference if the French persisted. He urged this course to Wilson before the latter's illness and was gratified at its results. Nevins, p. 436.

[49] Hamilton Holt has stated that four of Root's nine suggestions for the amendment of the Covenant were fully adopted, "with three partially recognized, six of Hughes' seven points were accepted, and all five of the proposals of Taft and Lodge were incorporated in the revised Covenant." Howland, *American Foreign Relations,* 1928, p. 261.

24, the Washington correspondent of the *London Times,* whose duty, it is to be presumed, was to report accurately the actual state of affairs, wrote to his paper that opponents of the proposed League of Nations were already engaged in a tremendous effort to affright public opinion "by raising all over the country a formidable array of political scare-crows. One of these scarecrows is intended to terrify labour. . . . The opponents of the League are stalking through the land with the spectre of Chinese coolie labour, which they say, Japan and China, through the League, will insist on importing freely to America. They are reinforcing this spectre with one proclaiming the certainty that the League, influenced by Japan, will decree that Japanese must be allowed to emigrate to the United States on the same terms as Euro-peans. The prejudices of the Irish the opponents of the League are seeking to foment by means of a phantom showing the Irish regiments in America employed by the orders of the League in suppressing rebellion in Ireland.

"These are the chief spectres. But there are many others raised for the purpose of frightening the ordinary American citizen with the idea that if the League is established Mexican bandits will be able to raid Texas and New Mexico, murder their inhabitants, and burn their cities while the American Government will be obliged, before defend-ing itself, impotently to wait until it receives a 'mandate' from the League of Nations, or until the League gives a mandate to police Mexico to some other nation. Mr. Borah's speech in the Senate yesterday was a most powerful appeal to fears such as these. With great ability he de-picted dangers to the Monroe Doctrine and to the traditional attitude of American aloofness from European quarrels. . . . President Wil-son will need all his ingenuity to defeat this campaign. A herculean task confronts him in his ten days stay in America."

If this was the situation as soon as the Covenant was proposed, what would it be three months later when the President finally re-turned with the treaty?

By March 5 the same correspondent had become impressed by the strength of the nationalistic feeling that the campaign against the Covenant was likely to arouse in the United States. The Senators were getting some conviction back of their opposition. Personal feel-ing against the President was a strong factor and especially his intima-tion that the Covenant would not be much amended. They resented the fact that no Senators sat on the Peace Commission and that the League would be in the treaty, but they especially attacked the President on the ground that the Covenant gave more than it got for the United States.

The Republican leaders felt, he said, that they could convince public opinion that this was the case. Feeling that the Monroe Doctrine should be recognized, or at least a statement made that the United States should be something of a mandatory for the peace and order of the Western World, was so general that the Republicans believed they could defeat the Covenant as it stood, because the pleas they were making against the Covenant were in accordance with American instinct. They argued that traditions imbibed at birth and cherished through adolescence were not abandoned over night, especially by a country which is still young. The strongest American tradition in the sphere of foreign relations, indeed the only one which counted, was the tradition that nothing but harm could come from meddling in extra-American, and especially European affairs, or from allowing Europe to meddle in the affairs of the Western Hemisphere. This tradition could be relied on.

There could be little doubt, continued the representative of the *Times,* March 7, 1919, that the Senate had surprised the country. "People had taken it for granted that the President would bring home a plan for a League. They had regarded the prospect with a vaguely sentimental benevolence. They had probably expected a sort of extension of all the harmlessly useful arbitration treaties which at one time and another the United States had concluded." Now they were told by leaders they were accustomed to respect that they ought to reject the Covenant as dangerous to their liberties.

What would the people conclude?

The Consequences of Repudiation. The reply to the argument that America would give to the League more than she would get was given (without intending such reply) by Frank H. Simonds in a dispatch from Paris published in the *New York Tribune* on March 6. Explaining the total inability of the peoples of Europe to distinguish between Mr. Wilson as President and as the leader of a party at home, he wrote that Europe was literally aghast at the possibility indicated by brief dispatches that the real views of America might be entirely different from the President's. It had "to an incredible extent risked all its future hope upon Mr. Wilson, not as an individual, but as President of the United States, and if the country repudiated what Mr. Wilson has done here, for domestic or political reasons which are wholly comprehensible to every American, the European tragedy will be stupendous. . . ."

"I have talked with many Republicans who are here," continued Mr. Simonds, "all of whom see the situation clearly, substantially as I have presented it here. Without exception they recognize the greatness of the American mission's opportunity and duty in Europe; with no dissenting voice they assert that to abandon the league of nations with its European responsibilities now will be little less than the abandonment of those who died in Europe to establish American ideals in the world. No country could deserve the admiration America receives in Europe today and no country could afford to surrender that position in the world which had been won for it by devotion and achievement, by unselfishness unparalleled in world history; and to withdraw from Europe now would be to sacrifice what seems to be the greatest opportunity for human service that has ever come to any single people."

To which appeal would the American people listen? Would they respond to the contention that membership in the League would be too dangerous and expensive? Or would they respond to the glory of a leadership such as no nation had ever had or mayhap would ever have again?

Press Support For the Opposition. The course to be taken could not then be predicted with certainty, but the shock of the Senate's opposition to the President and the Covenant had already indicated if not determined the attitude of many. The *Kansas City Star* and *Spokane Review* had already gone from the League camp over to the opposition [50] and the *New York Tribune,* another powerful Republican daily, felt compelled, apparently with reluctance, to follow.

On February 25 the *Tribune* had said: "The speech of the President in Boston neither in words nor in spirit contains anything to arouse controversy. . . . No sensible person now challenges, or has challenged, the sincerity of the President's allegiance to the idea of organizing the world for peace instead of for war. The war was to end war, and if this is not completely possible, then to set up some bulwarks for peace. If there is failure at Paris as to this, great indeed will be the failure. The discussion of the momentous problem must therefore be lifted above the plane of personality. To do other than this is to degrade a theme almost as lofty as that contained in the New Testament."

A week later, on March 5, just after the Round Robin, the lead-

[50] *London Times,* March 7, 1919.

ing editorial in the *Tribune* was entitled "The Covenant's End." It began by saying: "The quick finish that has come to the project that President Wilson brought home from Europe was inevitable. It never had a chance of ratification, and the Senate has done the world a service by frankly and openly making this clear."

This somewhat surprising disposal of the theme which a week before had been on a plane with the New Testament was explained on the ground that the scheme was so vague and nebulous that exactly opposite elements had attacked it. Those who were not afraid of surrendering enough sovereignty to safeguard adequately against war had "beheld a toothless and biteless plan that centered nowhere and which had no force behind it except that which might be subsequently assembled by unanimous consent." At the same time those jealous of national prerogatives had become alarmed. They feared for the Monroe Doctrine, tariffs, immigration, etc., and thought that in return for "these great sacrifices" we gained a practically sanctionless agreement that would be binding only on those who observed their treaties.

Senate Consultation Indispensable. The *Tribune* did not point out that if the Covenant displeased both extreme camps it must be a fairly moderate plan. Instead it proceeded to "other factors besides the demerits of the plan" which contributed to its rejection. The "other factors" simmered down to the President's political ineptitude in not appointing Senators to the Peace Commission. But the blunder could yet be repaired. "Let him summon to Paris representatives of the Senate and loyally accept their assistance in preparing a new instrument, and he may yet gain a great triumph." [51]

The *Tribune* was evidently convinced that the League was dead unless in some way the leaders of the Round Robin group, that is Senators Lodge and Knox, could be given co-authorship of it.

In his debate with President A. Lawrence Lowell of Harvard University, at Boston on March 19, Senator Lodge himself quite agreed with this conclusion, saying: "If the President had laid that draft before the Senate as these other Presidents have done, if he had said to the Senate, "I submit this draft to you for your advice, I hope for your approval, and for such suggestions as you may have to make," he would have had the amendments laid before him to present to the Peace Conference at Paris. The battle would have been more than half won by the mere submission."

[51] *New York Tribune*, March 5, 1919.

Calling again for specific exclusion of the Monroe Doctrine, immigration and the tariff from the jurisdiction of the League, and protesting again against being compelled to consider the Covenant as a part of the peace treaty, he expressed his belief that the Covenant would be amended "somewhere, and not in Paris." He also stressed Article 10 as the most important article in the Covenant.

A Proper League—or None. The likelihood that the Covenant could be revised in Paris to satisfy the Senator was indicated by his "hope" that "we shall have a league in proper form, properly prepared, free from doubts, excluding what ought to be excluded." He didn't want the American people to "go through a dark tunnel of umbrageous words, with nothing to see at the end except the dim red light of internationalism."

In spite of the innuendo which was evident in his hopes and fears one might have concluded, from the long cry to Washington and Monroe in his address, that Mr. Lodge was really the man to revise the Covenant, had he not included the usual demands for a harsh, vindictive peace that would bar completely the success of any league for peace. The thing to do, he made clear once again, was to "impose the reparations, build up the barrier states, put the monster where it cannot spring again, and bring the soldiers home." Panegyrics to the soldiers followed. [52]

A Ghastly Travesty. While Lodge was urging the country to consider the Covenant, George Harvey stopped calling it British long enough to say that by accepting amendments after opposing them Wilson "discredits himself save as a self-seeker equally ready to cry 'Good Lord!' or 'Good Devil!' so long as he can get something or anything adopted of his own devising."

Studying the Covenant, Harvey came upon the astounding fact that it gave control of the Council to the five great powers who had permanent seats upon it. "It would be a ghastly travesty" upon the ideal of the Fourteenth Point, he complained, "to say that while the

---

[52] *New York Times,* March 20, 1919.
There was widespread interest in the debate. Fully 40,000 people asked for seats and nearly 3500 were packed into a hall built for 2500. The crowd was with Lowell, but Lodge accomplished his purpose of giving the impression to countless readers throughout the country that here was something that attacked, or at least endangered, their fundamental liberties and that something drastic was necessary to save us —something which the Senate would do if public opinion would support him.
He admitted in the debate and in his letter to Henry White, saying that he had been aiming at the country, that the majority of the people wanted "a" League. But, he wrote to White, that "in the course of the discussion" the majority would come, he thought, to "insist on some very vital amendments." Nevins, *Henry White,* p. 413.

United States should have one delegate all her own, Argentina (and eleven other Latin American States enumerated) should have only one among them all." [53] Harvey's anguish if the United States had not been given one of the controlling voices can easily be imagined.

In his next issue, however, he was suggesting in a front page cartoon that Lloyd George shared the authorship of the Fourteen Points and condemning the President for resisting the French demand for the German provinces west of the Rhine, though he opposed the projected security treaty conceded to France by Wilson and Lloyd George in lieu of the Rhine boundary. A double page cartoon portrayed Wilson as the protector of the bloated Hun, alias "The Blond Beast." [54]

As the time for the extra session of Congress drew near Harvey bitterly called upon the Senate to remove "every vestige of the proposed League from the Peace treaty, approve the treaty and reject the League." The Senate could amend and ratify at the same time. [55]

Unified Action Urged upon All Senate Republicans. The Covenant was revised in Paris as described above, but when the amended draft was published, on April 28, Mr. Lodge still held to the opinion that it would be revised elsewhere than in Paris. Early on the 29th he united with Senator Curtis of Kansas, the Republican whip, in sending the following telegram from Washington to all Republican Senators:

> We suggest that Republican Senators reserve final expression of opinion respecting the amended league covenant until the latest draft has been carefully studied and until there has been an opportunity for conference.

Later in the day Mr. Lodge issued a statement to the press saying that he had no statement to make except that of course further amendment to the Covenant would be necessary. The statement said:

> I am not prepared to make a statement in regard to the new draft at this moment, because I desire to examine it carefully and compare it with the former draft, and also to confer with my colleagues, for it is obvious that it will require further amendments if it is to promote peace and not endanger certain rights of the United States which should never be placed in jeopardy.

[53] *Harvey's Weekly,* April 19, 1919, No. 16, Vol. 2, pp. 2, 4.
[54] *Harvey's Weekly,* April 26, 1919, No. 17, Vol. 2, pp. 1, 2, 10, 11.
[55] *Harvey's Weekly,* May 10, 1919, No. 19, Vol. 2, p. 2.

No Senator was to say hastily that the amendments to the Covenant really amended and that he was now in favor of the League. As the Washington correspondent of the *New York Tribune* put it: "In Republican circles the request made to Republican Senators was not interpreted as an attempt to 'muzzle' them, but rather a hint of the necessity of going slow in interpreting the new Covenant as an acceptable document. The debate on the new Covenant will proceed, it is predicted. However, the Lodge message, together with the Republican leader's statement that amendments to the Covenant are essential, will tend to guide the discussion along lines which will not embarrass the contemplated contest in the Senate to amend the revised draft." [56]

Editorially, the *Tribune* was pointing out on the same day how the Covenant could be changed by amendment or reservation without defeating the whole treaty, and on the preceding day it had indicated what would have to be done to it. It was still objectionable to both nationalists and internationalists, "a great hoax." The Monroe Doctrine article was "plainly a fraud," "merely a package covered with gold foil," and the "iniquitous Article 10" was still unchanged.

On the same day that Senator Lodge telegraphed to the Senators, a message which he maintained in the Senate later was a "strictly nonpartisan telegram," [57] he had a talk with Senator Borah, who characterized the conference as "entirely satisfactory." [58] This statement attracted attention in the press in view of Borah's known opposition to the Covenant, root and branch. Lodge had maintained in his debate with Lowell that he was not opposed to a league of nations, though he had been careful not to specify just what changes would make the proposed league satisfactory to him; that, only the Senate could do, *i.e.*, Mr. Lodge, at the proper time. What then could be "entirely satisfactory" about his plan of campaign to one whose only desire was to reject the Covenant entirely? Such a conference could not have been entirely satisfactory to Mr. Borah unless he found the majority leader either in complete sympathy with him or planning a course which he believed would lead to the failure of the League in the Senate.

After his talk with Lodge, Senator Borah issued a statement calling attention to some articles that ought to come out of the Covenant. He attacked Article 10 as the "most dangerous one in the

[56] *New York Tribune*, April 30, 1919.
[57] *Congressional Record*, Vol. 58, Pt. 1, p. 329.
[58] *New York Times*, April 30, 1919.

covenant." (Lodge, on March 19, had been sure it was the most important article.) Borah now gave it as his opinion that the adoption of the article would be treason.

He was sure, too, that the telegram urging Senators to withhold comment did not apply to him. "I do not regard it," he said, "as an attempt to stifle the criticism of those who have opposed it all along, and who have not hesitated to express their views." He had received no telegram anyway.

Neither, apparently, had a couple of western Senators who issued statements on April 29, presumably before the warning from Lodge had reached them. After expressing the opinion that the Monroe Doctrine article should be clarified and Article 10 amended, Senator Smoot of Utah said: "With the exceptions noted, I am pleased with the amendments agreed to but do not wish to express an opinion on the passage of the Covenant by the Senate until I have seen the official draft and given it careful study." Senator McNary of Oregon announced through the Associated Press that he would support the league Covenant as finally adopted at Paris. "In my opinion," he said, "the Covenant has been amended to meet all the legitimate objections raised against it." [59]

Dispatches from Washington of May 2 declared that Senators Borah and McNary as well as Senator Johnson of California, Senators Jones and Poindexter of Washington and Senator Kenyon of Iowa were opposed to making the League a party question. Senator Kenyon said: "It would be most unpatriotic as well as foolish to have any such line of division between parties. Further, it would be impossible, as many Republicans will support a League of Nations and some Democrats oppose it. Let us try to forget any politics and any feeling about the President in the solution of the momentous question." [60]

Senator Curtis reported the same day, however, that all but about six of the Republican Senators had agreed, in response to the telegram sent them, to keep silent about the League until after a party conference.

Could the Opposition Control the Senate? On April 29, the Washington correspondent of the *Chicago Tribune* reported to his paper that surface indications pointed strongly to the ratification of the Covenant by the Senate. Efforts would be made to amend it. "But even

[59] *Ibid.*
[60] *New York Times,* May 3, 1919: *Congressional Record,* Vol. 58, Pt. 1, p. 327.

if all attempts to amend or qualify adhesion to the covenant should be defeated it appears probable that the treaty will be ratified by more than the requisite two-thirds majority. Advocates of the revised covenant are predicting that not more than fifteen votes will be cast against it."

The feeling that the Covenant would be ratified was also reflected on the editorial page of the same issue of the *Tribune*. Concluding a discussion of the revised Covenant it said: "The covenant deserves to be considered sympathetically as a whole, to have its merits fairly balanced against such faults as it may be found to retain, and finally, judgment, while practical and reasonably cautious, should be broad. If defects are not deemed fatal, if on the whole the covenant is free from provisions perilous to the security and welfare of our country and offers substantial hope of producing a better system of international relations, pride of opinion and partisanship should not defeat it." [61]

On April 30 the League to Enforce Peace issued from Washington a tabulation of Senators which listed 64, or enough to ratify, as for the Covenant, 12 as opposed and 20 as doubtful. The prediction was based upon the attitudes of Senators as expressed in newspaper interviews, letters to the League and personal interviews. Senator Lodge was listed as one of the twelve definitely against the Covenant. [62]

THE FIUME AND SHANTUNG CRISES IN THE CONFERENCE

At the same time that Mr. Lodge issued his press warning that the Covenant would require further amendment (April 29), he also gave out a statement, addressed to the Italians in Boston, strongly supporting the Italian claim to the seaport of Fiume over which the President and the Italian delegation to the Peace Conference had just had a complete break. [63] On April 23rd the President had issued his famous public statement addressed particularly to the Italian people. This strong action was advised by the entire American delegation and supported by both France and Britain. The Italian delegates, having aroused Italian feeling to demand Fiume, now dramatically left the Peace Conference to appeal to it. As they caught their train for Rome, Balfour handed them a memorandum asserting the opposition of both

[61] *Chicago Tribune*, April 30, 1919.
[62] *New York Times*, May 1, 1919.
[63] *Chicago Tribune*, April 30, 1919.

France and Great Britain to their Fiume claims. This document was not published by either the French or the British, however, and it was carefully pocketed by the Italian chiefs. When Italian rage had been fully roused and vented in denunciation of Wilson, they returned to the Conference quite crestfallen, on May 7, just in time to sign the completed treaty before it was handed to the Germans. [64]

Lodge and Harvey for Italy. In his statement on the Fiume question Lodge had assumed that Fiume was as necessary to Italy as New Orleans had been to us before we acquired it. It was soon pointed out to him by the press, however, that the analogy must work the other way; it was the Jugo-Slavs, the Hungarians, Bohemians and Roumanians who must have an outlet on the Adriatic, as we had required it on the Gulf of Mexico. The Senator had also assumed that some other port could be given these peoples, whereas in fact none existed or could be built without the expenditure of great sums which none of the interested peoples had or could get, unless from us. Any such unnatural commercial outlet must be expensive because of the lay of the mountains, and possible, if at all, only after long delay. Italy on her part needed Fiume only to protect the commerce of Trieste and wished to compel the trade of the new central European states to flow through her hands.

Henry White had been doing his best to keep Lodge straight on this issue. When the latter's statement arrived in Paris, White was so exasperated that he wrote at once to him, "I cannot help feeling, after reading it, that my efforts to keep you accurately informed in respect to the situation have failed signally or you would have worded your letter somewhat differently, if indeed you had written it at all." Lodge, however, had acquired some information of his own that was quite satisfactory to him. He therefore replied with some heat that he had read histories of Dalmatia and knew perfectly well what he was talking about. The report of Rear Admiral Niblock portraying the "repressive, relentless, reactionary and malevolent" conduct of Italy in the disputed area—illegal as well—forwarded by White to Lodge on April 14, did not deter the latter. [65] He continued to advocate the Italian

---

[64] Nevins, *Henry White,* pp. 430, 433.

A minority of the American experts, under the influence of Colonel House, did for a time support the Italian claim. House argued "that Italy's support of the League must not be endangered." His desire for compromise on this clear issue was, in White's judgment, one of the principal factors which led the President to withdraw his confidence in him. See p. 427.

See also, Baker, Vol. II, pp. 166–180, for a vivid account of the lengths to which the Italian leaders went to frustrate the effect of Wilson's appeal in Italy.

[65] Nevins, pp. 429–32.

claim, to the great satisfaction especially of the large numbers of Italian-Americans in Boston and other cities.

Yet, in assessing the activity of Lodge in this case, and other similar ones, it would not be just to conclude that he was without any sincerity. The author of a leading history of American foreign policy has recently evaluated him, in these years, as "a sincere bigoted demagogue." [66] Lodge's conduct in the Fiume incident appears amply to support the latter part of this characterization. The desire for victory over Wilson overbore all other considerations, such as the fairness or propriety of trying to undermine the President at home and defeat him abroad, while he was making decisions of great difficulty in negotiations with foreign powers. At the same time, Lodge's opinion of Wilson was such that it was easy and natural for him really to believe that anything the President did was likely to be wrong, unwise, or both.

Harvey, also, found it easy to be deeply stirred by the cry of the Italians for Fiume. He performed his "painful and humiliating" duty by condemning the President for his stand in the strongest language. Not finding any direct ground for doing so, he argued that the Fourteen Points had indirectly turned Fiume over to Italy through points 1 and 9. There was "no more amazing example of self-reversal" in the President's career. [67]

The Shantung "Surrender." Aside from the Italian explosion, the last days of April were momentous ones for the President and his cause. He saw the revised Covenant formally and unanimously made an integral part of the Treaty of Peace in a plenary session of the Conference, on April 28, only to face on the two succeeding days the final crisis with the Japanese over the disposition of the German properties in the Chinese province of Shantung, which the Japanese had taken from Germany during the War and held not only by right of conquest but by the secret treaties of February, 1917, with Great Britain and France. The Japanese having lost one of their two major objectives at the Conference, a clause in the League Covenant recognizing racial equality, insisted with cold determination that they receive the German rights in full.

---

[66] Randolph G. Adams, "Henry White," *Current History*, January, 1931, Vol. 33, No. 4, p. viii.
[67] *Harvey's Weekly*, May 3, 1919, No. 18, Vol. 2, pp. 2, 4.
In the same issue Harvey made the startling announcement that the Covenant "does absolutely forbid any increase in force (army or navy) by any nation without the unanimous consent of the Council of the League" (p. 3).

President Wilson, well knowing that American opinion sympathized with China and suspecting that the Japanese in Shantung would
gradually absorb that province, opposed the Japanese demands to the
limit of his ability until it appeared that the withdrawal of Japan from
the Conference, following that of Italy and the serious disaffection of
Belgium, would break up both the Conference and the League of
Nations. On the morning of April 30 he agreed to the Japanese demands with the understanding, given by them to the Council of Three,
that:

> The policy of Japan is to hand back the Shantung peninsula in full
> sovereignty to China retaining only the economic privileges granted to
> Germany and the right to establish a settlement under the usual con-
> ditions at Tsingtao. The owners of the Railway will use special police
> only to insure security for traffic. They will be used for no other pur-
> pose. The Police Force will be composed of Chinese and such Japanese
> instructors as the Directors of the Railway may select will be appointed
> by the Chinese Government.[68]

In the midst of this crisis Admiral Grayson, the President's
physician, cabled to the White House, on April 29, "President putting
up great fight against odds"; and, on April 30, "Japanese situation
hanging by a thread. . . . These are terrible days for the President
physically and otherwise." [69] And indeed they were fateful days for
him. Not only were his opponents at home making sure that the changes
he had secured in the Covenant at heavy cost would be discounted or
ignored, but he was compelled to make a settlement at the same time
that would be seized upon by them as an immoral surrender of a weak
people's rights.

The Shantung settlement was a greater disappointment to the
President than it could be to any Senator of the opposition. He felt
as strongly as anyone could that the German concessions, which had
been extorted from China by force, should go back to China, but the
century of exploitation which China had been subjected to at the hands
of all the great powers could not be ended at one stroke. The Japanese
claim was completely buttressed by treaty, right of conquest and possession, and it was less immoral than other concessions wrung from
China had been. To Fiume, on the other hand, Italy could not advance

[68] Baker, *Woodrow Wilson and World Settlement*, Vol. II, p. 263. See the whole
of chapters 35 and 36.
[69] Tumulty, *Woodrow Wilson as I Know Him*, p. 535.

either legal, moral or possessional claims. Every consideration of necessity gave the port to the Succession States; Italy had no treaty promises to it, and was not in possession of it. Nevertheless the same Americans who publicly argued for the surrender of Fiume to Italy, for their own reasons, would hold up their hands in sustained horror at the immorality of recognizing the nearly impregnable Japanese claims as an alternative to disrupting the Conference. They would, too, use the case to show that the whole business, League of Nations and all, was bad, very bad—you could see from Shantung how rotten the foundations of the League were, and what all these claims of a New Order amounted to!

But the matter of Shantung would be only a vantage point in the general attack that would be made on the President's work at the Conference. The assumption would be widely spread that he had in fact failed all along the line, surrendered everything that he should not have surrendered to get his little league of nations—and now look at it!

The President's Failure. Such a failure indeed there never was! He had prevailed over the British (and the other Allies) in establishing the mandate system, with its principles of equal economic opportunity and responsibility to world opinion for the government of conquered peoples; he had resisted successfully through months of terrific strain the French demands for the Rhine and other safeguards that would have made such rapprochment with Germany as has since taken place, forever impossible; he had prevented the Italians from getting such a strangle hold on the East side of the Adriatic as would inevitably bring war between Jugo-Slavia and Italy; he had scaled down the Japanese demands until Chinese sovereignty in Shantung was much better safeguarded than it had been before and had the understanding with Japan left as a source of future supervision. In every one of these great contests and others his influence had moderated the settlements until a chance for a permanent peace existed. He had, too, it must be admitted, created a world association of the nations, which would alleviate injustices that inevitably remained, and provided a forum for the settlement of future grievances. Surely no other "stubborn," "hoodwinked," "visionary" statesman ever had such a failure!

It was scarcely to be expected, of course, that he should have complete success. The demands of many other nations had to leave some impress upon the treaty. Yet, if it had been possible for him to write a treaty perfectly just in all important respects, he would have been condemned around the world for "dictating" it. Moreover, dictation would have been necessary to secure such a settlement. The President "faced cold, practical politics as it had been played from time immemorial." [70] He achieved much because the power of his character and personality had given him the backing of a world-wide public.

His colleagues in the Conference accepted a large part of his program for this reason. Where they felt sure of their own ground they stood it. Sometimes, even then, the strength of the President's will gave him success; at others he was persuaded to accept settlements that might perhaps have been prevented. But before condemning the wicked diplomats of the Old World too severely, it should be remembered "that there was nothing politically immoral in secret bargainings, secret pledges and transfers of territory until President Wilson marshalled public opinion against this vicious practice." [71] And before too strongly castigating even the secret treaties which plagued the Peace Conference it would be well to remember the desperate nature of the war situations which dictated some of them.

In judging the success or failure of any of the leaders at Paris it is fair to bear in mind that they were all, in a measure, "helpless before the uncertainties, fears, doubts, hatreds of the war-exhausted publics behind them. The records are full of references by Wilson to American opinion, American constitutional limitations, the American Senate; and Lloyd George feared his own House of Commons not less than Clemenceau his Chamber. If anything grew clear to the observer at Paris it was that if democracies are really to control international affairs in the future a new technic of diplomacy, based upon a new knowledge and responsiveness on the part of the people must be devised. To expect a leader to achieve miracles and give him neither understanding nor support at home is the height of absurdity." [72]

---

[70] Harry Hansen, *The Adventures of the Fourteen Points*, N. Y., 1919, p. 370. Mr. Hansen attended the Conference for the *Chicago Daily News*.

[71] *Ibid.*

[72] Baker, *Wilson and World Settlement*, Vol. II, pp. 53-4.

The amount of work done by the leaders of the Paris Conference is indicated by the records of the Council of Four which "comprise 206 meetings on 101 days (including 15 Sundays) and occupy ten large foolscap volumes of typescript"—a pamphlet by Sir Maurice Hankey, *Diplomacy of the Conference*, p. 18; Howland, *American Foreign Relations 1928*, p. 258.

In addition to the labor here indicated, President Wilson heard privately many delegations present the claims of their peoples and led the intense work of the League of Nations Commission.

Each of the chief delegates had innumerable conferences with his advisers and experts.

CHAPTER VIII

THE ORGANIZATION OF THE SENATE

However complete the success of President Wilson at Paris may have been it was great enough to cause gloom in the band of men who had determined to deny him the creation of a League of Nations. The prospect before them was distinctly not encouraging as the time for the convening of the Senate drew near. The League had not only been created, but its Covenant had been amended to meet the principal American objections raised against it. The entire Treaty of Peace was also completed, and the President would soon be returning with the finished document containing the League of Nations so woven into its texture that it would, indeed, be impossible to separate the two.

Strategy Adopted and Funds Secured

Moreover, the Covenant had been so favorably received in the United States that it seemed out of the question to attempt to defeat it directly. A considerable body of opposition had been aroused and many doubts raised but the leaders of public opinion still stood overwhelmingly for the League.

Public Opinion For the League. Senator Lodge in his account of the succeeding events, published in 1925, says that as late as May 1, 1919, the great mass of the people "did not understand the treaty at all," though they tended to favor it because of a natural desire to see peace fully restored as quickly as possible. He continues, however, that "what I may call the vocal classes of the community, most of the clergymen, the preachers of sermons, a large element in the teaching force of the universities, a large proportion of the newspaper editors, and finally the men and women who were in the habit of writing and speaking for publication, although by no means thoroughly informed were friendly to the League as it stood and were advocating it."[1]

"The man in the street, to use a common expression," says Mr.

[1] Henry Cabot Lodge, *The Senate and the League of Nations*, N. Y., 1925, p. 147–48.

Lodge, didn't know what it was all about, "didn't understand the treaty at all," but the clergy, *i.e.,* "the preachers of sermons," the university teachers, the newspaper editors and all others who addressed the public were overwhelmingly in favor of the League "as it stood." That is, the leaders of American public opinion of every kind, all the people whose business it was to lead, to do in a large measure the nation's thinking—all these people were for the Covenant as it had been written and amended. Of course, in Lodge's view, the nation's leaders were "by no means thoroughly informed." His group had not been able to accomplish that yet. Would it be able to do so, if time could be gained? Could the convictions of all those elements in the nation best able to form a considered judgment on the subject be overcome?

Besides the ranks of leaders enumerated by Mr. Lodge there was still one important, powerful group that might turn the tide against the League if it chose—the business leadership of the Republic. Where did it stand? Surely its practical, hard-headed, dollar-minded leaders could be depended on to look after national interests without being much influenced by idealistic schemes to organize the whole earth against war. The business world was, moreover, mainly Republican and distinctly not pro-Wilson. Couldn't it be counted on? George Harvey replies, in his biography of Henry Clay Frick, published in 1928, that "of all classes none was so zealous, so determined and so active as the moneyed element of New York"—the commercial metropolis of the country. "Bankers noticeably and capitalists, though less aggressively, seemed to be literally unanimous in their advocacy." [2]

Indirect Attack Agreed Upon. With the influence and belief of the nation's leaders strongly behind the League there was only one recourse left, to arouse the masses by the persistent repetition of the cries already raised and any others that seemed likely to stir the emotions of a considerable bloc of people. If the nation would not think anti-League it must be made to feel so. Many antagonisms left smouldering by the war might be stirred to add to the concentrated hatred or dislike of Wilson that was known to exist. The nation, moreover, might be wearied eventually of the whole League business, if action on it could be delayed long enough.

In any event, time was the essence of the thing. "With these conditions existing," [3] records Senator Lodge in describing his conference

---

[2] George Harvey, *Henry Clay Frick the Man,* N. Y., 1928, p. 325.
[3] That is, the uninformed masses wanting peace and the "vocal classes" advocating the League.

of April 29 with Senator Borah, "I said to Senator Borah, it seemed perfectly obvious to me that any attempt to defeat the treaty of Versailles with the League by a straight vote in the Senate, if taken immediately would be hopeless, even if it were desirable." Thinking that "the interests and safety of the United States might be so protected by amendments or reservations that a large majority of the Republicans could vote for it," continues the account, "I told him that in any event there was only one thing to do and that was to proceed in the discussion of the treaty by way of amendment and reservation. He told me that he agreed entirely with my description of the situation, that he did not believe the treaty could possibly be beaten at that time by a direct vote, that he was against the treaty in any form whatever, whether with reservations or amendments or not, but that thinking I was right in my judgment of the conditions and the situation generally he would support any amendments or reservations which I and those who agreed with me should offer, although, of course, so far as he was personally concerned, after having voted for the reservations or amendments in the belief that they would make the treaty better and the League safer, on the final vote he would vote against the acceptance of the treaty by the Senate." [4]

In this fashion did two men professing to want irreconcilable results come to full agreement as to how to get them. Perhaps, though, their positions were not essentially different. Borah would discuss any number of amendments or reservations in the expectation that rejection would be advanced; Lodge must have amendments and would risk the rejection of the treaty in order to get them. One or the other must lose his professed objective, but they were wholly agreed that both would lose unless they united in a campaign of discussion and delay. If the treaty came swiftly to a vote the League would be accepted. Not even a third of the Senate would vote against it. This meant that in order to nullify a few Democratic negatives upwards of one half of the Republican Senators would decide either that the Covenant was not really dangerous or that the demand for it was so overwhelming that the country would have to take the consequences. The Round Robin even could not be depended on. Enough of its signers to ratify the treaty would take advantage of its escalator clause and contend that the Covenant had been acceptably amended.

This would hardly be a fitting end to the great defiance. Mr. Lodge wanted "the interests and safety of the United States . . . so protected

[4] Lodge, *The Senate and the League of Nations*, p. 147.

by amendments or reservations that a large majority of the Republicans could vote for it." He could not be satisfied to have only half of the Republicans vote for the League; the "large majority" of them must be enabled to do so, *i.e.,* all but Mr. Borah's dozen stalwarts. Borah, however, never even suspected that he was to be left in lonely isolation as the sole defender of the national heritage.

That was not strange either for it must have been evident to him that the new majority leader was deeply appreciative of his irreconcilable support. "To find him in agreement with me on the general situation," concludes Lodge, "therefore, confirmed me in the opinions which I had formed as to the proper way of dealing with the treaty when it came before us. This conversation, which was followed by many others with other Senators, gave to the course which I had suggested the assurance of the support of all those Senators who would not under any circumstances vote for the treaty but were willing to acquiesce in perfecting amendments or reservations, and, also the support of those who constituted the greater part of the Republican majority in the Senate and were anxious to adopt the treaty if it could be done with safety to the United States." [5]

The strategy here agreed upon was undoubtedly clever and it was most ably followed up in the months to come. It was, moreover, a good bargain for both leaders. If it could be executed, Lodge had the practical certainty that at the worst the Republican trademark would be stamped on the League; Borah knew from long experience that he need not have much fear of any treaty that Mr. Lodge set out to "perfect."

One first requisite was essential to success—control of the Senate machinery. This control was in their hands. The Foreign Relations Committee could take all the time that was necessary and when it was ready to move it could attach to the Covenant, by a bare majority vote of the Senate, such amendments or reservations as seemed likely to be effective.

A War Chest Necessary. The group might thus hope to prevail unless public support of the League continued to be so strong that it would be unsafe to delay the treaty or seriously to modify our adhesion to the League. To succeed it was necessary to expand the campaign to arouse popular sentiment against the League. This effort would require a great deal of money and the funds of the group were small. No one had yet been found who was willing to pour out

[5] *Ibid.,* p. 148.

large sums to defeat the achievement of a great coöperative endeavor of the nations to free themselves from the wholesale destruction by periodic warfare of life, wealth and the orderly virtues which constitute civilization. The immeasurable folly of continuing a state of international anarchy was so clear at the hour that contributions of money went to the cause of the League rather than against it.

The situation was very serious for the opposition "when, one evening in May, 1919," says George Harvey, "the group opposed to joining the League, assembled at their accustomed meeting place in Senator Brandegee's residence in Washington, [6] were apprized that their whole plan of campaign was seriously endangered. Their strategy had consisted of disseminating propaganda chiefly throughout the Middle West at mass meetings and by distributing quantities of 'campaign literature' for the purpose of starting 'backfires' upon wavering Senators."

"The campaign had progressed favorably," continues Harvey, "but the time had come when essential traveling and mailing expenditures required considerable sums, and the modest funds which the committee had been able to supply were completely exhausted. The problem of ways and means, to oppose successfully skillful antagonists suffering from no such handicap was poignant. The finding of a deeper reservoir upon which to draw for financial aid had become a paramount necessity." [7]

Frick and Mellon Appealed to. Various plans were rejected and "the outlook was lamentably gloomy" when, late in the evening Senator Knox suggested as a last resort an appeal to two multi-millionaires among his Pennsylvania friends, H. C. Frick and Andrew W. Mellon, "who were accustomed to act together in such matters." [8]

"Mr. Frick," according to his biographer, "was a staunch Republican of the type of George F. Edmunds, who held to his dying day that the Democratic Party never was, is not now and never will

---

[6] The home of Mrs. Nicholas Longworth, the former Alice Roosevelt, was also a meeting place for the group. Her assistance to them, in the opinion of many, was considerable. A recent article says: "With her own characteristic weapons she fought tooth and nail against the League of Nations and the World Court and she certainly helped to thwart American membership. Her house was a rallying place for the irreconcilables." H. H. Smith, "Alice in the Looking Glass," *World's Work*, August, 1930, Vol. LIX, No. 8, p. 80.

[7] George Harvey, *Henry Clay Frick the Man*, N. Y., 1928, pp. 325–26.

[8] *Ibid.*, p. 326.

According to Harvey, Knox had been returned to the Senate "largely through Mr. Frick's influence," and Knox was able later "to induce President-elect Harding to appoint their mutual friend, Mr. Andrew Mellon, Secretary of the Treasury" (p. 293).

be fit to govern the United States." [9] Support might therefore be expected from him if the matter could be properly put up to him. Circumstances, too, favored such a presentation of the case to him. Mr. Frick was giving a dinner in New York the next evening for General Leonard Wood to which "the New York representative" in the conference on ways and means, presumably Harvey, was invited. It was, accordingly, arranged that he should broach the matter to Frick and "fortunately for his design, the delegated conspirator," to use Harvey's phrase, was asked by his host to remain after the party and tell him about the contest over the League.

"Marveling at this auspicious fortuity, the eager propagandist set forth the stock arguments of the group of Irreconcilables with whom he was aligned as succinctly as possible, although at considerable length." After further explanation Mr. Frick characterized joining the League as "a crazy thing to do" and agreed to help fight it. [10]

A Deep Reservoir Found. "Three days later the New York member of the cabal" [11] received a note from Senator Knox, written in the Senate chamber, saying that he had been able to obtain "the same amount from Mr. Mellon" and that Senator McCormick (of Illinois) said he could now go to Chicago and "raise about twenty."

"The desired reservoir had been found and it was both deep and full. All anxiety respecting sinews of war was dispelled. Rejoicing pervaded the camp of the Irreconcilables, efforts were redoubled all along the line and the redoubtable little band pushed on to the victory which, whether desirable or not, presently was won in the Senate and ultimately was ratified by the people.

"Mr. Frick's interest became intense and never flagged for a moment during the seven months left to him of earthly existence. After listening, three days before he died, to an encouraging report of progress in what proved to be his last fight, he smiled contentedly and pronounced it 'GOOD.' " [12]

After his death, recorded Harvey in beginning the narrative thus

[9] Harvey, *Henry Clay Frick the Man*, p. 293.
[10] *Ibid.*, pp. 328–29.
While the war was on, Mr. Frick had been so moved by President Wilson's address at the opening of Congress in December, 1917, that he had sent him a letter, on December 7, saying that, "It is a great satisfaction to feel that we have in you a leader in whom we should be proud," and that, differences in politics aside, "I subscribe without reservation to all you are contending for." He even added, "It is my fervent wish that you may be spared to see the trouble ended satisfactorily . . ." (P. 318.)
[11] The word is Harvey's.
[12] Harvey, *Henry Clay Frick the Man*, pp. 329–30.

GEORGE HARVEY

concluded, appraisal of Mr. Frick's estate showed that his fortune "shrank many millions between the beginning and the ending of the war of the United States against the Central Powers." How much of this shrinkage of millions was due to Frick's intense share in the fight on the League is not made clear. The continuance of Mr. Mellon's support in sums approaching those of Frick is indicated by Harvey's statement that the two were the only multi-millionaires "who supported quietly, but effectively, the successful organized effort to prevent the inclusion of the United States in the League of Nations." [13]

An Educational Campaign Launched. The money reservoir of "the cabal" was to be henceforth "both deep and full." The second requisite of success was in its hands. The "organized effort" to arouse distrust of the League could now go forward on a nation wide scale backed by practically unlimited funds. Meetings could be advertised in many cities, for example, as in the *Boston Herald* and other Boston newspapers of July 8, 1919:

AMERICANS, AWAKE!

Shall We Bind Ourselves to the War
　Breeding Covenant?
It Impairs American Sovereignty!
Surrenders the Monroe Doctrine!
Flouts Washington's Warning!
Entangles Us in European and Asiatic
　Intrigues!
Sends Our Boys to Fight Throughout
　the World by Order of a League!
"The evil thing with a holy name!"

Mass Meeting,　　　　Tremont Temple
　　Tuesday, July 8, at 8 P.M.

Speakers:

SENATOR HIRAM W. JOHNSON
of California

GEORGE WHARTON PEPPER
of Philadelphia

Under the Auspices of the League for
the Preservation of American
Independence

Doors Open at 7 o'clock.
American Songs.

[13] *Ibid.,* p. 324

Control of the Senate Achieved

The opening of the special session of Congress, on May 19, thus found the conspirators, to use Harvey's term, as fully prepared by many quiet conferences, by the adoption of strategy and by the assurance of funds, as they could well be. This session, it will be remembered, had been made necessary by a Republican filibuster in March designed to force the calling of the Senate while the treaty was still in negotiation, in order that it might be used as a forum from which attacks on the League might continue. The President had avoided this compulsion about as long as he could and still get the throttled appropriation bills through by July 1, the end of the Government's fiscal year.

The Senate, therefore, came together on May 19, and its new Republican leaders made haste to recover lost time.

The Unfinished Treaty Demanded. On May 20, Senator Johnson, of California, introduced a resolution calling on the Secretary of State to transmit a copy of the Peace Treaty, then under discussion with the Germans, to the Senate. [14] Senators desired to begin the attack and wished at the same time to make it appear again that something was being withheld from them, and from the country. It mattered not to them that the treaty was not yet signed, nor finally agreed upon, and that by immemorial usage the Senate could act upon a treaty only after the President in the exercise of his judgment had submitted it to them. They proposed to drag the whole dark business out into the open. The resolution called upon the Secretary of State to transmit the treaty "forthwith," not under the usual qualification "if not incompatible with the public interest."

Pitiless Publicity Promised. In the course of the debate on this resolution, Senator Lodge served notice, on May 23, that he would demand that the Senate give the treaty "pitiless publicity." It was not to be debated in executive session as usual, it was to be "laid before the country without any secrecy."

The part of the treaty that was to receive the full force of pitiless publicity was indicated clearly: "The President," said Mr. Lodge, "brought over here a draft of a league and handed it to us; that is he handed it to the press. The general understanding was that we were to take that first draft. That is what was expected of us. It was a tentative draft submitted to the criticism of the world. Then he took it

[14] *Congressional Record,* Vol. 58, Pt. 1, p. 63.

back and they amended it. They made it much worse than it was before." [15]

Precedents of Rejected Treaties Mobilized. The suggestion in Lodge's opening remarks that the Covenant would have to be drastically altered at the very least, "and not in Paris," was clear. That the treatment to be accorded both Covenant and Treaty might be expected to go further was indicated, on June 5, by Senator George H. Moses of New Hampshire, who secured the printing of a two hundred page document setting forth the Senate's past record in disposing of treaties of which it disapproved. The title of the compilation was: "Proceedings in the Case of Treaties Rejected by the Senate, With some Examples of Amended Treaties, 1794–1901." [16]

The Amended Covenant Would not Do. The necessity of action by the Senate was made plain by Senator Lodge, on June 6, in explaining how much worse the hard won Monroe Doctrine amendment had made the Covenant. "In the first draft of the treaty that was presented to us," he said, "the Monroe Doctrine was left somewhere among the voices heard in the air and the visions that are seen by capable visionaries, and we were told that the doctrine was safe, because it had been extended to the whole world, which took away its entire meaning and all its characteristics. Now, however, there comes back a second draft with a direct statement in regard to the Monroe Doctrine putting it in a far worse position, in my judgment, than it was under the first draft, and that was bad enough." [17]

In March the Senators had cried out for protection for the Monroe Doctrine and the treaty now said, in direct response to their objections,

---

[15] *Ibid.,* p. 161.

[16] The account of treaties rejected occupied the bulk of the document. It was preceded by an extended account of "Methods and Procedure in Foreign Countries Relative to the Ratification of Treaties." This brochure showed that treaties had been questioned often in foreign parliaments. See *Senate Documents,* No. 26, 66th Congress, 1st Session, Vol. 14, pp. 1–280.

[17] *Ibid.,* p. 729.

Senator Reed, of Missouri, had meanwhile contributed a long speech to show that the League would be controlled by the dark peoples. A table listing most of South America along with South Africa and the Orient as "dark" gave him a population total three times as large as the white countries in the League would have. He then took up in turn some fifteen of these peoples, including Brazil and Japan along with Haiti and Liberia, and painted a lurid picture of their morals, religion, lawlessness, barbarity, etc., assuming that they would control the destiny of the United States. Why were these nations, "most of them the dregs of civilization," selected to sit around the council board? He openly warned the men of the West and South ("and I am making my argument to them") that the dark skins would impose racial equality upon them. (P. 235–46.)

Article 21 said: Nothing in the covenant shall be deemed to affect the validity of international engagements, such as treaties of arbitration or regional understandings, like the Monroe Doctrine, for securing the maintenance of peace."

that nothing in that Covenant shall be deemed to affect its validity. But no! It was never an international engagement cried Senator Lodge, and it is not an international understanding. It is ours. "It is all ours; and now it is carried into this league of nations. It is already interpreted by England, although it is wholly our affair, and it is to be determined in the future by the league of nations."

The English interpretation of the Monroe Doctrine of which he complained was an explanation of the propriety of Article 21. Mr. Lodge used this explanation as justification for his support of a resolution introduced by Senator Brandegee calling on the Peace Conference to take up the cause of Ireland. Well knowing the impropriety of thus interfering with the most intimate domestic affairs of a friendly nation and ally, he said that this action "might have been objected to in the past on the ground that those nations associated against Germany should not look into each others' affairs; but when it comes to those nations taking the Monroe Doctrine, our doctrine, our policy, and foisting it on the league of nations, and then telling us that they were going to interpret it"—then it was "quite legitimate and courteous" to make a few suggestions to them. [18]

A Definition of the Doctrine Which Excluded the League. But aside from his justification for supporting the Irish resolution, the Senator's remarks indicated the impossibility of satisfying the critics of the Covenant on the Monroe Doctrine. If you did not define the Doctrine it was true, as the English memorandum said, that the League would be there to define it, if it fell under dispute, in which case the United States would be supported by the plain letter of the Doctrine and a century of its application, plus Article 21 and our vast national power and influence. If you did attempt to define it in the Covenant no definition that you could make would satisfy the Senators unless it reserved this hemisphere for our domination and exploitation so completely that the effective membership of any American States in the League would be out of the question. Under no circumstances did the gentlemen intend to surrender their position as the defenders of the great American tradition.

As Senator Williams of Mississippi put it, with reference to Senator Lodge, "his objection to the exclusion of mention of the

---

[18] *Congressional Record*, Vol. 58, Pt. 1, p. 729.
    Owen Wister says in his friendly interpretation of Lodge: "He disliked the English through thick and thin. It would crop out anywhere." O. Wister, *Roosevelt, The Story of a Friendship*, N. Y., 1930, p. 157.

Monroe Doctrine increased to virulence when he was faced with the inclusion of it."

"What," asked Mr. Williams in soberer voice, "does the Senator want? Is he going back to old time days when we talked about a manifest destiny? I think he is. A manifest destiny to spread ourselves all over Central and South America. I do not know. But I never found any destiny in the world that was manifest except this: 'Whatsoever a man soweth that shall he reap.' If you sow the seeds of might and power and empire and unlimited sovereignty, the chances are that you will reap a harvest of that sort raised on some other people's field, not on your own; and if you sow the seeds of accord, harmony, peace, self limitation, then of those seeds some day you will reap the harvest, not only on other people's fields but upon your own. It is an awfully nice thing to reap the harvest that you planted, and it is the only destiny that I know of that is both good and manifest." [19]

Senator Williams' estimate of the kind of Monroe Doctrine the Senators were going to insist upon was amply confirmed a few days later by Senator Knox, who said of it, on June 17: "Its precise character, the extent, method, and time of its application, the means of compelling its observance, all are matters of our high and uncontrolled will and sovereign prerogative. We, the United States, cannot answer to any one else in respect of it. We use it when, as, and to what extent we need it. There can be no limitation upon it except our requirements, our will, and our force of arms." [20]

---

[19] *Congressional Record*, Vol. 58, Pt. 1, p. 796 (June 9, 1919).

Vice President Marshall wrote of Senator Williams, some years later: "Of all the men I have ever known John Sharp Williams had the most intimate knowledge of world history and world politics." Thomas R. Marshall, *Recollections*, Indianapolis, 1925, p. 301.

[20] *Congressional Record*, Vol. 58, Pt. 2, p. 1221.

Contrast these utterances with that of President Wilson to a group of Mexican editors, on June 8, 1918, in which, after describing the big-brother attitude we had assumed toward the other American republics, without asking their consent, he said: "That was all very well so far as protecting you from aggression from the other side of the water was concerned, but there was nothing in it that protected you from aggression from us, and I have repeatedly seen the uneasy feeling on the part of representatives of the States of Central and South America that our self-appointed protection might be for our own benefit and our own interests and not for the interest of our neighbors. So I said, (referring to his earlier Pan-American proposal) very well, let us make an arrangement by which we will give bond. Let us have a common guarantee, that all of us will sign, of political independence and territorial integrity. . . .

"Now, that is the kind of agreement that will have to be the foundation of the future life of the nations of the world, gentlemen. The whole family of nations will have to guarantee to each nation that no nation shall violate its political independence or its territorial integrity. That is the basis, the only conceivable basis, for the future peace of the world . . ." Lars P. Nelson, *President Wilson the World's Peacemaker*, Stockholm, 1919, pp. 214-15.

Such an assertion of "uncontrolled will and sovereign prerogative" was, of course, at the opposite pole from the idea of a partnership of nations which would take from the next imperial conqueror its right to enforce its own "requirements" and "will" upon its neighbors by force of arms "when, as, and to what extent" it desired.

The Real Monroe Doctrine. This exaggerated interpretation of our favorite national tradition appears also to have been due to the political exigencies of the hour more than to the imperial dreams of the wearers of the toga. In 1895, for example, at the time of President Cleveland's vigorous revival of the Monroe Doctrine, in the course of the British-Venezuelan boundary dispute, no one seconded him more heartily than Lodge. In his speech on this occasion, too, the same emphasis on the unilateral nature of the Doctrine appears, but the policy is stated clearly and without any additions whatever to its original intent. Said Lodge on December 30, 1895: "The Monroe Doctrine, as I have said, is very simple. It is merely the declaration that no foreign power may establish a new government, acquire new territory by purchase or by any method whatever, or seek to control existing governments in the Americas. That is the principle which Mr. Monroe declared." [21]

A Later View of Article 21. There was here no threat of a suzerainty to be imposed upon the Americas by the United States itself. Neither was any threat to the Monroe Doctrine discovered in the Covenant by Republican Senators after the war on the League of Nations had subsided. To illustrate, during the debate over our proposed entry into the World Court, in 1926, Senator Fess, of Ohio, at the present writing chairman of the Republican National Committee and long known for his aggressive Republicanism, said: "I notice that Article 21 of the Covenant of the League of Nations does recognize the Monroe Doctrine as exempt from any consideration by the League. I have wondered whether that is any consolation to those who claim that the Monroe Doctrine will be involved." To this his colleague from Ohio, Senator Willis, also a strong Republican, replied: "It would seem to me that that ought to find some consideration at their hands." [22]

Thus the Monroe Doctrine amendment to the Covenant when read by orthodox Republican Senators, apart from the fight on the Wilson League, aroused no protest whatever. On the contrary they accepted it as an adequate safeguard, if one were needed. Their re-

[21] *Congressional Record,* Vol. 58, Pt. 1, p. 420.
[22] *Congressional Record,* Vol. 57, Pt. 2, p. 1424.

marks do not even suggest any fear that the Doctrine needed either assertion or defense.

THE FOREIGN RELATIONS COMMITTEE DOMINATED

But to return to 1919, the Senate having been organized by the Republicans and the initial broadsides loosed against the Covenant, the leaders proceeded to the all important matter of reorganizing the Committee on Foreign Relations.

The result of their activity was made known on June 9 by Senator Hitchcock, who charged that the Committee had been packed with men certain to give an adverse report on the League. The Republican leaders, he said, had "filled the Committee on Foreign Relations with Senators practically pledged to oppose the league of nations and practically pledged to bring an amendment out of the Foreign Relations Committee."

"Do Senators think I have not talked with Republicans?" continued Hitchcock. "I know Republicans on the other side of this Chamber who feel just as I feel, indignant that agreement with the leaders on the treaty should have been made a test to decide whether a Senator should go on the Foreign Relations Committee or not. I am not the only indignant one. There are Republicans on the other side of this Chamber, and a number of them, indignant that their personal views on the league of nations should have been inquired into, and that it should have been necessary for them to pledge themselves on an issue which should be decided upon its merits and not on political considerations."

He charged that "as a matter of fact, at the present time the purpose of the recognized dominant Republican leadership on that side of the Chamber is to kill the league of nations, if possible, and to kill it by indirection."

These charges were not replied to, other than by an effort of Senator Fall, of New Mexico, to find out what determined the appointment of Democratic members to the Committee, although Senator Williams asked Senator Lodge to correct him "right now while I am on my feet" if he did not intend to make the League a party issue. Mr. Lodge sat silent. [23]

Taft's Warnings. Former President Taft had betrayed anxiety as to the situation two days earlier, in a speech before the Albany Cham-

[23] *Congressional Record,* Vol. 58, Pt. 1, pp. 791–2.

ber of Commerce on June 7, in which he explained that the Covenant was not a mere fad of Mr. Wilson; it had been demanded by the peoples of the world and by the necessity of leaving machinery to administer the peace. "The opponents of the league, however," continued Taft, "have aroused protest against the league among business men and partisan Republicans by asserting that Mr. Wilson is seeking personal credit and party advantage in making a league of nations and is sacrificing the interests of this country and delaying peace and prosperity to secure the league. The reasons for delay are now demonstrated to have been acute differences in respect to the terms of peace and not the covenant of the league, which was agreed to long before the treaty."

In the evening Mr. Taft returned to the same danger in concluding his address before the New York State Convention of the League to Enforce Peace, saying:

"This is not a partisan question. We should be for or against the league without respect to whether we are Democrats or Republicans. We should be for or against the league without regard to whether we think it will bring credit to our party or credit to any man. Personal and partisan considerations of this kind are reasons which should have no influence with us in determining an issue so fateful in the world's history and so likely to affect the future welfare of the people of the United States and of all mankind.

"When, therefore, you come to consider the question whether you are in favor of the treaty or not, you should search your hearts and souls and your consciences to see whether you are approaching it in the proper patriotic and humane spirit, or whether you are against it because Mr. Wilson is for it and you may fear that he will gain credit for its adoption, or because you may suppose that his party may gain party credit for it. These are small reasons for supporting or opposing the League." [24]

Mr. Taft's warnings indicated that the campaign of the Senate leaders was bearing fruit. The perfectly natural doubt that many Americans would have about the advisability of a new departure in foreign affairs was being stirred into something much more active.

Much Approval of the League Conditional. A poll of the press, published by the *Literary Digest* on April 5, had shown that while the majority favored the League as it stood, there was a very large body of opinion that would support conditional ratification. To the question

[24] *Congressional Record,* Vol. 58, Pt. 1, p. 899; *New York Times,* June 8, 1919.

"do you favor the proposed League of Nations?" 718 newspapers had answered "Yes," 181 "No" and 478 had given conditional replies. Since these figures included many small dailies, the circulation of the papers was also given, as follows:

TOTAL CIRCULATION OF REPLYING NEWSPAPERS

For 9,886,449
Against 4,326,882*
Conditional 6,792,461

DEMOCRATIC

For 4,886,449
Against 121,912
Conditional 508,384

INDEPENDENT

For 3,648,141
Against 2,955,706*
Conditional 2,447,660

REPUBLICAN

For 1,911,256
Against 1,249,264
Conditional 3,836,417

* Including the 2,488,976 circulation of the Hearst papers.

Each editor had been asked to interpret public opinion in his locality as far as he could, and every geographical division of the country had returned practically as many "Yes" replies as in the other two categories combined. Still, a good half of the readers of Republican papers was reported as "conditional" and the majority might be swung against the League. In the Independent group the influence of Mr. Hearst with his two and a half million circulation might also give an adverse majority. The likelihood was, of course, that the great lead indicated for the League could not be easily overcome, if at all. Hence the slowness with which the Foreign Relations Committee moved after it received the treaty.

The comments of the editors, many scores of which are printed in this issue of the *Digest,* give an interesting cross section of the state of public opinion after the Covenant had been first presented. The strength of the feeling against the League, and for it, on account of the President's connection with it, stood out clearly, as did the feeling stirred up by the Senate attacks. [25]

The Principle Clearly Favored. The influence of a majority of the political leaders of the people had also been so far thrown in favor of the League. Thirty-two state legislatures from all sections of the Union had endorsed the League by concurrent resolutions, and two others conditionally. [26] The names of 33 Governors of States who were supporters of a League of Nations were also published by the League to Enforce Peace. [27] These commitments were made, however, before the long sustained attacks upon the League and before the issue had been made one of conditional ratification *vs.* unconditional approval.

Treaty Publication Forced. Meanwhile the debate continued in the Senate as to whether the proposed Treaty of Peace should be published or not. Senator Borah charged, on June 3, that "special interests" in New York had copies of the treaty and Senator Lodge verified him, testifying that he had himself seen a copy of it in New York the day before. Senator Hitchcock thereupon offered a resolution demanding an investigation of the "leak" and the Senate passed it, on June 6, along with Senator Johnson's resolution, amended to read "if not incompatible with the public interest," asking the Secretary of State to send in a copy of the treaty.

President Wilson cabled in reply that he was unwilling to break his agreement with the Allied leaders that the treaty be not published until signed. [28] Senator Borah countered, on June 9, by presenting to the Senate a copy of the unsigned treaty, procured for him by the *Chicago Tribune,* and forcing its publication.

A few days later the Senate investigating committee established that the copy of the treaty seen by Mr. Lodge had passed from the

[25] *Literary Digest,* Vol. 61, p. 13 ff. Of the larger newspapers of the country who replied, 8 aside from the Hearst papers were against the League, 16 supported or opposed it conditionally and 33 supported it unconditionally.

[26] *Current History, June,* 1919, Vol. 10, Pt. 1, p. 509.

[27] *Kansas City Star,* December 24, 1918.

[28] According to Baker the French had wished to publish the treaty when it was handed to the Germans on May 7, feeling that publication would prevent any changes. Lloyd George, on the other hand, wished to prevent publication because he hoped for changes. The Italians also opposed publication and the President probably felt that the Senate would get hold of it soon enough. He, too, hoped for changes at the time, but later stood with the French against change. Baker, *Woodrow Wilson and World Settlement,* Vol. I, pp. 157–160.

Nevins says that the Allied leaders, fearing a storm of criticism at home, united in suppressing the document, and that Wilson certainly favored publishing it. Nevins, *Henry White,* p. 452.

He would have been wiser to have forced publication, for as soon as the Germans got it they did so, and the Senate could not thereafter be prevented from dragging the unholy thing out into the light.

hands of Mr. Thomas W. Lamont, financial adviser at Paris, to Mr. H. P. Davidson, of J. P. Morgan & Co., as head of the League of Red Cross Societies, who in turn had passed it on to Mr. Elihu Root who had shown it to Mr. Lodge. [29]

Suppression of the Covenant Again Demanded

On June 10, Senator Knox introduced one more resolution giving notice to the Peace Conference that the treaty should be divorced from the League. [30] It is difficult to believe that at this late date he hoped to gain any other ground than a vantage point for attack, although some of his followers in the Senate appeared to take the thing seriously, arguing that the Conference might still yield. The new resolution pushed the assumption of the Senate's right to "advise" as far as Senator Lodge himself had ever advanced it.

The Senate was represented as "gravely impressed by the fact that its provisions appear calculated to force upon us undesirable and far reaching covenants inimical to our free institutions . . . whereas the treaty may be easily so drawn as to permit the making of immediate peace, leaving the question of the establishment of a league of nations for future determination." It was therefore "resolved that the Senate would regard as fully adequate to our national needs and as completely responsive to the duties and obligations we owe to our co-belligerents and to humanity a peace treaty which shall assure to the United States and its people the attainment of those ends for which we entered the war (*i.e.* the repelling of German aggression), and that it will look with disfavor upon all treaty provisions going beyond these ends."

The second paragraph of the resolution warned against an assumed attempt to amend our constitution by passing the treaty, and the third explained with great care just how the Peace Conference could give the Senate a chance to vote on the Covenant separately— that document which "was obliterative of legitimate race and national aspirations, oppressive of weak nations and peoples and destructive of human progress and liberty." [31]

In the fourth paragraph the Senate "advised": "That this resolution indicates and gives notice of the limits of the present obligations

---

[29] *Current History,* July, 1919, Vol. 10, Pt. 2, pp. 53-4.
[30] *Congressional Record,* Vol. 58, Pt. 1, p. 894.
[31] Mr. Knox explained later, on June 17, that that characterization was meant for the Covenant, not the Treaty. *Congressional Record,* Vol. 58, Pt. 2, p. 1218.

against the United States in which the Senate of the United States is now prepared to acquiesce by consenting to the ratification of a treaty embodying peace conditions that may be found otherwise acceptable to its judgment, and that the adoption by the peace conference of the foregoing reasonable limitations and positions will facilitate the early acceptance of the treaty of peace by the Senate of the United States, will in no wise interfere with the league of nations as between these countries prepared to ratify the treaty without further consideration, and will offer such a manifestation of real respect for the wishes of a great people as cannot fail more firmly to cement the friendship already existing between ourselves and our co-belligerents."

The Conference had been warned by the Senator in December, before it ever met, not to attempt to make a league of nations; it had been sternly admonished to desist in January and February, and finally in March it had received notice supported by the signatures of thirty-six other Senators that the Covenant must not be included in the treaty. Yet, under the influence of the man whom the Senators hated, and under the compulsion of necessities of which the Senators still betrayed no knowledge whatever, the Conference had gone ahead to make the League the foundation of the peace, not an ornamental capstone or an annex added by some afterthought. Now, in June, still refusing to recognize anything that had happened, the Senator gave the Conference one more chance to "facilitate the early acceptance of the treaty of peace by the Senate of the United States," and afford "a manifestation of real respect for the wishes of a great people." If the Conference still thought that the President spoke for that people it would find out its mistake in due time.

A Promise to Consult Proposed. Yet Mr. Knox had made some progress, however reluctant. In his December resolution he had been willing to promise the Allies to help suppress the Germans, "the same necessity arising in the future." Now he proposed that it should be "the declared policy of our Government. . . . that the freedom and peace of Europe being threatened by any power or combination of powers the United States would regard such a situation with grave concern as a menace to its own peace and freedom" and would "consult with other powers affected with a view to devising means for the removal of such menace. . . ."

Here was a concession which many people would say was going far enough. The obligation was wholly general and there was absolutely nothing to determine when it should come into operation, but an obligation was undertaken and a stake in the world's peace recognized. "That will do quite well," many of the Senator's followers would say. It was going too far for the Senate Committee on Foreign Relations, however, which reported the resolution without the last paragraph containing this proposal. Even that indefinite commitment was too much for Borah. Lodge and Borah understood one another.

Renewed Protests from Taft. Taft realized fully the trend of these maneuvers and at once protested against them as strongly as he could. After commending chairman Will Hays of the Republican National Committee for refusing to be led by the Democratic chairman, Homer S. Cummings, into making a party issue of the peace treaty, he continued: "It is unfortunate that the action of the Republican committee on committees in the Senate should give color to a different view by a provision that the Foreign Relations Committee should have Republicans enough to give them a majority without the vote of Mr. McCumber, known to be favorable to the treaty, and by a careful selection of Republicans for that majority whose opposition to the treaty has been pronounced. Senator Kellogg would naturally have been taken before Senator Moses, a new Senator, and one whose term expires in two years. Senator Kellogg, however, had ventured to make a speech in favor of a league of nations, even before the covenant was agreed upon, and had refused to sign the 'round robin.'"

Noting the general expectation of Republican victory in 1920 among Republican Senators, as well as among others, he asked: "Can they afford to go before the country and uphold their course in defeating the treaty when there is a deep seated impression that they are in part, at least, prompted in their methods, unusual and not according to constitutional procedure, by personal and partisan motives? Will not many say that had this treaty been proposed by a Republican President or by a President who consulted the Senate or appointed on the Commission leading Republicans or Senators from the Foreign Relations Committee no such obstruction would have been offered?"

The Senators were reminded that Mr. Knox's claim that the Senate was a "co-equal" of the President in treaty making was not based on fact. The function of the Senate, unless invited by the President, did not begin until he laid the treaty before them for advice and consent. Only harm could come from the passage of the Knox resolution. The only possible effect on the other side would be to encourage the Germans to refuse to sign the treaty.

Moreover, maintained Mr. Taft, the whole attitude of the Senate leaders was contrary to Republican tradition. Republicans had always held that "this was a nation with a big N, able to meet every responsibility that nations should meet; able to do for its people and the world as much as any government, and courageous enough to do it." Always heretofore it had been the Democratic party which, as new problems arose, had sought to limit the sphere of our Government by nice interpretation and strained applications of the Constitution. The Republican party had pioneered in the Spanish War era in abandoning American isolation and in spite of the awful prophecies of ruin made by the Democrats the country was still safe. [32]

Censure for Delay Feared and Resented. Senator Knox, however, declared on June 13 that he would fight for his resolution "to the end." He did not know whether the Peace Conference would heed it or not, but if not the skirts of the Senate would be cleared of blame for delay. [33] And, although other Senators talked excitedly about finally forcing the Peace Conference to let them have a chance at the Covenant separately, a perusal of Senator Knox's speech of June 17 gives a strong impression that his major objectives were: time to arouse the country against the League and justification for taking it. Throughout the speech he asked most earnestly for time to consider the Covenant, even as Senator Lodge had done by the hour on February 28. Time, time to deliberate, time to consider was the plea.

It was important to the cabal to justify the long delay in ending the state of war that might be necessary to accomplish their purpose. They both feared and resented blame for this delay. That was what had been filling their souls with bitterness from the time they had told Mr. Wilson in December not to put any league of nations into the treaty. They were very little interested in the other terms of the treaty at any time, but they did appreciate the risk of delaying or defeating it. That they never wanted; they only wanted to spike the President in his wholly evident purpose to found a league of nations, and their wrath increased month by month as the chances of an unfettered opportunity to do so diminished.

Pleas for Abatement Unheeded. So consuming was their determination to thwart the President that no warnings of the ultimate consequences of their course could reach them, no matter how prophetic, how solemn or direct. Thus Senator McCumber appealed to

[32] *Congressional Record*, June 20, 1919, Vol. 58, Pt. 2, p. 1430.
[33] *New York Times*, June 13, 1919. Repeated threats of Senators to sign a new manifesto to let the Peace Conference know they meant business do indicate some remaining faith in the round robin tactics. See the *Times*, June 13, 14 and 17.

them quite vainly, on June 18, to take a long view, saying: "And I say candidly, Senators, that you may defeat the treaty, this league of nations; you may scatter abroad criticisms that are unjust or baseless; you may appeal to a national pride and to the selfish side of our natures and thereby destroy at this time the hope that has been in the heart of every thinking, feeling, loving human being for centuries that the time would come when the same law which governs the rights of individuals would be applied to shield the lives of nations. But as surely as this is defeated and the world suffers another such calamity, deeper than the hatred of the enemy will be the hatred toward the statesmen of the world who have failed in their great opportunity to league together to shield the poor, innocent human beings from such sufferings and calamities as have been visited upon them because there is no law to check a great, powerful nation from criminal aggression."[34]

Neither did the pleas of influential members of their party move them. The talk of a new round robin brought out the fact that a group of 28 prominent Republicans, lawyers, bankers and others of New York City had protested to the Senate that "political partisanship should have no place in the consideration on its merits of the Constitution of the proposed League of Nations" and urged "that the treaty and covenant be promptly ratified by the Senate without attempting to embarrass it by amendment." The statement was signed by two former Cabinet members, a Governor, a Senator, a former State Chairman, the President of the Chamber of Commerce, Federal and State judges, but the only effect it produced was a vehement attack from Senator Borah threatening that if the Republican party did not make a party issue of the League of Nations a new party would be created to do so, while a half dozen other Senators ridiculed the statement as coming from "the Taft crowd." [35]

A New Contribution Offered. At this stage in the proceedings Senator Sherman thought it time to cultivate a broad field of prejudice that had not yet been stirred. He had been preparing to inject a religious issue into the debate "through a long period, beginning last winter." [36] The openly avowed enemies of the League had first held up an awesome picture of the kings dominating the League; then it had been the British; a little later we were to fall under the sway of the negroes and other colored peoples; now it was to be the Pope.

[34] *Congressional Record*, Vol. 58, Pt. 2, p. 1266.
[35] *New York Times*, June 22 and 23, 1919.
[36] *Congressional Record*, Vol. 58, Pt. 2, pp. 1435–44.

After a column of justification for the high, patriotic and unselfish motives which prompted him, Mr. Sherman revealed that his researches had failed to find any evidence that the Papacy had abandoned any of its claims to temporal power over the nations. The portent of this could be seen in the fact that some twenty-four of the forty Christian nations in the League were "spiritually dominated by the Vatican." If the question of the jurisdiction of the ecclesiastical or civil power arose it would be "a matter of profound apprehension that one man at the head of a great religious organization controls, if he follows his own present as well as traditional convictions, or seeks to control the conduct of the delegates of the twenty-four member nations. And this power is proposed to govern the world!"

The Senator knew well that in both the Assembly and the Council of the League decisions were to be by unanimous consent. He knew also that the trend in the great Catholic states was toward a separation of church and state and that the little Catholic states would never dominate the great Protestant powers. He brought out that Italy had kept the Vatican out of the Peace Conference, and that the Papacy had no seat in the League, but suggested no safety in these facts.

Instead, he scouted the Pope's statement, after his interview with President Wilson on March 16, that "President Wilson put the matter so clearly that my doubts began to melt, and before our interview closed I agreed with him on the main lines of his plan." This was either a miraculous conversion or the deep traditional wisdom of the Holy See, which? The Pope gave no random interviews. Neither could one believe that "both the President's visit and the interview were not for a preconceived purpose."

Here was the President trafficking with the Pope! The Pontiff's not too friendly statement that "The President struck me as being more interested in his League of Nations than in fixing the problems of the newly created states" was quoted, but it was immediately inferred that the Pope and the President understood one another on Fiume—an understanding with the Pope who had essayed a mediation in 1917, at the instigation of Austria, that would have "left the Central Powers in possession of their plunder." This was the same Pope, too, that the *Masonic Chronicle* had charged with having a complete understanding with the Kaiser, according to an article reprinted by Mr. Sherman. There was nothing in the article to indicate opposition of the Masonic order to the League of Nations, but perhaps opposition from that great fraternity might be aroused.

The whole appeal would, of course, fail with informed people, but to countless others who were sensitive on the subject of papal power it would give a suspicion of danger in the League even if his inferences were not wholly accepted—as they would be by many. Not all, either, would see the incongruity of making the Scotch-Presbyterian President, who was founding a League of Nations around the city of John Calvin, the ally of the Pope.

THE LINES TIGHTENED

By June 21 it became evident that the Knox resolution could not be passed. Several Republicans refused to vote for it, enough, with the Senate evenly balanced, to defeat it. On the same day former Secretary Elihu Root appeared in the Senate wing of the Capitol and told the newspaper reporters that he had come "in expectation of getting an invitation to luncheon from some Senatorial friends." He got it. [37]

Reservations Advised by Root. The result was a change of tactics indicated by the publication the next day of a letter from Mr. Root to Mr. Lodge in which he advised dealing with the defects of the Covenant in a qualifying resolution of ratification. After commending the Covenant at length as containing "a great deal of high value that the world ought not to lose" he advised (1) that consent to Article 10 be refused, (2) that no qualification on the right of withdrawal be accepted and (3) that nothing in the Covenant "shall be construed as to imply a relinquishment by the United States of America of its traditional attitude toward purely American questions, or to require the submission of its policy regarding questions which it deems to be purely American questions to the decision or recommendation of other powers"—to cover the Monroe Doctrine and domestic questions more acceptably. [38]

The proposed resolution of ratification was to go into effect unless some of the other signatories of the treaty expressly objected. Silence

[37] *New York Times,* June 21, 1919.
[38] The difficulty of securing perfect words that will satisfy everybody has been brought out by Miller in examining these "stilted and obscure" phrases handed down from the First Hague Conference, and by now almost as sacred as the Monroe Doctrine itself to many. He objects that our foreign policy is based upon common sense, not upon a "traditional attitude," and that whenever we attempt to assert even the principle of the Monroe Doctrine the matter ceases at once to be "purely American." Miller, *The Drafting of the Covenant,* Vol. I, p. 381.
How, indeed, can any issue with any foreign country be "purely American," even though it arise out of a "domestic" question?

was to give consent. [39] It was received favorably by the opponents of the League as offering a way from the Knox resolution and by others as a moderate method of perfecting the Covenant. Senator Lodge announced, on June 23, that the Knox resolution would not be pressed because it might interfere with the passage of the appropriation bills. These would go through on time if the Senate had to sit night and day to do it. The radicals, however, thought that any reservations would be futile because the League Council would finally interpret them. Others believed that the elimination of Article 10 would throw the whole matter back into negotiation. [40]

On June 25 it was reported that the Knox-Lodge group had agreed with the Borah-Johnson faction to require the express acceptance of the reservations by all the allied signatories and to press the resolution introduced by Senator Fall, declaring peace by resolution, in advance of receiving the treaty. The Committee on Foreign Relations decided the next day, however, to let this resolution rest also. [41] It began to look as if the President would at least be allowed to submit the treaty to the Senate before final action on it was taken.

Chairman Hays, of the Republican National Committee, in Washington to attempt to reconcile the views of the various Republican groups, declared unhesitatingly to the newspaper men that he was for "a league of nations" and conveyed the same impression to the Senators. The country seemed to want it, he said, and conditions of unrest throughout the world argued for it. It did not appear, however, that Mr. Hays was successful in compromising the various views, particularly when Senator Borah strode into Senator Lodge's office and demanded to know why the Chairman was in town. [42]

On June 28, the Germans signed the treaty and the President issued an address to the American people in which he commended it to them as a great charter for a new order of affairs in the world. On the 27th, however, he had been reported by the Associated Press as opposed to amendments to the treaty for the reason "that if any one power seeks to make amendments then the war will not be over until every one of the twenty-one associated nations learns the results of the amendments. This can only be done through processes of negotiation and it is held that it would be a hopeless process of delay in restoring peace. It is also held that the effect of the amendments

[39] New York Times, June 22, 1919.
[40] New York Times, June 23, 1919.
[41] New York Times, June 25, 26, 1919.
[42] New York Times, June 27, 1919.

would be to keep the United States out of the treaty and out of the League." [43]

The President Opposed to Further Amendment. The President's viewpoint as to American changes in the treaty will not seem wholly strange or unreasonable to readers of the whole story in later years. He had steadily opposed changes in the treaty proper urged by Lloyd George during the last weeks of the Conference, changes of provisions which he had himself opposed earlier when Clemenceau and Lloyd George insisted on them—before the latter became alarmed as to the consequences—because he felt that the interminable business of altering or arguing decisions must some time stop. [44] To be faced then with a new prospect of indefinite negotiation and uncertainty arising from changes proposed by the Senate was the last thing he could be expected to desire. He knew as no one else did the difficulties that ensued while men were face to face, when a clause was reopened and the favor of changes asked. What would be the difficulty when diplomatic distances again intervened?

Moreover, he had spent himself to the limit to secure changes in the Covenant to satisfy the demands of his opponents and had sacrificed much to get them, only to have the amendments brushed aside as inadequate and still others demanded. Surely there must be a time with the Senate, as in the Conference, when negotiation and alteration would have to cease and the treaty be accepted or rejected. Certainly to one who was utterly weary from labors such as few men had ever performed, the prospect of seeing his work whittled away by his enemies could not seem attractive.

Senate Republicans United for Revision. As Senator Lenroot said, though perhaps from a different viewpoint, it was "the natural request for the President to make." Yet it seems to have unified completely the Republicans in the Senate behind the program of amendment by reservation. On the day after the publication of the President's statement the correspondent of the *New York Times* could not find a single Republican Senator who did not agree that changes in the Covenant would be necessary. He searched high and low and interviewed many but could not find one who did not maintain that there must be reservations. [45] After all the outcry of liberties endangered it was

[43] *Ibid.*, June 28. Presidential circles were reported to hold that the Root reservations were equivalent to amendment. Senator Lodge had also said, on June 21, that "One is as effective as the other." *New York Times*, June 22, 1919.

[44] *New York Times*, June 28, 1919.

[45] *Ibid.*, June 29, 1919.

simply incredible to them that they should do nothing directly to the Covenant. They must change or withhold acceptance to a few articles, at least, in order to justify all the commotion. Moreover, the idea of allowing the greatest treaty ever laid before it to go through the Senate without any changes being made in it was wholly unthinkable; the Senate had always amended important treaties. This one in particular had to be "Americanized."

Furthermore, the President had to stop telling the Senators what to do and what not to do. He had been doing that for six years and most of the time they had been compelled to obey, but it had irked many Democratic members of Congress as much as it had the Republicans. He had never cultivated them and as a result he had few warm friends in either House. "Weakness in personal contacts," as Professor Merriam has explained, "was one of the characteristics of the Wilsonian leadership. He produced an impression of coldness and aloofness, intensified by his limited number of contacts. Among his intimates a charming and delightful person, he was unable to project this picture on a larger scale, and appear as the genial friend of the people in general. In reality he did not possess the necessary strength and vigor for frequent contacts and conferences such as Roosevelt delighted in. They seemed to weary him, and he was obliged to choose between seeing many people and having no strength left for problems of state, or seeing few persons and reserving his powers for statecraft. He chose the latter course with the inevitable result that he acquired a reputation for exclusiveness and coldness. He himself realized this situation and discusses it keenly in his charming essay *On Being Human*. He did not in fact lack human sympathy, but strength for personal contacts." [46]

Maybe he had dominated the Peace Conference—maybe it hoodwinked him—there was disagreement about that, but he had intimated that the first draft of the Covenant would be very difficult to revise and now he was saying that the revised Covenant couldn't be amended. He would see! Moderate members of the opposition felt that they were not going to do any signing on the dotted line; the leaders knew that they were not. Their eight months' campaign against the President's effort to found a League of Nations was not going to stop when the treaty achieving his aim was laid before the Senate.

The President Coming Home. So, on June 29, the day after the signing of the treaty, the President sailed home to meet a more bitter

[46] C. E. Merriam, *Four American Party Leaders*, N. Y., 1926, pp. 54-5.

and implacable opposition than he had encountered in Paris—an opposition in which all the concentrated racial and personal and political hatreds engendered during the war, and his term preceding it, would be expressed. As he embarked, a meeting in Carnegie Hall addressed by a Democrat and a Republican, Senators Reed and Johnson, hissed his name and applauded a man who shouted that Wilson was a traitor. The two Senators were cheered as they painted the President's greatest achievement wicked and dangerous—more immoral than the Holy Alliance.[47]

"No human being, it seems," says David Lawrence, who observed the President through the Peace Conference, "could have survived the mental strain which rested upon Woodrow Wilson during the Peace Conference."[48] How far could he go against the bitter opposition organized against him at home and reinforced by the disappointments of powerful racial minorities in the United States with the results of the War and of the Conference?

[47] *New York Times,* June 28, 1919.
[48] David Lawrence, *The True Story of Wilson,* p. 267.
Another observer of the President at the Conference says that in the six months he spent in Paris hardly a moment of liberty had been his. Day after day he had most momentous decisions to make, the consequences of which might persist for generations to come. "When he was not in conference with other peace commissioners and subsidiary bodies of the Peace Conference he was counselling his experts, investigators and advisers; time and again he gave ear to unofficial delegations that came to plead their cause before him. There were formal bodies to address, and calls of state and courtesy to be made. Even on those few occasions when he enjoyed a drive over the boulevards of Paris his mind was busy." Hansen, *The Adventures of the Fourteen Points,* p. 361.

CHAPTER IX

THE TREATY BEFORE THE SENATE

As the President sailed home, the *New York Tribune,* the leading Republican newspaper, hoped, on July 1, that he would return prepared to let the Senate do something to the Treaty—that there would be "an abandonment of all attempt to deny to the Senate any real participation. Half the trouble the covenant has met has been because it has been presented as it was not, and the other half because the President would not counsel with his constitutional advisers. If representatives of the Senate had been members of the peace commission as heretofore, or if Senators had not heard themselves characterized as men of pigmy minds, a satisfactory adjustment might have been reached long ago."

"The country," concluded the *Tribune,* "had indicated its desire to join a league of nations; it has indicated that it deems the covenant as of sufficient value to warrant its ratification; it has also indicated it regards it as highly important to clear up all ambiguities as to what it is we pledge ourselves to do."

On July 3, Carter Field reported from Washington to the *Tribune* that the Senate would not hold any executive sessions on the Treaty. The Republican members were hotly opposed to any secret sessions of the Senate whatever. The sessions of the Foreign Relations Committee when it considered the Treaty and the Covenant, however, would all be executive.

On July 4, the text of the treaty with France, guaranteeing her against any unprovoked assault by Germany until the Council of the League should decide by a majority vote that the League offered sufficient protection to France, was published. The *Tribune* heartily favored this treaty.

On July 8, its Washington correspondent reported that it would be presented to the Senate in advance of the Treaty of Versailles. Senators were determined to probe deeply into the reported differences between the President and Secretary Lansing; and Senator Knox reiterated his intention of forcing a vote to separate the Covenant from the Treaty, in order to give more time for the consideration of the League.

An additional note in the day's news was the ratification of the Covenant by the Argentine Senate. The vote had been unanimous, and there had been no reservations or amendments. After all the din which had issued from Washington no Argentine Senator feared that he was voting away the right of the legislature to declare war, and none appeared alarmed at the propect of sending Argentine boys into all the fever zones of the world on bloody police errands. Were all the statesmen of Argentina devoid of the intelligence and imagination which animated Senators Knox and Lodge? [1]

The developments on July 9 included the arrival of the President in New York and a dispatch from Washington saying that the Senate was strongly opposed to considering the French treaty first. Also: "Indications that the Pacific Coast, until now one of the strongest sections of the country in favor of the league of nations, was beginning to get anxious about the necessity of a reservation safeguarding American control over immigration were welcomed by League opponents." [2]

The President's Reception in New York. The President's reception, as reported by the *Tribune,* was as hearty as he could have wished. He was treated to all the pomp the Navy and officialdom could offer, but "the greetings that seemed to mean most to him were the shouts and cheers of thousands of countrymen who lined the streets through which his automobile passed on the way to Carnegie Hall," where a crowd had been waiting for him three hours. "The enthusiasm of the crowds which came to greet him brought President Wilson to his feet a short distance from the Twenty-third Street ferry and did not allow him to take his seat again. . . . To the shouting, flag waving crowd it was not only the President coming home, it was the crowning incident of the war. For him they let loose the cheers that were suppressed on the day of the signing of the peace treaty. They saw in him the symbol of the victory and the peace, therefore the children shouted and white haired women leaned from the boarding

[1] George Harvey, who had been supporting the two with extravagant adulation, now plead, as the President started home, for "Calmness, Vigilance, Resolution." *Harvey's Weekly,* No. 26, June 28, No. 27, July 5.
[2] *New York Tribune,* July 9, 1919.

house windows with tears streaming down their cheeks to throw him a 'God bless you,' and soldiers in khaki straightened up with a salute which said they, too, had done their part to bring this day. Experienced persons said there had never been a demonstration like it.

"But the shouts and cheers of West Twenty-third Street and Fifth Avenue were as nothing to the prolonged din that came from nearly four thousand throats as he entered Carnegie Hall. The greatest demonstration, in strength and volume came when he stood on the platform of Carnegie Hall and earnestly declared that the peace concluded in Paris was 'a just peace which, if it can be preserved, will safeguard the world from unnecessary bloodshed.'

"The speech at Carnegie Hall was short, and the only recognition the President gave his opponents was when he said: 'I am afraid some people, some persons, do not understand that vision. They do not see it. They have looked too much upon the ground. They have thought too much of the interests that were near them, and they have not listened to the voices of their neighbors. I have never had a moment's doubt as to where the heart and purpose of this people lay.'

"There was another mighty roar of approval when that short talk was finished and Mr. Wilson was nearly overwhelmed by the rush of persons on the platform who sought to shake his hand or touch his coat."

The sincerity of the President's belief that the American people and all peoples everywhere wanted a better ordered world in which there would be some safeguard against war has been little questioned, though the extent to which he actually did represent American and world opinion has been much argued.

The Irish Revolt. But certainly he did not represent the Irish. While the Senators were condemning the President for creating a League which might consider domestic questions, the Irish were lambasting him for not wading into the British Philippine Islands and forcing an ally to grant the Irish independence. They had taken the doctrine of self determination to heart and were not disposed to recognize any limitations in its application. The President had not forced the independence of Ireland and her admission to the League, therefore away with both. Irish nationalism might be denied in Dublin and Paris; it would have its day in New York and Washington. Mr. De Valera might be a hunted rebel in Cork, but he was acclaimed as ruler in New York, two evenings after the President's return, by a crowd of 25,000, only 15,000 of whom could get into Madison Square Garden to hail him.

Escorted to the platform by fifty officers of the old 69th Infantry and as many Roman Catholic priests, Mr. De Valera heard the name of President Wilson frequently mentioned and hissed almost as loudly as his own was cheered.

Father Francis P. Duffey, wearing the uniform of a United States army chaplain, was the first to mention the President's name. He waited until the crowd had finished its jeering, but a little later when one reckless individual hissed the name of Archbishop Hayes he stopped in amazement and threatened to "turn loose about 500 boys of the 69th that I've got here." Thereafter there were hisses and boos only at each mention of the name of the President of the United States, the League of Nations, England and Sir Douglas Haig. [3]

THE TREATY LAID BEFORE THE SENATE

On July 10, the day following his return, the President laid the Treaty before the Senate. The address which accompanied its presentation was an attempt to explain again the nature and necessity of the basic settlements, and of the League in particular. He deemed it impossible to summarize or construe its manifold provisions in an address and suggested to the gentlemen who had been so long and so audibly groping in the dark that they had been daily cognizant of what was going on, as to be sure they had, for each crisis in the Conference had been mirrored in the American Press with a good deal of accuracy.

He expressed a desire, however, to give what additional informa-

[3] *New York Tribune,* July 11, 1919. Senator Johnson also spoke to a Boston audience, on July 8, which hissed Wilson's name. A "local celebrity," presided over this meeting of the League for the Preservation of American Independence; in Providence none could be found who would take the chair. In his address Johnson went so far as to say of Article 10 that "Under this article the British Empire can demand American blood to subdue Ireland." Perhaps a little more pardonable was the statement of a Boston physician, Dr. F. P. McCarthy, on July 7, that "This article makes it impossible for any nation subject to British rule to gain its independence. By it Ireland is to be in perpetual slavery."—The *Boston Herald,* July 8 and 9, 1919.

Irish partisans could hardly foresee that within the next decade the principle of self determination would win virtual independence for Ireland and Egypt and make great strides toward self government for India.

The *Herald's* description of the President's reception in New York was as vivid as that quoted above from the *New York Tribune.* Cheering thousands filled every available window, roof and sidewalk along the three mile route. In Carnegie Hall, after one great ovation as he entered, the national anthem was drowned in cheers as he arose to speak and the audience "refused to resume their seats until the President had signalled several times for silence."

tion he could, saying: "My services and all the information I possess will be at your disposal and at the disposal of your Committee on Foreign Relations at any time, either informally or in session, as you may prefer; and I hope that you will not hesitate to make use of them." [4]

The basis of our entry into the war and the part we played in it reviewed, the maze of secret treaties which appeared and the political reconstruction necessary in the larger half of Europe were described. It had not been easy to graft the new order of ideas on the old, and some of the fruits of the grafting might, he feared, for a time be bitter. Yet there had been opportunity to throw safeguards about the rights of racial, national, and religious minorities by solemn international covenant, to limit and regulate military establishments where they were most likely to be mischievous, to effect a complete and systematic internationalization of waterways and railways which were necessary to the economic life of more than one nation, to clear many of the normal channels of commerce of unfair obstructions of law or privilege and to secure for labor the concerted protection of definite international pledges of principle and practice.

The remainder of the address was an exposition of the development in the Conference of the League as a practical necessity and of the rôle of the American representatives. He closed by picturing the part which he would have his country play in the future. America had reached her majority as a world power. We had proved to the world in redeeming the pledges given in the Spanish War, and by our part in the World War, that we could be trusted. Weak peoples everywhere looked to us for guidance or protection. There could be no question of our ceasing to be a world power. The only question was whether we could refuse the moral leadership that was offered us, whether we would accept or reject the confidence of the world.

Our part in the war had established our position among the nations and nothing but our own mistaken action could alter it. The whole world had seen a great ideal asserted and vindicated by a nation they had deemed to be materialistic. They had seen in us the spiritual forces that must free men of every nation from unworthy bondage. "The stage is set," he said in conclusion, "the destiny disclosed. It has come about by no plan of our conceiving; but by the

[4] Further reflection seems to have suggested that it would not be wise to be "called" before a Congressional committee at the Capitol for when the invitation was renewed a few days later, the Senators were invited to the White House. *New York Tribune*, July 15, 1919.

hand of God who led us into this way. We cannot turn back. We can only go forward, with lifted eyes and freshened spirit to follow the vision. It was of this that we dreamed at our birth. America shall in truth show the way. The light streams upon the path ahead, and nowhere else." [5]

No Light for Republican Senators. The President's address, however, did not give the Republican Senators any light. They had joined heartily in applauding the President as he entered, but at the conclusion of the message the *Tribune's* correspondent observed that three Republican Senators, McNary, McCumber and Kenyon, clapped mildly. The others sat or stood silent. In statements afterwards, Senator Capper said, "It was merely a pleasant address"; Senator Norris, "A fine lot of glittering generalities"; Senator Spencer, "A most scholarly and general review of general conditions"; Senator Smoot, "Another Wilsonian essay, but not up to the standard"; Senator McCormick, "Soothing, mellifluous and uninformative"; Senator Brandegee, "Soap bubbles of oratory and soufflé of phrases." Senator Newberry was interested in the President's English, but disappointed in his advice; Senator Fall thought he had exhausted every argument for the League of Nations; in Senator Harding's opinion "it was utterly lacking in ringing Americanism. What the President said about America's moral leadership I thoroughly approve, but I do not regard it as necessary to write leadership into a covenant such as the proposed league of nations." [6]

All the Republican Senators united in deploring that the President did not answer the specific objections they had agreed to press against the League, and many Republican newspapers were similarly disappointed. After they had agreed upon four or five reservations to the Covenant, the President did not mention one of them. In fact he did not even allude to the subject of reservations, or suggest that such a thing was feasible. They felt that their specific attacks should have been recognized by reply; he wished to do nothing to dignify the thing he wanted to avoid.

The President's Attitude. He had explained to the press in the forenoon that reservations "presented a grave difficulty in that every nation joining the league would have to assent to them, and while this slow process was going on the United States would be at war with Germany." He believed that "even what seemed to be innocuous amend-

[5] Shaw, *Messages and Papers of Woodrow Wilson*, Vol. 2, pp. 698-712.
[6] *New York Tribune*, July 11, 1919.

ments or reservations may cause great trouble, since it can never be
stated that other nations will view a point as this country would.
There were occasions at Paris when every other nation took a view
opposite to the American commissioners."

This danger was scouted by his opponents throughout, and at
times their assumption that the signatories would accept us on our
own terms seemed substantiated. Yet to one who had felt—even
suffered—through months of negotiation the difficulty of securing
wide agreement to stipulations which seemed to be incontestably just
and advisable, the certainty of acceptance could not be so great.

The President's views regarding Shantung, Article 10 and the
Monroe Doctrine were explained in the same interview. On the subject of Article 10 the *Tribune* reported that "The President believes
that the League would be merely a debating society if Article 10
were eliminated. He does not think, however, that the League could
force the United States to go to war. On the contrary it was necessary
for him, as well as for the representatives of Brazil and certain other
republics, to point out time and again that they could not pledge their
countries to go to war in advance. The league, he believes, can only
propose military offensive measures after the commercial boycott has
been put into effect."

Opposition War Councils. After the President's address to the
Senate, Republican leaders conferred in the cloak room. "Those attending included Senators Lodge, Borah, Brandegee, Fall and McCormick." [7] The Treaty of Peace for which the Senators had been so
impatient had at last been signed and laid before the Senate for its
approval. Immediately Senator Lodge went into conference with the
leaders of the group of men who were to prevent the ratification
of the treaty, either with reservations or without, by voting first on one
side and then on the other.

Further conferences were held in rapid succession during the next
few days. Carter Field's dispatch of July 12 announced that "Republican members of the Senate Foreign Relations Committee, at a
meeting tonight discussed plans for their fight on the peace treaty
and the league of nations." The next day he reported that "the Republican lines were consolidated in a dozen scattered conferences
today at the houses of various Senate leaders." [8] Senator Gore, Democrat, of Oklahoma, had visited Senator Lodge and announced his ad-

[7] *New York Tribune,* July 11, 1919.
[8] *New York Tribune,* July 14, 1919.

hesion to the reservation program so that the reservationists now had a majority of the Senate.

An Appeal for Declaratory Reservations. Editorially, the *Tribune* argued powerfully on July 12 for ratification with reservations. Declaring that "the desirability and the need of a league of nations are not under debate, and attempts to make the contrary appear are deceptive," the *Tribune* quoted a long line of Republican leaders who had been conspicuous in the creation of a new international order. Congress in 1916 had by nearly unanimous vote authorized the President to invite the nations to a conference to consider organized peace. The New York Republican convention of 1918 had declared for the creation of a league and our entry therein. "If the question were now submitted, no major party, and probably no minor one would uphold the negative."

Neither was the desirability of adhering to the Covenant itself apparently under debate. A majority of the Senate was for it. The real argument was over what interpretative reservations were required; yet there was substantial agreement among the critics of the Covenant here. The defenders of the Covenant maintained that the things proposed in the reservations were already clearly implied. Then why not accept? We could confidently expect the tacit consent of all the powers to the reservations. They had so consented to our reservations to the Hague and Algeciras treaties.

No formalities even would be required. "Reservations by us do not require other countries to accept them as the true ones—they are merely binding on our courts and set forth the way we understand the covenant. . . . The league would function under one kind of ratification as well as under the other. The only difference would be that our people and the world would know our attitude toward attempts to interpret the covenant as confiding control of our destiny to alien hands." [9]

The Treaty a Contract. If the matter were as simple as this surely it would be a tragedy if agreement could not be reached. The weakness in the argument centered in the fact that the treaty was a contract of the first importance to which unilateral interpretations could not be so easily set up. A separate resolution embodying the reservations and publishing to the world the interpretations which we put on the

---

[*] On July 15, the *Tribune* called for action on the Treaty in "July, not October." The discussion had gone on for eight months. Not much new remained to be said. It would be as easy to decide now as three months hence.

Covenant would not impair the force of the contract and probably would not even arouse protests from the other contracting parties, though if several powers issued separate declarations construing the provisions of the Covenant various ways, in advance of its application, the chances for future friction would be obvious.

Such a separate declaration would, moreover, never satisfy Senator Lodge and his lieutenants. They either were obsessed with a desire to alter directly and visibly parts of the Covenant's anatomy for the sake of the personal pleasure and political profits to be gained from the operation, or they were deeply distressed by the fear that their patrimony was being filched from them. In either case, they could hardly be expected to be satisfied with action which merely advertised their fears further without binding the other contracting parties. Such an ending to all the alarums which had been sounded without ceasing for eight months would be bordering too near the comic. The Senators had made the woods ring with cries of "Wolf! Wolf!" so long that when the President's lamb was at last in their hands only the most powerful intervention could save it from at least being marked by their weapons.

The difficulty of depending on tacit consent to effect reservations in the present instance was brought out in a debate between Senator Pittman of Nevada and Senator Kellogg of Minnesota which followed the speech of Senator Swanson on July 14. Senator Kellogg readily admitted that "a contract cannot be changed by reservation or amendment without the consent of the other party to the contract," and that such change "must be directly or tacitly accepted by that country."

Then, replied Senator Pittman, "there is not a reservation or an amendment that we can place on this treaty that does not necessitate a renegotiation and reconsideration by every contracting power." We might not think that a change of language constituted any change of substance "yet no matter what the change is, the other contracting parties must agree, as we agree, that it does not change the substance of the contract or that such change is agreeable. Otherwise it is not a contract."

Senator Fall contended that if the amended treaty were deposited in Paris and acted upon by the other parties it would be binding on them, to which Senator Pittman replied that the matter was of too vital importance to this country, as well as to the rest of the world, for us to have anything but a definite understanding. We were not going to be bound by the treaty until we knew that the other nations to whom we assumed obligations were also bound. There was only one way to know, not by silence, not by lapse of time, not by mailing it to somebody, not by depositing it somewhere, but by open notorious assent to any changes that we made. The country would not stand for any arrangement which would enable other nations obligated to us under the treaty to arise when they saw fit and say, "We have never consented to such a change; we have never done anything that would bind us to such a change." If implied assent were relied on, what would constitute acting under the treaty? What acts would constitute an acceptance of the benefits of the treaty? And in the meantime what protection would our country have under the treaty? [10]

SENATOR SWANSON'S OPENING SPEECH

What would under normal circumstances have been the opening speech in the entire debate on the Treaty was made by Senator Swanson, of Virginia, on July 14, previous to the debate just quoted. In a speech filling ten pages of the *Record* he attempted to analyze the essential features of the Covenant and the objections raised against it. He believed no legislative body had ever before had dependent on its conclusions such important and far reaching consequences. Our social order itself had been shaken to its very foundations. Another such war bade fair to establish the rule of brute force and send us into a new Dark Age. Honor, prudence, self-interest and national prestige —invaluable assets—all demanded that we participate in the settlement of the disturbance of the world caused by a war in which we were one of the chief participants.

Laying aside all considerations except self-interest, our interests and commerce were so varied, so vast, permeating every quarter of the globe, that in the future it would be almost impossible for us to escape world embroilments. Prudence and wisdom demanded that we should be present to extinguish the embers that produce flames, and to see that flames, if started, did not become world conflagrations that would envelop us.

The Deterrent Power of Article 10. The guarantee by Article 10 of territorial integrity and independence against external aggression would act as a preventive of war as it was intended, not as a cause

[10] *Congressional Record,* Vol. 58, Pt. 3, pp. 2543–45. After Senator Fall had suggested that the President would be compelled to accept some things, and had condemned Senator Pittman for presuming to speak for the country, he closed the debate by insinuating strongly that somebody was getting some Carnegie Peace Foundation money.

of wars as the critics maintained. This guaranty made by four-fifths of the world including the dominant military and naval powers would be sufficient without the use of force to insure the peace of the world. "Reckless, indeed, would be that nation which would issue a challenge of defiance to so powerful a league and embark on the venturesome enterprise of conquest. Any nation would realize that it had more to lose than to gain by so dangerous an undertaking."

What had occurred under the Monroe Doctrine furnished convincing proof of this contention. The declaration of one lone power that it would protect from external aggression the territorial integrity and independence of all the nations in this hemisphere had been effective for a century without a single use of force. The British Navy, he might have explained, had enforced the Doctrine for many years, and it was true that we had been ready to use force against the French in Mexico, yet, as he pointed out, we had lately asserted it against the greatest powers, Germany and Great Britain, in Venezuela. If one nation had been able to make this doctrine effective for two continents without war was it not reasonable to suppose that the solemn guarantee of this powerful league would be even more effective? [11]

Its Defensive Value to Us. Moreover, the obligation of Article 10 was not one sided as was being assumed. Our own territorial integrity was protected by it. This fact simplified the immensely difficult problem of Philippine defense which had occasioned us great apprehension in the past, and at the same time offered a solution of the dangers inherent in carrying out our promise of independence for the Filipinos. The defense of the Panama Canal was even more vital to us and might be proportionately difficult and costly.

Its Authority Moral, Not Legal. Powerful as Article 10 would be as a deterrent against wars of conquest, each member of the League kept its right of judgment as to when and how the obligation should be enforced. The Council had power to advise what action it felt was necessary to enforce the guarantee; it had no power to issue an order

---

[11] It might have been replied that the certainty of the guaranty being swiftly upheld by force, if necessary, would not be as great in the case of the League. This would no doubt be true. Yet a deterrent of tremendous power was there and will be there in the future, in spite of the fact that the Senate's rejection of it robbed it of most of its force for the present years. One outstanding assertion of the vitality of the guaranty by the League in the future will be enough to serve its purposes for many a day—if even one assertion is necessary. Nor is it essential that the assertion be swift and unequivocal. The knowledge that the public opinion of the world will harden during a war enough to enforce the rule against the nation it has decided to be the aggressor may well be sufficient. But much more definite means of determining the aggressor than Article 10 provided may be expected.

Permission—Keystone View Co.

GILBERT M. HITCHCOCK
OF NEBRASKA

Permission—Underwood & Underwood

CLAUDE A. SWANSON
OF VIRGINIA

Permission—Underwood & Underwood

KEY PITTMAN
OF NEVADA

Permission—International News Photos, Inc.

JOHN SHARP WILLIAMS
OF MISSISSIPPI

THE LEAGUE LEADERS—DEMOCRATIC

legally binding. Law never advised action; it issued court decrees which became operative without the use of any discretion on the part of those affected.

The Council had no such power. Its advice could not even be given without the consent of our representative on it, and once given, it could not be carried out on our part without the consent of Congress. In acting on the advice of the Council, Congress would be bound by its own sense of honor and fair dealing. That was a great deal, but it left us a wide field of discretion as to the extent of our duty in the given circumstances, and as to how it should be fulfilled. No super tribunal was set up to issue dictatorial commands to us. [12]

Was There any Power in a Moral Commitment? The reply of the opponents of the Covenant to this statement of the case would be, of course, that if the League was not a dangerous super-power it was an innocuous farce. If it had only power to advise, each member would act solely as its self interest dictated, and nothing would be gained. Yet flying to the opposite conclusion ignored the facts that nations do habitually fulfill their obligations in the vast majority of instances, that the sense of international responsibility has been developing at an accelerated rate for centuries and that national pride itself is closely bound up with the honorable fulfillment of responsibilities assumed. That nations here and there would sometimes refuse to assume their proper responsibility in preventing an international raid from succeeding would undoubtedly be true. The latitude of discretion allowed would permit that, yet it would by no means follow that such action would be the rule. A narrow idea of self interest would sometimes give a restricted view of the action which a nation should take under the advice of the Council; an enlightened conception of self interest would more often lead to upholding the rules of order and security among nations. The War had proved, to anyone who would permit himself to see, that incalculable and widespread loss was likely to result at any time from the failure of collective action in an international crisis. It might be true enough that the mass of the American people, having been wounded so little by the war, might soon forget, but surely their statesmen would not. And surely, responsible leaders everywhere in the lands that had been bled white might be expected to remember.

If this was too much to expect, then no progress toward peace and security could be made. We could only wait for the next cataclysm

[12] *Congressional Record,* Vol. 58, Pt. 3, pp. 2532–42.

to overturn the whole social order in territories wider perhaps than Russia.

A Documentary Debate

Yet it is a matter of plain record that many of the Covenant's opponents absolutely ruled out the fact of the Great War and the terrific impact of its lessons. For them the war simply had not happened. It did not exist as a mountain of fact to be dealt with. Usually the implications of the war were silently overlooked, simply ignored, but occasionally they were disposed of consciously.

Humanity not Concerned. Thus a noted Pennsylvania lawyer, quoted in the *Congressional Record* on July 15 by Senator Knox, said: "The reasons put forward for the adoption of the League, or for the entrance of this country into the League, of the smallness of the world, of the cause of humanity, of the horrors of war do not seem to me to touch the question at all. The history of this country has not been one of oppression or of over-armament nor of seeking quarrels either on this continent or beyond the sea. . . . What possible call of humanity is there to lead us to undertake to constitute a part of the police force to guard the other side of the world?" It was perfectly apparent that the nations of the Old World, if they were of united purpose, could so make common cause against aggressive warfare that it would "cease even to be contemplated." [13]

Overlooking the assumption that the possible invocation of Article 10 was the same as policing the world—and the further assumption that its application need send us to the ends of the earth—there was not the slightest suggestion of any wisdom in our taking action to prevent or limit warfare. The sending of two million men overseas, a quarter million of whom became casualities, the spending of twenty-five billion dollars in two years, these little items in the case were not even suggested. It was even actually assumed that of course the thing to do both for us and for the world was to wait till the next catastrophe burst and then settle it for them. "But if, *unlikely as it may be,* (Italics mine) the cause of humanity (or of self interest?) ever should beckon us to give assistance to the peoples of the Old World, that assistance can be given when the time comes as readily and strongly as it has been done in the past. . . ." (Then followed an assumption that the League was to regulate and inspect all our soldiers,

[13] *Ibid.,* pp. 2581–83.

ships and armament.) Everything was to be argued from American history, and the fact that we had fought in every world war from the settlement of Virginia to date was accepted as the natural and desirable order of things.

The Representative Principle Would Break Down in the League. This gentleman evaluated the Assembly of the League as "its paramount body." Another distinguished member of the Pennsylvania bar, Mr. George Wharton Pepper, read into the *Record* the same day by Senator Frelinghuysen, was of the opinion, on the other hand, that "the so called assembly is a clumsy and superfluous institution. One doubts whether it will ever meet." [14] The best legal minds did not agree as to where the chief danger lay, but each could find a new one. In Mr. Pepper's case it was the inability of the nation to be represented in international affairs by one man. President Wilson had attempted "the absolutely impossible task of interpreting and expressing the mind and will of his fellow countrymen." Neither could any one individual sitting on the Council of the League represent the nation. If chosen by the President alone the danger would be at its maximum. "But if chosen by the Congress, or even by popular vote, he will still be placed in an impossible position with his own constituents the very first time a great world question comes before the Council for decision. When he undertakes to tell the Council and the world how the United States votes on the question at issue he will necessarily arouse the resentment and even the passion of millions of our own people."

Three Simple Amendments. Mr. Pepper also saw a delegation of sovereignty to the League and offered "three simple amendments" which would "transform the League from a war league to a peace league." The three amendments were:

First. Strike out the covenant which now binds member States to accept the action of the council or assembly and transform those bodies into useful international councils of conciliation.

Second. Create a court of international justice with a compulsory jurisdiction over all justiciable disputes.

Third. Eliminate from the covenant the blanket guarantees of Article 10 and incorporate in the treaty such definite and specific guarantees by the United States and other league members as are requisite to make the treaty settlements actually effective.

The extent to which these simple amendments would have altered the whole conception of the League will be readily apparent. On the

[14] *Congressional Record,* Vol. 58, Pt. 3, pp. 2581-2.

one hand the existing bodies of the League would have been reduced to mere "councils of conciliation" and a new judicial branch invested with a compulsory jurisdiction that the nationalistic opponents of the Covenant would have been the first to cry out against. A wholly different kind of league would have been created by these simple changes. But whatever happened there had to be amendments! "It will not do," said Mr. Pepper, "to refuse to make amendments on the ground that the evils at which they are aimed do not exist. The answer is that multitudes of wise, intelligent, and patriotic citizens actually perceive these grave elements of danger in the document. No group of men should indulge pride of intellect to the extent of declaring that there is only one side to the questions which I have been discussing. The alleged mechanical difficulties in the way of making amendments are purely imaginary. The document can be readily amended if people are in earnest about it."[15]

If all the dangers which were being shown to the "multitudes of wise, intelligent and patriotic citizens" by the opponents of the Covenant could have been eliminated by amendment, how much less than nothing would have remained!

Mr. Taft's View of the Consequences of Reservations. The probability that all the signatory nations would accept without negotiation such reservations on our part as that refusing to consent to Article 10 was discussed by Taft in an article printed in the same issue of the *Record*. The deep anxiety of France to strengthen the article rather than weaken it was cited as clear evidence that France would seriously object to the elimination of Article 10. Moreover, he continued, other and smaller nations would probably object. The importance of the article in the whole plan of the League was manifest. It was the inducement by which the weaker nations were brought into the League. It was the chief protection which the League offered them. The fact that the United States, with its great prestige, its disinterestedness, and its moral influence, as well as its military potentiality, was under the obligation of Article 10 constituted its great cautionary and miniatory effect, making it powerful as an agency in restraining wars of conquest. The nations great and small, therefore, would not pass over such an amendment lightly, but would naturally insist on a reëxamination of the whole Covenant when its character was thus materially changed.

Was the Hyphen to Control? The former President thought also

---

[15] *Congressional Record*, Vol. 58, Pt. 3, p. 2581.

that Mr. Root's argument that we should refuse to consent to Article 10 because some of our foreign born citizens might object to our helping to discipline their native countries was a curious one, in view of the lessons of the war just ended. Nothing had been more bitter than the denunciation of divided loyalty during the war. Should we now officially recognize and acquiesce in the generally condemned hyphenated Americanism? Was the Americanization campaign to fail? And must the continuance of this evil deter us from a course of world usefulness, from doing our duty and sharing the burden of the world in maintaining peace? [16]

Some Questions Asked by the Republican Publicity Association. Such questions were of no interest to the Republican Publicity Association, which on the same day called for investigation of a dozen questions, of which the first was whether Mr. Wilson was the author of Article 10. This question was being strongly pressed at the time. Familiarity with his utterances gave plenty of proof that he was closely identified with it, but the public had not been generally appraised of the fact. Bringing out this connection would concentrate a good deal of anti-Wilson hostility on the Covenant.

Other questions asked why Mr. Wilson insisted that the absurd language of Article 21 protected the Monroe Doctrine, why the British Empire had six votes, why it got four-fifths of the mandated territories, where Mr. Wilson got his authority to issue what amounted to an appeal to the Italian people to overthrow their government, what was the inside story of the French alliance treaty and of the Shantung settlement, what Peace Conference minutes were there and shouldn't the Senate have them? [17]

Another article by the same Publicity Association related that the advocates of the Covenant had "even gone so far as to characterize it as a 'league of peace.'" (Think of the effrontery!) The whole structure of the League centered about the idea of compulsion. It proposed to subject all the rest of the world to its will. It bristled with limitations and restrictions on independent nationalism. Almost every article save the purely administrative ones had in it "the essentials for the creation of friction likely to lead to war." Article 1, saying that two years notice and fulfillment of obligations should precede withdrawal, would operate so that the United States "once in would be compelled to remain a member, by international force of arms if necessary, if Japan or Spain or Greece chose to make us do so. The

[16] *Ibid.,* p. 2586.   [17] *Ibid.,* p. 2587.

resentment of red-blooded Americans to coercion from these sources would inevitably lead to war."

Article 4, giving each member an equal vote in the Assembly, was a fruitful source of irritation. It made Cuba, Liberia and Panama our equals. "Here the creator is controlled by its creations, which are given three times the voting strength of the power that made them." And other nations dependent for the maintenance of their "independent sovereignty" on the Monroe Doctrine were given equal voting power with the great protector. Haiti, Nicaragua, and Honduras were cases in point.

Wasn't the world topsy-turvy indeed! When such arguments could be seriously made, anything could happen. But the literal constructionists overlooked no possible reading that could paint the League as something exactly opposite to what it was. Thus under Article 5 Germany, soon to be a member, "could effectually veto any policy that we might formulate toward Mexico." And so on down through the articles; each one contained a grave threat or a great injustice. Article 10 breathed war from its first word to the last. It alone was "sufficient to damn the League covenant forever in the eyes of everyone who really wishes to see a step taken in the direction of future peace." Article 11 was "nothing more or less than an automatic declaration of war for every member of the League."

The opening sentence of Article 11 read: "Any war or threat, whether immediately affecting any of the members of the League or not, is hereby declared a matter of concern to the whole League." The last sentence in the Article said further: "It is also declared to be the friendly right of each member of the League to bring to the attention of the Assembly or of the Council any circumstance whatever affecting international relations which threatens to disturb international peace or the good understanding between nations upon which peace depends."

Two Portraits of Article 11. This is the clause that one of America's creative thinkers pronounced "the most precious in the whole document" because it strikes so deeply at the isolation which breeds arrogance. He recognized it as the most revolutionary idea which could be introduced into the comity of nations because a seal was put upon the truth that the peace of the world is of vital interest to all nations. "The active forces of peace are released by it. According to this new doctrine it will not be necessary for any people, neutral in a dispute, to sit helplessly by and see a conflagration prepared which may burn down its own homes. It abolishes those alleged private quarrels which in the end involve everybody. It states flatly that America, for example, is not to remain mute while some diplomat fixes up a war in the Balkans which cannot be ended until two million Americans are on foreign soil. It says that international duelling is over, and that every nation can discuss the causes of a fight before the fight takes place. Above all it enables any government in the League to arouse the public opinion of the world wherever a condition appears which threatens the peace. The faith is that no quarrel can grow big enough to justify war when the peoples who must do the fighting know about it soon enough." [18]

But to the Republican Publicity Association, Article 11, instead of being the most enlightened and promising idea in the Covenant, was the most damning. "Under this provision the United States, if a member, immediately becomes involved in every war of the future, no matter how remote from our shores, regardless of our relations with the parties to the dispute, or our desire to remain at peace. Our soldiers and sailors, to all intents and purposes, automatically become hirelings of the league, subject to orders to proceed to the scene of bloodshed and fight against the country that the council may deem to be in the wrong. Do you want to send your boys off on such a mission? What becomes of the 'league-for-peace' cry in the light of this article?" [19]

Did the League Mean More Overseas Service? This appeal to the mothers and fathers and to the boys themselves was apparently bearing fruit, for it was pressed with greater insistence as the bulk of the homesick armies returned from France "fed up" on foreign service and glad to get back to familiar and better conditions of life. The majority of them seemed to react without delay against any suggestion that they go back right away and whip the Emir of Afghanistan or the Llama of Thibet. Did this league of nations propose to send them off on such errands every few days? Then away with it!

Some would reason that it was infinitely better for a few who chose to serve to go abroad occasionally, if it should prove necessary, than for millions to be drafted and sent periodically. They could see that a little longer duration of our belligerency would the next time fill American homes with gold stars and our streets with maimed vet-

---

[18] Walter Lippman, *The Political Scene,* N. Y., 1919, p. 44.
[19] *Congressional Record,* Vol. 58, Pt. 3, p. 2588.

erans until the cry "It Must Not Happen Again!" would drown all pleas that it would be dangerous to try to prevent it. For countless others the business had merely been unpleasant enough to forget as soon as possible, or perchance for many profitable enough not to rise up against. Some, too, could recognize that a final trial by wager of battle might bankrupt our economic life as it had that of Europe, but for the most we were rich enough not to worry. Moreover, world wide, continuing economic depression growing at length out of the dislocations of the war had not yet engulfed even the great Republic.

The situation was becoming serious enough that Senator Underwood of Alabama, stable and conservative as he was, asked the Senate on July 15: "Has the suffering of the Great War taught us nothing? Must we lapse back to the barbarous national morals of the past, without an effort to reach out for a new ideal of national life that will make it as unmoral for a nation to murder, rob and plunder because it has the power as it has been for an individual to do so?" [20]

Shantung and Article 10. On the same day there was a long debate over Shantung, the opponents of the League assuming it to be the gift of 30,000,000 or 40,000,000 Chinese people to Japan and its defenders maintaining that only property rights had been given. Japan would keep her promise to hand back all political control to China. She had never yet broken her word.

On July 17 Senator McCormick, of Illinois, introduced into the *Record* a twenty page report of the Federal Council of Churches of Christ on Japanese atrocities in Korea, while Senator Sheppard, of Texas, inserted five editorials by Ex-Governor Hanly, of Indiana, Republican, explaining the fundamental character of Article 10. That article was the foundation of the Covenant. Its elimination would be in effect a rejection of the Covenant. The article did not stand alone; it was the preliminary assertion of solidarity on which Articles 11 to 17 were based. All this part of the League machinery would be used before Article 10 was resorted to. Even then the governments represented on the Council would most probably consult each other before agreeing to advise action under it, and finally, they could only advise.

SENATOR COLT FOR THE LEAGUE

The first speech on July 17 was given by Senator Colt, Republican, of Rhode Island. In his judgment, "the League of Nations in its

[20] *Ibid.,* p. 2600.

essence is simply an association of free nations. Its object is to prevent war through international coöperation. Broadly speaking, it covers three basic principles—obligatory conferences when war is threatened, compulsory submission of every international dispute to some form of arbitration or investigation and report before resorting to war, and reduction of armaments." All other means of preventing war had failed; there was no other conceivable solution of the problem except along the lines of a closer union of the family of nations based upon the principle of coöperation or federation. "Not to try this experiment would leave the world in the same condition of international anarchy as it was before the war—a world divided into jealous and competing national units, fully armed and dominated by the spirit of an aggressive nationalism. It is this form of nationalism which leads to war, and the only way to overcome this obstacle to peace and to install the reign of law among nations is through international coöperation. This does not mean the surrender of true nationalism. There is no antagonism between true nationalism and an internationalism which would substitute the reign of law for the reign of force."

Law or Force. Nothing would prevent war except the substitution of law for force. Compulsory conference was the best means of going over to the regime of law. The whole scheme rested finally upon good understanding and the exercise of good faith among the nations, and nothing would contribute more to these ends than conferences when the peace of the world was threatened.

He was unable to see the force of the arguments that a superstate destructive of our independence and sovereignty was being created. A superstate could not be formed when every material power that was exercised required the unanimous consent of the council or of the delegates. "By reason of this provision and the provision of retirement from the League upon giving two years notice, the league is more in the nature of a voluntary association. And in this connection it should not be forgotten that in a world composed of a family of nations there is no such thing as absolute sovereignty."

Nor was he impressed with the constitutional objections or the claim that the league should be separated from the peace treaty. He had always believed the two inseparable because the treaty could not be enforced except through the League. The treaty provided a basis of settlement; it actually settled little or nothing; it only provided a method of settlement which would take years to carry into effect.

To his mind "we must at least see through to the end the great undertaking upon which we embarked during the war, and as a part of this undertaking we must help to reëstablish a new world order by the establishment of the terms of peace, which can only be done by our becoming a member of the League of Nations. . . . And if it should then be found that this association of free nations is not accompanied by all the terrible consequences its enemies predict, and that it is really preventative of war, we could then decide to continue our membership in the League."

Merit Should Decide. He recognized that the enemies of the League fell into two groups, the isolationists who wanted to return to the traditional separation from European affairs and those who objected to the President's negotiation of the treaty and contended that he should have remained at home to consult the Senate and people. Yet, "however just this criticism may be, and however much it may tend to prejudice the minds of many, it really has no bearing on the question of the merits of the League as part of the treaty or its ratification by the Senate."

The great mass of the American people, he believed, was convinced that something must be done to prevent future wars, to prevent a recurrence of the frightful horrors of the past five years. They wanted something done and favored the League as the best solution. On the subject of reservations he reserved his judgment. [21]

Senator Sherman Followed. Mr. Colt was followed by Senator Sherman, who launched into an extended assault on Japan and the Shantung settlement, prefaced by observations on the political power of the papacy, and on a revolution in Peru, one of the members of the proposed League. He gave a detailed and bloody description of the Willard-Dempsey prize fight and wished to set it opposite Mr. Colt's address. Woodrow Wilson and the Japanese Emperor were two of a kind, and the League of Nations was "the colossal confidence game of the ages." [22]

Beck vs. Story. The insertions in the *Record* on July 21 included an address of Mr. James M. Beck of Philadelphia, exhorting the Senate to stand firm and the Republican party "to save again the Union, which Washington founded and Lincoln saved," and an article by Mr. Moorfield Story calling for the ratification of the treaty as it stood. Mr. Story suggested that if the provisions needed amendment these amendments could be made hereafter, and were far more likely to be

[21] *Congressional Record*, Vol. 58, Pt. 3, pp. 2721-2.
[22] *Ibid.*, pp. 2722-30.

made, "if we have shown toward our allies confidence and good will by agreeing to the compact which our representatives have made than if we exhibit suspicion of their honesty and selfish disregard of every interest but our own by refusing to unite with them." [23]

Our Obligation to the New Nations. Senator Pomerene, of Ohio, followed with a discussion of the questions of constitutionality and sovereignty and with an analysis of the objections of Knox, Lodge and Root. He, too, made the point that we did not enter the war with the intention of turning our backs upon our friends when it should suit some selfish purpose. We entered it to fight together, to win together, and to keep the peace together. Moreover, we had a responsibility to the new nations we had been instrumental in creating, that we could not now lay down. We had encouraged the Czecho-Slovaks, the Jugo-Slavs, the Poles and the Armenians to rise in revolt against their masters. Honor required that we should not desert them now before they were able to stand on their feet. Mr. Root himself, in his statement of March 29, 1919, had agreed that Article 10 should hold for a limited time, until order had been restored among the vast populations seething to the east of our Allies.

Senators who were continually fearing that we might be charged with breach of faith in the future, if Congress failed to carry out a decision of the League, were straining the gnat of future possible dishonor and swallowing the camel of present actual dishonor, while our friends were crippled even unto death. But if the signatory powers should attempt to exact from us something which was not dictated by a sense of justice and honor, he knew of no code of ethics that required any nation to perform their decrees.

For the League and the Monroe Doctrine. He thought, too, that there was blindness in placing the Monroe Doctrine above the League. "Who does not know," he asked, "that we are nearer to Europe today than we were to Central and South America at the time the Monroe Doctrine was announced? Who is not conscious of the fact that the dangers to the world peace and to our safety are in Europe today rather than in Central or South America? Why should we be so eager to assert our sovereignty over the Americas from which no evil has come to us, and at the same time blind ourselves to the dangers in Europe which well-nigh overcame the world? I want to

---

[23] *Ibid.*, pp. 2921, 2915. George Harvey now felt so sure that he proclaimed that the President "will get the advice; he will not get the consent. That is now the unescapable and unalterable fact." *Harvey's Weekly*, July 19, 1919, Vol. 2, No. 29, p. 2.

preserve the Monroe Doctrine in its entirety, but if I must choose between the preservation of the Monroe Doctrine and the League of Nations I shall prefer the latter. Sound statesmanship suggests our guarding against great dangers where they now exist and where they are likely to break out at any moment if we are not on our guard, rather than limit our concern to conditions in the Americas, present or future, from which even the most timid do not anticipate danger to the Republic. Fortunately we are not driven to choose between the two. We can have the protection of both the League of Nations and the Monroe Doctrine." [24]

CHARGES OF PARTISANSHIP

Democratic Indictment. The bitter partisan feeling that was governing the attitude of a section of both parties was veiled for the most part behind argument which was more or less related to the issue. Occasionally it flashed out into the open, as on July 21 when Senator Harrison, of Mississippi, charged that "Never before in the discussion of a great national question has deception been so lavishly practiced and misrepresentation so generously employed. Every alluring piece of sophistry that oratory could command, every cunning device that politicians could conjure, has been advanced by the opponents of the League here, that in the country reason might be dethroned and prejudice aroused. No argument has been too fallacious, no illustration too far fetched, for you to seize upon in your desperate efforts to becloud the issue."

Quoting the commendatory utterances of half a dozen Republican leaders made after the enunciation of the Fourteen Points, in January, 1918, he continued: "You do not object to the President going abroad as the head of our delegation in that great conference because of any doubt on your part of his ability to faithfully represent us. You knew, as the world knew, that he was at that time the most influential and commanding figure on earth, and that it was through his leadership that the war had been brought to an end. Your opposition arose simply and merely because he happened to be the spokesman and leader of another political party. I had never believed that partisanship could become so acute that jealous leaders would rather see the star of their country dimmed than to witness the ascendancy of an individual because he was of a different political faith." [25]

[24] *Congressional Record*, Vol. 58, Pt. 3, pp. 2927-38.   [25] *Ibid.*, p. 2939.

Republican Reply. To which the *National Republican* replied, in editorials published in the *Record* on July 23, that it was the President, and the Senators who served as phonographic records of his voice, who were playing politics with the League issue. "Of course, if it had been the desire of President Wilson or his party henchmen in the Senate to bring about the creation of a satisfactory league of nations, they would have accorded some consideration to the views of the majority members of the United States Senate, as anticipated in the national constitution, knowing as they did that ratification of the treaty by a two-thirds vote was vital to the very creation of the League. Instead of this they have taken just the position that would be expected of politicians not primarily anxious for the adoption of a league of nations, but to force the political opposition into what they believe would be a 'hole,' by attempting to make the public believe that the Republican Senators oppose any arrangement for forming a world organization to prevent war in so far as they may be accomplished by international action."

The President and his creatures had been "studiously insulting in their attitude toward all opposition to any feature of the proposals brought home from Paris" and were much more interested in their own political fortunes than in creating the League. "The meaning of the insistence of the administration that the Paris covenant must be accepted just as written or not at all is that it is not half so much interested in the adoption of a league of nations plan as in manipulating the situation to its own immediate political advantage. This is the meaning of the position taken by President Wilson that the treaty must be ratified without the slightest change or rejected in its entirety." Senators who were holding out against the "acquiescence in the sacrifice of American sovereignty and independence upon the altar of socialistic and imperialistic internationalism" could not be either intimidated by propaganda or bribed. [26]

The tremendous power of the spirit of partisanship was making itself felt more and more in the contest over the League. Some Democratic leaders undoubtedly felt that the League was so popular that the Republicans did not dare to tamper with it; other Republican leaders, equally convinced of the widespread desire for it, were just as sure that unless the Republicans could claim to have made it safe for America they were lost. Still other Republicans were certain that the reaction against President Wilson and his party was so strong

[26] *Congressional Record*, Vol. 58, Pt. 3, p. 3047.

that nothing could save them in the next election, while many Democrats preferred to see their party defeated rather than have it endorse
the League. Large numbers of Democrats were willing to follow the
personal leadership of Mr. Wilson to any conclusion however bitter,
and a powerful section of the Republican party was determined that
this time he should be finally destroyed regardless of the cost. And,
through the fury of the fight countless Republicans and Democrats
stuck by the issues of the debate and refused to follow their political
leaders in either direction.

Senator McNary's Plea for the League

One of the Senators who resisted great pressure from his colleagues
was Senator McNary, Republican, of Oregon. He explained his position to the Senate on July 22. He had repressed whatever desire he
may have had to discuss the treaty until it reached the Senate chamber
through conventional channels. The quicker we forgot our party affiliations the sooner we would be able to reach a proper solution of the
problem. The time for indulging in general statements of the sublimity
of peace, or indulging with owlish wisdom the ominous predictions
of a disgraced and destroyed Republic, had passed.

Article 10 a Moral Bond. The most serious objection had been to
Article 10. He had analyzed this section and could find no compulsion
in it to go to war in an unjust or unnecessary cause. In his opinion
"the extent and nature of the obligation imposed by Article 10 is not
involved by any doubt as to its proper solution. This nation is under a
moral bond to fulfill its obligations and go to war, if need be, whenso-
ever the fulfillment of the obligations is justified by the rules of morals."
Indisputably every member of the League was under an obligation to
protect an associate from invasion through external force, "but this
obligation is in no proper sense a legal one, but purely a moral obligation, entirely dependent upon the condition that the cause of the war
and the war itself is violative of the moral conscience of the American
people." Certainly the treaty making power could never cast any legal
obligation on future Congresses to declare war.

The moral force in the obligation imposed upon the nations of
the world, in his opinion, would do much to chill the ambitious designs
of nations that heretofore had been the cause of cruel wars, and for
that reason he would oppose by his vote the eradication of Article 10
from the Covenant. "It is the pillar section of the association of nations

contemplated under the League, and is the assurance of mutual support against any external aggression. It speaks the voice of freedom among the nations and guarantees to each its full share of sovereignty. It makes possible and encourages the reduction of armaments, as no nation will disarm unless assured that it will not be attacked by another nation. Nations which disarm or progressively deprive themselves of the weapons to repel an assault must protect themselves either by erecting a super-state, with an international armed force to guard them, or by entering into a compact to come to each other's aid when an outlaw nation threatens the use of force. This principle has been recognized by students of history from the time thought was first given to plans for the promotion of world peace. . . . In a world accompanied by an agreement for reduction of armament the necessity of a covenant containing the moral virility of Article 10 is manifest."

The truth here stated is one which received too little consideration throughout the whole debate on the League, but it remains and must compel recognition in the future.

All Could Demand Special Privileges. The demand for amendments and reservations came without proper regard for the results that would follow. [27] He was not interested in the term that was used. If luggage were added to the treaty it must of necessity go back to all the signatories and be re-accepted by them. To limit, alter, modify the moral obligation of Article 10 would in his judgment operate as an amendment. "We must not forget," he warned, "that if we attempt by general reservations or amendments to alter the splendid purposes of the Covenant or weaken it so far as it affects our duties, it cannot be expected that other nations will not follow our lead. Having demonstrated our altruism and unselfishness in this war and our overpowering strength and sublime heroism, is it not rather beneath our ideals to ask special privileges when the peace of the world and the welfare and happiness of mankind is involved?"

An Interpretative Resolution Proposed. We had been told "that our sovereignty had been dangerously diminished, the Monroe Doctrine endangered; that we have surrendered our control over certain vital domestic matters; that we could be plunged into war without a declaration of Congress." No one of these statements was believed by the advocates of the League to have a foundation in fact. He

---

[27] Senator Harrison had charged that the opponents of the Covenant proposed amendments as freely as they would make motions to add small town post office buildings to a public buildings bill.

proposed, however, that these questions be placed beyond the pale of controversy by an interpretative resolution restating the Monroe Doctrine, the international law governing domestic questions, etc. On the latter question, for example, he quoted a series of cases showing that the Supreme Court had uniformly applied the well understood rule of international law as applied to a nation's internal affairs. Since there was no disagreement at home or abroad as to what the law was, he could see no serious objection to annexing a resolution to the treaty redefining an established rule of the law of nations. That action he believed would not constitute an amendment to the treaty requiring action by the other powers. "While a work of supererogation, if found comforting, it would have its own reward."

The Covenant Not the Last Word. Although maintaining to Senator Knox that an explanatory statement of something already in the treaty would not require action by the other signatories, because it would not enlarge the scope of the treaty or amend its substance, Mr. McNary evidently preferred not to run the risk of attaching any sort of resolution to the treaty, for he plead that "The constitution of the League is not the final and unalterable judge of the world's opinion; it is the present repository of a world desire to create a moral and economic force calculated to act as an insuperable barrier against future armed conflicts. The constitution contains nothing of the finality of the historical laws of the Medes and the Persians. It is simply an instrument for the execution of some of the terms imposed by the treaty of peace—the establishment of a moral force to bring on this earth a permanent peace. Time opens the way and presents the opportunity for all needed amendments." The world was so impoverished in substance and wasted of man power that there would be ample time for amending the Covenant before the next serious conflict came on. The present crying need was for the introduction of the institution. Once started it would grow into "an international structure that shall protect humanity from the savagery of conflict so long as mankind and his institutions endure."

"You say this is a hope founded on faith," he concluded. "Yes; so long as faith abides, the fruits of faith ripen and flourish. The peoples of the world are heartstricken with sorrow, and upon their energies rest the burdens of a ponderous tax that will require many decades of patient toil to absorb. This occasion is too serious for anger and recrimination, too big for partisanship, too full of good for personal consideration. Let this country be committed to a step in the direction of everlasting peace, and it is my sincere belief that the League of Nations is the greatest step the world has ever taken toward peace; therefore I shall support the League, as it is the hope of the world." [28]

Was that Belief Justified? Where are the millions of American men and women who had that faith in 1919? Have they lost belief? Have they failed to inform themselves as to whether or not the League has justified their earlier faith? Have they abandoned the fight for it merely because of a reverse? Or is their conviction silently growing as the choice between coöperation and rivalry grows plainer each year?

Where Did Safety Lie? Senator Johnson, Democrat, of South Dakota followed Mr. McNary in support of the Covenant. What could be done to prevent future wars was the foremost question in the minds of the American people, yet after months of discussion the country was bewildered and confused by the attacks that had been made on the Covenant. He had always been a firm believer in agreements such as were proposed and would vote for any plan to keep the peace submitted by the leading statesmen of the world after six months deliberation.

He was old fashioned enough to believe that we reaped just what we sowed. If we relied on the doctrine that other nations needed us but we did not need them we would come to grief. That was a doctrine of selfishness which destroyed the morals of the people and encouraged wars such as we had just passed through. It was true that we were the greatest nation on earth, but no nation was strong enough to stand alone. Germany had to admit that at last. And no nation was strong enough to be safe from the future methods of warfare.

Should we Remove the Keystone? He was unable to see anything in Article 10 that was not perfectly plain and clear. Further, he could not see how it would be possible to have a covenant at all with any virtue or effect without the provisions which this paragraph embodied. Aside from our duty to the new nations we had helped to set up, suppose we refused to enter this League which had for its object the protection of the world from the aggressions of predatory nations. Why would we not be regarded with enmity and suspicion?

Was it possible that the bloodiest war in history had taught us nothing? Would we not profit by the experiences we had just passed through? The only hope he could see of directing the world into ways

[28] *Congressional Record*, Vol. 58, Pt. 3, pp. 2983-5.

of peace was in that League of Nations. Did those who opposed it have a better plan to offer? If so, what was it? The world looked to us for our answer as it did to no other nation on the globe. What would our answer be? [29]

Senator Moses Opposed to the Entire Treaty. On the same day Senator Moses, of New Hampshire, delivered an attack on the Treaty as a whole, with but little reference to the League, except that he came to the conclusion that after all it would be "neither a delicate nor a difficult task of dissection" to cut the League out of the Treaty. His main conclusion was that the Treaty itself was "infinitely worse for us than even the League of Nations, bad as it is." [30]

Senator Beckham's Appeal to the Fathers

Senator Beckham, of Kentucky, Democrat, followed immediately for the affirmative. Few participants in the debate, if any, were able to muster the kindly tolerance that seemed to fill his speech. One must realize, he said, that practically everything had been said about the League, for and against it that could be said, and in speaking upon it he did not indulge the hope of throwing any new light upon the subject or of producing any fact or argument that would change the opinion of anyone.

He had never for a moment doubted the sincerity and patriotism of the Senators who opposed the League; he recognized that they were just as good Americans as the advocates of the League. Beyond doubt they honestly believed in the apparent perils which their imaginations had conjured up and their eloquence so graphically pictured. Neither had he been inclined to believe that partisanship had exercised its malign influence in determining the attitude of Senators, though later he plead with them not to be misled by prejudice, dwarfed by partisan bias, or by some lurking ill will toward the person of the distinguished President of the United States. He knew that the best of us were not free from such influences operating frequently in an unconscious way upon us, but he hoped that each Senator would rise to a plane of broad statesmanship and look at the subject with a heart and mind so free that the real merit of the document would be considered and not the personality of anyone.

The Policy of Jefferson. If there were objections to the treaty he asked attention to the action of Thomas Jefferson, who, at first in-

[29] *Ibid.*, pp. 2985-88.   [30] *Ibid.*, pp. 2989-95.

clined to oppose the Constitution, fell into line behind it, in a letter of May 17, 1788, saying: "There are, indeed, some faults, which revolted me a great deal in the first moment, but we must be contented to travel onward toward perfection step by step. We must be contented with the ground which this constitution will gain for us, and hope that a favorable moment will come for correcting what is amiss in it."

Mr. Beckham knew of no better guide than this. The wisest and most far sighted statesman this country had produced had some objections to the Constitution, but he did not favor the rejection of it in whole or in part, thereby sending it into the chaos of another constitutional convention. He saw that the good in it outweighed what might be defective and that the defects might be removed by later amendments.

The Attitude of Patrick Henry and James Monroe. But there had been others also who could not be guided by the vision of a Jefferson. In Wiet's life of Patrick Henry he found that the Virginia patriot had arisen in the ratification convention of his state to oppose the Constitution "with that awful solemnity and look of fearful portent by which Mr. Henry could imply even more than he expressed and that slow, distinct, emphatic enunciation by which he never failed to move the souls of his hearers." (Mr. Beckham did not need to recall to his hearers the effects lately produced by Senator Knox.)

"This proposal," said Patrick Henry, "of altering our Federal Government is of a most alarming nature. Make the best of this new Government—say it is composed by anything but inspiration—you ought to be extremely cautious, watchful, jealous of your liberty; for instead of securing your rights you may lose them forever. If a wrong step be made now the Republic may be lost forever. If this new Government will not come up to the expectation of the people, and they shall be disappointed, their liberty will be lost, and tyranny must and will arise. I repeat it again, and I beg gentlemen to consider, that a wrong step made now will plunge us into misery and our Republic will be lost."

Again, it was not necessary to remind the Senate how Senator Lodge had cautioned us by the hour, before the Covenant was ever written, and again while it was being drawn, to be careful, deliberate, beware of the consequences! Instead, Senator Beckham cited the very earnest and sincere alarm which James Monroe had expressed about the Constitution. The fears which the misguided leaders of those days so earnestly felt and eloquently expressed were never realized. What would have happened if the solemn warnings of those patriots had prevailed?

Should we now listen to the prophets of evil? Should we be frightened by the ominous picture of gloom which they painted so luridly before our eyes? No, he believed not. The common sense of the American people would prevail. No one could say the document was perfect, "but it at least comes to us with a promise that if given a fair trial, if improved where improvements may be found necessary later on, and if supported by the civilized governments of the earth, it will certainly be a tremendous advance over all previous plans, and one that may in reality fulfill the dreams of its most enthusiastic advocates, a world-wide and an enduring peace." [31]

[31] *Congressional Record,* Vol. 58, Pt. 3, pp. 2995-3000.

CHAPTER X

JULY DEBATES

THE debate was continued on July 23 by Senator McKellar, Democrat, of Tennessee, who could not refrain from calling the roll of the decades to show that from the time that Washington announced his doctrine of entangling alliances no President had ever taken a constructive step without incurring the opposition of reactionary Senators. But where were these men now? Search the pages of the country's history and you would find only the names of the builders remaining.

SENATOR McKELLAR'S COUNTER-ATTACK

The shifting of ground on the part of the opponents of the treaty to suit the purposes of opposition also drew McKellar's fire. When it was reported, as the Peace Conference met, that President Wilson wished to insert the League of Nations in the peace treaty and the Allies wished to postpone it, Senator Lodge had been all for Allied harmony, declaring in a public statement that "To attempt in any way to separate us from our Allies now or to prevent perfect unity of action is as harmful as such efforts were when we were fighting in Northern France and on the plains of Flanders. To encourage or even permit any serious differences to arise between the United States and Great Britain, or with France, or Italy, or Belgium would be a world calamity of the worst kind. Any serious difference among English-speaking people would be deplorable in the highest degree. Any thought of war among them would be as abominable as it is inconceivable. To differ greatly from France, bound to us by so many ties of faith and affection, or with Italy or Belgium, is unthinkable."

What had since come over Mr. Lodge and his colleagues? The Allies had all agreed upon the treaty. The utmost harmony prevailed. Apparently they were now united in doing just what Senator Lodge and his associates wanted done. But now the only discordant note, the only criticism, the only fight, came from Senator Lodge and his associates. The only attempt to break up cordial relations with the Allies and to stir up serious differences between the English-speaking peoples was coming from them. In all the world no other faction, except possibly one in China, was making any trouble. Why this change? If perfect harmony and unified action was a good thing in December, why wasn't it a good thing in July? If it was a bad thing to encourage such differences then, why was it not now?

The Knox Doctrine. The speaker then adopted the tactics of the opposition and viewed with alarm the Knox doctrine, the only proposed substitute for the Covenant which had ever been offered. As refined in the last Knox resolution, introduced on June 10, it had read: "it shall be the declared policy of our Government, in order to meet fully and fairly our obligations to ourselves and to the world, that the freedom and peace of Europe again being threatened by any power or combination of powers, the United States will regard such a situation with grave concern as a menace to its own peace and freedom, will consult with other powers affected with a view to devising means for the removal of such menace, and will, the necessity arising in the future, carry out the same complete accord and coöperation with our chief cobelligerents for the defense of civilization."

This was obviously a pretty far reaching commitment. It was so inclusive that Senator McCumber had declared to the Senate that he would be satisfied if those words, without elimination or addition, should be the only compact between the nations. If this declaration were signed by the nations it would in his judgment prevent unjust wars as effectively as the Covenant. [1] He evidently felt that the commitment was just as strong as that of Article 10.

This had been the view of Senator Beckham. Did Article 10 go any further in principle? asked Mr. Beckham. Did it put a stronger obligation on us to go to war? The only practical difference that he could see was that Article 10 was backed by all the machinery necessary to cope with the situation if it did arise, whereas the Knox substitute was not. [2]

These had been sympathetic interpretations of the Knox proposal. Senator McKellar indicated what could be done by the critical method. What did this plan mean? Was there any attempt to settle wars in a peaceful way? Was there any attempt to arbitrate differences? Was there any attempt to adjust and compromise and settle international

[1] *Congressional Record,* Vol. 58, Pt. 3, p. 2997.   [2] *Ibid.*

disturbances and disputes? None whatever! The doctrine was just a rehash and a restatement of the Monroe Doctrine, applying it to Europe. If it were carried out we would become simply the chief of police for Europe, "Mind you, not with agreements that war should not be made, but with an agreement that Europe can stir up all the wars she wants and we will be the policeman to stop them." If that solution should become law "it would take 5,000,000 American soldiers on guard in Europe all the time to preserve the peace; it would take the largest navy in the world, a larger navy than all the other navies in the world, to preserve the peace of Europe."

No wonder the Foreign Relations Committee had turned this proposal down, he said, "because it would involve us in war. It provides no agreement to keep us out of war. Instead of being a peace treaty it would be a war treaty, a treaty to incite, to produce, war throughout the world. The remarkable thing about it is that the junior Senator from Pennsylvania, after introducing a resolution like that, is against extending the Monroe doctrine to the world. If we extend the Monroe doctrine to Europe, it seems to me, everybody would say it might as well be extended to the world, as it is in this peace treaty." [3]

If the reader's attention wandered a moment in reading this characterization of the Knox plan he would suppose that he was merely reading another excoriation of the dangers of that war-breeder, the League of Nations. The criticism is not quoted as a wholly judicial appraisal of the Knox plan—it was hardly intended to be that, though it appears to have some validity—but only as a suggestion of the slant that can be given to the simplest kind of proposal. Mr. Knox no doubt felt that he had perfected a formula for satisfying our obligation and interest in world peace that was as safe and sane and inexpensive as could be devised.

The Feeling of Final and Irrevocable Action. Yet fears that appear strained to us now seem to have really troubled some of the best men in the Senate in 1919. Thus the proviso that a nation might withdraw at any time on two years notice, provided it had fulfilled its international obligations, probably would excite little alarm now. The likelihood that we would have any unfulfilled obligations about which there would be dispute strikes us as remote, and the danger that other nations would attempt to hold us in the League by war on such a pretext seems still more unreal. However, this problem seems to have really disturbed so progressive and forward looking a man as Senator Ken-

[3] *Congressional Record,* Vol. 58, Pt. 3, pp. 3022-32.

yon, of Iowa. Senator McKellar was not able to prove to him that there was no possibility of any trouble on this score in the future. All he could do was to point out that every sentence and phrase in our Constitution had had to be construed by the Supreme Court and that no quantity of reservations adopted in advance could prevent the necessity of future construction of the League's clauses, for the reason that nobody could tell how each and every one of them would work out.

The long campaign against the President's mission must have subconsciously convinced many that scrutiny must be minute and insurance certain.

The President had been determined that lawyers should not write the treaty, but he could not prevent them from passing upon it in the Senate, and even the most unbiased of them discovered possibilities that no one could prove did not exist, however unlikely their materialization was. Added, then, an all-pervading sense of the overwhelming importance of their action and you had an atmosphere for solemn objection even when an isolationist bent or partisan bias did not supply the motive power. It would be difficult to exaggerate the importance of the action which the Senators were faced with and of the results which have followed from it, yet one cannot help wishing that they could have felt occasionally that great as was their hour they could only determine the main lines of future action at the most.

Robinson on Shantung. The high moral indignation of the Senators over the Shantung settlement was by this time exciting such a widespread popular response that one of the minority leaders, Senator Robinson, of Arkansas, felt it necessary to make, on July 24, an exhaustive analysis of the Shantung case. The history of the case, he maintained, did not justify the violent attacks which had been made upon Japan in the Senate. The treaty whereby the Germans obtained the Tsingtao lease, in 1898, in express terms agreed to the exercise of sovereign rights in the leased area by Germany. Japan had displaced Germany by conquest during the war and had been guaranteed the German rights by treaties with the Allies. These treaties had been war measures made to secure greater military activity from Japan and to prevent the campaign of Germany for a separate peace with Japan from succeeding. We ourselves had concluded the Lansing-Ishii agreement recognizing Japan's special position in China at the same time and for the same reasons. The cause of the Allies was trembling in the balance and engagements made then could not be lightly disregarded now.

He then quoted a page of statements by Japan wherein she had on a half dozen different occasions promised to return the leased territory to China in accordance with the treaty of May 25, 1915, with China. This treaty also could not be thrown out on the ground that it was exacted from China by duress. Practically all foreign intercourse with China was carried on under treaties extorted by force.

Japan had a claim which the Peace Conference could not fail to recognize. She was unalterably committed to the obligation to restore the leased territory to China. No good effect could come from assuming that she was acting in bad faith and intended to break her word. [4] China herself could better afford to rely on her treaty rights for a return of the territory than to herself breach that treaty and thus provoke Japan to insist on her claim acquired from Germany through conquest, for that involved no obligation to restore the territory before the expiration of the lease.

At the conclusion of the speech, Senator Williams assisted Mr. Robinson in bringing out that the United States instead of protesting against the original and much more reprehensible rape of Shantung by Germany had quite cordially recognized the transaction. Senator Williams wanted the people to know that Woodrow Wilson was not President then and that the Senatorial wolves were not abroad at that time.

SENATOR LENROOT'S JUSTIFICATION OF RESERVATIONS

After this little byplay Senator Lenroot spoke again for the mild reservationists. The country ought to know that the real issue was not whether the League should be ratified but whether it should be ratified with reservations. The members of the Senate "with very few exceptions" were, irrespective of party, in favor of a league of nations. That a league of nations following the war was desirable seemed so clear as not to permit of argument. He sincerely hoped that the Committee on Foreign Relations to whom the treaty had been referred would make a report to the Senate very soon so that the country might know what the issues were.

---

[4] Senator Beckham had brought out that if the Allies had refused to confirm Japan's title to Tsingtao they would have cast an aspersion upon her trustworthiness and national honor which no proud and sensitive people could be expected to rest under, particularly when they had never broken a treaty and had already had their pride deeply wounded by the Conference on the racial equality issue. *Ibid.*, p. 2998. For Senator Robinson's speech, see pp. 3084-90.

We Had Fought in Our Own Interest. He took the President sharply to task for saying that we went into the war "not because our material interests were directly threatened" and demonstrated at length that that was exactly why we had gone in. Therefore in now considering the interests of America first we were not violating any obligations to our associates in the war. We were absolutely free to consider our own interests first.

This conclusion was reached also by a consideration of the Fourteen Points serially which convinced him that they had not been applied; only six had been complied with, leaving eight either violated or undetermined. He had no quarrel with the Points as a peace program nor with the President for failing to secure their execution. He had done his best. And if the Fourteen Points had been fully complied with he conceded that we would be under at least some obligation to guarantee the peace thus made. Since they were not faithfully carried out we were under no such obligation.

We had been the only unselfish nation around the peace table. While other nations were striving to secure assets for themselves President Wilson was striving to secure liabilities for the United States. In "seeking no material advantages for ourselves he truly represented the people of the nation," but we were certainly not obligated to guarantee the others in their gains.

Many Had Doubts. Four of the six principal objections to the Covenant which he had discussed in his address of February 28, he felt had been removed wholly or substantially by the Conference in revising the document. [5] Doubts still remained about two or three provisions. One was the matter of withdrawal. He agreed with Senator Swanson that in case of any difficulty over our withdrawal the dispute would be with the League itself and not with any of the members composing it. We would be on an equality with the League and the League was nowhere given any power to decide such a dispute or to exercise compulsion upon us. Therefore there was no danger to us in the withdrawal clause, but other Senators on both sides of the aisle feared it, so why not all agree on a reservation which would remove the fears?

The same consideration applied to the Monroe Doctrine. All the

---

[5] The greatest value of the revised Covenant, he felt, would come from the machinery which compelled delay in going to war. There could be no war suddenly arising over an honest dispute.

The next most beneficial provision, in his judgment, was Article 11 which declared that any threat of war was a matter of concern to the whole League—*Ibid.,* p. 3093.

supporters of the League insisted that the Monroe Doctrine was fully protected, while other equally eminent statesmen and lawyers expressed grave doubt upon the subject. He felt certain that at the proper time the Senate would agree upon a reservation removing the doubts.

Article 10 Did Bind us to Fight in Unjust Causes. Coming to Article 10, there was real necessity for a reservation because that article obligated us to fight for unjust causes. It would have prevented the liberation of Cuba, and it would bind us to go to war against China if China should fight Japan to recover Shantung—and Senator Robinson had not convinced him that Japan was not the receiver of stolen property in this case. "Can it be possible," he asked, "that there is a Democrat so partisan that he does not see the necessity of a reservation as to Article 10 relieving us of the obligation of declaring war in an unjust cause? I am profoundly convinced that if partisanship be forgotten and only Americanism remembered we can agree upon a reservation to this article, now so dangerous to the cause of true liberty, so destructive of American ideals and principles. I care not in what form the reservation is made so long as it does not obligate us to engage in war irrespective of the justice of the cause."

Altogether, "if Senators across the aisle would only forget that President Wilson is the leader of the Democratic party, and remember that this is an American question so crucial, so important to our country, so fateful to its future that consideration of political advantage should not have the weight of a feather in our deliberations—if this could be done, Mr. President, I am confident that we would come to an almost unanimous agreement as to reservations for the protection of the United States." [6]

Thus when the charge of partisanship was reversed it appeared that the stubbornness of President Wilson coupled with a Democratic desire to make political capital out of the League was preventing the ratification of the Covenant. [7]

---

[6] *Congressional Record,* Vol. 58, Pt. 3, pp. 3092-96.

[7] Senator Fletcher, of Florida, who followed Mr. Lenroot, replied that: "Before the league of nations was formulated there were those who were sneering at it, criticizing the idea, and raising objections to it. After the first draft was prepared they were loud in their denunciation. One cannot escape the impression that many of those were prompted by personal animosity toward the President and others by partisan bitterness, and both these groups by a desire to paralyze his leadership at whatever cost, and that at a time of a commanding world crisis. . . .

"Others doubted because they lacked vision; withheld approval because they did not grasp the subject. Others, since they could not lead themselves, were disposed to criticize all effort and thwart all accomplishment. They demanded that they should

SENATOR PITTMAN ON THE EFFECT OF RESERVATIONS

Senator Pittman, of Nevada, who was the first speaker on July 24, devoted his entire time to the subject of the effect of reservations. The fate of the treaty was in the hands of the group of Senators who desired interpretative reservations. If reservations could be adopted with a reasonable certainty that they would not lead to the reopening of the whole peace negotiations such reservations would be approved by two thirds of the Senate. What was to be expected?

Every Word Attached to the Treaty Was Binding. In the first place everything in the resolution of ratification became a part of the treaty, if accepted by the other signatories. Chief Justice Taney in ruling upon the Florida Treaty with Spain in 1821 had stated: "For it is too plain for argument that where one of the parties to a treaty, at the time of its ratification, annexes a written declaration explaining ambiguous language in the instrument or adding a new and distinct stipulation, and the treaty is afterwards ratified by the other party with the declaration attached to it, and the ratifications duly exchanged, the declaration thus annexed is a part of the treaty and as binding and obligatory as if it were inserted in the body of the instrument. The intention of the parties is to be gathered from the whole instrument as it stood when the ratifications were exchanged."

"It is immaterial," continued Senator Pittman, "whether the Senate considers the reservation as changing the treaty or not, for that is a question under the law of contracts that the other party has an equal right to determine. It is immaterial whether the change be accomplished in the body of the treaty or by interpretative clauses annexed to the treaty. The question is, Is the wording of the treaty changed? If it is, the construction to be placed upon such words and their effect upon the terms of the treaty are questions to be determined by all the parties to the treaty. The treaty is a contract; it is an agreement that requires the meeting of the minds of the contracting parties upon the terms. Agreements may be only expressed in words and words are subject to various constructions . . . and the words

---

be consulted, even though the Constitutions vested the authority to conduct negotiations exclusively in the Executive.

"They continued their attacks while the negotiations were in progress when they knew the only effect would be to embarrass those having the matter in hand. They discussed 'leaks' which amounted to nothing, but which they endeavored vainly to magnify into a public scandal. They offered resolutions and had them cabled to the peace conference—and then let them rest. Finally the time came to specify, and the burden of complaint was directed to Article 10."—*Ibid.*, p. 3098.

once agreed upon cannot be changed without the consent of each of the parties to be bound by the contract."

The Supreme Court had further made it clear in connection with the Treaty of Peace with Spain that the Senate could not pass a separate resolution which would have any binding effect upon the other parties to the treaty. (The Case of the Diamond Rings, 183 U. S. 182).

Every Qualification Would Have to be Accepted by the Signatories. Any qualifications or interpretations whatever, then, added to the treaty by the Senate would have to be accepted by the treaty ratifying power in every state signatory to the treaty. The right to ratify treaties was variously exercised in the different countries, but the governments of Great Britain, France and Italy had already declared that this treaty should be binding only after approval by their parliaments. The Parliament of Great Britain had already ratified the treaty by a nearly unanimous vote. The other parliaments were about to act. If we changed or qualified the treaty in any way it would have to be resubmitted to these parliaments again for their approval.

Were we justified in assuming that these other parliaments and governments would accept without further interpretation our definitions of the articles of the Covenant as affecting our own obligations? Was it natural to suppose that, after the results of the long and tedious labors of the peace conference and its painful efforts at compromise had once been set aside by the United States Government, other governments would hesitate to attempt to secure privileges and protections which they had sought during the negotiations and failed to obtain?

Did Senators think that after Japan's bitter disappointment over the failure of her racial equality clause she would neglect an opportunity to insist upon a reservation to this effect if the negotiations were opened again? Would the Italian Parliament hesitate to insert a reservation to advance their interests in Fiume and Dalmatia, once we had set the example? The French Chamber of Deputies had already demanded of Clemenceau his justification for signing the treaty without provision for a standing army under the League to protect the borders of France. Would they fail to seize the opportunity in a reopening of negotiations? And would it then be cause for surprise if, under the circumstances, the British Parliament should have something further to say about the limitation of naval armaments?

Every Foreign Reservation Would Have to Be Approved by the

Senate. Then, if a single nation followed our lead and attached a reservation to the treaty, or failed to assent unqualifiedly to ours, the treaty would have come back to the Senate for its further assent. This had been made clear in the case of the Florida treaty referred to. The Senate in approving the treaty, February 22, 1819, had attached a reservation annulling certain land grants. In assenting to this reservation the King of Spain had stated that it was the positive understanding of the negotiators on both sides that these grants should be annulled. Thereupon the President resubmitted the treaty to the Senate for its approval. The King of Spain's declaration was merely interpretative of the Senate's interpretative reservation, and did not in any wise change the purpose or effect of the treaty as previously ratified by the Senate, but the Senate was entitled to determine that question for itself. So it would be of any interpretation of its reservations, in the present case, or of any new ones imposed by other countries.

Every addition to the treaty made by the Senate would have to be approved by the ratifying authority in each of the other signatory countries, and every sentence added by these countries would have to be re-submitted to the Senate for its approval. Mr. Root's statement that our reservations would become binding upon other countries unless they expressly objected, was, he respectfully insisted, not founded in law. Neither was his suggestion that the President ask the assent of the four principal Allied powers practicable. Would not the consent of the other twenty-two associated powers signatory to the treaty be necessary before the treaty would be binding upon them? Was it proposed to eliminate them from the treaty? What would be the result upon the League if the new treaty as proposed by the Senate were ratified by only four powers? Was it not evident that we would have only an alliance and not a league of nations?

Either Deadlock or Interminable Re-negotiation Would Ensue. Where, therefore, did the course of attaching reservations to the treaty lead us? Who could give assurance that the other twenty-two nations would accept our reservations unequivocally? Some of the counter reservations he had suggested as in all human probability due to be made by them, and no doubt many others, our Government certainly would not approve—nor would the Senate. So, without end, changes might be made by the various parliamentary bodies ratifying the treaty, and without end they must be returned to the other parliamentary bodies for their consideration and approval. Once the reservation program were embarked on, the only alternative to abandoning efforts for future peace would be long, uncertain and dangerous re-negotiations between all the parties to the treaty.

Even Germany would have to assent to any changes in the treaty, and under the new German laws such assent would have to come from their parliamentary body. But the real peace treaty was not with the enemy, but between us and our friends. And there was no precedent for such a treaty. We might force any treaty upon a defeated enemy, but we must compromise a treaty with friends. The ablest and most patriotic statesmen in the world had given their lives for months to arrive at such a compromise and at last a compromise which they all agreed was the best that could be obtained had been reached.

It Was Better to Reject the Treaty Than to Reopen Contention. Meanwhile, the governments of Europe could not wait; they must act. They must bring peace and order out of chaos and anarchy or they would be swept away. They had an almost superhuman task in meeting the wants and allaying the impatience of their people. They were holding them together, waiting for our Government to act, while our Senators slowly debated technical questions and future vague possibilities. "If you are against the League of Nations," he pleaded, "then say so and vote against it; kill it openly and quickly, but do not give it a slow poison that must result in its death."

Like nearly every other Senator he had never seen an instrument drawn by someone else that he did not feel he could improve upon, but in the last analysis we must trust the nations of the world to do justice to us. And if they would violently misconstrue the articles of the League against us they could accomplish their purposes outside a League and would be more likely to combine against us in such attempt. [8]

His Position Endorsed by Senator Borah. At the conclusion of Mr. Pittman's speech, Senator Borah completely agreed with his position that no interpretations made by the Senate would have any legal effect unless accepted by the other signatories to the treaty. He said: "I thoroughly agree with the Senator. I have no doubt that view is correct, and I hope the Senate will take that view. The idea of the United States putting in an interpretation and Brazil putting in an interpretation which may be in conflict with it, and another nation putting in an interpretation, and assuming that those interpretations are going to have any effect ultimately unless accepted, is perfectly absurd to my mind. I agree entirely with the Senator from Nevada

[8] *Congressional Record,* Vol. 58, Pt. 3, pp. 3130–35.

that any interpretation or amendment, or any construction or reservation, must go back and be accepted by those nations before it is worth
the paper it is written upon."

Bearing in mind that from first to last Senator Borah desired
only the complete defeat of the League, the reader may judge as to
what chance Mr. Borah thought the League would have of withstand-
ing a siege of reservations begun by the United States.

Mr. Borah's Restatement of the Isolationist Position

A little later in the same day he maintained, in reply to Mr. Taft's
charge of partisanship, that no such consideration influenced himself
and others. His position had always been clear. He had voted against
the acquisition of the Philippines and wanted to turn them loose now.
He wanted no "entangling alliances" of any kind with either Europe
or Asia. No matter what you put on paper or how beautifully you
phrased your League covenants the result meant war for our people
about things which had remote concern for them. It meant that our
young men would be called upon to suffer and sacrifice in those racial,
territorial and dynastic quarrels, twenty-three of which were now
going on. "Your league will not bring peace. The causes of war cannot be removed by the writing of a covenant, nor can those causes be
controlled by any five or nine men. The causes of war lie deep in the
structure of European society, and this treaty which lies before us
has done much to perpetuate and keep alive those causes."

Here was the fundamental lack of faith in the whole movement
to limit warfare that would make any support of the League impossible. If you did not believe in any probability of preventing war, then
the complete freedom of choice which Mr. Borah demanded for us in
entering future wars was logical. With reference to Article 10, the
commitment under it was moral and not legal. He would "accede to
the proposition that technically the Congress of the United States
could refuse to declare war, yet the moral pressure which would be
brought to bear upon Congress to comply with the action at Geneva
would practically deprive it of its legal power to do so."

The kind of moral pressure Mr. Borah was thinking of is clear.
He did not explain, however, how it could force us to take part in
a war we felt to be immoral, or to bear an unreasonable share in one
we felt to be righteous.

League Membership Meant Loss of Strength and Liberty. Mr.

Borah had, it is true, another pillar for his position in the League debate; *i.e.,* the belief that we could not enter any league "without losing some of the self governing powers of the American people, without forfeiting some of the independence of this Republic." It would make no difference at all, for example, what was put on paper about the Monroe Doctrine. If we intermeddled in the affairs of Europe, Europe would inevitably help to settle affairs in these continents.

"If I have had a conviction throughout my life," he said, "with which it has been possible for me to be consistent at all times, it has been the conviction that we should stay out of European and Asiatic affairs. I do not think we can have here a great, powerful, independent, self-governing Republic and do anything else; I do not think it is possible for us to continue to be the leading intellectual and moral power in the world and do anything else. I do not think we can achieve the task now confronting us, that of establishing here an industrial democracy, as we have achieved a political democracy, and do anything else."

This was a position which the advocates of the League were compelled to respect. They believed we should lose our world leadership if we didn't join the League and that far from robbing us of any essential element of independence and self government the League would become the best protection for our peace and domestic safety. Somebody was wrong; both could not be right; but there was nothing equivocal about Senator Borah's denial of the whole League case.

We Should Either Go in or Stay out. Aside from a common desire to further the interests of their country, the two camps could agree upon nothing except their mutual aversion to reservations. "Let the people of this country who are opposed to entering into an alliance with Europe," said Mr. Borah, "who are opposed to surrendering the policy of Washington and the doctrine of Monroe, understand that reservations, like political platforms, unless they are conditional upon acceptance by the other powers, are made to get votes, and not for the purpose of standing upon them after they once get in. The tactics now is to get votes, and, as Mr. Taft in effect says, we will bait our hook with interpretations."

He was "not interested in any form of interpretations or amendments or reservations. . . . It is either fundamentally right to enter into this enterprise or it is fundamentally wrong, as I view it. If it is fundamentally right, I do not expect the President of the United States or any other man to perfect the instrument in the first instance; no one but the divine power Himself can, without experience, perfect a thing out of mind; and, if it is fundamentally a correct proposition, I am not going to waste my time with reference to details in regard to it." [9]

SENATOR SMITH ON CONSTITUTIONALITY

Mr. Borah thus escaped the growing bitterness among the Democrats which had been expressed by Senator Smith, of Arizona, just before Mr. Borah spoke. The Covenant had been criticized in sincerity by some, said Mr. Smith, and grossly misrepresented by others. These latter critics were "professedly, devotedly in favor of *a* league, but not *this* one. Not one of them has presented even the skeleton of *the* league that would suit him and save the world. A league of nations for the future peace of the world was one of the famous 14 points set forth by the President in his message to Congress, on which a just and abiding peace must be made. Not one word of objection or dissent was heard then. Why this uproar and clamor now? Oh, you answer, 'It is not the kind of league we wanted.' What kind do you want? It is high time to give us a sample of your superior wisdom by presenting a model. Your good faith is at stake. It is easy to tear down what you cannot build."

Why all this hypercritical interpretation of the terms of the Covenant? The amendments suggested by the leaders of the opposition had been made by the President, "but no sooner had he done that than we began to hear of the unconstitutional provisions of the League —that it took from Congress the power to declare what tariff taxes should be collected, or at least affected seriously the constitutional powers of Congress in that regard; that in certain emergencies it took from Congress its constitutional power to limit and control appropriations on the happenings of certain fancied events which might occur under the covenants contained in the treaty. What wet nurses of the Constitution these great fault finding leaders have recently become."

Congress had often (in cases cited) conformed its action to the provisions of our treaties without any cry of unconstitutionality being raised. "Why, then, this persistent assault on Article 10 of this Covenant and the loud declamation against its unconstitutionality? . . . Section 10 of the Covenant is the very heart of the League of

[9] *Congressional Record,* Vol. 58, Pt. 3, pp. 3141-45.

Nations and promises the only forceful safeguard in carrying out the purpose of preserving the world peace by using the common, mutual force of the world, if necessary. . . ."

The Monroe Doctrine Pledge was Equally Strong. Moreover, the guaranteeing of other nations against external aggression was no new experience with us. "The Monroe Doctrine, to the preservation of which such useless and fervid appeal has been made of late, is itself a striking example. I say *useless* appeal for the reason that the Monroe Doctrine is not now, and never has been in jeopardy by reason of any provision in the Covenant. Is the Monroe Doctrine violative of the constitutional power of Congress to declare war? It simply warns the world that Congress will declare war if the doctrine is questioned by assault of any trans-oceanic nation. The Monroe Doctrine would be a silly threat if the world doubted that Congress would, when occasion arose, raise armies and pay bills in its maintenance and support. The world knows Congress has said so. Congress always has and always will keep faith with the treaties we make, but the whole diplomatic world knows that Congress has the power to refuse supplies whenever it shall so determine, and every treaty made with us is executed in the light of this knowledge."

The Panama Treaty Bound Us Legally. Besides the general guarantee against external aggression which we had maintained for a century over two continents we had also guaranteed one American republic even against its American neighbors. The first clause of our treaty with Panama declared that "The United States guarantees and *will maintain* the independence of the Republic of Panama." That bond of ours was "a direct defiant declaration of war in advance against any and all nations daring to interfere with or destroy the independence of this little home-made republic of ours."

Neither the Monroe Doctrine nor the treaty with Panama were attacked as unconstitutional.

"Why," he asked again, "all that clamor about a treaty amending our organic law? Why all this vociferous exaggeration about this covenant changing our form of government? Why this desperate delusion of a supersovereignty being erected on the ruin of our revered constitution? A super-state, a supreme sovereignty! What is meant by such declamatory catch words? Do Senators think they are fooling anybody by constant reiteration of them? A super-state indeed! Without a citizen or subject, with no local habitation or name, no geography, no army or navy, no treasury, no power to declare war or levy taxes. And yet such is the scarecrow of a super-state that political prejudice or personal hate is holding up to the frightened gaze of those who are ofttimes willing victims of this miserable cheap political camouflage."

Why Not Meet the Issue of Policy? Yet he appreciated the danger of the attack on the Covenant as unconstitutional. The great mass of genuine, patriotic American citizens, said Mr. Smith, revered the Constitution as the palladium of their liberties as well as the source of our marvelous prosperity and power. To the unread and busy of this noble class the disingenuous appeal was going forth to defeat, or amend, or qualify this great document because it violated the constitution. "Why not," he appealed, "quit trying to scare the people with these specters and hobgoblins scurrying among the ruins of our once glorious Constitution and meet the question fairly on the ground of policy? Is it better for the United States and for the peace of the world that we ratify this treaty just as it is?"

Every criticism of the League made in the Senate and elsewhere was based on the postulate that all the burdens imposed by it were to be borne by us alone. "All imagined injustice in it is to be visited on us alone. One moment's consideration of the mutuality of the Covenant—that each must bear his part in what is done and each must refrain from doing prohibited things—would greatly relieve much of the fear expressed for our safety and the preservation of our rights under it. Whatever we have to do, England and France and Italy and Japan and some thirty other nations are also bound to do; and everyone who joins the League must likewise become bound materially to do with us the same things exactly. All being obligated to the same results it follows that there is not one chance in one hundred that much will be required, and not one in a thousand that resort to arms will be necessary. Therein lies both the virtue and the force of the whole scheme. . . ."

Our interest, moreover, lay in a partnership with the nations to keep the peace. We were an essential and very important part of the world from now until the end of all human government. "Whether we will or not, our interest, our trade, our industries, touch every port and every transportation line on earth, and every consideration of all these demands that peace, not war, shall be the normal condition of mankind. Our premier position makes the peace of the world more important to us than to any other people. We have it in our hands now to accomplish this, backed as we are by the common consent and eager acquiescence of all the decent peace-loving nations of the earth." [10]

As soon after Mr. Smith had finished as he could obtain the floor, Senator Borah accepted his challenge and, as noted above, met the issue squarely on the ground of policy. European wars could not be stopped. Therefore we had nothing to gain from attempting to stop them; and we had everything to lose.

SENATOR WALSH ON ARTICLE 10

On July 28, Senator Walsh, of Montana, spoke on Article 10 and its implications. He emphasized the persistent ignoring of the phrase "against external aggression," and held it to be a perfectly gratuitous assumption that the political map of the world could never undergo any change unless nations were permitted to wage aggressive warfare against each other. He listed many examples of changes of sovereignty made by other means. Conquest, for example, accounted for little sovereignty in this hemisphere aside from the first Mexican cession to us.

The right of revolution was clearly preserved in the Covenant, a fact which set it apart from the Holy Alliance about which so much had been heard in the debate. Everybody knew that the object of the Holy Alliance was to put down revolt. But it was held that Article 10 prevented us from going to the aid of rebels in other countries—even made us fight those who did go to their aid.

Even if the charge were true what did it amount to? It was contended that we could never have won our independence without the aid of France which Article 10 might have prevented. He denied the allegation and quoted English statesmen and historians who agreed that England lacked the power to prevent our secession. Moreover the French Government in aiding us had expressly declared that its purpose was to diminish the power of England, not to aid us.

History in fact disclosed almost no examples of the unselfish intervention of foreign states in behalf of rebels fighting for freedom. Our intervention in behalf of the Cuban insurrection had been proclaimed as unique in that respect, and yet we came out of that war with Porto Rico and the Philippines to balance its cost. On the other hand, ambitious monarchs with imperialistic aims had often excused

[10] *Congressional Record,* Vol. 58, Pt. 3, pp. 3135-40.

their invasion of the territory of friendly neighbors upon the pretext that they came to assist rebellious subjects struggling against oppression to regain their ancient rights and liberties, and in many instances the uprising was fomented from abroad in order to afford an excuse for intervention that culminated in conquest.

It was necessary to remember that the League was not created to operate in a world ruled by intriguing monarchs, exercising autocratic power and dominated by the idea of conquest; it was created to function in a world ruled by self-governing democracies. This made a vast difference.

Who Would Fight England to Free Ireland? It was true that Article 10 would prevent any member of the League from warring with England to free Ireland. But where was the armed help for Ireland to come from? The effort, usually insidious, but not infrequently direct, to arouse the prejudices of our citizens of Irish birth and descent against the League was apparent. "But it is worthy of remark that those who most stoutly assail this feature of the Covenant avow with equal vehemence and insistence that we must 'keep out of the quarrels of Europe.' In one and the same breath they assert, in effect, that if Ireland should rise in revolt against the tyranny of Great Britain we would violate the most sacred precepts of the fathers by participating in the strife, even in aid of the Irish; yet they declaim against Article 10 because by it we agree not to do so."

It was plain, then, that the Irish could expect no armies from the United States, even if the opponents of the Covenant won. Neither could they expect them from impotent Germany, or England's ally France or illiberal and weak Spain. France and Spain had tried repeatedly in general wars to free the Irish, but had never succeeded. Ireland's freedom did not lay in the armed force of other nations.

But the League did offer hope of Irish independence by enabling, through Article 11, any friendly power to bring Ireland's case before the League for discussion, and through Article 10 by removing the supposed military menace in a free Ireland which England always professed to fear.

The case of Shantung offered a similar situation. Article 10 had also been condemned as perpetuating the Shantung settlement. This settlement was condemned as a part of the campaign to defeat the League because, it was maintained, the President agreed to it to save the League. That was what hurt. "Wilson saved the League by giving Shantung to the Japs" expressed equally malice toward the builder and his creation. Yet, again, how was China to be helped by defeating Article 10? What nation was going to send armies and navies to take Shantung away from Japan? Yet Article 10 offered China a guarantee against further aggression which she had sadly needed for a century and certainly needed still.

The Soul and Spirit of the Covenant. But perhaps too little attention had been paid to the criticism of Article 10 and too little to its merits. It was the soul and spirit of the covenant. It was the greatest guaranty of peace which the document afforded. "It is because it is such that those who for one reason or another wish to see the proposed plan defeated or rendered ineffective, if adopted, desire to emasculate Article 10 by 'Amendments'."

The effect of the article had been made plain in a recent debate wherein it was asserted that if Bulgaria attacked Roumania American boys would have to go over and fight Bulgaria. If this were true "the boys of Great Britain would equally have to go—indeed, the boys from every part of the far-flung British Empire, as well as the boys of France and Italy and Spain and Norway and Denmark, of Brazil and Argentina, with those of half a hundred lesser nations—and Bulgaria, in that situation, would probably take council with herself and determine that after all it would be more profitable to submit whatever differences she may have with Roumania to the arbitrament of the executive council of the League."

Senators lost sight of the fact, purposely or otherwise, that under the operation of Article 10 there could not be the recurring wars of which they declaimed. Inadvertently they admitted this even in the midst of their denunciations. A Senator had lately declared that "The Monroe Doctrine has done more to preserve peace for 100 years than all the leagues of nations ever formed." "Yes," replied Mr. Walsh, "and how has the Monroe Doctrine preserved peace? Because through it the United States declared in effect its purpose to make war upon any European nation that should attempt to violate the soil of an American republic; because we voluntarily and without any reciprocal agreement or other consideration bound ourselves and avowed our purpose to 'preserve as against external aggression the territorial integrity and political independence' of the republics of the Western Hemisphere."

The League was denounced as a "war trust," a treaty for war. In exactly the same sense the treaty guaranteeing the independence of Panama was a war treaty. But peace was the result.

Congress Must Weigh the Facts in Each Case. Neither did the operation of the article take from Congress its power to declare war. It was morally bound, though not legally, to follow the advice of the Council, but in each case it would be for Congress to determine whether the occasion for carrying out the obligation had or had not actually arisen. Our diplomatic representatives in the troubled area might advise that the obligation was not present under the circumstances. Nobody but Congress could determine the fact of its existence. Senators knew perfectly well that oftentimes one nation having a treaty of alliance with another would call upon the other to make good its obligation under the treaty of alliance, and the other would say, "We do not think the conditions require it," as for example the refusal of Italy to fight with her allies, Germany and Austria, in 1914.

Furthermore, if Congress decided that the obligation existed in the light of all the evidence before it, it would still be free to determine how the obligation should be enforced on our part. Perhaps only participation in an economic boycott would be required—that was a mighty weapon. Congress certainly would decide whether the army should move or not, in what numbers and under what conditions.

Senator Lodge had truly said, in his Union College address of June 9, 1915: "Turn it back and forth as we may, there is no escape from the proposition that the peace of the world can be maintained, as the peace and order of a single community are maintained, as the peace of a single nation is maintained, by the forces which united nations are willing to put behind the peace and order of the world." There were just two ways by which the forces of the united nations could be put behind the peace of the world—either by the creation of an international force, against which public opinion outside of France was generally arrayed, or by an agreement such as that evidenced by Article 10, in which the nations agreed to provide the force as occasion should arise.

One group was attacking the League because it contemplated war; another because it was founded on wholly impractical notions of human perfection. "In truth," said Mr. Walsh in conclusion, "it recognizes the inveterate character of greed, vanity, selfishness, and allied vices in humanity—in nations as well as in individuals. They now assert themselves, restrained, only feebly, perhaps, by the precepts of the Gospel or an intelligent perception of self-interest. The League attempts only to add, in the case of nations, the coercion which even

Permission—International News Photos, Inc.

JOSEPH T. ROBINSON
OF ARKANSAS

Permission—Underwood & Underwood

THOMAS J. WALSH
OF MONTANA

Permission—Keystone View Co.

ROBERT L. OWEN
OF OKLAHOMA

Permission—International News Photos, Inc.

KENNETH D. McKELLAR
OF TENNESSEE

STRONG LEAGUE ADVOCATES—DEMOCRATIC

primitive man found essential to his welfare in the case of members of his little community." [11]

Two Views of What Could Be Accomplished

Senator Williams on the Consequences of the Untrammeled Choice. When Senator Walsh had finished, Senator Williams was moved to an impromptu speech which attacked both the reservationist and the irreconcilable positions. The isolationist position he termed chauvinism, "this dead-set, mean, selfish, egotistical idea that leads a man, as a citizen of a nation to say: 'I want my nation left free and untrammeled to do whatever it pleases. I do not want to enter into any entangling agreement with anybody to do anything, whether it is right or wrong. I want to be left free at the time to judge for myself.' What would become of a municipal society composed of individuals founded upon that sort of basis?"

"Suppose the Senator from Utah, as a citizen of the State of Utah, went out and said: 'I decline to be trammeled; I decline to enter into an agreement to abide by the pistol-toting law, or by the homicide law, or by the thievery law, or by anything else. I will do right myself. I am my own sovereign, responsible to nobody but God, and at the right time I will do the right thing, and I want to be free to say when I shall do it and where I shall do it and how I shall do it.' Could you get civilization in a State out of citizens of that persuasion? Suppose each State in the Union said that to the other States of the Union? Could you get civilization in the American Union out of that? Why is it that thus far you have never gotten any civilization in the international world? Just simply because one nation after another, in blind chauvinism, has uttered that infernal, stupid selfishness. What is the difference between the American who says it and Bernhardi and Treitschke and those other Prussians who preached the unlimited and illimitable right of a State to do whatever it pleases, whenever it pleases, and who have said that the only limitation upon the right of a state is the power and might of the State?"

Human Nature Not Unchangeable. Another favorite argument against the League, that it was human nature to make war and you could not change human nature, roused Mr. Williams to equally vigorous expression. "You cannot change human nature! What a stupid, barbarous utterance that is! If human nature had not been changed

[11] *Congressional Record,* Vol. 58, Pt. 4, pp. 3222–28.

from the day our ancestors were drinking mead and beer out of the skulls of their enemies, this world would have been in a mighty bad fix; . . . and if the human nature had not changed from the day of Jesus Christ, and the precious leaven that He had thrown in to leaven the whole lump, from what it was then to what it is even now, as bad as the world is even now, we would be in a much worse fix. Why there is no way of securing progress, there is no way of going forward from savagery to barbarity, and from barbarity to civilization, and from civilization to enlightenment except by changing human nature. . . . And every nation upon this globe that is not willing to change its human nature far enough to leave questions in controversy to fair arbitral determination, instead of going around and cutting one another's throats by way of settlement, will be kicked out of the civilized arena, and ought to be. . . . It is a lie to say you cannot change human nature. With God's help, you can change it upward and upward, and onward and onward more and more."

All Nations and Institutions Were Fallible. For the reservation-ists his observations were equally clear cut. It was said that the League might decide against the United States. He imagined it would. We were not infallible. But he undertook to say that whenever the Council by unanimous vote, excepting the disputants, decided against us it would be because we were plainly and palpably and obviously wrong.

Still it was contended that they might decide wrong. Of course they might. He had represented a dozen clients in lawsuits where in his opinion the court went wrong, but it was a great deal better even then for the court to decide the issue than for the disputants to cut each other's throats. The chief good about municipal law and about international law for the preservation of peace was not that the decision should always be right but that there should be a decision and an end of litigation.

What Was Important? Gentlemen in criticizing the treaty looked through smoked glasses at the sun and noting a speck upon it ex-claimed, "My goodness, George, that is the sun itself; do you not see it?" Everything outside of it was only a rim of radiance, and of visions and of idealism while we looked at the dark spot, the speck. But, "Senators, however finespun your webs, you cannot get away from the common ethics and common sense and common morality of this proposition of bringing about a measure of world peace by a world agreement. You can take up the treaty and quarrel with this provision and that, and so can I. I do not like the Shantung provision.

I do not like the idea of trying the Kaiser, though most of you do. . . . I can find some other things there that I do not like; but when I compare the specks on this sun with this sun itself, which, as I hope, shall shed light to all mankind, giving men courage, giving women hope, giving children a promise of the future, giving education in the world a chance, giving progress an opportunity, under the wings of the angel of peace, a chance to grow from one generation to another, adding the fruits of one generation to the fruits of those gone before, and inviting the new generations to forget the ugly past, what care I about Shantung, and what care I about the Kaiser?" [12]

The Opposite View. The almost complete antithesis of Senator Williams' belief in the progress of mankind and in the inevitability of international enforcement of the peace was presented to the Senate the next day, July 29, by another Democratic Senator, Mr. Thomas, of Colorado. His speech was apparently the result of long thought and aside from hopeful interludes was almost as depressing as a judicial indictment of human weakness could be.

The desire for permanent peace had been expressed in all ages and had been vitalized by the carnage of every great war. Parchment restraints had been imposed at the close of all wars and the people had turned aside to find absorption in the more prosaic and profitable pursuits of trade, industry and politics. If the present treaty would do what all past treaties had been powerless to achieve it should be ratified at once.

Morality Was Static and Human Nature Unchanging. But what warrant did history furnish for the optimism of the hour? Had the recent war effected transformations in man that all previous ones had not? The war had been fought by the foremost Christian nations on earth and each side had proclaimed that the Almighty was on its side. "Morality, like every other natural condition, is static; its laws are unchanging and unchangeable. That which they were in the beginning they are now, and they ever will be." Moreover, moral motives and moral instinct had exercised but little influence over the progress of

---

[12] *Congressional Record,* Vol. 58, Pt. 4, pp. 3230-35. He started to say "What care I about the Monroe Doctrine?" But he would not say that because the Monroe Doctrine was absolutely protected; it was excluded from the operation of the League by specific name. But they said it was misdescribed. What if it were? If he named Mark Smith and described him inaccurately as having a pale countenance would that keep him from being Mark Smith? "and would the fact that some people said that the Monroe Doctrine was 'not a regional understanding' keep it from remaining the Monroe Doctrine any more than Mark would cease to be Mark because I had said his countenance was pale?"

civilization. How could we rely on either religion or morals to prevent future conflicts?

Were man's "ambitions so softened, his greed, avarice, and selfish competitions so permanently dissipated, that appeals to the sword may now be replaced by appeals to conscience, by tribunals of arbitration, and by conventions of similar import?" The twenty-three wars reported in progress at the hour gave conclusive answer. The passions and discontent of men rocked the world. Wars could not be avoided by any plans, leagues, or precautions unless the minds of men became averse to war; and he was unable to accept the theory that men could be made merciful, wise, and moderate, that their ambitions could be stifled and their jealousies curbed by treaty regulations. France knew that the German of the twentieth century was identical with the Hun of the fifth century, coveting his neighbor's possessions and restrained only by the power of visible force. Italy wanted peace, as we did, but not without Fiume and in getting it was willing to give the new Jugo-Slavia a wound that naught but war could heal.

Internationalism a Menace if it Were Not Unattainable. The Covenant presupposed internationalism. Could internationalism be relied on to banish wars? Racial instincts and tendencies were the infallible antidotes of internationalism. They asserted themselves with a vigor and persistency that no barriers could suppress. They survived every obstacle they encountered. Internationalism would be a menace if it were not an unattainable dream. Bolshevik Russia asserted its cause.

"Ours is a material world and man is a fighting animal. . . . Bernhardi was not far wrong when he said that war was the continuation of foreign policy by non-diplomatic means. And foreign policy now concerns itself with commercial intercourse more largely than with purely political problems. . . . The manufacturing powers are facing the dawn of their fiercest and most relentless industrial contention for the world's markets and materials."

He had been studying the causes of war since the beginning of the late war, and the effect of treaties upon war and peace. His studies had convinced him, much against his inclinations "that the optimism of those in times past and of those now living regarding the establishment of permanent international relations of any sort, and particularly for the regulation of their political affairs, however high the purpose or propitious the occasion, might prove disappointing." Yet he was aware that armaments tended to war and that we could not return to the old conditions and expect to avoid the old consequences. He was as desirous as anyone of reducing the probabilities of war. Hence his address was not a plea toward treaty rejection. It might be better in operation than it seemed in theory. [13]

LATE JULY APPEALS FOR THE LEAGUE

To Senator Nelson the Entanglement Argument Came too Late. Senator Thomas was followed at once by the venerable Republican Senator from Minnesota, Knute Nelson. The first part of his address was largely an exposition of the stake we had in the world. Our resources and activities were so vast that we required a world for their development and expansion. A fifth of the world's trade was ours. The most distant countries were now our near neighbors. Nations could no longer say with safety and immunity, "I am not my brother's keeper." Europe in particular absorbed half of all our foreign commerce. We needed Europe and Europe needed us.

"I confess," he said, "that I can not take much stock in the 'entangling alliance' argument. When we sent our soldiers to Europe to participate in the war with the Allies, we jumped that fence. It seems to me that was to a considerable extent an entanglement in European Affairs. And having entangled ourselves to that extent, why should we not entangle ourselves to secure the full results of our victory and avoid being entangled in another war? But it is claimed by some over-nervous people that the league will breed war. Can any sane man believe that if the representatives on the League of the United States, Great Britain, France and Italy, through the machinery of the League, should forbid Germany to enter upon a war, Germany in the face of that admonition would venture to cross the Rubicon? The League is the first concrete and substantial effort that has been made looking to the prevention of war and the maintenance of international peace. It may be that some of the provisions are crude and vague and could well be improved upon. We can hardly expect perfection in a first effort in a new field. Time may develop the necessity for amendments, and provision should be made therefor in the covenants."

With reference to reservations he thought that since there was doubt and controversy over the effect of Article 10 on the power of

[13] *Congressional Record,* Vol. 58, Pt. 4, pp. 3316-20. However true the conclusions noted above, Senator Thomas seems to have been right in tracing a fundamental conflict between the spirit of the Covenant and the harsher terms of the treaty.

He would have much preferred a league of the English-speaking peoples only, and predicted such a league eventually. If these peoples could not save the world it was past all redemption.

Congress to declare war it was better to explain to the League in a reservation just what we could do. So for the dispute over domestic questions; he thought the contention that Article 12 might compel us to arbitrate such questions was to a great extent neutralized by the second paragraph of Article 13 and the eighth of Article 15, but if there was any serious doubt about it let there be a reservation. This applied to the Monroe Doctrine and withdrawal.

He showed no enthusiasm for these reservations, but like many others assumed they were necessary because of the contention, and apparently thought they would be accepted by all the powers without difficulty.

Except in one particular, the provisions of the treaty proper seemed to him just, fair and reasonable. It would never do to leave Japan in full control of Shantung, with full right of exploitation. It would tend to put her in full control of the East, and ultimately lead to the dismemberment of China.

His deep sympathy with the League appeared in closing. "I have not groped around to find objections to defeat the treaty, for I am imbued with the faith that fundamentally the general purpose of the league is sound and fully warranted. . . . It seems to me that our country is, and ought to be, as much interested in preventing the recurrence of any similar war as in entering the war in the first instance. We ought to be as much interested in securing permanent peace results from the war as in making war. It surely cannot be more dangerous to 'entangle' us in securing a permanent peace in Europe than to 'entangle' us in a war in Europe." [14]

Senator Ransdall Reviewed the Costs. Senator Ransdall, of Louisiana, speaking on July 31, sought to review the costs of the war in human suffering and economic loss with such completeness that they could not be ignored in the further discussion of the League. He included tables compiled by Col. Ayers, Chief Statistician for the General Staff, and others, showing that the deaths from battle alone had been 7,500,000, and the direct monetary cost $186,000,000,000. The combined military and civilian deaths due to the war were estimated at from seventeen to twenty millions and the total cost between two hundred and two hundred and fifty billions.

Why was it that any considerable number of people could fail to be moved by the overwhelming necessity of avoiding similar waste of youth and wealth in the future? This question recurs to the writer

[14] *Congressional Record,* Vol. 58, Pt. 4, pp. 3320-23.

again and again. The phenomenon can only be explained by recognizing the extent to which the hatreds and fears aroused by the war still filled men's minds. For the United States, aside from this condition, it must have been possible only because we were so prodigiously wealthy that we could afford our huge slice of the cost, and because death losses had not actually forced into each home in the country a realization of what the war meant to the major section of the white race. To large numbers of elderly Americans the war had apparently been an exciting and profitable interlude ending pleasantly and gloriously.

Progress in Destruction was Plain. Mr. Ransdall next marshalled the evidence that burned itself into the consciousness of so many in 1919 that the next great war would be destructive beyond the power of imagination. If the art and means of killing progressed only in the same ratio as in the past, nothing but divine interference could prevent the world from destroying itself. Just as the present war had far exceeded in blood and treasure the great wars of the past so would future wars exceed this one. Civilization must end war or be ended by it.

The unbelievable acceleration in inventing destruction, evident from 1914 to 1918, convinced millions of Americans in 1919 that civilization must end or control warfare if it was to survive. Why was it that other legions of Americans could never be moved by the danger? Was it because they did not comprehend the power of science to destroy? Was it because they so lacked the power to visualize that the warnings of ultimate doom struck them as merely imaginary? In either case it was also because American cities had not been under constant shell fire from Big Berthas and in nightly terror of bomb and gas attacks from the air—because the composure of Americans had never for one moment been disturbed by the presence of a single invader or the sound of a hostile shot. The "sixth German city of the world" was safe enough at the foot of Lake Michigan. Its most influential press and official leaders felt—how mistakenly the future will tell—that it could afford to become the capital of isolated Americanism—if only it could get waterways dug to the Gulf and to the North Atlantic!

Some Conclusions. Senator Ransdall summarized the results of his study of the Covenant in twenty-three conclusions, the first six of which follow:

1. That the formation of a league of nations is a problem that cannot be evaded, and the experiment can never be tried under more favorable conditions than now.

2. That the present system for maintaining peace by international alliances has failed, and a strong league of nations is the only means for preserving the peace of the world.

3. The possession of a powerful international police force, as contemplated under the League, would serve as an effective preventive of war. The success of the Monroe Doctrine for ninety-three years without the need of armed intervention in a single instance fully illustrates the effect of a threat of force upon the conduct of the world without the necessity of its exercise.

4. A league of nations would mean the end of secret diplomacy and secret alliances based upon dynastic ambitions, and it would tend to create a strong feeling of international comity and good will.

5. It would secure material limitation of armaments by guaranteeing the different nations against sudden aggressive warfare, thereby excluding the main motive for military preparedness.

6. It would bring to bear upon international disputes and difficulties the organized public opinion of the world—the strongest force on earth.[15]

How true were these conclusions in 1919? How true are they today? Would they be any more true if the United States had thrown its weight to the League? What could the United States still add to their realization? These are questions which the reader of any later day may well consider thoughtfully. [16]

Senator Owen: the Dangers in the Monroe Doctrine and Article 10. Senator Owen, of Oklahoma, argued that the political enemies of President Wilson should not throw themselves in blind fury against the Covenant on the theory that it was his child, and therefore deserving of slaughter. It represented the best opinion of the whole civilized world. It was a child conceived by all the lovers of men. [17]

Without a gleam of humor opponents of the League had had the

---

[15] *Congressional Record,* Vol. 58, Pt. 4, pp. 3397-3404.

[16] Senator Gay, of Louisiana, spoke, on July 29, in a vein somewhat similar to that of his colleague. The art of destruction was still in its infancy. Could we as a nation stand out alone and say to the world that we refused to join in the plan to have world peace simply because the plan had a few features that were not to the liking of some people?

America could not, and would not, go to war unless a majority of her chosen representatives so affirmed. Article 10 simply put a stop to the land grabbing of greedy nations. It would do more to preserve the peace than any other article in the Covenant. Pp. 3313-16.

[17] Senator Owen's eulogy of the President was one of several warm ones which the Democratic Senators gave him in the speeches of this period.

hardihood to confront the intelligence of mankind with the astonishing proposal that the Covenant would abolish the Monroe Doctrine.
These unhappy statesmen thought the Monroe Doctrine was a charter
establishing suzerainty over the Central and South American Republics and that it was a species of overlordship by which the United
States had a right to manage and control the policies of those republics.
This un-American conception had been highly mischievous just to the
extent that it had had the temerity by mysterious innuendoes to
formulate itself. It had caused the Latin republics to look upon us as the
Colossus of the North, ready to invade their territory and their existing political independence whenever a pretext arose for the purposes
of profit—commercial, financial, or political. [18]

Article 10 was a powerful confirmation of the true principle of
the Monroe Doctrine, but the Covenant went further. It specifically
recognized the Monroe Doctrine in terms which ought to satisfy any
reasonable man. Instead of weakening it, the Covenant would
strengthen it, confirm' it, and cause it to be acknowledged by all the
world.

In connection with the proposed reservations it was to be remembered that sovereignty in the United States is vested in the people; any
Congress merely occupied a position of temporary authority. No Congress could bind a succeeding Congress. And any Congress could repeal
any treaty in existence at any time. That was the law of the United
States as repeatedly construed by the Supreme Court.

If it was feared that Congress in the exercise of its judgment might
give to the other members of the League, at some future time, an
impression of moral delinquency, this contingency could be guarded
against by a separate resolution passed by the Senate explaining the
constitutional situation to future as well as present governments. [19]

A One Minute Speech. The last speech of the month on the Covenant, and probably the shortest speech on the League ever made in

---

[18] It is interesting to note one of the irreconcilable Senators complaining of this
attitude toward us in 1927, and ascribing it to European propaganda, chiefly Bolshevik.
Former Senator Poindexter, of Washington, who on his defeat for reëlection to the
Senate was sent by President Harding as the American Ambassador to Peru, was
much concerned over the situation in an interview with the press on November 2, 1927.
The alleged propaganda had weakened American prestige in South America and
aroused apprehensions as to American intentions toward Latin-speaking republics.
"Active steps to counteract this propaganda should be taken by the United States,
Mr. Poindexter said. In his opinion, every effect should be made to convince the
South American people that this country not only intends to respect their sovereignty
but at all times has their best interest at heart." *Chicago Daily Tribune,* November
3, 1927.
[19] *Congressional Record,* Vol. 58, Pt. 4, pp. 3404–10.

the Senate, was made by Senator Sheppard, of Texas, the author of
the Eighteenth Amendment to the Constitution. After noting a report
in the press that he would offer an amendment looking to international
prohibition, he said: "Mr. President, this is an error. I have never
at any time had any intention of offering an amendment to the Covenant of the League of Nations. I regard it as the sublimest document
in history since the Declaration of Independence and the American
Constitution, and I regard the opposition to it as one of the most
unfortunate and depressing episodes in American or world annals.
I am for the Covenant without amendment or reservation." [20]

Other Developments in the Last Half of July

Meanwhile, efforts to advance and retard the cause of the League
went on outside the Senate chamber as well as in it. On July 16 the
headlines in the *New York Tribune* featured Senator Lodge as calling Shantung the "Price paid to Japan," and on July 17 they told
that President Wilson himself wrote Article 10.

Conferences With Republican Senators. On July 17 the President began having conferences with Republican Senators friendly to
the League, conferring with seven of them in two days. This brought
out strong protest from Senator Borah who attacked these "secret
conferences," and, talking of "a new crisis," demanded a national
referendum on the League.

In these conferences the President did not defend the Shantung
settlement on its merits; he simply said it could not be helped. Neither
did he offer any objections to the proposed reservations, much to the
alarm of his opponents. The Washington correspondent of the
Tribune reported on July 18 that "the President's plan of not opposing
the ideas underlying the reservations proposed to the League Covenant came as a bitter disappointment to opponents of the Covenant.
They had been eager to drive the President to oppose the reservations
on their merits, believing they could quickly convince the country they
were right in any such controversy.

"The President however did not even discuss the reservations.
He did not ask the three Senators to vote against them. He con-
cedes frankly that the ideas underlying them are good. He would
have no objection to their language instead of what exists in the Covenant, were the language already 'riveted in.'

[20] *Ibid.,* p. 2410.

"On the contrary, he dwelt on the dangers of opening up the Covenant to reservations from other countries about to join the League. If the United States adopts any reservations, he pointed out, the other nations might do likewise, and the result might easily be chaos. The path so started, he told his callers, might easily lead to the upsetting of the delicate balance of conflicting interests achieved at the peace conference only after weary months of negotiations, during many periods of which there was almost despair of any hope of finally reconciling the opposing interests and views of the representatives of the different countries."

On July 23, the President was headlined as the author of the unpopular Shantung section of the treaty. He had revealed this fact in discussing that settlement with Senators. The following day the President issued a statement denying the authorship, and saying that he had exerted all the influence he felt at liberty to use to get the terms modified.

The two Senators who had spread this report felt themselves unnecessarily thrust into the Ananias Club. [21]

Taft Convinced That Reservations Would be Attached. Ex-President Taft's proposal of reservations was also published on the same date. He wished to emphasize that the Senate might well ratify without any reservations. He was confident that the operation of the treaty would give exactly the same results as under the reservations, but it was the part of a statesman "to recognize the exigencies, personal, partisan and political." Condemning vigorously Mr. Wilson's course in handling the treaty, he wished to make it possible for enough Republicans to vote for it to ratify.

The League to Enforce Peace issued a statement on July 25 saying that a meeting of its heads in New York had been unanimously against any reservations.

The French Treaty Demanded. On July 24, Senator Brandegee reported to the Senate that the President had violated the treaty with France by not submitting it at the same time he laid the Treaty of Versailles before the Senate. He read an article from *Harvey's Weekly*, including a copy of the treaty as if it had never been published before. There could be no doubt about the violation. Senator Lodge gravely read Section 4 of this treaty from the Paris *Figaro* in both French and English so that there might be no mistake. Senator Brandegee held up the *London Times* of July 4 with the treaty in it, and had the

[21] *New York Tribune,* July 24, 1919.

British copy of the treaty read into the *Record*. All the world knew about the treaty except us, said the Senator. Why was it not sent to the Senate?

One would have thought that the Senators wished to ratify the treaty, or that it had not been published in full in the American press on July 3 and 4. In his message accompanying the Treaty of Versailles the President had said: "I shall presently have occasion to lay before you a special treaty with France. . . . I take the liberty, however, of reserving it, because of its special importance for special explication on another occasion." [22]

Why was it withheld? Perhaps for any one of several reasons that naturally suggest themselves; perhaps for the reason that the main treaty was enough to keep the Senate busy for a while; certainly because the President did not want it ratified if the League were defeated. But here was the President holding out on the Senate again! So Senator Lodge introduced a resolution about it. [23]

On July 29, the President transmitted the desired treaty to the Senate with a message explaining why he had signed it.

The Polish Treaty Obtained. On August 1, Mr. Lodge presented to the Senate the treaty between the Allied and Associated Powers and Poland, known as the Minorities Treaty, explaining that it had been submitted to the British Parliament two weeks ago and was for sale in London. [24]

Evidently the President could no longer choose his own time in the submission of treaties; the chairman of the Foreign Relations Committee had taken over that duty. He wanted to give the Senate instant information on all these matters, yet he was sometimes impeded. He was having much difficulty in getting desired information from the President about the Treaty of Versailles. [25]

The Treaty of Versailles Read. However the Foreign Relations Committee was going ahead anyway, according to a dispatch of July 29, which said: "The Foreign Relations Committee, which had not yet received the information it requested from the President, completed today the formal reading of the treaty. Chairman Lodge began reading

[22] *Congressional Record*, Vol. 58, Pt. 3, pp. 3075–83.
[23] *Ibid.*, p. 3083.
[24] *Ibid.*, Pt. 4, p. 3465.
[25] Three resolutions asking the President for a copy of the alleged separate treaty of peace between Japan and Germany, asking him to inform the Senate by what constitutional or legal authority he had acted in Paris, and desiring to have the protests reported to have been made by the other members of the American Peace Commission on Shantung had not brought much information. (See pp. 2271, 2276, and 2398 for texts.)

aloud when the committee convened. One by one the Senators slipped
out of the committee room, until finally Senator Lodge looked up to
see that he was reading to Charles F. Redmond, clerk of the committee,
and no one else. Without comment, Mr. Lodge continued. A little
while later, his eyes again lifting from the pages, he noted that Mr.
Redmond had slipped out to attend to some mail and he was reading
alone. Continuing to read, Mr. Lodge completed the formal reading
for the committee." [26]

The treaty of course had to be read, if it did take the committee
two weeks to do it. And some time was necessary to perfect the program of reservations.

Senators Pledged to Reservations or Rejection. On July 27, Carter
Field reported in the *Tribune* that Senator Lodge was highly indignant with Senator Borah because of the latter's speech arguing that
reservations would be worthless. "The significance of Mr. Borah's
statement lies," he wrote, "in the fact that strong efforts have been
made to secure the word of Senators that they would vote to reject
the entire League and if necessary the treaty unless reservations
should be obtained. If the 'Bitter Enders,' who want to kill the League,
it is pointed out, should succeed, by joining with the Democrats, in
preventing reservations being made, Senators who had entered into
such an agreement would find themselves bound to vote against the
League."

This was a probability apparently that was beginning to dawn on
Senators who really wanted to see the League ratified and who had
taken the vow "Reservations or Rejection!" chiefly with the idea that
it would make ratification with reservations certain. Many of them
apparently had not expected that the rejection part would become effective, nor had they calculated the full destructive effect upon public
opinion of prolonging the fight on the League. But the Irreconcilables had anticipated these developments, as the report of July 27
shows. "Senator Borah was non-committal as to the strength of the
fight to smash the league altogether when questioned today as to this
development. 'If we had time enough I would state positively that
we could beat the whole League idea,' he declared."

On July 28, the President gave Democratic Senators the impression that he was not sure he would make his proposed speaking trip
for the League. [27] He was continuing his daily conferences with Re-

[26] *New York Tribune,* July 29, 1919.
[27] *Ibid.*

publican Senators, seeing now some less friendly to the whole League idea. Nearly all of them declared to him without solicitation that they were for various reservations.

On July 30 he received Senators Fernald, of Maine; Harding, of Ohio; Dillingham, of Vermont; and Lenroot, of Wisconsin. His visitors told him that if he would accept reservations ratification would be speedy; if not, the Senate would force them on the treaty anyhow after a long fight. The President continued to hold that reservations would cause international complications. [28]

What should his course be? Should he accept reservations and risk the results of renewed negotiations with the signatories to the treaty? Or should he appeal to the people and undertake a long, bitter fight for simple ratification?

That was the choice he had to make in August. To him it was a choice of evils. Which would be considered the lesser?

[28] *New York Tribune*, July 31, 1919.

CHAPTER XI

THE TREATY IN COMMITTEE

THE beginning of August brought evidence of strength in both the irreconcilable and mild reservationist camps. A group of seven Republican Senators agreed to support a draft of reservations covering withdrawal, Article 10, domestic questions and the Monroe Doctrine. While the proposed resolution was intended by most of its signers as an interpretation which would not change the meaning of any provision of the Covenant it was to be incorporated into the Treaty at ratification.

Both Mild and Implacable Opposition. The Senators who sponsored these mild reservations were: McNary, Oregon; McCumber, North Dakota; Colt, Rhode Island; Spencer, Missouri; Cummins, Iowa; Kellogg, Minnesota; and Lenroot, Wisconsin—all Westerners except one. They did not present their reservations to Mr. Lodge for approval, but were in negotiation with Administration leaders. Their purpose was to hold a balance of power that would compel one or both of the other groups to modify its position. [1]

The chance of agreement with the ratification group seemed best, for the irreconcilables were increasing steadily the scope of their attacks. The *Tribune* noted editorially on August 1 that Senator Borah, apparently satisfied with the results of the shooting at Article 10, was bringing Article 11 under fire as equally dangerous. The deduction seemed a forced one. Surely there was no offense against sovereignty or complete liberty of subsequent action in agreeing to meet to consider a problem. It was incumbent on the critics of the Covenant to be reasonable. The document was entitled to fair treatment. A threat of war was already deemed a matter of common concern. Surely to discuss the matter at Geneva instead of at the various capitals was no great or objectionable matter.

[1] *New York Tribune,* August 2, 1919.

The irreconcilables, however, were in a perfect position for future offensive, due to their control of the Senate Foreign Relations Committee. Thus the Washington Bureau of the *Tribune* reported, on August 3, that "those definitely in that class on the Foreign Relations Committee" were Senators Knox, Brandegee, Hiram Johnson, Moses, Fall and Borah, while Senator New almost qualified and the spirit of Senator Harding was declared to be willing. Senator Lodge was not accounted for.

Entrenched on the Committee, the irreconcilables believed that time was working in their favor. Senators Spencer, of Missouri, and McCormick, of Illinois, reported that the opposition to any league at all was growing in their states, and Senator Walsh, Democrat, of Massachusetts, was reported as having gone over to the reservationists. On the other hand, the President was said to believe that the sentiment for outright ratification was growing. [2]

The Foreign Relations Committee's Quest for Information

The Foreign Relations Committee, having completed the reading of the treaty, proceeded, on July 31, to hold a series of hearings in order to find out how the treaty was made and for other purposes. [3]

Mr. Bernard M. Baruch, one of the economic advisers of the American Peace Commission, was called first. He explained to the Committee how the Economic Commission of the Conference worked, and answered questions on the economic clauses during three days. He was followed, on August 4 and 5, by Mr. Norman H. Davis, one of the American financial advisers.

Secretary Lansing Examined. Secretary Lansing was asked, on August 6, about the American draft of the Covenant. He denied to Senator Brandegee that it was written by two New York lawyers and destroyed at Paris because it was so absurd. Asked if the President had not recently cabled to Premier Clemenceau requesting him not to

---

[2] *New York Tribune,* August 5, 1919.
[3] The *New York Times,* of August 5, editorially described the activity of the Committee in July as follows:
"The Foreign Affairs Committee has laboriously read the document, line by line, paragraph by paragraph, to the end of the eighty-seven thousand words it contains. It conducted the reading not in the spirit of men intent upon a sympathetic examination of the great charter of peace and liberty for all nations, but rather like a body of the Inquisition hunting through an Erasmian pamphlet for heterodox utterances, or a gimlet-eyed church committee bent upon convicting the parson of heresy. The members of the committee are no wiser than they were before. The hearings go on, the speechmaking continues. . . ."

give the minutes of the League of Nations Commission to the French Chamber of Deputies, he brought out that the President had concurred in his own reply to Clemenceau that in view of the great freedom of debate in the League Commission it would cause irritation to publish the minutes. The query had come from Clemenceau. [4] The reported protest of the other American commissioners to the President on Shantung, which the Committee had been trying to get, he testified to be a memorandum of advice on the issue prepared at the President's request.

Other long sessions with Mr. Lansing, on August 6 and 11, dealt with a wide range of subjects. Mr. Lansing expressed the opinion that the President need not have yielded on Shantung to secure the signature of Japan to the League and Treaty, but failed to give the Committee any assurance that the records of the Peace Conference would be brought from Paris before the treaties with the other enemy powers were finished.

Replies From the President. At the close of the session of August 11, Mr. Lodge introduced into the record two replies of the President to the requests for information. The first, replying to the Senate Resolutions of July 15 and 17, stated that he knew of no Japanese-German negotiations during the war. The Bliss memorandum on Shantung, prepared for his confidential use, contained references to other governments which made it inadvisable to transmit that letter. He had no information as to any attempt of the Japanese peace delegates to intimidate the Chinese delegation.

A letter of the same date to the Committee replied to its request for all drafts or forms presented to or considered by the peace commissioners relating to the League of Nations, all proceedings, arguments, and debates on the League including the stenographic report of the same, and all data bearing upon the treaty with Germany. No formal drafts of a league constitution except that presented by the American commissioners were in his possession. This document he enclosed along with the formal reports to the Conference of the League of Nations Commission. No stenographic reports were taken of the debates of this Commission, and it had been agreed that the minutes should be kept confidential. The reason for regarding as confidential intimate exchanges of opinion on many delicate matters would of course occur to them. The mass of data used in connection with the treaty itself was so enormous that it would be impossible for him

[4] *Senate Documents,* Vol. 10, 66th Congress, 1st Session, 1919, pp. 145-6.

to supply it without bringing from Paris the files of the American Commission which included many memoranda that on grounds of public policy it would be unwise to make use of outside the Conference. [5]

The Senators, then, were not to have the intimate record of the multitude of differences and compromises of which the treaty was the result. Aside from the international friction and ill will certain to result from the publication of such differences, in the atmosphere of the moment, there was from the President's standpoint no reason for putting into the hands of his enemies starting points for further attacks on the Covenant.

As stated by the Senators, they were compelled to grope on in the dark not knowing how "this thing" was made. They had obtained, to be sure, the point they wanted most, evidence connecting the President with Article 10, but there were so many more possibilities they would like to have explored. They had asked for all the records. Was it not a most reasonable request? And the President had sent them only one document. Was not the President still holding out on the Senate?

D. H. Miller Grilled. Disappointed in their quest for access to further ammunition, the Committee on August 12 fell upon Mr. David Hunter Miller, one of the legal advisers to the American Commission, to wring from him some admissions of danger in the Covenant. He was questioned quite closely about his previous work and experience; the Committee did not seem to have heard of him. Mr. Lodge questioned him at length as to what became of the American plan for a league and attempted to show that the League Commission made the British plan the foundation of its work. Then Senator Brandegee asked him another page of questions about his experience as an international lawyer, before attempting to make him say that Article 10 originated in the American plan. A long colloquy followed as to exactly when Article 10 would come into force, during which Senators Hitchcock and Swanson intervened a couple of times to protect the witness.

A long series of questions, designed to show that there was no debate at the plenary session of the Conference which approved the first draft of the Covenant, came next, succeeded by questions from Senator Harding aimed at the conclusion that the League might exert pressure to alienate American territory. Senator Moses then brought out that

[5] *Ibid.*, pp. 252-3.

Mr. Miller and Mr. C. J. B. Hurst of Great Britain had drafted the final form of the unamended Covenant, after which Senator Fall engaged in a lengthy attempt to make the witness admit that the League could take territory from the United States and give it to Mexico. This again brought Senators Hitchcock and Swanson to his defense.

A further line of questions by Senator Fall argued that a status of peace already existed with Germany or could be created without ratifying the treaty. Senator Brandegee then attempted to bring out that the Englishman, Mr. Hurst, was a pacifist radical. Mr. Miller had not heard it, but wrote the Committee later that Mr. Francis W. Hirst must have been meant. After further questions by Senator Moses as to his legal connections, three Senators joined in an unsuccessful effort to compel the witness to say that the six British votes in the Assembly might be used against us in case we had a dispute with Great Britain. After Mr. Miller had refused to agree that the stipulations of the Covenant were not sufficiently clear, the Committee adjourned. [6]

Action Demanded by Senator Hitchcock. The next day Senator Hitchcock demanded that the treaty be reported to the Senate. Asked after the Committee session if he did not think it would advance the cause of the treaty to have Colonel House come from Paris and give further information, Senator Hitchcock replied: "The point is just this, I do not believe that any testimony which could be produced would change one vote in that Committee either way. Every member has his mind made up just how he will vote on every question. Frankly I expect the treaty to be manhandled in committee. It will be amended or reserved to death. But the Committee is not fairly representative of the Senate. In the Senate we will undo the harm which has been done the treaty in committee. A majority of the Committee is actually in favor of killing the League of Nations." [7]

What did not appear in this statement was the lack of votes in the Senate to compel the Committee to report, and the fact that the sentiment in favor of the Covenant had passed its zenith. The importance of controlling the Committee became increasingly evident. The initiative was in its hands. It could delay any action as long as it felt that opposition to the Covenant was being created, and when it did decide to strike it could choose any method it desired.

[6] *Ibid.*, pp. 379-429.
[7] *New York Tribune*, August 14, 1919.

EARLY AUGUST SPEECHES

The speeches in the Senate during the first half of the month were made by those who were in some degree opposed to the treaty. They followed, in the main, the forms already laid down.

Would the Millennium Ever Come? Senator Fall spoke on August 1, dealing extensively with the historical expressions of American patriotism. The League had "every element of sovereignty and government" because it dealt directly with the people of the Saar valley, the Rhine provinces, and German colonies. It would even "be the duty of the President of the United States, without calling Congress, to make war in enforcing the orders of the League," and the League would have "the right to inspect, pass upon, and drag us into an international court to ascertain the meaning" of every act of Congress.

He admitted that "there is no questioning the fact that aside from the well organized propaganda in that direction there does exist in the minds of a great majority of the people of the United States and of the world the keenest desire that some means should be discovered and worked out by which such wars . . . should be rendered impossible of repetition in the future." The desire was as old as Confucius; it took the form of the idea of a millennium in Christian times and in turn this doctrine was largely responsible for the popular feeling of the moment. Alexander the First had tried to bring it about in the Holy Alliance and now "another great chiliast" was commanding us to yield our sovereignty, surrender our freedom and subvert our government. If we yielded and joined the League we would have "not only destroyed the government of our fathers but, in my mind, we have committed a crime against the nations of the earth, against civilization itself, and retarded more than a thousand years that reign of Christ which we all hope will eventually bring the people of the earth together." [8]

Could We Ever Get Out of the League? Senator Sterling, on August 4, joined Mr. Fall in rejecting the claim that the opposition to the League was factious or partisan and cited a half dozen speeches of the President during our period of neutrality holding up America first.

He could not agree with Mr. D. H. Miller's construction of the withdrawal clause. The right to withdraw was contingent not only on the fulfillment of all obligations under the Covenant, but of all other

[8] *Congressional Record,* Vol. 54, Pt. 4, pp. 3492-99.

international obligations. "Any covenants which we have entered into in the long years since we became a sovereign nation, and which are continuing covenants or obligations, must be fulfilled before we can withdraw from this supreme covenant—this lord over all." This construction would of course make withdrawal forever impossible. Maybe, suggested the Senator, the clause was not meant to be binding, but only inserted as "so much camouflage, meant to deter whom it might, with the smaller nations or those inclined to be recalcitrant especially in mind." [9] He evidently was privately inclined to this view for he added that were it not for other objections he might, notwithstanding this one, vote to ratify the covenant. His main plea was for reservations preserving our freedom of action under Article 10 and the Monroe Doctrine. [10]

On August 5, Senator Watson, of Indiana, reviewed Japan's course in Korea, Formosa, and Shantung and asked if in the light of her record anyone expected her to retire from Shantung. China's entry into the war vitiated Japan's title by conquest and her subsequent treaty with Japan was void because based on fraud. Yet we would have to send troops to subdue China if she fought Japan to recapture Shantung. [11]

Was it Constitutional? Senator Kellogg spoke on the constitutionality of the Covenant on August 7. That document had been discussed over the whole country for six months and had been before the Foreign Relations Committee for a month. Without criticising the Committee he believed the country wanted the treaty disposed of and that every Senator had made up his mind how he intended to vote.

An examination of many judicial decisions convinced him that we had, and had used, the power to make treaties guaranteeing the inde-

---

[9] The withdrawal clause read: "Any member of the league may, after two years' notice of its intention to do so, withdraw from the league, provided that all its international obligations and all its obligations under this covenant shall have been fulfilled at the time of its withdrawal."

Mr. Miller, in a memorandum prepared at the request of Senator Swanson, held that the proviso in the article instead of qualifying the right of withdrawal introduced an obligation binding up to the date of withdrawal. Charges of nonfulfillment of obligation, he maintained, would have to be based on the fact of withdrawal.

Neither could any jurisdiction for the Council or Assembly over withdrawal cases be found, either express or implied.

Moreover in no other part of the Covenant could the slightest purpose to keep an unwilling member in the League be found—any member could resign by expressing its dissent from any amendment however slight. In fact the proviso, instead of preventing departure, made expulsion legal during the two years interval where otherwise it might have been contested. *Congressional Record,* Vol. 58, Pt. 4, p. 3606.

[10] *Congressional Record,* Vol. 58, Pt. 4, pp. 3607-11.

[11] *Ibid.,* pp. 3633-46.

pendence of other states, limiting armament and affecting trade and commerce. Similar review of the history of reservations and amendments to treaties led to the conclusion that a reservation which changed the meaning of the treaty would have to be submitted to all the signatory powers.

Reservations were, he felt, needed to clarify the matter of withdrawal, to reserve for us the right to decide what were questions within our domestic jurisdiction and to establish the action of the Council under Article 10 as purely advisory. He felt personally that the Monroe Doctrine was sufficiently excluded, but since others did not concur he added a reservation on this score to the draft submitted at the close of his speech.

The exceptions offered were not in any manner designed to defeat the Covenant nor to suggest that he was opposed to it. He firmly believed that they would in no way detract from the influence which the United States would exercise in the League and that they would make us an even greater factor in world affairs. He could not accept the view that any change in the treaty whatever was a reflection on our representatives at Paris. If this was correct then the Senate had no function to perform in this the most important treaty ever submitted to a deliberative body.

Mr. Kellogg also appreciated "the aversion which exists for European entanglements and alliances, which should, however, be overcome by the realization that no more disastrous results can ensue from a league of nations than have been wrought by the great conflict which has just closed during which we have been compelled to ally ourselves with the nations of Europe.

"The future, as it develops, will coördinate more and more the activities and interests of nations, and there is every reason to believe that, in the nature of things, an international court or league must sooner or later be established to advise upon and regulate the sum of human affairs and interests." [12]

---

[12] *Congressional Record*, Vol. 58, Pt. 4, pp. 3681-90.

Senator Brandegee included in the *Record* on the same day an article by W. J. Jordan on "What Every American Should Know About the League of Nations," in which 41 points of danger, vagueness, weakness, etc., were set forth. In this document it appeared, among many other things, that the method of admitting new members was not democratic; we could never withdraw from this supergovernment; there was doubt about our being represented in both Council and Assembly; the Council was the most dangerous body in history; yet expecting unanimous action in the Council was futile; no quorums were prescribed; the proposed disarmament would be futile; nations abrogated all right to settle their own disputes; all five of the League's methods of preventing war were weak; it proposed to override non-members; the matter of amendment was in a hopeless muddle; the mandatory system

In the debate after Mr. Kellogg's speech, Senator Borah served notice that his group would never consent to any reservations which rested for their vitality on the mere silence of other powers. Senator Brandegee agreed, but rejected the idea that the reservations would have to be submitted to all the 42 nations. Senators like Lodge and Knox had told him that it wouldn't do any harm to specify the consent of four or five of the great powers; we cared little about the others.

Renewed Assault by Senator Lodge. On August 12 Senator Lodge delivered his first prepared utterance since the treaty was submitted to the Senate. He, too, began with an extended history of the doings of the Czar Alexander and the Holy Alliance, suggesting that history was largely repeating itself. The preamble to the Covenant, which nobody had thought to attack yet, he saluted with: "Brave words, indeed! They do not differ essentially from the preamble of the Treaty of Paris, from which sprang the Holy Alliance."

But the "Covenant of this League" went farther than the Holy Alliance; it actually gave the League the right to interfere in the internal conflicts of its members in the clause of Article 3 which said: "The Assembly may deal at its meetings with any matter within the sphere of action of the League or affecting the peace of the world." No revolutionary movement, no internal conflict of any magnitude could fail to affect the peace of the world. Could anyone say that our Civil War didn't? Moreover, the letter of Clemenceau to Paderewski on the Polish Minorities was a practical demonstration of what could be done under Articles 3 and 11.[13] If Europe desired such an

---

was dangerous; the Covenant was irreconcilably antagonistic to the Constitution and the Monroe Doctrine; the Senate could not ratify it in any form without plunging into the dark, entailing appalling penalties, and granting a monopoly to one plan for ending war.

No statement in condemnation of the Covenant was too strong for the school of opponents which this writer represented to make. But when it came to hinting of an alternative method of gaining the ends sought in the League they were vagueness itself. This, said Jordan, was "neither the time nor the place to present even an outline of the better way"; but it could be quickly and easily set up. "Never was the world so safe from any serious war, for a year at least, as at the present time. One single year would be long enough to have the world practically guaranteed against war by the better way. . . ." (pp. 3670–80).

Once the Covenant was defeated it would all be so simple. Many men, carrying more responsibility than Mr. Jordon, who were engaged in arousing the fear and distrust of the American people against the Covenant, were to leave the assumption —even the definite promise—of "a better way."

[13] One of the conditions upon which the Allies created Poland as a State was the protection of her minorities, a condition exacted of the other succession states.

The whole purpose of Article 3, of course, was to preserve international peace, not internal order, yet no one could prove that the Assembly might not sometime consider a great internal struggle. How it could "deal with" the same would require much more ingenuity to determine.

alliance or league with power of this kind, so be it; if England wished to abandon the policy of Canning and join he had not a word to say; but he objected in the strongest possible way to the United States being drawn into these internal conflicts.

He could see no distinction whatever between legal and moral obligations in connection with Article 10. Moreover, he asserted that any member of the League could appeal to the United States directly, without going through the Council. We might have to help Japan whip China in Shantung. If at any time the United States did not fulfill both the letter and the spirit of the Covenant, we would be dishonored and the League would crumble into dust, leaving behind it a legacy of wars. He did not like the prospect.

Furthermore, Article 11 carried this danger still further. "Any war or threat of war" meant both external aggression and internal disturbance. Suppose King Hussein of Hejaz, then being attacked by the Bedouins, appealed to us for aid, we should be bound to send American soldiers to Arabia. It wasn't relevant to say that it was unlikely to occur. Congress would have no honorable choice but to send the troops. "There would be no escape except by a breach of faith, and legislation by Congress under those circumstances would be a mockery of independent action."

Then there was "the insuperable difficulty" of Article 15, which began: "If there should arise between members of the League any dispute likely to lead to a rupture." That would enable Japan to hail us before the Assembly on immigration. Was it too fanciful to think that it might decide against us?

The contention of the British that any question that arose under the Monroe Doctrine would be passed upon and interpreted by the League was absolutely correct. That meant its extinction. Why in the name of peace should we extinguish it?

In the matter of withdrawal also we must be protected. Were we deliberately to put ourselves in fetters and be examined by the League as to whether we had kept faith with Panama or Cuba before we could be permitted to leave the League? That seemed to him humiliating, to say the least.

Altogether, there was no doubt whatever in his mind that American troops and ships might be ordered to any part of the world by nations other than the United States. It must be made perfectly clear that not even a corporal's guard could ever be ordered anywhere except by the constitutional authorities of the United States. The lives of American soldiers must never be otherwise sacrificed. They had never failed us.

So far as the question of isolation went it was impossible to isolate the United States. Our part in the war also disposed of the charges of selfishness.

He would go as far as anyone in world service, but the first step to world service was the maintenance of the United States. "You may call me selfish, if you will, conservative or reactionary, or use any other harsh adjective you see fit to apply, but an American I was born, an American I have remained all my life. I can never be anything else but an American, and I must think of the United States first, and when I think of the United States first in an arrangement like this I am thinking of what is best for the world, for if the United States fails the best hopes of mankind fail with it. I have never had but one allegiance—I cannot divide it now. I have never loved but one flag and I cannot share that devotion and give affection to the mongrel banner invented for a league. Internationalism, illustrated by the Bolshevik and by the men to whom all countries are alike provided they can make money out of them, is to me repulsive. National I must remain, and in that way I, like all other Americans, can render the amplest service to the world."

After paying his respects to "the rhetorician," visions, visionaries and idealists, the accumulated grievance of months was packed into his question, "Are ideals confined to this deformed experiment upon a noble purpose, tainted, as it is, with bargains and tied to a peace treaty which might have been disposed of long ago to the great benefit of the world if it had not been compelled to carry this rider on its back?"

His closing peroration was, in part: "No doubt many excellent and patriotic people see a coming fulfillment of noble ideals in the words 'League of Peace.' We all respect and share these aspirations and desires, but some of us see no hope, but rather defeat, for them in this murky covenant. For we, too, have our ideals, even if we differ from those who have tried to establish a monopoly on idealism. Our ideal is our country. . . . We would have our country strong to resist a peril from the West, as she has flung back the German menace from the East. We would not have our politics distracted and embittered by the dissensions of other lands. We would not have our country's vigor exhausted, or her moral force abated, by everlasting meddling and muddling in every quarrel great and small, which afflicts the world. Our ideal is to make her ever stronger and better and finer, because in this way alone, as we believe, can she be of the greatest service to the world's peace and to the welfare of mankind." [14]

Reply From Williams and Taft. When Mr. Lodge had finished, the galleries, packed with women's organizations and veteran marines, filled the capitol with shouts and cheers for three minutes. No one could remember such cheering before. [15] The cheers changed to hisses as Senator Williams, essaying to reply to Mr. Lodge, made a personal reference to him.

Senator Willams in the heat of his reply flayed the trend of Mr. Lodge's remarks and his general attitude mercilessly. In some of his milder moments he said: "All the crossing of 't's' and the dotting of 'i's' that the Senator from Massachusetts has recourse to does not make me forget that he has neglected 'the weightier matters of the law.' What is the weightier matter of the law here? It is peace amongst the nations of the world! . . . Has he shown the slightest heart sympathy with the desire of the world to have peace?" With "an absolute, cold, New England, Brahmin cynicism" he had made fun of the idea of breaking the heart of the world, but the question presented to the American people today was "not whether you would, if you could, amend Article 10, or Article 11, or Article 22, or Article 25 of this treaty; the question is, Take it all in all, as a measure for the advancement of civilization and peace and humanity and justice, does it meet with your approval or does it not?" He had listened carefully to the speech and he made bold to say that it never touched the question of the peace of the world.

Coming to the most serious of Mr. Lodge's carefully made statements he said: "The Senator from Massachusetts speaks of 'the right of all the powers to call out American sailors and soldiers.' I want to appeal especially to the Senator from Idaho (Mr. Borah), because however mistaken he may be, however radical he may be, I pick on him as a man on the other side of the Senate who is honest; at any rate who has intellectual integrity—and I do not mean by that that there are on his side no others who have, of course. But the Senator from Massachusetts speaks of the right of all the powers to 'call out American soldiers and sailors.' I wish that the Senator from Idaho would tell me when he gets the floor—or now, if he chooses—where that treaty at any place gives any right to the League to 'call out American soldiers or sailors.' He cannot do it, because it is not in the

[14] *Congressional Record,* Vol. 58, Pt. 4, pp. 3778-84.
[15] *New York Times,* August 13, 1919.

treaty, and the Senator from Massachusetts knew it was not in it. He knew it as well as I do. . . . " [16]

Taft in his press reply to Lodge used more considered terms, but was hardly less severe. It needed no profound knowledge of history to realize how lacking in force and fairness Mr. Lodge's Holy Alliance analogy was. The view that Article 3 gave the Assembly unlimited power could not be sustained by an examination of the Covenant. Neither could the suppression of an Irish rebellion be brought in under Article 11. The clause put in to safeguard domestic questions was not put in to deceive as Mr. Lodge intimated, and the claim that the King of Hejaz could call on us to help defend his boundary was not a fair construction of Article 10.

It was very difficult for him to understand the attitude of Senator Lodge and others toward the Monroe Doctrine. They objected to its definition or to its recognition by anyone else. Yet how could it become "immutable international law" unless it had definition and terms? The Monroe Doctrine certainly affected the relations of all American states with others. It was a limitation upon them all. It was not a mere domestic policy; it related directly to international relations. The doctrine of Senator Lodge, if he could understand it, was to refuse to define these relations in advance, but to decide when the occasion arises what we thought they ought to be. This was not to make the Doctrine immutable international law, but an arbitrary decree, *ex post facto*. It was the language of absolutism. It made the Doctrine as offensive as possible to non-American nations, and to American nations other than ourselves.

When we had full recognition of the Doctrine for the first time we even resented the recognition and declined to say what the Doctrine was.

Further, the Senator's position that we could better contribute to peace by keeping entirely free from obligation ignored the central feature of any useful league to secure peace. The object of such a league was to convince those who would disturb the peace that they would be restrained. It was this cautionary effect of the League that was essentially and highly important. It was this feature of the Monroe Doctrine that had made it so successful. But if the United States was to refuse its might and sanction to the League, much of its power would be gone, while we would be merely drifting and waiting to be

[16] *Congressional Record*, Vol. 58, Pt. 4, pp. 3784-88.

driven into a position in which we must fight, as we had been driven into the Great War. [17]

THE SECOND WHITE HOUSE CONFERENCE

On August 10, the *New York Tribune* reported that the Foreign Relations Committee was eager to question the President in public, but its members did not want to be put in the position of guests or to be bound in confidence.

Failing to get access to the records of the Peace Conference, they were more anxious than ever to question someone who had heard the league debates and the Shantung discussions. They would like to have questioned Colonel House, but as he seemed likely to be abroad indefinitely the President was the only chance.

This desire became so strong that on August 14 Mr. Lodge asked the President for a public conference, and received an immediate acceptance. The President fixed the date for Tuesday, August 19, at 10 A.M. The Foreign Relations Committee also voted on August 14 to call five men connected with the American Peace Mission who were reported to have resigned because of objections to some part of the negotiations.

On August 15, the President reiterated to Senator Hitchcock his objection to the attaching of reservations to the treaty. The adding of reservations would encourage other nations to make them and would drag out the negotiations interminably. It would also indicate a half-hearted acceptance of the League which would not impress foreign nations with any confidence in its peace preserving possibilities. If the Senate amended the treaty textually, the President said he would send Senators Lodge and Knox to Berlin to negotiate a new treaty with Germany. [18]

The conference between the President and the Committee, on the 19th, took place in the East Room of the White House with the Senators seated around the President in proper order of precedence. A group of stenographers relayed the proceedings to a small army of newspaper men in the basement, from which the verbatim report of the conference went out while it was still in progress.

The President's Statement. The President first read a prepared statement in which he urged the early approval of the treaty, to permit

[17] *Washington Post*, August 27, 1919; *Congressional Record*, Vol. 58, Pt. 5, p. 4404.
[18] *New York Tribune*, August 16, 1919.

the reopening of trade with Central Europe and to stabilize conditions everywhere. The Committee was reminded how the Covenant had been amended to meet their objections as to the Monroe Doctrine, domestic questions and the right of withdrawal. Article 10, he felt, was in no respect of doubtful meaning when read in the light of the whole Covenant. The advice of the Council, which must be unanimous, was advice only. Each government was free to reject it. The article was the very backbone of the whole Covenant, and without it the League would be hardly more than an influential debating society, but the obligation was moral, not legal. It was a very grave and solemn obligation, but Congress was left absolutely free to put its own interpretation upon the obligation in all cases which called for action. It was binding in conscience only, not in law.

Most of the interpretations of the Covenant which had been suggested embodied what seemed to him the plain meaning of the Covenant. There could be no objection to such interpretations accompanying the act of ratification provided they were stated in a separate resolution. "If the United States were to qualify the document in any way," he concluded, "I am confident from what I know of the many conferences and debates which accompanied the formulation of the treaty that our example would be followed in many quarters, in some instances with very serious reservations, and that the meaning and operative force of the treaty would presently be clouded from one end of its clauses to the other."

General Discussion. Mr. Lodge then asked when the other treaties might be received by the Senate and proceeded to the question as to who wrote the Covenant. The President replied with the whole story of his drafts and freely admitted his connection with Article 10.

After that the discussion covered a wide range of subjects, the Senators asking him some hundreds of questions during a period of three hours and a half. Some of the topics covered included the reparations clauses, the island of Yap, the secret treaties, mandatories, when the treaty came into force, how the Peace Conference operated and what records were kept. In a few cases the President asked to be excused from answer, but only where he was asked about the delicate issues of the Peace Conference or to express an opinion about other countries. Several times he was pressed for an admission along a given line for a considerable period, but only once was he driven to an apparently untenable position. In this instance he had been contending that changes in the treaty would have to be submitted to Germany, but when confronted with the question as to why Germany should consent to amendments to the Covenant before she was allowed to belong to the League, he admitted readily that she would not have to consent— an admission which he might have refused to make had he reflected that the Covenant was as much a part of the Treaty as any other section in it, and that Germany had a strong future interest in the terms of the Covenant.

On the subject of Shantung he said simply that he had worked for China, and accepted the settlement only because he felt it was the best that could be obtained at the time. He explained the full details of the promise Japan had made to the Conference.

Congress Retained its Discretion. The debate as a whole centered on Article 10, the basic element of the Covenant. The President took the position early in the discussion that the guaranty was moral and not legal, and that it left to the judgment of Congress our acceptance of any recommendation that the Council might make under it. Again and again different Senators returned to the point and sought to make him admit that Congress would be bound in the legal sense in which a national law binds, or that there was little difference between the two, but his replies only served to make the distinction clearer. A legal obligation specifically bound you to do a particular thing under penalty. This was the familiar rule of national law. There was no element of judgment in it. A moral obligation was superior to a legal obligation and had greater binding force, but there always remained in it the right to exercise one's judgment as to whether under the circumstances he should act. Between nations where no superior power existed to enforce the obligation a legal obligation could not exist; it must be moral. The article created an attitude of comradeship and protection among the members of the League which by its very nature was moral, not legal.

He agreed that the guaranty was strong, so strong that in practically every case we would probably act under the advice of the Council given by unanimous vote, but that was not the question. His confidence that the nation would fulfill it did not remove from each individual case the element of judgment which we would be free to exercise at two different stages. We were, first, free to exercise it in the vote of our representative on the Council, who would of course act under the instructions of the home government; and in the second place we were to exercise it when the President acting under the advice of the Council submitted a recommendation to Congress. At that time Congress would exercise its judgment as to whether the instructions of the Executive to our member in the Council were well founded, and whether the case was one of distinct moral obligation.

When repeatedly presented with the omnipresent objection that if we did refuse to accept the advice of the Council other nations would reproach us, he replied that, in his belief, such a refusal would very seldom occur and only on the gravest grounds—and in case Congress was right he was indifferent to foreign criticism. The Covenant was built in the consciousness that the nations concerned had popular government. The moral and practical judgment of each nation would have to rule.

In the face of the evident truth of this interpretation of the article which was the backbone of the Covenant, neither Mr. Lodge nor any of his associates had the temerity to suggest that other nations would order out our soldiers and sailors at will. Neither did one of them attempt to show on any other ground that the League was a super-state.

The Right to Exercise Judgment Did not Destroy the Power of the Guaranty. Not finding that line of attack productive, they did take the diametrically opposite course which was always open to them, and said it would be futile, "a rope of sand and not an effective tribunal which would result in promoting peace," said one. "If there is nothing more than a moral obligation on the part of any member of the League," asked another, "what avail Articles 10 and 11?" [19] "What permanent value is there, then, to this compact?" And, "Would it not be quite as moral for this Republic itself to determine its moral obligations?"

"Undoubtedly," replied the President, "but in the meantime the world would not have the knowledge before it that there will be concerted action by all the responsible governments of the world in the protection of the peace of the world. The minute you do away with that assurance to the world you have reached the situation which produced the German war. . . . Without such notice served on the powers that may wish to repeat the folly that Germany commenced, there is no assurance to the world that there will be peace even for a generation, whereas if they know beforehand that there will be concert of judgment, there is the most tremendous guaranty. Joining

[19] This question brought the only trace of impatience with the Senators that was reported, though the color mounted to his face when Secretary Lansing's opinion to the Committee that Japan would have signed anyway, if defeated on Shantung, was read to him. *New York Times* and *Tribune,* August 20, 1919.

in it we steadied the whole world by our promise beforehand that we would stand with other nations of similar judgment to maintain right in the world." [20]

New Phraseology Could Always be Debated. Pressed on the advisability of reservations, he maintained that only we could interpret a moral obligation. A legal obligation could be enforced by such machinery as there was to enforce it. We were certainly at liberty to interpret the sense in which we undertook the obligations of the Covenant, but he pleaded that other governments be not called upon to act upon our interpretations. The League Commission had spent more than half its time discussing phraseology rather than ideas. The acquiescence of the other members could not be counted on.

Reminded that other noted men thought reservations attached to the treaty necessary, that the framers would not always be there to interpret the Covenant, and that after all it was only his opinion that reservations were not needed, he replied that you could not use any language, he assumed, that could not possibly give rise to some sort of dispute, but that with reference to the Covenant it was not a question of being confident of an opinion; it was a question of being confident of what language meant." [21]

Results. The *New York Tribune* reported the occasion as "probably the most searching inquiry ever directed, for a public record, at any President of the United States, or for that matter any other head of a great power," yet the proceedings had been very pleasant. "Senator Hitchcock praised the Republicans for their attitude, and the Republican Senators admitted that the President had been most frank." He entertained the Committee at luncheon afterwards, and all the Senators emerged from the White House in good humor.

However, "A careful canvass of the Committee on the return of

[20] On December 1, 1927, as these lines were first written, the world had steadied itself, for the time being. The Preparatory Disarmament Commission of the League was meeting in Geneva. The representative of Russia, joining actively for the first time (only for propaganda purposes?), had indicted the Western World for spending more on armament in the previous year than in 1913, and for preparing to use every power of science in the next war. The French had pointed out that local security pacts were becoming so numerous as to threaten the peace by the old alliance and division route, and had called again, in effect, for a revitalization of everything that Article 10 stood for.

[21] For full report of the conference see *Congressional Record,* Vol. 58, Pt. 4, pp. 4013-30; also the *New York Times* and *Tribune* for August 20, 1919. A study of the record of the conference, long as it is, will repay anyone wishing to get to the bottom of what happened in 1919.

Senator Fall had prepared twenty long questions which he advanced two or three times during the debate, and eventually left with the President for later reply, which was made on the day following.

the Senators to their offices showed an absolutely unchanged alignment. The President did not convince any Senators who are opposed to the League or Treaty, or any of those who want reservations. But, on the other hand, he inspired with more enthusiasm, apparently, those who favor ratification without change."

This seemed to be the effect upon editorial supporters of the League also. The *New York Times* declared editorially, on August 20: "In his address and in his frank answers to innumerable questions it seems to us, and we are altogether confident it will seem to the country, that Mr. Wilson met and disposed of every reasonable objection that has been advanced against particular provisions of the treaty. Our withdrawal from the League at any time is subject to no other decision than our own. As the *Times* has repeatedly pointed out, the question whether our obligations have been fulfilled is one for our own determining in the light of conscience and honor. Action under Article 10 is again subject to our own judgment; Congress has unquestionable authority to determine whether we do or do not take part in active resistance to aggression upon the territory of League members. The Monroe Doctrine remains above and beyond the League jurisdiction; it is sustained by the whole principle of the League, and in terms recognized. Questions of domestic policy are as free from any foreign dictation or meddling as they ever were, and the other nations are equally interested with ourselves in maintaining that exclusive jurisdiction. If the President's interpretation of the letter and spirit of the treaty, of the purposes of its authors, and his straightforward replies to the questions of the Senators have not removed from their minds all reasonable doubts and misgivings, then evidently nothing can remove them, and the country will be forced to the conclusion that the grounds of their objection do not lie in the treaty or in the League covenant, but somewhere outside. If that be true, then the people must deal with the Senatorial obstructionists, for the President has exhausted the resources of reasoning and exposition."

On the other hand, the *Chicago Tribune* headed its report of the conference "U. S. Arms at League's Beck, Wilson Admits." A two inch headline, "Plane Fires on Mexicans" stood above, and the first paragraphs of its account of the White House discussion read: "If it enters the League of Nations the United States will be expected to maintain its 'moral obligation' to employ its army and navy and other resources in any part of the world in which it may be called upon by the executive council to aid in preserving the territorial integrity of a member state from external aggression. This is the big, outstanding feature of the admissions made by President Wilson in the course of the cross-examination to which he was subjected by members of the senate committee on foreign relations for three hours and a half at the White House today."

The cross examination of the President by his foes had, in fact, been a severe disappointment to them. They had hoped to secure confirmation for a number of the charges of their campaign. They came away practically empty handed. Wilson had met them in close personal encounter, had subjected himself for hours to their attack and had frustrated it by the simple, direct replies of a man whose cause only needed opportunity to speak for itself.

An Interlude in the Contest

The month of August was a time of grave domestic unrest. Prices were still rising and wage demands to meet the increased cost of living were insistent. The President urged 80,000 striking railway shopmen to return to work at the same time that the street car men of New York went on strike. The railway brotherhoods and the labor world generally demanded the nationalization of the railways in terms that made the newspapers talk of "rebellion." Strikers rioted in Peoria, and even the actors of Chicago and New York struck and were later joined by the stage hands and musicians. Serious negro race riots occurred in Chicago and Washington resulting in considerable loss of life and increase of tense feeling. The passion generated by the war expressed itself in more than one manner.

Finally, on August 25, the President felt compelled to issue an appeal to the public to support the government in its denial of the wage demands of the railway employees. He was sympathetic with their need of higher wages, but felt that the cost of living could never be reduced or even checked by wage increases. The sounder plan was to attack the cost of living by other means. His position was at once endorsed by President Stone of the Locomotive Engineers. The increases were averted.

The Federal Trade Commission reported a close combination among the packers, and prosecution of them was ordered. The price of livestock fell 30%. On August 8, the President addressed Congress asking for a law to punish the profiteers, urging the supreme need of peace, discussing the hoarding of food, the regulation of cold storage, discouraging strikes and attempting generally to focus public opinion on the reduction of living costs. Army food stores were thrown upon the market in an effort to stop the ascent of prices. The Attorney General started a fair food price campaign. [22]

The situation was much worse in Europe where none of the belligerents were richer for the war, and want, starvation, disease and sporadic fighting were widespread.

For a week in mid-August the domestic unrest received the attention of Congress. There was a lull in the treaty debate during which a very interesting pair of arguments written by veterans of the war was inserted in the *Congressional Record.*

Hawes for Congressional Control of Future Negotiators. One was written by Major Harry B. Hawes, of Missouri, later elected to the Senate from that state. He began by urging full discussion of the League and the adoption of reservations. He had been much impressed by the power of recall which the people of the European countries having parliamentary government had over their negotiators at Paris and thought the power of our Executive to negotiate was entirely too great. The President did the negotiating himself and the American people would have been helpless but for the Senate.

He quoted the remarkable plaudits which the Tsar Alexander, an advocate of a league of nations, had received in Europe after the Napoleonic wars and suggested that there was a familiar ring in the description. It seemed highly improbable that Europe could recover enough to fight another great war in twenty-five years, so we could proceed slowly and with circumspection before "irrevocably" binding ourselves in a world compact. This was especially true since we had so many European stocks in our population. The various minorities would be stirred up when their home lands were under consideration by the League.

For What Did We Fight? Finally, we had not gone to war for various "fine reasons," but to punish German attack on our commerce. We had simply seen red. Did "sensible men believe that our draft would have worked smoothly, that our millions would have gone cheerfully to slaughter, simply to demonstrate the theories of the doctrinaire? The violation of international law, the brutal treatment of Belgium, and the thought that our turn might come made America see red; and seeing red, she went to war, and went to war for punishment

[22] *New York Times,* August 7-10, 1919.

and not for the purpose of participating in the government of Europe after the war was over!" [23]

Two days later Senator Williams put into the record an article by Frederick Palmer, one of the most widely known of American war correspondents. Mr. Palmer had followed and seen at close range almost every war of importance from 1896 to 1919. He wrote, in part: "We are making the League of Nations a partisan question when it is no more partisan than fresh air for school children. . . . It no more revolves around a single statesman's personality than the president of a railway is indispensable to the daily schedule of trains. Woodrow Wilson is one man, and 10,000,000 men have died on the Continent of Europe. He is 60 years old, with perhaps 20 years of life before him. The League of Nations concerns the life and livelihood of billions of human beings for generations to come and the whole structure of world civilization.

"I have voted the Republican ticket, and I may connect the responsibility of the Democratic administration with the management of the post office, but I refuse to rely exclusively on this administration or on any political party, grooming for the campaign of 1920, for the future welfare of American humanity or humanity in general.

"We are told that the World War was inevitable. If so, it was the product of the old system. Do we want to continue the old system in order to make another world war inevitable? Or are we going to try a new system? Many observers in Europe hold that if the new system— the league of nations—had been in existence in 1914 we would have avoided the cataclysm which has immersed the wreckage of nations in the blood of their sons. This supposition itself calls to the imagination of every progressive human being.

"The soldiers who fought in Europe were fighting to preserve their children from another such war, as I have heard them say again and again. That was their sense of self-preservation, the preservation of humanity from a repetition of the late orgy of human slaughter. The cry of the Allied cause was not loot, as in the old days, but to end war. All Allied propaganda in this modern antitoxin age found it must avoid any reference to the glory and adventure of war, which once had its appeal to that human nature which the cynics say cannot

---

[23] *Congressional Record*, Vol. 58, Pt. 4, pp. 3616-19. The article was presented by Senator Reed on August 13. It suggested further that 1,500,000 American soldiers did disagreeable training camp duty in Europe for months after the Armistice largely because the League was being discussed.

be changed. Shall we be true in action to the thought which was the inspiration of the Allied cause, now that the cause is war?"

Were We for the Old System? Then in equally vibrant sentences he described the vast differences between the Congress of Vienna, intent on restoring the fallen kings upset by Napoleon, and the Paris Conference looking forward to a universal era of counsel and democracy in which each nation should be made secure in self government in its own land. To be sure there had been at Paris a mighty struggle between the old system and the new in which the United States had played an arbitral, pacific and mighty part. The new spirit had won.

What now was our part to be? Were we to invoke the Monroe Doctrine against the very spirit it was meant to defend? And where was the danger in Article 10? He had not been able to see it. As the common law did not permit one man to overrun another's property, and the Constitution of the United States did not permit the big state of Pennsylvania to overrun the little state of Delaware, the League would not permit a stronger nation to override a weaker. If reservations had to be made, then make them without weakening the great principle which was the guiding force of the League.

But to start making reservations was to undermine world confidence in the League at the start. We could not expect the first draft to be perfect, and we could not be the kind of partner that suspected all his other partners of trying to take advantage of him. It was a plain issue between peace and war. If we were, after all, for the old system then let us arm.

But would we not have to police Esthonia and Armenia? That was supposing the old system. Moreover was it really sensible that European pride would welcome our soldiers to police their domains?

Could We Afford to Stand Aloof? If for no other reason we should support the League for selfish reasons. The world's creditor nation had nothing to gain and everything to lose in war. (This would not prevent classes from profiting, of course.) Any system which secured us in our possessions without extra expense for armament was good business for us. For us who had long preached loudly for peace to show little faith in practice would not only give the adherents of the old system in Europe an impetus to excite fresh animosities and new alliances, it would make us a partisan of the old system and compel us to make good our claim that we could stand alone.

Then he asked a question which is well worth reflection still. Did we want to excite the predatoriness of all the world against us when we had a land capable of supporting five times our population? That was not an idle question, as anyone who had lately been in Europe well knew. It was a burning question.[24]

But does this warning move the average American of later years, even though he knows that in Europe and Asia, and Latin America alike, the ruling feeling toward us tends to be one of resentment or fear, of envy or suspicion? Hardly. Until world-wide economic suffering engulfed him, he seemed little concerned. We could whip the world anyway. Perhaps. At any rate, if the League, lacking our support, fails to organize the world into a safe place for our global commerce and investments we may expect to have future opportunities to defend our interests when allies are not as numerous as they were in 1917.

[24] *Congressional Record,* Vol. 58, Pt. 4, pp. 3911–13.
Mr. Palmer added his conviction, twelve years later, that "An important motivating influence in the public acceptance of the draft in 1917 had been that it was a means to win the 'war to end war.'" Frederick Palmer, *Newton D. Baker, America at War,* N. Y., 1931, Vol. II, p. 64.

CHAPTER XII

AUGUST AMENDMENTS

In support of his campaign to preserve us untainted by further association with our atrocious allies Senator Borah presented to the Senate, on August 18, detailed charges of horrible atrocities by British soldiers in Egypt.[1] Senator McCormick, of Illinois, followed, on August 20, with "a review of the perfidy and aggression which has been the basis of empire in Africa and Asia." His effort was mainly to present Japanese aggression on China.[2]

Discretion Under Article 10. In line with the willingness of the President, expressed at the White House Conference, to accept Senate reservations to the treaty stated in a separate resolution, Senator Pittman introduced such a draft on the same date.

The debate following contains a very interesting exchange on Article 10, in which Senator Borah and Mr. Pittman agreed that it was the heart of the Covenant. Borah also stated that he had never at any time contended that you could take away the right of Congress to declare war, and he agreed that it could exercise discretion as to whether to send a small force or a large one, whether to blockade or to exert economic pressure, but he maintained that we could not exercise our discretion as to guaranteeing the integrity of the country assailed in some manner. Senator Pittman added that the section plainly left it to us to determine whether the fact of aggression existed.[3]

At times the outspoken men in the opposite camps came near indeed to agreeing exactly as to what the vital article called for. It was the group who had long before determined that amendments of some kind

---

[1] *Congressional Record,* Vol. 58, Pt. 4, pp. 3934‒38.

[2] *Ibid.,* pp. 4041–47. Senator Lodge submitted the Allied Protocol on the Military Occupation of the Rhine to the Senate on the same day. He had not noticed it in the papers and was sure it had not been sent to the Senate. He had obtained a photostat of the British copy as it had been submitted to Parliament. (P. 4033.)

[3] *Congressional Record,* Vol. 58, Pt. 4, p. 4054.

Senator Owen had also introduced a draft of reservations, to be passed separately, on the same day. Compare them, pp. 4013 and 4054. Both covered the disputed points in substantially the same way that the critics of the Covenant desired.

must be made who would never agree as to what this article or that meant.

Reservations Must Bind. All shades of the reservationists, however, even including those whose faith in the League greatly overbalanced their fears of it, now agreed that reservations in a separate resolution would not do. The irreconcilables together with their near allies insisted that the reservations must be fastened to the treaty and consented to by the other signatories, and the mild reservationists seemed impelled by party loyalty to concede that point.

Senator Nugent, Democrat, of Idaho, spoke in behalf of the treaty on August 25. He called attention to the fact that the Covenant was mutual; it didn't bind us alone; all subscribed to the same terms. But if through our failure to ratify the treaty the League died aborning, the responsibility for the next great war would be clearly on us.

Moreover, the principle of the League was not new to us. We had originated it and practiced it for a century and a half. Neither were the objections to it new. Delegate Smith had said of the Senate itself, in the New York Convention which ratified the Constitution of the United States, "Can the liberties of 3,000,000 people be securely trusted in the hands of twenty-four men? Is it prudent to commit to so small a number the decision of the great questions that shall come before them? Reason revolts at the idea." Delegate Nanson, too, had said to the Massachusetts Convention: "We have sworn that Massachusetts is a sovereign and an independent state. How, then, can we vote for this constitution that destroys that sovereignty?"

Sovereignty. Mr. Nugent knew of no reason why a distinction should be drawn between the "sovereign right" of a nation to plunder its weaker neighbor and the "right" of an individual to do so. It was true that if we joined the League we would lose certain "rights" known as sovereign, but all the other members would lose identically the same rights, so we would be in exactly the same relative position as before. Moreover, the "sovereign right" to declare war exactly when it pleased us had already been given up in the twenty-eight Bryan peace treaties ratified by the Senate.

The issue was between the League and armament, which always eventually led to war. If we joined the League we did lose our "sovereign right" to arm to the teeth and make ourselves an arsenal like Germany was for forty years.

Referring to the frequent invocations of the shade of Washington, he described vividly the total difference between his world and ours and held that nations like individuals could not stand still. We had to move with progress or against it. To pretend that the Covenant was akin to the alliances between kings and despots of Washington's day, born of a desire for power and conquest, did not obviate the necessity of our choosing to go forward or backward.

The statement that Article 10 was the heart of the Covenant was absolutely correct. Without it there could be no assurance that we would not again have to mobilize millions of men and billions of money. If 50,000 American soldiers were needed in Europe for some years to preserve peace it was a thousand times better to keep them there than to send millions to suffer and die after war had broken out.

He closed with a statement that he would do all that it was possible for him to do to bring the League into existence in order that when his summons came to join the innumerable caravan he might not hear the moans of men stricken in battles that he might have averted, the weeping of women that he might have prevented and the rebuke of a multitude of voices for being faithless to humanity and to reason.[4]

To the satisfied "realist" this was, of course, mere appeal to sentiment, wholly unjustified. But every Senator had to select the judgment that he would hold himself liable to, and they all ran the risk of submitting themselves to the wrong court. Perhaps Mr. Nugent in appealing to the judgment of humanity and of the victims of the next war did not appeal to the tribunal of the weightier jurisdiction. But certainly the men who labored incessantly to create the impression that the rest of the world would combine in the League to take unfair advantage of the United States and subject her to undue burdens cannot complain if their case is appealed to other courts than the voters of the 1920 election.

The Power of Our Good Example. Yet it would not be fair to assume that there were not men, then as now, believing that the policy of aloofness was the best way to protect the United States, and even to serve the world.

Senator Townshend, of Michigan, speaking on the League for the first time, on August 28, visioned little but dangers and burdens in the Covenant. "We are," he said, "to be linked up with a league of more than thirty nations, of which not more than one besides the United States is unquestionably solvent. If trouble occurs in Europe, which under the League and the treaty the United States is bound to enter, our government must settle the trouble and pay the bills, even though

---

[4] *Congressional Record,* Vol. 58, Pt. 5, pp. 4259–65.

a majority of its men are sacrificed and its whole treasure is exhausted, for morally we cannot turn back or surrender when we enter the contract. In a partnership each partner is responsible for all the obligations of the firm."

Here indeed was unlimited liability! And American boys taken from American homes would have to serve in both Europe and Asia for many years. "Something other than hazy dreams or untried theories should form the foundation for such a sacrifice." The reasonable possibilities for irreparable injury to the country were so great that strong reservations or amendments must be adopted. "If we remain aloof from international complications and properly solve the problems of this Republic, we will be the one hope of a world looking and longing for peace. If we engage ourselves with all the Bolshevist, monarchical, revolutionary, territory-grabbing nations of the Old World, we will not only be unable to help them but we may destroy ourselves." [5]

In some manner the United States was apparently to serve best the peace of the world by setting it a good example—an example, no doubt, of order and industry and prosperity. The supposition that such an example will have a profound effect upon the "Bolshevist, monarchical, revolutionary, territory-grabbing nations of the Old World" is not to be laughed at. The effect of such an example is and must be tremendous. But the very striving of the other democracies of the world, not to mention the peoples controlled by dictators, after the wealth and standards of life that we enjoy may lead to wars before we are well aware of it.

Furthermore, the assumption of moral superiority over the other peoples involved in the terms applied to them by this speaker, and many others of the period, cannot be calculated to establish a régime of peace. Even the assurance, often implied in our policy of leading by example, that we will probably settle the next great war for them as we did the last is not a palatable morsel for the European. There cannot be good feeling between any given parties, individual or national, where one arrogates an attitude of moral superiority over the others. Such a national attitude is as unwise as it is un-Christian.

Senator Owen in replying to Senator Lodge's speech of August 12, acknowledged that the prevailing appeal to the sentiment of "America First" was popular. The galleries always applauded when a Senator

<hr>

[5] *Ibid.*, pp. 4453-55. Mr. Townshend felt that the President had treated the Senate and the country unfairly in handling the question, that he should not have been practically our sole representative at the Peace Conference, and that the League should have by no means been joined to the Treaty.

struck an oratorical pose and thundered forth his sturdy Americanism. Yet a man could be a good citizen of a town, of a county, of a state, of a nation and of the world without any inconsistency. He could love his home, be a glorious American, and yet favor international good neighborliness and the means of attaining it.[6]

Knox for Rejection. It remained for Senator Knox to close the month's debate by going on over into complete opposition to the whole treaty. He scarcely deigned to allude to the Covenant, but condemned the whole treaty as spelling "not peace but war—war more woeful and devastating than the one we have but now closed." It was one of the calamities of the situation that but few of the one hundred million Americans upon whose backs "this great promissory note" would place "its mighty burdens" would be able to read it before signature. His only reason for speaking again was to let them know what was in it.

He then proceeded to condemn generally the way the treaty handled Germany. "Lacking the wisdom to go forward and inflict a military punishment (upon the Germans) that would have uprooted their philosophy of force . . . ," the treaty makers had written a treaty of peace which his long analysis showed was too harsh and severe.

The nationalistic aims which the President had asserted in advising our declaration of war having been achieved, he proposed that this treaty be rejected and a status of peace be declared by Congressional resolution. The approval of the Executive would be superfluous. "Nothing in all our history," he said in conclusion, "has called for a clearer perception of our present and future, a keener and juster understanding of our free institutions, a clearer vision of the mighty mission of our great nation in the world, or the dedication of a purer and loftier patriotism than the consideration of this treaty. Unless, sir, we shall have the guidance of the infinite wisdom we shall fail in our duty, and, wrecking our beloved country, earn the odium of its treasonable betrayal." [7]

A Western Campaign to Defeat Ratification. On August 21, Senator Knox invited a group of the irreconcilables to luncheon to lay plans for a speaking campaign in the West to bring about the complete defeat of the League. The Senators, besides Knox, who attended the council

[6] *Congressional Record,* Vol. 58, Pt. 5, pp. 4547–51. Senator Owen spoke on Aug. 30. He defended Article 10 as vital to the peace of the world and opposed its modification.

[7] *Congressional Record,* Vol. 58, Pt. 5, pp. 4493–4501. Having rejected the treaty he proposed that we proceed with his old, original plan of organizing a league of nations at a different time and place. (p. 4500).

were Johnson of California, Fall, Borah, Moses, Poindexter, Brande-gee and Reed.

The plan adopted was to send members of the group on speaking tours designed to cover all of the Middle and Far Western states, especially the states in which there appeared a good chance of winning Senators from reservations to outright rejection. The Senators felt that they could stir up a wave of opposition among the people that would give them enough votes in the Senate to bring about rejection, only a third of the Senators being necessary to that end.

The speakers would start as soon as the treaty was reported out by the Committee. Senator Knox planned to assure them that their votes would not be needed in the Senate while they undertook this campaign.[8]

EVENTS IN THE FOREIGN RELATIONS COMMITTEE

On August 23, the Foreign Relations Committee, on motion of Senator Lodge, voted 9 to 8 directly to amend the treaty by substitut-ing the word "China" for "Japan" in the Shantung clause, thus nega-tiving that settlement completely. Senator Knox also moved that no further action be taken until the treaties with Austria, Hungary, Bul-garia and Turkey were completed and submitted to the Senate.[9]

Senator McCumber's Indictment. The Shantung Amendment was adopted in the committee over the vote of Senator McCumber, who gave the Senate his view of the aims and consequences of the proposal on August 26. "Why," he asked, "did the majority of this Committee pause in the midst of their hearings to make this particular amendment and then proceed with the usual leisure to lay out dates for further hearings which will consume a week or so more? The purpose is ap-parent. It is to signify to the country that the Senate is hostile to this treaty. It is to put Japan in a position where she cannot without an ap-pearance of being coerced do what she has promised to do. It is to create trouble between this country and Japan and thereby send the first dagger thrust into the body of this treaty. I cannot but believe that the plan will fail because I know it ought to fail.

"Is it an act of true friendship toward China or a mere political move to defeat the treaty? If its sponsors now fail to come forward and openly pledge that if Japan is driven out of this treaty then the

---

[8] *New York Tribune,* August 22, 1919.
[9] *Ibid.,* August 24, 31, 1919.

United States will proceed single-handed and alone to drive Japan out of China, will renew the World War and send our soldiers into the Orient to fight for her, then by this act they are betraying China with a false kiss.

"If, on the other hand, they declare they will make war to drive Japan out of China, to prevent Japan receiving only those rights which the other great nations of the world have received, then they are proclaiming a policy which they have assailed as being the most wicked part of the League of Nations—a policy of interference with the quarrels of the Old World. Worse than that, while they violently condemn a joint agreement with the other great white nations of the world to shield the greater white races from annihilation they would send our sons to death to defend the inferior yellow races whom we claim to be so inferior as to be unfit to associate with us from a like self-destruction. . . .

"By this amendment we, a third power, whom the opponents of the League insist should never interfere with the affairs of the Eastern Hemisphere, proceed to set aside a compact entered into between two nations of the Eastern Hemisphere in which we are in no way connected and performing this act with an arrogance no white nation would ever submit to so long as it had a drop of blood left to shed for its national honor. By this amendment you declare that Japan cannot be trusted to keep sacred her word, given not only to China alone but also given to the United States and every other important nation by reiterated declarations. The act is not only grossly discourteous, but it is the act of a big bully intent on either forcing war or compelling a disgraceful surrender."

He knew they would declare that this wound to the treaty would not be fatal, but their purpose was death. The dagger was poisoned and if the poison acted as was expected, it did mean death to the treaty.

There was but one honorable course to pursue—cease attempting to annul the treaty between China and Japan, to set at naught a treaty made between Japan and the Allies during the stress of battle before our entry, and bring both Japan and China into the League where China would receive both complete present justice and assured future protection.[10]

No stronger arraignment of the methods and purposes of the dominant faction on the Senate Foreign Relations Committee in handling the Treaty of Versailles could well be phrased, coming as it did from

[10] *Congressional Record,* Vol. 58, Pt. 5, pp. 4345–48.

one of the older Republican members of the Senate who had nothing to gain from exposing the inner workings of the war which his colleagues waged on the treaty.

Few Americans liked the Shantung settlement, and some thought it so immoral that we should risk any consequences rather than accept it. Yet equally few could suggest anything practical to do about it. With some exceptions it was the opponents of the League, or of the President, who felt consumed with righteous indignation over the affair.

Borah's Defense. Senator Borah, in reply to Mr. McCumber, called a long roll of Japan's promises to respect the independence of Korea as evidence that Japan could not be trusted, and held up the Shantung affair as the iniquity incomparable. It is, he said, "indefensible from any standpoint of morals or international justice or common decency. It is one of those things so immoral and unrighteous that we wish to approach it with deaf ears and closed eyes. We dread even to think about it. We loathe to be forced to attempt to defend it. It will dishonor and degrade any people who seek to uphold it. War will inevitably follow as the result of an attempt to perpetuate it. It is founded on immorality and revolting injustice. It is outside the pale of respectability even according to ancient standards. It shocks the conscience even of European diplomacy. Naked, hideous, and revolting it looms up before us as a monster from that cruel and shameless world which all had hoped and prayed was forever behind us. It smacks of all the iniquities of European adjustments. Indeed perhaps it has no parallel when all its features are considered." [11]

On the same day the Foreign Relations Committee adopted fifty amendments to the treaty designed to remove the American members from nearly all of the commissions set up to enforce the various provisions of the treaty.[12]

An American Peace Conference Instituted. The Committee had been engaged in questioning two Americans who had been advisers to China, Mr. Thos. F. Millard and Mr. John C. Ferguson, at the time of the White House Conference. Two days later, on August 21, it replied to the President's plea for action on the treaty by voting, in the words of the *Chicago Tribune*, "to grant 'a day in court' to all the subject peoples denied a hearing at the Paris Conference."

The Senators would thus hold a peace conference of their own.

[11] *Ibid.*, p. 4355.
[12] *New York Tribune*, August 27, 1919.

Denied the privilege of sitting at Paris, they would make themselves into a tribunal to review the complaints of all those racial groups who were outside the scope of action of the Paris Conference, or dissatisfied with its results.

Sensing the Senate's profound interest in the enforcement of the President's doctrine of self-determination, seventeen such peoples had already established their headquarters in Washington to "ascertain whether President Wilson's self-determination principle has any more weight in the American conference than it had at Paris." The "American Conference" would hear the subjects of Great Britain first. What the Committee would do in response to these protests was "largely a matter of surmise," but it was regarded as "inevitable that the subject peoples will present issues that must be voted on in the Senate." [13]

The Committee then proceeded gravely to hear the complaints of purported representatives of the various disappointed peoples of the earth, as if they actually had the power to do something for them besides assist in airing their grievances. Egypt on August 25, was followed by representatives of the Negro-Americans on the 28th, who presented amendments designed to provide guarantees for the colored American "minority," accompanied by the appeals they had addressed to the Peace Conference. The record does not include what the Committee would have said if the Peace Conference had attempted to legislate in behalf of the American Negro. [14]

The Negroes were succeeded, on the 29th, by the American Mid-European Association, representing Lithuania, Latvia, Esthonia and the Ukraine. They prayed recognition of their new governments as independent countries, just as if recognition were not an executive function and the Committee could give it to them. The President had maintained the attitude that recognition of the new states carved out of Russia in her disorganizaion should not be too hasty. This session was enlivened by moving pictures showing German atrocities committed on the Lithuanians. It also witnessed an American lawyer with an Indian at his elbow arguing for freedom for India and maintaining "that this is not fiction—this argument."

Before the Committee proceeded to break up the British Empire, however, it heard a delegation of Irish-Americans present the case of

---

[13] *Chicago Tribune*, August 22, 1919. Even a Scottish National Committee, pretending to speak for "organizations representing majority of constituents of Scotland," was on the ground to present its case.—*New York Tribune*, August 24, 1919.

The Committee did require the dissatisfied groups to present their case through American citizens.

[14] *Senate Documents*, No. 10, 66th Congress, 1st Session, pp. 628–700.

the proposed Irish Republic on the 30th. The territorial claims of Greece were presented on the same day, but the Committee did not fix the Greek frontiers at that session.[15]

On September 2 the Committee heard extended arguments of the Hungarians against the dismemberment of the kingdom they had maintained for a thousand years, *i.e.*, against the freeing of their subject peoples. The Committee, however, left the delimitation of the Hungarian boundaries to the Paris Peace Conference. Instead, it listened to representatives of Albania plead for the establishment of their independence. They were followed by a gentleman who had surreptitiously obtained a copy of an alleged treaty just concluded between Great Britain and Persia which was said to hand over to the English the total sovereignty of Persia. He read it to the Committee to see if they didn't think it sounded authentic, and desired them to make a ringing protest against it. Additional Irish, Lithuanian and Japanese briefs were incorporated into the record of the day.

September 3 saw the Swedish claim to the Aaland Islands presented by a man who said he could not speak for Sweden, and a delegation of American Czechs refute the Hungarian claims.

September 4 brought friends of Jugo-Slavia who contended that any port for Jugo-Slavia on the Adriatic other than Trieste or Fiume was out of the question due to the prohibitive cost of piercing the Dinaric Mountains. The Italians came, on the 5th, and maintained that the people of Fiume were Italian and must remain so.[16]

Some Explanations of the Committee's Course. What purposes did these hearings serve? They were ostensibly carried on to give the Committee information about the treaty, and of course they were not unprecedented. Listening to all those who wish to argue is a common device of Congressional Committees when controversial questions come up. The Committee got a good deal of interesting general information, too, about the territorial and racial disputes, in all of which it had little interest.

Otherwise the hearings gave further time for developing opposition to the League. They were also "good politics." They gave a number of large groups of Americans of foreign extraction a feeling that the Senate Committee on Foreign Relations was a friendly and sympathetic body ready to listen to the grievances of their home lands, if it couldn't do anything about them. Some of the groups clashed, of course, but all felt that they had had a good chance to publish their argument.

[15] *Ibid.*, pp. 701-934.   [16] *Ibid.*, 947-1159.

The results for the anti-League cause seem to have been good. The effect upon our national unity and ideals is a different matter. One bitter critic of the time charged that "The forces of hyphenation were boldly called into being and no effort spared to revive and exaggerate the divisive prejudices of American life." [17] The indictment is a serious one.

The operations of the Committee, however, were apparently generally accepted as strategic maneuvers. Most of the observers still took it for granted that the treaty would be ratified in some form. Thus the *New York Times* of August 27 could hardly believe that Senator Lodge, "with all his carefully cultivated art of incandescent partisanship," expected to see his Shantung amendment adopted by the Senate. He could scarcely want to see the United States exposed to the humiliation and shame of making a separate peace with Germany. The purpose was pretty clear. It was to make sure, for 1920, of California and all the other Far Western states where the anti-Japanese bugaboo could be used to advantage, and elsewhere to attract the various racial groups who were angry or dissatisfied over the outcome of the war. Incidentally, the President might be driven to accept reservations to avert amendments.

In similar vein, if not by way of reply, the *New York Tribune* advised its readers the next day to discount the resolves to do this or that which were coming out of Washington, however loudly advertised. The action of the Committee in adopting the Fall amendments was, it thought, strategic rather than definitive. The President had begun the encounter by boasting that he would entangle the treaty and the Covenant so that they could not be separated. This was in "disregard of the spirit of the Constitution," and the Senate had set about devising ways to defeat the President's design. It had "not been a pleasing business," but the Senate could say the President began it and had not desisted from effort "to win a personal and party victory without scruple as to method." In this contest of wits the Senate had so far outplayed the White House.

The President, continued the *Tribune,* had several times been seemingly on the verge of accepting the principle of reservations. Perhaps he still intended to do so, but strategy forbade him until the Senate was firmly committed to a particular form of reservations. The Pittman separate resolution reservations offered a springboard from which to vault to public acceptance of reservations as soon as the Senate

[17] George Creel, *The War, the World and Wilson,* N. Y., 1920, p. 330.

majority uncovered its precise program. So far the position of the Senate had steadily grown stronger, but should it appear that the purpose was to defeat ratification altogether, the sentiment might change.

The *Times* of the same date addressed itself to the situation that would result if the Committee were sustained. It held that that body in tearing up the Covenant was also destroying the actual League built up by the war. Their Shantung amendment expelled either Japan or the United States from the Allied powers. Could it be seriously contended that by destroying the association of powers thus built up the United States would not deserve to lose its friends?

Moreover, if this Committee could repudiate the work of a great Peace Conference by maiming and transforming the whole meaning of the treaty at the rate of fifty amendments a day, what respect and consideration could be shown to plenipotentiaries of the United States in future serious negotiations? The fact was that several of the Republican members of the Committee were aspirants for the Presidential nomination the next year. For this reason and others they would destroy Woodrow Wilson politically. Because this group insisted that the way must be made clear for the election of one of their number or of their party as President, we must withdraw from the world-wide organized peace movement. We declared that we did not care whether peace was preserved and war abolished; we were concerned only with party plans and triumphs.

WILSON'S DECISION

In whatever way one looked at it, the treaty's chances were not improving. The very situation that the President had feared and had sought to avert a year before in his appeal to the people for a Democratic Congress had occurred. Organizing the Senate by two votes, including that of Mr. Newberry of Michigan, later forced from that body by public opinion, the President's bitterest enemies sat securely astride the treaty in the Committee. The majority leader, Mr. Lodge, offered an amendment that must exclude the United States from the League, if adopted. His principal aid, Senator Knox, came out for complete rejection and planned a great speaking campaign in the West to stir the fears of the people to that end. The other members of the Committee majority attacked daily, wherever an opportunity seemed to offer.

Furthermore, instead of proposing the final mutilation to the League which it was evident they wished to administer, they deliberately awaited a more favorable opportunity while they encouraged a medley of racial elements to attack the Treaty and the League. In response to the President's request for action, they solemnly heard a lady with an Irish name argue the claim of Italy to Fiume. She had not been officially connected with the Peace Conference, but she had been an unofficial secretary to somebody who was.

In this situation it appeared to the President that the treaty was lost, or at the best due to receive indefinite emasculation, unless the power of public opinion could be stirred to insistent intensity behind the Senators. Believing as always that the people wanted the League and would demand it if they knew the facts, he made his final decision to appeal to Cæsar, to go into the West which had elected him in 1916 and had since stood by him in more than one crisis.

It was a fateful decision, the wisdom of which is questioned by many. Should he not have remained in Washington, conciliated the opposition and made the best terms he could with it? It may be so. It is less easy, however, to say just what more he could have done to advance the treaty unless he had sought the mercy of his implacable enemies. He had talked individually with many Senators who were known to favor the League in some degree, without result. Several had said to him that they knew the treaty should go through, but were pledged to defeat it. [18] He had conferred collectively with his opponents in the Second White House Conference, hoping to make his "whole position as clear as possible" and "to clear the air in a sober and wholesome way." [19] This effort also had been unproductive. Furthermore, Wilson could not have followed the course of his leading opponents in the Senate during the year preceding without knowing that they would accept no settlement which would leave him in a tenable position. Every move of the chief leaders of the opposition from September, 1918, to September, 1919, had indicated that nothing could be expected from them.

Could Reasoning Turn the Scale? No gain, moreover, seemed likely to come from waiting. The initiative was in the hands of the opposition and they were appealing not only to the passions of the foreign born, but to instincts and ideas, not to say prejudices, that were deeply embedded in the earlier American stock. Senator Lodge himself represented the original American stock of the Republican North

[18] A letter of July 21, 1931, from Mr. Norman H. Davis.
[19] H. H. Kohlsaat, *From McKinley to Harding*, N. Y., 1923, p. 220.

which, while it might be glad to use the newer immigration at the moment, was determined at all odds to control it and to continue to rule the country.

As R. L. Duffus, wrote in the *New York Globe,* a paper friendly to the League: "Underneath the flood of the new immigration there still stands, solid as a rock, the pioneer race of the old immigration, maintaining stubbornly the old American ideals. And among those ideals are two that apply to this crisis: diplomatic isolation, political particularism. We are the chosen people and can have no traffic with the Philistines. To deepen this insular consciousness, a homesick army of three million men has poured back from France, irritated, disillusioned, and only too glad to shut the front gate and stay at home for a while.

"An appeal to this deep sentiment might carry an election against Mr. Wilson and smash the League, root and branch. I think it can be demonstrated that the arguments such an appeal would carry are all easily answerable. But something more than arguments will be necessary. Mr. Wilson and his supporters will have to create anew a moral fervor as intense as that which carried our armies to France." [20]

Could it be done again so soon? Woodrow Wilson believed it could. Until the votes in the 1920 election were counted, he never doubted that the people would stand by the League. Even then his faith was not destroyed; its justification was, he thought, only postponed. His belief that the American people presented with a moral issue would decide it rightly was profound.

Should Wilson Risk the Effort? A serious doubt did exist as to his ability to carry the case to the people. Returning from the Peace Conference seriously depleted in vitality, the heat and pressure, both of events and of the Washington summer, had left him little opportunity for recovery. It was, nevertheless, difficult to restrain him from carrying his cause to the people in midsummer, regardless of the cost, as the tactics of the opposition continued.

A visitor on July 25, finding the President weak and trembling, told him that he was too ill to make the trip, that he would break down before he reached the Rockies. His Cabinet, too, warned him that the effort might be fatal, but in each case he promptly replied that he would be glad to give his life for the cause.[21] "The President," adds Kohl-

[20] *Literary Digest,* August 30, 1919.
[21] Kohlsaat, *From McKinley to Harding,* p. 219; David F. Houston, "The War on Wilson," *World's Work,* September, 1926, Vol. 52, p. 542.

saat, "indulged in no heroics." He did not need to. The War had been to him a tragedy mitigated only by the hope of some effective insurance emerging from it that would prevent the repetition of such colossal folly.

While striving to find some way of bringing the carnage to a close, he had resisted being pulled into its vortex as long as it seemed possible. In spite of the complexity of his mind and character, he had been "moved by the old American feeling that America is a new land which must not be entangled with Europe. The sympathy of his mind was pro-Allies though chastened by a certain irony about their moral pretensions, a suspicion of their motives, and a conviction that unfortunately they too were mad; in this period his heart was always neutral and non-European. His real judgment he expressed several times, to the horror not only of the Allied spokesmen but of Colonel House; it was that the war arose out of obscure causes that were hatched in a sinister system and a tortuous diplomacy. Wilson never accepted the official propaganda even when it blew the hottest; he never respected it, and could hardly bear to listen to it. What he wanted above all things was to keep out of the hideous mess." [22]

He had hated the decision to go in with all his soul. For some two weeks he had fought the matter through in solitary agony. "The day before he went to Congress he told Frank Cobb of his horror and cried out to him, 'If there is any alternative, for God's sake, let's take it!' " [23]

In the months that preceded this final hour, his growing allegiance to a league of nations had not been a passing sentiment; it had been "the one good he might be able to promote and defend in the face of the oncoming disaster. It was the one compensation, it was the one reasonable ideal, it was the one moral justification, it was the one balm to his conscience for the plunging of a great people into the red madness of Europe." [24]

It had not been for oratorical effect that he had placed at the highest point in his war message to Congress the declaration that we would fight "for a universal dominion of right by such a concert of free peoples as shall bring peace and safety to all nations and make the world itself free." It had been his pledge to the legions who would not come back. "Think what it was they were applauding," he said after his return to

[22] Walter Lippman, *Men of Destiny*, N. Y., 1927, pp. 121-2.
[23] *Ibid.*   [24] *Ibid.*

the White House, "my message today was a message of death to our young men. How strange it seemed to applaud that." [25]

How much more strange, it seemed to him in August, 1918, that after the great sacrifice had finally ceased some of the same men who had applauded his war message should oppose bitter opposition to the one permanent compensation that not only might come from it all but was actually at the point of realization. It was incredible that the people, once roused to the danger, would not make the Covenant effective.

Such, at least, was Wilson's faith and his background of deep experience when he faced Admiral Grayson, his physician, as the latter came in, on the morning of August 28, to make a final request that he refrain from incurring the hazard, the seriousness of which Grayson knew better than anyone other than Wilson himself. With a foreground of tremendous endeavor filling his mind, and a long training of strict devotion to principle behind him, it was inevitable, too, that the President should say that he must go. Walking first to the White House windows for a long look out to Washington's monument, he returned, to rejoin, with evidences of emotion which his Scotch-Presbyterian heritage seldom permitted, that with the fate of the treaty in the balance he could let no personal consideration be decisive, no sacrifice that he could make to see it through was too great. [26]

[25] Tumulty, *Woodrow Wilson as I Know Him,* p. 256.
[26] From a personal statement by Admiral Grayson.

CHAPTER XIII

WILSON'S APPEAL TO THE PEOPLE

THE President left Washington on the evening of September 3, eager to carry his case to the people. He had no speeches prepared, and severe headaches did not contribute to the effectiveness of his first addresses.

THE JOURNEY

Central States Apathetic. Correspondents traveling with the party described Ohio and Indiana as not aroused about the League one way or the other. The *Columbus Evening Dispatch,* of September 4, 1919, reported that cheers and applause greeted the President "throughout his entire visit." There had been tumultuous applause from the 4000 hearers in Memorial Hall who repeatedly interrupted him with cheers. The *Indianapolis News,* of September 5, said likewise that his audience of 12,000 in the State Fair Coliseum broke into frequent applause. The setting for the Indiana address had not been favorable. Hundreds of Fair visitors, there to see all things new or unusual, were satisfied as soon as they had seen the President. Thousands of others trying to get into the enclosure caused such confusion that the speaker could not be heard in the outskirts of the crowd, which naturally continued restless. Hostile observers described the coming and going as indicative of what the Hoosiers thought.

Illinois, with its two irreconcilable Senators, was passed over in silence. Its great city, Chicago, was already becoming known as the country's chief center of isolationist influence. Led by the *Chicago Tribune* and Mayor "Big Bill" Thompson, robust if peculiar types of America-Firstism were becoming popular in that region. A quarter of a million dollars had not then been spent by a traction magnate to defeat a Senator who did not share these creeds, and a city election had not yet actually been won on opposition to King George of England, but the ground was being prepared for the time when the purging of the Chicago Public Library could be seriously proposed and enthusiastically applauded by the devotees of the jingoistic type of patriotism that was then being developed.

The Plains Divided. Missouri was found to be keenly interested and sharply divided on the issue, due largely to the activities of Senator Reed. Charles H. Grasty reported to the *New York Times,* of September 6, however, that after the President's talk to a St. Louis Chamber of Commerce group of 1200, he had interviewed forty or fifty of those present and found them all in favor of unconditional ratification. Those who were really opposed to the treaty had probably not attended.

In the evening, an audience of 12,000 gave Mr. Wilson a "tumultuous ovation" lasting five minutes, while thousands fought to gain admission. Cheering along the Presidential route had been "general and liberal." "The President was tremendously pleased with the friendly demonstration from Republican St. Louis and showed it." He was working at his typewriter as the train pulled out. [1]

There was "real enthusiasm" in the audience of 15,000 at Kansas City[2] and Iowa, though a heavily Republican state, gave him a really triumphal welcome in Des Moines. The strong support for the League in Iowa was due in large part to the conviction of leading Republican newspaper editors that the world must be organized for peace instead of war. Mr. Harvey Ingham of the *Des Moines Register* and Mr. John Kelly of the *Sioux City Tribune* were particularly responsible for the belief in the League which the President found—and which still continues in that state.[3]

In Omaha the President's automobile was brought to the hall, with the greatest difficulty, through a "humming maelstrom of people." He checked a second ovation from the audience,[4] as he frequently did, to speak as seriously as he could.

There was much hostile sentiment in Nebraska. The heavy German-American population of that state had not forgotten the mental suffering which the war had cost them.[5] They had also read widely and

---

[1] *St. Louis Globe Democrat,* September 6, 1919. Although he spoke without manuscript before him, Wilson worked late and early to organize his next address before parades and receptions made it too late.

[2] "His prediction of victory for the League of Nations was the signal for a wild demonstration, many leaping to their feet. . . . They seemed eager to cheer."—*Seattle Daily Times,* September 7, 1919.

[3] *New York Times,* September, 6, 7, 8, 1919.

[4] *Omaha Daily Bee,* September 9, 1919.

[5] This was still true in 1930. Prominent Germans touring in behalf of the League the regions of the United States inhabited by German-Americans found that they were not only cold to the League of Nations, but wanted to hear nothing of the German Republic as well. The glorious Fatherland they had become proud of having been destroyed, they preferred to live in their memories—both bitter and sweet.

sympathetically Senator Knox's speech indicating that the treaty laid heavier burdens on Germany than she could bear. Neither the fact that the Knox faction would have ravaged Germany to Berlin, crushing her utterly, nor that of Wilson's long effort to give the new Germany a fair chance, now seemed to count. Wilson had brought about the defeat administered to Germany. The League, moreover, was said to be British.

Minnesota appeared well satisfied with the attitude of her Senators, Nelson and Kellogg, who supported the League strongly but were committed to mild reservations. The *St. Paul Dispatch,* of September 9, thought the reception given the President moderate, though it noted "full throated cheering" as he passed under the victory arch. It also carried a Washington dispatch from Clinton W. Gilbert saying that "All accounts reaching here represent the people of the West as tired of the delay in ratifying the treaty, desiring formal peace and inclined to blame business uncertainty upon the tactics of the Republican leaders who are obstructing the treaty."

Stronger Commitments for Reservation. The President's journey, however, seemed to be stirring some of the mild reservationists into more active opposition. Senators Spencer of Missouri and Kenyon of Iowa delivered much stronger utterances than were expected after the President had passed through their states.

Three Democratic Senators also announced that they would vote for reservations and perhaps even introduce some of their own. To these three, Senators Hoke Smith of Georgia, Shields of Tennessee and Thomas of Colorado, Walsh of Massachusetts and Meyers of Montana were commonly added. The promise of Democratic support was so encouraging in fact that Senator Lodge was reported as convinced that he could muster enough votes to ignore the mild reservationists, ten of whom had notified him that they would not support his reservation to Article 10. Their support of all the other reservations, however, presaged agreement.

Senator Ashurst of Arizona, Democrat, was even quoted as convinced that sentiment was overwhelmingly against the treaty without radical reservations and as saying that "The future is what President Wilson must look to for his vindication. . . . We may be winning elections about 1940 on the strength of Woodrow Wilson's memory, but not in the near future." He could count only twenty-seven Democrats who would stand to the end against reservations.[6]

[6] *New York Tribune,* September 7, 8, 1919.

A Clear Verdict on the Pacific. On the other hand the increasing enthusiasm which the President met as he traveled through Montana and Idaho to the coast encouraged him to believe that he could still count on the West to stand by him. Some 30,000 people turned out to give him an uproarious welcome in the Stadium at Tacoma, and in Seattle he was met by a continuous and riotous uproar akin to fanaticism. It was doubtful if in the history even of recent political campaigns a more remarkable demonstration had been witnessed. Police, soldiers and secret service men were nearly overwhelmed in trying to keep the crowds from the President's automobile. The reception accorded him in the Armory was "comparable in every way" with that received earlier in the day. Oregon, too, was pronounced as sound league territory. The Republican press was supporting the League and little opposition was evident.[7]

In San Francisco hundreds of thousands of people waved and roared a continuous chorus of cheers. "The ovation was unexpected in its exuberance and magnitude," said the *Chronicle.* For half an hour the President was compelled to stand in his automobile. Oakland, too, gave him "a spontaneous welcome." A crowd of 12,000 in the Auditorium, with half as many outside, gave him "four successive salvos of greeting into each of which was injected a fervor that was dynamic." A man in the gallery asked, "Are we with him?" "We are!" was hurled back by thousands of voices. The *Chronicle,* however, still continued to oppose the Covenant on the ground that it subjected "all small nations to the rule of the great powers." It "explicitly" did that.[8]

Nothing had been lacking in the San Francisco and Oakland receptions, yet Southern California was, if possible, more enthusiastic. An audience of 50,000 at San Diego, to which the President spoke through amplifiers, repeatedly interrupted him with applause, and Los Angeles was apparently whole hearted for his cause. Both the great Republican papers, the *Times* and the *Express,* were backing it warmly. The climax of the President's sojourn in the city came when Lyman J.

[7] *New York Times,* September 14, 15, 1919; *Seattle Daily Times,* September 13, 14, 1919. A part of this fervor was probably due to the simultaneous visit of the newly created Pacific fleet. At the same time, the *Tacoma Daily Ledger,* of September 14, reported that "The response in the armory was instant upon the utterances of the President's address which carried particular meaning." The audience had risen as one man to cheer as he came on and "each sound that swept the big auditorium during the address was full, decisive, in keeping with the manner of address of the President."

[8] *San Francisco Chronicle,* September 18, 19, 1919. The President's "departure was marked by friendly acclaim." He had spoken to 1500 women at a luncheon on September 17 and a like number of men on the 18th, in addition to his two tremendous evening meetings and two long street ovations.

Gage, Secretary of the Treasury in President McKinley's cabinet, said to him, "I think I express the sentiment of the great mass of the people when I say 'God bless President Wilson. Go on with the work.' " [9]

The Senators Also Stirring Great Crowds. Be that as it might, Senators Johnson and Poindexter would not be moved from opposition. They could say, too, that public opinion was with them, for Senator Johnson and other Senators, who were much more clever as popular orators than the President, were out speaking to immense audiences and eliciting even stronger emotions than Mr. Wilson could stir. Attacking him bitterly, these men appealed to deep-seated traditions, prejudices and passions that he could not enlist if he would. Or they touched the true instincts and noble patriotism of their hearers. At least they did not rely on appeal for a new order.

Senator Johnson was having such success on his tour that friends of the League declared he was running away with the Republican Presidential nomination. Even the official leaders of the fight on the treaty appear to have decided that he ought to be at Washington again. A conference on September 18, in which Will Hays, Chairman of the Republican National Committee, Senators Lodge, Brandegee, Borah and Knox participated, decided to send for Mr. Johnson to return and lead the fight for his amendment designed to give the United States six votes in the Assembly. Senator Penrose was also to be summoned from Pennsylvania to assist in the strategy.[10]

Johnson hurried back, and, describing the terrific response he was getting, begged for more delay, saying, "If we could just get sixty days before the final vote, the American people would make their desires known in such unmistakable terms that nothing would be left of this treaty." The defeat of his amendment, however, seeming to be certain, it was announced on the day the President's trip ended that the Senator would set out again, this time to continue to the Pacific.[11]

Triumph in the Mountains. The President on his part was so encouraged that as he turned east from Los Angeles he resolved to carry his campaign into the New England States. Yet while winning undoubted support for his cause by commending the League to his fellow-country-

[9] *New York Times*, September 18, 19, 21, 1919.

[10] *New York Tribune*, September 19, 1919. Confidential reports reaching the *Tribune*, on September 22, indicated that the President was weaker than the League, and that he had not gained a single vote in the Senate. At the same time his candidacy for a third term was assumed.

The *Times*, of September 17, charged that fear of his reëlection was the great motive power back of the opposition to the League.

[11] *New York Tribune*, September 24, 25, 26, 1919.

men "with all his old eloquence and moral fire, with all the fine lucidity of thought that had given many of his utterances a classic distinction," he had been losing his battle with pain and strain. "He appeared to grow older by years with the passing of each day," [12] though Dr. Grayson now began to hope that he would pull through the journey.

Between addressing great audiences at Reno and Cheyenne, Wilson had further confirmation in Salt Lake City of his belief that the West would stand behind him in his fight for the League. The *Salt Lake Tribune,* of September 24, reported that every available point was occupied for his welcome to the Utah capital. The cheers along the route could be heard blocks away and they traveled ahead of him long in advance of his appearance. As the dense throngs at the monument were reached "the cheers became a great roar," swelling as the President appeared "into a tumult which shook the air."

Reaching the Tabernacle, he found the greatest throng which it had ever held. "Fifteen thousand persons heard the President and more than that number were turned away from the doors. After a five minute ovation when he entered, another almost as great in volume was given when he rose to speak. Then, "crowded and uncomfortable as they were, the immense gathering by their attention and applause gave overwhelming evidence that a vast majority of them agreed with what the President had to say about the Covenant. They interrupted him time and again with handclappings; they shouted favorable answers to his questions and demonstrated at every climax which the President reached that they wished to see the ratification of the treaty and the League of Nations."

"The President's sincerity," commented the *Tribune,* "the care with which he weighed his words, and the ease of his address made his message simple and at the same time tremendously effective." [13]

Going on to Denver, Wilson found the same warm welcome. The cheering swept along Seventeenth Street into his hotel, where hundreds waited to greet him. The *Rocky Mountain News* thought that the larger part of the adult population of the city waited along the way to the Auditorium, in addition to 32,000 school children. Thousands stood outside during the address to acclaim him as he came out.

[12] P. H. Box, *Three Master Builders and Another,* Philadelphia, 1925, pp. 385-6.
[13] The *Salt Lake Tribune,* September 24, 1919. This was one of the addresses about which the President's foes made the most charges of violence and intemperance.
The *Tribune* was another Republican paper which was supporting the League strongly.

As he spoke, "a demonstration even greater than he received when he first entered the great hall was accorded the President when he asserted that, because the treaty embodied American principles, he felt that he had a right to say that he had the support of the people of the United States. Cheers broke loose, women waved handkerchiefs and flags, the enthusiasm mounting until it took expression in a tumultuous outbreak."

The speaker himself was calm. "He spoke dispassionately, earnestly. He appealed almost not at all to the emotions of his hearers." [14]

The visit convinced the *News* not only of the President's moderation and sincerity but also that he was winning. It observed, on September 26, that "Yesterday President Wilson disposed of a lot of pettifogging objections that have been made to the League of Nations Covenant and he gave a broader definition of what the League stands for than is usually credited to him. . . . If the other side does not have a care Mr. Wilson will be choosing his own battleground and the weapons that are to be used."

The President had indeed chosen his battleground. He was appealing to all the reasonable people of his day and of future generations. But his course was almost run. Before it was finished he made a final magnificent appeal, one in which he poured out his own soul as he had never done before.

Perhaps it was the pull upon him of the myriads of school children he had lately seen, whose future he felt to be involved; perhaps it was from presentiment that his voice would soon be stilled that he spoke from his heart to the hearts of his hearers, as well as to their heads. He had doubted his ability to go on when he stood up to speak in Denver. This was also true in Pueblo, where an immense assemblage awaited at the new Auditorium to give him one of the most tremendous welcomes he had ever received. When he appeared, "the entire audience arose and cheered for fully ten minutes," and as he pleaded an hour for fulfillment of the high aims of the war the audience roared its approval "time and time again." [15]

Journey's End. Wilson had given his valedictory. Sleep did not come that night, and alarming signs of collapse appeared. After a walk into the country the next morning had failed to give him a margin of

---

[14] The *Rocky Mountain News*, September 25, 1919. The President's reception at Cheyenne was captioned, "A Wild Welcome Given Wilson at Cheyenne. People Jam Streets and Thousands Turned Away at Theater."

[15] The *Rocky Mountain News*, September 26, 1919.

strength for another speech, he was obliged to cancel the six remaining addresses of his schedule. It took Dr. Grayson's full power, however, to compel him to submit, after the city of Wichita had filled with people to greet him. Fearing that his enemies would say he was a quitter, and thus injure the cause that was so close to him, he resisted long before acquiescence.

His fear, moreover, was not without basis. The *New York Sun,* which, on September 26 had described his Colorado audiences as "pretty cold," now said, on the 27th, that "Early this morning as the train was nearing Wichita, the President admitted his breakdown. He said to Dr. Grayson and Secretary Tumulty: 'I can't go on with this. I shall have to give up the rest of the tour.' This was precisely what Dr. Grayson had intended to order. . . ."

This announcement was substantiated by the following: "Late this afternoon as the Presidential special slid along the Kaw River toward this city one of the President's traveling companions sought official information from the President's own cook:

" 'Boy, how is the President's appetite?'

" 'He suttenly made a fine lunch, sah!' which was taken without any further corroboration from Dr. Grayson to indicate that the President was feeling a little better already."

Instead of quitting his campaign with a good appetite, the fact was that the President ate no lunch and took nothing but liquids during the entire day. [16] Far from expecting him to eat heartily, those on his train were surprised that he was able to walk from it on reaching Washington and to take a short motor ride the next day before he was stricken with partial paralysis.

His crusade was ended, though not before he had delivered thirty-seven speeches averaging an hour in length during the space of twenty-two days, traveled more than 8,000 miles and participated in a dozen wearying parades during which he was compelled to stand in a swaying automobile for an hour at a time.

The correspondents on his train had discussed from the start the question whether a slender man of 63 years, living more on his nerves than on his physique, could complete the 10,000 mile itinerary. On one or two occasions they had talked of it with the President

---

[16] A letter of August 6, 1931, from Admiral Cary T. Grayson.

The *Sun* revealed the true situation quite accurately on the 28th, indicating even that the President had taken little food.

Both dispatches were accompanied by gracious editorials, the one of the 28th assuming with great finality that he had lost his fight.

himself, only to find him always smiling and refusing to put a long face on his difficulties. He admitted that his constitution might be exhausted, but jokingly said that he had his by-laws left and could live on them for a while. [17]

Testifying that his tour had been "a fine mettlesome performance," Charles H. Grasty wrote at its close: "Woodrow Wilson has the true Spartan quality. Not another man aboard could have stood the mere physical strain, to say nothing of the intellectual activity. Throughout the entire peace program the President has been sustained by his faith in and zeal for his cause. With all his enthusiasm he has committed no excesses of oratory. He has left behind no potentialities of reaction. The figure that will stand out in the memory of the Western people is that of a man burning with a restrained passion for a great purpose, for the accomplishment of which he would gladly lay down his life." [18]

There need be no appeal to sentiment in adding that it would have been a miracle indeed if Woodrow Wilson had completed the trip and retained his strength against all the assaults upon it to the end of his term. Starting into the Presidency far from a strong man, he had been confronted by tasks such as no man, perhaps, had ever met. First, he had attempted domestic reorganization and reform on a sweeping scale, with a success that alone would have made the administration of any President distinguished. Blending into this first campaign was the stormy period of neutrality with its succession of crises and its hue and cry for intervention in Europe and in Mexico. The strain had been long, and the test of reëlection had not lessened it.

Once in the war, Wilson had led the country triumphantly through an effort of unparalleled intensity, and, with scarcely an hour's delay, had plunged into the even more wearing undertaking of persuading the victors to frame a peace that would last. During this long ordeal, his fourth sustained trial, he was subjected to constant and unrelenting fire from his rear. Returning eventually with such a promise of world stability as the ages had dreamed of and world chaos demanded, he found the opposition at home securely entrenched in the Foreign Relations Committee of the Senate and showing every disposition to reject as much of his work as it dared. Tiring of a war of attrition that boded no good for the treaty, he felt constrained, without rest which his labors had earned, to take up yet a fifth ordeal of

[17] *New York Times*, September 27, 1919.
[18] *Ibid.*

appalling proportions—no less than to tell the people directly what the Treaty and the League amounted to.

That after responsibilities and struggles such as these he completed five-sixths of his exhausting appeal to the people must be evidence enough that no man fighting an unrighteous battle either could or would have borne up so long.

Wilson had staked everything on his long held belief that the people need only to be aroused to a just cause. He had not expected to win all those who saw him. He knew well that a large proportion of great crowds come to see and to hear, even to cheer, without supporting the speaker afterwards. When the Italian multitudes were giving him ecstatic acclaim, and burning candles to him in thousands of churches, he agreed that it was tremendous but asked what it would be like if he disappointed them in the Peace Conference. He could sense the fury of the later hour. [19]

His own people he trusted, more than he should, to perceive the moral quality of a problem, as he saw it, and to see it in the short run as well as the long—even in the face of skilful and confusing counter appeals. [20] He perhaps expected a too quick and clear comprehension in the slower moving masses of the people, masses in considerable degree alienated from him in the course of the war.

Nevertheless, if he could have kept his feet a few weeks longer, the growing power of his campaign would have been a force to reckon with indeed.

THE APPEAL

Early Errors. It would not be truthful to suggest that the President made no mistakes in judgment or errors in reasoning during his western tour. He began his first speech with the statement that the people were the only ones to whom he owed any report. His feeling can be understood, but it would have been well if he had phrased his idea differently. At Indianapolis on the same day, too, he made the more unfortunate statement that under the Covenant we could mind other people's business. He was explaining that it was the friendly right of every nation to call the attention of the League to anything likely to affect the peace of the world, but it was inept to furnish the Senators with such a juicy morsel. In fact he later frequently up-

[19] Statement from Admiral Cary T. Grayson.
[20] David F. Houston, "The War on Wilson," *World's Work,* September, 1926, Vol. 52, p. 539.

held Article 11 and the inviolability of domestic questions with equal vigor, without making it wholly clear that there was no conflict in the two contentions. Doubtless there is no fundamental conflict, but his analysis did not make that plain to a reader of all the speeches. [21]

As David Lawrence has pointed out, he also explained at St. Louis that "this was a commercial war" and soon asserted at Des Moines that the bankers and business men of Germany did not want war. Probably both statements were true, but they appeared to be contradictory. He was in error, too, in saying in early speeches that the secret treaties giving Japan the German rights in Shantung were made to induce Japan to enter the war. They came much later, to secure a fuller participation of her navy. After Senator Norris had called attention to this misstatement the President wired him an admission of the fact.

He won high applause in St. Louis by his confession that he sometimes heard politics until he wished both parties were smothered in their own gas, but he probably did not please the politicians thereby. Certainly his invitation to his opponents, at Kansas City and other places, to "put up or shut up" might have been omitted. He had much justification for feeling that way, but the scholarly President was not expected to fight back in the vernacular. His statement in the same speech that "when at last in the annals of mankind they are gibbeted, they will regret that the gibbet is so high" may have been prophetic, but it won no votes in the Senate. It gave some Senators, too, a chance to give the impression that the President actually wanted to see them hanged in the flesh, instead of "in the annals of mankind."

Obviously, it would not be fair to overemphasize these lapses in a man laboring under his circumstances and speaking extempore day and night. The remarkable thing is that they were so few. He repeatedly said that he had not come to debate but to explain the plain meaning of the Treaty. The Covenant, he insisted, meant what it said, not what anybody chose to read into it. It was written in plain English.

The Critics Viewed Details. He characterized the Treaty as a great human document, but declared that after one had heard it talked about in Washington a while he would conclude that there were only about three clauses in it—something about the Monroe Doctrine, Shantung, and a certain Article 10. The few criticized articles of the Covenant

[21] The speeches of the President's Western tour are printed in Albert Shaw's edition of the *Messages and Papers of Woodrow Wilson*, N. Y., 1924, Vol. II.

were, he often repeated, only a small part of the whole. There were twenty-five other articles, all important. Had they been told about them? It was a matter of unaffected amazement to him that there should be men in high station who devoted their scrutiny to a few details and forgot the majesty of the plan.

The essential of the matter was that all the great fighting nations promised "that they will never go to war without first either submitting the question at issue to arbitration and absolutely abiding by the decision of the arbitrators, or, if they are not willing to submit it to arbitration, submitting it to discussion by the Council of the League; that they will give the Council six months in which to consider it and that if they do not like the opinion of the Council, they will wait three months after the opinion is rendered before going to war. And I tell you my fellow citizens, that any nation that is in the wrong and waits nine months before it goes to war will never go to war."

Reminding his hearers that the Senate had already accepted the principle of a cooling-off period in the twenty-eight Bryan treaties, he contended almost daily that the nine months cooling period would be effective. War was a process of heat; exposure a process of cooling. What was proposed was that every hot thing should be spread out in the cooling air of the opinion of the world, while the nations concerned decided whether they would fight about it or not. "The only thing you cannot face," he said at the close of his Salt Lake City speech, "is the truth. The only thing that will get you sooner or later, no matter how you sneak or dodge, is the truth. No nation is going to look the calm judgment of mankind in the face for nine months and then go to war." [22]

Agreement or Armament. Conference was the healing influence of civilization. World opinion was its greatest force and this power was to be organized as it never had been. The world forum which the League provided and the obligations of the Covenant were the means of redeeming and protecting the weak peoples of the earth. Frequently calling the roll of the infant nations which would need its protection, he reminded the partisans of other small peoples that they could not ask a better forum from which to submit their legitimate grievances to the common judgment of mankind—the most tremendous moral compulsion that could be devised.

The functions of the League in preventing secret treaties, by pub-

[22] Shaw, *Messages and Papers of Woodrow Wilson,* Vol. II, pp. 775, 784, 1038, 1084.

lishing them all to the world, and in quieting international land titles, were as often stressed. What would happen, he asked in state after state, if every farmer in the commonwealth felt his land titles to be insecure? They would all be defending their boundaries with shot guns against squatters and invaders. The much mooted Article 10 simply proposed to give the same security against illegal aggression to national landholders. There could be no prospect of settled peace without it. The old system was based upon the principle that no power was obliged to respect the territorial integrity of any other power if it had the force necessary to disregard it. Article 10 cut at the very heart of that system and it was the only instrument which would do so, he told his St. Louis hearers.

But would such guarantees not require war for their enforcement? No, he maintained throughout, because the economic boycott would be effective. The blockade had fatally undermined the German armies from the rear. For most nations an absolute boycott would be worse than war. Few aside from the United States could stand it. If the covenant breaking state still insisted on running amuck, civilization would know that it had an outlaw to deal with.

The world, he agreed, was at the mercy of men's passions. The League proposed to organize and mobilize the fine passions of men. If it failed, the world would have to contend with some nation dominated by evil passion just as soon as recovery came. Was it not better, he often asked, to accept 75% insurance, or 50%, or even 10%?[23] In his judgment the League offered a much higher percentage of safety than any of these figures.

The only alternative was to arm and to submit to the dominance of a military class. Again and again at Paris a civil government had found it dared not promise what its general staff would not approve. We might say what we pleased about the Imperial German Government, yet it was the only sort of government that could handle an armed nation. It made no difference, said the President at Kansas City, what your form of government was. If you were determined to be armed to the teeth you must obey the orders and directions of the only men able to control the great machinery of war. Elections meant little, because back of the political policy they determined was the

[23] His question was answered by a prominent Republican, five years later, as follows: "The League of Nations Covenant is only 70% perfect; sometimes I think it is much less than that, but it is the big thing of the Peace Conference, the most significant thing west of the Ganges since the crucifixion, and it is all Wilson's work. If it were only 10% perfect it would still be a step in the right direction." William Allen White, *New York Times*, October 24, 1924.

constant pressure of powerful bodies of men disciplined in arms and wondering if they were never going to be allowed to use their education and skill. The spirit of armaments was as burdensome as the cost.

The Common Objections. Taking up the common objections to the Covenant, he described the attitude of many of those who professed to be alarmed over the right of withdrawal as one of sitting close to the door with hands on the knob as if to say, "We are in this thing but we are in it with infinite timidity; we are in it only because you overpersuaded us and wanted us to come in, and we are going to try this thing every now and then and see if it is locked, and just as soon as we see anything we don't like, we are going to scuttle." Now what was the trouble? The Covenant set up no tribunal to judge whether we had fulfilled our obligations at the time of withdrawal. The only thing restraining us was the opinion of mankind. Were the gentlemen afraid we should cut a poor figure before it?

Then they did not like the way the Monroe Doctrine was mentioned. Well, he would not stop on a question of style. The new meanings that the English language seemed to have acquired puzzled him. He did not know what dictionaries—or what manuals of conscience they could possibly resort to. The Monroe Doctrine was adopted and for the first time expressly authenticated by all great nations of the world. What more could you ask?

The proposal to enumerate specifically certain questions as exclusively domestic he pronounced as dangerous, because you were almost sure to leave out some that you would wish later were included. He saw no way to overturn or escape the long-established world understanding as to what domestic questions were. Fears that such a thing could be done were groundless because all the other nations were just as jealous of their sovereignty as the United States. Not one of them had the slightest idea of surrendering control over its domestic concerns. [24]

Discussing the Shantung settlement throughout the trip, and from one end of the Pacific coast to the other, he freely admitted that he was not satisfied with it. Instead of defending it as a perfect resolution of the problem, he reviewed the whole history of the spoliation of China from 1898 on, gave the facts which he had to face at Paris and left his hearers to judge whether a better decision could have been secured. He left it to them, too, to determine whether China's best

---

[24] Perhaps a typical discussion of the four objections to the Covenant is found in the Kansas City speech.

interests could be served through the League or by scrapping the settlement. [25]

Replying to the attacks upon the section of the treaty creating the International Labor Office as an attempt to pull down American labor standards, he referred to it consistently as a great Magna Carta for labor, designed to improve labor conditions everywhere, not to pull them down for any man.

For Our Own Advantage. Frequently, but always with an apology, he agreed that it was to our selfish advantage to join. We could make more money out of friendly traders than hostile traders, out of men who trusted us than from men who feared us. We could bring about a state of mind where by every possible device foreign markets would be closed to us.

On the other hand, we could be the senior partner in the family of nations. The financial leadership would be ours, the industrial primacy and the commercial advantage. The other countries of the world were looking to us for leadership and direction. If he was to act as a selfish American he wanted to get in as quickly as possible, to be on the inside, know how the thing was run and help to run it.

Our Glorious Destiny. But he was much happier in picturing the glory of leadership that would be ours than in dwelling on the national benefits of membership. This was, perhaps, his favorite theme, and one of the most popular with the crowds. The most touching and thrilling thing that had ever happened to him occurred in Paris, when delegations from all over the world came to solicit the friendship of America, with a trust and confidence they could place nowhere else. If by any mysterious influence of error America should fail to take the leading part in the League, the world would experience one of those reversals of sentiment, one of those penetrating chills of reaction, which would lead to a universal cynicism.

The peace of the world could not be organized without America. The American people were the makeweight in the fortunes of mankind. Yet we could not bring peace by ourselves. No small group of nations could do it. The concurrence of all was necessary. The nations looked to us for leadership. They had built their peace largely upon the basis of our suggestions. Was it conceivable that we should refuse the leadership offered us? Must we have in the future the same dangers, suspicions and distractions ending in disastrous armed conflict? Or should we look forward to a world that would sit down at

[25] See the San Francisco addresses.

the council table and delay the use of force until there was time for judgment to rule?

He refused to admit a conflict between nationalism and internationalism in this connection. "The greatest nationalist," he said, "is the man who wants his nation to be the greatest nation, and the greatest nation is the nation which penetrates to the heart of its duty and mission among the nations of the world. With every flash of insight into the great politics of mankind, the nation that has that vision is elevated to a place of influence and power which it cannot get by arms, which it cannot get by commercial rivalry, which it can get by no other way than by that spiritual leadership which comes from a profound understanding of the problems of humanity." The only question which the opponents of the League could ask us to decide was whether our influence in the future should be profound and controlling, whether it should be exercised at a great advantage, or at a profound disadvantage.

He besought his hearers to look at it as a fulfillment of the destiny of the United States, for it was nothing less. At last after a long century and more of blood and terror the world had come to the vision that we had had in 1776. Men in Europe had laughed then at the little body of men who talked dogmatically about liberty, but the fire kindled had at last consumed every great autocratic government in the world. He believed more profoundly in the destiny of the United States than in anything else human. He believed that she had a spiritual energy in her which no other nation could contribute to the liberation of mankind, and that this nation loved its honor better than it loved its interest.

He had not a moment's doubt as to what our final action would be. Our character was undergoing a heroic test, but he did not fear the results, for he knew that "at heart this people loves freedom and right and justice more than it loves money and material prosperity or any of the things that anybody can get but nobody can keep unless they have elevation of spirit enough to see the horizons of the destiny of man." We were going in and not to sit by the door. We were going to sit in the high seats and our counsels would be the prevailing counsels. If we were to sit humbly by the door at the outset we would be asked to go up and take the chair. [26]

[26] Shaw, *Messages and Papers of Woodrow Wilson*, Vol. II, pp. 755, 790, 791, 823, 857, 967-8, 1012, 1025, 1047, 1076.

Far from granting that we should be passive in foreign affairs because some of our foreign born citizens might become agitated, he held that the very fact that we

No Special Privileges for the United States. His speeches from the start at Columbus had been full of confidence that the cause could not fail. In San Francisco, he declared he did not believe that there was any body of men, however they might concert their power or their influence, that could defeat this great enterprise of divine mercy and peace and good will. If he did not believe in Divine Providence and thought the direction of the disordered affairs of this world depended on finite intelligence, he should not know how to reason his way to sanity. [27]

After his great reception on the Coast he turned to the East again with even greater confidence, declaring that of all the objections only that against Article 10 was still seriously pressed. And yet as his strength diminished from day to day a somber note came into his speeches. His increasing distress may also have had something to do with the firm position which he took on reservations to Article 10, yet it is not necessary so to assume. He had explained at Omaha that he had found some of the people at Paris as ingenious as any American in attaching unexpected meanings to plain words, and having gone through the mill on the existing language, he didn't want to go through it again on changed language.

At Salt Lake City, in September 23, he read a compromise reservation drawn by some Senators and forwarded to him by an official of the League to Enforce Peace. The reservation was as follows:

> The United States assumes no obligation under the provisions of Article 10 to preserve the territorial integrity or political independence of any other country or to interfere in controversies between other nations, whether members of the League or not, or to employ military and naval forces of the United States under any article of the treaty for any purpose, unless in any particular case the Congress, which under the Constitution has the sole power to declare war or authorize the employment of the military and naval forces of the United States, shall by act or joint resolution so declare.

---

drew our blood from every civilized stock in the world fitted us by sympathy and knowledge to understand the peoples of the world, their interests, their rights, their hopes, their destiny. No other nation had that equipment. The others were set in a mold; we were not. No other nation could so sympathetically lead the world in organizing peace. (P. 847.)

[27] He disclaimed any authorship of the League for himself repeatedly. He did not originate it. It was not his handiwork. It had originated out of the conscience and thought of men who had wanted justice and loved peace for generations. See, for example, Shaw, Vol. II, p. 917.

That, said the President, was rejection of the Covenant. It was an absolute refusal to carry any part of the same responsibility that the other members of the League carry. The obligation of Article 10 was a moral one only, but this resolution would destroy even that obligation, declaring that when a case arose Congress might take it up as if no Covenant existed. The effect was to give the United States a special standing, to exempt it from the obligations the other members assumed, or to put a special interpretation upon our duties under the Covenant. It was unworthy of the United States to ask any special privilege of that kind. He was for going into a body of equals or staying out. The proposal violated the very principle we had been proud to fight for—that the rights of the weak nations were just as sacred as those of the strong. [28]

He knew that some of the gentlemen quoted as approving a reservation of that sort were high-minded and patriotic. He had talked with them about the treaty and knew them to be men whose character and judgment he entirely respected, and whose motives he respected as much as he respected the motives of any man, but he begged them to look further into the matter. It was, he explained at Cheyenne, as if we refused to join the League definitely but might join it occasionally; we promised nothing, but we might coöperate; if you got into trouble come around and we would see about it.

At Denver he closed his address with a demand that when the Senate approved the treaty it do so in such a form that he would know whether the treaty had been approved or rejected. He did not wish to draw doubtful conclusions. He did not wish to do injustice to the process of any honest mind, but when the treaty was acted upon he must know whether we had ratified it or rejected it.

We Fought For a New Day. As the President neared the end of his journey he had at least made it as clear as lay within his power that we fought in the Great War for something more than the protection of our ships upon the sea. He reminded his first audience at Columbus that we had taken by processes of law the flower of our youth from every household, and had told their loved ones that we were taking them to fight a war that would end business of that sort. If we did not end it, if we did not do the best that human concert of action could do to end it, we were of all men the most unfaithful, the most unfaithful to the loving hearts who had suffered in the war, the most unfaithful to those households bowed in grief and yet lifted with

[28] Shaw, *Messages and Papers of Woodrow Wilson,* Vol. II, pp. 1071, 1074, 1104.

the feeling that the lad laid down his life for a great thing and, among other things, in order that other lads might never have to do the same.

At Indianapolis he put it in the record that we had promised both the boys in khaki and the world itself that we would not conclude the conflict with a mere treaty of peace. "We entered into solemn engagements with all the nations with whom we associated ourselves that we would bring such a kind of settlement and such a concert of the purpose of nations that wars like that could not occur again. If this war has to be fought over again, then all our high ideals and purposes have been disappointed, for we did not go into this war merely to beat Germany. We went into this war to beat all such purposes as Germany entertained."

At St. Louis, calling the country to witness that Article 10 was not only the inevitable, logical center of the whole Covenant, but the fulfillment of his promise to the boys who fought, he declared that if the article should be impaired in any important respect he would feel like asking the Secretary of War to assemble in one field all the boys who went over, so that he could go to them and say that he had done his best to fulfill the promise, but he was obliged to come in mortification and shame and say to them that he had not been able to fulfill it, that there must still hover over the nations the nightmare of dread which lay upon them before the war came.

Then he warned the American people with all the earnestness that a life study of history could give, that if the promise were broken "There will come some time in the vengeful Providence of God, another struggle in which, not a few hundred thousand fine men from America will have to die, but as many millions as are necessary to accomplish the final freedom of the world."

The time for the fulfillment of this prophecy is still young, but if the greatest people in the world sit idly and complacently by while the world drifts into another orgy of bloodletting, in which science shall unerringly speak the last word of destruction to still more numerous millions, those words will ring in American homes far louder than did the warnings of 1919 that there was danger of our being entangled in foreign affairs.

The Boys Did Not Turn Back. The treaty, said the President at Reno, was not written, essentially speaking, at Paris. It was written at Château Thierry and in Belleau Wood and in the Argonne. Our men did not fight there with the purpose of coming back and letting the same thing happen again. They expected that kind of thing to be finished, and it would be. They had never thought of turning back, he continued at Denver, or of saying "we are going to do this much of the job and then scuttle and leave you to do the rest." Our fighting men had never gone any direction except forward, and in helping to complete the task which they began he was not going to turn back any more than they did. Neither did America fail to finish things which she began. She would meet the test of honor and courage and endurance in the League or on the battlefield.

And in the last great speech of his life he used the final remnant of his strength in a plea for fulfillment that moved both the men and women of his Pueblo audience to tears, as it must dim the eye of generations to come if the full extent of the tragedy he sought to forestall unfolds.

Telling how again and again mothers who lost their sons in France had taken his hand and shed tears upon it saying, "God bless you, Mr. President!" he asked, "Why, my fellow citizens, should they pray God to bless me? I advised the Congress of the United States to create the situation that led to the death of their sons. I ordered their sons overseas. I consented to their sons being put in the most difficult parts of the battle line, where death was certain, as in the impenetrable difficulties of the Forest of Argonne. Why should they weep upon my hand and call down the blessings of God upon me? Because they believe that their boys died for something that vastly transcends any of the immediate and palpable objects of the war. They believe, and they rightly believe that their sons saved the liberty of the world. They believe that wrapped up with the liberty of the world is the continuous protection of that liberty by the concerted powers of all civilized people. They believe that his sacrifice was made in order that other sons should not be called upon for a similar gift—the gift of life, the gift of all that died. . . . These men were crusaders. They were not going forth to prove the might of the United States. They were going forth to prove the might of justice and right, and all the world accepted them as crusaders, and their transcendent achievement has made all the world believe in America as it believes in no other nation organized in the modern world. There seems to me to stand between us and the rejection or qualification of this treaty the serried ranks of those boys in khaki, not only those boys who came home, but those dear ghosts that still deploy upon the fields of France."

The final judgments of history or of God cannot be known, but it will take many cynics indeed to remove the evidence that throughout the long months of the war the true soul and spirit of America fought for the great ends which Woodrow Wilson voiced and which he continued without faltering to voice until the end. His countrymen, confused by many cries and impulses, stopped short of the goal which they had helped to hold mountain high in the view of all men during the great struggle. Wilson never turned back nor hesitated.

The Truth Would Lead Us. A few minutes after he had avowed his eternal fidelity to those who died to give us a safer and better ordered world, he predicted once again that the arrangements of justice would receive the support of the combined power of the great nations of the world, and closed both the Pueblo address and his active career with the words: "Now that the mists of this great question have cleared away, I believe that men will see the truth, eye to eye and face to face. There is one thing that the American people always rise to and extend their hand to, and that is the truth of justice and of liberty and of peace. We have accepted that truth and we are going to be led by it, and it is going to lead us, and through us the world, out into pastures of quietness and peace such as the world never dreamed of before."

But there were not soon to be any pastures of quietness and peace for him. Like the staunchest of the men who had served under him, he had fought on until his last ounce of strength was spent, and, like the countless legion of maimed men whose sacrifice he had sought to make supremely fruitful, he was to spend the rest of his days as a wounded veteran of a great cause. Yet, unlike them, he could not quit the field even then, but must continue for months to face a relentless attack that scarcely paused as he fell.

The Commander-in-Chief of the American armies in the Great War had led them as far as he could, farther than they could go. He had been struck down far in advance, within sight of the high goal which he had set for them, and they for him. Other hands would have to take up the standards of reason and sanity and carry them on by slow and painful stages, with the great objective seeming at times to recede into the darkness which succeeded his fall.

"The world has known few finer speeches," said the Swiss journalist William Martin, in retrospect, speeches "better suited to their audiences, more reasonable, more convincing, more elevated in tone, than those delivered by President Wilson in the course of his famous tour through the United States. If illness had not struck him down, if he had been able to keep on and continue kindling public opinion as he had done so often, the face of history would have been changed."[29]

"Now Let the Senate Act." "In his unapproachable egotism," wrote George Harvey, tireless leader of "the cabal," several days after Wilson's breakdown, "he is quite capable of believing anything that he wishes to believe; even that his tour has been a triumphal march. . . . He has gained the immense gratification of holding the center of the stage for a time, in full glare of the limelight. . . . He has received a considerable share of the adulation which is ever so dear to his heart . . . . Undoubtedly he had the time of his life 'slangwhanging' the United States Senate and insulting every American citizen who ventured to disagree with him, in circumstances when he was safe from direct reply. . . . He rushed about the country like a howling dervish. . . . He uttered again and again what he knew was untrue.

"He has had his say. He has shot his bolt. He has done his worst. He is no more to be considered. Now let the Senate act." [30]

[29] William Martin, *Statesmen of the War,* 1918-1928, New York, 1928, p. 232.
[30] *Harvey's Weekly,* October 4, 1919, Vol. 2, No. 40, pp. 1-2. A cartoon filling two entire pages pictured the President as a threatening, glowering, sinister figure.

CHAPTER XIV

COMMITTEE REPORT

THE Senate Foreign Relations Committee had felt itself impelled to begin to act soon after the start of the President's tour. It was not happy over the necessity. In its report, made September 10, it recited that in the two months since the treaty was presented to the Senate the Committee had met on every working day it was possible to meet. Compared with the six months that had been taken to frame the treaty, this time did not seem excessive. This was mentioned because there had been "more or less clamor about delay in the committee." The demand for haste was largely artificial, coming from the Administration and its supporters and from certain great banking firms. They had been aided by "the unthinking outcry of many excellent people" who for the most part had scarcely read the treaty beyond the words "league of nations."

The committee was also hampered by the impossibility of securing information from the negotiators, it explained at length. The clamor for speedy action had not been directed against those of the Allies who had not yet ratified. "Persons afflicted with inquiring minds have wondered not a little that the distressed mourners over delay in the Senate have not also aimed their criticism at the like shortcomings on the part of France, Italy, and Japan, an act of even-handed justice in fault-finding which they have hitherto failed to perform."

The emptiness of the demand for haste in order that we might trade with Germany, a plea now rather faded, was shown by the fact that we had shipped $11,270,624 worth of goods to Germany since the Armistice. It was "a mere delusion" to argue that we needed a new treaty of amity and commerce with Germany and the reëstablishment of our consular system there to enable us to trade with Germany.

Before leaving this subject, continued the report, it might not be amiss to remark that Mr. Lloyd George, while recently expressing grave apprehension about social and economic conditions in England, had failed to point out how the ratification of the League Covenant by England had relieved the situation. "He was apparently equally remiss in omitting to suggest that prompt action by the Senate of the United States in adopting the covenant of the league of nations would immediately lower the price of beef."

In introducing the fifty odd amendments which were proposed, it was observed that nothing was "more groundless than the sedulously cultivated and constantly expressed fear that textual amendments would require a summoning of the peace conference and thereby cause great delay." There would be no necessity for that because the conference was still in session in Paris. Textual amendments made by the Senate could be considered at once, "and the conference would be at least as usefully employed in that consideration as they now are in dividing and sharing southeastern Europe and Asia Minor, in handing the Greeks of Thrace over to our enemy, Bulgaria, and in trying to force upon the United States the control of Armenia, Anatolia and Constantinople through the medium of a large American army."

Still more unimportant was the bugbear which had been put forward of the enormous difficulties of securing the adhesion of Germany. But "no great amount of time need be consumed in bringing German representatives to Paris. The journey is within the power of a moderate amount of human endurance, and it is also to be remembered that Germany is not a member of the league and need not be consulted in regard to the terms of the covenant. When Germany enters the league she will take it as she finds it."

The spirit of the report was further expressed in the reservations proposed, of which No. 2 is typical. It read:

> The United States declines to assume, under the provisions of Article 10, or under any other article, any obligation to preserve the territorial integrity or political independence of any other country, or to interfere in controversies between other nations, members of the league or not, or to employ the military or naval forces of the United States in such controversies, or to adopt economic measures for the protection of any other country, whether a member of the league or not, against external aggression or for the purpose of coercing any other country, or for the purpose of intervention in the internal conflicts or other controversies which may arise in any other country, and no mandate shall be accepted by the United States under Article 22, Part I, of the treaty of peace with Germany, except by action of the Congress of the United States.

Here, at last, was the final form of the negation which Senator Lodge had agreed upon in his conferences with Roosevelt and Knox in December, 1918.[1] Then only the central idea of the league that the President would try to create was known; now all of the supporting features of the idea could be condemned along with it. The condemnation, too, was put in such form that to "the unthinking" it would appear to be a proper preservation of American safety. The responsibilities which the Committee declined to assume sounded quite dreadful as they were listed.

The rejection seemed complete, but it was not quite total. Appended at the end of the "reservation" was a clause which might make it possible for Congress to commit all the fearful interferences which were expressly abjured in the body of the declaration. To be sure the discretion of Congress seemed to extend only to the acceptance of a mandate, yet it could be argued that we might go back of the word "and" to assume all the abhorred obligations. At the very best, the gentlemen who had so long criticized the Covenant for its ambiguous language made it certain that their action upon it could be interpreted both ways. They made the spirit and purpose of rejection too plain to doubt, but left a glimmer of hope which the party members who believed in the League might grasp, if they liked.

Finally, after denouncing the League once more as an alliance and a war-breeder, the possibility that the other nations would not accept the Committee's fiat was contemptuously brushed aside. So was the idea that there was any kind of compulsion operating upon us. "Equally unfitting is the attempt to frighten the unthinking by suggesting that if the Senate adopts amendments or reservations the United States may be excluded from the league. . . . That is the one thing that will certainly not happen. . . . The other nations will take us on our own terms, for without us their league is a wreck and all their gains from a victorious peace are imperilled."

We exacted nothing selfish for ourselves, but only insisted that we be the judges, the only judges, as to the preservation of our rights, our sovereignty, our safety, and our independence.[2]

[1] See Chapter III. The majority report was signed by Senators Lodge, Borah, Brandegee, Fall, Knox, Harding, Johnson, New and Moses.

[2] *Congressional Record*, Vol. 58, Pt. 5, pp. 5112–14.

Under the head "Jingoism Gone Mad," the *Seattle Times* of the same date said: "Had the committee set out with deliberate intent to antagonize international public opinion, it could not have drafted a more provocative or scornful document. . . . It would be better—infinitely better—for the peace of the world and the security of America that this country should remain forever in its position of 'splendid isolation' than that it should seek association with other sovereign states after the adoption by

The Minority Report. The minority report, signed by the six Democratic members of the Committee, Hitchcock, Williams, Swanson, Pomerene, Smith (of Arizona) and Pittman, urged the ratification of the treaty without change. The adoption of direct amendments could only have the effect of defeating our participation in the treaty. They could not even be dictated to Germany. The skeleton of the Peace Conference did still exist, but it had no further power to bring German representatives to Paris and compel their signature to new terms. The power of compulsion had been exhausted. The Germans had been told to sign and had done so. There must be a finality to ultimata in a treaty of compulsion. Neither could the Covenant be changed without Germany's consent, except through regular amendment by the League itself. The Covenant had been accepted by Germany; it vitally concerned her, and it expressly stated that it could only be amended in one way.

The reservations proposed were of such a character as to at once betray their authorship. They were the work of Senators organized for the purpose of destroying the League and, if possible, defeating the Treaty. They were in no sense interpretative reservations, to be used to make clear language in the treaty that might be considered doubtful, but were so framed as to receive the support of Senators who desired the defeat of the treaty. While masquerading in the guise of reservations they were in fact alterations of the treaty. Presented in the resolution of ratification they would result in its defeat. The opponents of the League realized that it was invincible on a square fight and hoped to destroy it by this indirection.

The decisions of the majority of the Committee could have been made as well in July as in September and would have been the same.[3]

the Senate of a statement so insolently asserting American greatness, American independence of all restraint and American superiority in all things." *The Seattle Daily Times*, September 10, 1919.

The judgment of the *Times* was probably correct. It would hardly be possible to explain to the Allied peoples that the language of the report was really not directed against them.

In its succeeding issue the *Times* decisively rejected the minority report also, contending that moderate reservations had become necessary. Other newspapers, too, began to take the same position, arguing that the people of the United States always favored the middle ground.

[3] *Congressional Record*, Vol. 58, Pt. 5, pp. 5213–14.

The *New York Times*, on September 11, declared that the Committee report set the world back a hundred years. It destroyed the gains of victory and annihilated the League. The Allies had fought that nations and men might be free, that the world might be governed by law and justice, not by the will of autocrats anywhere. The Versailles Treaty organized one world at peace; the Senate Committee would call into being a world divided, always necessarily armed for war, and frequently engaged in war. The peace of the world might be thrown to the dogs, but these perversely minded men must have their way.

McCumber's Report. Still another minority report was filed by Senator McCumber, the lone Republican friend of the League on the Committee, in which he flayed the report of the majority in terms which must always rise up to confound any assumption that the course of that Committee was dictated by real fear of the League. Noting that a committee report usually explained the object of a bill or treaty, he said:

> The majority of the Committee on Foreign Relations have deviated from this rule in reporting this treaty. The great purposes of the covenant upon which 27 nations, the great and the small of the world, studied and labored for six months in an attempt to formulate a plan that would tend to insure good fellowship among the nations of the world and prevent another such catastrophe as we have just passed through have not been alluded to. Not one word is said, not a single allusion made, concerning either the great purpose of the league of nations or the methods by which those purposes are to be accomplished.
>
> Irony and sarcasm have been substituted for argument and positions taken by the press or individuals outside the Senate seem to command more attention than the treaty itself. It is regrettable that the animosity which centers almost wholly against the league of nations provisions should have been engendered against a subject so important to the world's welfare. It is regrettable that the consideration of a matter so foreign to any kind of partisanship should be influenced in the country as well as on the floor of this Senate by hostility toward or subserviency to the President of the United States. No matter how just may be any antagonism against President Wilson, the aspirations and hopes of a wounded and bleeding world ought not to be denied because, under our Constitution, the treaty must first be formulated by him.

Since the United States had played an important part in bringing the war to a close, he could scarcely understand this studied effort on the part of the majority of the Committee to eliminate the United States as a factor in determining any question relating to the final settlements. He recalled the eloquent words in which some of the same gentlemen had urged in the Senate the necessity and duty of the United States to assist in the re-mapping of Europe and Western Asia, and could not understand why the new nations created in so doing should now be cast adrift. To his mind such an attitude was "most selfish, immoral, and dishonorable."

> Neither can one understand why a country whose whole history has been devoted to the advocacy of the peaceful settlement of international

disputes is suddenly to have its policy reversed and to become, in effect, an opponent of the only means that has ever been attempted to assure world peace, namely, an agreement, not between two nations or between two groups of nations that they will settle their difficulties by arbitration, but an agreement among all nations that they shall not resort to war without first submitting their controversies, either for arbitration or discussion, to a council of all; that no nation shall begin a war of aggression against another without such submission, and that if such recalcitrant nation does attempt a war of aggression and wrong, the other nations to the compact will prevent the consummation of such felonious policy.

The instrument was not as complete and binding as a constitution. It depended chiefly upon the moral sentiment of each nation for its enforcement. But it was a mighty step in the right direction. Every sentiment of justice and morality was on its side. Some of its provisions were yet crude and uncertain, but the whole purpose was most noble and worthy. As we had been compelled to depend on the right of amendment to perfect our own Constitution, so would experience undoubtedly necessitate many changes in the Covenant.

The spirit of the compact was the principle "that the same code of morality which governs people in their relations to each other in every highly organized state of the world shall govern nations in their relations to each other; that no nation shall rob another nation of its territory or its independence; that no nation shall have the right to murder the people of another nation for the selfish purpose of extending its own domains." No statesman, no philosopher had ever yet given a single reason why nations should not be governed by the same code of ethics that regulated great communities in their internal relations. "All of these noble and lofty purposes have been ignored in the majority report or treated with sarcastic disdain or jingoistic contempt."

The Committee's reservation number 2, quoted above, he analyzed as follows:

> The second reservation recommended by a majority of the committee is objectionable for several reasons. First, it is an amendment pure and simple, and an amendment of the most important article in the league of nations. Its purpose is to take the United States as a power for the peace of the world out of the league entirely. Our disinterestedness, our freedom from the ordinary jealousies that affect the European mind, our power and our resources place us in the front rank of influence in this council of nations. We are the keystone of the arch upon which must rest the superstructure of a successful league of nations. So situated

PORTER J. McCUMBER

we ought not only to be willing but eager to help a distracted world which so needs the moral assistance of our membership and the potential assistance of our known power. Second, it places this country in a false and wrong position, an attitude of encouraging powerful countries to inflict or impose any wrong upon weaker nations, by our declared policy of non-intervention. The better policy and the right policy is to let the world understand that in all probability the United States will not stand idly by and allow a great wrong to be perpetrated by one country against another. Third, that policy of non-intervention is asserted in a dictatorial and offensive way. It is not couched in the language which should govern friendly nations in answering proposals one to another.

Other pages of McCumber's report patiently digested again the story of the Shantung case and the impropriety of the amendment giving us six votes in the assembly, to balance the votes of the British dominions. The necessity of recognizing the equality of all nations somewhere in the League was pointed out, and the foolishness of giving a voice to Haiti, while denying one to Canada, explained. In reality the United States could always overbalance the Dominions with her own satellites. If any one had a right to complain it was Continental Europe, which could well protest against the big block of American votes that we would be likely to wield. But action was taken in the Council, where it must be unanimous and one vote decisive. More important still, if we got six additional votes, surely France and Italy would demand as many, with results which anyone could foresee.[4]

If there had ever been any basis for the Committee's statement that no reason why we should not have six votes had ever occurred to it, it could never so declare again.

The Bullitt Hearing. On September 12, the Committee played the

[4] *Congressional Record,* Vol. 58, Pt. 6, pp. 5356-59.
The Committee's assumption that anything the Senate voted would be accepted, he dealt with as follows:
"No one, so far as I know, has asserted that delegates of this conference are not still in Paris. They are there for the purpose of carrying out certain provisions that are in the treaty itself. It required six months of arduous labor to bring the minds of all the signatory nations to a point where they could sign this treaty. It was important that every provision in the treaty should satisfy every signatory member. The treaty has been consummated. The hundreds of experts and advisors who assisted in making the treaty have returned to their homes. Only the skeleton form of the conference remains.
"What is claimed by the opponents of these amendments is that they would require a reconsideration of the whole treaty because they present a new and different treaty. And realizing the difficulties which had to be overcome in order to secure the assent of these 27 nations, we cannot fail to recognize the added difficulties and uncertainties that would arise in a resubmission of the whole question to the peace conference."
At the conclusion of his report he presented a draft of reservations designed to allay the fears that had been raised without giving offense or destroying our opportunity to function in the League on a basis of equality.

trump card of its series of hearings. William C. Bullitt, who had resigned from the staff of the American Peace Commission because of general dissatisfaction with the treaty, testified on that date. He came armed with a sheaf of documents which he had collected at the Conference, and in connection with his Russian trip, some thirty-two of which were printed in the record as "Bullitt Exhibits." One was the President's proposition for a league of nations, in his own typing, which Colonel House had given Bullitt as a souvenir. Others were later drafts. They indicated that the only one of the President's original proposals which remained more or less intact was Article 10.

The witness had a complete record of the Russian transaction, too, and of the terms of peace which the Soviet Government was alleged to have agreed to accept, terms which the French opposed, which Lloyd George dared not identify himself with, and on which the President had not felt able to proceed.

Bullitt had been employed in the State Department during the war and had been in the confidence of both House and Lansing, who had joined in selecting him for the secret mission to Russia, and with whom he had had daily conferences as a part of his duties during most of the Conference. He had talked with them at length after his resignation and had immediately made a written record of the conversations. He was, therefore, in a position to tell the Committee that Secretary Lansing said to him at 2:30 on May 19: "I consider that the league of nations at present is entirely useless. The great powers have simply gone ahead and arranged the world to suit themselves." These powers would see to it that the weaker peoples did not get unanimous consent in the League to alter the unjust clauses of the treay.

They had then talked of the possibility of ratification, Lansing saying: "I believe that if the Senate could only understand what this treaty means, and if the American people could really understand, it would unquestionably be defeated, but I wonder if they will ever understand what it lets them in for." Evidently, Lansing had been almost as despondent for the future that day as Bullitt was. But he did have some hope. "He expressed the opinion that Knox would probably really understand the treaty, and that Lodge would; but that Lodge's position would become purely political, and therefore ineffective. He thought, however, that Knox might instruct America in the real meaning of it."[5]

[5] *Senate Documents*, 66th Congress, 1st Session, Vol. 10, pp. 1161–1291. It was stated that Bullitt would have testified on August 23 had he been available. For some

The most damaging statements that the President's Secretary of State could have made thus came out in the midst of the President's explanation of the treaty to the people as a just and humane settlement. When Lansing made these comments to a dissatisfied official— not to say a disillusioned or disgruntled one who had resigned two days before, convinced that effective labor for a new world order was no longer possible as a servant of the American government—he had not, of course, intended that he should later be quoted at a critical time. Yet when it was thus publicly revealed that he was totally out of sympathy with everything that the President was fighting for, and that he was depending for the defeat of his chief upon the gloomy mind of Senator Knox, the Senator who had from the start warned the President not to try to create a league of nations, Lansing did not resign. Nor did any statement issue from him, except that on September 20 he did come out strongly for the ratification of the Treaty and Covenant as written. His position was unquestionably difficult.[6]

September Oratory in the Senate

From Unconditional Surrender to Unconditional Peace. While these events took place, the speech-making, of course, went on in the Senate. Senator Hitchcock, on September 3, listed the substantial advantages which Germany accorded us in the treaty and which would be lost by its failure. He reminded the Senate how a year ago the President's opponents in the Senate had shouted until the rafters rang for "unconditional surrender" by Germany, when the bare possibility of a negotiated peace was suggested. Now they blandly proposed an "unconditional peace." Then they protested it would be an outrage for the President to act independently of the Allies; now they denounced him because he had made peace in agreement with them and compelled Germany to accept it.

Senator Knox, on October 28, 1918, had said: "The league of nations which now challenges our solicitude is the league of nations of which we are now a member—the glorious present alliance of the many powers with whom we are now fighting as a league to enforce

reason no administration Senators were present at the later hearing, otherwise the Lansing memorandum could have been kept out of the record. Bullitt read only half his notes, saying afterward that he gave the dynamite but withheld the nitroglycerine. *The Independent,* September 27, 1919.
    [6] Wilson had stated to Norman H. Davis shortly before leaving Paris that he wanted to bring Lansing back to help get the treaty through the Senate.—A letter of July 21, 1931, from Mr. Davis.

peace and to maintain peace from disturbance by the German menace."
Now, Knox condemned the treaty on the ground that it "provides
merely and simply for an alliance." In October he had said: "If we
should allow that league to fall apart or to be pried apart by German
machination, who can say when this world will ever again be so near to
having a general league to enforce peace as it is today?" Now he was
deliberately trying to pry apart the glorious alliance and make a separate peace with Germany. In October he had sought "to perpetuate
the league we have, already embracing the majority of the population
of the globe, as a league for one single purpose of enforcing peace";
now, because the President had done this very thing, he sought to dis-
rupt it. In October Knox had not feared the enforcement of peace.
Then he had said: "The function of such a league, as I take it, would
be to examine any controversy that threatened war and then to throw
its weight to the side of such controversy where justice and equality
lay, and also to suppress with its overwhelming power any war that
might break out and to indicate the just solution of the contentions."
Where was his fear of the principle of Article 10 then? At that time
he had declared: "Such a league, like any league, will demand some
encroachment upon the conception of complete and independent sovereignty." Now he was all for protecting American sovereignty from
any contamination by the treaty.

Quoting further to the same effect from Senators New, Cummins,
Poindexter and Lodge, Hitchcock showed that the position of the
latter had been, "The Republican stands for unconditional surrender
and complete victory, just as Grant stood." He now called upon the
Senators to rise in their places and explain why they had come down
from the heights of unconditional surrender to the depths of unconditional peace.[7]

Replies to the President. Senator Poindexter, on September 8,
spoke in reply to the President's early addresses. He dwelt upon the
great army and the billion dollars it would take to protect Armenia,
holding that we should have to police all Turkey to do it. And how
then should we perform our "obligations" in Mexico, if sending
armies to Turkey and Germany and Siberia? Wouldn't economic
blockades be a sure cause of war, and didn't the Covenant unconstitu-
tionally give the supervision of our trade in arms to the League?

In reply to the President's contention that the League would have
prevented the invasion of Belgium and the war itself, he magnified

[7] *Congressional Record,* Vol. 58, Pt. 5, pp. 4730–31.

the treaty of 1839, neutralizing Belgium, into a "league of nations" and asked if the new one would be any more effective.[8]

Senator Spencer, of Missouri, maintained on September 9 that the President had presented a false issue in his state. The issue was not between acceptance or rejection, but between acceptance with reservations and rejection. He had no sympathy with proposed changes, under whatever name they might be called, which were offered mainly in the desire and with the intention to kill the treaty, or so to complicate the situation as to destroy or endanger its ratification. There were too many commendable provisions in the Covenant that deserved a confident trial, and too many treaty provisions that were essential to the interests of this government, to have the treaty itself killed; but he had every sympathy with and a clear conviction in favor of such reservations as would safeguard the essential rights of our country.

There were millions of people who believed, as he did, that these rights were in real, not imagined, jeopardy. Reservations were therefore necessary to insure confidence at home, as well as out of candor and fairness to the nations abroad.

The real need of reservations he demonstrated by saying that Japan could buy Magdalena Bay, in Lower California, from Mexico, and that Article 10 would then protect her in possession of it. If this were true, then of course, the Covenant, instead of safeguarding the Monroe Doctrine, had destroyed its central principle—the protection of our security.[9]

Kenyon for Reservations. On September 10, after the Foreign Relations Committee report, Senator Kenyon, of Iowa, made a strong speech for reservations which had all the more weight because Kenyon had not previously spoken on the League, "feeling it better to wait until the matter was before the Senate." Far from beginning to oppose the League before it was written, and at every stage in its making, he had continued working effectively on domestic questions until the treaty had been negotiated, laid before the Senate, considered by the proper committee and reported back to the Senate for action. His name had not appeared on the Round Robin and his voice had never been raised in obstruction.

When, therefore, politely paying tribute to those who had informed the country, he delivered a rousing speech charging the Democrats with making a political issue of the question, it came with especial

[8] *Ibid.*, pp. 5024–31.
[9] *Ibid.*, pp. 5078–79.

weight. He was wholly opposed to the Shantung clause, terming it as infamous and unholy as anything in history. The President would need a lot of gibbets upon which to put his opponents, but he doubted if we had really reached one-man power in this country. The Senate would not be bulldozed. Nor would it be a mere automaton.

When the treaty first came up, 80% of the people in his state were for the League. A majority of them might still be for it exactly as written, but he knew there were many who now wanted it modified, though a great majority still favored "some league to carry out the terms of the Paris Conference." However, he said deliberately that if every person in Iowa were for the Covenant without reservations he would not support it. He had waited long and thought much, and his mind had reached a fixed conclusion that he would be a traitor to his convictions and do an injury to the nation if he voted for the Covenant without reservations. He would keep faith with his conscience. If that were State treason, make the most of it.

The first essential reservation should be to make clear just how we could get out of the League upon proper notice. That was the most important of all reservations. Domestic questions should, of course, be protected, and, he assumed, would be. The Monroe Doctrine was a good deal of a fetish with the American people. He was not particularly alarmed about it, because there was reference to it in the treaty; it might not be a regional understanding, but there was basis for us to claim it was excluded.

He favored strong reservations on Article 10. Didn't it preserve to the great powers everything that they had acquired, and thus stifle the voice of oppressed people everywhere? The article meant just what it said. Our peripatetic Executive might ride through the country in his palatial de luxe train, at the expense of the public, and tell the people that it did not mean sending their boys to repel an invasion of Hedjaz, but the people could read and understand what the article called for. If Article 10 was the keystone of the arch of the Covenant it was a rotten keystone, a war breeder.

He trusted that the gentlemen on the other side of the Chamber would come out of the valley of stubbornness and recognize that the votes were not there to ratify the treaty as it stood, that they were available to ratify it with substantial reservations, and that "the votes are here to defeat the whole treaty regardless of consequences if reservations are not adopted."[10]

[10] *Congressional Record,* Vol. 58, Pt. 5, pp. 5149–55.

Harding's Dilemma. Senator Harding, of Ohio, followed on September 11. He too agreed that, "It was the truth, last year, two years ago, three and four years ago, the people of this country were heedlessly and overwhelmingly for a league of nations, or a society of nations, or a world court, or some international association which should develop a fraternity of action among civilized peoples and save humanity not only from the sorrows and sufferings like those which came with the war now ended, but from the involvements of which we are not yet emerged." He had helped to write a Republican party platform in Ohio voicing the aspirations of the people of that state. Nobody stopped to think of the cost then. People were only learning the involvements now. Each day of discussion, presidential utterances included, persuaded him that the venture was full of peril for the Republic.

It would have been well to have counseled with one another before the Covenant was fashioned. The people had voted such a preference most emphatically in November. Yet he had found no fault with the President's going to Paris, nor with his failing to take Senators with him. He understood, too, the perfectly laudable and natural ambition of the historian to do the superlative thing, "but it needed penetrating vision to meet the pressing, practical problems which were awaiting solution, by very practical men." The "glory of the league of nations—an appealing conception—filled the American commission's vision, while distinctly American interests—aye, sacred American interests—were ignored or forgotten in a new and consuming concern for the world."

After this charitable explanation of what had happened, the Senactor came to define his position, and he found himself almost unable to decide whether the League was to be feared because it was too strong or because it was too weak, saying: "It is my deliberate conviction that the league of nations covenant, as negotiated at Paris, and signed at Versailles, either creates a super-government of the nations which enter it or it will prove the colossal disappointment of the ages. Though it would be vastly more serious as the former, I cannot believe this Republic ought to sanction it in either case. Why proclaim a promise that will embitter the world's disappointment?"

This was a new turn of the Senatorial mind. The Covenant had been condemned often as a super-state, or as a farce, but the critic had never displayed any hesitation about calling it one or the other—even if he took the other tack on a different occasion. Harding, however, added later in the address that he believed it "designed" to establish super-government, and no explanation or apology had altered his opinion. It would have been better to have said, " 'We do not mean to mix in again, unless some bully in making a row infringes our rights and murders our citizens and destroys our lawful property. In that event we will be forced to come back, but we will come more promptly the next time.' That would have left a good impression, and we would have been at peace, and so would Europe, months ago."

He quoted a number of the President's utterances before our belligerency, which condemned those who would have us depart from "our habitual and traditional policy." Protecting Armenia was "the avenue to unending war." Nobody was a quitter, and nobody would shut up. He would vote for the amendments. In closing, he liked "to think, sirs, that out of the discovered soul of this Republic and through our preservative actions in this supreme moment of human progress we shall hold the word American the proudest boast of citizenship in all the world." [11]

Super-government. Senator Jones, Democrat, of New Mexico, analyzed, on September 15, the charges of a super-state which half a dozen Senators, whom he quoted, had made. After careful and analytical consideration, he failed to find anything which even tended to justify these invectives. Taking up in sequence all the provisions which were supposed to establish the super-state, he showed that they only gave the Council and Assembly specific authority to effect settlement through negotiation, to "formulate plans," "make inquiry," "advise," "submit," "report," "propose," "recommend." He could find in these terms no attributes of government or foundation for "the impassioned oratory which would present to the public gaze the specter of an overreaching power destined to destroy American institutions and make vassals of American citizens." Moreover, it must not be forgotten that whatever restrictions were imposed upon us were also imposed on all the other signatories. Surely we should hesitate before concluding that the representatives of 26 other nations would bring upon their governments and fellow countrymen all the calamitous results which it was said our representatives would impose on us.

He had expended much mental effort to discover the processes which would lead to such declamations of danger. Maybe it was because the

---

[11] *Congressional Record,* Vol. 58, Pt. 5, pp. 5219–25. Harding's hostility to the League was thus established long in advance of the election of 1920. Super-state or farce, he would not sanction it, "in either case."

failure to secure desired Federal appointments had aroused such hostility in Democratic Senators that any peace document proposed by the President would provoke instant and withering scorn. Perhaps others, convinced of their unequalled fitness to negotiate a treaty of peace, were unable to believe that any treaty of merit was possible unless they had had a hand in it. Or again, it might be due to the conviction that the conclusion of a treaty contributing to the future peace of the world, following a victorious war, would give to the President's party an assured advantage in approaching political contests.

Certainly the negotiations at Paris had hardly commenced, before the idea was disseminated throughout the country that a United States of the World would be created, and that Woodrow Wilson was anxious to become its first President. Then nearly every day, following what seemed to be a definite program, Senators had reviewed in fantastic horror provisions which it was assumed had been created at Paris. Certain newspaper organizations (especially the Hearst papers) took up the hue and cry, and daily sought to impress the public that all our cherished institutions were to be subjected to the domination of a superforce. Even a Republican publicity organization had conducted a systematized campaign to further this impression, so that the very name "league of nations" should be brought into popular disfavor and disrepute.

He could not see the necessity for reservations that other Senators demanded so strongly. If it were thought necessary to safeguard the right of Congress under Article 10, it could be done at any time by instructions to our representative on the Council.

The proposal to reserve to the United States the sole right to determine for itself whether or not a question was one of wholly domestic concern might easily render the whole scheme of no avail. All international questions were in a sense of domestic concern, and all nations would have the right to make the same reservation. In clear cases, such as immigration and the tariff, the council could decide against us only by purely arbitrary action. Such action against us by one nation was much more likely. But if the often quoted supposition of the adverse decision of the Council on an issue of Japanese immigration were followed through, it would be found that we could appeal to the Assembly, where a majority of the nations not on the Council would have to be against us. If this came to pass, we could keep the Japanese out by changing our legislation, and no penalty would hold against us so long as we did not go to war.

On the Monroe Doctrine, if some doubtful question as to what came under it some time arose, wouldn't it be better to submit to the unanimous decision of the Council than go to war about it? The essential meaning of the Doctrine was certainly clear. No individual had a right to be a law unto himself, and no nation had a right under all circumstances to be a judge in its own case. Civilization meant association, and, if nations were to join in any plan looking to peaceful intercourse, each must be prepared to submit to the enlightened and organized opinion of the world. It was unthinkable that the American people wanted to perpetuate the old idea that each nation was privileged to take and hold what it could. We had just sent millions of men and expended billions of treasure to defeat that doctrine.

Even if it were true that we assumed large burdens and received no direct or material benefit, we should join the League. The peace of the world meant so much to mankind that we should be justified in making even greater sacrifices than were now ascribed to membership. If direct benefits were looked for, they could be found in securing the assistance of the League in pacifying Mexico without war.[12]

Here was treason indeed to the Senators who looked upon the whole western hemisphere as our own domain and to the newspapers who desired to pacify Mexico by conquest. No proposal could have been more repugnant to leaders like Albert J. Beveridge, former Senator from Indiana, who believed firmly that Wilson must be broken, whether he were right or wrong, because if he were not broken he would involve the United States in closer associations with Europe which would thwart the United States in her Mexican and Latin American policies.[13]

Treaty Reading. At the conclusion of Jones's speech the reading of the Treaty of Peace with Austria was begun, at the instance of Senator Lodge, not the treaty with Germany which was before the Senate. Neither had the President hurriedly sent the treaty with Austria for quick action by the Senate, as might be supposed. The *Chicago Tribune* had just supplied Lodge with a copy of the Austrian treaty, obtained in Austria, and he wanted the Senate to know about it at once. He consented under pressure, however, to permit this document to go into the *Record* without taking some days for its reading.[14]

[12] *Congressional Record,* Vol. 58, Pt. 6, pp. 5390–5400.
[13] From a statement of July 8, 1930, by Dr. William E. Dodd, of the University of Chicago, quoting statements by Beveridge.
[14] *Ibid.,* pp. 5400–5448.

The next day, September 16, the reading of the Treaty of Versailles was begun. It was finished on October 20.

War Objectives. Senator Overman, of North Carolina, speaking in the place of Senators who were absent because they thought the Austrian treaty would be read, followed Jones. He recalled to the Senate that when the President had declared, in his war message, that "we shall fight for the things which we have always carried nearest our hearts—for democracy, for the right of those who submit to authority to have a voice in their own governments, for the rights and the liberties of small nations, for a universal dominion of right by such concert of free peoples as shall bring peace and safety to all nations and make the world itself at last free," Congress had declared war without a single protest by any member against these principles and purposes.

That keynote, sounded by the President, had rung around the world, thrilling the hearts of people in every warring country and inspiring them with hope and aspiration for a new order of things in which peace should reign and men should be free. That slogan had been sounded upon every stump, in every pulpit, and upon every platform in the land, in meetings held for the sale of liberty bonds, thrift stamps, for the raising of funds for the Red Cross, Y. M. C. A., Salvation Army and other war purposes.

All the people were made to understand the purposes of the war. It was not our intent to send our soldiers to a foreign land simply and only to whip Germany; it was also for a higher and nobler purpose— to fight for justice, humanity, liberty, freedom and the future peace of the world. This was the eloquent sentiment which had thrilled the hearts of the people, stirred their patriotism, caused them to open their purse strings as no one had ever dreamed they would, and with the greatest enthusiasm do everything they could to help win the war.

This keynote, furthermore, was echoed and re-echoed by the leaders of all the countries at war with Germany. Lloyd George had said: "The world will then be able, when this war is over, to attend to its business in peace. . . . The best security for peace will be that nations bind themselves together to punish the peace breaker." Balfour spoke it again, saying, "Here we come face to face with the great problem which lies behind all the changing aspects of this tremendous war. When it is brought to an end, how is civilized mankind to reorganize itself that similar catastrophes shall not be permitted to occur?" Premier Viviani had added for France: "Our task will be—I quote the noble words of President Wilson—to organize the society of nations. After material victory we will win the moral victory."

Should it all go for nothing, asked Overman. Should all the blood shed and the treasure expended go simply to have helped the Allies whip Germany? Should our boys have died in a foreign land for that purpose only? No, the victory won on the battlefield must extend farther than that. After all our promises and pledges and the prayers of our people for peace, for fifty years, we could not afford from the standpoint of honor to defeat it. With more than two-thirds of the world willing to join hands with us we could not afford to block the way to the fulfillment of that which we had advocated, hoped for, and dreamed of for years.

We were told that this was all altruism and idealism. That was what the Tories of England and America had said about the sentiments of equality, liberty and self government contained in the Declaration of Independence. Faced with the first opportunity in the world's history to bring about a new order of things for the people of the earth, should we not at least try it, as the doubting colonists tried our Constitution? Benjamin Franklin, speaking from the wisdom of eighty years, had confessed that there were several parts of the Constitution which he did not approve, but he was not sure he should never approve them, for he had experienced many instances of being obliged by better information or fuller consideration to change his opinions, even on important subjects. On the whole, therefore, he had said to the Pennsylvania constitutional convention: "I cannot help expressing a wish that every member of the convention who may still have objections to it would with me, on this occasion, doubt a little of his own infallibility, and to make manifest our unanimity, put his name to that instrument."

It was easy to find fault, easy to see ghosts and make evil predictions. Yet the objections then centering on Article 10, that our soldiers would have to suffer and die in wars waged for remote countries, had no terrors for him. The constitution would follow our representatives in the League as it did the flag. Moreover, while it was all but inconceivable that the powerful deterrents to war in the other articles would fail, still Article 10 was the very cream and crux of the Covenant without which it would have very little vitality.

He would not object to statements in the resolution of ratification as to what we thought the disputed articles meant, but reservations that would throw the whole matter back into conference would bring chaos.[15]

Impossible Idealism. Senator Sherman, on September 16, ridiculed the idea of our being deserters and retorted that nothing required us "to scatter our strength over earth's seven seas and dissipate our energies and resources in crusading in the affairs of every warring people, except an impossible idealism, drunk with phrase-making and cajoled by European diplomacy into spending our national strength to underwrite the war risks of Europe, Asia and Africa." [16]

Safeguards Required. In somewhat different spirit, Senator Thomas, with his somber belief that human nature could not be changed, wrote the Democratic State Executive Committee of Colorado, that it was his opinion "that that is a victor's treaty, a treaty of force, a treaty of punishment, a treaty of partition, a treaty burdened with conditions accepted by the vanquished only at the point of the sword." Doubtless, Germany deserved its punishment and much more, but the treaty was nevertheless "freighted with a ghastly cargo of future wars, only awaiting opportunity for their bloody development." Describing the widespread turmoil in Europe and visualizing a combination between Russia and Germany, he asked if they didn't see "that when one of these storms breaks from three to five thousand miles distant from America, the burden of their suppression under the league must fall upon us because ours is the only great power still possessed of the financial and military sinews of war."

He had naught but admiration for the President and sympathy with his ideals and purposes, and had never failed to say so. He had denounced the "miserable naggings and reflections upon the President's motives, his abilities and his judgment" more than once upon the floor of the Senate. He knew that he performed his great task as well as any man similarly circumstanced could have done. It was with sorrow that he found himself compelled to differ from him on a great question of international concern lying so near his heart, but he could not cast his vote for the treaty in its present form.[17]

The Possibilities. On September 19, Senator Spencer introduced a twelve page plea from the "Republic of Korea," and Senator Wadsworth, of New York, explained the grounds for his aversion to the

---

[15] *Congressional Record,* Vol. 58, Pt. 6, pp. 5448–52.
[16] *Ibid.,* p. 5491.
[17] *Ibid.,* pp. 5674–5. Senator Lodge had defended himself against the charge of inconsistency, on September 16, by citing many of the President's utterances during our neutrality. (Pp. 5502–10).

treaty. He protested against poisoning the political life of the people. Some block of our people would be writing letters to the Senators every time their home land in Europe was dealt with. And if Greece attacked Bulgaria, no American citizen could buy anything of the several hundred thousand Greek citizens in the United States. He could have no financial dealings with a Greek. Every little store kept by a Greek in this country would have to be closed. What would become of them? Presumably they would all have to be interned somewhere and fed and clothed. If Austria should attack Hungary some day, then every Austrian in the United States would have to be ostracized. "One might go on and multiply the possibilities." [18]

Indeed they might, if this much could be drawn from the provision for the boycott of an aggressor nation. But what must the average Greek or other foreigner think, when thus solemnly told by a United States Senator that the operation of the Covenant might throw him into an internment camp any day?

Dishonor. Senator Nelson, following, defended the presence of the American troops then in Russia, and pointed out that the treaties closing the Napoleonic wars were not akin to, or even suggestive of the League of Nations, as had been so often maintained. He could not, either, view it as anything but dishonorable to abandon the new nations we had helped to create, as the Foreign Relations Committee proposed to do in its second reservation. "This reservation," he said, "in its entirety throws overboard and scatters to the four winds by its disavowals the whole moral weight and influence of the United States." [19]

Destruction. Senator Reed, on September 22, collected all the references to his enemies which the President had made on his tour and delivered a bitter sixteen page attack upon him and upon almost every conceivable aspect of the League. [20] Senator Frelinghuysen continued, on September 24, with a speech voicing his opposition to the "unwise policy and monstrous provisions" of the treaty, labelling the President an autocrat, and deploring the fact that he had apparently convinced the people of Europe that we in this country demanded "his league of nations." He would not follow him because "approval of the treaty means destruction of our beloved country." [21]

Superstition. Senator New, of Indiana, gave his opinion of the President and the treaty on September 25. The President said he be-

[18] *Congressional Record,* Vol. 58, Pt. 6, pp. 6518–25.
[19] *Ibid.,* pp. 5622–25.   [20] *Ibid.,* pp. 5700–16.
[21] *Ibid.,* pp. 5841–48.

lieved the League would prevent war. That was quixotic. Many a man had believed in fiction. Mirages seemed real. Many people believed firmly that a potato carried in the pocket would prevent rheumatism, that a silk thread around the neck would prevent sore throat.

Dwelling on our polyglot population as a reason for abstention from the League, as most opposition speakers now did, he maintained that the Knox declaration was all the peace proposal that was needed.[22]

Why Dissipate the Strength of the Compact? Senator Smith, of Maryland, had never for an instant doubted the wisdom and duty of ratifying the treaty, as promptly as possible, without amendments or reservations. Our Constitution was a tissue of compromises, yet it had stood every strain. Similarly the treaty was a result of the compromising of widely conflicting views, and of an assimilation of motives, interests, and forces that in extent girdled the earth. Necessarily it did not meet the judgment and wishes of everyone, but it was most certainly the best the world could then get.

So, he asked, "why set a demoralizing example to the less enlightened nations of the world, nations prone to selfishness, by writing reservations in the treaty? Reservations made by one nation, to that degree and extent weaken or cancel the otherwise reciprocal obligations of the other nations, parties thereto. So that by a series of reservations it is clear that the strength of this compact will be dissipated, the treaty made ineffective. We then inevitably face a return to the dishonored system of arms piled upon arms, taxes upon taxes, warships added to warships, slaughter, deaths innumerable throughout the world —a return to the whole wretched and ancient competition to destroy. For if, under the very sting and impetus of the recent great battles, it took the Peace Conference, guided by the finest brains and characters existing, so many weary months to effect this present proposed agreement among nations, it seems perfectly idle to hope for a better or more enlightened document, if any at all, from a future conference." He would, therefore, vote for no reservations, unless convinced of the absolute necessity of so doing in order to save from failure the tremendous principle involved.

What a reproach to the minds and hearts of men, he thought, that the ultimate determination of international controversy still depended on the exercise of brute force in personal combat, a method despised in private controversy since lawgivers and judges first sat.[23]

[22] *Ibid.,* pp. 5899–5902.
[23] *Ibid.,* pp. 5902–3.

Egotism. Senator Cummins, on September 26, ascribed full patriotism to everybody. All the Senators, on both sides, were equally patriotic. The trouble grew from "the one great irremediable error" which was made when the President outlined the terms of peace. For years and years to come the country would feel the weight of "that crowning mistake of overpowering egotism." Then, after an interval, he explained just exactly what the President should have done. In brief, he should have stayed just long enough to have helped disarm Germany completely, without helping to fix a single boundary anywhere, and long enough to have made a compact with the nations to arbitrate all "arbitrable" questions, submitting all others to a council which should have neither the power to decide nor to recommend, but only to discuss. Then "everything that mortal wisdom and foresight can do to prevent war would have been done."

Having demonstrated the difference between Presidential and Senatorial egotism, Mr. Cummins announced, "with some gratification," that the opinions of the Covenant which he now entertained after six months of diligent study and constant reflection were in exact accord with those he had expressed six months earlier.

Recognizing the compulsion which all the opponents of the League felt to insist upon the narrowest interpretation of our war aims, he declared we had "just one object" in the war—to whip Germany and remove the peril that threatened to overcome us. [24]

Faith. Later in the same day, Senator Williams arose to pay again his respects to all the various types of opposition. He pitied the man who spent three or four months out in the country crusading against the cause of world peace and then came back and made a speech of three or four hours to emphasize his opposition—to what? To an attempt to perpetuate peace as fully as poor fallible human nature could do it. He warned the reservationists, too, that they could not force the President to carry on negotiations for an emasculated and impotent instrument, and appealed to them: "If you want to beat this treaty and beat the league of nations, come out in the open like men. . . . Do it like men, open and above board. Just say you will not have it, you do not believe in it."

While the President was speeding back to Washington, a broken

---

[24] *Congressional Record,* Vol. 58, Pt. 6, pp. 5952–64.
He appended an article by F. H. Simonds describing the dispute between the Roumanians and the Serbs over the Banat as an admirable example of the dangers in the League and the fallacy that the principles of the 14 points or of the League would control. (Pp. 5964–5).

WARREN G. HARDING

OF OHIO

HARRY S. NEW

OF INDIANA

ALBERT B. FALL

OF NEW MEXICO

ALBERT B. CUMMINS

OF IOWA

STRONG RESERVATIONISTS—REPUBLICAN REGULARS

man physically, Williams warned the Senators that they could not break him down by questioning his intellectual integrity. It had ever been the history of the world that a prophet was apt to be somewhat without honor in his own country, sometimes overwhelmingly without it, enough so to be crucified. "But at any rate you cannot tear down this man. He is too big a man, too great a man, he is too much of an idealist—just the very thing that you curse him for being; the best thing in the world that a man can be; a thing bringing him nearer the angels than any other human characteristic can bring him. Sordid politics cannot hurt him; hyphenated Americanism cannot hurt him; over-hasty, undigested expressions even from good men cannot hurt him; and whether the league of nations is adopted this year, or 4 years from now, or 5 or 10 years by the United States . . . and time is of small import in comparison with the great question itself . . . whatever may be the lapse of time, the time will come when there will be a league of nations and when we will be members of it, substantially, if not identically according to the very provisions of this treaty." [25]

The Campaign at Its Height

Incessant War on Wilson. All that Senator Williams said might be true. There was a ring of faith in it that gave conviction. His words showed that he had little hope in any constructive action by the existing Senate, but that he banked on the future. He would need to, for the President's enemies would be satisfied with nothing less than his annihilation, and no cause that he was identified with would be allowed to succeed while they could prevent it.

The campaign to arouse the country to "the crimes of Wilson" went on incessantly. The treaty was used as a means of enlisting the passions or sympathies of most of the newer racial elements in the country, not already aggrieved by the war. Even the negroes were persuaded that he hated them and was their enemy. To the older stocks in the North the offense of his reëlection in 1916 was enough, but to make assurance doubly sure his "autocracy" was stressed daily, and he was held up continually by great Northern papers as a narrow-minded Southerner, bent on plundering the rest of the country to enrich his own section. Boasts of Southern newspapers about Wilson and his

[25] *Congressional Record,* Vol. 58, Pt. 6, p. 5974.

Senator Edge, Republican, of New Jersey, delivered a strong plea for the League with reservations on September 30. He was firmly convinced of the mission of the League and the impossibility of isolation, but desired equally the safeguards of the reservations.

work were especially reproduced in the North. The income tax law, including the excess profits taxes, had given many a deep grievance. Did not these laws shift the chief burden of taxation, which the whole country had formerly paid in customs and internal revenue taxes, to New York and Pennsylvania and Illinois? And was not Wilson responsible for the new tax base? It was often said that the South had asked for "self-determination" in 1860, and eminent men even went so far as to announce that it would have been better to have given the South her self determination than to have endured Wilson.[26]

Powerful Support for the League. Yet at the close of the President's Western trip it appeared that he might win one more victory, in the ratification of the treaty. He was still supported in his fight so strongly by the intellectual classes of the nation that continued opposition to the League seemed likely to give his party a chance for victory that nothing else could. The teachers and preachers of the country had their convictions strongly enlisted, and the chief leaders of the industrial and commercial classes felt that the League should go through. Judge Gary, head of the U. S. Steel Company, publicly advocated its ratification. The American Bar Association, meeting in Boston, voted for ratification without change, and the Associated Advertising Clubs of the World adopted a resolution supporting it. The same action was taken by the American Bankers Association and the American Federation of Labor. Even the Massachusetts Republican State Convention, under Senator Crane's leadership, passed a motion favoring our entry.[27]

An appeal to the Senate to ratify the treaty at once, with only such explanatory reservations as should not require resubmission, was made by 250 leading Americans and laid before each Senator on the morning of the day the treaty came up for official consideration. Taken almost entirely from Northern states, they included a dozen Governors and ex-Governors, a larger number of university presidents, a score of great bankers, and many lawyers, besides judges, bishops, publishers, labor leaders, merchants and capitalists. It was signed by Lyman Abbott, John Burroughs, Luther Burbank, Irving Bacheller, Alexander Graham Bell, Thomas A. Edison, Roger Babson, Cyrus H. K. Curtis and other noted individuals. Beseeching the Senate to give the country peace and certainty, the statement held that delay in the Senate had

[26] Dodd, *Woodrow Wilson and His Work*, pp. 377–85.
[27] C. P. Howland, *Survey of American Foreign Relations 1928*, New Haven, 1928, p. 270.

"resulted in indecision and doubt, bred strife and quickened the cupidity of those who sell the daily necessities of life and the fears of those whose daily wage no longer fills the daily market basket." Dissensions were being sown between us and our former allies, and the world was put in imminent peril of new wars by the lapse of each day.[28]

These considerations, together with the strength of the feeling for the Covenant, led many Republicans not interested in the League to believe that continued opposition might make the country angry enough to give the Democrats a chance. With victory a certainty, they said, why imperil it?[29] It was even reported that Senator Lodge required a good deal of bolstering to prevent his acquiescence. When you come to think of it, the responsibility for defeating the great experiment that bade fair to change the course of history, let alone the risks attendant upon imperilling the Treaty of Peace itself, was enough to make the stoutest of hearts falter. But the men who had convinced a large part of the people of the North that Wilson had created a super-government for them, and that he had tried to abrogate the Constitution, could not turn back. They had to go on telling the country that internationalism was now the great sin, and that all patriots should fly to their tents to save the country.[30]

Moreover, they were still bitter over the necessity of considering the League with the peace treaty. That was the thing they had feared of all things from the start. They had fought against it with might and main from the outset. Having lost in that strategy, they would not yield the President a place of honor at Geneva. Besides, might he not use the prestige of a success with the treaty to secure another term of the Presidency? Fear of him was almost as great as their hatred. Fear and hate usually go together.

Violence and Unrest at Home. Events also worked in their favor. The country was nervous and jumpy. Fear of the I. W. W. was widespread. Working secretly and destructively, what might they not do? Troops fought race rioters in Knoxville on September 1. On the 10th the police of Boston struck, and sections of the city were sacked by hoodlums while the streets witnessed every known form of assault in broad daylight. A nation wide steel strike was inaugurated on the 22d. As the month closed a mob stormed the new Omaha County building, set it on fire, and lynched the negro they sought in the most savage

[28] The *New York Times,* September 15, 1919.
[29] *Ibid.,* September 27, 1919.
[30] Dodd, *Woodrow Wilson and His Work,* pp. 370, 386.

fashion. The Mayor of the city, attempting to intervene, escaped the same fate only after being cut down by police a couple of times. Passions stirred by the war smoldered everywhere.

In such an atmosphere any alarm spread. Every new charge against Wilson and his League received some credence, whether it warned that he would keep 150,000 American boys permanently fighting in Turkey or that the League was likely to lead to the internment of all the Greek restaurant keepers in the United States.

Continued Strife and Turmoil Abroad. Events abroad, too, gave the opposition much opportunity to cite evidence of the immorality of the old world. With the Poles attempting to conquer great reaches of Russia, the Roumanians in possession of Hungary, and Fiume seized by an expedition of Italian irregulars, there was much occasion to point out the dangers of trying to pacify Europe and to ridicule the peacemaker. He was widely jeered abroad as well as at home. The very fires of lawless force loosed by the war were cited as arguments against the establishment of counsel and arbitration and law in international affairs.

It would not be just to lay even the major part of the blame for the domestic unrest in the country upon the Senate Foreign Relations Committee and the fight against the Treaty. But, as the statement of the 250 indicated, the contest did nothing to solve the pressing problems of the hour and it did further inflame the country. Neither would it be true to ascribe the land grabbing in Central Europe to the fight of the Senators to canonize the Farewell Address and the Monroe Doctrine. This factor is not needed to explain these forays. Still, the paralyzing of the strong hand that had sought to prevent in the settlements the creation of new wars did not contribute to the suppression of exaggerated nationalism. With him fighting at home for his pacific program, his back to the wall, the opportunity to upset his decisions in Europe was at least open, if not inviting.

Our Fears Not Shared. Yet some progress toward settlement had been made. Great Britain and Belgium had ratified the treaty. The Spanish Senate voted unanimously to join the League and the Foreign Relations Committee of the Chilean House of Representatives voted without a dissenting voice for adhesion.[31]

Was it possible that there were no patriots in the Spanish or Chilean legislatures! Surely it was not possible that the dangers in the Covenant cried by the American Senators had failed to be reported in

[31] *Current History,* September, 1919, pp. 388–9.

those lands. Or did the Covenant fail to affright in the Spanish language as it did in the English? Spain had maintained her neutrality to the very end of the war. Surely if the Covenant meant that Spanish boys must now begin to fight in all parts of Europe, some Spanish Senator would have risen to oppose it. The Spaniards were much closer to the "cauldron" than we, and they knew European conditions at least as well as our Senators. Moreover, they had fought the Moors enough to know what war in Siam or Madagascar might be like. If the Covenant were a dangerous "war breeder" that once you got in you might not be able to get out of, surely some Spanish legislators would have sensed the facts and opposed the step with all their might. They had observed closely the framing of the Covenant, and they had everything to lose by adhesion, if it was as dangerous as represented.

What, too, is to be thought of Chile? The Chileans are a live, virile people. They could not have failed to know what dangers to their liberty the American Senate saw in the Covenant. Their constitution, like ours, gave the Congress the right to declare war. Were they all willing to surrender that right to "nine men sitting in Geneva," none of them likely to be Chileans? If the Covenant took away their discretion and condemned them to send their boys to the ends of the earth in endless wars, surely some Chilean statesmen should have seen it. Their boys had never had to go to Europe to fight in wars other people had started—and they would have much farther to go than ours. Why should they subscribe to a scheme which our leaders said would cost them more than they could ever get from it?

They could not have escaped knowledge, either, that the Monroe Doctrine, which had protected them for a century, was said to be abrogated. It had been called a "regional understanding" and that finished it! Were they so blind as to fail to perceive that the benevolent arm of the United States was a better protection to them than any league could be? If joining the League meant trading assured security for dangerous entanglement, the legislatures of Chile and Argentina and Brazil and a dozen other American republics must have been composed only of spineless internationalists, willing to vote lightly for "the destruction of our beloved country."

Unkind questions, these? Perhaps, but they are questions which will have to be faced in the future, should the League succeed in its mission without our great aid, or fail without our powerful support and leave us to tread the path of blood again. It is the business of the strong to lead.

CHAPTER XV

NOVEMBER RESERVATIONS REJECTED

THE beginning of October found the Democratic supporters of the treaty almost leaderless. The President, instead of coming back to Washington to exert his full power upon the contest, backed by the aroused pro-League sentiment, had returned helpless to lift a hand. The force of his personality was not available to head a determined drive for outright ratification or to attempt to secure a two-thirds majority for interpretative reservations. He was in no condition to lead a fight to the finish or to be convinced that compromise was inevitable and had better be made at once.

Wilson had been compelled to take to his bed a few days after his return from Pueblo, and by October 2 his condition was serious. Four specialists were called into consultation, and bulletins of October 3 called his condition grave, though his cheerful frame of mind was an encouraging symptom. He was "profoundly exhausted and very weak."

Thereafter bulletins issued each day noted slight improvement, but on October 11 the country was warned that he must have a long rest in bed. Rumor ran rife in Washington as to his condition. A letter from Senator Moses to a constituent was published, on October 13, saying that he might live, but if he did he would not be "any material force or factor in anything." This brought a statement from Dr. Grayson, on the 14th, that the President's mind was as "clear as a bell." He was sufficiently improved by October 26, that the daily announcements of his condition were omitted. [1]

---

[1] See the *New York Times* or *Tribune* on the dates following those quoted.

In response to speeches describing the great riches which the President and Mrs. Wilson had received as gifts while in Europe, a list of these gifts was published from the White House on October 6. Senator Sherman had stated that "cloakroom gossip had the value of these gifts at $500,000." Senator Penrose had been informed that the presidential party "brought back to this country presents from crowned heads and foreign governments amounting to several million dollars." Representative Rodenberg of Illinois had presented a Congressional resolution on the subject. The supposed mil-

This situation, leaving the Democrats in the Senate scarcely knowing how to proceed, was further accentuated by the illness of Senator Martin of Virginia, the Democratic leader in the Senate. Sick for months, he died a week before the first defeat of the treaty in November. During many critical weeks Senator Hitchcock, the acting leader for the minority, was sitting in a dying man's shoes, a fact which had an important bearing upon the course of the struggle. After Martin's death, too, a contest between Hitchcock and Underwood for the permanent leadership lasted for weeks. Hitchcock had the responsibility of leadership without the actual authority to lead having been given him, either from above or below. In this situation he was confronted, in Senator Lodge, by one of the most adept parliamentarians of a generation.

Lodge, also, was heavily embarrassed, not by lack of authority but by the necessity of holding the two opposing wings of his party in line. It was a difficult job, though time was on his side. He knew that the campaign against the League was producing a widespread "attitude of uneasy scepticism and suspicious criticism." [2] "Senator Lodge is now in full control of the situation," wrote Harvey on October 11, under the head "Put it up to the President." [3]

While Lodge's control of the situation may not have been complete at the beginning of October, he greatly strengthened it by fighting stubbornly through the entire month, and the first week of November, for the proposed direct amendments to the treaty, particularly his own on the subject of Shantung. This campaign bound both the anti-League and the pro-League wings of the Republicans in the Senate more closely to him. The amendments failed, as Lodge had probably anticipated.

Amendments Defeated. The first test of strength came on the Fall amendments designed to take the United States out of the various commissions provided for the execution of the treaty. These amendments were all defeated by votes varying but little from that on the first, 30 for to 58 against. After other long speeches, a vote on the six

---

lions of jewels, said the *Tribune,* dwindled to a few pieces of lace and offerings of small intrinsic value. The President had planned to ask Congress for the right to retain these gifts.—*New York Tribune,* October 7, 1919.

[2] Rask Ørsted Fondet, *Les Origines et l'Oeuvre de la Société des Nations,* Copenhagen, 1923, p. 315.

[3] *Harvey's Weekly,* October 11, 1919, Vol. II, No. 41, p. 2.

Attacking Admiral Grayson for not giving more news of the President's condition, Harvey remarked that "The whole country is deeply sympathetic with the President in the great affliction that has come upon him in his marvelous career."

amendments purporting to restore the economic privileges on the Shantung Peninsula to China was reached on October 16, and they were
rejected 35 to 55. [4]

The majority on both occasions had been composed of about 40
Democrats and from 14 to 18 mild-reservationist Republicans. The
minority was made up also of two groups, one of about 20 organization Republicans upon whom Senator Lodge could depend at all times,
and another of some 12 or 13 irreconcilable Republicans. The Republicans were thus divided into three sections, all of which were
necessary to the success of any motion. The one or two Democratic
bitter-enders and four or five reservationists voted with the Republican factions with whom they sympathized.

After the decisive defeat of the Fall and Lodge amendments, no
hope was held out for any of the others except the Johnson amendment, giving the United States as many votes in the Assembly as the
British Empire. The press had so often carried the statement of League
opponents that Great Britain would have, in every international dispute, six votes to our one, that support for the proposal to equalize
that matter was widespread. Senator McCumber testified, on October
6, that of all the many false declarations concerning the Covenant
none had been so persistently reiterated and none had lodged deeper
in the public mind. [5] A majority of one or two was, therefore, still
counted for the Johnson proposal. This majority disappeared before the vote came, on October 27, however, and the amendment was
defeated 38 to 40. [6]

Amendments with the same purpose by Shields and Moses were
defeated, on October 29, by majorities of 9 and 17 votes. A pious
proposal of vitriolic Senator Sherman to invoke "the considerate judgment of mankind and the gracious favor of Almighty God" was also
lost on the same day, as was another Johnson amendment on voting
in the League. [7]

A motion by Lodge to strike the Shantung articles from the treaty
was lost, on November 4, 26 to 41; one by Senator La Follette to
strike out Part 13, creating the International Labor Office, was also
voted down on November 5, and a final textual change, moved by

---

[4] *Congressional Record,* Vol. 58, Pt. 7, p. 7013. The *New York Tribune* complained,
on October 16, that in his Shantung speech Senator Lodge had "prejudiced the case
against Japan in a manner calculated, it would seem, to prejudice good relations between Japan and the United States."
[5] *Congressional Record,* Vol. 58, Pt. 7, p. 6439.
[6] *Congressional Record,* Vol. 58, Pt. 8, p. 7548.
[7] *Ibid.,* pp. 7679–80, 7683.

Senator Gore on November 6, to require a vote of the people of any member of the League before going to war, ended the efforts to amend the treaty directly. [8] Thereafter, the majority Republicans sought to accomplish by reservations what they had failed to do directly, the middle-grounders tried to weaken the force of the blows aimed at the treaty, and the Administration forces sought to preserve it intact.

The Democrats on the Defensive. The Democrats were reported, on October 5, as especially determined to oppose to the last any requirement that reservations be positively approved by the Allies. Such a course would inevitably cause each nation to ponder on what reservations it ought to propose. [9] On October 6, Senator Hitchcock left word at the White House that if drastic reservations were adopted the Democratic Senators would vote against the treaty. This was a mere bluff, said Senator Lodge on the 7th. If it was intended as a warning to the mild reservationists it at least brought a meeting between them and Senator Hitchcock on the 9th. Results were not recorded.[10]

A conference of fifteen Democratic Senators, held on October 21, revealed some divergence of view, but it was agreed to maintain opposition to all treaty changes for the time being. The Democratic leaders were reported now to be quite willing to let the treaty take a slow course in order that the President might gain in health enough to take the responsibility of deciding finally whether reservations should be accepted.

Domestic Strife Increasing. His first effort after his collapse was directed to a situation at home which was even more urgent than action upon the treaty. On October 21, against the will of his physicians, he sent a letter to the Industrial Conference, which had been meeting at his call since October 6, in an effort to compose the nation-wide conflict between labor and capital which had broken out. His plea was without avail. Two days later the labor representatives to the Conference withdrew and it ended without result on the 24th.

The industrial situation was disquieting indeed. The great steel strike dragged along for many weeks to failure. A dock workers' strike, starting on October 10, spread along the Atlantic coast. All expressmen in the East were ordered out on the 16th. Book and job printers in the New York area locked out their pressmen on October 1, and

[8] *Congressional Record,* Vol. 58, Pt. 8, pp. 7942, 7969, 8013.
[9] *New York Tribune,* October 5, 1919. Taft was also reported in conference with Senators McCumber and McNary. On October 12, the ex-President was quoted as favoring compromise in order to save the treaty.
[10] *New York Times,* October 6, 7, 9, 1919.

magazines appeared in strange form, if at all. Strikes occurred every-where. An appeal from the President, and all other efforts, failed to avert a national strike of soft coal miners on November 1, and the government set itself to break the strike by the use of injunctions, protection of strike breakers and other means. A general strike was threatened in Pennsylvania and talk of industrial revolution was heard in conservative quarters. The President's strength had been rarely more needed. He had, moreover, administered so much power personally, in the exigencies of the war or by his own choice, that it was difficult for others to act with authority in an emergency. His effort to avert the spread of industrial warfare having failed, his ad-ministration was now compelled to fight classes of the people which were in sympathy with his policies and usually supporters of his party.

Adding to the turmoil, race rioting continued at intervals, par-ticularly at Elaine, Arkansas, where fifteen people were killed. Even Senator Reed was a victim of mob violence at Ardmore, Oklahoma, where he was egged from the platform and denied the right to speak against the League and its sponsor. [11]

Force Still the Arbiter Abroad. In Europe violence continued to flourish. A German army of uncertain status, led by General Von der Goltz, captured the Baltic city of Riga and it appeared for a while as if the power of the German Junkers might be restored at once. The Roumanians, flouting the mandates of the Peace Conference, got what they wanted and did as they pleased in Hungary. Italy, following these examples, was rejoicing in the seizure of Fiume and the French reactionaries were in a mood to overturn Clemenceau and follow suit, seizing what of Germany they liked. Poland was similarly minded and Greece might at any time work her will on Bulgaria. A few more lawless seizures would wreck the Treaty of Versailles completely. The President's policy of insisting that new Alsace-Lorraines be not created seemed about to fail entirely.

His fall, and the continued onslaught of his foes upon the treaty, emboldened sponsors of conquest and demoralized the advocates of moderation. Both exultation and apprehension spread through Europe. "Throughout the Old World there was a feeling that the American government was impartial because disinterested; that its representa-tion would be almost indispensable on the commissions created by the treaty; and that the removal of its steadying hand would be a serious

[11] *New York Times,* October 2, 3, 1919.

misfortune." [12] Anxiety was keen in Germany and the French were only less dismayed.

The latter now began to understand the import of the election of 1918. Listening in that year to the outcries of Roosevelt and Knox and Lodge against the President's negotiations for the Armistice, and to their shouts for smashing the Germans back to Berlin, unless we got "Unconditional Surrender," the imperialistic and military elements in France concluded that the Senate Republican leaders would make the President march along the paths they desired to take. When it now appeared that they had not only been mistaken in this estimate but that the Republican leaders were going to withdraw support from the concessions which the President had made, they assailed Lodge through the press as strongly as they had Wilson earlier in the year. [13]

The next reaction was naturally a revulsion to old methods. "If there was no possibility," wrote Frank Simonds, "of winning American sympathy and support by accepting American ideas, as expressed by the President, at real sacrifices of national security and aspiration, then Europe was prepared to reject them—was already rejecting them. Had the United States Senate accepted the Treaty of Versailles without delay and by a unanimous, or approximately unanimous, vote, the European reaction would have been far different from what it now is." [14]

This statement was not made in condemnation of the Senate. It nevertheless recorded the probability that while Wilson was being laid low by his own people, the forbearance introduced into the settlements by so many months of blood sweating would be wiped out by lawless force, acting in the old short-sighted manner.

Senators Unmindful of the Spread of Violence. Did such a prospect alarm the Senators leading the attack in Washington? Not at all. Senator McCormick inserted the Simonds review just noted in the *Congressional Record* as an argument for rejection, and as "an addition to the sum total of literary provender." [15] Senator Penrose found himself, on the first anniversary of the Armistice, still "outraged and humiliated" by the conduct of the President in "going to Paris without authority, obsessed with an egotistical idea about a

[12] Nevins, *Henry White*, p. 471.
[13] Nevins, *Henry White*, pp. 471, 472, 477. A leading French journalist told White that he never regretted any action of his life more bitterly than his participation in the earlier press attack, for he now saw that Wilson had been the truest friend of France (p. 477).
[14] *New York Tribune*, October 5, 1919.
[15] *Congressional Record*, Vol. 58, Pt. 7, pp. 6547–49.

peace covenant which no one wanted or cared about." [16] Senator Lodge openly stood for conquests by the Allies that would make new wars a certainty. He celebrated the Armistice by ridiculing the efforts to moderate the settlements which the President had made. By our "meddling" we had "deprived Poland of her issue to the sea"; we had "put our clumsy hand into Italy and brought on by so doing all the difficulties of Fiume"; our last performance was "to take Thrace from the Greeks" to whom it properly belonged. The sooner a country so unfacile in dealing with the affairs of other countries took itself out of any relationship to the affairs of other nations the better it would be for that country and the world. [17]

The leaders of the drive to destroy Wilson, already broken physically, were in no mood to halt their campaign, whatever the consequences might be. They were so far committed, moreover, that it would have been difficult for them to draw back, even in the event of his death. With the initiative fully in their hands, they were too busy saving the country, by gesturing in behalf of China and protesting Canada's status in the League, to heed the repercussions of their course abroad or to care if the settlements were upset thereby.

"Take all the time in the world, if need be," advised the *New York Sun,* "to get to the bottom of this dangerous compact, and to trace out with infinite care every word, every little hidden word that could in any circumstance work to our disadvantage as a free and independent people." The Senate had a solemn responsibility to "take the necessary time to fathom this monstrously impudent thing, and to acquaint the American people of the meaning of all the hideous possibilities." To which Harvey added his bravo, saying of the *Sun:* "Its course has conformed precisely to that of Senator Lodge—keenly judged, neither too rapid nor too slow, but shrewdly timed to the essentials of ultimate achievement." [18]

Reservations Agreed Upon. Backed by Harvey's steel determination and organizing ability, Lodge, by supporting the drive for amendments, was paving the way for the "ultimate achievement." The mild-reservationists had demonstrated by the middle of October that few

---

[16] *Congressional Record,* Vol. 58, Pt. 8, p. 8273.
Shortly before, Senator Spencer had introduced into the *Record* a long estimate of the probable expenses of the League of Nations, prepared by an accountant, purporting to show that the annual expense would be $1,194,591,000. This "audit" included such items as 6,505 salaries at $10,000 and 166,310 at $2,000 each. (Pp. 8190–92.)
[17] *Congressional Record,* Vol. 58, Pt. 8, p. 8296; *New York Tribune,* November 12, 1919.
The President celebrated the Armistice by leaving his sick bed for an invalid chair.
[18] *Harvey's Weekly,* November 1, 1919, Vol. 2, No. 44, p. 2.

direct amendments, if any, could be adopted, but at the same time they made it equally clear that they would insure the adoption of reservations. While the Fall and Lodge amendments were being voted down, the entire group of middle-grounders had pledged themselves, one after another, to vote for reservations on the same subjects. The Foreign Relations Committee therefore returned to the framing of reservations. To the four which it had originally proposed, new ones on minor points were added until a total of fourteen had been reached. The President had stated his fourteen points; the committee would have its fourteen counter-points. The original reservations had not been numerous enough to get a majority; enough would now be added.

As a concession to the mild-reservationists the language of the reservations was toned down somewhat, made a little less abrupt, but the basic content was not changed. Senator Lodge stated, on October 23, that the 14 reservations would have the value of amendments, and Senator Hitchcock said with emphasis that if they were adopted the Democrats would vote against ratification.[19]

The reservation program went through without a hitch, in the period November 7th to 19th. On the 7th, a preamble requiring the written assent of three of the Associated Powers was adopted, 48 to 40. On the 8th, the first reservation passed 50 to 35, and on the 13th, the key reservation on Article 10 was adopted 46 to 33. After that, cloture was invoked and twelve reservations were put through, on the 15th, by votes approximating 53 to 40.[20]

The leaders were now ready for the final decision. A long list of reservations had been adopted by majority votes. Those who had opposed them were now to be confronted with the alternative of accepting what they had lately voted against or of seeing the treaty fail of approval for lack of the constitutional two-thirds majority, a situation which always works against preserving a treaty intact in the Senate and for those who would change or defeat it.

The Campaign Local. Little effort to qualify or reject the League Covenant was existent, even at this late date, outside the United States. The National Assembly of Guatemala gave its approval in early October; in the latter part of the month the Uruguayan Chamber did likewise and Paraguay gave notice of her unconditional entry.[21] As the American objections to the treaty finally came to a head in the Senate,

---

[19] *New York Times,* October 20, 24, 1919.
[20] *Congressional Record,* Vol. 58, Pt. 8, pp. 8074, 8139, 8437; Pt. 9, pp. 8546–71.
[21] *Le Temps,* October 6, 1919; the *Times,* (London.) October 18, 1919; C. A. Kluyver, *Documents on the League of Nations,* Leiden, 1920, p. 236.

it was ratified by the Brazilian Chamber, on November 10, and by the Senate of that republic, November 12. On November 18, the Parliament of Colombia authorized its government to give notice of adhesion and the Peruvian National Assembly unanimously ratified the treaty.[22] The other American republics deliberately walked toward the destruction of national liberty and safety which was said to lurk in the League of Nations. They seemed to prefer the perils of Article 10 to the protection of the hegemonic Monroe Doctrine proclaimed by the leaders of the North American Senate.

Final Appeals. Nothing, however, now stood in the way of the "ultimate achievement" of the latter, except the possibility that the pro-League Republican Senators might at the final moment decide that they would rather have the League and the Treaty than the reservations. This contingency was forestalled by two events. First, Will H. Hays, Chairman of the Republican National Committee, asked William H. Taft for "a confidential expression of his views and Taft complied with the request by a frank and full exposition in a letter marked 'confidential.' Excerpts from this letter admitting imperfections in the Covenant were published in the press on the next day in such a way as to stamp Mr. Taft as advocating the modification of the League and thus as favoring the reservations. Notwithstanding Mr. Taft's indignation at this breach of confidence, the letter served the ends of the Republican party machine, and his name was now used in support of the Republican reservations." [23]

This move was soon followed by a decision of the executive committee of the League to Enforce Peace, under Taft's chairmanship, to accept the Lodge reservations. Their conclusion was announced on November 18 and read into the *Congressional Record* by Senator Mc-Nary shortly before the Senate voted. It reiterated that some of the reservations were harmful but argued that they left the Covenant equal to the task of preserving the peace, continuing:

> The treaty, even with the reservations now adopted, can accomplish the purpose and should be ratified. There is no adequate reason why it should not be. The world waits. Delay is perilous. Any action which casts the covenant . . . into the politics of a presidential election will delay peace and halt political reorganization and economic rehabilitation of nations sorely smitten by war, by winter, and by famine.

[22] *Le Temps,* November 10, 1919; *Deutsche Allgemeine Zeitung,* November 12, 1919; *La Paix par le Droit,* December, 1919, p. 533; League of Nations *Official Journal,* 1920, pp. 13–16, 259–60.
[23] C. P. Howland, *American Foreign Relations 1928,* New Haven, 1928, p. 278–9.

The League to Enforce Peace, speaking for the great multitude which has labored for this supreme end, sensible of its responsibility, calls for the immediate ratification of the treaty, even with its reservations, but it is most important that the preamble be changed by removing the necessity for positive action on the reservations by nations definitely named and contenting ourselves by acceptance in the ordinary way by silent acquiescence in a time limited.

Failure to ratify now would defeat the world's hopes for peace now and always. Such a failure would throw the world back into worse than pre-war conditions by re-establishing a balance or hostile grouping of powers with a burden of armaments. If the League be once established and permitted to function with our country as a member the foundations of a new world order would continue to grow in beneficent steadibility, securing for all nations, great and small, peace with justice.[24]

This advice from the great organization which had been laboring so powerfully for a league of nations for years was counteracted, so far as the Democratic Senators were concerned, by the following letter from President Wilson to Senator Hitchcock, read at a conference held before the Senate assembled to vote.

MY DEAR SENATOR:

You were good enough to bring me word that the Democratic Senators supporting the treaty expected to hold a conference before the final vote on the Lodge resolution of ratification and that they would be glad to receive a word of counsel from me.

I should hesitate to offer it in any detail, but I assume that the Senators only desire my judgment on the all-important question of the final vote on the resolution containing the many reservations of Senator Lodge. On that I cannot hesitate, for, in my opinion, the resolution in that form does not provide for ratification, but rather for nullification of the treaty. I sincerely hope that the friends and supporters of the treaty will vote against the Lodge resolution of ratification.

I understand that the door will then probably be open for a genuine resolution of ratification.

I trust that all true friends of the treaty will refuse to support the Lodge resolution.

Cordially and sincerely yours,

WOODROW WILSON.[25]

[24] *Congressional Record,* Vol. 58, Pt. 9, p. 8773: The Executive Committee argued that its decision would lead Wilson to accept the reservations. Howland, *American Foreign Relations* 1928, p. 279.
This result might have been considerably advanced if they could have had a conference with him before announcing their decision.
[25] *Congressional Record,* Vol. 58, Pt. 9, p. 8768; *Current History,* December 1919, p. 383. The *New York Tribune* of December 28, 1919, quoted Senator McNary as

As the hour for voting approached, Senator Brandegee, author of the Round Robin, reminded its signers of that compact by putting it before them again. He himself had sworn to vote against the League, if it were included in the Treaty, and he meant to keep his vow. He would not vote for "this contraption." He would consider himself "a candidate for the madhouse if he voted for any such thing." [26]

Rejection. In accordance with these conflicting appeals, the League Republicans voted with the regulars for approval of the treaty, with the Lodge reservations, and the Democrats, joined by the irreconcilables, opposed it. The vote was 39 for, 55 against. A vote for unconditional ratification was then permitted and it failed by a vote of 38 for to 53 against, the bitter-enders voting nay, together with seven Democrats, Gore, Reed, Shields, Smith (Georgia), Thomas, Trammell and Walsh (Massachusetts). Senator McCumber, Republican, voted aye.[27]

Press Comment. "Jubilation reigned in some quarters," began the *Literary Digest* in reporting the rejection of the treaty, "as a sensational climax to one of the most bitterly fought political battles in our history." Senator Borah was heard proclaiming the result as "the greatest victory since Appomattox." "Thanks be to God which giveth us the victory," said the *Boston Transcript,* "may well become the language of a reverent and grateful people!" A "twin victory of independence and democracy," said the *Cleveland News* (Republican).

It may have been a victory and the destroyers of the Treaty and the League might exult in their triumph, replied the *Springfield Republican* (Independent), "but they will go into history as having constructed nothing and selfishly leaving the world to its darkness and woe." To the *St. Louis Star* (Independent), too, the Senate had destroyed our prestige and given us the rôle of "the chief international cynic." Asking where we would be if the other American nations joined the League, it concluded that the best we could hope for was "that the Senate's action will destroy the League, weaken our former allies and leave us dominant in a disillusioned world."

---

saying that Oscar S. Straus of the League to Enforce Peace had shown him a list of seventeen Democratic Senators who had signed a pledge to vote for the Lodge reservations. Straus later said that he had added enough Democrats to make the two-thirds majority. The President's letter had made it impossible for them to fulfill this pledge.

[26] *Congressional Record,* Vol. 58, Pt. 9, pp. 8774–75.

[27] *Congressional Record,* Vol. 58, Pt. 9, pp. 8786, 8787, 8803. The Swiss National Commission voted in favor of entry into the League on the same day by a vote of 128 to 43. The States Council of Switzerland came to the same decision, on November 21, 33 to 6. Kluyver, *Documents on the League of Nations,* p. 249.

As to who was responsible there was similar disagreement. To the *New York Times* it was only necessary to ask: "Who has supported the Treaty of Versailles from the moment of its submission to the Senate, who has toiled and striven for its ratification? Who has opposed ratification, who has piled Ossas and Pelions of obstruction across its pathway. Who has engrafted upon it reservations that blast and destroy it?" "The United States Senate under the bankrupt leadership of Senator Henry Cabot Lodge has killed the peace treaty," said the *Rochester Times-Union* (Independent), and in consequence "millions today are bitterly disappointed, sick at heart, disgusted with politicians and their tricks."

But Republican papers of all shades of friendliness and hostility to the League joined in laying responsibility at the door of the stubborn, imperious "autocrat" in the White House. It was plain enough, said the pro-League *St. Louis Globe Democrat,* when the President returned with the League that it could not be ratified without reservations, "yet with unbending egotism and amazing tactlessness he stood in the way of conciliation and compromise."

Others held that the responsibility would have to be shared by both sides. The President, said the *Philadelphia Inquirer,* a pro-League Republican paper, "has been egotistical and has ignored the Senate," while the "opposition to the treaty has been malicious and with mighty little honesty in it." The *New York Globe* (Republican) also suggested that both were to blame and perhaps, also, the people at large. A natural reaction from the idealism of the war period had played a part that it would take prolonged campaigns of education to overcome. Many refused, however, to believe that the rejection could be final and predicted a compromise. "There is simply no acceptable alternative to a peace based on the principles of the Covenant," said the *Chicago Daily News* (Independent). "Necessity will force the Administration and the Republican friends of the Covenant to reach an agreement." [28]

ATTITUDES TOWARD COMPROMISE

The strategy of the Administration forces as indicated in the President's letter, and as appraised by the press, was to bring about a double vote on the treaty, with reservations and without them, and from the complete deadlock thus established to work out compromise reservations which both sides could accept. The Republicans had demonstrated

[28] *Literary Digest,* November 29, 1919.

that the treaty could not be ratified without reservations; the Democrats would show in turn that it could not be ratified with the Lodge reservations. Senator Hitchcock stated after his final conference with the President, on November 17, that the President was not opposed to all of the Lodge reservations, but he would pocket the treaty unless the preamble were omitted and the reservation on Article 10 altered. [29]

In line with this policy Senator Hitchcock, on November 13, had introduced into the Senate a list of five reservations dealing with withdrawal, Article 10, domestic questions, the Monroe Doctrine and the votes of the British Dominions in the Assembly.[30] The mild-reservationists, however, excepting Senator McCumber, stood solidly against the Hitchcock reservations, at the close of the session on November 19, and prevented their consideration. They also defeated a motion by Senator Pomerene that the President of the Senate appoint a committee of conciliation, headed by Senator Lodge and including Senator Hitchcock, whose duty it should be to report a resolution of ratification that not less than two-thirds of the Senate would support. The vote was 48 to 42. [31]

The Pro-League Republicans Committed. The Democrats apparently had delayed too long to make terms with the Republicans most friendly to the League. The latter had hoped for a long time that the Administration would agree to enough of the mild reservations, which they favored, to enable the two-thirds vote to be mustered. They had expected, on more than one occasion in October, that such an agreement would be forthcoming, only to be disappointed.

They were thus driven, in the words of a foreign observer, "into the unenviable position of having to negotiate with the Republican majority in order to mitigate the reservations as much as possible, without any hope of winning the Democrats over to vote for these reservations." [32] At the same time they were embarrassed by the necessity of voting down the deadly amendments pressed by their Republican brethren, and so deterred probably from toning down the reservations as much as they might have with some assurance of Democratic support, or with the opportunity of coalition with the Democrats open to them.

The Democrats thus repudiated allies who were sincerely for the

[29] *New York Times,* November 18, 1919.
[30] *Congressional Record,* Vol. 58, Pt. 8, p. 8433.
[31] *Ibid.,* Pt. 9, p. 8800.
[32] P. Schou, in Rask Ørsted Fondet, *Les Origines et l'Oeuvre de la Société des Nations,* Copenhagen, 1923, p. 319.

FRANK B. KELLOGG

OF MINNESOTA

KNUTE NELSON

OF MINNESOTA

CHARLES L. McNARY

OF OREGON

IRVINE L. LENROOT

OF WISCONSIN

MILD RESERVATIONISTS—REPUBLICAN

Covenant and willing to put aside party considerations to a very considerable extent for it. Occupying the middle ground in the dispute, it was difficult for the League Republicans to see why both sides should not yield something to their mediation. If the Democrats would not budge, they could see no reason why they should again split their own party, not yet fully restored to power, to save the Covenant, when the Democrats might do it by what seemed to them reasonable concession.

The mild-reservationists felt that they had done about all that could be asked of them. Senator McCumber in his final plea to the Democrats, made just before the vote was taken, said: "Every one of these reservations represents a compromise between conflicting opinions. You have known from the very beginning that reservations were necessary, and with the possible exception of the preamble, these reservations are just as mild and inoffensive as could possibly be obtained and yet command enough votes on this side of the chamber as, added to all you can muster on that side, would make the necessary two-thirds vote for ratification." [33]

The Democrats Unconverted. The leaders of the League to Enforce Peace had, no doubt, come to the same conclusion. Its capitulation at this point, however, won no Democratic votes for the reservations. The Democratic Senators could not forget that Taft had been one of the first to expose the packing of the Foreign Relations Committee with opponents of the President and of the League, and they could not throw off the conviction that the terms they were asked to accept had been dictated by the League's worst foes. They were told time and again by Senators like Kellogg and Lenroot that the reservations, particularly those on Article 10, had been framed by the treaty's friends, the mild-reservationists, but they could not believe that the influence of the nullificationists had not been determining, particularly when not a single reservation could have commanded a majority vote of the Senate without the aid of the bitter-enders. [34]

The Democrats were convinced, moreover, that they faced in Senator Lodge a leadership that would capitalize to the limit every concession made. Senator Hitchcock as late as December 16 invited the mild-reservationists to submit reservations. If the Democrats offered definite terms it "might be seized upon by the foes of the treaty as material for demanding further compromise." [35] Some of the leaders

---

[33] *Congressional Record,* Vol. 58, Pt. 9, p. 8786.
[34] See, among others, the statements of Senators Robinson, Owen and Hitchcock on November 19. *Congressional Record,* Vol. 58, Pt. 9, pp. 8769, 8774, 8779.
[35] *New York Times,* December 17, 1919.

of the League to Enforce Peace also had resigned, for the same reason, when the League accepted the Lodge reservations.[36] With this conviction it seemed useless to begin to compromise.

Moreover, to accept numerous reservations of a serious character would place the Democratic party in the weak defensive position into which Lodge and his colleagues had been laboring for many months to drive it. Serious concessions would clinch the claim of the Republican leaders that Wilson had sacrificed and endangered American interests and enable them successfully to pose "as the saviors of Democratic negligence." [37]

Believing that such a claim was wholly unjustifiable, the Democrats could not see the virtue of compromising their defense of the League. Some foresaw the outcome, but others found it incredible to conclude that the people would repudiate so great an achievement as the League, even though the propaganda against it continued indefinitely. Aside from the League, the political capital of the Democratic Party was running low. Its administration of tremendous affairs for seven years had accumulated a heavy accounting. Why should the President's party aid in beclouding the great achievement which might snatch victory from defeat?

The Leaders in Control. The Lodge Republicans, likewise, could not now be deterred from affixing their brand on the Covenant in large and unmistakable letters. They had not toiled for an entire year, first to keep Wilson from rearing the structure and then to share in its architecture, to abate their efforts now when even the League to Enforce Peace, which had been so long a thorn in the side, had endorsed their work. If the League of Nations was to be, it would have the Republican trademark affixed plainly and solidly upon it.

The seven years which had just passed had been bitter indeed for the elder Republican Senators, used to sitting in the seats of the mighty. Their dethronement had not only been longer than ever before but it had covered the most stirring and momentous period of modern times. The lean years, however, seemed to be about over. All signs now pointed to a sure resumption of power—unless a supreme achievement of world statesmanship, climaxing a mighty career, should enable the great leader of the opposing party to save it. It could happen. No orthodox Republican can be blamed for fearing the possibility. If it did occur, their exile might be long. No chances must be taken.

---

[36] Howland, *American Foreign Relations,* 1928, p. 279.
[37] Schou, in *Les Origines et l'Oeuvre de la Société des Nations,* p. 316.

Therefore, the reply of Senator Lodge, made on November 14, to the report that the Democrats would reject his reservations and create a deadlock, was: "Once the Democrats vote down the ratifying resolution the treaty may be considered as dead. It may lie in the Senate but the breath of life will never be put in it again." [38] No compromise was to be permitted. The 14 reservations constituted the final terms, the consummation of a year of opposition to any Wilson-made League of Nations. They could be taken or left. "The door is closed," said Lodge to Senator Swanson as the vote was taken. [39] "Take it or leave it," said Senator Edge, "that or nothing." [40] Even the mild-reservationists felt that the time for compromise had passed.

Thus, when the demand for a compromise presently swept the country so strongly that even Lodge felt compelled to go into conference, he could do so feeling that he need concede nothing whatever. He need only hold his ground. The Democrats would have to accept his terms to save their treaty. If they did, all the responsibility would then be upon the President who had "ignored" the Senators so long; if the Democrats did not capitulate, the responsibility would at least be divided and the country would know who had saved it. [41]

[38] *New York Times,* November 15, 1919.
[39] *New York Times,* November 20, 1919.
[40] *Congressional Record,* Vol. 58, Pt. 9, p. 8779.
[41] Ten days after the Senate had rejected the reservations, and with them the treaty, Senator Newberry, whose election over Henry Ford by a vote of 220,054 to 212,487, had given the Republican leaders control of the Senate, was convicted of violating the Federal Corrupt Practices Act and sentenced to two years in prison. The law limited his campaign expenditures in the primary to $3,750, whereas almost $200,000 was admitted to have been spent in his behalf. Sixteen of his aids were also sentenced.

From the standpoint of the Senate leaders the reward of Newberry's election had been obtained, however, and court appeals served to keep him out of prison until the Supreme Court freed him, on May 2, 1921, by declaring the law under which he was convicted unconstitutional. Before that time the fight on the treaty was safely concluded.

Popular opinion eventually compelled Newberry's resignation from the Senate, in November 1922, after Senators defending him had fared badly in the elections of that year. Repudiated in his own state by the election of a Democrat to the Senate on the issue, and faced by a clear majority of the Senate pledged to unseat him, Newberry preferred not to endanger further his supporters in the Senate.—Howland, *American Foreign Relations, 1928,* p. 246; *New York Times,* March 21, 1920, July 5, November 9, 15, 20, 1922.

Public opinion gave a clear and sustained condemnation of the means by which the Republican Senate majority of 1918 was obtained, without attaching the same censure to the chief use to which it was put.

CHAPTER XVI

THE COMPROMISE NEGOTIATIONS

THE view of the Democratic leaders that public opinion would force a further consideration of the Lodge reservations, once they had been defeated, was well founded. The failure of the Senate to approve the Treaty struck the multitudes who resented or regretted the reservation campaign as a world tragedy such as had seldom happened. To still larger numbers, who did not feel the sense of epochal decision, it seemed simply incredible that the dispute should not be compromised in such a way as to allow the United States to participate in the liquidation of the war and the establishment of peace, on a somewhat more stable basis at least. [1]

These feelings were so strong that Lodge himself, who had been so sure that the treaty was dead on November 19, found two weeks later the following situation:

> In that brief interval I went to Massachusetts for a few days and while there and after I reached Washington at the opening of the regular session I found that a situation had developed, both in the Senate and in the country, which was caused by the continued assertion of the friends of the League that the reservations had been added and the defeat of the treaty had been brought about by disputes between the two parties on what were merely verbal differences. The statement was false, but I thought its falsity should be publicly exhibited. It seemed to me very clear, after considering the new conditions thus presented that, in order to make it perfectly plain to the world that the differences between those who supported the treaty and those who opposed it were not verbal but vital and essential, it was most desirable to make an effort, at least, to come to some agreement between the two sides; that is, between the opponents of the reservations and of the treaty and those who favored accepting the League substantially as it was offered. . . . [2]

[1] See Howland, *American Foreign Relations 1928*, pp. 280–81.
[2] H. C. Lodge, *The Senate and the League of Nations*, N. Y., 1925, pp. 192–93.

Positions Maintained. Lodge did not, however, at once move to make it perfectly plain to the world that the differences were vital and essential. He insisted instead that the President must withdraw the treaty from the Senate and re-submit it before anything more could be done, to which claim Senator Underwood replied that such a course would put the treaty in the hands of the Foreign Relations Committee again. [3] The President, disclaiming any intent to touch the treaty, was no more conciliatory. He had "no compromise or concession of any kind in mind," but intended that the Republican leaders of the Senate should continue to bear "the undivided responsibility." [4]

Senator Lodge was soon after quoted as "standing pat" on the reservations. He called a meeting of the Foreign Relations Committee, on December 18, to act upon the Knox separate peace resolution. The Committee favorably reported the proposal on the 20th. Senator Underwood offered a counter resolution calling for the appointment of an official conciliation committee of ten Senators, but consideration was blocked by Lodge, a proceeding which was reported to have angered the mild-reservationists, who conferred with him on the 21st. Senator Underwood also talked with Lodge. [5]

On the 27th the press carried reports of a serious conference of the middle-grounders. The *Times* reported that the dozen Senators present had decided to notify Lodge that they would ignore his leadership and deal with the Democrats, if action looking to a compromise was not begun. The *Tribune* denied the threat of revolt, but reported the conference and the projected meeting with Lodge. Talk of compromise was incessant. Conferences were numerous.

Wilson for a Solemn Referendum. The President did not participate in any of these discussions. Several new diplomatic representatives of foreign countries waiting to present their credentials to him were not able to do so. His isolation did not prevent him from thinking of the treaty, however, and his opinion of the Lodge reservations did not change. On January 8, he sent a message to the Jackson Day dinner of Democrats in which he refused to accept the action of the

---

[3] *Congressional Record*, Vol. 59, Pt. 1, pp. 533–34; *New York Times*, December 13, 1919.
[4] White House statement of December 14. *New York Times*, December 15, 1919. The Chicago Board of Trade and the Cleveland Chamber of Commerce urged agreement on the treaty on December 17. The latter realized that a "legalistic interpretation" of the Covenant might involve some sacrifice of national tradition, but felt that even if it cost something the great gain at stake was worth the price. It believed that "with the exception of an unimportant minority" the people of the United States desired the League.—*New York Times*, December 18, 1919.
[5] *New York Times*, December 19, 21, 23, 1919.

Senate as representative of the nation and declared his willingness to submit the issue to the people in the approaching election. He wrote, in part:

> Personally, I do not accept the action of the Senate of the United States as the decision of the nation. I have asserted from the first that the overwhelming majority of the people of this country desire the ratification of the treaty, and my impression to that effect has recently been confirmed by the unmistakable evidence of public opinion given during my visit to seventeen of the States.
>
> I have endeavored to make it plain that if the Senate wishes to say what the undoubted meaning of the League is, I shall have no objection. There can be no reasonable objection to interpretations accompanying the act of ratification itself. But when the treaty is acted upon, I must know whether it means that we have ratified or rejected it. We cannot rewrite this treaty. We must take it without changes which alter its meaning, or leave it, and then, after the rest of the world has signed it, we must face the unthinkable task of making another and separate kind of treaty with Germany. But no mere assertions with regard to the wish and opinion of the country are credited.
>
> If there is any doubt as to what the people of the country think on this vital matter, the clear and single way out is to submit it for determination at the next election to the voters of the nation, to give the next election the form of a great and solemn referendum, a referendum as to the part the United States is to play in completing the settlements of the war and in the prevention in the future of such outrages as Germany attempted to perpetrate.
>
> We have no more right to refuse now to take part in the execution and administration of these settlements than we had to refuse to take part in the fighting of the last few weeks of the war which brought victory and made it possible to dictate to Germany what the settlements should be. Our fidelity to our associates in the war is in question, and the whole future of mankind.[6]

The reading of the letter at the gathering of Democrats was interrupted time and again by "the wildest enthusiasm," the greatest outburst coming on the suggestion of letting the people settle the issue in the coming election. The next day, however, Senators and Representatives of both parties were cool to the idea. Apart from the bitter-

[6] Shaw, *Messages and Papers of Woodrow Wilson*. Vol. II, p. 1163.
This letter was considerably revised by a member of the President's cabinet, David F. Houston, before it was issued. Houston doubted whether Wilson dictated the first draft.—D. F. Houston, "The War on Wilson," *World's Work*, September, 1926, Vol. 52, p. 546.

enders, neither side appeared to want the dispute in the campaign. No one had suggested how a "yes" and "no" vote on the question could be taken, especially when complicated by domestic issues. [7] William J. Bryan had combated the proposal at the Jackson dinner and he continued strongly to advocate letting the Republican majority, small as it was, have its way. Senator Owen, of Oklahoma, labored also to secure agreement. He invited all the Democratic Senators to his home for conference. Twenty came on short notice, January 11th, and agreed upon a reservation to Article 10 that would not destroy its moral obligation. The *Times,* editorially, thought "Agreement in Sight." [8]

The Demand for Adjustment Insistent. With public opinion urgently demanding some solution of the impasse, it did seem unthinkable that none could be found. Even Senator Lodge appeared hopeful when visited by a massed body of official representatives from twenty-six great national organizations whose combined membership totaled 20,000,000 voters. This delegation, calling in turn upon Lodge and Hitchcock, urged immediate ratification of the treaty on a basis "that will not require its re-negotiation." [9]

Some sort of conference between the opposing sides could no longer be delayed. Lodge had accepted the President's challenge to an electoral decision and he continued to maintain that the pressure should be put upon Wilson, not upon himself, but he could not avoid at least the appearance of an effort to compromise. The treaty had been ratified by enough of the Allied powers to put it into effect on January 10. President Wilson called the first session of the Council of the League of Nations on January 13. The next day Senators Kenyon and Owen were reported as uniting to call a joint conference of Senators. [10]

The Bi-partisan Conference. The conference met on the 15th, after Owen persuaded Hitchcock to go with him to Lodge's office and "to invite Walsh, Simmons and McKellar to accompany them." [11]

---

[7] *New York Times,* January 9 and 10, 1920.

[8] *New York Times,* January 12, 13, 1920. On January 9, President A. Lawrence Lowell advised the Democrats to abandon Article 10 and Judge George Gray stood strongly for the article. *The Times,* January 10, 1920.

[9] *New York Times,* January 14, 1920.

A referendum vote taken in 410 colleges on the sentiment of students and professors, after rejection, was announced about this time. Of 158,078 ballots cast, 61,494 favored a compromise between the Lodge and Democratic reservations that would ratify the treaty, 48,423 opposed any reservations, 13,943 favored killing the treaty and the League and 27,970 expressed themselves for the Lodge program. *Current History,* February, 1920, p. 204.

[10] *New York Times,* January 11, 14, 15, 1920.

[11] *The Washington Post,* January 15; *New York Times,* January 16, 1920; *New York Tribune,* January 16, 1920.

The effort of which this step was the culmination has been described by Senator McKellar as follows:

Senator Le Baron Colt of Rhode Island, now dead, was a thoroughgoing advocate of the League. He wanted some reservations but was not particular about them. He had an office on the same floor with me and we were great friends. Drawing his arm through mine, one day, returning from the Senate, and on our way to our offices, he said, "You and I could get together and adjust the differences about reservations and we could confirm this treaty, including the League."

We went into his office and talked it over carefully, taking the controverted points up in order. We discussed it in this way,—not what he wanted or what I wanted, but what he believed would get the approval of two-thirds of the Senate and what I believed would get the approval of two-thirds of the Senate. We finally reached a tentative conclusion and he suggested that we call in others. He called in Senator Kenyon and I called in Senator Kendrick, and it was not long before the four of us reached a tentative conclusion, and we decided to call in others. He called in Senator Lenroot and I called in Senator Simmons, and this enlarged informal committee agreed tentatively. Then the conference called in Senator Walsh of Montana and Senator Kellogg and with this enlarged conference, reached a tentative understanding.

We had made such progress that it was concluded that we should call in our respective leaders, and so our Republican friends on the conference called in Senator Lodge and my Democratic colleagues and myself called in Senator Hitchcock.

Both thought good results might come from the conference, but unfortunately Senator Lodge did not get along well with Senator Colt, nor do I think he was pleased to have Senator Kenyon. So, when the matter thus got into the hands of our leaders, a little different bi-partisan committee was arranged. The result was that our respective leaders took the matter out of our hands and Senator Lodge called in Senator Lenroot and Senator Kellogg of the old committee, but left off Senators Colt and Kenyon,—I recall distinctly to my very great surprise, as both Senators Colt and Kenyon were earnest advocates of a compromise and had been very active on the informal committee.

There was some reason why Senator Kendrick could not serve, and Senator Hitchcock named Senators Simmons, Walsh, Owen and myself.[12]

---

[12] H. Maurice Darling, "Who Kept the United States Out of the League of Nations?", *Canadian Historical Review*, September, 1929, Vol. 10, pp. 196–211. Reports in the *New York Times*, of December 17, and January 11, and on the intervening dates, follow the thread of this narrative.

"After much discussion among individual Senators," says Lodge, "I called together what was known as the 'Bi-partisan Conference.' " [13]

In substituting New for Colt and Kenyon, Lodge had undoubtedly weakened the prospect of compromise, but it cannot be said that the Republican delegation as remodeled was not representative of the Republican reservationists. The Lodge regulars, represented by Lodge and New, were never far from the irreconcilables; Lenroot and Kellogg could speak for the more conservative of the mild-reservationists.

Mr. Lodge's attitude, as the conference opened, appeared to the *Times* correspondent "to be that of tolerance and amusement about the whole matter. He indicated that he would do nothing to stop the pleasant proceedings by becoming blunt." [14] Several discussions were held, however, and there appeared to be agreement on minor modifications of the lesser reservations. Senator Hitchcock demanded, on the 17th, that no more publicity be given the proceedings, and a motion that the conferees bind themselves to keep the discussions secret was adopted by a party vote, 5 to 4. A delegation of mild-reservationists also visited Hitchcock to protest his stand that President Wilson must be consulted before any compromise was finally agreed upon. [15]

Article 10 having been reached, the dispatches reported the parleys stalled. The mild group threatened again to call the treaty up on the floor, but McNary, after a talk with Lodge, agreed to give the conference further time. Hitchcock was blamed. Senator Lodge, however, was quoted, on the 21st, as saying that he felt progress had been made. [16]

"Senator Conferees May Compromise." The news of the 22nd was very optimistic. The *Tribune* and other papers ran large heads presaging agreement. While nothing was actually settled, "the language of the compromise program is regarded as distinctively milder in its terms than the Lodge reservations." Lodge was again said to be looking for results. [17]

The morning of the 23rd naturally found the bitter-enders thoroughly alarmed. All the reports from the conference, supposed to be operating secretly, agreed that a compromise was about to be adopted that would probably command the two-thirds majority. Action was de-

---

[13] Lodge, *The Senate and the League of Nations,* p. 193.
[14] *New York Times,* January 17, 1920.
[15] *New York Tribune,* January 18, 1920.
[16] *New York Tribune, New York Times,* January 21, 22, 1920.
[17] *Washington Post,* January 22; *New York Tribune,* January 23; *New York Times,* January 23, 1920.

manded. Borah and Johnson circulated "energetically" among their fellows, stirring them to action. McCormick and Brandegee were "greatly disturbed." Threats of revolt from Lodge's leadership and from the party began to be heard right and left. Frelinghuysen issued a statement declaring that he would not be bound. Sutherland, of West Virginia, declared that he was irreconcilable at heart; he had voted for the Lodge reservations with great reluctance. Sherman vowed that he would bolt. [18]

As the hour of two o'clock approached, when the conferees were to assemble, the embattled bitter-enders gathered in Senator Johnson's office. Knox, Borah, Johnson, Moses, McCormick, Sherman, Brandegee and Poindexter were there. Lodge was summoned to them as he entered the door of the conference room that might see the long battle ended. He excused himself "temporarily." The conference waited an hour before adjourning. Lodge did not emerge from communion with his left wing for three hours.

Senator Lodge in his considered account was not able to "give a report of the views expressed by all those present at this gathering." He had made no notes. But he "assured them, and Senator New joined with me, that there was not the slightest danger of our conceding anything that was essential or that was anything more than a change in wording." [19]

Lodge did not have much to say immediately after the conference, but Senator Johnson talked. No poll of the Senate had been produced, it was said, but a total of thirty-eight Senators had been claimed who would permit no modification of the "Lodge" terms. The conclusion of the *New York Tribune* representative, on January 24, was that "Certainly, if the Senators interpret the views of their colleagues correctly, no reservations would be accepted by the thirty-eight which would meet the approval of President Wilson." [20]

Republican Conflict. On the other hand, "The revolt of the irreconcilables was not taken so seriously by some of the mild-reservationists, who professed to see it a move on the part of the majority leader to have the country understand that a further compromise had

---

[18] *New York Tribune*, January 24; *New York Times*, January 24, 1919; Darling, *Canadian Historical Review*, September, 1929, Vol. 10, p. 205.

[19] Lodge, *The Senate and the League of Nations*, p. 194.

[20] Senator Johnson told the Senate, six years later, that "the job was perfected and we were right at the entrance of the League of Nations when those sixteen men," he did not care what you termed them, "called the thing off through the then leader of the Republican party in this chamber." *Congressional Record*, Vol. 67, Pt. 3, pp. 2349 ff.

PHILANDER C. KNOX

OF PENNSYLVANIA

HIRAM JOHNSON

OF CALIFORNIA

MEDILL McCORMICK

OF ILLINOIS

JOSEPH I. FRANCE

OF MARYLAND

BITTER-ENDERS—REPUBLICAN

been rejected by more than a sufficient number of Senators to kill a treaty that carried them, and that as a consequence no such reservations could possibly be put through." [21]

Numerous conferences were held the next day and many Republicans were still hopeful. The mild-reservationists grew impatient again at the continuing parleys between Lodge and the bitter-enders. Lodge was trying to commit them to vote for his November reservations, [22] not as a means of killing the treaty in the Senate but of putting it up to the President. If he could persuade the sixteen irreconcilables to agree to support, on a final vote, the reservations that they were so passionately forcing him to stand by, he could be practically certain that enough Democrats would join to make up the two-thirds vote. It was not an unreasonable demand for him to make, and, if he had been able to make it with sufficient force, it might have succeeded. He could then have ignored the Democratic leaders, including Wilson, and put the responsibility for accepting his terms squarely upon the President.

It was an attractive opportunity, but lacking conviction for the League and faced with a division in his party, Lodge was content to hold what he had won. He had been driven into conference by the mild-reservationists, backed by public opinion; he would now be driven out by the bitter-enders, supported by the dread specter of party schism.

The total opponents of the League were, moreover, not idle. They did not rest on threats alone. On the 25th the bitter-enders were telling their regular Republican colleagues that by standing pat on the Lodge reservations the Democratic party might be split. The pressure for ratification would force the Democratic Senators to surrender. The President would thereupon drop the treaty and there would be "a rift in the ranks of the Democratic party which would be entirely favorable to Republican chances in the forthcoming campaign." [23]

For those who strongly desired the approval of the treaty the reasoning was somewhat changed. The next day, "Some of the irreconcilables were trying tonight to make the mild-reservationists look at the situation as they view it. They feel that it is not merely a question of changing the wording of the reservations, but changing with the words the political party which would get credit for those reservations. So long as the reservations bore Lodge's name, the country, these Senators feel, would remember them as Republican reser-

[21] New York Tribune, January 24, 1920.
[22] New York Tribune, January 26, 1920.
[23] New York Times, January 26, 1920.

vations, but the minute they were changed they probably would become known as the Hitchcock reservations, and the country might eventually come to believe that they were the result of Democratic effort. Even Senator Lodge himself was said tonight not to have realized the political significance of this Democratic plan until it was pointed out to him by the irreconcilables." [24]

Financial Obligation. The bi-partisan conferences continued, meanwhile, without further success. The Democrats maintained, then and ever afterwards, that the Republicans had agreed tentatively to accept the Simmons reservation on Article 10 (to be quoted later) when the irreconcilables delivered their ultimatum to Lodge. [25] Kellogg and Lenroot supported the regulars in denying this claim. [26] Then, "the Republicans suddenly discovered that they had omitted the question of financial assistance and retired to a caucus of their own." [27]

Nobody, apparently, had ever thought heretofore that the League might make us pay for its policing operations, even though we had refused to send any forces or to take part in an economic boycott. Here was a new danger that made it necessary to stiffen the disavowal of Article 10, rather than weaken it. The other members of the League must not be sending the United States the bills for wars incurred in defense of the Covenant. Financial obligation, the Republicans said, "would be likely to prove as much of a burden to the United States as any military obligation, and its fulfillment could be dictated, they held, by the Council of the League of Nations." [28]

"There can be no compromise of principle," declared Senator Lodge, on January 26, adding that in his judgment it would be impossible to secure two-thirds of the Senate if any change was attempted in the reservations relating to Article 10 or the Monroe Doctrine. [29] "I had made up my mind at the beginning," added Lodge in 1925, "that if the conference was to break up it should be on Article 10, which was the

---

[24] *New York Tribune,* January 27, 1920. Senator Colt was quoted in the same report as saying: "Senator Hitchcock doesn't want a compromise. He wants to throw the blame for beating the treaty on the Republicans."

Senators Sherman and Borah voted with the Democrats, January 27, on a party measure, a motion calling for investigation of the Navy Department, as an earnest of what they would do if Lodge yielded. Sherman said he was on a "political hunger strike."—*New York Times,* January 28, 1920; *Congressional Record,* Vol. 59, Pt. 1, p. 2094.

[25] See the statements of Hitchcock, *New York Tribune,* January 27, 1920; McKellar in Darling's article, *Canadian Historical Review,* September, 1929, Vol. 10, p. 207; Walsh, *Congressional Record,* Vol. 59, Pt. 5, p. 4583.

[26] *Omaha World Herald,* January 28, 1920; *New York Times,* January 28, 1920.

[27] *New York Tribune,* January 27, 1920; *New York Times,* January 28, 1920.

[28] *New York Times,* January 28, 1920.

[29] *New York Tribune,* January 27, 1920.

crucial point throughout the contest over the Covenant of the League of Nations." [30]

The final break came on January 30, when the Democrats gave notice that they would try to call the treaty up in the Senate on February 9. [31]

Lord Grey With Lodge. The next day Lodge received an important public endorsement of his position, one which he had probably known was coming before the conciliation conference began its sessions. He had been on intimate terms with Viscount Grey, sent over four months earlier by the British Government as its Ambassador, when it became evident that the treaty might fail in the Senate, to see if he might be of service in composing the differences. Being unable to see the President, due to the latter's illness, Grey had spent four months in estimating public opinion and in close conference with Senators of various groups, especially that of Senator Lodge. [32]

In January he returned to London convinced that the reservations were inevitable and that they should be accepted. Shortly after his arrival home he threw his influence to that end in a letter to the *London Times,* published February 1, 1920, in the *New York Times.* Disappointment and regret over the deadlock between the President and the Senate were just as keen in the United States, he wrote, as in England. Europeans should recognize, too, that the Senate was an independent element in the treaty-making power. No charge of bad faith or of repudiating signatures could therefore be brought against it. Nor was it fair to represent the United States as holding up the treaty solely from motives of party politics or even of self interest. These factors were not the sole or even the prime cause of the difficulty.

There was in the United States a real conservative feeling for the traditional policy. The League was not only a plunge into the unknown but a plunge into something of which historical advice and tradition had hitherto positively disapproved. The country did not refuse to make the departure, but desired time to feel its way.

In addition to this major consideration he had been impressed

---

[30] Lodge, *The Senate and the League of Nations,* p. 194.

[31] *New York Tribune,* January 31, 1920.

[32] Secretary Houston wrote that Grey commented sympathetically to Lodge on his handling of the treaty situation in Houston's presence, at a dinner in Washington. Darling quotes a Republican member of the bi-partisan conference as saying that Lodge had told the committee of Grey's assurance that Great Britain would accept his reservations.—D. F. Houston, "The War on Wilson," *World's Work,* September, 1926, Vol. 52, p. 547; Darling, *The Canadian Historical Review,* September, 1929, Vol. 10, p. 209.

with another, that it would be possible, as the Covenant stood, for a future President to commit the United States through the American representative on the Council to a policy which the Congress of the time might disapprove. They had reason and, if they desired, the right to prevent that.

Fears Would Disappear in Practice. Moreover, the idealistic spirit of the American people was still there, he wrote, continuing:

> It is as much a part of the nature and possibilities of the American people as any other characteristic. It is not possible for such a spirit to play such a part as it did in the war and then to relapse and be extinguished altogether. It would be a great mistake to suppose that because the citizens of the United States wish to limit their obligations, they therefore propose to themselves to play a small part in the League of Nations. If they enter the League as a willing partner with limited obligations, it may be much more fruitful than if they entered as a reluctant partner who felt that her hand had been forced. It is in this spirit, in this hope, and in this expectation that I think we should approach, and are justified in approaching, consideration of American reservations.
>
> I do not deny that some of them are material qualifications of the League of Nations as drawn up at Paris or that they must be disappointing to those who are with that covenant as it stands and are even proud of it, but those who have had the longest experience of political affairs and especially of treaties know best how often it happens that difficulties which seem most formidable in anticipation and on paper never arise in practice. I think this is likely to be particularly true in the working of the League of Nations. The difficulties and dangers which the Americans foresee in it will probably never arise or be felt by them when they are once in the League. And in the same way the weakening and injury to the League which some of its best friends apprehend from the American reservations would not be felt in practice.
>
> If the outcome of the long controversy in the Senate is to offer co-operation in the League of Nations it would be the greatest mistake to refuse that co-operation because conditions are attached to it, and when that co-operation is accepted let it not be accepted in a spirit of pessimism.
>
> The most vital considerations are that representatives should be appointed to the Council of the League of Nations by all the nations that are members of the Council, that these representatives should be men who are inspired by the ideals for which we entered the war, and that these representatives should be instructed and supported in that same spirit of equity and freedom by the Governments and public

opinion of the countries who are now partners in peace. If that be the spirit in which the Council of the League of Nations deals with the business that comes before it there need be no fear that the representative of the United States on that Council will not take part in realizing the hopes with which the League has been founded.

Even in the matter of the British Dominion votes in the Assembly, Grey argued that in practice no dispute would be likely to arise.

This letter, endorsed by the British and French press with practical unanimity, greatly strengthened the position of the reservationist Senators. They could point to it as evidence not only that they were right, but that their terms would be accepted abroad. It gave Lodge strong reason for believing, too, that at the worst he would accomplish one of his principal objectives. Said he, in 1925: "There was another object which I had very much at heart, and that was that if he were successful in putting on reservations we should create a situation where, if the acceptance of the treaty was defeated, the Democratic party, and especially Mr. Wilson's friends, should be responsible for its defeat, and not the *opponents* of the treaty who were trying to pass it in a form safe for the United States." [33]

The Hitchcock Reservations Acceptable to Wilson. The President, on his part, had agreed to accept interpretative reservations four days before the publication of Lord Grey's letter. In a letter of January 28 to Senator Hitchcock he also stated definitely his attitude toward the Lodge reservations, saying:

MY DEAR SENATOR HITCHCOCK:

I have greatly appreciated your thoughtful kindness in keeping me informed concerning the conference you and some of your colleagues have had with spokesmen of the Republican Party concerning the possibility of ratification of the treaty of peace, and send this line in special appreciative acknowledgment of your letter of the 22d. I return the clipping you were kind enough to enclose.

To the substance of it I, of course, adhere. I am bound to, like yourself. I am solemnly sworn to obey and maintain the Constitution of the United States. But I think the form of it very unfortunate. Any reservation or resolution stating that "The United States assumes no obligation under such and such an article unless or except" would, I am sure, chill our relationship with the nations with which we expect to be associated in the great enterprise of maintaining the world's peace.

That association must in any case, my dear Senator, involve very serious and far-reaching implications of honor and duty, which I am

[33] Lodge, *The Senate and the League of Nations*, p. 164. Italics added.

sure we shall never in fact be desirous of ignoring. It is the more important not to create the impression that we are trying to escape obligations.

But I realize that negative criticism is not all that is called for in so serious a matter. I am happy to be able to add, therefore, that I have once more gone over the reservations proposed by yourself, the copy of which I return herewith, and am glad to say that I can accept them as they stand.

I have never seen the slightest reason to doubt the good faith of our associates in the war, nor ever had the slightest reason to fear that any nation would seek to enlarge our obligations under the covenant of the League of Nations, or seek to commit us to lines of action which, under our Constitution, only the Congress of the United States can in the last analysis decide.

May I suggest that with regard to the possible withdrawal of the United States it would be wise to give to the President the right to act upon a resolution of Congress in the matter of withdrawal? In other words, it would seem to be permissible and advisable that any resolution giving notice of withdrawal should be a joint rather than a concurrent resolution.

I doubt whether the President can be deprived of his veto power under the Constitution, even with his own consent. The use of a joint resolution would permit the President, who is, of course, charged by the Constitution with the conduct of foreign policy, to merely exercise a voice in saying whether so important a step as withdrawal from the League of Nations should be accomplished by a majority or by a two-thirds vote.

The Constitution itself providing that the legislative body was to be consulted in treaty-making and having prescribed a two-thirds vote in such cases, it seems to me that there should be no unnecessary departure from the method there indicated.

I see no objection to a frank statement that the United States can accept a mandate with regard to any territory under Article XIII, Part 1, or any other provision of the treaty of peace, only by the direct authority and action of the Congress of the United States.

I hope, my dear Senator, that you will never hesitate to call upon me for any assistance that I can render in this or any other public matter.

Cordially and sincerely yours,
WOODROW WILSON.[34]

Final Rejection. After the breakdown of the bi-partisan conference the Senate voted, on February 9, to reconsider the treaty and

[34] Shaw, *Messages and Papers of Woodrow Wilson*, Vol. II, pp. 1166-68.

referred it again to the Committee. It was reported back the next day with the Lodge reservations. Debate was resumed on February 16, and continued for a month during which the reservations were made more objectionable to the President, rather than less, and finally crowned with a declaration in favor of self-determination for Ireland.

The culmination of the opposition to the League did not bring any overtures of conciliation or of surrender from Wilson. On the contrary, he wrote to Senator Hitchcock, March 8th, that deliberation convinced him that "practically every so-called reservation was in effect a rather sweeping nullification of the terms of the treaty itself." He heard of reservationists and mild-reservationists but he could not understand the difference between "a nullifier and a mild-nullifier." Our responsibility in this turning point of history was an overwhelming one and if he had the opportunity he "would beg every one concerned to consider the matter in the light of what it is possible to accomplish for humanity, rather than in the light of special national interests." [35]

It was the voice of Wilson, somewhat sharpened by adversity, but only the Democratic Senators from the Southern States felt that they could stand by him on the final vote, which came March 19, 1920. Joined by Senators Hitchcock, of Nebraska, and Johnson, of South Dakota, together with three irreconcilable Democrats and twelve bitterend Republicans, the total of votes against approval of the treaty with the Lodge reservations was 35. The Northern Democrats, with the exceptions noted, combined with the reservationist Republicans and four Southern Democrats to give a poll of 49 votes for the Lodge resolution, seven short of the required two-thirds majority. Twelve Senators did not vote. [36]

The reservation campaign had both won and lost. It had alienated enough of the Democratic voters of the North that the Democratic Senators from this region were finally swept along with it, some by conviction; it had broken and discredited their leader to such an extent that none could rely upon his aid. Yet the drive for reservations had failed to put the Treaty into his hands stamped as a dangerous venture, which might be permitted under many enumerated safeguards. The Treaty went back to him as it came, without either amendment or approval, and those who had fought so long to qualify it could never claim more than a preservative action. They might still reap political

---

[35] *Current History,* April, 1920, pp. 27–28.
[36] *Congressional Record,* Vol. 59, Pt. 5, p. 4599. Twenty-three Democrats voted against approval; twenty-one for it.

victory on this ground, but such constructive achievement as had weathered the storm of eighteen months' unrelenting criticism remained with Wilson, dimmed though it might be by his refusal to accept the Lodge terms.

It was difficult to see a clear victory for anyone except the battalion of death, as the Senate moved to pass a resolution for separate peace with Germany. The triumph of the bitter-enders, too, would have to stand the test of the future.

CHAPTER XVII

THE RESERVATIONS

MEANWHILE, the Covenant had gone into force on January 10, 1920, with twenty-three original members in the League. By March 10, the number had increased to thirty-three, including all of the American states except Costa Rica, Santo Domingo, Mexico and the United States. All the states invited to join had done so. Cuba, Panama, Salvador, Venezuela, and Columbia had given their ratifications since November.[1] They did not have much to lose, it may be said, and perhaps a good deal to gain.

In a sense this may have been true of the small neutral states of Europe, which cast their lot with the League in February and March while the Senate was sharpening its resolve that the mighty republic should not be imposed upon. Yet the people of the European neutrals had known what the war was like as few Americans had. They had stood hard by it for four years, never safe from being drawn into its

[1] Manley O. Hudson, "Membership in the League of Nations," *American Journal of International Law*, July, 1924, Vol. 18, pp. 436 ff.; *Current History*, April, 1923, p. 67.

Costa Rica was not asked to become a member of the League in order to avoid recognition of her government, of which the United States disapproved. She was later admitted by vote of the Assembly on December 16, 1920. Secretary Lansing advised against the inclusion of Costa Rica, but favored that of Mexico and Santo Domingo. The latter came in during the 1924 Assembly, on September 29 of that year.

Mexico was not originally invited because of the opposition of the United States and Great Britain. Wilson was still distrustful of Mexican stability, and Lord Cecil was similarly minded. His government, having withheld recognition from the existing Mexican government, did not wish to grant it indirectly through an invitation to join the League. Probably both statesmen were wrong in holding Mexico out. The decision hurt Mexico without providing any assistance in pacifying the country.

The omission was recognized as an error by the Twelfth Assembly, in 1931, which frankly apologized for it and invited Mexico to enter. Cecil joined in the invitation, saying that since he was, he supposed, in part guilty of it, it gave him "particular pleasure to take part in remedying an omission which should never have been made."

By accepting the invitation Mexico increased the League membership, at the close of 1931, to fifty-five nations.

See D. H. Miller, *The Drafting of the Covenant*, Vol. I, pp. 318, 466–67, Vol. II, p. 116; Denys P. Myers, *Nine Years of the League of Nations*, Boston, 1929, pp. 14–15; *Current History*, October, 1931, p. 105.

destruction themselves and sometimes in grave danger of it. Some profits they had made; many losses had they suffered. But they had kept out. Wouldn't it be wise to put their continued trust in free and unconfined neutrality? The neutrals did not think so.

In Switzerland there was a real struggle of opinion. Her neutrality, respected as it had been and protected by mountain defenses, was dear to her. She once voted to join on condition that the five principal Allied and Associated Powers go in, a proviso that was later withdrawn, as the United States continued to demur, and the question was not finally settled until a national referendum had ratified her entry by a vote of 416,870 to 328,719, [2] the only real "solemn referendum" held anywhere in the world upon the question of joining the League.

The statesmen of Switzerland, after long and patient analysis of the Covenant, could not find in it the dangerous obligations which the United States Senators thundered so many months in behalf of. In a book of 409 pages analyzing the Covenant, prepared by the Swiss Federal Council for the Federal Assembly, Article 10 was assessed as "not a very heavy obligation to the members of the League." It would come into operation only in extreme cases, and even then there was no automatic action, for "the Council can, according to this article, only give advice and not direct orders." [3] Swiss leaders looking down on one side into the cockpit of the Balkans and on the other across the age-old battlefields of Flanders, saw nothing in the Covenant of peace that would keep detachments of their sons endlessly marching, along with American armies, to preserve a hundred unjust boundaries and to suppress a succession of wars at the ends of the earth.

It would have been nothing short of criminal for the responsible leaders of Switzerland, or of Holland and Denmark, to have failed to ward off a danger so deadly. There was sober thinking and some dissent in Holland also, but the alarm at involvement only registered 5 votes out of 59, on February 19, 1920, in the upper house of the Dutch Parliament. In Denmark the votes in the Folketing, February 27, and the Landsting, March 4, were unanimous. It is true that the neutral states were invited to accede to the Covenant "without reservation." There was, therefore, no opportunity for a Dutch Knox or a Danish Lodge to plan a long and intricate campaign of opposition by indirection. But some patriotic Reed or Brandegee might have

[2] Hudson, *The American Journal of International Law,* Vol. 18, p. 440.
[3] *New York Times,* January 26, 1920.

arisen to stir the masses and to fight the "monstrous contraption" to the bitter end, if it had been so regarded.

To be sure, the Parliaments of Norway and Sweden could not be called upon by the League Council to send in the huge sums of money, to pay for the suppression of League wars by other nations, that it was alleged the United States would be liable to, but these countries would have to pay their proportionate share of such sums. Strange was it then that the second chamber of the Swedish Parliament should vote for entry, March 4, 1920, 152 to 67, and the lower house 86 to 47, March 5, while the Norwegian Storting polled 100 votes for adherence to 20 against, on March 4. The Borahs and Johnsons of the Scandinavian peninsula, enjoying a relatively safe degree of geographic and political isolation, did not have open to them the chance of promoting reservations expected to prevent entry into the League—if they had the desire.

The attitude of the Scandinavian peoples, who have a habit of acting like mature, grown-up nations, internationally, was indicated by the motion of the Konstitutions-Komite of the Storting which proposed, March 4, 1920, "That in accordance with its traditions it associates itself entirely with the great idea upon which the League of Nations is based, and that the Storting considers this League as being the most important endeavor that has ever been made to further the reign of justice between nations and, further, that the future of the League depends essentially for its development on the basis of the adhesion of all civilized peoples, of a general reduction of armaments and of an obligatory peaceful settlement of all disputes in order to prevent war." [4]

How different in spirit and purpose from the Senate Foreign Relations Committee report of September 10, 1919—and how clearly marked out the path along which civilization must eventually go however reluctantly.

Reservation No. 1. What indeed were the reservations over which eighty United States Senators who professed to be for the treaty and the League could not agree?

The first concerned withdrawal. It read:

> 1. The United States so understands and construes Article 1 that in case of notice of withdrawal from the League of Nations, as provided in said article, the United States shall be the sole judge as to whether all

[4] C. A. Kluyver, *Documents on the League of Nations,* Leiden, 1920, p. 236. For the parliamentary votes quoted above, see pages 232, 240.

its international obligations and all its obligations under the said Covenant have been fulfilled, and notice of withdrawal by the United States
may be given by a concurrent resolution of the Congress of the United
States.

The principal objection to this reservation was that it attempted
to deprive the President of a voice in case withdrawal were proposed,
a concurrent resolution not requiring his signature. This was Wilson's
view, as noted in his letter of January 26 above. He therefore proposed that a joint resolution be indicated, but the Senate refused, on
February 21, to agree to this amendment. It was contended that the
President through his power to terminate treaties could take us out
of the League at any time he saw fit, and that Congress should have
the same right. Lodge moved to recognize specifically the President's
independent power, on February 21, by amending the clause to read,
"and notice of withdrawal by the United States may be given by the
President or by Congress alone whenever a majority of both houses
may deem it necessary," but the change was defeated 33 to 32, the
bitter-enders voting nay. [5]

The terms of the reservation were generally taken as a slap at
Wilson, though this was denied. Senator Nelson, in attempting an
amendment when it was first passed, on November 8, protested that
Mr. Wilson might be mistaken, he thought he was in many particu-
lars, "but the President is now lying on a sick bed, and we are asked
here in the Senate to put a slight upon him by putting in this provision in regard to a concurrent resolution in order to cut him off, as it
is viewed here in the Senate. That goes against my grain, Mr. President. I am a Republican and have been all my days—but I do not
approve of the intense partisanship that at this moment would put a
slight upon the President of the United States, and would say to
him, 'We do not trust you to have anything to do with denouncing
this treaty.' " [6]

Lodge replied that it was much more likely to apply to Republican
Presidents than Democratic, and was only inserted to prevent the Executive power from expanding too greatly as a result of our League membership. How the President could expand his power by taking us out
of the League was not explained. Others insisted that he must never
be able to prevent withdrawal.

Aside from the very doubtful constitutionality of such a pro-

[5] *Congressional Record,* Vol. 59, Pt. 4, p. 3241.
[3] *Ibid.,* Vol. 58, Pt. 8, p. 8136.

vision, it would seem to be of highly questionable wisdom to put it
in the power of either branch of the government to take so important
a step alone. It is true that the exercise of the President's veto would
require a two-thirds vote of Congress to overcome it, but if we could
not get into the League without a two-thirds vote of the Senate it
would seem that a similar majority should be required for withdrawal,
or at least that the President should have the discretion of calling for
such a majority.

It should not be considered strange, either, if the sick man in
the White House should resent the form of the reservation as both
an affront to him personally and an attack upon his office. Perhaps
he should have left it to the Supreme Court to declare his veto un-
assailable, in a step of such national importance, as it would have done,
in all probability. There is nothing merely procedural about such a
step that would justify its being taken by concurrent resolution of
Congress.

As for the reservation itself, it was neither necessary nor un-
acceptable. There was nothing in the spirit of the Covenant nor
in its provisions that gave any organ of the League the right to hold
a member in the organization against its will. Article 1 properly laid
upon a retiring member the duty of looking to its obligations when
resigning, but the interpretation in the Senate reservation was as
correct as it was unnecessary. There was nothing that could prevent
American withdrawal from the League, if the American government
came to a sober decision that the step must be taken. Nothing less
than the gravest consideration of both the Executive and Congress
should ever have been considered.

No. 3, Mandates. The reservation on the acceptance of mandates
read:

> "No mandate shall be accepted by the United States under Article 22,
> par. 1, or any other provision of the treaty of peace with Germany, ex-
> cept by action of the Congress of the United States."

It is difficult to see how the President could administer a foreign
territory over a term of years without the consent of Congress, particularly if the great armies, which the critics of the Covenant invariably predicted, were actually needed, although President Roosevelt
had gone pretty far on his own authority in the Caribbean. Unlikely
as the assumption that the President alone would attempt to undertake the heavy and continuing responsibilities involved in any man-

date was, it was most difficult to refuse to condemn such a possible contingency when it was held up for disapproval. The final vote on the Clause, on February 26, was 68 to 4. [7]

No. 4, Domestic Questions. Similarly, it was risky indeed for any Senator to refuse to agree that the League should not "meddle" in our domestic affairs. The likelihood that such interference, forbidden in international law from its inception, would be instituted by action of any group of strongly nationalistic states may be judged from the fact that in all the earth no fear of such a happening was generated, except in the United States. Among the fifty-seven states who joined the League no single one became alarmed about interference with its domestic affairs. They were just as jealous of their domestic integrity, too, as we could be—and many of them a hundred times less able to protect it in case of infringement. Yet when the possibility was held high in the Senate it seemed unreasonable not to forestall it, particularly when it always came down to the plausible insistence that, "If the League does not mean to do these things, it surely won't do any harm to say so." Therefore the Senate voted 56 to 25, on March 2, that:

> The United States reserves to itself exclusively the right to decide what questions are within its domestic jurisdiction and declares that all domestic and political questions relating wholly or in part to its internal affairs, including immigration, labor, coastwise traffic, the tariff, commerce, the suppression of traffic in women and children and in opium and other dangerous drugs, and all other domestic questions, are solely within the jurisdiction of the United States and are not under this treaty to be submitted in any way either to arbitration or to the consideration of the Council or of the Assembly of the League of Nations, or any agency thereof, or to the decision or recommendation of any other Power.[8]

This declaration could not vitiate the fact that many important domestic questions have international aspects that sometimes become controlling. It ignored the consideration, too, that as the common law of nations evolves under the impact of the machine age, no one nation is likely to find advantage in blocking its advance, even if it could. But the anxiety of the Senators of 1919 to keep as many questions as possible "domestic" was so great that they even decreed that nobody should question the way we handled our traffic in women and children, in opium or other dangerous drugs, before any arbitration court,

---

[7] *Congressional Record,* Vol. 59, Pt. 4, p. 3514.
[8] *Ibid.,* p. 3741.

council or assembly. These also were matters that we would handle exactly as we pleased.

The unwisdom of thus laying down a list of untouchable domestic questions, and of Congressional fiats in diplomacy, soon became evident in connection with the regulation of the traffic in opium. In 1924, Congress, forgetting the domestication of the opium traffic by the Senate, sent delegates to the League's International Opium Conference of that year under rigid instructions to "sign no agreement which does not fulfill the conditions necessary for the suppression of the habit-forming narcotic drug traffic. . . ." Not being able to secure from the other countries the sweeping measures for the suppression of the traffic, involving the regulation of their crops and trade, which their instructions and convictions demanded, the American representatives withdrew from the conference, stating as they did so, however, that "The United States recognized that the world-wide traffic in habit-forming drugs can be suppressed only by international cooperation," and would not cease its efforts in that direction.

Within five years we had not only abandoned our sacred right to regulate the traffic in opium and other drugs, but we were insisting that the production of these drugs be subject to international regulation. What problem could be more domestic than the regulation of agricultural production? [9]

At bottom the reservation was a renewed expression of the Senate's antagonism to arbitration. Strange as it may seem, the Senate still insists, in 1931, upon setting itself up as a tribunal to scrutinize first every proposed arbitration before the question can be submitted to arbitration. [10] As Miller has pointed out in his penetrating analysis of the reservations, Reservation No. 4 is logically indefensible. If a question relates "in part" to internal affairs, must it not relate also to foreign affairs to some extent? The question is conclusively answered by the fact that the United States had already ratified treaties regulating all seven of the subjects "reserved" in the reservation. [11]

Harshly and illogically as the reservation was expressed, it probably would not have done extensive harm in practice, except as it supported the Senate's claim to scrutiny of every arbitration *com-*

---

[9] See Quincy Wright, "The American Withdrawal From the Opium Conference," *American Journal of International Law*, Vol. 19, pp. 348–55.

[10] D. F. Fleming, *The Treaty Veto of the American Senate*, N. Y., 1930, pp. 272–74.

[11] David Hunter Miller, *My Diary at the Conference of Paris*, N. Y., 1926 (Limited edition), Vol. 20, pp. 577–80. Examples of past treaties on all the forbidden subjects are cited.

promis. It would have been something concrete to point to in justifying this practice and thus might have served as a continuing justification for it in the minds of some Senators. This would have been a most unfortunate result, but the reservation would not have prevented the Executive from continuing to attempt to send disputes to arbitration, even if they happened to fall within the broad zone proscribed by the reservation.

The Hitchcock reservation on domestic questions attempted to cover the subject in more general terms, and in less offensive language, as follows:

> That no member nation is required to submit to the League, its Council, or its Assembly, for decision, report, or recommendation, any matter which it considers to be in international law a domestic question, such as immigration, labor, tariffs, or other matter relating to its internal or coastwise affairs.[12]

No. 5, The Monroe Doctrine.

> The United States will not submit to arbitration or to inquiry by the Assembly or by the Council of the League of Nations, provided for in said treaty of peace, any questions which in the judgment of the United States depend upon or relate to its long-established policy, commonly known as the Monroe Doctrine; said doctrine is to be interpreted by the United States alone and is hereby declared to be wholly outside the jurisdiction of said League of Nations and entirely unaffected by any provision contained in the said treaty of peace with Germany.

The antecedents of this reservation have been given in sufficient detail that the reader has no doubt long ago made up his mind as to its necessity and wisdom. The writer can only record his conclusion that the real Monroe Doctrine—the legitimate protection of our security by excluding old-world aggression from this hemisphere—was never in danger from the League which sought to prevent all aggression. This would be true even if the League should assist in settling disputes between American states. In all reason why shouldn't it, even though the United States be a party to the dispute? Have we grown so good and great that we are above the law, infallibly right? "It is unquestionable," moreover, that under many of our treaties "a dispute involving an interpretation of the Monroe Doctrine would properly be the subject of international inquiry." [13]

---

[12] *Congressional Record*, Vol. 58, Pt. 9, p. 8800.
[13] Miller, *My Diary at the Conference of Paris*, Vol. 20, pp. 580–81.

Then, as now, a willing deference on the part of the League to our leadership in settling Western Hemisphere controversies, to which we were not a party, was much more probable than European or Asiatic attempts to undermine our safety by machinations through the League, which would be utterly foreign to its spirit and purpose.

What is on trial is the perversion of the Monroe Doctrine of which this reservation is the expression—the presumption that the Doctrine covers any imperialistic or arbitrary action which we ourselves may at any time desire to take in Latin America. The ex-president of a South American republic may misrepresent the purpose of most Americans when he says that the Monroe Doctrine is "the will of the United States Government, supported by its army and navy, to do as it pleases, when it pleases, on the American continent," [14] but he is accurately interpreting many of the speeches which led to the above declaration that all questions are excluded from adjudication which "depend upon or relate to" a doctrine which we will define as we please and discuss with nobody.

When the American nations are so strong that the probability of trans-oceanic aggression grows more remote every year, what must our southern neighbors think of a policy of expanding the Doctrine when by every criterion of necessity or expediency it should be left to occupy the historic place of honor and dignity which it deserves? Fortunately, the good will tours of President Coolidge, to the Pan American Conference at Havana early in 1928, and of President-elect Hoover around Latin America at the close of the same year, have repaired much of the damage done abroad by the backward looking and provocative pretensions of 1919. It may be a harder task to deflate the exaggerated ideas spread among the American people.

The Hitchcock substitute reservation read:

"That the national policy of the United States known as the Monroe Doctrine, as announced and interpreted by the United States, is not in any way impaired or affected by the Covenant of the League of Nations and is not subject to any decision, report, or inquiry by the Council or Assembly." [15]

This statement, which was accepted by President Wilson, though phrased more moderately, seems at first glance to go almost as far as the committee reservation in excluding Latin American questions

[14] *The Christian Century,* January 19, 1928.
[15] *Congressional Record,* Vol. 58, Pt. 9, p. 8800.

from the jurisdiction of the League. It traveled a long way in that direction. The uncompromising Wilson in accepting it had receded far from the time when he set out to found the League on the central principle of the Monroe Doctrine. And for all the good it did him, he might just as well have stood his ground, first and last, on the proposition that the Covenant did extend the Monroe Doctrine to the world.

No. 6, Shantung. The terrific war on the Shantung settlement ended in November with the adoption of the following statement: "The United States withholds its assent to Articles 156, 157, and 158, and reserves full liberty of action with respect to any controversy which may arise under said articles between the Republic of China and the Empire of Japan," and in March the words "between the Republic of China and the Empire of Japan" were struck out on motion of Lodge.

The declaration thus boiled down was likely to serve two purposes, to lay a moral censure upon Japan, mildly stated it is true after all the fulminations upon the subject, and to make it difficult for President Wilson to accept the reservations by repudiating his signature to the Shantung articles as something immoral and unnecessary.

Aside from challenging also the honor of the Japanese and Allied statesmen who had agreed originally to the settlement, thereby imperiling their acceptance of the reservation if the President swallowed it, the statement was of little or no practical value. In view of Japan's promise to the Peace Conference to return the province to China the United States was perfectly free to support China in the case without the reservation.

No. 7, Appointment of Representatives.

The Congress of the United States will provide by laws for the appointment of the representatives of the United States in the Assembly and the Council of the League of Nations, and may in its discretion provide for the participation of the United States in any commission, committee, tribunal, court, council or conference, or in the selection of any members thereof and for the appointment of members of said commissions, committees, tribunals, courts, councils or conferences, or any other representatives under the treaty of peace, or in carrying out its provisions, and until such participation and appointment have been so provided for and the powers and duties of such representatives have been defined by law, no person shall represent the United States under either said League of Nations or the treaty of peace with Germany or be authorized to perform any act for or on behalf of the United States thereunder, and no citizen of the United States shall be selected or appointed as a member of said commissions, committees, tribunals, courts, councils, or conferences, except with the approval of the Senate of the United States.

The purpose of this reservation apparently was to prevent the unconstitutional appointment of representatives by the President, and to keep him from participating in League activities without the consent and direction of Congress. Such a provision must have made our participation very halting and irregular, unless Congress had soon passed blanket laws permitting large Executive discretion. If the President had to go down to ask the Congress every time a representative on a commission was to be appointed, and secure the passage of a law saying exactly what he could and could not do, settlements and investigations would not advance very fast, particularly if Congress happened to be on vacation. What the situation might be if the Presidency happened to be in the hands of one party, and Congress controlled by the other, is also worth remembering. The League activities of the United States might be hampered under such a régime for a term of years.

The propriety of confirmation by the Senate of our representatives in the Council and the Assembly is unquestionable. Nor would such confirmation have been avoidable, as many Senators seem to have supposed, since these offices were created by treaty which is also law in the United States. [16] Beyond scrutinizing the fitness of our representatives in the League and of any other officials whose offices were created specifically by the treaty, was it wise for Congress to attempt, or be conceded, a right to direct minutely our participation in the League, and in the administration of the Treaty? Could Congress, moreover, prevent the President from conducting these phases of our foreign relations, in part at least, by the use of his regular diplomatic representatives, or even of his cabinet officers?

Congress could not be deprived of its right to pass upon important commitments calling for the expenditure of money, the conclusion of treaties or war. Beyond that, if any attempt was to be made further to control the Executive officers engaged in League or Treaty activities, it was surely a matter for act of Congress, not for proclamation by one house of Congress to the world at large.

A much shorter substitute, moved by Senator Walsh, of Montana,

[16] Miller, *My Diary at the Conference of Paris*, Vol. 20, p. 583.

was accepted in March as fully accomplishing the end sought. It read:

> No person is or shall be authorized to represent the United States, nor shall any citizen of the United States be eligible, as a member of any body or agency established or authorized by said treaty of peace with Germany, except pursuant to an act of the Congress of the United States providing for his appointment and defining his powers and duties.

No. 8, Reparations Commission. The eighth "reservation" asserted a veto over certain acts of the Reparations Commission:

> The United States understands that the Reparations Commission will regulate or interfere with exports from the United States to Germany, or from Germany to the United States, only when the United States by act or joint resolution of Congress approved such regulation or interference.

This stipulation was both harmless and unnecessary. The possibility which it envisaged was extremely remote, and in any event unanimity would have been necessary to undertake such direct control of Germany's foreign trade. [17] Naturally the indirect effects of reparations upon that trade could hardly be controlled by any reservation.

No. 9, Payment of Expenses.

> The United States shall not be obligated to contribute to any expenses of the League of Nations, or of the Secretariat, or of any commission, or committee, or conference, or other agency, organized under the League of Nations or under the treaty or for the purpose of carrying out the treaty provisions, unless and until an appropriation of funds available for such expenses shall have been made by the Congress of the United States.

The League was notified that it need not try to saddle its expenses on us, and the Allies that they need count on no contribution at any time toward the cost of administering the Treaty, until Congress had actually made the appropriation. The bad grace of this declaration, which fortunately was not copied by any other parliament, was somewhat modified in March by an addition, by Senator Kellogg, saying:

[17] Miller, *My Diary at the Conference of Paris*, Vol. 20, p. 584.

Provided, That the foregoing limitation shall not apply to the United States' proportionate share of the office force and salary of the Secretary General.

This amelioration still left a proposed statement that the United States having joined in the war decisively would assume no responsibility whatever for the expense of administering the peace treaty. Congress might, indeed probably would, grant as a bounty the comparatively trivial sums that would be required, but no duty to do so was to be admitted, and no jobbery was to be practised upon the United States.

No. 10, Arms Limitation. The tenth article assumed that the reduction of armament might infringe upon the inherent right of self defense. As adopted in November it read:

> If the United States shall at any time adopt any plan for the limitation of armaments proposed by the Council of the League of Nations under the provisions of Article 8, it reserves the right to increase such armaments without the consent of the Council whenever the United States is threatened with invasion or engaged in war.

In March it was amended, on motion of Senator New, to require the approval of Congress for any limitation, reading:

> No plan for the limitation of armaments proposed by the Council of the League of Nations under the provisions of Article 8 shall be held as binding the United States until the same shall have been accepted by Congress, and the United States reserves the right to increase its armament without the consent of the Council whenever the United States is threatened with invasion or engaged in war.[18]

The acceptance by Congress of any limitation of armament is, of course, thoroughly proper, so much so that the enforcement in the United States of any disarmament proposal is quite inconceivable without the consent of Congress. The right of Congress to provide for the army and navy could not be bartered away in any treaty, nor indeed abolished by a law of Congress itself. The presumption indulged in so freely by the reservation makers, that in some occult way the treaty which contained the Covenant of the League of Nations could abrogate the Constitution, was passing strange.

The attempt, moreover, of the reservationists of the hour "to re-

[18] *Congressional Record,* Vol. 59, Pt. 4, p. 4006.

serve rights to the United States under an agreement *not yet entered into,"* was an absurdity. Except as an indication of policy, the words were "a nullity, for if Congress in the future chooses to agree to any plan for the limitation of armament, it will not be limited in the extent of its agreement by any previous declaration of our Government, however made." [19]

No. 11, The Boycott.

The United States reserves the right to permit, in its discretion, the nationals of a covenant-breaking state, as defined in Article 16 of the Covenant of the League of Nations, residing within the United States, or in countries other than that violating said Article 16, to continue their commercial, financial and personal relations with the nationals of the United States.

This stipulation grew out of the fact that Article 16 of the Covenant did not provide for all the possibilities that might occur in the complex situation which would arise in applying an economic boycott to a covenant-breaking state. The reservation, therefore, knocked down the assumption that the article would require American citizens to boycott the nationals of a covenant-breaker who happened to live in their midst. Then, in their extreme anxiety to prevent any imputation of bad faith being laid upon Congress at any future time, the reservationists made the more questionable suggestion that it might be proper for our citizens to trade with nationals of the state breaking the Covenant who resided abroad, but not in the United States.

No government of the future, again, could be bound to adopt either of the suggestions of Senators in 1919, nor could it be compelled by the League to take the contrary action in either case. Its common sense and good faith would have to be depended upon to put the blockade into force with a measure of completeness calculated to accomplish its purpose.

In any event the reservation helped to make up the number fourteen.

No. 12, Debts of Nationals.

Nothing in Articles 296, 297, or in any of the annexes thereto, or in any other article, section or annex of the treaty of peace with Germany, shall, as against citizens of the United States, be taken to mean any confirmation, ratification or approval of any act otherwise illegal or in contravention of the rights of citizens of the United States.

[19] Miller, Vol. 20, p. 586.

The treaty confirmed the validity of the acts of the Alien Property Custodian. This confirmation, says Miller, had no bearing upon the legality of such acts as against American citizens, but Senators fearing that the treaty might be otherwise construed, insisted upon this clause. The reservation, though unnecessary, was not otherwise open to criticism. [20]

No. 13, The International Labor Organization.

The United States withholds its assent to Part XIII (Articles 387 to 427, inclusive) unless Congress by act or joint resolution shall hereafter make provision for representation in the organization established by said Part XIII, and in such event the participation of the United States will be governed and conditioned by the provisions of such act or joint resolution.

This reservation reflected suspicion, perhaps justified at the time, of the effects of one of the most beneficent provisions of the treaty. At the same time it withdrew from the President the power to help start another part of the treaty machinery.

No. 14, The British Dominion Votes. The declaration on the score of the British votes in the Assembly, as phrased in November, was perhaps as mild as any statement could be, after the months of protest against the Dominion votes. It read:

The United States assumes no obligation to be bound by any election, decision, report or finding of the Council or Assembly in which any member of the League and its self-governing dominions, colonies or parts of empire in the aggregate have cast more than one vote, and assumes no obligation to be bound by any decision, report or finding of the Council or the Assembly arising out of any dispute between the United States and any members of the League if such member, or any self-governing dominion, colony, empire or part of empire united with it politically has voted.

In March the clause was amended, on motion of Lodge, by saying that this should be the case:

Until Part I being the Covenant of the League of Nations shall be so amended as to provide that the United States shall be entitled to cast a number of votes equal to that which any member of the League and its self-governing dominions, colonies, or parts of empire, in the aggregate shall be entitled to cast.[21]

[20] Miller, Vol. 20, p. 587.
[21] *Congressional Record,* Vol. 59, Pt. 4, p. 4061.

The Hitchcock reservation on this subject provided that in case one of the British countries was involved in a dispute all of them should be considered as parties and barred from voting. In all other questions their votes were to be valid.

No. 15, Irish Self-determination. Shortly before the final vote in March, a combination of Democrats and Republicans spoiled the symmetry of the Fourteen Reservations by adding a fifteenth, on the subject of Ireland. Introduced by Senator Gerry, Democrat, of Rhode Island, it was frowned on by the Lodge Republicans as an effort to hold the Irish vote and to complicate the reservation program. It was doubtless both, but it passed by a vote of 38 to 36, with the bitterenders enthusiastically voting yea. The Republicans divided 18 for and 20 against; the Democrats split 20 for and 16 against.

The last of the reservations set forth that:

> In consenting to the ratification of the treaty with Germany the United States adheres to the principle of self-determination and to the resolution of sympathy with the aspirations of the Irish people for a government of their own choice adopted by the Senate June 6, 1919, and declares that when such government is attained by Ireland, a consummation it is hoped is at hand, it should promptly be admitted as a member of the League of Nations.

An effort was made by Senator Thomas to kill the reservation, by attaching an amendment to express the same sympathy for Korea, but it was not successful. Neither was an amendment by Senator Lodge, to take out the statement that we adhered to the principle of self-determination. Senator Kellogg opposed the reservation, not only because it violated every principle of international law and the rights of sovereign states, but because its adoption would prevent the ratification of the treaty and its acceptance if ratified. But Senator Norris contended that Ireland was about to have "her destiny sealed and her subjection extended for all time." [22]

So the Senate in one reservation dared anybody even to consider anything that we might label a domestic question, and in another encouraged a separation movement in the territory of a friendly ally. In one reservation it inveighed against the six British votes in the Assembly, and in another prayed for the creation of a seventh. Strangely enough, too, this last wish of the Senate is the only one that was granted. The Irish Free State has been a proud and active

[22] *Congressional Record,* Vol. 59, Pt. 5, p. 4501.

member of the League of Nations since 1923, and in 1931 is also a member of the Council.

No. 2, Article 10. The most disputed reservation, as adopted in November, read:

> The United States assumes no obligation to preserve the territorial integrity or political independence of any other country or to interfere in controversies between nations—whether members of the League or not—under the provisions of Article 10, or to employ the military or naval forces of the United States under any article of the treaty for any purpose, unless in any particular case the Congress, which, under the Constitution, has the sole power to declare war or authorize the employment of the military or naval forces of the United States, shall by act or joint resolution so provide.

On March 12, Senator Lodge, in consonance with his often expressed desire not to cause the defeat of the treaty on a mere question of phraseology, offered a substitute for the above reservation which stiffened it by adding "its resources or any form of economic discrimination." In so far as the article was a refusal to assume obligations, the use of the economic boycott which the President had so often said would prevent the use of armed force, was also abjured. To this extent the claim of the mild-reservationists that the reservations left the economic boycott in full force was invalidated.

But with this sharpening of the reservation the irreconcilables set up a wail that the new draft was really a surrender by Lodge; it was ever so much weaker than the original reservation. So the phrase, "including all controversies relating to territorial integrity or political independence," was inserted to make sure that the article really negatived. The final form of the reservation was, therefore:

> The United States assumes no obligation to preserve the territorial integrity or political independence of any other country by the employment of its military or naval forces, its resources, or any form of economic discrimination, or to interfere in any way in controversies between nations, including all controversies relating to territorial integrity or political independence, whether members of the League or not, under the provisions of Article 10, or to employ the military or naval forces of the United States, under any article of the treaty for any purpose, unless in any particular case the Congress, which, under the Constitution, has the sole power to declare war or authorize the employment of the military or naval forces of the United States, shall, in the exercise of full liberty of action, by act or joint resolution so provide.[23]

[23] *Congressional Record,* Vol. 59, Pt. 4, p. 4211; Pt. 5, p. 4322.

The Hitchcock substitute, which the President agreed to accept, stated:

> *That the advice mentioned in Article 10 of the covenant of the league which the council may give to the member nations as to the employment of their naval and military forces is merely advice which each member nation is free to accept or reject according to the conscience and judgment of its then existing Government,* and in the United States this advice can only be accepted by action of the Congress at the time in being, Congress alone under the Constitution of the United States having the power to declare war.[24]

The Simmons substitute, which the Democratic members of the Bi-partisan Conference thought was about to be accepted when Lodge was called to account by the irreconcilables, provided that:

> The United States assumes no obligation to employ its military or naval forces or the economic boycott to preserve the territorial integrity or political independence of any other country under the provisions of Article 10, or to employ the military or naval forces of the United States under any other article of the treaty for any purpose, unless in any particular case the Congress, which, under the Constitution has the sole power to declare war, shall, by act or joint resolution, so provide. Nothing herein shall be deemed to impair the obligation in Article 16 concerning the economic boycott.

Still another alternative, known as the Taft reservation, said:

> The United States declines to assume any legal or binding obligation to preserve the territorial integrity or political independence of any other country under the provisions of Article 10 or to employ the military or naval forces of the United States under any article of the treaty for any purpose; but the Congress, which under the Constitution has the sole power in the premises, will consider and decide what moral obligation, if any, under the circumstances of any particular case, when it arises, should move the United States in the interest of world peace and justice to take action therein and will provide accordingly.

At this distance it is difficult for the reader of the Lodge and Simmons reservations to distinguish any difference in their legal effect, aside from the question of the economic boycott, and the conclusion

---

[24] The italicized part of the reservation was adopted by the League Assembly, September 25, 1923, as the true interpretation of the intent of Article 10.—Howland, *American Foreign Relations 1928*, p. 281.

intrudes itself that maneuvering for party advantage must have prevented agreement upon one or the other. There was, however, a distinct difference in the mental approach of the contending Senators to the reservation. The Senators who strongly believed in the principle of Article 10, desired to limit the reservation to a statement of the powers of Congress which might allay enough of the fears aroused, without invalidating the obligation of Congress to start from the premise that it ought to support some action, however mild, if the article were violated. The strong supporters of the League, therefore, did not wish to go beyond the Taft or Hitchcock drafts.

The majority of the Republican Senators, on the other hand, wishing to disavow the obligation as completely as possible, gave the impression that their reservation accomplished this purpose quite efficaciously, and apparently convinced both themselves and their opponents that it did. It was possible, accordingly, for men of opposing opinions to look at virtually the same words with far different feelings, depending upon the supposed intent back of them.

Even the reader of today tends to get lost in that "extraordinary specimen of Congressional English," the Lodge draft. It is, to be sure, only one sentence, but "cumbersome and involved in form and 137 words long." To "untangle this mass of verbiage" [25] and understand clearly what it meant was not simple. One reads down through nearly 100 words to the word "unless," without finding anything except the letter and spirit of negation. Contrariwise, by commencing at the end of the reservation, stressing "unless" as the key word and reasoning up through the sentence to the beginning, a strong case can be made for the position that the reservation would not have seriously hampered the United States as a League member, in practice.

The chief result of the long campaign against the League might have been shortened to the Simmons form, sheared of its last sentence on the boycott, without losing any of its effectiveness. The declaration, for example, that Congress under the Constitution has "the sole power" to "authorize the employment of the military and naval forces of the United States" added nothing. The statement was, moreover, wide of the fact. The President as commander-in-chief of the armed forces of the United States had too often employed them, as in the Boxer uprising, without authority of Congress. [26]

Furthermore, in spite of the undoubted intent of its authors to limit

[25] Miller, Vol. 20, p. 571.
[26] *Ibid.*

the obligation of Article 10, the reservation did not completely destroy the effect of the joint guarantee against aggression. The duty of *respecting* the territorial integrity and political independence of all nations was left, and, unless the aggression came from outside the League, the sanctions of Article 16 were substantially unimpaired. If the critics of the League had been really in mortal fear of the mutual obligations of the Covenant, they should have concentrated their fire upon Article 16 in its entirety, instead of pecking querulously at a possible, far-fetched interpretation of one of its clauses (in Reservation No. 11). But, in lieu of a policy so consistent, they talked incessantly about Article 10, because it was the one article whose authorship could be fastened definitely upon President Wilson, and because it was felt that he, regarding it as the keystone of the whole structure, would not compromise nor surrender upon it. In this confidence the leaders were justified by events. The President, taking his final position in a letter, of March 8, to Senator Hitchcock, said:

> Any reservation which seeks to deprive the League of Nations of the force of Article X cuts at the very heart and life of the covenant itself. Any League of Nations which does not guarantee as a matter of incontestable right the political independence and integrity of its members might be hardly more than a futile scrap of paper, as ineffective in operation as the agreement between Belgium and Germany which the Germans violated in 1914.
>
> Article X as written into the Treaty of Versailles, represents the renunciation by Great Britain and Japan, which before the war had begun to find so many interests in common in the Pacific; by France, by Italy, by all the great fighting powers of the world, of the old pre-tensions of political conquest and territorial aggrandizement. It is a new doctrine in the world's affairs, and must be recognized, or there is no secure basis for the peace which the whole world so longingly desires and so desperately needs.
>
> If Article X is not adopted and acted upon, the Governments which reject it will, I think, be guilty of bad faith to their people, whom they induced to make the infinite sacrifices of the war by the pledge that they would be fighting to redeem the world from the old order of force and aggression. They will be acting also in bad faith to the opinion of the world at large, to which they appealed for support in a concerted stand against the aggressions and pretensions of Germany.
>
> If we were to reject Article X, or so to weaken it as to take its full force out of it, it would mark us as desiring to return to the old world of jealous rivalry and misunderstandings from which our gallant soldiers

have rescued us and would leave us without any vision or new conception of justice and peace. We would have learned no lesson from the war, but gained only the regret that it had involved us in its maelstrom of suffering. If America has awakened, as the rest of the world has, to the vision of a new day in which the mistakes of the past are to be corrected, it will welcome the opportunity to share the responsibilities of Article X. . . .

Every imperialistic influence in Europe was hostile to the embodiment of Article X in the covenant of the League of Nations, and its defeat now would mark the complete consummation of their efforts to nullify the treaty. I hold the doctrine of Article X as the essence of Americanism. We cannot repudiate it or weaken it without at the same time repudiating our own principles.

The imperialist wants no League of Nations, but if, in response to the universal cry of the masses everywhere, there is to be one, he is interested to secure one suited to his own purposes, one that will permit him to continue the historic game of pawns and peoples—the juggling of provinces, the old balance of power and the inevitable wars attendant upon these things. The reservation proposed would perpetuate the old order.[27]

The President's conviction as to the indispensability of the principle of Article 10 was too strong to permit him to realize that the reservation, long and inclusively nugatory as it seemed to be, did after all leave him and his successors real power to make the positive obligation of Article 10 effective. The reservationists did quite effectively cut away the obligation mutually to preserve, as against external aggression, territorial integrity and political independence by means of armed force, the application of the economic boycott, or the use of our "resources."

Although the *right* of Congress to apply these great weapons was preserved at the same time that the duty to use them was disavowed, the invalidation of the article appears at first study, and even on second scrutiny, to be quite complete. The President did, however, retain the power on his own initiative to make every kind of protest to a recalcitrant nation under the treaty promise given by all signatories of Article 10 to respect the integrity and independence of their neighbors. [28] Senators might arise to say that their predecessors of 1919 had solemnly reserved to Congress, in a reservation to Article 10, the right "to interfere in any way in controversies between nations," but

[27] *Current History,* April 1920, pp. 27–28.
[28] Miller, *My Diary at the Conference of Paris,* Vol. 20, p. 575.

the effect upon the President's effort to assist in the solution of the crisis would not likely be great.

Moreover, the power of the President would not be limited to upholding the negative obligation of the article. The positive obligation to oppose international aggression to the extent that it could be done by means *other than those enumerated* in the reservation remained, and these means were not so inconsiderable as would at first appear. If the Council, for example, advised the sending of a note to the offending state or states, the United States could still join in such warning or admonition, and, if the aggression still continued, the President could break off relations with the offending state and urge Congress to enforce the further sanctions which the reservation disavowed any duty to apply. [29]

The issue whenever it arose would have to be settled by public opinion, reservation or no reservation, and in such a crisis no influence is so powerful in determining the result as that of the President and his Secretary of State. [30]

In the last analysis, therefore, the gem of the collection of reservations was likely to be of little practical importance, except as it expressed, or as the campaign to get it generated, a feeling that we are not our brother's keeper, and that we are not going to have anything to do with anyone's wars, until they have run their course to the extent of treading heavily upon our toes.

Perhaps Wilson was justified in combating such suggestions with his remaining strength. Quite probably he should have trusted that the reaction which confronted him, even if shortsighted and misinformed, would pass before the League was put to its ultimate test. The emotions of the hour so filled men's minds, however, that few plumbed the practical consequences of either the Covenant or the reservations to the bottom. It is most unlikely, too, that any of the few who did so were ever able to try to help Wilson, in his invalid condition, to see that the reservation to Article 10 was likely to be of ephemeral importance in practice.

Aside from the actual value of the reservation, or of Article 10 itself, there can be no doubt that the sustained opposition against what was believed to be the central principle of the League made some sort of reservation to it attractive to most Americans. Even the final form of the reservation, read with emphasis on the latter clauses, appeared

[29] *Ibid.*, p. 572.
[30] *Ibid.*, p. 574.

so reasonable that it would have been difficult for any politician to oppose it.

As for its real necessity, a perplexed observer of the period asked: "Does it not seem incredible that a Peace Commission in which the best legal minds of all nations joined would put into the most important document ever written—a document on which the peace of the world must hang for many years—those crude attacks on the national constitutions of its members which we are asked to believe lie concealed in the Covenant of the League?" Supposing that its provisions did violate the Constitution, he continued, they would have no effect. The Covenant might be hurt thereby; the Constitution could not be. [31] Moreover, if the powers of Congress were imperiled by the Covenant so were those of dozens of parliaments which hold similar powers, most of them under written constitutions as specific as our own.

The reader who still feels in doubt as to the dangers in the Covenant which beset the United States may well read and re-read that document with the reservations beside it, if he would find that which would stamp as foolish or unpatriotic those 55 nations which have entered the League of Nations without reservations. [32]

The Preamble. Consideration of the enacting clause of the proposed resolution of ratification has been left to the last, because of its vital importance in determining how the reservations might become effective. As passed in November, the preamble stipulated:

Resolved (two-thirds of the Senators present concurring therein), That the Senate advise and consent to the ratification of the treaty of peace with Germany concluded at Versailles on the 28th day of June, 1919, subject to the following reservations and understandings which are hereby made a part and condition of this resolution of ratification, which ratification is not to take effect or bind the United States until the said reservations and understandings adopted by the Senate have been accepted by an exchange of notes as a part and a condition of this resolution of ratification by at least three of the four Principal Allied and Associated Powers, to wit, Great Britain, France, Italy and Japan.

The attitude taken in November was that if England, France and Italy accepted the conditions we could ignore the other powers. The insult to Japan was open and contemptuous. Assuming that she would

[31] Pierrepont B. Noyes, *While Europe Waits for Peace,* N. Y., 1921, p. 77–78.
[32] See *Ibid.,* p. 78.

reject the Shantung reservation, the reservationists disdainfully took it for granted that the other Associated Powers, allied to the Japanese by treaty long before the United States "associated" herself, would leave Japan isolated and branded by strong implication as an evildoer, not lifting a voice to indicate their own positions. It is to be hoped that it will be long before the Senate again so arrogantly insults a friendly power and at the same time sets a low value upon the honor of others.

But what of the other 28 nations signatory to the Covenant and the Treaty? Need they be consulted? Not in the view of Senators blinded by the goal ahead of them to all sense of international propriety. What did the feelings of some 30 nations toward the work of the Senators upon the treaty matter? Whatever pleased the United States would, of course, be accepted by them.

The interval between the two votes brought impressive support for this assumption in the Grey letter and its widespread endorsement. The evidence was even clearer, however, that the Senate could not prevent the reservations from being considered and acted upon by all the signatory powers. All studies of the precedents indicated that any declaration limiting or defining the terms of a treaty had to be accepted by the other signers, in some clear manner, before becoming effective. Moreover, by the express language of the final clauses of the treaty a certified copy of each *procès-verbal* was to be transmitted to all of the signatories. The American *procès-verbal,* then, including the reservations, would have had to go to each and every signatory for its consideration, and every one of these powers would have had the right to disapprove and refuse to accept. [33]

Consideration by all Treaty Signatories Essential. The inevitability of this procedure seems finally to have impressed itself upon the managers of the proposed ratification, after the November vote, for on March 19, Lodge moved to amend the preamble by saying that our ratification should not take effect

> until the said reservations and understandings adopted by the Senate have been accepted as a part and a condition of this resolution of ratification by the Allied and Associated Powers, and a failure on the part of the Allied and Associated Powers to make objection to said reservations and understandings prior to the deposit of ratification by the United States shall be taken as a full and final acceptance of such reservations and understandings by said powers.

[33] See the Memorandum by D. H. Miller in the *New York Times,* October 26, 1919.

In presenting the change Lodge did not acknowledge the affront to the 28 nations of trying to prevent their acting on the proposed limitations upon the treaty. The "sole purpose" of the amendment, he explained, was "to secure the acceptance of our reservations by all the signatories prior to our deposit of ratification."

The avowed purpose of the amendment was thus to make more certain that the reservations would go into full force and effect internationally. Whether there was an intention to make our final entry into the League easier or more difficult, in the event that the President decided to accept the reservations, is difficult to say. The bitter-enders evidently assumed that it made our entry less probable for they accepted the new provision without a roll call. But so did the friends of the treaty. They evidently felt that silent acquiescence by the powers might be given.

The irreconcilables, however, soon sensed that the provision gave the President some room in which to maneuver for our entry into the League. Senator Norris at once asked what the situation would be if the President should immediately file our ratification, as provided in the treaty, without giving the other powers notice or time to protest. Lodge had thought of that but deemed the danger to be "extremely remote." Brandegee agreed with him. What the latter was afraid of was not that the President would obtain the necessary silent acquiescence by rushing the process, but that he might obtain the affirmative acceptance of protesting powers by long negotiation. [34] He therefore moved to amend the preamble to provide that our ratification should not take effect or bind the United States unless the instrument of ratification were filed within 60 days (later made 90) of the final action of the Senate. This amendment was defeated by a vote of 42 to 41, the Republicans, with two or three exceptions, voting for it. [35]

Was Tacit Assent Sufficient? If the nations, or one of them, did not at once object to the proposed reservations, then all would be bound by them, according to their architects. "It is customary," said Lodge, "when reservations are made for a tacit assent to be all sufficient, and that must come before our deposit of ratification. If objection is not made before this time, their acceptance is final and complete of all our reservations. If objection is made, the United States stays out until they are accepted."

The last of these assertions was unquestionably true; the others

[34] *Congressional Record*, Vol. 59, Pt. 5, pp. 4568–69.
[35] *Ibid.*, p. 4574.

were by no means so certain. The Senate in the past had successfully proposed amendments to many treaties, sometimes unsuccessfully, but it had not had much experience in imposing its will upon great treaties signed by many powers. Reservations, it is true, had been made to a number of multilateral treaties by various nations but in all except two or three cases the treaties dealt with non-political matters (sanitation, communication, etc.) and in almost all cases the consent of the other powers to the reservations was either given or fairly implied at the time of signature. [36]

As a practical proposition, if the President presented all the signatories to the Treaty of Versailles with a set of Senatorial reservations they might have had difficulty, if objection were not made, in contesting the position of the United States in the League later, but if a serious crisis arose and the United States refused to recognize any responsibility whatever for its solution, other members of the League might have refused, very humanly, to regard their former failure to protest as debarring them from challenging the reservation whose protection was claimed. The "tacit assent" of all the nations "must come before our deposit of ratification." How, one may ask, does tacit assent "come?" How can its departure and arrival be certainly accounted for? And what would have been the situation if many of the signatories of the treaty had sent around a set of provisos, some conflicting with others, to be tacitly assented to?

Some more definite means of modifying the contractual rights laid down in multilateral treaties would appear to be called for, as the Senate realized when, in 1926, it came to compose the customary list of reservations to our entry into the World Court. Express, written acceptance was then demanded. [37]

WOULD THE RESERVATIONS HAVE BEEN ACCEPTED BY THE POWERS?

It was thus established that every signatory power would pass upon the reservations adopted. Would the 32 signatories, without exception, have accepted each and every one of the 15 reservations?

[36] See H. M. Malkin, "Reservations to Multilateral Conventions," *British Yearbook of International Law,* Oxford, 1926, pp. 146–62.

[37] It is not self-evident that in addition to the 32 signatories of the treaty the 12 neutrals invited to join the League would have had a vote upon our reservations. Still, the neutrals who had already accepted membership would seem to have been entitled to consider any reservations to the Covenant made by any state. Having been required to accede to the Covenant *without reservation* themselves, they would surely have been in position to insist that others do the same. At least they must have had a right to know and consider the qualified terms of membership proposed by others. The principle of the equality of states upon which the League was founded would give them that right.

That some of them would have failed to protest against any of the reservations is most probable. Many of the small states would have taken them entire. That some nations would have accepted all except one or two is quite probable. That one or more nations might have refused to accept any of them is not beyond the bounds of probability. It is surely not less difficult to secure unanimous acceptance of a proposal, be it ever so simple, among 32 nations than it is among 32 individuals. Who that has ever attempted to get the unanimous agreement of 30 people to a series of legally phrased statements would predict confidently that it could be done by mail among 32 nations—or 44, if the neutrals should be consulted?

The Chance of Total or Group Rejection. With the nations still flocking into the League, it would not have been altogether strange if some country had said: "We do not see the necessity for the special position in the League which the United States asks. Moreover, we believe that the acceptance of the qualified obligations proposed would go far to destroy the effectiveness of the League. Since, therefore, no other country has asked for special privileges, though all have been aware of the American objections, we object to the acceptance of the conditions proposed by the United States." The prestige of the United States was so high at the time, however, and the desire for her great weight in the League so universal, that such an outright rejection of our terms would have been unlikely. Still, it would have taken only one disgruntled power, or perhaps a single irritated Minister of Foreign Affairs, to have vetoed our entry flatly.

What was more likely to occur was that a group of States would confer and agree to oppose a given reservation, as for example, the Latin American powers our declaration on the Monroe Doctrine, or the British states our voting proviso.

This contingency, too, does not seem a probable one in the conditions of the time, though when we later proposed to join the World Court with reservations which weakened or destroyed one of its most useful functions, the nations almost unanimously agreed not to accept our adhesion on such terms. Yet it required neither concerted action nor a complete rejection by any one power of our conditions of adhesion to the League. All that was necessary was for one country to refuse to accept one reservation. In terms of single reservations the acquiescences might run into the hundreds, but a single refusal would keep our ratification from becoming effective.

Would the Individual Reservations Have Passed Scrutiny? What was the likelihood that objection to single reservations would be made? The first, establishing the interpretation that each nation on withdrawal was to be its own judge of whether it had fulfilled its international obligations would doubtless have been accepted by all. So also might the second, dealing with Article 10. And yet statesmen representing foreign countries who were anxious above all things for their own security could have looked long at the body of that reservation without seeing anything in it except the spirit of disavowal of any common responsibility. They might have hoped that, in practice, the power of Article 10 to protect them would not be destroyed. But it would have been strange if the French government had not asked whether, in case the reservation were accepted, the Franco-American Treaty guaranteeing France temporarily would be approved by the Senate. This treaty, which the Foreign Relations Committee had been at such pains to force the President to send to it promptly, had never been so much as discussed by the Committee and, according to Lodge, the Committee scarcely even considered taking it up. [38] The desire for American cooperation on any terms was strong in France, however, and would have militated in favor of accepting the best terms that could finally be obtained. If France eventually came to an understanding upon the subject, the group of nations profoundly concerned with the problem of security would have tended to follow the French lead.

Reservation 3, on mandates, and many others would have passed as merely a proclamation of forms which the Senate was attempting to lay down to govern our dealings with the League.

The Monroe Doctrine. Reservation No. 5, on the Monroe Doctrine, might have been challenged by any of the South American republics which believed that the day for a paternalistic Monroe Doctrine had passed, let alone an overweening one. The opportunity to put the United States in an embarrassing position was wide open. That is not to say that any of them would have kept us out of the League by seizing the opportunity, though the temptation to leave us standing isolated on the issue of American hegemony might well have proved too much to resist. The Chilean government in adhering to the Covenant reserved the right to pass upon such amendments or modifications of its stipulations as might be made by states which had not yet ratified,[39] and Costa Rica actually had the temerity later to ask the League to define

[38] Lodge, *The Senate and the League of Nations*, p. 156.
[39] Kluyver, *Documents on the League of Nations*, p. 231.

the Monroe Doctrine, a definition, needless to say, which the League did not attempt, saying that to do so might extend or limit it.[40]

Shantung? The withholding of our assent to the Shantung settlement could not fail to offend deeply a large section of the Japanese people, coming as it did after months of bitter public denunciation of Japan in the United States. The changing of the disavowal from the amendment offered by the Committee to the reservation form created a bare possibility that the Japanese government might remain silent, but on grounds of national pride it would have had every urge to refuse to accept the reservation as a reflection on Japan's good faith and an invitation to controversy in the future. The statement that we reserved full liberty of action with respect to any controversy which might arise under these articles was plain notice to China that if she wished to raise the issue we would support her.

Japan had her full quota of sensitive nationalists at the time, not to say militarists and jingoes, who could not be expected, if opportunity offered, to do other than retaliate against the moral castigation which Senators had been giving Japan for many months. When the Japanese delegates to the Peace Conference returned to Japan, on August 26, 1919, they were met by a mob of Japanese chauvinists who made a hostile demonstration against the envoys because they had not put through the racial equality clause. [41] This element would have been supported by large sections of even liberally minded Japanese in demanding that their government stand firm on the acceptance of the Shantung settlement as signed. No nation is more sensitive on matters touching its national pride and honor than Japan. It would have taken an outstanding expression of Japanese statesmanship indeed to have withstood public sentiment on the issue, even if the government itself had been disposed to acquiesce in the reflection upon its conduct and integrity of which Reservation 5 was the final expression.

Of scarcely less importance is another consideration. With a protest of Japan against the withdrawal by the Senate of our agreement to the Shantung settlement almost certain to come, what would have been the position of England and France? Could they in honor have remained passive before such an issue? In the stress of the war they

[40] D. P. Myers, *Handbook of the League of Nations since 1920*, Boston, 1930, pp. 17–18. Costa Rica's note was dated July 19, 1928. Mexico refused to recognize Article 21 of the Covenant, concerning the Doctrine, when entering the League, in 1931.

[41] *Current History*, November, 1919, Vol. XI, p. 219.

The situation had changed sufficiently ten years later that when the Japanese delegates returned from the London Naval Conference a crowd of 100,000 went to cheer the returning delegates for limiting competition in arms.

had promised to Japan all that the treaty gave her. They could hardly fail now to support Japan in the assertion of her claims under two treaties.

Reparations Commission Veto? The eighth reservation, giving our Congress a veto over any control of Germany's foreign trade established by the Reparations Commission was one of the possibilities which the Allied governments would have scrutinized most carefully.

The proviso set up a very remote contingency, but it touched a thing which to them was of vital and urgent importance. If in the atmosphere of the moment any one of the beneficiaries of reparations had fancied its ultimate chances of recouping its losses to be imperiled, the reservation would have had to be discussed. The United States has never had a monopoly on national sensibilities and suspicions.

Ireland? Consider, to illustrate further, what the reaction of the English Unionists must have been to the Irish reservation, calling upon England to give the people of Ireland "a government of their own choice." The "die-hards" on that question were far more numerous in England than the irreconcilable isolationists were in the United States. They were totally opposed to turning the Irish loose, or to giving in to them appreciably. What, therefore, must have been their feelings at the prospect of swallowing this intervention of the American isolationists in their most intimate, domestic affairs? Nor could it be expected that the mass of more moderate Englishmen would appreciate the encouragement to Irish rebellion and secession which was inherent in the "reservation." Far from desiring to oppress Ireland, they believed themselves striving for a solution that would give the Irish liberty without sacrificing British safety. Were they not vexed and troubled enough by the Irish situation, without America stirring the fires in Ireland anew, and telling them what to do? American popular audiences were not the only ones that could be stirred to anger by suggestions of interference in their own business. Neither were all the politicians who were ready for an issue that would rouse a strong popular reaction confined to our shores. At the moment, also, the British government was headed by Mr. Lloyd George, who had an unexcelled reputation for sensing popular feeling and conforming himself to it.

To have expected that the British government would accept the Irish article would have been the height of assumption indeed. Not even Lord Grey had anticipated that the Senate would put the explosive Irish question into the treaty.

One Vote for the British Empire or Six for Us? Friendly as he was, also, to acceptance of the original reservation on voting in the Assembly and Council, Grey had not been able to guarantee the acceptance by the Dominions of the November draft. For the United States to hold itself free to disavow any "election, decision, report or finding" in which the Dominions had voted, would operate in practice to leave the United States unbound by any action of the Assembly, if it abstained from voting. We could hardly vote and then repudiate the result, but on any occasion that an action threatened to displease us we could be in a position to say, "We do not accept it." In practice such repudiation would never be likely to occur, for the spirit of those trying to qualify the treaty would not long continue to rule the conduct of the United States in the League. Still, the possibility would always exist that the vote of one or all of the Dominions could be condemned or challenged, and the Dominions, be it remembered, were proud and jealous of their new recognition in the family of nations.

The original reservation, moreover, furnished the basis for a claim for more votes for the United States. The March version formally incorporated this claim into the reservation. Its acceptance would have pledged the signatories by plain implication to give us as many votes in the Assembly as the British Empire had. Yet this action would have destroyed the theory of the equality of sovereign states upon which the League rests and must rest, however much weight the great powers may have in its practical operation. The step would, in addition, have over-represented the United States, from the standpoint of every considerable group of nations in the League. From the position of the Dominions, viewing themselves as distinctly national entities, it would have given one nation the voting power of six clearly differentiated states. From the viewpoint of the European states, the United States was already too well represented, in the votes of its dependent states in the Caribbean, plus Liberia. To give us five more votes might be to surrender control of the Assembly entirely, particularly if some of the British Dominions themselves came to gravitate in our orbit. To the South American countries, not interested in increasing our preponderance, the same objections would appeal. If, too, we had five additional votes, powerful Japan would be entitled to claim at least three extra votes to cast for Asia—or China, if area and population were to count, could ask for a dozen. France, though also controlling a block of smaller states, would have at least equal right to, and greater need than we, of two or three added votes. And so on; once you discarded the principle of equality, the way for endless disputes over representation—and the destruction of the League itself—was wide open.

The conclusion seems inescapable that even if the Dominions had agreed, the members of the League could have given the United States no encouragement for its claim to six votes, and if the claim had been pressed, as political tactics in the United States would have demanded for some time, the results upon the development of the infant League of Nations would have been deplorable, if not disruptive. It is not to be concluded, however, that these young and vigorous countries would have accepted the reservation. Soon after its final form was approved by the Senate, the President of the Privy Council and Acting Secretary of State for External Affairs in Canada, Mr. Newton W. Rowell, issued a statement saying that if the reservation were accepted by the other powers Canada would withdraw from the League. [42]

Nations Do not Readily Accept Propositions thus Laid Down. There were limits beyond which foreign nations could not be expected to go in placating the United States Senate, particularly when it was the almost universal impression that the campaign against the treaty was primarily a political and personal fight against the President. Those limits would certainly have been discovered in any attempt to secure the acceptance of the Senate reservations. The response would hardly have been as humiliating as it was when a later Senate asked the forty-eight nations belonging to the World Court to accept, in forty-eight separate notes, its terms of adhesion to the Court, embodied in a long ten-paragraph document. In the latter case instead of acceptances rolling into the State Department, as many naïve Senators had apparently expected, welcoming letters from Cuba, Greece, Liberia, Albania and Luxembourg finally trickled in, while sixteen countries sent polite notes merely acknowledging the receipt of the Senate's condescension.

Naturally, when a conference of twenty-one Court members, called

---

[42] *Current History*, April, 1920, p. 29; Associated Press dispatch of February 16, 1920.

Miller's analysis of the reservation showed that it would come into practical operation only when questions were decided in the Assembly by a majority vote and we were in the minority. That would mean that all votes in the Council were against us and a majority of the Assembly. Even then he thought that complaint could be made only if the Assembly were almost evenly divided. His conclusion was, therefore, that the reservation was of almost no practical importance.—Miller, Vol. 20, pp. 587 ff.

Probably this was true, and patient negotiation might have finally persuaded the British nations to acquiesce in a wholly needless affront to their feelings, on the ground that, after all, threatened trouble would not materialize. But should other nations be compelled to restrain or abase themselves in order that United States Senators may not only twist the Lion's tail but those of her cubs grown to maturity?

by the League to rescue the Senate's proud move from utter sterility, sent back conditional acceptance to some of the Senate's reservations, Senators were shocked. The possibility of reservations being offered to reservations had not been considered in the Senate debates, except by one Senator. [43]

It does not follow, of course, that a similarly cool yet tolerant reception would have met the Senate reservations to the Covenant. It was true that the nations had full cognizance of the fears raised in the Senate without sharing them, but our aid and leadership were then thought to be so indispensable that the impulse to overlook in us a fit of post-war reaction would have been world wide.

When all is said, however, the passions aroused by the war were still alive abroad, as well as at home. The nations refusing our grudging, suspicious coöperation would not have been so numerous as in 1926, but it would not have been strange if they had been sufficiently so. Nations whose interests and whose pride were both deeply touched by the Senate's course could not have accepted its terms meekly.

It is difficult to avoid the conclusion that, at the very least, several of the reservations would have been subjected to long diplomatic discussion, and that the Senate would have had to abandon one or two entirely and accept modifications of others. Would it have done so when invited through the medium of Woodrow Wilson or his Secretary of State? How could the embattled advocates of China and Ireland and six votes for Uncle Sam have abandoned their sacred trusts? How, on the other hand, could the nations who felt vital rights infringed or questioned by the Senate's action be expected to be properly solicitous for the anti-Japanese, the anti-English and anti-Wilson vote in the United States?

Would the President Have Accepted Them? In the light of his months and years of negotiation with the principal powers concerned, it is similarly difficult to conclude that the President would have accepted the proposed reservations, if the treaty had received a two-thirds vote of the Senate with them attached. [44] After the ordeals to secure international agreement which he had been through, his opinion of the chance of securing acceptance for the Senate's terms was bound to be

[43] *United States Daily*, December 31, 1927; D. F. Fleming, *The Treaty Veto of the American Senate*, N. Y., 1930, Chapters IX and X.

[44] Most readers will be familiar with the fact that under the Constitution it is the President who ratifies all treaties. He must first have the "advice and consent" of the Senate, but the initiative in finally putting the treaty into force, as in making it in the beginning, is with the President.

low. Moreover, every public utterance which he made on the subject to the day of his death expressed a certain belief that the Senate had effectively nullified his work, for the time being, so far as the United States was concerned. Believing that, and passionately adhering to the principles upon which the League was founded, the utility of advancing the objectives of the opposition leaders by asking the powers to accept the Lodge Reservations was likely to appear small, especially when they carried certain affront to some powers, implied suspicion and distrust of all, and, in his view, repudiated settlements which he felt himself in honor bound to uphold.

The *New York Times* had said as early as July 25, 1919, assuming that the President would accept interpretative reservations: "Beyond that he will not go. He has not labored all these weary months with the high, sincere, and unselfish purpose to establish the reign of law and justice in international relations with so little conviction that he will now consent to annul the beneficent achievements of the Peace Council and insult his distinguished co-laborers by begging them to assent to a dwarfed and maimed version of the treaty, an instrument upon which the Republican Senators have committed mayhem as a means of expressing their spite against himself."

Needless to say, the President, with his conviction only hardened by physical collapse, would be still more likely to take that position in April than in July.

There is little evidence that Wilson would have accepted the Lodge resolution of March, 1920, yet no one can say with finality that he would not have done so in time. If it had been presented to him, and the Treaty thus approved had reposed on his desk, as he grew somewhat stronger in the spring of 1920 he might have been led to try out negotiation for its acceptance.

The prospect would have been at least as good as would that of persuading the Senate leaders to abandon enough of their embattled positions to make possible agreement with the powers, during Wilson's remaining year.

CHAPTER XVIII

THE SOLEMN REFERENDUM

THE Senate having twice failed to approve the treaty, it was returned to the President and the majority leaders moved a joint resolution, April 1, 1920, which attempted to end the legal state of war with Germany by the same method which inaugurated it. This resolution passed in both houses by substantial majorities, was vetoed by President Wilson, May 27th, and failed of passage over his veto by a vote of 220 for repassage to 152 against. [1]

CHICAGO

The contest then passed to the Republican National Convention, meeting in Chicago, of which Senator Lodge was both temporary and permanent chairman. In his keynote speech Lodge strongly condemned "the man and his associates who have thus endeavored to turn us from the right road into dark and devious ways which with all nations lead to destruction." This man, said the orator solemnly, "had apparently but one aim—to be the maker of a league of nations of which he should be the head." He had, however, created "an alliance and not a league for peace" which had had to be opposed. But during all the tedious weeks and months of the discussion "party was scarcely ever mentioned nor was the effect of our action upon the party considered." [2]

Crane's Fight for the League. The time to consider the effect of the action taken upon the party having apparently come, Lodge threw his influence against approval in the platform of the reservations he had labored so long to secure and perfect. The battle in the resolutions sub-committee over the League of Nations plank was described by the correspondent of the *Times* as "one of the most stubbornly

[1] *Congressional Record*, Vol. 59, Pt. 5, p. 5129; Pt. 8, pp. 7447, 7805-9.
[2] *New York Times*, June 9, 1920.

maintained struggles incidental to conventions of recent times." [3] The fight for the League was led by ex-Senator Murray Crane, Lodge's former colleague from Massachusetts. He was supported by Kellogg, McCumber, Lenroot and others. As the leader of the League forces, Crane met the threats of Borah and Johnson to bolt the party, if the platform contained any approval of the League, by saying flatly, "If there is going to be a split in the party over the treaty, let it come now." [4]

For a time it looked as if irreconcilable positions would not be compromised, but just at the time when, according to Taft, the committee seemed about to approve the reservations,[5] Mr. Ogden L. Mills of New York, who had been supporting Senator Crane, drew from his pocket a compromise plank prepared by the party adviser who never failed it in a great emergency.

This statement, said Mr. Mills, "was accepted just as it was received three weeks ago from Mr. Root." [6] It had to meet first, however, a stubborn fight on the part of Senator Crane. The conference which accomplished his isolation was attended by Lodge, Crane, Mills, George Wharton Pepper, Senators Borah, Brandegee, McCormick and Smoot together with George Harvey, the chief organizer of the fight against the League. [7] Perhaps others were there, but they were likely to be of little importance when confronted in the same room by three or four of the utterly determined group of men who had declared unrelenting warfare upon the League as soon as its barest outlines could be determined. One or two were not there, but they were not needed. The advocates of a declaration for ratification acquiesced to the call of harmony, until Crane only held out.

At this point Lodge declared that he would leave the chair and fight from the convention floor any attempt to declare for ratification of the League with his reservations. [8] It was clear that he had no intention of having his success in holding his party together through months of controversy jeopardized. The bitter-enders he feared; the League advocates would hardly bolt. They would have to be satisfied with a noncommittal platform.

Even Senator Crane was at length convinced of this, and the

[3] *New York Times*, June 11, 1920.
[4] *New York Tribune*, June 10, 1920.
[5] *Boston Transcript*, June 16, 1920.
[6] *New York Tribune*, June 11, 1920.
[7] *New York Times, New York Tribune*, June 11, 1920.
[8] *Ibid.*

Permission—Keystone View Co.

ELIHU ROOT

Permission—Keystone View Co.

MURRAY CRANE

Tribune reported that, "Discounting the possibilities of a blow-up on the floor of the convention, those on both sides of the treaty fight asserted that, in their opinion, another great party crisis, which last night had threatened for a time a repetition of the disastrous division of 1912, had been averted." [9]

The Platform. The plank which averted a repetition of the disaster of 1912 said: "The Republican Party stands for agreement among the nations to preserve the peace of the world. We believe that such an international association must be based upon justice and must provide methods which shall maintain the rule of public right by development of law and the decision of impartial courts, and which shall secure instant and general conference whenever peace shall be threatened by political action, so that the nations pledged to do and insist upon what is just and fair may exercise their influence and power for the prevention of war."

The Covenant signed by the President in Paris, said the platform, "contains stipulations not only intolerable for an independent people but certain to produce the injustice, hostility and controversy among nations which it proposed to prevent."

For the group of men who had directed the fight on the League, and who dominated the convention, there was high praise and, in the same sentence, for the disappointed advocates of the League a promise of hope for the future, as follows: "The Senators performed their duty faithfully. We approve their conduct and honor their courage and fidelity, and we pledge the coming Republican administration to such agreement with the other nations of the world as shall meet the full duty of America to civilization and to humanity in accordance with American ideals and without surrendering the right of the American people to exercise its judgment and its power in favor of justice and peace." [10]

The usual aim of the platform-maker to carve a plank for a controversial question upon which all could stand was thus achieved in remarkable degree. The first paragraph read well to those who wanted the League. It promised at the very least a consultative pact with the

[9] *New York Tribune,* June 11, 1920.

Crane, always delicate in health, suffered a collapse during the Convention and died a few weeks later, October 2, 1920.

During the fight in the Senate, he had exerted, at times from his bed, all the influence he could command in favor of the Covenant, warning his friends that they were wrong to let the Republican party be put in a position of opposition to the League—wrong morally and in the end, they would find, politically. *Springfield Republican,* October 3, 1920.

[10] *New York Times,* June 11, 1920.

nations whereby "instant and general conference" should be had whenever the peace was threatened—a pledge which is still unfulfilled.

The second paragraph denounced the Covenant in words grave
enough to suit any bitter opponent of the League as "certain" to
produce "the injustice, hostility and controversy among nations which
it proposed to prevent"—a promise of failure for the League which
also has never been realized.

The most violent opponents of the League and the strongest be-
lievers in the Covenant having been provided with places upon the
platform, it but remained to gather in the reservationists and at the
same time suggest that perhaps the coming administration would
form a new and better "association" of nations which would doubtless
be both Republican and American. "Such agreement with the other
nations of the world as shall meet the full duty of America to
civilization and to humanity"—with reservations, of course. This
might mean the League with many reservations or a new league. In
fulfillment it has meant neither. The "full duty of America to civilization and to humanity" is now said to be satisfied by an agreement on
our part not to engage in war—unless it be a defensive one.

The Candidate. Given this platform and the continued dominance
of the Republican party by the faction which opposed the League
loudly enough to inspire fear of a bolt, there was but one hope for
the League Republicans, namely the nomination of a candidate for
President who would have the courage and the will to interpret the
platform liberally and defy the little band of bitter-enders. Bolting
would prove to be rather unprofitable business after the election.

Instead of such a leader, however, the Republicans who stood
for the League received a Senator, one of the few ever nominated,
who had been distinguished chiefly by his complete regularity in the
treaty fight, a regularity shading toward irreconcilability. Senator
Warren G. Harding, of Ohio, was not among the leading candidates.
His initial poll of 65½ votes was doubled or quadrupled by the strength
of each of the three chief contenders, Wood, Lowden and Johnson.
Several ballots showed small gains for all except Harding, but none
even approached a majority. The leaders, therefore, again went into
conference with George Harvey who had come to the conclusion a year
before that Senator Harding would be the candidate.[11]

The time for action having arrived, Harvey fittingly consulted
Brandegee first, then Lodge and Smoot joined them and Watson,

[11] W. F. Johnson, *George Harvey,* Boston, 1929, pp. 278–79.

McCormick, Wadsworth and Calder—Senators all, were sent for. Joseph R. Grundy, of Pennsylvania, came in unannounced, but agreed to the decision instantly.

Harding was then called in and asked for reassurance concerning rumors circulating by whisper which created some doubt in Harvey's mind as to his availability. Informing Harding of his prospective choice, Harvey said: "But, first, Senator Harding, I wish you to assure these gentlemen and myself upon your sacred honor and before your God, that you know of no reason, arising out of anything in your past life, why you should not stand with confidence before the American people as a candidate for the highest office within their gift."

Asking to be alone a while before replying, Harding returned fifteen minutes later to answer firmly, "Gentlemen, there is no such reason," and within an hour the tenth ballot in the convention gave him 692 votes. "He was nominated," said Harvey afterward, "because there was nothing against him and because the delegates wanted to go home." [12]

Harmony. The Republican convention left many Republicans strongly dissatisfied, but in the main each interpreted the platform to suit himself, as was intended. Taft declared that "nothing but approval and promise of the League with the Lodge reservations can be inferred from the resolution," while Herbert Hoover, after accepting an invitation to visit Senator Harding, stated somewhat less confidently that "Nothing prevents the compromise planks on labor, the League, etc., from being given a forward looking interpretation." Mr. Hoover defended these compromises on the ground that we had "not arrived at an era of new political and social tendencies" and that the two party system must be preserved. [13]

San Francisco

The Democratic Convention, convened in San Francisco, faced similar difficulties in taking its stand and choosing its candidate. Senator David Walsh, of Massachusetts, led a long fight in the resolutions committee for such amendment of the League of Nations declaration as would permit Democratic Senators who voted for the Lodge reservations to justify their action during the campaign. If Senator Lodge would not defend his reservations, his Democratic colleague from Massachusetts would. He was as anxious to avoid condemnation by his party as the Republican bitter-enders were.

[12] *Ibid.*, p. 278.   [13] *New York Times*, June 19, 20, 1920.

The position of Democratic Senators who had actively supported the reservations was recognized by an amendment to the League resolution, accepted during a tempestuous session which lasted from 7:30 P.M. until 3:30 A.M., when a committee of nine was appointed to prepare the final draft on the subject. [14]

The completed platform, commending the President for his courage and good faith and charging that the Republican Senate refused to ratify the treaty "merely because it was the product of Democratic statesmanship," declared for the League of Nations "as the surest, if not the only practicable means of maintaining the permanent peace and terminating the insufferable burden of great military and naval establishments."

The attitude of the Democrats toward reservations was defined as follows: "We endorse the President's view of our international obligations and his firm stand against reservations designed to cut to pieces the vital provision of the Versailles Treaty, and we commend the Democrats in Congress for voting against resolutions for separate peace which would disgrace the nation. We advocate the immediate ratification of the treaty without reservations which would impair its essential integrity, but do not oppose the acceptance of reservations making clearer or more specific the obligations of the United States to the League Associates." [15]

The Democrats, also, had no outstanding candidate for the Presidency, and no controlling mind nor Senatorial junta to decide the problem for them. Hailing the platform as a declaration of conquering purpose which nothing could defeat, President Wilson refused to indicate any preference as to his successor. Starting, like the Republicans, with four leading candidates, the convention therefore fought it out for several days. Governor Smith, the last of the quartet, soon dropped out, leaving the contest between McAdoo and Cox, with Attorney General Palmer a strong third—sometimes second. His delegates, released on the 38th ballot, went largely to Cox who was nominated on the 44th poll. [16]

HARDING AND COX

The two presidential candidates selected proceeded to define their personal attitudes toward the League in somewhat different fashion.

---

[14] *Springfield Republican*, July 2, 1920. Newspaper men at a considerable distance could hear the shouts of combat coming through the closed doors.
[15] *Ibid.*, July 3, 1920.
[16] *Ibid.*, July 4–6, 1920.

Harding, in his acceptance speech, advised by George Harvey, as Lodge had been in his keynote speech, [17] said: "It will avail nothing to discuss in detail the League Covenant, which was conceived for world super-government. . . ." Thus construing the purpose of the Covenant and brushing the League aside, he proceeded to say that the way was "very simple." Explaining how simple it was, he continued: "With a Senate advising as the constitution contemplates, [18] I would hopefully approach the nations of Europe and of the earth, proposing that understanding which makes us a willing participant in the consecration of the nations to a new leadership. . . ."

The Senator was evidently to make an ideal candidate for the platform prepared for him. Naturally he had to have some time to produce something better than Wilson had proposed, but he hinted that there was a program, saying: "If men call for more specific details I remind them that moral committals are broad and all inclusive, and we are contemplating peoples in concord of humanity's advancement. From our point of view the program is specifically American, and we mean to be American first of all to the world." [19] How a specifically America first program could satisfy all the nations, or solve the problem of world peace, he did not elucidate. Perhaps he was already hinting at "outlawry." [20]

Reference to the League in Harding's speech was brief; in that of Governor Cox, accepting the Democratic nomination, it occupied one third of the address. His position was as clear cut as that of Harding was cloudy. Declaring the League question to be the supreme issue of the century, he stated unequivocally that the first duty of the new administration would be the ratification of the treaty. His complete willingness to accept interpretative reservations was clearly expressed. [21]

---

[17] Johnson, *George Harvey*, p. 274. "Although he was still nominally a Democrat," says Johnson, "the Republican leaders with one accord looked to him to be the chief inspirer and director of their campaign, both at the National Convention, and in the subsequent electoral canvass; precisely as they had accepted his leadership in the senatorial fight against the Covenant of the League."

[18] He little knew how later he would implore the Senate not to defeat the treaties of the Washington Naval Conference.

[19] *New York Times*, July 23, 1920.

[20] In a speech of September 3, he called for "a newer understanding" and declared, "We would lead the world to outlaw war." *New York Times*, September 4, 1920.

Senator Johnson was much pleased by Harding's "firm and emphatic stand against the proposed league." *Springfield Republican*, July 24, 1920.

[21] *Springfield Republican*, August 8, 1920.

Answering the alarm of Republican leaders at entanglement in foreign affairs he charged that "the present senatorial cabal, led by Senators Lodge, Penrose, and Smoot," was formed in the midst of the war. He recalled, further, that the same

This position was maintained by Governor Cox, and his running mate, Franklin D. Roosevelt, throughout the campaign. Realizing the heavy odds against them, they battled sturdily for the League of Nations to the end, hoping that the moral fervor of enough people might be stirred to enable them to escape impending defeat. But, although very large numbers of voters undoubtedly did respond to their clear call, the hope was vain.

REPUBLICAN TRENDS

The majority of the people were now so tired of the League wrangle that they could not be aroused to affirmative support of the ideal that had originally appealed to nearly all. As Colonel Frederick Palmer, the leading American war correspondent of the period, pointed out, the giving of a bad name to the League at the very start had made public opinion skeptical. "Faith is a great factor in the affairs of nations, no less than in the affairs of individuals." Things are not usually accomplished unless we believe they can be done. [22]

Never-ceasing questioning of the perils in the League had not only generated much lack of confidence; it had aroused active prejudice as well. But even more important, perhaps, the incessant dispute over the Covenant had tired the nation until the majority of people were so sick of the whole squabble that the Republican managers could safely temporize with it.

The Democratic candidates, realizing that the League issue was already old, were at first strongly inclined to subordinate it, but after paying a visit to Wilson, whom Cox had never met, they decided to carry on the struggle which he could no longer wage. Finding him sitting gaunt and broken, but confident that "the fight can still be won," they could do little else but go out to continue the battle for him and they left him with a high resolve to do so. [23]

It would have been futile, moreover, for the Democrats to have waged a defensive, apologetic campaign in the face of the multitude of active resentments which clamored for expression. The two Wilson administrations had disturbed nearly everybody. The great business

---

leaders who were "now inveighing against our interest in affairs outside of America, criticized President Wilson in unmeasured terms for not resenting the invasion of Belgium in 1914."

[22] *New York Times*, June 16, 1920.

[23] Milton MacKaye, "Governor Roosevelt," *The New Yorker*, August 15, 1931, p. 22.

interests and labor both felt themselves too much repressed. Excessive cost of living, profiteering during the war and speculation after it had all aroused unrest. Western farmers were disgruntled over price regulation, and its abandonment at the close of the fighting, while Eastern manufacturers were dissatisfied with a lower tariff which they desired to change quickly. Earlier high prices were resented by many and the falling prices of the time by others. The "exactions" of labor during the war and rising unemployment generated strong feeling in different quarters. According to custom everyone blamed the business depression of the time upon the party in power. [24]

The Promise of a Republican League

These were by no means all of the forces composing the mighty desire for a change which existed. In the presence of them the only thing that could prevent Republican victory was the possibility that large numbers of Republican voters might place their convictions about the League above everything else. This danger had been largely forestalled by the platform and it was carefully guarded against in the same manner all through the campaign. Senator Harding's speeches usually condemned the League, and at the same time almost invariably held out strong hope that something effective would be done to replace it. In his Marion speech of August 28, for example, he held that if the United States had ratified the Covenant it would have had to suppress the war then raging between Poland and Soviet Russia. The absence of the wealthy United States from the League in this emergency had prevented that infant organization from functioning, it was suggested. "The original League" had therefore "undoubtedly passed beyond the power of restoration."

New Machinery Proposed. In the place of it Harding proposed "a world court of justice supplemented by a world association for conference." He would begin by taking the old Hague tribunal and putting "teeth" into it. Then he would add machinery, wherever found, that seemed desirable. If, even, "in the failed League of Versailles there can be found machinery which the tribunal can use properly and advantageously, by all means let it be appropriated. I would even go further. I would take and combine all that is good and excise all that is bad from both organizations."

[24] See the analysis of the *New York Evening Post* and others, in the *Literary Digest*, November 13, 1920.

The League Revised Might Do. Lest this operation might possibly not seem to be simple, he held out the hope that the League might be retained and used after some revision. Continuing, in the next sentence, he added: "This statement is broad enough to include the suggestion that if the League, which has heretofore riveted our considerations and apprehensions, has been so entwined and interwoven into the peace of Europe, that its good must be preserved in order to stabilize the peace of that continent, then it can be amended or revised so that we may still have a remnant of world aspirations in 1918 builded into the world's highest conception of helpful co-operation in the ultimate realization." [25]

The new thing, moreover, might even be called by the old name. He had already declared in the same address that he did not care what it was called. "Let it be an association, a society, or a league, or what not, our concern is solely with the substance, not the form thereof." [26]

The League Rejected and Association Proposed. Again at Des Moines, on October 7, Harding stated flatly: "It is not interpretation but rejection that I am seeking," a statement which, it would seem, could have no double meaning. It was immediately modified, however, by a promise to consult with the "best minds" in the country after the election "to the end that we shall have an association of nations for the promotion of international peace."

Paying tribute to the astuteness with which Harding's speeches were composed, Chester H. Rowell, former Republican National Committeeman from California, has described them as follows: "One half of the speeches were for the League of Nations if you read them hastily, but if you read them with care every word of them could have been read critically as against the League of Nations. The other half were violent speeches against the League of Nations if you read them carelessly, but if you read them critically every one of them could be interpreted as in favor of the League of Nations." [27]

Confusion Complete. Faced by a campaign so cleverly directed, the feelings of the League Republicans were naturally mixed. Contradictory interpretations of the same Harding speech appeared simultaneously in leading Republican papers. The Republican press in the main attempted to extricate itself from confusion by deprecating Hard-

[25] Harding's expressions were often somewhat unusual. They have been reproduced here with care.
[26] *New York Times*, August 29, 1920.
[27] C. H. Rowell, "The Foreign Policy of the United States Since the War," in *The Problems of Peace*, Oxford, 1927, p. 177.

ing's anti-League pronouncements and apologizing for his evasions as being politically necessary. [28] The terrible Hiram Johnson might bolt a pro-League stand. Had not his coolness permitted the election of Wilson in 1916?

The Appeal of the Thirty-One. Signs that individual Republicans were angered by such a policy were numerous enough to give some concern, but not sufficient to cause a change of policy. The danger of defection and the necessity of reconciling pro-League beliefs with support of the highly doubtful or anti-League candidate did lead to a remarkable expression of faith and hope by a group of prominent Republicans which has become almost as famous as the Round-Robin of March 4, 1919. The statement of the Thirty-One, however, was not conceived by a bitter opponent of the Wilson League but by that eminent attorney for the Republican party who, having written the platform which Harding was interpreting so expansively, now felt it incumbent upon him to give the League interpretation what support it was possible to muster. Root's statement of October 14, affirming a desire to have the United States do her "full part in association with the other civilized nations to prevent war," phrased the issue as "not whether our country shall join in such an association," but "whether we shall join under an agreement containing the exact provisions negotiated by President Wilson at Paris, or under an agreement which omits and modifies some of those provisions. . . ." [29]

[28] C. P. Howland, *American Foreign Relations 1928*, New Haven, 1928, pp. 297, 299.

[29] The full statement is as follows:

The undersigned, who desire that the United States shall do her full part in association with the other civilized nations to prevent war, have earnestly considered how we may contribute most effectively to that end by our votes in the coming election.

The question between the candidates is not whether our country shall join in such an association. It is whether we shall join under an agreement containing the exact provisions negotiated by President Wilson at Paris, or under an agreement which omits or modifies some of those provisions that are very objectionable to great numbers of the American people.

The paper signed by thirty-eight Republican Senators in March, 1919, before the League covenant was adopted at Paris, advised the President that the signers could not approve a treaty in the form then proposed, although it was their sincere desire that the nations of the world should unite to promote peace and general disarmament.

A majority of the Senate voted to ratify the League amendment with modifications, which there is good evidence to show would have been accepted by the other nations; but Mr. Wilson refused to accept these modifications, and insisted upon the agreement absolutely unchanged, and Democratic Senators sufficient in number to defeat the treaty as modified followed Mr. Wilson by voting against ratification.

That is substantially the difference between the parties now. The Democratic platform and candidate stand unqualifiedly for the agreement negotiated at Paris without substantive modification.

Reciting the failure of President Wilson to heed sufficiently the Round-Robin or to accept the reservations proposed, the statement proceeded to put itself in unity with the entire campaign against the League by condemning Article 10 and calling for its deletion. This

---

On the other hand, the Republican platform says: "The Republican Party stands for agreement among the nations to preserve the peace of the world. We believe that such an international association must be based upon international justice and must provide methods which shall maintain the rule of public right by the development of law and the decision of impartial courts; and which shall secure instant and general international conference whenever peace shall be threatened by political action so that the nations pledged to do and insist upon what is just and fair may exercise their influence and power for the prevention of war."

Mr. Harding said in his speech of August 28: "There are distinctly two types of international relationship. One is offensive and defensive alliance of great powers. . . . The other type is a society of free nations, or a league of free nations animated by consideration of right and justice instead of might and self-interest, and not merely proclaimed an agency in pursuit of peace, but so organized and so participated in as to make the actual attainment of peace a reasonable possibility. Such an association I favor with all my heart, and I would make no fine distinction as to whom credit is due. One need not care what it is called. Let it be an association, a society or a league, or what not. Our concern is solely with the substance, not the form thereof."

Mr. Harding has since repeatedly reaffirmed the declarations of this speech in the most positive terms.

The question accordingly is not between a league and no league, but is whether certain provisions in the proposed league agreement shall be accepted unchanged or shall be changed.

The contest is not about the principle of a league of nations, but it is about the method of most effectively applying that principle to preserve peace.

If the proposed changes in the Paris agreement were captious or without substantial grounds, one might question the sincerity of their advocates. This, however, is not the case.

The principal change proposed concerns Article X, of the League Covenant as negotiated at Paris. Mr. Wilson declares this to be "the heart of the League" and the chief controversy is about this.

Article X provides that the nations agreeing to the treaty shall "preserve as against external aggression the territorial integrity and existing political independence of all members of the League."

That is an obligation of the most vital importance and it certainly binds every nation entering into it to go to war whenever war may be necessary to preserve the territorial integrity or political independence of any member of the League against external aggression.

It is idle to say that Congress has power to refuse to authorize such a war, for whenever the treaty calls for war a refusal by Congress to pass the necessary resolution would be a refusal by our Government to keep the obligation of the Treaty. The alternative would be war or a breach of the solemnly pledged faith of the United States.

We cannot regard such a provision as necessary or useful for a league to preserve peace.

We have reached the conclusion that the true course to bring America into an effective league to preserve peace is not by insisting with Mr. Cox upon the acceptance of such a provision as Article X, thus prolonging the unfortunate situation created by Mr. Wilson's insistence upon that article, but by frankly calling upon the other nations to agree to changes in the proposed agreement which will obviate this vital objection and other objections less the subject of dispute.

For this course we can look only to the Republican Party and its candidate; the Democratic Party and Mr. Cox are not bound to follow it. The Republican Party is bound by every consideration of good faith to pursue such a course until the declared object is attained.

The conditions of Europe make it essential that the stabilizing effect of the

action was asked for under an interpretation of the article which excluded any right of a future Congress to consider all the circumstances in a case and decide whether the advice of the Council should be accepted wholly or in small degree. Maintaining that war was called for, it was affirmed that "It is idle to say that Congress has power to refuse to authorize such a war, for whenever the treaty calls for war a refusal by Congress to pass the necessary resolution would be a refusal by our government to keep the obligation of the treaty."

---

treaty already made between the European Powers shall not be lost by them and that the necessary changes be made by changing the terms of that treaty rather than by beginning entirely anew.

That course Mr. Harding is willing to follow, for he said in his speech of August 28: "I would take and combine all that is good and excise all that is bad from both organizations" (the Court and the League). This statement is broad enough to include the suggestion that if the League which has heretofore riveted our considerations and apprehensions has been so entwined and interwoven into the peace of Europe that its good must be preserved in order to stabilize the peace of that continent, then it can be amended or revised so that we may still have a remnant of the world's aspirations in 1918 builded into the world's highest conception of helpful co-operation in the ultimate realization.

We therefore believe that we can most effectively advance the cause of international co-operation to promote peace by supporting Mr. Harding for election to the Presidency.

Lyman Abbott
Nicholas Murray Butler, President, Columbia University.
Robert S. Brookings, President, Washington University, St. Louis.
Paul D. Cravath.
Charles W. Dabney, University of Cincinnati.
William H. P. Faunce, President, Brown University.
Frank J. Goodnow, Johns Hopkins University.
Warren Gregory, San Francisco.
John Grier Hibben, President, Princeton University.
Herbert Hoover.
Charles Evans Hughes.
Alexander C. Humphries, President, Stevens Institute of Technology.
Ernest M. Hopkins, President, Dartmouth College.
William Lawrence, Bishop of Massachusetts.
Samuel McCune Lindsay, President, Academy Political Science, Columbia University.
A. Lawrence Lowell, President, Harvard University; Chairman, Executive Committee League to Enforce Peace.
John Henry MacCracken, President, Lafayette College.
Samuel Mather, Cleveland, Ohio.
George A. Plimpton, President, Board of Trustees, Amherst College.
Henry S. Pritchett, President, Carnegie Foundation for Advancement of Teaching.
Charles A. Richmond, President, Union College, Schenectady, N. Y.
Elihu Root.
Jacob Gould Schurman, former President, Cornell University.
Henry L. Stimson.
Oscar S. Straus, member Executive Committee, League to Enforce Peace.
Henry W. Taft, member Executive Committee, League to Enforce Peace.
Isaac M. Ullman, New Haven, member Executive Committee, League to Enforce Peace.
William Allen White, editor, Emporia, Kansas.
George W. Wickersham, member Executive Committee, League to Enforce Peace.
W. W. Willoughby, Professor of Political Science, Johns Hopkins University.
Ray Lyman Wilbur, President, Leland Stanford Jr. University.

New York Times, October 15, 1920.

The Thirty-One, therefore, reached the conclusion that "the true course to bring America into an effective league to preserve peace" was frankly to call upon the other nations to amend the Covenant. "For this course we can look only to the Republican Party and its candidate; the Democratic Party and Mr. Cox are not bound to follow it. The Republican Party is bound by every consideration of good faith to pursue such a course until the declared object is attained."

This was strong language. It even implied that Harding had a right to give only one interpretation to the cover-all platform with which he had been provided. The platform was actually quoted in the statement and insistence also made that the Covenant be amended only. It was essential "that the necessary changes be made by changing the terms of that treaty rather than by beginning entirely anew."

But Root was too late. He could not now undo what he had done earlier, in order to repress the issue in the convention. George Harvey and more subtle dialecticians than Root were now expounding the platform. They had, moreover, just as much right to interpret its call for "an international association . . . which shall secure instant and general conference" to mean a new Republican league, which they would fashion after their own desires in due time, as the platform maker himself had to say that preservation of the shell of the existing League was intended. Furthermore, they had equal right to interpret the strong denunciation of the Covenant in the platform as justification for no action or for rejection. In his desire for party harmony Root had overreached himself.

He did his best, it is true, to check the trend of the Republican campaign which his ambiguous platform plank had invited, cabling from Europe in August, when the Republican managers began to refer to the League as "dead," that it was unwise to call it dead for it was not true. He warned, moreover, that "a new deal here from the beginning by abandoning the Versailles treaty is impossible." But it was futile for him to appeal, as he did in the same dispatch, to the Chicago platform. [30] When you fight something piecemeal and in detail for a long time, you come naturally and perhaps insensibly to combat the whole thing. You cannot be both for it and against it at the same time.

Nevertheless, the appeal of the Thirty-One bravely quoted the statements from Harding's speech of August 28, expressing willingness to "take and combine" the good parts of everything that existed, and

[30] New York Times, November 9, 1920.

called for his election as "most effectively advancing the cause of international co-operation to promote peace."

One leader did foresee clearly that the pro-League Republicans had lost all control of Republican policy. Dr. H. N. MacCracken, President of Vassar College, stated at the time: "Although I have been asked to sign the statement of Elihu Root in behalf of Senator Harding's candidacy, I cannot do so, for the reason that the names of those signing it will not in my opinion have any influence on Senator Harding's foreign policy after election. It seems to me that the same group of Republican Senators will control Republican policy who have controlled it in the past, and that nothing is to be expected from them in the way of international coöperation." [31]

It is not probable, however, that this conclusion was reached by more than a minority of Republican League advocates. When threescore of the most prominent and most respected Republicans in the country, former high officials and eminent intellectual leaders, united in a sober statement urging that Republican victory offered the best way into "an effective league to preserve peace" a very large number of troubled and hesitant Republican voters must have been confirmed in their desire to support the party nominee. It must be assumed, moreover, that the thirty-one leaders themselves put some confidence in Harding's pro-League manifestations. At the very least they must have hoped to commit him to what they desired so publicly that he could not turn back after the election. It is not credible that men of such standing were interested only in winning an election. They had the deepest kind of conviction that "an effective league to preserve peace" ought to be created. [32]

The Private Assurances of Harding. Furthermore, there is reason to believe that Harding personally gave them assurances that the pro-League half of him was really the better half. Professor Irving Fisher,

[31] *New York Times,* October 15, 1920.
Dr. Charles W. Eliot, of Harvard University, characterized the Root statement as "an extraordinary demonstration of partisanship." *New York Evening Post,* October 25, 1920.
[32] The statement of 121 Republicans and Progressives urging support of Cox on the League issue hardly offset the appeal of the Thirty-One. The signers were noted people and they were more numerous, but most of them did not have the national standing and influence that the Thirty-One had. The counter statement did show that fifteen out of twenty Republican officers of the League to Enforce Peace, who had declared themselves, were for Cox. *Springfield Republican,* October 18, 1920.
Herbert Parsons, Republican National Committeeman from New York, 1916 to 1920, resigned his party offices on October 19, to work for Cox and the League. *New York Evening Post,* October 20, 1920. The number of individual Republicans who left their party temporarily on the issue was undoubtedly large.

of Yale University, has testified publicly that in an interview with Harding, in July, 1920, the latter said, "I want the United States to get into the League just as much as you do. Of course I am opposed to the Wilson League, as I have always said, but the League can be changed. My idea is to call the nations together and ask them to make such amendments as are necessary to secure the approval of the United States."

Questioned on the score of feasibility, Harding gave the usual reply that the nations would be "only too glad to get us in on any terms" and explained that for reasons of political strategy his real views must not be published. The information was to be "personal but not confidential." Express permission was given Mr. Fisher "even in this campaign to tell your friends." [33]

It was only natural that Harding should supplement his public statements looking both ways on the League issue with private assurances to all those who came to sound him on either side of the question. Thus, again, after a visit to Marion, former Attorney General George W. Wickersham issued a statement saying that "Harding does not wholly or finally reject the League." [34]

Even after the election, and further public repudiation of the League, Senator Harding continued to inspire confidence in the Republicans desiring an effective league to preserve peace who talked with him personally.

The New York Times of January 4, 1921, for example, contains a statement by President Nicholas Murray Butler, after a seven-hour conference with Harding, expressing his confidence for the future, while Paul D. Cravath after an hour's talk with the President-elect said: "I return to New York with the feeling that those friends of international co-operation to promote peace who supported Senator

---

[33] New York Times, September 3, 1923; C. A. Berdahl, "The United States and the League of Nations," Michigan Law Review, April, 1929, Vol. 27, pp. 619–20. Ex-President Taft is quoted in the Times, of September 4, 1923, as having received this information from Mr. Fisher during the campaign. The same editorial notes that Taft later signed the statement of the Thirty-One.

[34] New York Times, September 6, 1920.

Speaking the next day with reference to the Wickersham statement Harding publicly held out hope, but not too definitely, that the good results achieved would be built upon. "It is folly to talk about a specific program," he said. "The specific thing must be evolved out of a conference of the best thought and highest capacity which can be brought together, not the diction of one spokesman. We are all agreed now that amendment or revision or reconstruction is possible and vastly better than reservations. Moreover, Europe is in accord, and has suggested that we lead the way. Manifestly the path is opening clearly and we shall play America's big part and hold fast to all America holds dear. There can be no lack of clarity about that!" New York Times, September 7, 1920.

Harding because they felt their cause was safest in his hands made no mistake."

Senator Hiram Johnson, on the other hand, defended Harding throughout the campaign from any League taint. Speaking at Los Angeles on September 25, he declared that he had received private assurances from the highest authority that the election of Harding meant the death of the League. Amplifying the point he referred not only to "the public records" but asserted that "the demonstration might be otherwise made." [35]

WILSON REPUDIATED

However large the number of Republican advocates of the League who were held in line by the Harding promises to remodel the League of Nations or provide an effective substitute—and they must have made a great army—there can be no doubt of the torrent of anti-Wilson support which flowed into Harding headquarters.

Racial Revenge. The editor of an Italian daily newspaper in Chicago called to assure the Senator that "The Fiume question has made all Americans of Italian extraction Republicans," [36] and George Sylvester Viereck, known nationally as a leader of militant German-American sentiment, headed an organization to deliver the five or six million votes of German-Americans to Harding. Governor Cox might be an estimable gentleman, "We do not know; neither do we care. As long as he is a supporter of the Wilson policies we are determined to defeat him. We have decided that there must not be another Democratic President for a generation." [37]

[35] *Springfield Republican,* October 3, 17, 1920; *New York Times,* October 2, 4, 9, 12, 14, 15, 17, 1920.

[36] *New York Times,* September 6, 1920.
The editor, also, was filled with confidence after his interview. "After talking with Senator Harding," he said, "I know that Italy will have an understanding friend when he is President. He knows the problem of the Adriatic. . . ."
An Italian newspaper in New York exhorted its readers that "not to vote for the adversary of Cox, the legatee of Wilson, is a betrayal of the mother country. Let Italians bear this in mind and consider the day of the presidential election as a day of sacred and imperative revenge." *Springfield Republican,* October 30, 1920.

[37] *New York Times,* September 5, 1920.
The *New York Sun* declared that "not one prominent German daily stands behind Governor Cox . . . and against him are added hundreds of German weekly and monthly periodicals which are rapidly coming into the field again." *Literary Digest,* September 18, 1920, p. 11.
Writing in 1930, Viereck said: "German-Americans were doubtless opposed in great numbers to the League as a matter of principle, but most of them were drawn into the fight not by that proclaimed motive but by the unproclaimed motive of punishing Wilson." George S. Viereck, *Spreading Germs of Hate,* N. Y., 1930, p. 266.

Irish partisans, while not so determined to punish the Democratic party, were equally resolved to overthrow Wilson and his works because of the President's refusal to take up the cause of Irish freedom. Following the President's refusal to see Daniel F. Cohalan, one of the most violent Irish leaders, the latter had pursued him, on his return from Paris, "like a gadfly." On his Western trip Wilson had been heralded by full page advertisements sarcastically attacking the League of Nations, and as he turned to another town another advertisement assailing his arguments had appeared in the local press. The advertisements were paid for by the Friends of Irish Freedom. [38]

War Resentments. Many other Americans for the moment were equally willing to dispose of Wilson and his Administration. The acts of the government during the war were inevitably an issue in the election, and a legion of minor irritations incident to it clamored for expression. Necessarily, too, the personality of the man who had led the nation's mighty war effort could not be kept out of consideration even though he was now retiring, an invalid. But aside from occasional half-apologetic references to Wilson's condition there was no effort to mitigate the storm of hatred which beat around him. On the contrary it was fanned, as the campaign proceeded, by rising denunciation of the "dictator" and "autocrat" in the White House. [39]

Party Feeling. From the hate of Wilson that burned through the land one might have concluded that he was a supreme enemy of his

---

[38] G. S. Viereck, *Spreading Germs of Hate,* p. 227.

With his eye to the future Viereck wrote soberly, ten years after the election of 1920, "Both the Allies and the Central Powers have joined hands at Geneva. Let us hope that their protagonists in the United States will permit the United States to decide our own course with regard to the League of Nations on purely American grounds." (P. 269.)

Suggesting a mature view of Wilson's attitude toward the war, Viereck records, incidentally to various parts of his story, his belief (1) that Wilson was sincere in his desire to see neither side crushed—a peace without victory, (2) that in the light of events it would have been better for Germany if the United States had entered the war at the sinking of the *Lusitania,* "before Germany was completely exhausted and the Allies too embittered to permit the peace envisaged by Woodrow Wilson," and (3) that "war madness, fanned still further by Allied intrigues" thwarted Wilson at the Peace Conference. (Pp. 266–68, 210–11.)

[39] When Governor Coolidge, the Republican candidate for Vice President, in one of his addresses toward the close of the campaign, expressed sympathy for Mr. Wilson and hope for his recovery, the *New York Times* considered it so notable that it asked who else had done likewise and added: "When the President was first stricken down a year ago, and during the weeks when he hung between life and death, not a word, not a whisper of concern or condolence came from the Republican Congress. And since then the attitude of his political opponents has been one of thinly concealed gloating over his breakdown. Never have they made a magnanimous gesture toward his sickroom." *New York Times,* October 29, 1920.

The same issue of the *Times* contains a further speech by Coolidge declaring his willingness to take the League of Nations amended, or a new one, but affirming his own belief that the Covenant was a compact, not a super-state.

country. The fury of local grievances and of racial masses merged into that deep resentment of the Republican ruling class which Dr. Randolph G. Adams, of the University of Michigan, has described as "based not upon any understanding of the world situation, not upon an outraged sense of fair play, not upon disgust with Europe's relapse into Metternichian diplomacy, not upon a feeling that Wilson was trying to behave like a Prime Minister who had lost his majority and was still trying to act as Prime Minister, but upon the underlying fact that jealousy was a predominant Republican emotion from 1912 to 1920. Fussy old gentlemen sitting in Union League Clubs in America never could and never would be able to reconcile themselves to the fact that at the greatest moment in world history the Presidential chair was occupied, not by one of the many second-rate mentalities whom the Republican party have so frequently considered worthy successors of Abraham Lincoln, but by a Democrat and the son of a Rebel." [40]

This sentiment, dormant at first because of the split in the Republican ranks and repressed by the tragedy of the world conflict, burst out as military victory came into sight, and, fed by the war on the League, rose to a climax in the "solemn referendum" which was to be its last chance of expression. Emotional cries and responses filled the air until it was electric with hate—not that such appeals were unusual in a political campaign; the soil had seldom been so ready for them before.

A Mountain of Malice. The reaction against Wilson was so violent that the *Springfield Republican,* at the close of the campaign, questioned whether "the systematic piling up of hatreds against a public man until a mountain of malice disfigures the national landscape" might not "finally serve as the demonstration of his future greatness." The large number of people moved by the anti-Wilson obsession were "themselves evidence of the tremendous impression the object of their fury has made upon this period." His most malignant enemies had, more-

---

[40] R. G. Adams, "Henry White," *Current History,* January, 1931, p. x.

Mark Sullivan, foremost of American political correspondents for a long period, writing also from the perspective of several years, described the situation as follows: "The League as we looked upon it in the Senate fight and in the Presidential campaign of 1920, was bound up with the personality of Woodrow Wilson and his political position. It carried the liability of the partisan bias against him and of the unwillingness of the opposing political party to take a step which would have exalted him in history, which would have labelled him as a great leader and his work as a success, and would have implied such an approval of him as should logically have been followed by keeping his party in power. All that burden the League question carried in 1920." Mark Sullivan, "America and the League: Six Years After," *World's Work,* January, 1926, Vol. 51, p. 289.

over, "by their assaults compelled the perpetual identification of the President's name with an ideal of international organization that is simply deathless." Even the killing of "Wilson's League" in a tempest of passion would insure his own survival as an idealist and prophet, for when war next came on a large scale the thought that it might have been prevented by the assassinated "Wilson League" would capture the imagination of posterity. [41]

Overwhelming Defeat. But the opponents of Wilson were little interested in the verdict of history. Their joy was complete when the election returns gave them the unheard of electoral victory of 16,152,-220 votes for Harding to 9,147,553 for Cox—a triumph which they interpreted as a smashing repudiation of the "Wilson League." William H. Taft denied any such result, [42] and the newly elected Vice President, Calvin Coolidge, said soon after the election: "I doubt if any particular mandate was given in the last election on the question of the League of Nations and if it was the preponderant issue." [43]

---

[41] *Springfield Republican,* October 30, 1920.
The *New York Evening Post* held editorially, on October 26, 1920, that the desire to punish was the only cement that held the Harding ranks together.
[42] *Springfield Republican,* November 4, 1920.
The Senatorial returns in a number of States showed that candidates opposing the League ran considerably behind Harding while their Democratic opponents fared noticeably better than Cox. Thus in Connecticut, Brandegee received 12,446 votes less than Harding while his opponent was 11,103 votes ahead of Cox. In New Hampshire, where the total vote was less than 100,000, Moses was 5,610 votes behind Harding and his opponent 2,363 ahead of Cox. In New York, while 1,869,911 votes were cast for Harding, Wadsworth received but 1,451,225, and the Democratic candidate ran 117,331 votes ahead of Cox (897,999 to 780,668).
Similar results were also to be found in the West. In Idaho, the Democratic Senator Nugent, who had stood for the League, received 17,937 votes more than Cox (64,513 to 46,576), while the successful Republican, Gooding, had 12,336 votes less than Harding (88,321 to 75,985). Similarly, in California, Senator Plehan, standing for the League, ran 152,389 votes ahead of Cox while Shortridge, who strongly opposed the League, ran 217,057 votes behind Harding, though elected by a substantial majority. In Colorado, again, Nicholson received 16,671 votes less than Harding while Scott was 8,354 ahead of Cox. *World Almanac,* 1921, pp. 686, 687, 688, 690, 704, 705-7.
So many factors entered into the various State contests, of course, that these figures do nothing more than indicate that opposition to the League probably reduced considerably the majorities of some Republican candidates for the Senate and that advocacy of it did not prevent Democratic Senatorial candidates from making a good showing in the face of the anti-Administration landslide.
[43] Statement of November 23, 1920, to a group of business men in Boston. *New York Times,* December 10, 1923.
Walter Lippman has summarized the elements making up the Republican avalanche as follows: "The Republican majority was composed of men and women who thought a Republican victory would kill the League, plus those who thought it was the most practical way to procure the League, plus those who thought it the surest way offered to obtain an amended League. All these voters were inextricably entangled with their own desire or the desire of the other voters to improve business, or put labor in its place, or to punish the Democrats for going to war, or to punish them for not having gone sooner, or to get rid of Mr. Burleson, or to improve the price of wheat, or to lower taxes, or to stop Mr. Daniels from outbuilding the (naval)

Both League and Association Abandoned

The President-elect, however, expressed no doubts about the significance of the vote. Speaking to a victory celebration of fellow-townsmen, November 4th, he said, "You just didn't want a surrender of the United States of America; you wanted America to go on under American ideals. That's why you didn't care for the League which is now deceased." [44]

Habit and the vague belief which he may have developed that he could somehow provide a substitute led him to go on to promise once more "to ask for nations associated together in justice"—an association which he had often admitted he did not know how to bring about, and which he was to discover that the "best minds," whom he did proceed to consult, would not provide him with. [45]

There is no record that Harding regretted that failure. No effort that has come to light was made to modify the League of Nations to meet Republican objections. The growth of the League from 33 members on March 10, 1920, to 48 by the time the first meeting of the Assembly adjourned, late in 1920, was evidence enough that trial of international "association" was going to be made through the existing organization, but no attempt was made to achieve association through the pro-League half of the Republican platform and of the Harding campaign promises.

The new Administration was not bound to take such action, of course. It was entitled, if it chose, to interpret the election returns as the result of its anti-League commitments. It might have reasoned that the anti-Wilson, anti-Administration vote was by no means all

---

world, or to help Mr. Harding to do the same thing." Walter Lippman, *Public Opinion*, N. Y., 1922, pp. 195–6.

For a thorough discussion of the election of 1920 as a mandate on the League see the book by Samuel Colcord, *The Great Deception*, N. Y., 1921.

[44] *New York Times*, November 5, 1920.

[45] In addition to the men mentioned earlier in this chapter, Charles E. Hughes discussed the outlook with Harding on December 10. George Harvey unexpectedly joined the conference. Herbert Hoover urged the revision of the League rather than its scrapping, on December 13. He recommended this policy to prevent the reopening of "ten thousand questions closed in documents already executed." Colonel Harvey, still a guest in Harding's home, was not on hand to greet Mr. Hoover. William H. Taft conferred on December 24. He found Harding "properly chary of a definite program," but "in an accommodating state of mind." December 29 found Senator McCumber, concluding that the League was dead, advising a new association and Oscar S. Straus, former Secretary of Commerce and Labor, suggesting the contrary. Senator Knox apparently closed the association of the best minds, on December 30, by picturing to the coming President in graphic fashion the possibilities of a factional fight if the Administration asked for any sort of membership in the League. Knox issued from the conference confident that no such recommendation would be made. *New York Times*, December 11, 14, 25, 30, 31, 1920.

opposed to the League by conviction, but the demand of Wilson for a decision of the League issue in the election did give ample ground for letting the returns speak for themselves.

It was easier, moreover, and for the time being politically safer to adhere to the anti-League pledges given during the canvass. "In compliance with its pledges," said Harding after his inauguration, "the Administration which came into power in March, 1921, definitely and decisively put aside all thoughts of entering the League of Nations. It doesn't propose to enter now, by the side door, back door, or cellar door." [46]

Though entitled to take this position, if he elected to do so, the decision left the whole siege of the Republican leaders for reservations under a permanent cloud. If the League was something so dangerous that membership in it could not be accepted under any circumstances, the leaders should have followed Borah and Johnson from the beginning, fighting the thing root and branch. No palliative "reservations" would be of avail. If, on the other hand, the reservations did make American co-operation in the League safe, as was contended so incessantly for many months, if their purpose was really to safeguard American membership rather than to prevent it, then strong considerations of honor demanded that the constructive yet truly conservative course be adhered to.

The plea that circumstances were changing too rapidly to admit of any action would not do. The Covenant had not changed, though an effort of Canada, in the first Assembly, to have Article 10 struck out offered a splendid opportunity for the new Administration to push the Republican claim to membership without that obligation. The Republican leaders, moreover, could no longer make use of the cry that only Wilson's stubbornness prevented the acceptance of the Republican reservations. This could not continue to be true when power was passing to them. Suffice it to say that when the Treaty came into their hands no effort was made to ratify it with the Lodge reservations, or any others. Instead, a separate treaty of peace was eventually negotiated, after further months of delay, which any careful analysis must show retained all the benefits of the Treaty of Versailles that it could, without assuming any of its responsibilities.

Not only did reaction ride so far, but it was characterized by a persistent hope that the "Wilson League" would die in its infancy. It was avoided as if pestilent. It was repeatedly referred to by the Presi-

[46] Howland, *American Foreign Relations 1928*, p. 300.

dent and others as "dead," though they continued to denounce it as a "super-government." [47] Repeated announcements of decease, so contrary to evident fact, were also accompanied by a refusal even to acknowledge receipt of communications from the League. These documents, dealing mostly with humanitarian questions, but including proposals to change the Covenant which might have been warmly welcomed, piled up in the State Department for more than six months before acknowledgment of their receipt was finally given by circuitous means. [48]

The triumph of the Senate cabal was complete. "Normalcy" held sway in both foreign and home affairs, with results of which there is now little disposition to speak.

[47] Clarence A. Berdahl, "The United States and the League of Nations," *Michigan Law Review*, April, 1929, Vol. 27, p. 620.
Mark Sullivan, speaking especially of the bitter-enders (into whose ranks the regular reservationists had been largely merged), observed later that while their fight was nominally against joining the League, "actually it was a fight against the League itself. It was impossible (for men of their temperament certainly) to fight against America joining the League without fighting the League itself, impossible to fight the League without hating the League, and impossible to hate the League without wishing it to die. They were not able to say to the League, 'We will not join you, but God bless you anyhow.'" "America and the League: Six Years After," *World's Work*, January, 1926, Vol. 51, p. 291.
[48] *Ibid.* (Berdahl), p. 622–25; *New York Times*, July 18, 1921, October 19, 1924.

CHAPTER XIX

WILSON AND LODGE

Further lapse of time will be needed to establish the full effects of the failure of the United States to enter the League of Nations in 1920. The view of many still continues to be that the United States was saved from destruction in that year and that its safety still forbids any regular participation in the world's councils. "Political" association, they believe, is not necessary to American prosperity or world stability, and we can continue indefinitely without participation in anything resembling world government.

The view of this group is tacitly shared by a larger number, who, comprehending vaguely the forces which led to the result, take it for granted that the decision must have been a wise one. Did not the people decide to stay out—and by a huge majority? To those who assume that majorities are always right, and who further assume the clearness of the verdict of 1920, the impression that there must have been something dangerous about the Covenant comes easily. To a people worshipping bigness, the suggestion of a huge majority against a proposal carries its own answer.

The working of technological and economic forces, however, steadily reduces the number of people so minded, and increases the ranks of those who feel that a mutually effective and reasonably satisfactory relationship, economic, political, and moral, between the United States and the rest of the world will work itself out—or be compelled by events—in time to save modern civilization from economic collapse related strongly to the moral and material destruction of the Great War, and from the almost certain catastrophe to life as we know it which would come from an attempt on a considerable scale to change present unsatisfactory conditions by military means.

A third group of serious people believes, that the very limited participation of the world's greatest nation in international political life for a generation following the disorganization of the war, will prove to be a disaster for which few parallels in history can be found and one which can never be retrieved.

We cannot certainly know which of these attitudes will be vindicated. The answer can only be given by the working out of forces which no man, no political party, or no nation can wholly control. In the same measure we cannot pass a wholly complete judgment upon the work of the leaders of the great controversy of 1918 to 1920. Many facts are still unknown, and the ultimate, final wisdom of the stand of either side is still to be fully demonstrated.

In the meantime, some further facts and observations concerning the activity of the two leading actors in the struggle appear to be relevant.

The Attitude of Lodge

The position of Senator Lodge in the long controversy was sufficiently veiled that his close associates, and direct descendants, now disagree as to what he really sought to do. Some say he attempted to help take the United States into the League and others that he sought only to emasculate it.

Thus Mrs. Corinne Roosevelt Robinson, a sister of President Roosevelt, at a meeting of the Foreign Policy Association, in New York City, January 4, 1930, declared that as a guest in his house, she had breakfast with Senator Lodge on the day of the final vote on the League, March 19, 1920, and that "He told me that he was going to come back that afternoon with the promise of the signing of the League (of our going into the League with reservations), and I asked him if he was sure of it. He said that he was sure of a certain number of Democrats who would vote with a certain number of Republicans for the United States to go into the League with strict reservations, but to go into the League."

After the vote in the Senate, continued Mrs. Robinson, "I was at the door to meet him when he came back, and he went into his library with a very heavy brow. He said, 'Just as I expected to get my Democrats to vote with my Republicans on going into the League, a hand came out of the White House and drew back those Democrats, and prevented our going into the League with reservations.'" [1]

[1] See the report of the 121st New York Luncheon Discussion.

Some weeks later Mr. Henry Morgenthau, former Ambassador to Turkey, who had participated in the Foreign Policy Association discussion, published in the *New York Herald Tribune,* of March 7, 1930, a letter from Mrs. Clarence C. Williams, a daughter of Senator Lodge, which stated that she had been in close association and conference with the Senator during the struggle and that "My father hated and feared the Wilson league and his heart was really with the irreconcilables. But it was uncertain whether this league could be beaten straight out in this way, and the object of his reservations was so to emasculate the Wilson pact that if it did pass it would be valueless, and the United States would be honorably safeguarded. My father never wanted the Wilson league, and when it was finally defeated he was like a man from whom a great burden had been lifted."

Shortly thereafter, there appeared in the same newspaper a statement from Henry Cabot Lodge, a grandson of Senator Lodge, which read as follows:

The current discussion with regard to the attitude of Senator Henry Cabot Lodge at the time of the League of Nations debate has just come to my attention and in order to keep the historical record perfectly clear I should like to make a few observations. Mrs. Corinne Roosevelt Robinson is right when she says that no interpretation of Senator Lodge's attitude is necessary since he has himself stated for all time what his attitude was. As he has said, he gave the League with reservations "genuine support" and was surprised when President Wilson drew away enough Democrats to prevent its ratification on that basis. Whether he was disappointed or not is, of course, a matter of personal impression. He certainly had favored some sort of machinery for international co-operation earlier in his career and in the last years of his life he inclined to the belief that fate had been good to the United States by keeping it out of the League altogether.

There is certainly no foundation in fact for the statement that he was "an irreconcilable at heart," although my personal feelings are such that I should be proud to think that he was. This thought, however, cannot be sustained. Mrs. Robinson, who was one of Senator Lodge's most intimate friends, deserves to be heeded when she discusses this question because, in addition to her friendship, she was staying in Senator Lodge's house in Washington in March, 1920, when the debate reached its climax and was in closer touch with actual events than almost anyone else. [2]

[2] *New York Herald Tribune,* March 25, 1930.

The record as to Senator Lodge's advocacy of a league to enforce peace is clear, as is that of his change of position soon after President Wilson espoused the same cause. It does not necessarily follow, however, that Lodge changed his mind for no other reason. It is well known that in the early part of the Wilson period Lodge successfully resisted the temptation to alter his stand when Wilson came to the same ground, and that he defended himself in words that are still memorable. In his famous "water's edge" speech of April 9, 1914, delivered during the Panama Canal Tolls debate, Lodge said:

> I am not blind to the political temptations which the situation at this moment presents. I am a strong party man. I believe in government by parties and in party responsibility. I have for many years fought the battles of the Republican party, alike in days of sunshine and in days of storm and darkness. If life and strength continue, I shall to the best of my ability oppose President Wilson if he is a candidate for re-election and the party which he leads. The allurements of political advantage appeal to me as strongly as they can to any man. But when the relations of my country with other nations are involved I cannot yield to them. My politics has always stopped at the water's edge.

Saying that this feeling had twice at least led him to oppose treaties submitted by Presidents of his own party (arbitration treaties) and to support a Democratic President in the Venezuela controversy, Lodge defined the limits of legitimate political warfare in connection with foreign affairs in terms that have never been excelled. Continuing, he said:

> I voted and spoke against the toll exemption embodied in the canal act. I cannot change now merely because a Democratic President recommends the repeal of that clause which I earnestly resisted. Within our borders Mr. Wilson is the leader and chief of the Democratic party. In the presence of foreign nations he is to me simply the President of the United States. If in his high responsibility as the representative of the nation before the world he does or tries to do what I believe in my conscience to be wrong I shall resist him, no matter what his political faith may be. But if he is doing or trying to do what I conscientiously believe to be right he shall have my support without regard to

party or to politics. To thwart the purposes or to discredit the policies of the official head of a political party is legitimate political warfare. To discredit or break down the President of the United States upon a question of foreign policy is quite another thing, never to be undertaken except for very grave reasons. In the one case we overthrow a party leader and political chief within the arena where the American people alone sit in judgment, in the other we break down and discredit the representative of the whole country in the great forum of the nations of the earth and paralyze his future power and usefulness in that field where he and he alone can declare and represent the policies, the honor, and the dignity of the United States. Conditions may arise where this last resort must be accepted, but it can only be justified by grim necessity. [3]

Much had happened between 1914 and 1918. The whole course of the Great War had been run, in the midst of which President Wilson had been unexpectedly re-elected. He had then led the United States into the struggle and through it to victory. Much had transpired, too, to change the relations between the two men. The correct principles governing the attitude of Senators toward the Executive conduct of foreign affairs had not altered.

What then was the "grim necessity" which led the Senate leaders to demand suddenly that the Paris Conference propose no League of Nations? What grim necessity drove them to insist passionately that if such a project were drawn up it should be an afterthought of the Conference—by no means a part of the treaty of peace? What pressing need led Roosevelt and Lodge to hold a consultation, before the Conference had decided even to attempt the creation of a League, in which a programme of reservations was agreed upon? Did the national safety demand agreement upon the efficacious way to attack the Covenant before a word of it was penned?

What, moreover, were the "grave reasons" which led Lodge to attempt to send, by Henry White, to the President's prospective opponents in the Conference, a store of information for use against "the representative of the whole country in the great forum of the nations?" [4] The necessity must have been grave which led Lodge to

[3] *Congressional Record*, Vol. 51, Pt. 7, p. 6456.
[4] Rabbi Stephen S. Wise, who was in Paris while President Wilson was negotiating the treaty, has described an active press campaign against the President in the Parisian press, directed from the United States. For a considerable time a series

father a written demand of Senators, after the first draft of the Covenant was approved by representatives of fourteen nations, that the project be suppressed. Grave need, indeed, must have impelled Lodge to telegraph all Republican Senators to express no opinion of the revised Covenant, pending conference, and to secure the assistance of the total opponents of the League for his reservation campaign.

It is true that Wilson took no outstanding Republicans with him and that he lost a close mid-term election. Did this omission and this failure constitute sober ground for a sustained effort to "paralyze his future power and usefulness in that field where he and he alone can declare and represent the policies, the honor, and the dignity of the United States," when he was striving to achieve a universal aspiration so powerful that the Senators, by their own admission, dared not attack it openly in their own country? [5]

Surely nothing less than profound alarm at the consequences of American leadership in a mutual effort of the nations to establish peace and security could have justified a long and carefully planned advance organization against a treaty, before it could be submitted to the Senate for its approval. What, in fact, led Lodge and his associates to conclude, at the close of a war in which the United States had helped to destroy the political system in all central Europe, that their country could play only a carefully restricted part in future world politics—if any? What had happened which would destroy their confidence in the ability of their country to play a part of leadership in the world?

In the address lately quoted from, Lodge had stated his pride in the limited pre-war leadership of the United States, as follows: "When the year 1909 opened, the United States occupied a higher and stronger position among the nations of the earth than at any period in our history. Never before had we possessed such an influence in interna-

---

of articles by Judson C. Welliver appeared in the *Echo de Paris* and *Le Matin* arguing that any ultimate negotiations would have to be made with the Republican members of the Senate Foreign Relations Committee. The President had passed from power and was negligible.

The articles, the cabling of which cost a good deal of money, became so bitter, both personally and politically, that Clemenceau had to order them stopped.

Mr. Welliver turned up later as press agent to Harding in the Republican campaign of 1920. *New York Evening Post,* October 20, 1920.

[5] The testimony of one of the strongest opponents of the League may be added. Dr. David J. Hill, in *The Problem of a World Court* (N. Y., 1927) wrote: "It will be recalled that when, in 1919, the Senate of the United States was invited to ratify the Treaty of Peace made in Paris and signed at Versailles, the whole country was at the moment favorable to ratification" (pp. 88–89).

tional affairs, and that influence had been used beneficently and for the world's peace in two conspicuous instances—at Portsmouth and at Algeciras. . . . A world power we had been for many long years, but we had at last become a world power in the finer sense, a power whose active participation and beneficent influence were recognized and desired by other nations in those great questions which concerned the welfare and happiness of all mankind." [6]

What had happened after 1914 to destroy Lodge's pride in his country's international leadership? Was he opposed to American intervention in the war? If so it was never suspected. No one was more stern in its prosecution than the Senator and his associates. They enjoyed it so much in fact that they opposed its cessation. Smash them back to Berlin! No soft peace!—was their cry, as the German lines and morale crumbled and the enemy appealed to President Wilson for peace. No one could have been more filled with confidence in American power and resourcefulness than the group of leaders of whom George Harvey assumed the direction at this juncture.

What in truth did suddenly chill these men with fear when the President of the United States, in fulfillment of his incessant pledges, and "in his high responsibility as the representative of the nation before the world," moved to make permanent the position of the United States as "a world power in the finer sense, a power whose active participation and beneficent influence were recognized and desired by other nations in those great questions which concerned the welfare and happiness of all mankind?"

In 1914 no one had deplored the loss of such a position more than Lodge. He said with regret that the leadership of the Roosevelt era had been lost, both in the old world and the new. "Rightly or wrongly," he added, "they have come to believe that we are not to be trusted; that we make our international relations the sport of politics and treat them as if they were in no wise different from domestic legislation."

What had transpired since 1914 that made it proper for the Senate leaders to handle the greatest treaty ever laid before them much as they

---

[6] *Congressional Record*, Vol. 57, Pt. 7, p. 6455.
The instructions of Secretary Root to White and Gummere, the American delegates to the Algeciras Conference, had said: "The complete dissociation of the United States from all motives which might tend to thwart a perfect agreement of the powers should, in case of need, lend weight to your impartial counsels." *Foreign Relations of the United States*, 1905, pp. 678–80.

would treat a rivers and harbors appropriation bill? The multitude of direct amendments to the treaty failed, truly enough, to be later translated into "reservations," but they were defeated in spite of the leaders.[7]

Few things are clearer than the determination of Lodge and his collaborators, formed before the creation of the Covenant, that it should have reservations attached to it. This resolve never gave way to the strongest pressure. "If the president adheres to his position that we must ratify it without crossing a 't' or dotting an 'i'," wrote Lodge to White on July 2, 1919, "my best judgment is that he will fail. The treaty will be sent to him with reservations, and then it will be up to him to hold it back. I am giving a good deal of time and thought to it." [8]

To two visitors later in the same month Lodge gave a clearer idea of the situation in which the President would be when the reservations were presented to him. On July 21, 1919, the majority leader was visited by Mr. James G. McDonald, Chairman of the League of Free Nations Association, and Mr. Allen T. Burns, President of the National Conference of Social Work, in behalf of the treaty. Mr. Burns' account of the interview is as follows: "In our discussion of the treaty situation with Senator Lodge he summarized his attitude and purpose in the following manner: Taking from the shelves of the foreign relations committee room a copy of the general arbitration treaty with Great Britain negotiated by President Taft in 1911, the chairman pointed out the amendments and reservations made by the Senate. Exultingly he remarked: 'And President Taft never saw fit to return the treaty to Great Britain. We shall deal with the Versailles treaty in the same way. If President Wilson does not see fit to return it to our allies that is his responsibility.' Then with a snap of his jaw and a bang of his fist, 'That is the way to handle such treaties!'" [9]

"Such treaties!" The yearning of the race for some insurance of

---

[7] Referring to the defeat of the direct amendments, Lodge said later: "Personally I never could see the force of this objection because just as much time would have been consumed by the consideration of reservations by each of the Powers as by the consideration of amendments." Lodge, *The Senate and the League of Nations*, p. 162.

[8] Nevins, *Henry White*, p. 455. On May 20, he wrote: "And what the final judgment of the people will be I do not know. There is no doubt the hostility to the League of Nations has grown, and if they adopt it, it will be a sorry day for the country in years to come which you and I are not likely to see" (p. 451).

If this expression represented a matured judgment, and a true prophecy, Lodge may be vindicated in the future for having sought to kill indirectly what he was not strong enough to prevent openly.

[9] The *Springfield Republican*, October 31, 1920. Previously published in the *New York Evening Post*, after careful consideration by its editor, Edwin F. Gay. Verified by an interview with Mr. Burns on August 26, 1931.

settled international order made no more impression upon Lodge than had President Taft's constructive attempt to make arbitration something more than a name, or a method of settlement occasionally used for minor disputes.

The purpose of the reservations, moreover, that would encumber the treaty when it reached the President, could not have been more clearly stated, and, needless to say, the determination to affix them grew as popular opinion approved. "Strong and effective reservations will be put on," wrote Lodge again, on October 2, as Wilson returned to Washington from the West. "I feel very sure that there is now a decisive majority for them, not only Republicans, but some Democrats; and this is certain: if they are not put on, the treaty will be killed on the floor of the Senate." [10]

But the likelihood that this method of execution would be necessary was already small. Reservations would be put on. As time passed the likelihood that Wilson would be able to keep them from coming up to him, by two-thirds vote of the Senate, increased, but in any event, as Lodge assured White on March 11, 1920, "the President would receive the blame for defeating the treaty." [11]

To bring about such an astonishing reversal of positions was indeed an ambitious plan. To turn the tables on Wilson entirely, to leave him condemned for having defeated his own treaty, required strategy both bold and subtle. The risk was great but the stakes were high. If success came, not only would the one threat to the re-establishment of Republican supremacy be removed, but it would be possible to ascribe to Wilson failure as great as his achievement then loomed. It would be possible for future historians to say, as Lodge himself later wrote in the concluding words of his book, that Wilson "was given the greatest opportunity ever given to any public man in modern times, which we may date from the Revival of Learning in Europe. Having this opportunity he tried to use it and failed. The failure necessarily equalled the opportunity in magnitude and the failure was complete and was all his own. No one could have destroyed such a vast opportunity except the man to whom it was given, and in this work of destruction unaided and alone Mr. Wilson was entirely successful. Difficult as such an achievement in the face of such an opportunity was, it does not warrant describing the man who wrought the destruction in any sense as a 'very great man.' " [12]

[10] Nevins, *Henry White*, p. 467.   [11] *Ibid.*, p. 486.
[12] Lodge, *The Senate and the League of Nations*, p. 226.

To be able to lay the blame for the "destruction" of the greatest opportunity ever given to modern man upon Wilson, "unaided and alone," it was essential to gauge with great care just what Wilson himself would do. If the reservations were mild he might accept them and put them into effect; if they were too drastic, on the other hand, he might be able to rally public opinion to his side so strongly as to give him victory. If they could attack, in a sufficiently offensive manner, things which he would be sure to defend, and at the same time seem moderate to the public in aim, the proper mean would be achieved.

Hence Lodge devoted himself tirelessly to the task of anticipating, at every stage of the fight, just what Wilson's reaction would be. Lodge explains with great clearness, in that strange defense which he left behind him, how he performed this function. "As the final vote drew near," he records, "I felt convinced that it was quite possible that the treaty with the reservations would be adopted by the Senate because it was obvious to me that on this final and crucial test a majority of the Democrats would be unwilling to vote against ratification. But I also felt convinced that President Wilson would prevent the acceptance of the treaty with reservations if he possibly could. I based this opinion on *the knowledge which I had acquired as to Mr. Wilson's temperament, intentions and purposes.* I had learned from a careful study of the President's acts and utterances during those trying days —and it was as important for me to understand him as it was for his closest friends—that the key to all he did was that he thought of everything in terms of Wilson." [13]

To give a supreme demonstration of his key to Wilson's character, Lodge continues: "The most striking illustration of his absorption in himself to the exclusion of everything else was shown at the time of the last vote in the Senate on the Versailles treaty. After the vote had been taken and the treaty defeated, Senator Brandegee, an 'irreconcilable,' turned to me and said, 'We can always depend on Mr. Wilson. He never has failed us. He has used all his powers to defeat the treaty, because we would not ratify it in just the form which he desired.' I replied, 'That is quite true. Without his efforts the treaty would have been accepted by the Senate today.' " [14]

There can be little doubt that this final vote was both a victory and

[13] Lodge, *The Senate and the League of Nations*, p. 212. Italics supplied.

"Lodge from his grave," wrote Mark Sullivan in 1926, "is still emitting undying hate against his rival in the shape of a book conceived as a self-justification but unable to avoid being partly an *apologia pro vita sua* and partly a last thrust of malevolence." "America and the League: Six Years After," *World's Work*, January, 1926, Vol. 51, p. 289.

[14] Lodge, p. 214.

a defeat for Lodge. The number of votes cast for the reservations, plus those of the irreconcilables who had made them possible, probably insured political victory, but the responsibility was less clearly upon Wilson, "unaided and alone," than Lodge would have liked. Knowing that he was within a few votes of sending the treaty to Wilson, and knowing that the tide flowed his way, Lodge believed that when the final die was cast he would get the two-thirds majority and place the onus squarely upon Wilson. If Wilson did accept the reservations, under these circumstances, the achievement which the League represented would do his party little good in the election. But Wilson was depended on not to accept them, in which case both his historical and political position would be more doubtful than it was now to be with his rejection of the reservations veiled in the votes of Senators.

The historical advantage thereby lost did not weigh long upon Lodge; the immediate victory was the main goal. But as a student and writer of history he was not unmindful of the future placing of responsibility for the "destruction" of the greatest opportunity of the age. He had plenty of reason to return to his home with "a very heavy brow" and with regret for the complete victory of which he had been deprived.

It is probable, too, that given the immediate victory Lodge would have been glad to escape the rôle of going down as one noted only for his obstructive power, even though his negative attitude toward great treaties might prove eventually to be preservative. But again the certainty of his conviction that he knew what Wilson would do forbade that hope, if the President retained any real influence in the Senate. "This conviction held by me as to the governing quality of Mr. Wilson's mind and character," he reiterates, "was reached very slowly and only finally arrived at when I found myself confronted with a situation, the gravity of which in its public importance could not be exaggerated, and *when a correct analysis of Mr. Wilson's probable attitude was an element of vital moment to me* in trying to solve the intricate problem which I and those with whom I acted were compelled to face." [15]

And on the last page of the book Lodge states once more: "As the strenuous days which were filled by the contest over the League of Nations passed by, almost every one bringing its difficulty and its crucial question, I made no mistake in my estimate of what President Wilson would do under certain conditions." [16]

[15] Lodge, *The Senate and the League of Nations*, pp. 218–19. Italics supplied.
[16] *Ibid.*, p. 226.

HENRY CABOT LODGE

The purpose of this persistent re-emphasis was, of course, to drive home Lodge's explanation of Wilson's character, not to make clear the key to his own action and that of his associates who fought under the direction of George Harvey. But Lodge did inadvertently leave it to be explained why, if the campaign against the Covenant was waged only to protect American future safety, it should be of such moment to know exactly what Wilson would do. If the Covenant, amended as it had been, represented an attempt at world statesmanship the "destruction" of which would be of colossal consequence, it was the duty of the Senate leaders to approve it. If, on the other hand, it contained danger so grave as to justify rejection, the leaders should have either rejected it or set forth their terms without reference to what Wilson would do about them. There would be no need to study his every word and act to see what their own next move should be, or to determine confidently just what their action would bring from him. No refinement and shading of terms would then have been necessary.

To the pursuance of a course of sincere and single minded devotion to national duty, regardless of consequences or of the stand of others, it may be objected that Lodge was the leader of the Republican Party, and that with his followers split, as completely as they could be, a shrewd policy was necessary to hold the party together. This is true. No party leader, either, ever labored harder or more successfully than did Lodge in the party crisis which confronted him. It is doubtful if any man ever performed a more difficult political feat. In skill of parliamentary maneuver, in ability to manipulate factions against each other, and to his own purpose, Lodge may never be excelled. If devoted service to party is a claim to grateful remembrance, the name of Lodge should never be omitted from any mention of party heroes.

Lodge's service to his party in 1919 and 1920 cost him much. In dashing from first one end of his line to the other, to hold back the over zealous and stimulate the reluctant, he incurred perpetually the resentment and suspicion of one faction and sometimes of all. Moves to ignore him or to unseat him were bruited repeatedly.[17] People who wanted to charge ahead, to move cautiously and to move not at all

---

[17] See *The Mirrors of Washington*, N. Y., 1921, p. 207. Referring to the violence of the pressure exerted upon him by the irreconcilables, Lodge once said plaintively that they addressed him in language which "no man of my age should be obliged to hear." Mark Sullivan, "America and the League: Six Years After," *World's Work*, January, 1926, Vol. 51, p. 291.

naturally resented being drawn along at a common pace. Yet in the end Lodge made them sing essentially the same battle song. To change the figure slightly, he tuned the roar of the lion down to the maximum pitch of the dove until the resultant chorus, while somewhat discordant, possessed the elements of harmony.

The difficulties of this accomplishment, and its aim, have been excellently epitomized by Senator Lodge in a letter of May 25, 1920, to Harvey, accompanying a draft of the keynote speech he expected to make at the Chicago convention, "subject to your revision." "In regard to the League," wrote Lodge, "no one knows better than you what a narrow channel I have to navigate in, with rocks on both sides. I want to condemn Wilson and all his works. That is comparatively easy, and I think I have done it. I also want to get the Convention to give a full approval of all that the Republican Senators did, drawing no distinctions between their differing opinions as to the final result. That is, I seek to make my speech, and I hope the platform, so broad that those of us who have fought the treaty for a year in the Senate can all stand upon it without any difficulty, and that we can use every argument, from Borah's down to McCumber's. I think the bulk of the Convention and the mass of the people at the present moment are in favor of the treaty with the reservations which bear my name. But I do not want to make any pledge as to the future." [18]

Even after his success in holding the Republican Senators together one might have doubted the feasibility of "using every argument from Borah's down to McCumber's" in the campaign, for if Borah got what he wanted McCumber was bound to be disappointed, and if McCumber's beliefs were recognized Borah's position was hopeless. No platform and no action could possibly express the convictions of both. Nevertheless, as we have seen, the miracle was performed, to the extent at least that was necessary. From the standpoint of political strategy the only criticism that can be made of Lodge and his associates is that they performed their work too well. The prevailing political winds, measured with fair accuracy by most observers of the time, were so strong that a clear position for the League, with the reservations, might have been taken without serious risk of the resulting defection being decisive. [19] The leaders did not certainly know this, however, and they meant to make sure.

[18] Johnson, *George Harvey*, p. 274. Lodge gives the swiftly shifting scene in Europe as his reason for not wishing any definite commitment.

[19] Charles D. Hilles, Republican National Committeeman from New York in 1920, warned on July 8, 1919, as the treaty was laid before the Senate, that "There

They did so. But in the process they cast overboard without a qualm the reservations which they had labored so many months to "perfect," and which they had convinced the American people were necessary to safeguard their ancient liberties. The conviction having been generally established that the League might be safely entered, under the protection of the Republican reservations, these precious phrases in whose behalf the nation had been rocked for months were *spurlus versenkt* without a sign of regret from the coterie of Senators who had become the nation's rulers.

The election being won, Senator Lodge was content to state that "The people of the United States have declared that they will not accept or enter upon Mr. Wilson's League of Nations which he brought home from Paris and laid before the Senate. So far as the United States is concerned that League is dead." [20]

THE POSITION OF WILSON

In contrast to the subtle attitudes of Lodge, the position of Wilson in his contest with the Senate leaders is usually assumed to be simple. He negotiated a treaty, it is said, presented it to the Senate and demanded its acceptance, without any qualification or reservation. Stubbornly insisting, the charge runs, that not a line of it should be altered, and taking all opposition as a personal insult to himself, he preferred to see the treaty die rather than yield an inch. After having compromised heavily with the foreigners, in negotiating the treaty, he refused to concede anything whatever to his own people.

Woodrow Wilson will always remain a secondary figure, we are told, because he would not compromise. The names of the great who became so through a talent for compromising are not quoted. The ability to compromise at the proper time and in the right degree is a high gift which few statesmen have had. Much more frequently the habit of compromising has led to a willingness to agree when the proper course was to stand and fight. There are some issues that cannot be compromised and no amount of desire to be accommodating can make the wrong course the right one. At such times compromise

---

is no danger that President Wilson will perpetuate his power through his advocacy of the League unless the Republicans make a partisan issue of the Covenant. The League is an idea born out of the agony of the war, out of the determination that the incalculable waste of life and treasure shall hereafter be neither the aim nor the fate of civilized nations. McKinley, Hay, Roosevelt, Root, Choate and Taft sponsored it before Mr. Wilson came into power." *New York Times,* July 8, 1919.

[20] *New York Times,* November 21, 1920.

only means surrender. The two men, for example, both famed for their ability at compromise, who at different times tried to save the League by compromising with the opposition did it far more harm than good.

A reputation for agreeability, moreover, breeds popular distrust in a leader. To compromise is easy. Few can refuse to do so. Woodrow Wilson could. He was at times, also, too hard a fighter, a fact which makes the charge that he refused to make any concession to sincere opposition to the League of Nations a serious one.

To this accusation Wilson never replied. He left no apologia for his part in the conflict. Although frequently urged to do so, he steadily refused to make any statement of what he had tried to do, maintaining that he could add nothing to what he had already publicly said. In a unique sense this was true, for in all probability no man ever lived who left in print such an extensive record of what he stood for, a record in the main taken from the lips as he spoke to the widest audience he could reach. This was peculiarly true of his fight for the League of Nations from May 27, 1916, onward.

There was little that he could have added, unless he had penned some of his reactions after he was confined to the White House, and even here his conclusions had gone out in the form of statements. Wilson, moreover, was never interested in what he had done. His intimate associates agree that he could never be induced to make any record of something upon which he had already acted. He was tremendously interested in what he wished to do in the future, but hardly at all in what was past. Documents he kept as he went, which evidenced his acts, tons of them. Beyond that he would not go.

Apart from the volumes of his formal public statements, however, it seems fairly clear from his acts and his informal utterances that his attitude toward the reservations proposed was dominated by two convictions. The first of these was that he faced in the group of leaders headed by Roosevelt, Lodge and Harvey, opponents who would give small quarter and to whom concession would be of little use[21]; the second was a belief that serious qualification of the treaty would re-

---

[21] This conviction was not peculiar to Wilson. Among the many who shared it, Vice President Marshall, who was in closer touch with the public aspects of the struggle than any other person, later recorded his "fixed opinion that nothing would be done. . . . The long and weary months of discussion over the treaty, after he returned in June and laid it before the Senate, was to my mind simply a waste of raw material. There never was a moment when those who had said they would not stand for the League of Nations could have been induced, under any circumstances, to vote for the ratification of the treaty. No difference what the effect might be upon the world; no difference how public opinion may have changed; no difference what

open the whole world settlement, with consequences which would be calamitous—more destructive even than abstention from the treaty by the United States.

The first of these beliefs took root during the war. It received marked confirmation shortly before the issuance of his appeal for a Democratic Congress, and much additional substantiation immediately thereafter. It may be that Wilson should have suppressed his distrust of what these men would do to his peace program, if they could, and have concentrated his efforts upon conciliating them. Opinions will vary as to whether he could have succeeded. The moment at which he could have begun such conciliation would certainly be difficult to name. Certain it is that instead of seeking terms with them he long broke the force of their shafts, some of which reached him through private channels, by ignoring them as fully as his official position would permit. Nothing irks able men who have an animus more than to be ignored.

It might have been better if Wilson had given still less thought to the results of their activity than he did. As it was, he had work of crucial importance and pressing urgency to do, before the war, during it, and after, and he spent the great bulk of his time going about it, leaving his enemies aside. In the midst of his last and greatest task of salvaging from the waste of the war and the conviction of the hour a rallying point for future civilization in time of danger, and a perpetual meeting place for counsel on the issues of the world's common life, the violence of the attack of his foes, when he returned to Washington in February, compelled him to pause.

Should he stay in the White House, attempting to control American opinion, or return to Paris to exert his full power upon the settlement of the complex issues before the Conference? It was a vital decision. Wilson made it quickly, adhering to his plan to return. In so doing he made one of his chief mistakes, in the opinion of some of his friends and advisers at Paris. The Covenant, they feel, had then been written and the Conference started off in applying the President's principles. All was gain so far, and if Wilson had stayed away he might have avoided some of the compromises which he later made at Paris, at the same time exerting greater influence over the situation at home.

---

new light they had upon the subject, they had said they would not stand for it and they did not. It was pride of opinion, as I saw it." Thomas R. Marshall, *Recollections,* Indianapolis, 1925, p. 364.

A reading of the various accounts of the Conference, however, suggests that the Treaty might probably have been much worse than it was in the event of the President's absence. In the first place, without his powerful presence in Paris the Covenant might not have been raised from the submergence into which it fell when he left—it might even have been separated from the Treaty. This would have greatly facilitated its defeat or complete emasculation at home, in which case it would almost certainly have been abandoned by the Allies, if not imbedded in the treaty of peace as it actually was, with many parts of the Treaty dependent on it for execution. The blow of American rejection would surely have killed the League if the great powers had had any choice about setting it up. It was four long years before they turned to it and began really to give it their confidence after they had created it. The consequences of American rejection, as it finally came, were grave enough, but they are not irreparable; to envisage the world trying to function without the League is to contemplate blind groping away from chaos. Wilson was wise in keeping the building of the new institution close under his eye and following it step by step as far as his strength would permit. He came to tragedy as it was, but long indeed would be the world's woe if his effort had failed sooner.

We can never know how fewer his errors in the other settlements would have been, if he had remained in the White House after February. We do know that he felt to the full the responsibility resting upon him, as the Chief Executive of the nation which he had led in decisive intervention in the War, to make the new settlements as safe as he could make them. Aside from the creation of the League no other task that confronted him was so important. He faced it on the spot where the decisions were to be made and spent himself without stint to get a workable peace. Errors he made, sometimes under the persuasion of his fellow negotiators; other serious mistakes he undoubtedly avoided by his personal touch with the contending forces. [22]

It was hardly possible for the President to grasp the full import of situations at the end of a 3,000 mile cable as often as he did on the ground. In some cases his veto would probably have been more effective if delivered indirectly through negotiators, who would thus have had a simple position of not being able to go further. On the other hand the leaders of the Conference might soon have rebelled against a distant potentate who, informed imperfectly at best, vetoed everything

[22] See Nevins, *Henry White*, pp. 423, 427.

from his seclusion. In all probability the limits to this kind of dictation to the Conference would have been reached sooner than some commentators have anticipated. Moreover, in the most important crisis of the Conference it seems to have been essential that Wilson's will should operate on the spot, backed by as full an understanding of the facts and personalities involved as he could get. "Few of the men around him," in the opinion of one foreign observer, "were really capable of seeing what he saw, of understanding what he understood; not one of them could *will* what he willed with the same forces as he." [23] Whether or not this evaluation of Wilson's vision and power of understanding be accepted, there can be little doubt that his great will was supremely needed at Paris, and that it dominated the Conference as it could hardly have done from a great distance.[24] The world has but begun to appreciate what it owes to the combination in Woodrow Wilson of power to see ahead and strength of will to drive toward what he saw.

After a decade of opportunistic drifting, the might of Wilson's unfaltering leadership stands out ever more clearly. Called to lead the nation in time of peace, he reorganized and revivified it as none had ever done before. With responsibility for the peace, even the existence, of many nations laid upon him at the close of the war by humanity itself, he strove without hesitation or ceasing to execute a trust such as no man before him had borne. His achievement was not complete, but the road which the nations must take was so clearly marked out that it can hardly be lost in the future. [25]

Returning to Paris convinced that the attack would continue re-

[23] William Martin, *Statesman of the War 1918–1928*, N. Y., 1928, p. 224.

[24] "He was without question the dominating figure in the Conference," wrote the special observer for the *London Daily News*, and, "As to the nature of the influence the President exerted there is no conflict of opinion. He was there to make a Fourteen Points peace, and he did his best to make it. He failed in part, but he did not fail for want of trying. All through the Conference, except, perhaps, during the revision of the German Treaty, when Lloyd George suddenly took the field as an apostle of moderation, Mr. Wilson was the one force on the Council of Four making consistently for "a clean peace." H. Wilson Harris, *The Peace in the Making*, N. Y., 1920, pp. 48–49.

"Of course," says Melville E. Stone, later head of the Associated Press, "in a case of such magnitude some compromises were necessary, but as a whole the American President won a victory from his point of view." Melville E. Stone, *Fifty Years a Journalist*, N. Y., 1921.

The existence of a perfected transatlantic telephone would have put the President in Washington into considerably closer touch with the negotiations.

[25] If the President could have secured the amended Covenant, and as good a treaty, by staying in Washington, then, of course, he would have been fresh for his struggle with the Senate, or to make, at the proper moment, a compromise with his opponents that would have permitted entry into the League in some form. Most probably

gardless of his course, Wilson resolved so to cut the ground from under it by amendments to the Covenant, to meet the common objections, that moderate opinion would give him the victory. The amendments, secured at real sacrifice, he found discounted and his foes thoroughly organized to demand still further conditions. [26]

The tactical situation which confronted Wilson after he had put the treaty into the Senate's hands was one of the greatest difficulty. The initiative was now with his opponents and they gave every sign of continuing their campaign to arouse the country against the treaty as long as it should be necessary.

In this emergency the President had two courses open to him, to make what terms he could or to appeal to the only force which could possibly move the leaders of the Senate, the people themselves. The first course he tried, offering in his public conference with the Committee, to accept interpretative reservations which could be communicated to the powers without reopening the treaty. This offer being rejected, he talked with many individual Republican Senators, finding them all bound to party action.

At this juncture the difficulty of compromising becomes apparent. The President might have gone to Lodge and surrendered. Surrender was not in him. Any offer of terms on his part would have led him to capitulation, and Lodge showed no disposition to formulate terms of his own. Therefore, the President took his case to the people.

The attitude of the pro-League Republican Senators later in the struggle indicated that if the President had bided his time he might have been able to win them to his side, before it was too late, but there was nothing in the days when he made his decision to indicate that.

His experience with the Senators had convinced Wilson that some kind of reservations would have to be accepted. Before setting out on his tour, therefore, he drew up a draft of interpretative reservations which he would be willing to accept and gave it to Senator Hitchcock for use during his absence. This draft was as follows:

---

he would have still felt compelled to make his appeal to the people, but he would have been more likely to survive it physically. Certainly, the opposition of his foes would have been but little less determined and sustained, if any.

[26] He was prepared when he came back to accept further interpretation of the terms of the Covenant. Immediately after his return he dictated to the journalist Kohlsaat, on July 10, 1919, the following statement, "The President is open-minded as to every proposition of reasonable interpretation, but will not consent to any proposition that we scuttle." H. H. Kohlsaat, *From McKinley to Harding*, N. Y., 1923, p. 218.

SUGGESTION

THE WHITE HOUSE
Washington

The Senate of the United States of America advises and consents to the ratification of said Treaty, with the following understanding of the Articles of said Treaty mentioned below; and requests the President of the United States to communicate these interpretations to the several States signatory to said Treaty at the same time that he deposits the formal instrument of ratification with the Government of the French Republic at Paris.

Inasmuch as Article ONE of the Covenant of the League of Nations provides no tribunal to pass judgment upon the right of a member State to withdraw from the League, the Government of the U. S. understands the provision of Article ONE with regard to withdrawal as putting no limitation upon the right of a member State to withdraw except such as may lie in the conscience of the Power proposing to withdraw with regard to its having fulfilled "all its international obligations and all its obligations under the Covenant" in the sense intended by the instrument.

It understands that the advice of the Council of the League with regard to the employment of armed force contemplated in Article TEN of the Covenant of the League is to be regarded only as advice and leaves each member State free to exercise its own judgment as to whether it is wise or practicable to act upon that advice or not.

It understands that under Article FIFTEEN of the Covenant of the League no question can be raised either in the Assembly or in the Council of the League which will give that body the right to report or to make any recommendations upon the policy of any member state with regard to such matters as immigration, naturalization, or tariffs.

It understands, also, that the reference to the Monroe Doctrine in Article TWENTY-ONE of the Covenant of the League means that nothing contained in the Covenant shall be interpreted as in any way impairing or interfering with the application of the Monroe Doctrine in the American hemisphere. [27]

This document explains the origin of the Hitchcock reservations. Hitchcock later expanded them somewhat and offered them in the

---

[27] Received from Senator Hitchcock, May 2, 1929. The original copy is now among Wilson's official papers.

Senate. He permitted them to be known by his name, not through a desire to claim credit for himself, but through a hope of securing acceptance before Lodge, watching intently for every sign of Wilson's hand, was aware of their authorship. Reasons of strategy prevented the Wilson reservations from ever becoming known to the people at all, whereas the Lodge reservations were served at every breakfast table for months on end.

Wilson had, nevertheless, committed himself to the framing of reservations, and there is no reason to suppose that if he had kept his feet he would not have attempted to develop a compromise between what was probably his own minimum proposal and those advanced by his opponents. In his Western campaign he repeatedly affirmed his willingness to accept reservations, though opposing firmly, as his strategy required, some of those announced by his opponents. [28]

It is true enough that Wilson was standing for reservations to be attached to the resolution of ratification, but not incorporated in it. From the legal standpoint there was a considerable difference, but both gave clear notice that we would insist upon certain interpretations of the Covenant, and, given sincere good will upon both sides to achieve this purpose, agreement might have been reached.

The President's breakdown certainly altered the prospects for compromise. There was inaction on his side when there should have been alert effort to secure agreement, if possible. In this period the best opportunity for a compromise passed. There was then serious concern in the Republican organization, lest the opposition to the treaty go too far, and the pro-League Senators were tired of too caustic treatment of the treaty and anxiously desirous of seeing the Covenant made a reality. In such circumstances there is no reason to suppose that Wilson would not have conceded everything that could be conceded without destroying the principles at stake.

The issue would then have depended upon the balance of pressures upon Lodge. He had studied the mind of the President and continued to do so, according to his own account, with the greatest intentness. He knew, therefore, the points beyond which Wilson would not go. There was not the same necessity for Lodge and the men back of him to agree with Wilson, furthermore, that faced the leaders with whom he compromised in Paris. The latter needed agreement, and speedily, even more than he did; lacking great party pressure, Lodge could wait

---

[28] See his speech at Coeur d'Alene, Idaho, September 12, 1919. *Senate Document* No. 120, 66th Congress, 1st Session, p. 162.

indefinitely and profit by the delay. The Allied leaders at the Peace Conference had no desire or motive to overthrow Wilson politically; his chief opponents at home had a consuming desire and an imperative motive for his political destruction.

Wilson's colleagues in Paris, moreover, granted his sincerity and high purpose, whereas the followers of George Harvey did not. They interpreted his greatest conceptions in terms of egotism. The men of Paris, too, knew that he voiced an universal desire, and even if they doubted, they recognized that he might be right; the men of Washington long recognized that enlightened American public opinion stood for the League, but they never admitted that a "Wilson League" could be either wise or desirable.

With his best effort Wilson might have failed to compromise with Lodge and his backers. But if he had kept his health Woodrow Wilson would have left no stone unturned in his effort to secure ratification of the Treaty of Versailles. He later believed that in spite of the odds against him he would have succeeded. He was too intelligent not to know, moreover, that he had to satisfy the great segment of public opinion led by the Senators who sincerely wished the Covenant further interpreted in a friendly manner. Wilson recognized again and again, in words the frankness of which can hardly be doubted, that much of the concern over the implications of the Covenant was sincere, and his own desire to see the League succeed was too deep to permit him to refuse any reservations that did not appear gravely to endanger the establishment of the League or its effectiveness if instituted. The survival of the League was more important to him—and to humanity —than the immediate entry of the United States.

With the initiative fairly well recovered into the hands of Wilson, "the intricate problem" which Lodge "and those with whom" he "acted were compelled to face" would have been much more difficult than it was. Lodge and his supporters would have had still greater difficulty than they did encounter in preventing pro-League Republican opinion from agreeing to interpretative reservations. As events moved after Wilson's fall, the supreme struggle for the support of the moderate reservationists proved relatively one-sided. Wilson's breakdown robbed him of the opportunity which October and the weeks succeeding offered. Thereafter, pain and sickness inevitably colored his mental attitude, particularly toward the opposition which he had combated until he fell. Body paralysis and nervous collapse might have led a different type of man to surrender in any fight in which he was engaged outside the sickroom, but in Woodrow Wilson it only steeled his spirit to cling tighter than ever to the ideals and principles for which he had been ready to die. He was only more willing to rest his case in time and eternity upon them.

The influence of this element in the situation was widely overlooked or incorrectly estimated by the American people at the time. This was partly due to the decision which prevented his physicians from saying, for a while, just how seriously he was stricken, and it was partly because people had become so used to Wilson the ruler that as long as he spoke at all they visualized the Wilson of old. But to attempt any interpretation of the course of the treaty struggle, between September, 1919, and March, 1920, without taking the President's invalid condition heavily into account is to produce inescapably a distorted picture.

This is true not only because illness accentuated in Wilson the qualities which were at once the source of much of his greatness and of his enmities, but because his precarious strength cut him off from contact with the bulk of his friends and advisers when he most needed them. Always limited in personal contacts by his normal strength, there were now weeks at a time when no one entered his room except his caretakers, perhaps his private secretary and an occasional Senator for a brief period. So the treaty situation dragged into deadlock and thereafter the reservations were made more drastic, instead of less so, more unpalatable to him and to the other nations instead of more acceptable.

Simultaneously, the President received counsel from a very few persons only, and these the people most likely to sympathize with his stand and believe in its impregnability. A leading journalist who followed him from Princeton days to the end of his career has declared, without qualification, that "the United States would today be in the League officially if the President had been able to get the advice he so much needed in his enfeebled condition. On his sick bed he almost agreed to accept the Lodge reservations, but someone urged him to make an issue of it in the 1920 campaign and in January, 1920, he asked that a solemn referendum be taken." [29]

This conviction presupposes, of course, that later additions to the November reservations would not have been made. Instead, the additions were facilitated by the President's further letter of March 8, which discouraged Democratic Senators working for compromise and cracked the party whip over their heads, confirmed the irreconcilables

[29] David Lawrence, *The True Story of Woodrow Wilson*, N. Y., 1924, p. 299.

and consolidated the "mild-nullifiers" firmly into the Lodge organization. [30]

The doubt as to the authorship of the Wilson letter of January 8, expressed by Secretary Houston, who revised it, may have been justified, but the later letters of January 28, and March 8 appear to summarize fairly the position which Wilson maintained throughout. The former, agreeing to accept the "Hitchcock" reservations entire, and suggesting certain modifications of the Lodge reservations, offered a basis of compromise from which a set of reservations safeguarding every legitimate interest might have been worked out. It is true that the Democratic strategy of first defeating the Lodge draft, adopted while Wilson was prostrate, made this offer come too late politically speaking, yet it came.

The defiance of six weeks later reflected Wilson's clear conviction that the reservations, then in the process of stiffening, effectively nullified American membership in the League of Nations. He may have been wrong; he may have been cleverly outmaneuvered and trapped by carefully shaded and sharpened words. If so, the vengeance of his opponents, who had cried out against his "words" so long, was complete. The "analysis of Mr. Wilson's probable attitude," which, said Lodge, was "an element of vital moment to me, in trying to solve the intricate problem which I and those with whom I acted were compelled to face," had justified, from the standpoint of Lodge and his confederates, all the time and care devoted to it. They could rest certain "as the strenuous days which were filled by the contest over the League of Nations passed by," in the knowledge that they had "made no mistake" in their "estimate of what President Wilson would do under certain conditions." They had, they believed, finally led Wilson to destroy himself. But they had not conquered the spirit which had ranged the earth to its deepest recesses, calling men to a life of liberty and of co-operation together for the common safety and the common good. The visible Wilson, the Wilson of clay let us say, was no longer to trouble those of his countrymen who, weary of the pace he had set them, desired less disturbing leadership. But the mighty spirit which, for the first time in human annals, had been able to stir the people of every nation and race could not be prevented from moving in all lands where nationhood was still to be achieved; neither could it be stopped from stirring all nations toward a union in which liberty might live.

[30] *Ibid.*, p. 294.

It is probable that Wilson attached too much importance to the Republican reservations. Most of his contemporaries did. The fate of the nation hardly hung on whether this shade of meaning or that should prevail on most of the disputed points, as it seemed to at the time. The weight of opinion in later years strongly inclines toward the view that the President should have accepted the reservations, as finally refined in March. By advising his supporters in the Senate to give way at the last minute, when further additions would be impossible, it is said, he could have demonstrated by negotiation that some of the reservations would have to be abandoned and, perhaps, have secured the moderation of others.

Much reason certainly argues in favor of such an attempt. It does not follow, however, that his opponents, in the midst of a presidential campaign, would have permitted the abandonment or modification of any of their work through Wilson's agency, least of all the very reservations which gratified the anti-British, anti-Japanese voters. Of all the reservations these would have received the stoutest defense in the Senate. The Senate leaders would totally abandon all the reservations themselves, without a qualm, but they would hardly have modified any of them at Wilson's hands.

After the election in November, moreover, they would have preferred to deal with the matter themselves. It may be that in the campaign they would not have stigmatized the League so thoroughly as a dangerous Wilson concoction, if the Democrats had abandoned the League in the canvass. Our way into the League might have been found sometime in the administration of Harding, if he had desired to find it. The prospect would have been better in the era of Coolidge, who believed in the League. The conclusion of A. J. Beveridge, in 1926, that if Wilson had accepted the reservations we would then have been a member of the League is tenable, [31] but not probable, for in that same year a less sensitive Senate was so nonplussed by the qualified acceptance of its World Court reservations that we are still out of the Court six years later.

Beveridge's further opinion that the reservations would not have amounted to anything as a practical matter is now widely shared by both friends and foes of the League. Thus Borah, in 1925, said emphatically, "I do not care to discuss the Lodge reservations, but if we had gone into the League with the Lodge reservations, that would have

[31] *Congressional Record,* Vol. 67, Pt. 3, p. 2686.

been the last that there would ever have been heard of the Lodge reservations." [32]

Many supporters of Geneva, also, assuredly now share the conclusion of David Hunter Miller in 1920 that a sympathetic trial of the League would make it a living force, and would date the beginning of a new era, in which the millions of words wasted upon the language of particular clauses would be forgotten by all except students of the curiosities of literature. [33]

Given a sympathetic trial of the League, the present would doubtless bear out this prediction—perhaps the future. But could the League have been given a sympathetic trial by the United States in the years after 1920? Had it not been pilloried too thoroughly to make such trial possible? And would a suspicious trial have been better than none? Wilson thought not. He believed that we had better go in right or not at all.

He clung tenaciously, too, to the last possible minute to his belief that the people would decide the issue rightly, as he saw it. Seeing an issue clearly himself, he "trusted the masses of the people too implicitly to see it clearly and see it as he did, in the short run as well as the long run"—even in the face of skillful arguments. [34]

When members of his Cabinet sought to prepare him, some two weeks before the election of 1920, for what was coming, he tried to reassure them instead. The people were a good jury, he said, especially on moral causes. Trying again, in the Cabinet meeting of November 2, on the very eve of the election, to break the force of the blow that he was about to receive, Secretary Houston met only confidence in the outcome. A great moral issue was involved, insisted the President. The people could and would see it. "You need not worry," was his parting assurance. "The people will not elect Harding." [35]

The blow fell and the day following found Wilson calm in defeat. He felt that the nation stood disgraced in the eyes of the world, yet it was a difficult thing "to lead a nation so variously constituted as ours quickly to accept a program such as the League of Nations." Describing then, with a good deal of penetration, what had happened, he left the people "to learn now by bitter experience just what they have lost."

[32] *Congressional Record*, Vol. 67, Pt. 1, p. 1074.
[33] Miller, *My Diary of the Paris Conference*, Vol. 20, p. 588.
[34] David F. Houston, "The War on Wilson," *World's Work*, September, 1926, Vol. 52, p. 529.
[35] David F. Houston, *Eight Years With Wilson's Cabinet*, N. Y., 1926, Vol. II, pp. 94-5.

A suggestion that the defeat of the hour might prove to be the best thing for the Democratic party brought the quick rebuke that he was "not thinking about the partisan side of this thing. It is the country and its future that I am thinking about." [36] Similar concern for the future, expressed at the Cabinet meeting of November 9, drew another suggestion that all he need do to put Harding and the Republican party in a hole was to return the treaty to the Vice President's desk. Reply was again instant. The situation was too serious. He wished, moreover, to help Mr. Harding and hoped that every good citizen would try to do the same. [37]

In the twilight that remained to him, Wilson saw the League of Nations pass the critical period of its infancy and he came to believe that later entry of the United States would be better, when a more sober perspective prevailed. From the conviction that truth was mighty and would prevail he never faltered—a belief that was equally strong in those who had seen what he saw.

"If the reaction triumphs," said the *Springfield Republican* as that movement reached its climax, "its triumph will be temporary. The leader of the cause may become its martyr, yet the moral forces he mobilized and threw as best he could into the face of the world's war-makers, on the heels of the world's greatest war, must ultimately have their victory or civilization will meet its end on a bleeding and smoking earth." [38]

Sane vision and realistic action are never in conflict.

[36] Joseph Tumulty, *Woodrow Wilson as I Know Him,* N. Y., 1921, pp. 501–2.
[37] Houston, *Eight Years With Wilson's Cabinet,* pp. 94–5.
[38] *Springfield Republican,* October 30, 1920.

WOODROW WILSON

CHAPTER XX

TOWARD THE FUTURE

At the time, and for some years afterward, the struggle over the League of Nations was generally considered to have advanced distinctly the power of the Senate in treaty making. The Senate had killed the most important treaty ever presented to it. Hereafter it would surely play an important rôle even in the making of treaties.

RESERVATIONS TO TREATIES

In the general awe which was inspired by the mighty struggle over the League the fact that the result was sterile from the standpoint of the Senate, as well as from that of the Executive, was widely overlooked. What was evident was a consistent and ever more destructive emasculation in the Senate of treaties designed to keep the peace. The Olney-Pauncefote Treaty of Arbitration with Great Britain, supported by both the Cleveland and McKinley Administrations, had been amended and then rejected by the Senate in 1897. The Hay Arbitration Treaties of 1904 similarly had been nullified in the Senate and dropped by President Roosevelt, who wished "either to take part in something that means something or else not to have any part in it at all."

Roosevelt was, however, persuaded by Secretary Root, in 1908, to yield to the Senate its demand that every *compromis* for an arbitration be approved by the Senate, a surrender which greatly weakened their effectiveness. The political scene having shifted, Roosevelt became the bitter opponent of the more effective Taft Arbitration Treaties of 1911, and, with the assistance of Senator Lodge, secured such amendment of the treaties in the Senate that President Taft dropped them. This contest having taught those desiring to oppose "such treaties" exactly how to dispose of them, with apparent safety to themselves, the technique learned had been applied, with world-resounding results, to the Treaty of Versailles.[1]

The Senate had indeed asserted itself, under skilled leadership, with rising crescendo. That was clear. What escaped attention was the fact that the Senate had not yet come to grips with the signatories of a modern multilateral treaty. This the Senate confidently did in framing the inevitable reservations to the Executive proposal for joining the World Court. It was taken for granted by both the Senate and the public, as it had been in 1919 and after, that of course the powers would accept any reservations which the Senate proposed, "in order to get us in." Great was the astonishment, therefore, except among the shrewder opponents of the Court, when of the forty-eight nations to whom the Senate's terms were sent, but five of the smallest and weakest accepted unconditionally. The feeling of injured dignity which arose was not improved, moreover, by the counter reservations proposed by the September, 1926, conference of twenty-two League states. Both the Senate and the Executive retired into silence for two years before deciding to accept the invitation to negotiate which had been given.

Then came the Paris Peace Pact, in January, 1929, and a distinctly different atmosphere prevailed in the Senate. Reservations were offered, of course, but the qualificationists were so frowned upon that they soon let it be known that they would be satisfied with the sending of a separate document rejecting the various implications which Senators feared might reside in the treaty. Even this extra-legal form of reservation, however, did not meet with favor. President Coolidge was unable to see why the United States should be super-safeguarded against this peace treaty. Senator Borah, too, now in charge of the treaty, was not willing to do anything "which could be represented abroad as a change or reservation." Even the suggestion of a separate resolution, he declared, had been "used to our detriment abroad." It had "produced a serious situation."

The objectors then indicated that they would accept a report of the Committee on Foreign Relations, if adopted by the Senate but not circulated to the states signatory to the Pact, then approaching fifty in number. To their astonishment this kind of proclamation was also rejected. The Committee was willing to present the desired report provided that it should not be acted upon. Finally, after practically every Senator had privately promised not to move its passage, the report was

---

[1] The Senate's handling of the series of arbitration treaties referred to has been traced in the author's, *The Treaty Veto of the American Senate*, pp. 77–108.

brought in and read, "solely for the purpose of putting upon record what your committee understands to be the true interpretation of the treaty, and not in any sense for the purpose or with the design of modifying or changing the treaty in any way or effectuating a reservation or reservations to the same." [2]

To be sure, the effort to attach conditions to the resolution of ratification would have been much more intense if the Pact had committed us to any positive action. Nevertheless, the invention of a kind of reservation which would give dissenting Senators something to point to, without incurring any risk whatever of killing the treaty under consideration, demonstrated that Senators can grow in knowledge both of the amenities and mutual concessions of international intercourse.

The Advice and Consent of the Senate. These considerations would probably operate more consistently if it were not so easy to precipitate controversy concerning the exact limits of the Senate's power over treaties. Argument can be made easily from the phrase of the Constitution, "by and with the advice and consent of the Senate," for Senate participation in treaty making at all stages. Disputes over the implication of these words is perennial and likely to be perpetual. The one thing certain about the clause is that the method of intimate secret conference intended by the Fathers was never established.

The debate on the London Naval Treaty, concluded on June 21, 1930, was largely dominated by an especially long chapter in the recurring discussion of the Senate's relation to the negotiation of treaties. It also furnished another example of the type of reservation often made which does not require any dissent on the part of the other signatories because it merely reiterates what is generally taken for granted. The reservation to the London Treaty consented to it with the "distinct and explicit" understanding that no secret agreements modified its terms.

Such a reservation, and others of a more drastic nature, are always in the background of the usual campaign of Senators to reconstruct the intimate details of the negotiations—an effort largely foredoomed to failure, but good opposition tactics. Thus the solemn, emphatic and reiterated statements of President Hoover that the Naval Treaty had not been modified by any agreement withheld from the Senate were not enough. Neither did the equally positive denials of Secretary Stimson, who headed the American delegation in the conference, or the repeated, face to face, pledges of the two Senator-negotiators, David A. Reed and

[2] *Congressional Record,* Vol. 70, pp. 1537, 1717–19, 1724, 1783.

Joseph T. Robinson, give assurance. Senators had to make absolutely certain that nothing compromising lurked behind the treaty.[3]

The assumption that the Executive officials, as well as any Senators that may help to negotiate a treaty, are ever subject to foreign blandishments, or blind to the real interests of the country, leads naturally to the demand for perfection.[4] Some Senators always find it easy to take for granted that the American delegates should have secured the best possible treaty that could be written, whereas all they can ever do is to get the best terms obtainable under the stress of the many conflicting forces centering in the conference from which the treaty results.

Such considerations do not yet prevent the legislative habit of mind from continuing to operate in Senators who sincerely wish to support a forward looking treaty and are not seeking its defeat by indirection. Senators are used to offering amendments to laws freely. Treaties are also legal documents. Most of the lawyers of the Senate can find a clause in any treaty that is not ideal. "The treaty is not perfect, is it?" Why not improve it?

This query seems reasonable enough if it is not reflected that every great treaty is a delicate adjustment of conflicting claims and keen sensibilities, or of divergent principles and different legal systems. It has been made with great labor and much compromising, after which it cannot fail to nettle the other parties to find concessions made by the American negotiators withdrawn in the Senate or new advantages claimed. There are almost invariably some Senators so busy asserting the sovereignty of the United States that the sovereignty of other nations escapes them completely. Demands are laid down in what seems to the other signatories the form of an ultimatum, without any opportunity on their part to controvert or ameliorate them. Moreover, when the Senate has acted in its wisdom it does not expect its revisions to be modified. They are to be accepted.

So long as our chief treaties were bilateral, the consequences of these habits were occasionally serious but not disastrous. Now that our great compacts are negotiated in international conferences, under conditions of deep complexity, and signed by several powers, or by scores

[3] *Congressional Record*, Vol. 72, Pt. I, pp. 4, 24–6, 35, 41, 45, 46, 50–6, 64, 89–91.
[4] Isolationist newspapers are as prone to deplore the gullibility of American negotiators in international conferences. Thus the *Chicago Tribune* of September 17, 1931, closes an editorial with comment upon the obvious "influence of subserviency upon those who have represented us in most of these international contests. Only in the counsels of the United States are the vital interests of a nation in the hands of men more anxious to win the applause of foreigners than to stand strongly and self-respectingly for the interests of their own nation."

of states, their free modification in the Senate has become immensely more dangerous. Fortunately, other legislative bodies have not adopted widely the Senate's custom of subjecting treaties to legislative routine.[5] If they should do so, the adjustment of the vital international issues, increasingly complex and requiring the agreement of many peoples, would be brought to a standstill. The legislative alteration of multilateral treaties is a game that only one parliament can play, or at most a small number, unless a second conference is to be called to consider the reservations and amendments proposed by the various parliaments, many of them doubtless conflicting. Such procedure may be feasible for treaties upon subjects of continuing but not immediately urgent importance, such as transit conventions or opium treaties. Where the business is pressing, or important political agreements are at issue, the necessity of a re-negotiation is likely to defeat the very objectives of the treaty. When really important issues are at stake a conference which settles nothing may well be worse than useless; it may only intensify rivalries and jealousies, and by venting them in national parliaments set back international agreement rather than advance it.[6]

The business of adjusting the frictions and promoting the mutual

[5] In reply to a question as to whether the House of Commons had the right to modify the Treaty of Versailles, Bonar Law said: "I am really surprised that the right honorable gentleman should put the question. Does he really think it possible that any treaty could be arranged in the world if something like twenty Powers are to discuss the details of it? It seems to me quite impossible."

In the French Chamber of Deputies, dissenting members in the main put their objections against the treaty on record by "motions of regret," after voting for ratification.

The four votes cast against the treaty in the House of Commons, and the 53 votes in the Chamber of Deputies, by no means registered the amount of opposition in those bodies to particular provisions in it. C. P. Howland, *American Foreign Relations 1928*, pp. 287–88.

[6] The First Committee submitted a report to the 1930 Assembly of the League recommending that conventions be signed in the future under a proviso empowering the Council to call a second conference, which all would agree to attend, if by a given date the ratifications of certain enumerated powers had not been received.

This procedure would make it possible for the first time to achieve a new meeting of minds in order to appease parliaments objecting to certain articles of a multi-party treaty, so long as the objections were not too antagonistic to each other. Its use might, however, demonstrate the necessity of withdrawing many objections made without full thought of the consequences. Much would depend upon the amount of congressional or parliamentary *amour propre* that came to be involved.

A greater gain from giving the Council power to summon a new conference would seem to accrue from its ability to stimulate more effectively governments that are merely dilatory, or chary of asking parliamentary approval of treaties to which there may be objection and upon which action may be delayed. The proposed procedure probably offers more hope for the reasonably prompt and widespread ratification of multilateral treaties in this direction than it does as a means of reconciling the objections of independent legislatures, acting without references to executive policy or to each other. See "The Ratification of International Conventions Under the Auspices of the League of Nations," *League of Nations Publications, V Legal 1930*, Vol. 25. (Official No. A. 83. 1930. V.)

concerns of a world of nations more closely knit together each year must go on, even if our governments have to resort to executive agreements and gentlemen's understandings. It will proceed with much more smoothness in the future if the Senate can come to understand that it is not primarily a legislative body in dealing with treaties, but an executive council whose duty it is to weigh proposed international agreements in the large, and with the purpose of sympathetically promoting executive policy if grave objection be not found to its main lines.

This realization should counteract the ever-recurrent feeling in the Senate that something must be done to every leading treaty. Senators will no longer feel that they are mere "rubber stamps" unless they can affix some imprint upon the treaty that will be visible to the country. Politics will continue to be played in considering treaties. We may as well accept that as settled. So long as popular favor or party advantage may be expected from attacks upon an executive policy of agreement with Great Britain or the League, such attacks will reverberate from the floor of the Senate, through the microphone and the columns of newspapers, especially those jingoistic journals which dominate in some cities and states.

This can hardly be otherwise, but may we not expect that the minority of Senators surrendering to such influences will become steadily smaller, as our hard experience in the school of international discord proceeds? Is it not reasonable to expect, also, that the fears of small groups of Senators may be recorded in documents not attached to our treaties, as in the committee report on the Peace Pact, or in statements clearly calling for no action on the part of other signers, such as the anti-secrecy declaration in the resolution of consent to the London Naval Treaty?

In the latter debate it was asserted with regret that the Senate had come to have only the right to accept or reject treaties. If the growing intricacy of international agreements precludes the legislative alteration of vital treaties after signature, is this evolution really to be deplored? Is it not more probable that the development will conserve both the time and dignity of the Senate, without interfering with its primary and indispensable function in the scrutiny of treaties? Whether any amendment to a treaty voted by the Senate, and made effective by the Executive, has ever been of striking value or lasting importance is at least highly debatable. But even if some exceptions be established, the gain of knowing when the Senate has finished with a treaty whether it has rejected it or not will more than compensate for any refinements of advantage which the Senate might get for us as the price of its consent.

After all, why should the basic power of the Senate need extension? In all our high places there are few rights of honor or importance equal to that of a United States Senator to sit in judgment upon the greatest of contracts proposed for the United States, to weigh its advantages and disadvantages in the light of searching debate and to register his judgment as to whether its terms are on the whole for the benefit of the nation. We do not undervalue the veto powers of the President or of the Supreme Court. Why should that of the Senate over treaties be considered as anything less than a vast and significant power? If a Senator's verdict be negative he can nullify the decision of any two of his colleagues who approve a treaty, and his vote may have consequences reaching farther than could the veto of any law.

What of the League?

With the United States Senate apparently evolving away from the captious stoppage of peace treaties, in what direction has the League of Nations developed? Has it become the dreaded super-state which was said to be inevitable from the terms of the Covenant? The answer is clearly in the negative. The fears of the post-war reaction have not been realized. The League, to be sure, has achieved a great influence over the world of nations, but whatever power it wields flows from them and must continue to do so. Geneva has become a great clearing house for international conference and coöperation of almost every kind, but it has not become the capital of a world state.[7]

Nor is any other development normally to be expected. Appreciation is clearer now of the fact that internationalism depends for its very existence upon the preservation of strong nations. Once the member nations of the League cease to exist, or become seriously weakened in their power or ability to govern themselves, the League must correspondingly decline. The gradual decay of the nations is much more likely to yield world anarchy than it is to produce a global state. Instead of being antagonistic principles, Nationalism and Internationalism are necessary and complementary to each other, in the high-speed world of the present and future.

Yet to see the League as the servant of the nations, not their master,

[7] See William E. Rappard, "The League as It Seems Likely to Develop," in *Problems of the Peace,* Oxford, 1927, p. 45 ff.

does not remove the necessity of building it into an effective stabilizer to regulate their disputes and to promote the finding of common interests among them. Circumstances and conditions alter, but the fundamental need of the peoples for peace and security does not change. The words of President Hoover, spoken at Stanford University on October 2, 1919, will be just as true in the future as today. The League of Nations, he said, is "an aspiration which has been rising in the hearts of all the world. It has become an insistence in the minds of all those to whom the lives of our sons are precious, to all those to whom civilization is a thing to be safeguarded, and all those who see no hope for the amelioration of the misery of those who toil if peace cannot be maintained." [8]

A Place for Conference. Realization of the necessity of international organization was deep in the minds of intellectual leaders everywhere in 1919. It may be doubted, however, if the masses of the people anywhere grasped the need for constant co-operation as clearly as they felt the need for curbing war. The gradual growth of comprehension among the peoples of Europe that the League of Nations offered the only hope of escape from the developing chaos left by the war, deepened only by traditional methods of diplomacy, is nowhere better described than in Frank H. Simond's illuminating book, *How Europe Made Peace Without America.* Finding that ultra-nationalistic governments "had failed in every single effort to restore order," even though no political groups "had ever been allowed greater latitude in the application of their ideas," the peoples turned to the League, making it "the first principle in all Liberal and Democratic political groups in Europe." [9]

Without attempting to foretell the outcome, the veteran foreign observer felt that "it is clear that the single conceivable basis of hope for the future, which has emerged from the catastrophe of our own time, is the idea which is instinct in the popular conception of the meaning of the League of Nations. Geneva may fail, but the experiment of European peace is to be made there and nowhere else." [10]

[8] *New York Times,* October 3, 1919. It does seem odd now that it should have been necessary for Mr. Hoover to say, in answer to "the cry that the League obligates that our sons be sent to fight in foreign lands," that "the very intent and structure of the League is to prevent war."

[9] F. H. Simonds, *How Europe Made Peace Without America,* N. Y., 1927, pp. 267, 373. Mr. Simonds' further judgment, in 1927, was that "despite temporary reactions, it is not merely patent that liberalism is gaining ground in Europe, but also that nationalism finds itself, even in periods of temporary success, unable to reverse the movement toward Geneva" (p. 376).

[10] Simonds, pp. 379–80. The growth of solid popular belief in the League has perhaps been slower in non-European lands. The younger generations in every

In attempting to explain the growing influence of the League, Mr. Simonds said: "As an institution the League of Nations has evolved slowly and, after all, slightly, but as an idea and a place its expansion has been well-nigh incredible." [11]

This development arises from the fact that the League has transformed international conference from an extraordinary occurrence into the customary, proper method of settling international affairs. The Foreign Ministers of Europe instead of writing clever and suspicious notes to each other year after year, now go to the annual meeting of the League Assembly, or to the quarterly sessions of the Council, and clear up misunderstandings face to face before they have accumulated dangerously. Some of them leave home breathing fire and thundering loudly the positions they mean to maintain in particular controversies, but the atmosphere of Geneva, and the force of world observation focused upon them, lead to acceptance of settlements of some kind that neither would nor could have been made under the cross fire of nationalistic controversy between two or more capitals.

The value of personal discussion that every business man knows is one which diplomats could appreciate but seldom under the old diplomacy. Pilgrimages to other capitals were occasionally undertaken, in times of comparative calm or to cement alliances for a storm, but speculation and fear were almost sure to arise in other chancelleries, and when the need was greatest, political and nationalistic outcries at home usually made such journeys impossible.

Ministers, therefore, nursed the suspicious attitudes which a fencing correspondence breeds, whereas they now measure each other in Geneva and discover that much confidence in the other's motives is justified. Thus, while little may be decided in the formal meetings

---

country, however, see it continually as a working force in the life of the world. Education in the aims and purposes of the League is, moreover, systematic in many nations.

The mental approach in the United States has of necessity changed, perhaps more markedly than elsewhere. As expressed by Mark Sullivan, "The League of 1920 was a conception; to-day it is an institution in being. That is a most important distinction, for much of our hesitation to join was distrust of the unknown, fear worked up by the anti-ratification Senators through putting the unforeseeable possibilities of what the League would become and do in terrifying terms of responsibilities and even dangers, whose very vagueness inspired caution. Now we know what the League is. Will anyone question the statement that the 'Irreconcilables,' the 'battalion of death,' could not to-day work up as much fear of a concrete institution we can look at and examine, as they were able to work up against an abstraction whose indefiniteness permitted them to paint their own picture of what it might become?" "America and the League: Six Years After," *World's Work*, January, 1926, Vol. 51, p. 289.

[11] *Ibid.*, pp. 379–80.

of the Assembly, much understanding may be achieved in the incessant private meetings of the statesmen.

A Focus of World Opinion. The public Assembly Sessions, however, provide for the first time a recognized and respected forum to which every nation gives ear. Here the smallest nation can effectively air its grievances, and on one or two occasions a great Power has been made distinctly less bellicose by a few speeches from men who know the power of a world public opinion informed of the facts. It is a startling thing, but apparently true, that no nation is powerful enough now to face without serious concern a general condemnation of its policy, or its tactics, in the Assembly of the League of Nations. Even militant Russia, in its increasingly frequent appearances at Geneva, plays to world opinion, and the United States, in its approach to the World Court, expressed great concern at the possibility of condemnation incidental to some advisory opinion of the Court which the Council might request.

The presence of some four hundred representatives of the world's leading newspapers and press services in Geneva, during an Assembly session, makes it certain that news of national misdoings and of international understandings will go out immediately to the most remote nations. The same charges or the same proposals for agreement have a good chance of reaching the people of every nation at the same time. The possibilities of widespread reaction to the messages from such a sounding board are not likely in the long run to be lost upon any nation, so long as memory recalls how world public opinion crystallized against Germany in 1914 and after.

Of scarcely less importance, moreover, is the mingling of the newspaper men themselves. Friendships are formed, viewpoints corrected and information gained which tend constantly to mitigate, in some degree, the follies of the press wars between countries that have been such a prolific source of grave friction.

The searchlight of world observation plays less brilliantly, but still powerfully upon the more frequent sessions of the Council as they occur during the year. They are scarcely less important also as gatherings of statesmen for conference upon their own problems.

A Permanent Watch Tower. The Council is not so impressive a body as the Assembly, but it is much more mobile. It is always in existence and can be summoned without delay if any serious disturbance arises anywhere. No agonizing waiting to learn if a conference can be gotten together can occur again while the League of Nations continues to function. Neither can any powerful nation again prevent a conference from taking place. The Council is the world's insurance against the repetition of the tragedy of 1914. It will meet in time of future danger, clothed in advance with authority to speak for all the members of the League, the Great Powers by virtue of their permanent membership and the lesser ones through their elected representatives.[12]

The Council can meet quickly. The Secretariat of the League is always in session. It is daily studying the problems that vex and trouble the nations, preparing for conferences, managing them, following up the recommendations made. For the first time the nations have a body of trained men whose business it is to serve the common interests of all. For the first time, too, the world possesses a body of able men, neutrally placed, whose prestige is involved in preventing international disagreements from going too far. As an emergency lookout the Secretariat is of first importance, yet its principal labors are directed toward removing or minimizing international frictions before they become dangerously acute. Few things have surprised the members of the League more than the efficiency of the Secretariat in assisting the world to perform its international chores, little and big.[13]

A World Court. Of less conspicuous importance than the other organs of the League, but significant of immense hope for the future, is the judicial arm of the League, the Permanent Court of International Justice. Made possible for the first time by the creation of the electoral machinery of the League, the Council and the Assembly, the World Court has so far rendered its greatest service in giving rulings upon disputed points of International Law, or treaty interpretation, referred to it by the Council. This phase of the Court's activity, so useful in clarifying and securing sober consideration of the serious disputes coming before the Council, has somewhat overshadowed for the time being its strictly judicial decisions. As time goes on, however, the truly judicial work of the Court promises to become one of the League's

---

[12] When one looks back to 1914 the words of Raymond B. Fosdick do not seem to be too strong when he says that "the world seems to have leaped a whole century since then." "The year 1914," he continues, "stands for all time as the indictment of a civilization that was unprepared. No machinery, no institution was ready. There were no rules and no precedents and in those few frantic days of July, just seventeen years ago, new expedients could not be devised. A handful of hasty, misunderstood telegrams plunged the world into the greatest tragedy ever visited upon the human race." *New York Times Magazine*, July 12, 1931, p. 19.

[13] The excellence of the service performed by the Secretariat is in no small measure due to the fact that the failure of the United States to enter the League led those who had little faith or courage to decide not to risk their fortunes in its service. Gilbert Murray, "The Real Value of the League," *Harper's Magazine*, September, 1930, p. 446 ff.

greatest contributions to international order. Time will be required to develop a new system of procedure and to promote the habit of resorting to the Court directly. It may well prove necessary to extend its jurisdiction to important cases between individuals and to create continental or regional courts under it to induce a steady and habitual resort to its facilities.[14] The possibilities inherent in the development of the World's Court should certainly stimulate all those who would like to reduce the field of "political" controversies between nations.

The League of Nations, in short, has developed into a working system of continuing co-operation and perpetual conference.[15] Its benefits have so far largely gone, in first effects at least, to the European nations, although every continent has continued to be actively represented.

A European League? The development of the League by the European and Latin American states may in the long run prove a real compensation for the absence in the early formative years of the people whose aroused conscience gave to the League its original spark of life. It does not follow, however, that the League can be commended for its good work in Europe and left standing aside as something that is all very well for the parent continent. This evasion of the issue of our own relationship to it cannot be permanently maintained, for two reasons, the first of which is that the center of the world's life is still in Europe. This is true in the realms of culture, religion, politics, economics—even of finance in essential respects. The center of gravity in all these aspects of human life may move, but until it does so, what contributes to a tranquil, orderly Europe is of more than indirect concern to the rest of the world.

Moreover, should the centers of power shift to North America, or to the Orient, the situation would not be essentially different, because of the unity of a world of nations bound together by complex ties and forces which never weaken; they only grow stronger alike in times of prosperity and of adversity. This is an evolution which is motivated at bottom by the progressively rapid advance of science, the fruits of which cannot be confined. It is a development which fills many people

---

[14] See P. B. Potter, *Introduction to International Organization,* N. Y., pp. 355-372.

[15] Space does not permit even a summary view of the work of the International Labor Organization, the Transit and Communications Organization, the Health, Financial, Economic and Mandates Services, to mention only the more important of the subsidiary bodies of the League, whose services only occasionally create news because they work quietly to remove disagreeable or prosaic impediments to human life.

with real uneasiness amounting to fear, but it is a situation beyond the power of any nation to control; it is a job for world intelligence of the highest order.

"Sixty nations cannot span the earth with their ships and airplanes and systems of commerce, and expect the business to run without some centralized technique of understanding and supervision. The new integration of economic interests demands an integration of control. Economic internationalism cannot live without some measure of political internationalism." [16]

International Politics. Comprehension of this truth naturally comes slowly to a people dwelling largely in the interior of a vast continent, from whom leadership was not demanded until yesterday. It is perhaps not to be wondered at that their political leaders continue to hide behind the fiction that co-operation with the rest of the world can take every form except "political" collaboration. "Political" association with the other nations is dirty business, we are reminded incessantly, in which we can not, need not engage.

All the politics with which the American politician is familiar is beyond dispute somewhat dirty. Local politics in the cities from which he comes are at least periodically rotten; graft and favoritism flourish and crime breeds apace. Corrupt machines also rise and fall in the States of the American Union, headed at times by governors who are knaves and mountebanks. Public funds by the millions are misappropriated and squandered. Even the national government itself now and then falls into the hands of a gang, and a cabinet minister eventually goes to jail. "Politics" everywhere wears, periodically, soiled habiliments. Most of the good citizens cannot permit themselves to be contaminated by her and few of the young look forward to a public career.

Shady doings also take place in international politics. Occasionally the players are nothing more than local politicians elevated beyond their sphere. Intrigue and attempts to manipulate situations to national or partisan advantage occur perpetually. There is, nevertheless, among international politicians a constant display of honesty and sincerity, of efficiency and breadth of view, of ability and sacrificing toil, just as all these virtues are practiced continually in municipal, state and national

---

[16] Raymond B. Fosdick, "The New World Co-operation," *New York Times Magazine*, July 12, 1931, p. 19.

It should be added that if an economic union of the European nations should grow out of the League, the United States will be much better off as the political collaborator and friendly associate of those nations than she would be as the superior power holding aloof and facilitating combination against her.

politics. The probability is, indeed, that as the stage enlarges the men who play upon it are freer from taint, both of deed and of motive, and the certainty is that in a world economically unified we can no more abolish international "politics" than we can dispense with national politics.

What, after all, is politics, except the determining of social and economic policies and their administration? How, furthermore, can the regulation and advancement of the conditions of human life be an indispensable and praiseworthy task up to a national boundary line, but disreputable and unnecessary as soon as the effort reaches over the border—even though its primary motive be to advance the interests of those living behind it?

It is, of course, true that the whole of life is not regulated and determined by the methods which we call political. This truth, which will continue to apply to international dealings as well as to national affairs, supplies another point of departure for those who shrink from assuming the duties and responsibilities of international statesmanship. Adjustment of international relations must go on, they admit, but not by political methods. Hence the tendency of the reluctant to fly for refuge to the World Court—as a place of intellectual retreat, of course, not for the actual settlement of serious issues. Our disputes might possibly be trusted to a court of judges, it is said, but never to a council of politicians, insistence being at once made that we be bound to submit no cases unless we choose to do so—which reveals the whole situation.

The fact is that few of the nations are yet ready to resort to judicial means to settle the important international issues, though most of them are far ahead of the United States in this respect. They prefer, and will continue to elect for the predictable future, to trust their fortunes to the discussion and recommendation of the Council, to its temporizing, compromising, "political" methods, supplemented perhaps by resort to the Court for rulings on legal phases of the questions at issue.

This preference, moreover, is not due to mere human perversity, but to the fact that the judicial method is nowhere recognized as suitable for the determination of policies, even in nations where it has centuries of growth behind it. Courts sometimes encroach upon the functions of legislatures but no one proposes to dispense with the legislature, at least not until the framing of international policies is reached. It may be confidently expected, therefore, that the legislative and executive functions of the Assembly and Council, however rudimentary in form, will continue to be performed by these bodies, or by successors which would be very similar to them. The United States as a member of both the League and the Court might exercise great influence in promoting the increasing resort of the nations directly to the Court, influence of which succeeding generations would be justly proud, but it would be the last to wish to abandon Geneva in favor of compulsory, universal submission to The Hague.

World Economics. Underneath all the insistence that international political action need not, for the United States, be organized and continuous, and beneath all the repeated assertions that "political" and economic questions can be separately handled, to our resulting benefit, there has persisted the feeling that the United States, having been thrown back into political isolation by the reaction from the war, was still self-sufficient enough to be able to pursue its own prosperous way.

Then came adversity, and as usual it has proved to be a great teacher. President Hoover, undertaking in his Indianapolis speech of June 15, 1931, the necessary task of bolstering up our confidence in the undoubtedly large degree of self-sufficiency which we do possess, took the occasion to state plainly that it was beyond the power of the strongest of nations to cope fully with world-wide business depression. "As we look beyond the horizons of our own troubles and consider the events in other lands," he said, "we know that the main causes of the extreme violence and the long continuance of this depression came not from within but from outside the United States. . . . A large part of the forces which have swept our shores from abroad are the malign inheritances in Europe of the great war—its huge taxes, its mounting armaments, its political and social instability, its disruption of economic life by the new boundaries. Without the war we would have had no such depression. Upon these war origins are superimposed the over-rapid expansion of production and collapse in price of many foreign raw materials." [17]

[17] *Baltimore Sun,* June 16, 1931. Leading economists and bankers of the principal countries, meeting in the International Chamber of Commerce at Washington, a few weeks earlier, had one after another traced the troubles of 1931 to the wastes and dislocations of the war. See *The New York Times,* May 5–9, 1931.

Continuing the record of adverse international factors, President Hoover recorded that "Some particular calamity has happened to nearly every country in the world, and the difficulties of each have intensified the unemployment and financial difficulties of all the others. As either the cause or the effect, we have witnessed armed revolutions within the past two years in a score of nations, not to mention disturbed political life in many others." Political instability had affected three fourths of the population of the world and the fear and discouragement thus generated in our own business men had been no small factor in our own decline.

It was well for the nation to be reminded that the consequences of the war, and of future wars, could not be avoided by any amount of political head burying. Mr. Hoover did not have time to do more. Returned to the White House, he was in conference instantly with congressional and executive officials to devise ways to save Germany, the erstwhile enemy, from financial collapse. The next day, June 21, found him proposing, with general assent, that all "intergovernmental debts, reparations and relief debts" be postponed for one year. Though hailed around the globe as a generous act of statesmanship, the Hoover moratorium was not based upon altruism. Involving a loss to our own empty treasury of some $236,000,000,[18] it had stronger foundation than that. It was declared in order to save American investments in Germany, variously estimated between one and a half and three billion dollars, and, more important still, to prevent an economic, social and political collapse in the Reich that would shake all Europe upon its none too secure foundations. A nation can hardly endure a second national bankruptcy within ten years, with its consequent destruction of the investing classes and wholesale wrecking of individual lives.

We might continue to carry on, it is true, after the disintegration of social order in Europe, but Mr. Hoover and his advisers knew that it would be a changed world in which we would live, involving perhaps a serious depression of our standard of living and ultimately a change of our own social and political institutions. Mr. Hoover's warning of 1919[19] that "We cannot fiddle while Rome burns" was even more true in 1931.

His warning of the earlier year had not been heeded. The United States had retired into the position of war debt collector, continued lender and unofficial adviser as to what to do about reparations and other matters, though no connection between the Allied war debts and German reparations was ever admitted until the moratorium pointedly raised the question in the minds of all as to whether the effort of the participants in the war to collect its costs from each other was likely to be attended with much success in the future. Certainly some new means of enabling the payments to be made appeared to be necessary. With Britain, the strongest of war debtors, forced off the gold standard, carrying a train of other nations with her, and with some three quarters of the world's gold already in the hands of the two great

[18] *New York Times*, May 1, 1931. A Treasury statement.
[19] *New York Times*, October 3, 1919.

war creditors, the United States and France, the payment of the war debts in gold could hardly continue.

The moratorium was not, of course, an isolated phenomenon. Though largely made necessary by world conditions, it was precipitated by the French financial drive against Austria and Germany, designed to prevent the proposed customs union between them—an economic proposal of far-reaching political implications fought by economic means with profound political consequences.[20]

The moratorium was followed, too, by conferences with France in which it became clear that the sudden projection of American plans, however impelled by events suddenly realized, could no longer be assured of success. The sitting of the two ranking American Cabinet Ministers, Henry L. Stimson and Andrew W. Mellon, in the London Seven Power Conference of July 21, and the earlier negotiations of Secretary Mellon in Paris, did, however, give tangible evidence that the era of attempting to disentangle economics and finance from politics is drawing to a close. We shall continue, doubtless, to talk in the phrases of the last decade for some time, but the continuing urgency of salvaging the wreckage of 1914 to 1918, and of warding off new disaster, is not likely to permit us to retire into inactivity again.

The Issue of Security. Just as the British financial crisis, and many others, succeeded the German panic, so the London Conference of July, 1931, had not adjourned before the carefully prepared memorandum of France, looking to the World Disarmament Conference of 1932, asked with undiminished insistence the old question, "What will states do if war breaks out and a crime of aggression is committed?" Reaffirming her readiness to consider all general solutions: "Universal pledges of mutual assistance, combination of focal agreements, constitution of international armed forces," the French Government reiterated once again that "insecurity for one state means insecurity for all" and that no one could "deny, in the domain of politics, a solidarity daily promoted in the domain of economics. By reason of the danger threatening the weaker or more exposed states, the general reduction of armaments lays upon the stronger or less threatened powers fresh responsibilities which they cannot elude. The government of the republic is

---

[20] See *The New York Times*, March 23, 24, 27, 29, May 6, 19, 20, June 4, 21, 22, July 21, 22, 24, 1931. Conforming to the ideology of the time, Secretary Stimson announced, on March 27, that the only interest of the United States in the proposed customs union was in its effect on trade—a statement which no doubt appeared impeccable to nearly all Americans who read it.

convinced of the necessity of a security guaranteed to every state by assistance which should be mutual, effective and prompt." [21]

Declaring the real task of the conference to be "the organization of a solid and durable peace," the French thus challenged another defensive thesis of the American government, laid down at the London Naval Conference, that no guarantees can be given in connection with the reduction of arms. The reluctance of nations protected by oceans, and the absence of covetous neighbors, to recognize the need for political security of nations placed in the opposite circumstances is easily understandable. We are not afraid of attack; why can't they settle down, disarm and be quiet? Canadians ask this question only less tartly than Americans, and the query rises strongly in Britain.

Yet we should be able to understand that the defeat of the League of Nations in the United States, following as it did the perpetual hammering of the principle of mutual guarantee, did much to perpetuate this issue. The vitality of both Articles 10 and 16 of the Covenant was at least temporarily destroyed by the onslaughts of American Senators. Faced with the defection of the world's most powerful state, the other geographically protected members of the League themselves sought, in succeeding Assemblies, to weaken the obligations of the guarantees. They succeeded, in large measure, morally, though not legally.

Every line of the Covenant is still "the complete negation of militarism," as President Hoover believed it to be at the time it was written. His appraisal of the opposition to it in the Peace Conference as arising "entirely from the representatives of the old militaristic régimes and from the reactionaries of the world in general" was also sound, as was his judgment that these elements saw in it "truly the undermining of militarism. They had the vision to see, and even openly to state, that it would mean the ultimate abandonment of military force in the world." [22]

Unfortunately, this result of the Covenant is still to be realized, but the first great test of its fruition in this vital direction is soon to be made. The United States, too, can hardly stand in the coming Disarmament Conference, and its successors, fortified alone by the splendid example of its leadership in naval limitation. The testimony of Herbert Hoover, following his visits to the capitals of the states newly created by the powerful aid of American arms in the war, stated that "the first anxious question of their officials was, 'Will America ratify the League?' and their invariable comment was that without it their only course was

[21] *New York Times*, July 22, 1931.   [22] *New York Times*, October 3, 1919.

the hopeless effort to arm themselves against stronger neighbors; to do it in the midst of misery; to endeavor to set up groups and military alliances, and all the old treadmill of oppression of arms and ultimate war." [23]

That American abstention from the post-war organization of peace has been predominantly responsible for the partial revival of the old treadmill is not clear. It is plain, however, that the United States did nothing to assure security to the nations arising maimed from the war and that if a new balance of power, presaging the final eclipse of European civilization, has not arisen, no credit therefor belongs to us. We invited that result. Beyond that, from our relatively secure and unpledged situation we have even begun to denounce strongly the nations who ask to know our intentions for the future before they disarm.

These nations may be foolishly unwilling to trust with finality their security to a League of Nations which is not universal, and from which two giant nations, the United States and Russia, hold aloof, but they are not utterly fatuous. The League, also, may have been timid in facing the issue of reducing the arms of the victors or permitting the increase of those of the defeated powers, but its weakness in this direction is not wholly its own. The paralyzing doubt as to what the most powerful industrial nation would do in case the security of nations hung upon the application of the League guarantees has haunted every effort definitely to outlaw war and will continue to do so until we make our position unequivocally clear. We are additionally bound to take our stand, moreover, by the obligation assumed toward Germany, both in the Treaty of Versailles and in our separate treaty of peace with her, to make her disarmament the prelude to general disarmament.

National Interest. The writer, however, has no desire unduly to emphasize the duty of the United States to join in the organization of peace. He does believe that in throwing their whole effort into the demolition of empires and political systems, in demanding the creation of new states and in backing throughout the war new principles of international conduct and morality, the American people incurred obligations to assist in the stabilization of the new Europe, and the establishment of a better political system, which no super-patriotic washing of hands could eradicate. Nevertheless, nations, like individuals, do not always take the high view of their duties and it is certainly possible to argue convincingly that the American people did enough.

It is not possible, moreover, to show that they have any duty to

[23] *Ibid.*

shoulder the responsibility for, or to arrogate to themselves the settling of every petty quarrel or knotty problem which the follies and passions of European peoples give rise to. Such paternalistic regulation, furthermore, is assuredly not what the peoples of the Old World desire, nor is it necessary to the collaboration of the United States in world politics. The peoples who are caught in the tangle of nationalistic aspirations which criss-cross Europe do want the impartial voice and the pacific influence of the United States exerted as a factor in the achieving of settlements, but no complicated set of reservations is needed to tell the American government when to use its full influence in the Council, the Assembly or in League committees. Nor could any reservations tell it when it ought to keep silent or play a minor part. The conduct of our world relations, through whatever channel, must be left to the common sense of future governments and to their estimate of what the real interests of the United States are. The contention that American representatives cannot be trusted to exercise good judgment and to know what our interests are, is one of the strangest arguments ever invented by Americans who glory in the leadership of American mentality in every other avenue of human endeavor. Only less to be marveled at is the claim that in some mysterious manner the most neutral and most powerful member of the League would be oppressed or bullied by other members, whereas the actual tendency, in most cases, is for the American representative to possess more than his proportionate share of influence.

The interests of the people of the United States will determine the extent of their future participation in the work of the League of Nations. With our investments by the billion scattered over the earth, and sure to flow again if the economic development of the world and our own prosperity are to continue; with long term investments abroad a foolish gamble if any new competition in armaments is allowed to develop; with the decline of our export trade permeating back through our whole economic structure—weakening it far more than the export loss figure can indicate; with international intercourse of every kind increasingly accelerated, American participation in whatever machinery exists for keeping world life running as smoothly as possible cannot be delayed indefinitely.

If War Comes. The interest of the United States in that most disastrous of all breakdowns in world economy, modern war, is particularly deep, though it appears to be now partially forgotten. It is conceivably possible that the United States might escape the direct effects of another general European or Asiatic war, although there is no historical warrant for such a hope. We have taken part in every world war that has occurred since Jamestown was settled in 1607, usually quite against our will. While we were still a part of the British Empire we fought regularly in wars which centered in Europe. Three times, world war swept the outposts of England and France in North America. Whether it was "King William's War" with Louis XIV (1689–97) or the War of the Spanish Succession, which we domesticated into "Queen Anne's War" (1702–13), or the Seven Years' War which really began in North America as "The French and Indian War," spreading across the ocean until all Europe was involved (1756–63), our participation in the world's wars had always materialized up to 1776. Then came independence, and we said that that kind of business was ended. We would fight no more, simply because of dynastic or national rivalries abroad.

Napoleon followed swiftly, and a struggle mightier than any known before developed. Both sides harried our commerce and interfered with the liberty of our citizens upon the seas. Attempting to enforce some respect for our rights, we resorted to an embargo, in 1808, which resulted only in the further wholesale seizure of our ships, particularly by Napoleon. Other measures failing similarly, we finally drifted into war, in 1812, with the side that we felt had outraged us the most, just as we did in 1917.[24]

In both cases forbearance had persisted about as long as it could, if any rights were to be maintained in the face of a death struggle in Europe which made the stoppage or control of neutral commerce seem imperative to survival. It is possible, of course, that the might of our effort of 1918 may enable us to awe and intimidate future belligerents who believe themselves fighting for existence, but the temptation to try to achieve victory by using new death-dealing devices, multiplying according to all observers at an accelerating rate, appears likely to overbalance the dread of an intervention that is not certain to come, or that might come too late. The possibilities, further, for bringing the war to our own shores, through the perfection of new offensive weapons, will certainly be seriously considered on both sides of the ocean in the future.

Neither, also, is it necessary for the weapons of the future to provoke American intervention by wholesale attack or arrest of our seagoing commerce in order profoundly to modify the democratic, capital-

[24] See H. C. Hockett, *Political and Social History of the United States*, N. Y., 1929, Vol. I, pp. 104–12, 293–304.

istic civilization that the centuries have built up. A short savage war in the heart of Europe, opened by thousands of airplanes and long range guns and supported by all the resources of science, particularly chemistry, may well do irreparable damage to the social and economic system that we value, as well as wipe out quickly some billions of dollars of American property. Those Americans who are nervous about the spread of Communism, or the rule of dictators, should be constantly in the watch tower of Geneva, scanning the horizon for every war cloud as big as a man's hand. All their efforts to maintain the present ways of life are likely to prove futile, if the folly of 1914 is allowed to be repeated.

The cry that we must wait to see what the fracas looks like before we decide what to do about it seems also to be dangerously short-sighted in our own interest. No man likes to commit his action in advance, though life in any country would be chaotic if people did not do so continually. It is pleasant to feel untrammeled for the future, yet the business world could not operate a day if people did not bind themselves incessantly to do what later may be painful to perform. Some men are so fond of pursuing freely the desires of the moment that they never tie themselves down with any social responsibilities, but most people do not prefer that kind of liberty. Similarly, it would be pleasant indeed to wait for future wars to develop, observe the amenities with which they might be conducted on both sides, weigh all the rights and wrongs that skillful propaganda could deliver to us, sense all the advantages and disadvantages of this course or that and then issue our fiat in the full consciousness of duty performed in complete wisdom. Such deliberation was, perhaps, possible in the past. It is perilous in the extreme for the future.

From such a conclusion it is not necessary to fly to the assumption that full responsibility for the suppression of every conceivable kind of war, no matter how unrighteous in origin, must be undertaken in detailed terms. No such anticipation is possible, even if it were desirable. Neither is it desirable or safe to wait until the storm breaks before constructing a shelter, or until the fire comes before organizing a fire department and purchasing an insurance contract. The general policy that a nation is going to pursue in the face of an emergency which has been repeatedly experienced before, and whose manifestations have been adequately studied, can be laid down in advance much more safely than it can be improvised under the conflicting strains and stresses set up by the disaster itself. A nation of 130,-

000,000 people may be able to make up its mind, before it is too late, as to what its long interests as well as the short ones demand, but it promises to be much cheaper and safer for it to take its stand definitely and positively on the side of international law and order before the emergency occurs. The ability of selfish or partisan groups to paralyze action will not only be thus considerably reduced, but the full power of American influence can be thrown into an effort to prevent the conflict rather than to suppress it, or to limit its effects if sudden outbreak cannot be prevented.

Even more important is it that American influence should be steadily exerted in the League toward the reduction of the international sore spots before they cause acute difficulty. The true function of the League is not to await the arrival of dangerous crises, but to forestall them, to relieve them before heroic measures are required. The League, once it becomes universal, will have nearly failed if any major conflict of interest develops into war.[25]

The Place of Force. There are very competent observers, indeed, who confidently believe that the facilities for mediation, investigation and delay which the League offers make it practically impossible for war to occur again. Their demonstration of the steps any nation would have to take before it would dare to confront world opinion with war is startlingly convincing. If it be actually true that the operation of the Covenant of the League of Nations has made war almost impossible in the first decade of its existence there has been no greater miracle performed in the story of the race. If the most destructive of deep-seated human institutions, established for thousands of years and glorified for centuries, has been uprooted without the use of any force, other than the organized opinion of mankind, there can scarcely be again a development so stupendous.

The fact seems to be, however, that the bulk of the peoples are unable to believe that they are free from the dangers of a scourge which has embittered and dwarfed the lives of many millions of people who are still young. The conviction, now in process of modification, that the Great War was criminally plotted by one or two nations, has something to do with it, but, aside from that impression, belief persists unavoidably that national word may fail, or national ambition run riot, and that wars of sudden passion do occasionally occur.

Until popular faith in the sure efficacy of the conference method

[25] See Gilbert Murray, "The Real Value of the League," *Harper's Magazine,* September, 1930, pp. 446–53.

is well grown, and supported by long experience, it follows that nations not geographically protected will not radically disarm without assurance that they will be effectively supported if attacked. People are not secure until they feel that they are safe. The proper place of force in keeping the peace is a factor as elusive in the international domain as in the national. In both areas it unquestionably belongs in the background and quantitatively considered governs little activity. In all areas of life, moreover, the steady aim should be to reduce the occasions requiring the use of force, but there is no indication that the acts of predatory individuals can be ignored in any future that is worth considering. Correspondingly, we certainly have no sure guarantee that national aggression is no more to be contemplated. Quite to the contrary, the impression is general in the Winter of 1931–32, that we are witnessing a major exhibition of it in Manchuria.

Some assurance of safety, or at least of strong support in the ultimate emergency there must be, if the evolution away from dependence upon national armies and navies is to move forward with the rapidity that world recovery and future peace demand. A *Pax-America,* supported by overwhelming force of every kind, military, economic and financial, might remove, for a time, from the rest of the world the incubus and danger of heavy armaments. Short of a solution so hopelessly out of date, none other than a mutual guarantee seems possible. Such guaranty may be regional or limited to friendly groups only; it appears to be much safer and more effective when as universal as possible. If there is to be any "sanction" at all, the more overwhelming it is the less the likelihood that it will ever need to be applied. What nation could defy a completely universal sanction?

At the best there would be some risk in adding our great weight to such a guarantee, but is there not more risk without it? There are those, it is true, who conceive that the simple promise of the nations, made in the Pact of Paris, that they will not go to war, is assurance enough, particularly for a naturally protected country of great power. No one should depreciate the vast importance of the brand of illegality which the Pact has put upon war. Neither, also, should any assume that the signatories to that epochal document can keep silent when the Pact, negative as it is in terms, is broken. Least of all can the United States, its main sponsor, remain passive. The chief prestige in the world of nations that it has regained since 1919 is bound up in that small document. "Any international war anywhere is now a diplomatic defeat for the United States." Unnecessary as the Pact would have been if the United States had gone originally into the League, it is now our way back into the organized effort of the nations to establish peace. It must be followed up and supported, if we are not to stand before the world clothed in thin futility. It must be followed up if we are not in the long run to be the authors of a step backward from the Covenant, instead of an advance from it.

Hence the desire of much of our sober leadership—up to October, 1931—to implement the Pact by an agreement to consult instantly with its signatories when it is broken. Our experience in the Russo-Manchurian embroglio of 1929 taught us that no one nation, however loftily placed, can define, after hostilities have started, whether "war" is in progress or not and that any such unilateral intervention is quite sure to be resented and rebuffed.

A Consultative Pact? Strangely enough a much more serious outbreak of trouble in Manchuria, the Sino-Japanese crisis of 1931, seems to have brought the movement for a new consultative pact to its logical end, and to have terminated it years before it would have expired otherwise. When the impact of the overnight seizure of the heart of Manchuria by the Japanese army was felt, realization that no international agency other than the Council of the League of Nations could hope to cope with the situation came almost as quickly. The Council might fail, but if so no consultative conference of signatories of the Pact of Paris that could be called together would be likely to succeed.

The strong support promptly given by the Executive arm of the United States government to the Council's effort to restore the peace was the natural action which any "realistic" government would have taken, unless it wished to give the Pact a mere lip service. To ignore its existence and either hold entirely aloof or pursue solely the old policy of applying independent diplomatic pressure would be to confess the impotence of the Pact and frankly abandon all effort by the United States to limit international disorder.

If the necessity of using the machinery of the League to maintain the vitality of the Pact be doubted, let the alternative be considered. With whom should we consult, when any violation of the Pact occurs?

A conference of the signatories of the Pact, some sixty in number, would be slow to assemble and difficult to secure action from when it did gather. Yet every member has the same right to a voice in the action to be taken and none can be denied it. It would not do to leave the consultation to the Great Powers; smaller states must be at least represented. It would hardly be feasible or desirable to call only the Powers most directly interested; the counsel and weight of those not so concerned in the issue is needed. Who, in any event, is to call the conference? Shall the duty rotate, and if so how far? It is hardly likely that the United States either would or should be entrusted with a discretion of such universal importance.

It cannot be said that no system of consultation apart from the machinery of the League of Nations could possibly be worked out, but if it could be done the result would be another league of nations— a weakening duplication which even the United States itself does not desire. Meanwhile the Council of the League is ready at a moment's notice to perform the service. It was created for the express purpose and is clothed with representative authority by nearly all the signatories of the Pact to act for them in time of stress. It is equipped with a consultative agreement, in Article 11 of the Covenant, which has been invoked with a fair degree of success more than twenty times.

Granting, however, that another council might be instituted to give life and continuity to the Pact, what would it do when it met? It would meet to consult, but would the conclusions agreed upon, or the measures advised, be designed to restore the peace by simple persuasion only? It is hardly likely that governments could fail to consider, in all soberness, the recommendations made, or that they would refuse to support them in any degree. The conference, like the Monroe Doctrine, would be an idle futility indeed if there was no intent whatever to back it up. The situation would be morally no different than that arising when the League Council is the consultative body. In either case wide discretion would remain to each government as to just how far it should co-operate, but it could only rarely refuse to co-operate at all.

Practically there would be a great difference between the operation of an *ad hoc* league of nations and a permanently organized one. In the first case all action would have to be improvised when improvisation is time-consuming and dangerous; in the latter a gradation of carefully matured measures, ranging from simple mediation up through the application of an economic boycott to the asking of military or naval forces, can be ready for consideration and selection.

If the crisis be serious the task will require all the experience that the Council of the League and the permanent officials of the Secretariat have been able to accumulate. Even then mistakes in judgment will occasionally occur, as in any humanly controlled agency. The technique of the League, however, is already developed enough to be well understood, and it is available for immediate application. Its primary task is to stop fighting, its chief resource in the emergency, if important nations are involved, being the rapid mobilization of world opinion.

Economic Pressure? The weight of neutral opinion will usually be sufficient to enable peace to be restored, perhaps by patient negotiation. Experience strongly suggests, however, that we shall never have real assurance of settled peace until a powerful and determined aggressor has been restrained, in the common interest, by stronger means. The direct use of force may in the end have to be resorted to, but it would seem wisest first to prepare in all seriousness for a major trial of the economic boycott. Preparations for the application of this arm of the law have often been discussed. (See page 540.) They should be pushed to practical conclusion. Such a use of economic power in support of international order will bring loss to all concerned and suffering to some, but it is not too soon to face the issue squarely as an alternative to the recurrent, violent destruction of life, of wealth and of all confidence in the establishment of law and security among nations.

The very least that the United States can do is to make it illegal, in advance of the occurrence, for Americans to trade with a power which has violated our own Kellogg Pact. Needless to say the effectiveness of such action will be greatly increased by our membership in the League Council which declares the Pact broken. The chances of making aggression a disastrous undertaking will be much greater, too, if the members of the League, or some of them, join the boycott.

Certainly no important boycott can be attempted without the participation of the United States. The decision to support the League in such a grave test may be made, to be sure, by the United States as a non-member, but the chances of a crisis proceeding to the point where drastic action must be taken would be much less than they are now if all future belligerents faced the probability that the United States, as a member of the League, would both help to direct the League's handling of the crisis and shoulder its share of whatever measures might be necessary to restore the peace.

The League, hampered as it has been, has tremendous progress to the credit of its brief moment of existence. Its future evolution is a matter of the most vital concern to every nation. We shall either go on to the perfection and establishment of the machinery for keeping international intercourse reasonably orderly, or we shall go backward to the quite hopeless chaos which is inherent in a return to the jungle era of international relations.

The American people should ask themselves in all seriousness, not only whether they actually want to have competitive armaments reduced the world over, but also whether they really wish to see the League of Nations fail in a final test of the chief reason for its existence—its ability to give security against aggressive war.

Effective Disarmament? The impracticability of avoiding participation in the consultative machinery provided by the League is made equally clear by consideration of the insistent problem of disarmament. No treaty, whether covenant, or disarmament convention, can be allowed to attempt a freezing of conditions when all know that change is the one certain law of life. It was, therefore, a wise initiative of the American delegation in the League's Preparatory Disarmament Commission which led to the inclusion into the draft convention, which the World Disarmament Conference is called to consider, of an escape clause whereby when national safety is threatened national armament may be increased.[26]

In order to prevent the abuse of this necessary right, however, Article 50 of the proposed treaty provides that whenever any one Power suspends the treaty, giving "full explanation" of its reasons, the others "shall promptly advise as to the situation thus presented." The right of suspension is, further, to be strictly limited by "a change of circumstances" constituting, in the opinion of a signatory, "a menace to its national security." Articles 54 and 59 remove every ground for suspending the treaty except the threat of war or revolution and indicate clearly that by a menace to national security war is meant.[27]

The invocation of the escape clause thus calls for immediate consultation, as does the violation of the treaty by the increase of arms without giving notice of suspension. Article 51 recognizes that any violation is "a matter of concern to all the parties," and Article 52 provides that any nation may cause the investigation of a suspected violation of the treaty, by complaining to the Secretary General of the League, who will report to the Permanent Disarmament Commission, the advisory body to the Council.

If the threat of war thus raised proves to be real, the Council is, of course, bound to take action, when members of the League are concerned, under Article 10 of its own charter, and this duty of the Council is naturally expressly recognized in Article 52 of the draft

[26] See the excellent analysis of the problem by Clarence K. Streit under "The United States and World Consultation," in the *New York Times*, May 5, 6, 7, 1931.
[27] Preparatory Commission for the Disarmament Conference, *Draft Convention*, IX. Disarmament, 1930. IX 8 (Official no: C. 687, M. 288, 1930, IX.)

convention. Article 10 of the Covenant thus promises to be greatly strengthened, if not restored to full vitality, by the disarmament treaty. It is a remarkable fact that any serious approach to the problem of world peace and security leads back to its vital principle.

Article 11 of the League's charter, moreover, bids fair to have its present great importance increased by the addition of the function of bringing to the attention of the Council the situation resulting from a threat of war to non-members of the League. The League is not bound to move to protect the territorial integrity or political independence of non-members, of course, but if their co-operation with the League comes to approximate membership, it may decide to do so. The larger interest would indicate such a course, just as the interest of the non-members impels them to claim that protection as a right by accepting membership.

The obligation of the non-members to consult with the Council of the League is not expressly stated in the draft disarmament treaty. It may be, too, that some screen will be erected in the final treaty to veil the inescapable step toward working partnership in the League which must be taken, if we are to have disarmament. Strong resistance to the inevitable requirements of any effective international organization may still be expected from the isolationists of the United States Senate, especially from some of the Senators who are still strongly influenced by the old continental attitude of the great interior of the country, but surely few reservationists will have the temerity to propose soberly, at this late date, the expansion of the Permanent Disarmament Commission from the small body necessary for any efficiency into a congress of sixty delegates, divorced from the League.

The Issue of Change Without War. The best thought at the capital is needed, instead, for the serious consideration of a further advance toward concerted action to remove the deep grievances that grow into wars. We shall not be able to keep from going farther in this direction. If force is to be barred as a means of correcting situations which seem to peoples permanently intolerable, some other means of eliminating or ameliorating the worst sources of friction will have to be developed. We shall have to come to the point of correcting an occasional boundary even, if it becomes and remains clearly unjust. Neither does this mean the action of a super-state. The Covenant again provides a safety valve, in Article 19,[28] that can be used as a vehicle to convey the deepening judgment of the League that a rectification of exist-

[28] See Appendix.

ing conditions is to the interest of all concerned. This provision read literally means exactly nothing, but the voting of a resolution by succeeding Assemblies, and by increasing majorities, declaring it to be the sense of organized humanity that a revision of boundary and treaty ought to take place is not likely to be without effect.[29] Better methods of correcting outworn conditions may be worked out. The task cannot be permanently evaded.

The Place of a Great Nation. In the never ending endeavor of the world's peoples to perfect a working relationship between themselves that will establish civilization and law where anarchy has hitherto too often prevailed, the share of the American people cannot be a small one. No mission to "save the world" need be laid upon the United States, but its great wealth and power must give it a responsibility for the smooth running of international life that is second to none. Power and responsibility can hardly be separated, if either is to continue, and neither inertia nor faction should be allowed to stifle for long the voice of the world's "greatest" people in the councils of the nations.

Neither should such participation be spasmodic or intermittent. Wherever world problems are to be discussed, an American representative is entitled to a seat. Further than that, American delegates of the highest rank have a right to talk man to man with the statesmen of the world as they meet in the regular sessions of the League Council and Assembly. Our dignity is not advanced, nor our interests adequately protected, by the occasional, casual trips of American Cabinet Ministers abroad, supposedly on vacation, during which they happen to pick up much needed information and understanding. It does not follow that the American Secretary of State and his colleagues at Washington need to travel abroad habitually, but when it is desirable that they go, their journeys should be taken as a matter of course.

It should never have been necessary for Secretary Stimson to say on returning to the United States, August 28, 1931: "It was my privilege to meet the Foreign Ministers of Great Britain, France, Germany and Italy, as well as high officials and the executive heads, and we had a chance to talk matters over. Better still, we became personally acquainted, and that is a great thing in the present state of the world. It is my profound view that these personal meetings with the representatives of different countries must lead to an enormous amount of good, and I believe in them thoroughly. I feel better equipped for

[29] A suggestion made by Dr. William E. Rappard, at the 1931 Williamstown Institute of Politics.

THE NEW LEAGUE OF NATIONS BUILDINGS

ERECTION BEGUN IN 1929. ESTIMATED COST, $5,000,000

my own duties, for I have a better knowledge of these European problems." [30]

It is high time that an American statesman had the courage to tell his countrymen what their own welfare demands. His example may well be followed by the leaders of public opinion generally. The American people may rebel against vigorous leadership occasionally but they cannot do without it. They are too vast in number and varied in character to stir quickly, but they are not too ponderous to respond to strong initiative in their own interest, nor too self-centered to quicken to no other appeal.

If the people of the United States do desire to see a de-militarized world, in which the rules and guarantees of civilization shall apply to the most important of all groups of men, the nations, it is not too soon for them to begin to resume the rôle of leadership which none can play in their stead. Unity of opinion may still be difficult to achieve. It can hardly be completely attained, any more than national politics can be fully excluded from the question, but in a cause which touches every man's welfare a preponderance of support for constructive action may surely be expected to develop, and rapidly, if courageously led.

The leadership, moreover, may be expected from either political party. The tradition of powerful championship of the orderly adjustment of international relations, built up through long years of devoted labor by Hay and Root, Roosevelt and Taft, Hughes and Kellogg, Hoover and Stimson, together with a host of leaders only less great, can hardly fail to reassert itself powerfully among Republicans, especially under the propulsion of distresses and dangers common to all peoples.

Correspondingly, it would not seem credible that the Democrats should much longer fail to respond to the pull of Woodrow Wilson's far-seeing statesmanship. The temptation to try to win elections for themselves by rousing isolationist sentiment, against the returning international leadership of Republican Executives, will be strong for a time. Some Democratic Senators have already given deplorable evidences of surrender to it. In a party that has produced as many indomitable leaders as have risen from its ranks, however, the emergence of a successor to Wilson may be expected with a good deal of confidence.

In a future in which the welfare of every citizen is more and more dependent upon the success or failure of international statesmanship, the emergence of the next world figure must be a matter of keen moment to both Republicans and Democrats. This will be true not only because

[30] *New York Times*, August 28, 1931.

those with pride in their party will wish it to write the next great chapter in our history, and not alone because capacity to grapple with world problems is likely to encompass constructive leadership in domestic affairs, but because it is imperative that American leadership shall be powerfully revived in time to buttress the League of Nations against the grave tests which still face it.

The struggle to establish international order has been splendidly begun; it must continue incessantly, with every enlightened nation shouldering its full share of the burden of each engagement. Stable world organization will not be established without courage nor achieved without putting something into it. It may even be necessary, at least once, for the nations to pay the price of suppressing by force a strong aggressor. Better that, by far, than submission to never-ending wars which must be suffered with small compensation, if any. No nation can longer live in security in a lawless world, and no international organization can maintain the peace unless its members will defend each other against arbitrary attack.

To dismiss such common action in defense of law as "war," and to maintain that neither "aggression" nor "defense" can ever be defined, is to deny that civilization can establish itself and to challenge the continued existence of law in any field of human relations.

Entanglement? Yes, in the ringing words of President Hoover's Stanford University address of October 2, 1919, spoken from the shadow of the fall of the first world statesman, "Our expansion overseas has entangled us for good or ill, and I stand for an honest attempt to join with Europe's better spirits to prevent these entanglements from involving us in war. We are not dealing with perfection, we are dealing with the lesser of evils. These are reasons of interest."

"There are also reasons of idealism," continued Mr. Hoover, "and true national interest lies along the path of practical ideals. . . . It was with the hope of ending war that we went into it. To fix peace in international law—that idea dominated our representatives at the Peace Conference. We have expended the lives of our sons and an enormous portion of our wealth, hoping to see these ends made secure. For us to refuse to enter into a joint attempt with the well-thinking sections of a large part of the world to establish a continuing moral conscience against war is the utmost folly in our own interest." [31]

Involvement? Certainly, involvement in every effort to prevent the involvement of war. That is the only real entanglement from which

[31] *New York Times*, October 3, 1919.

there is no retreat—an entanglement from which there is no escape by the order to cease firing, but whose effects run on like a malignant disease through the world's economic body, persisting as does the memory of the agonies which were endured, and poisoning international relations for long periods to come.

Surrender of "sovereignty"? By no means! No sovereignty is lost by agreements voluntarily entered into to secure co-operation and to prevent the recurrence of world anarchy. An undertaking to join with other nations in a common defense of the right of all to live in peace and security is the highest expression of sovereignty. Neither, also, is the sovereign power of a nation, when faced with such an issue, to be defended by putting it into storage for future possible use. Two things may be expected with confidence, if the entanglements of war are permitted to continue: either the civilization that we love, in spite of its imperfections, will be long submerged by the consequences, or the League of Nations that will eventually arise from the ruins will have powers to enforce the peace that will leave the present mutual association of nations standing merely as the historic symbol of the failure of the sovereign state.

SELECT BIBLIOGRAPHY

RAY STANNARD BAKER, *Woodrow Wilson and the World Settlement,* Volumes I, II and III, Doubleday, N. Y., 1922.

WILLIAM E. DODD, *Woodrow Wilson and His Work,* Doubleday, N. Y., 1922.

GEORGE HARVEY, *Henry Clay Frick the Man,* Scribners, N. Y., 1928.

CHARLES P. HOWLAND, *American Foreign Relations, 1928,* Yale Press, 1928.

WILLIS FLETCHER JOHNSON, *George Harvey, A Passionate Patriot,* Houghton Mifflin, Boston, 1929.

HENRY CABOT LODGE, *The Senate and the League of Nations,* Scribners, N. Y., 1925.

DAVID HUNTER MILLER, *The Drafting of the Covenant,* Volumes I and II, Putnam's, N. Y., 1928.

ALLAN NEVINS, *Henry White, Thirty Years of American Diplomacy,* Harpers, N. Y., 1930.

CORRINE ROOSEVELT ROBINSON, *My Brother, Theodore Roosevelt,* Scribners, N. Y., 1921.

OWEN WISTER, *Roosevelt, The Story of a Friendship,* Macmillan, N. Y., 1930.

APPENDIX

THE COVENANT OF THE LEAGUE OF NATIONS

WITH AMENDMENTS IN FORCE AUGUST 1, 1929[1]

(See note below)

THE HIGH CONTRACTING PARTIES,

In order to promote international cooperation and to achieve international peace and security

by the acceptance of obligations not to resort to war,

by the prescription of open, just and honorable relations between nations,

by the firm establishment of the understandings of international law as the actual rule of conduct among Governments, and

by the maintenance of justice and a scrupulous respect for all treaty obligations in the dealings of organized peoples with one another, agree to this Covenant of the League of Nations.

ARTICLE 1

Membership and Withdrawal

1. The original Members of the League of Nations shall be those of the Signatories which are named in the Annex to this Covenant, and also such of those other States named in the Annex as shall accede without reservation to this Covenant. Such accessions shall be effected by a declaration deposited with the Secretariat within two months of the coming into force of the Covenant. Notice thereof shall be sent to all other Members of the League.

2. Any fully self-governing State, Dominion or Colony not named in the Annex may become a Member of the League if its admission is agreed to by two-thirds of the Assembly, provided that it shall give effective guaranties of its sincere intention to observe its international obligations and shall accept such regulations as may be prescribed by the League in regard to its military, naval and air forces and armaments.

3. Any Member of the League may, after two years' notice of its intention so to do, withdraw from the League, provided that all its international obligations and all its obligations under this Covenant shall have been fulfilled at the time of its withdrawal.

ARTICLE 2

Executive Organs

The action of the League under this Covenant shall be effected through the instrumentality of an Assembly and of a Council, with a permanent Secretariat.

---

[1] Edited by the World Peace Foundation, 40 Mt. Vernon St., Boston, Mass., sole American agents for all League publications. The notes in this reprint have been somewhat shortened.

ARTICLE 3

Assembly

1. The Assembly shall consist of representatives of the Members of the League.

2. The Assembly shall meet at stated intervals and from time to time, as occasion may require, at the Seat of the League, or at such other place as may be decided upon.

3. The Assembly may deal at its meetings with any matter within the sphere of action of the League or affecting the peace of the world.

4. At meetings of the Assembly each Member of the League shall have one vote and may have not more than three Representatives.

ARTICLE 4

Council

1. The Council shall consist of representatives of the Principal Allied and Associated Powers [United States of America, the British Empire, France, Italy and Japan], together with Representatives of four[1] other Members of the League. These four[1] Members of the League shall be selected by the Assembly from time to time in its discretion. Until the appointment of the Representatives of the four Members of the League first selected by the Assembly, Representatives of Belgium, Brazil, Greece and Spain shall be Members of the Council.

2. With the approval of the majority of the Assembly, the Council may name additional Members of the League, whose Representatives shall always be Members of the Council;[2] the Council with like approval may increase the number of Members of the League to be selected by the Assembly[2] for representation on the Council.[1]

2 bis.[3] *The Assembly shall fix by a two-thirds majority the rules dealing with the election of the non-permanent Members of the Council, and particularly such regulations as relate to their term of office and the conditions of re-eligibility.*

3. The Council shall meet from time to time as occasion may require, and at least once a year, at the Seat of the League, or at such other place as may be decided upon.

4. The Council may deal at its meetings with any matter within the sphere of action of the League or affecting the peace of the world.

5. Any Member of the League not represented on the Council shall be invited to send a Representative to sit as a member at any meeting of the Council during the consideration of matters specially affecting the interests of that Member of the League.

6. At meetings of the Council, each Member of the League represented on the Council shall have one vote, and may have not more than one Representative.

ARTICLE 5

Voting and Procedure

1. Except where otherwise expressly provided in this Covenant, or by the terms of the present Treaty, decisions at any meeting of the Assembly or of the Council

---

[1] The number of Members of the Council selected by the Assembly, by application of the second clause of Art. 4, par. 2, was increased from four to six on September 25, 1922, and from six to nine on September 8, 1926.

[2] By application of this clause Germany was designated as a permanent Member of the Council on September 8, 1926, the appropriate action of the Council having been taken on September 4.

[3] This paragraph came into force on July 29, 1926, in accordance with Art. 26. The regulations were adopted by the Assembly on September 15.

shall require the agreement of all the Members of the League represented at the meeting.

2. All matters of procedure at meetings of the Assembly or of the Council, including the appointment of Committees to investigate particular matters, shall be regulated by the Assembly or by the Council and may be decided by a majority of the Members of the League represented at the meeting.

3. The first meeting of the Assembly and the first meeting of the Council shall be summoned by the President of the United States of America.

ARTICLE 6

Secretariat and Expenses

1. The permanent Secretariat shall be established at the Seat of the League. The Secretariat shall comprise a Secretary-General and such secretaries and staff as may be required.

2. The first Secretary-General shall be the person named in the Annex; thereafter the Secretary-General shall be appointed by the Council with the approval of the majority of the Assembly.

3. The Secretaries and the staff of the Secretariat shall be appointed by the Secretary-General with the approval of the Council.

4. The Secretary-General shall act in that capacity at all meetings of the Assembly and of the Council.

5.[1] *The expenses of the League shall be borne by the Members of the League in the proportion decided by the Assembly.*

ARTICLE 7

Seat, Qualifications of Officials, Immunities

1. The Seat of the League is established at Geneva.

2. The Council may at any time decide that the Seat of the League shall be established elsewhere.

3. All positions under or in connection with the League, including the Secretariat, shall be open equally to men and women.

4. Representatives of the Members of the League and officials of the League when engaged on the business of the League shall enjoy diplomatic privileges and immunities.

5. The buildings and other property occupied by the League or its officials or by Representatives attending its meetings shall be inviolable.

ARTICLE 8

Reduction of Armaments

1. The Members of the League recognize that the maintenance of peace requires the reduction of national armaments to the lowest point consistent with national safety and the enforcement by common action of international obligations.

2. The Council, taking account of the geographical situation and circumstances of each State, shall formulate plans for such reduction for the consideration and action of the several Governments.

3. Such plans shall be subject to reconsideration and revision at least every 10 years.

---

[1] This paragraph came into force as an amendment on August 13, 1924, in accordance with Art. 26. The original provision was as follows:
"The expenses of the Secretariat shall be borne by the Members of the League in accordance with the apportionment of the expenses of the International Bureau of the Universal Postal Union."

4. After these plans shall have been adopted by the several Governments, the limits of armaments therein fixed shall not be exceeded without the concurrence of the Council.

5. The Members of the League agree that the manufacture by private enterprise of munitions and implements of war is open to grave objections. The Council shall advise how the evil effects attendant upon such manufacture can be prevented, due regard being had to the necessities of those Members of the League which are not able to manufacture the munitions and implements of war necessary for their safety.

6. The Members of the League undertake to interchange full and frank information as to the scale of their armaments, their military, naval and air programs, and the condition of such of their industries as are adaptable to warlike purposes.

ARTICLE 9

Permanent Military, Naval and Air Commission

A permanent Commission shall be constituted to advise the Council on the execution of the provisions of Articles 1 and 8 and on military, naval and air questions generally.

ARTICLE 10

Guaranties Against Aggression

The Members of the League undertake to respect and preserve as against external aggression the territorial integrity and existing political independence of all Members of the League. In case of any such aggression or in case of any threat or danger of such aggression, the Council shall advise upon the means by which this obligation shall be fulfilled.

ARTICLE 11

Action in Case of War or Threat of War

1. Any war or threat of war, whether immediately affecting any of the Members of the League or not, is hereby declared a matter of concern to the whole League, and the League shall take any action that may be deemed wise and effectual to safeguard the peace of nations. In case any such emergency should arise, the Secretary-General shall, on the request of any Member of the League, forthwith summon a meeting of the Council.

2. It is also declared to be the friendly right of each Member of the League to bring to the attention of the Assembly or of the Council any circumstance whatever affecting international relations which threatens to disturb international peace or the good understanding between nations upon which peace depends.

ARTICLE 12 [1]

Disputes to Be Submitted for Settlement

1. The Members of the League agree that, if there should arise between them any dispute likely to lead to a rupture they will submit the matter either to abitration *or judicial settlement* or to inquiry by the Council and they agree in no case to resort to war until three months after the award by the arbitrators *or the judicial decision,* or the report by the Council.

2. In any case under this Article, the award of the arbitrators *or the judicial decision* shall be made within a reasonable time, and the report of the Council shall be made within six months after the submission of the dispute.

[1] The text as printed came into force as an amendment on September 26, 1924, in accordance with Art. 26. Revision indicated by italics.

ARTICLE 13 [1]

Arbitration or Judicial Settlement

1. The Members of the League agree that, whenever any dispute shall arise between them which they recognize to be suitable for submission to arbitration *or judicial settlement,* and which can not be satisfactorily settled by diplomacy, they will submit the whole subject-matter to arbitration *or judicial settlement.*

2. Disputes as to the interpretation of a treaty, as to any question of international law, as to the existence of any fact which, if established, would constitute a breach of any international obligation, or as to the extent and nature of the reparation to be made for any such breach, are declared to be among those which are generally suitable for submission to arbitration *or judicial settlement.*

3. *For the consideration of any such dispute, the court to which the case is referred shall be the Permanent Court of International Justice, established in accordance with Article 14, or any tribunal agreed on by the parties to the dispute or stipulated in any convention existing between them.*

4. The Members of the League agree that they will carry out in full good faith any award *or decision* that may be rendered, and that they will not resort to war against a Member of the League which complies therewith. In the event of any failure to carry out such an award *or decision,* the Council shall propose what steps should be taken to give effect thereto.

ARTICLE 14

Permanent Court of International Justice

The Council shall formulate and submit to the Members of the League for adoption plans for the establishment of a Permanent Court of International Justice. The Court shall be competent to hear and determine any dispute of an international character which the parties thereto submit to it. The Court may also give an advisory opinion upon any dispute or question referred to it by the Council or by the Assembly.

ARTICLE 15 [2]

Disputes Not Submitted to Arbitration or Judicial Settlement

1. If there should arise between Members of the League any dispute likely to lead to a rupture, which is not submitted to arbitration *or judicial settlement* in accordance with Article 13, the Members of the League agree that they will submit the matter to the Council. Any party to the dispute may effect such submission by giving notice of the existence of the dispute to the Secretary-General, who will make all necessary arrangements for a full investigation and consideration thereof.

2. For this purpose the parties to the dispute will communicate to the Secretary-General, as promptly as possible, statements of their case, with all the relevant facts and papers, and the Council may forthwith direct the publication thereof.

3. The Council shall endeavor to effect a settlement of the dispute and, if such efforts are successful, a statement shall be made public giving such facts and explanations regarding the dispute and the terms of settlement thereof as the Council may deem appropriate.

4. If the dispute is not thus settled, the Council, either unanimously or by a majority vote, shall make and publish a report containing a statement of the facts

[1] The text as printed came into force as an amendment on September 26, 1924. Changes made provide for resort to the World Court.

[2] On interpretations of pars. 1 and 8, see *Official Journal,* V, p. 524, and for the replies of the Governments, Document 1926. V. 12.

of the dispute and the recommendations which are deemed just and proper in regard thereto.

5. Any Member of the League represented on the Council may make public a statement of the facts of the dispute and of its conclusions regarding the same.

6. If a report by the Council is unanimously agreed to by the Members thereof other than the Representatives of one or more of the parties to the dispute, the Members of the League agree that they will not go to war with any party to the dispute which complies with the recommendations of the report.

7. If the Council fails to reach a report which is unanimously agreed to by the members thereof, other than the Representatives of one or more of the parties to the dispute, the Members of the League reserve to themselves the right to take such action as they shall consider necessary for the maintenance of right and justice.

8. If the dispute between the parties is claimed by one of them, and is found by the Council, to arise out of a matter which by international law is solely within the domestic jurisdiction of that party, the Council shall so report, and shall make no recommendation as to its settlement.

9. The Council may in any case under this Article refer the dispute to the Assembly. The dispute shall be so referred at the request of either party to the dispute, provided that such request be made within 14 days after the submission of the dispute to the Council.

10. In any case referred to the Assembly, all the provisions of this Article and of Article 12 relating to the action and powers of the Council shall apply to the action and powers of the Assembly, provided that a report made by the Assembly, if concurred in by the Representatives of those Members of the League represented on the Council and of a majority of the other Members of the League, exclusive in each case of the Representatives of the parties to the dispute, shall have the same force as a report by the Council concurred in by all the members thereof other than the Representatives of one or more of the parties to the dispute.

ARTICLE 16

Sanctions of Pacific Settlement

1.[1] Should any Member of the League resort to war in disregard of its covenants under Articles 12, 13 or 15, it shall *ipso facto* be deemed to have committed an act of war against all other Members of the League, which hereby undertake immediately to subject it to the severance of all trade or financial relations, the prohibition of all intercourse between their nationals and the nationals of the covenant-breaking

---

[1] The Assembly has voted in favor of the following amendments to Art. 16, to replace paragraph one, and the Members are now deciding upon their ratification:

"Should any Member of the League resort to war in disregard of its covenants under Articles 12, 13 or 15, it shall *ipso facto* be deemed to have committed an act of war against all other Members of the League, *which hereby undertake immediately to subject it to the severance of all trade or financial relations and to prohibit all intercourse at least between persons resident within their territories and persons resident within the territory of the covenant-breaking State and, if they deem it expedient, also between their nationals and the nationals of the covenant-breaking State, and to prevent all financial, commercial or personal intercourse at least between persons resident within the territory of that State and persons resident within the territory of any other State, whether a Member of the League or not, and, if they deem it expedient, also between the nationals of that State and the nationals of any other State whether a Member of the League or not.*

"It is for the Council to give an opinion whether or not a breach of the Covenant has taken place. In deliberations on this question in the Council, the votes of Members of the League alleged to have resorted to war and of Members against whom such action was directed shall not be counted.

"The Council will notify to all Members of the League the date which it recommends for the application of the economic pressure under this Article.

"Nevertheless, the Council may, in the case of particular Members, postpone the coming into force of any of these measures for a specified period where it is satisfied that such a postponement will facilitate the attainment of the object of the measures referred to in the preceding paragraph, or that it is necessary in order to minimize the loss and inconvenience which will be caused to such Members."

State, and the prevention of all financial, commercial or personal intercourse between the nationals of the covenant-breaking State and the nationals of any other State, whether a Member of the League or not.

2. It shall be the duty of the Council in such case [1] to recommend to the several Governments concerned what effective military, naval or air force the Members of the League shall severally contribute to the armed forces to be used to protect the covenants of the League.

3. The Members of the League agree, further, that they will mutually support one another in the financial and economic measures which are taken under this Article, in order to minimize the loss and inconvenience resulting from the above measures, and that they will mutually support one another in resisting any special measures aimed at one of their number by the covenant-breaking State, and that they will take the necessary steps to afford passage through their territory to the forces of any of the Members of the League which are cooperating to protect the covenants of the League.

4. Any Member of the League which has violated any covenant of the League may be declared to be no longer a Member of the League by a vote of the Council concurred in by the Representatives of all the other Members of the League represented thereon.

ARTICLE 17

Disputes Involving Nonmembers

1. In the event of a dispute between a Member of the League and a State which is not a Member of the League, or between States not Members of the League, the State or States not Members of the League shall be invited to accept the obligations of Membership in the League for the purposes of such dispute, upon such conditions as the Council may deem just. If such invitation is accepted, the provisions of Articles 12 to 16, inclusive, shall be applied with such modifications as may be deemed necessary by the Council.

2. Upon such invitation being given, the Council shall immediately institute an inquiry into the circumstances of the dispute and recommend such action as may seem best and most effectual in the circumstances.

3. If a State so invited shall refuse to accept the obligations of Membership in the League for the purposes of such dispute, and shall resort to war against a Member of the League, the provisions of Article 16 shall be applicable as against the State taking such action.

4. If both parties to the dispute, when so invited, refuse to accept the obligations of Membership in the League for the purposes of such dispute, the Council may take such measures and make such recommendations as will prevent hostilities and will result in the settlement of the dispute.

ARTICLE 18

Registration and Publication of Treaties

Every treaty or international engagement entered into hereafter by any Member of the League shall be forthwith registered with the Secretariat and shall as soon as possible be published by it. No such treaty or international engagement shall be binding until so registered.

---

[1] The Assembly on September 21, 1925, adopted a resolution providing that the words "in such case" shall be deleted. The amendment has been submitted to Member States for ratification.

Article 19

Review of Treaties

The Assembly may from time to time advise the reconsideration by Members of the League of treaties which have become inapplicable, and the consideration of international conditions whose continuance might endanger the peace of the world.

Article 20

Abrogation of Inconsistent Obligations

1. The Members of the League severally agree that this Covenant is accepted as abrogating all obligations or understandings *inter se* which are inconsistent with the terms thereof, and solemnly undertake that they will not hereafter enter into any engagements inconsistent with the terms thereof.

2. In case any Member of the League shall, before becoming a Member of the League, have undertaken any obligation inconsistent with the terms of this Covenant, it shall be the duty of such Member to take immediate steps to procure its release from such obligations.

Article 21

Engagements that Remain Valid

Nothing in this Covenant shall be deemed to affect the validity of international engagements, such as treaties of arbitration or regional understandings like the Monroe doctrine, for securing the maintenance of peace.

Article 22

Mandatory System

1. To those colonies and territories which as a consequence of the late war have ceased to be under the sovereignty of the States which formerly governed them and which are inhabited by peoples not yet able to stand by themselves under the strenuous conditions of the modern world, there should be applied the principle that the well-being and development of such peoples form a sacred trust of civilization and that securities for the performance of this trust should be embodied in this Covenant.

2. The best method of giving practical effect to this principle is that the tutelage of such peoples should be intrusted to advanced nations who, by reason of their resources, their experience or their geographical position, can best undertake this responsibility, and who are willing to accept it, and that this tutelage should be exercised by them as Mandatories on behalf of the League.

3. The character of the mandate must differ according to the stage of the development of the people, the geographical situation of the territory, its economic conditions and other similar circumstances.

4. Certain communities formerly belonging to the Turkish Empire have reached a stage of development where their existence as independent nations can be provisionally recognized subject to the rendering of administrative advice and assistance by a Mandatory until such time as they are able to stand alone. The wishes of these communities must be a principal consideration in the selection of the Mandatory.

5. Other peoples, especially those of Central Africa, are at such a stage that the Mandatory must be responsible for the administration of the territory under conditions which will guarantee freedom of conscience and religion, subject only to the maintenance of public order and morals, the prohibition of abuses such as the slave

trade, the arms traffic and the liquor traffic, and the prevention of the establishment of fortifications or military and naval bases and of military training of the natives for other than police purposes and the defense of territory, and will also secure equal opportunities for the trade and commerce of other Members of the League.

6. There are territories, such as Southwest Africa and certain of the South Pacific islands, which, owing to the sparseness of their population or their small size, or their remoteness from the centers of civilization, or their geographical contiguity to the territory of the Mandatory, and other circumstances, can be best administered under the laws of the Mandatory as integral portions of its territory, subject to the safeguards above mentioned in the interests of the indigenous population.

7. In every case of mandate, the Mandatory shall render to the Council an annual report in reference to the territory committed to its charge.

8. The degree of authority, control or administration to be exercised by the Mandatory shall, if not previously agreed upon by the Members of the League, be explicitly defined in each case by the Council.

9. A permanent Commission shall be constituted to receive and examine the annual reports of the Mandatories, and to advise the Council on all matters relating to the observance of the mandates.

ARTICLE 23

Social and Other Activities

Subject to and in accordance with the provisions of international conventions existing or hereafter to be agreed upon, the Members of the League:

(*a*) will endeavor to secure and maintain fair and humane conditions of labor for men, women, and children, both in their own countries and in all countries to which their commercial and industrial relations extend, and for that purpose will establish and maintain the necessary international organizations;

(*b*) undertake to secure just treatment of the native inhabitants of territories under their control;

(*c*) will intrust the League with the general supervision over the execution of agreements with regard to the traffic in women and children and the traffic in opium and other dangerous drugs;

(*d*) will intrust the League with the general supervision of the trade in arms and ammunition with the countries in which the control of this traffic is necessary in the common interest;

(*e*) will make provision to secure and maintain freedom of communications and of transit and equitable treatment for the commerce of all Members of the League. In this connection, the special necessities of the regions devastated during the war of 1914–1918 shall be borne in mind;

(*f*) will endeavor to take steps in matters of international concern for the prevention and control of disease.

ARTICLE 24

International Bureaus

1. There shall be placed under the direction of the League all international bureaus already established by general treaties, if the parties to such treaties consent. All such international bureaus and all commissions for the regulation of matters of international interest hereafter constituted shall be placed under the direction of the League.

2. In all matters of international interest which are regulated by general con-

ventions but which are not placed under the control of international bureaus or commissions, the Secretariat of the League shall, subject to the consent of the Council and if desired by the parties, collect and distribute all relevant information and shall render any other assistance which may be necessary or desirable.

3. The Council may include as part of the expenses of the Secretariat the expenses of any bureau or commission which is placed under the direction of the League.

ARTICLE 25

Promotion of Red Cross and Health

The Members of the League agree to encourage and promote the establishment and cooperation of duly authorized voluntary national Red Cross organizations having as purposes the improvement of health, the prevention of disease and the mitigation of suffering throughout the world.

ARTICLE 26 [1]

Amendments

1. Amendments to this Covenant will take effect when ratified by the Members of the League whose Representatives compose the Council and by a majority of the Members of the League whose Representatives compose the Assembly.

2. No such amendment shall bind any Member of the League which signifies its dissent therefrom, but in that case it shall cease to be a Member of the League.

[1] The Assembly voted in favor of the following amendments to replace Art. 26, in 1921, and the Members are now deciding upon its ratification:

"*Amendments to the present Covenant the text of which shall have been voted by the Assembly on a three-fourths majority, in which there shall be included the votes of all the Members of the Council represented at the meeting, will take effect when ratified by the Members of the League whose Representatives composed the Council when the vote was taken and by the majority of those whose Representatives form the Assembly.*

"*If the required number of ratifications shall not have been obtained within twenty-two months after the vote of the Assembly, the proposed amendment shall remain without effect.*

"*The Secretary-General shall inform the Members of the taking effect of an amendment.*

"*Any Member of the League which has not at that time ratified the amendment is free to notify the Secretary-General within a year of its refusal to accept it, but in that case it shall cease to be a Member of the League.*"

ANNEX

Original Members of the League of Nations, Signatories of the Treaty of Peace

*United States of America	Haiti
Belgium	*Hedjaz
Bolivia	Honduras
*Brazil	Italy
British Empire	Japan
Canada	Liberia
Australia	Nicaragua
South Africa	Panamá
New Zealand	Perú
India	Poland
China	Portugal
Cuba	Rumania
*Ecuador	Serb-Croat-Slovene State
France	Siam
Greece	Czechoslovakia
Guatemala	Uruguay

States Invited to Accede to the Covenant

Argentine Republic	Persia
Chile	Salvador
Colombia	Spain
Denmark	Sweden
Netherlands	Switzerland
Norway	Venezuela
Paraguay	

States Admitted to Membership

Abyssinia	Finland
Albania	Germany
Austria	Hungary
Bulgaria	Irish Free State
*Costa Rica	Latvia
Dominican Republic	Lithuania
Esthonia	Luxemburg
	Mexico

* Not a Member state, 1931.

INDEX

Abbott, Lyman, urged ratification, 382
Adams, Randolph G., quoted, 201, 469
Alexander I, Czar, 302, 305, 317
Algeciras Conference, the, 4, 480n.
Alsace-Lorraine, 174
Amendments to the Covenant, necessity evident, 172–3; made by Peace Conference, 179–90; rejected by Lodge, 213–14
Amendments to the treaty, 326, 328, 341; defeated, 387–89
American Bankers Association, 382
American Bar Association, 382
American Federation of Labor, 382
American press opinions on Covenant, 165–71
Annexations, issue of in Peace Conference, 106–9
Appeal of the Thirty-One in 1920 campaign, 461–4
Arbitration, Republican fostering of, 82–3; Senate's antagonism to, 423
Arbitration treaties, Bryan, 6; Taft, 17n., 481, 501; Olney-Pauncefote with Great Britain, 501; Hay, 501
Argentina, Senate ratifies Covenant, 233
Armistice, the, 27, 53, 57, 173
Arms limitation, reservation as to, 429–30
Army of Occupation, American, in Germany, 93, 139, 146
Article 10, see Security, the mutual guarantee of
Article 11, 111, 113, 123, 248–9, 529
Article 21, adoption of, 187–88; declared insufficient to defend the Monroe Doctrine, 213–14; a later view of, 216
Articles of Confederation, the, 8
Ashurst, Senator Henry F., 339
Assembly of the League of Nations, 510
Austria, sues for peace, 27; treaty with, 374
Axson, Dr. Stockton, 7 and n.

Babson, Roger, 382
Bacheller, Irving, 382
Baker, Newton D., 126
Baker, Ray Stannard, quoted, 188, 189, 204, 220n.
Balfour, Arthur, 106, 199
Baltimore Sun, quoted, 166
Bartholdt, Richard, 3
Bartlett, Vernon, quoted, 189n.
Baruch, Bernard M., 298
Beard, C. A., cited, 51n.

Beck, James M., 252
Beckham, Senator J. C. W., speech for the League, 260–2
Belgium, ratifies peace treaty, 384
Bell, Alexander Graham, 382
Bernhardi, 286
Beveridge, Senator Albert J.: in conference on *Harvey's Weekly,* 27; objections to a league, 66–7; urged opposition to League in its entirety, 117; belief that Wilson must be crushed, 374; opinion that reservations would have been ineffective, 498
Bitter Enders, *see* Irreconcilables, the
Bliss, Gen. Tasker H., member American peace delegation, 58, 59; his amendment to Article 10 accepted, 113; for swift demobilization, 174
Bolshevism, 98, 177
Borah, Senator William E.: 18; attacked whole idea of League, 94–5; speech in opposition to, 122; attacked Article 10 as the most dangerous in the Covenant, 197–8; agreement with Lodge on indirect attack, 207–8; forced publication of unsigned treaty, 220; on necessity of assent of other signatories to reservations, 273–4; restatement of isolationist position, 274–6; on Article 10 and rights of Congress regarding war, 321; on Shantung affair, 328; opinion as to unimportance of Lodge reservations in practice, 498–9; objected to any change or reservation in case of Paris Peace Pact, 502
Boston Transcript, quoted, 70 and n., 71, 72n., 396
Bourgeois, Leon, 110
Boycott, economic, as a sanction, 161, 282; reservation to, 430; in the future, 527
Brandegee, Senator Frank B.: Wilson cross-examined by, 133; and the Mad Hatter, 134; conceived the Round Robin, 153, 159; his house the rendezvous of "the cabal," 209; author of Irish resolution, 214; demanded that the Round Robin now be kept, 396; did not fear acceptance of reservations by Wilson, 441; ascribed defeat of treaty to Wilson, 483
Brazil, ratifies League, 394
British-Venezuelan boundary dispute, 216, 242
Brooklyn Eagle, quoted, 167

Lodge, Senator Henry Cabot—*Continued*
son to withdraw and resubmit treaty,
403; accepted Wilson's challenge to an
electoral decision, 405; in the bi-partisan conference, 406 ff.; in Republican
National Convention 1920, 451, 452,
454; attitudes during League controversy, 475–87; revealed purpose of
reservations, 481–3; his study of Wilson's character, 483–5; his difficulties,
485–6; and success, 486–7
Lodge, Henry Cabot, grandson of the
Senator, on his attitude toward the
League, 476
London Daily Mail, quoted, 67
London Daily News, 167
London Naval Treaty, 503–4
London Times, quoted on the campaign
against the League in the United States,
191–2
Longworth, Mrs. Nicholas, 209n.
Lowell, President A. Lawrence, 187, 194,
195, 405n.
Lowell Courier-Citizen, quoted, 167
Lusitania, the, 13, 60

McAdoo, William G., 456
McCarthy, Dr. F. P., 235n.
McCormick, Senator Medill, 210
MacCracken, Dr. H. N., 465
McCumber, Senator Porter J.: his answer
to the demand for postponement, 84–7;
reply to critics of the Covenant, 148–
52; account of the first White House
Conference, 151; 223; warning of the
consequences of defeating the Covenant, 224–5; arraignment of methods
and purposes of League opponents in
committee, 326–8; minority report filed,
363–5; voted for unconditional ratification, 396; pleaded for acceptance of reservations, 399; concluded League had
been killed, 471n.
McDonald, James G., 481
MacDonald, Ramsay, 60
McKellar, Senator Kenneth, speech for
League, 263–5; on origin of bi-partisan
conference, 406
McKinley, President, electoral appeal to
voters in 1898, 48–50; 57, 58, 179
McNary, Senator Charles L., satisfied
with the amended Covenant, 198; 237;
appeal for the League, 256–9; for mild
reservations, 297; exerted pressure for
compromise, 407
Magdalena Bay, 79, 369
Makino, Baron, Japanese delegate to
Peace Commission, 114
Manchester (N. H.) *Union,* quoted, 166
Manchuria, 524, 525
Mandate system, the, 106–7, 108–9, 116,
131–2, 176, 184, 203, 421–2
Marshall, Vice President Thomas R.: on
Wilson's electoral appeal, 45; on John
Sharp Williams, 215n.; shares belief

of Wilson that treaty opponents were
irreconcilable, 488–9n.
Martin, Senator Thomas S., 387
Martin, William, Swiss journalist, on
Wilson's western addresses, 357–8; on
Wilson's achievement at Paris, 491
Massey, Mr., of New Zealand, 109
Mellon, Andrew W., contributes funds to
campaign against League, 209, 210, 211
Merriam, Prof. C. E., 230
Mexico, 123, 147, 417n.
Mild Reservationists, *see* Reservationists,
mild
Millard, Thomas F., 328
Miller, David Hunter: on obligation under
treaties, 109–10n.; on deference to Wilson in League Commission sessions, 111;
as American legal adviser at Paris, 112;
on Wilson and adoption of Monroe
Doctrine amendment in the Conference,
188; on feeling of the French that
their safety was of primary importance
to the world, 189n.; on phrasing of
references to Monroe Doctrine, 227n.;
in Senate Foreign Relations Committee
hearings, 300–1; on withdrawal clause,
303n.; on reservations 10 and 12, 430–
1; analysis of reservation to Article
10, 435–6; on Dominion votes reservation, 448n.; opinion in 1920 as to result
of a trial of the League, 499
Mills, Ogden L., 452
Minneapolis Tribune, quoted, 169
Monroe, James, 18, 261
Monroe Doctrine, the: in plans for opposing the Covenant, 54, 76, 290, 309,
350; invoked by Lodge, 79; the essence
of the Covenant, 86, 90, 242, 253; 123;
as an alternative to the Covenant, 138;
applicable to us also, 151; protects only
territory and independence, 161; amendment concerning in the peace conference, pleas for and struggle to adopt,
183–90; amendment to Covenant not
accepted, 213–14, 311; defined to exclude the League, 214–15; as defined in
1895, 216; the Covenant greater, 253–4;
to allay alarm for, 257–8, 287–8; and
the Knox doctrine, 265; existence at
stake, 275; close kin to the Covenant,
277; strengthened by the League, 291;
inflation of, 309; Wilson's reply to
fears for, 350; not purely our own affair, 374; abrogation not feared below
the Rio Grande, 385; reservation concerning, 424, 444; effects of the campaign, 424–6
Moratorium of 1931, 516–17
Morgenthau, Henry, 476
Moroccan crisis of 1911, 4
Moses, Senator George H., mobilized the
precedents for amendment and rejection
of treaties, 213; for rejection, 260
Mowrer, Paul Scott, 80
Multilateral treaties, 504–6